# WRESTLING WITH THE ANGEL

*For
(again)
Bill Brown
and
John Money*

WRESTLING WITH THE

# Angel

a *life* of janet frame

**M I C H A E L   K I N G**

COUNTERPOINT
WASHINGTON, D.C.

First Published by Penguin Books (NZ) Ltd, 2000

Library of Congress Cataloging-in-Publication Data
King, Michael, 1945–
Wrestling with the angel : a life of Janet Frame / Michael King.
    p.    cm.
Includes bibliographical references (p. ) and index.
ISBN 1-58243-069-1
    1. Frame, Janet.    2. Women and literature—New Zealand—History—
20th Century.    3. Authors, New Zealand—20th century—Biography.
I. Title.

PR9639.3.F7 Z75    2000
823'.914—dc21
[B]
                                                                                    00-026861

Jacket design by Wesley Tanner

Printed in the United States of America on acid-free paper
that meets the American National Standards Institute
Z39-48 Standard.

COUNTERPOINT
P.O. Box 65793
Washington, D.C. 20035-5793

Counterpoint is a member of the Perseus Books Group

10   9   8   7   6   5   4   3   2   1

# Contents

| | | |
|---|---|---|
| Author's Note | | 8 |
| Prologue | | 9 |
| One | *Railway People* | 11 |
| Two | *Kingdom by the Sea* | 24 |
| Three | *Like Cousin Peg . . .* | 42 |
| Four | *An Unravelling* | 58 |
| Five | *Out of the Depths* | 72 |
| Six | *Except through Storm* | 91 |
| Seven | *Into the World* | 107 |
| Eight | *Sorcerer's Apprentice* | 121 |
| Nine | *Traveller's Joy?* | 144 |
| Ten | *In the Warm South* | 155 |
| Eleven | *Towards Sanctuary* | 171 |
| Twelve | *A Home in the Maudsley* | 183 |
| Thirteen | *A Career Resumed* | 200 |
| Fourteen | *On the Rock of Her Self* | 214 |
| Fifteen | *A Roots Crisis* | 231 |
| Sixteen | *Return of the Prodigal* | 255 |

| | | |
|---|---|---|
| Seventeen | *Exiled at Home* | 265 |
| Eighteen | *Dunedin and the Messrs Burns* | 283 |
| Nineteen | *Home and Away* | 301 |
| Twenty | *Utopia Discovered and Postponed* | 314 |
| Twenty-One | *Cherishing America* | 330 |
| Twenty-Two | *Lonely for Her Own Kind* | 350 |
| Twenty-Three | *Away from Civilisation* | 367 |
| Twenty-Four | *The Mansfield Connection* | 380 |
| Twenty-Five | *In Search of Silence* | 392 |
| Twenty-Six | *State of Siege* | 407 |
| Twenty-Seven | *A Change of Direction* | 431 |
| Twenty-Eight | *Gathering Fame* | 451 |
| Twenty-Nine | *Ascending Angel* | 477 |
| Thirty | *An Allegiance to Origins* | 503 |
| Acknowledgements | | 520 |
| Bibliography of Janet Frame's writing | | 523 |
| Bibliography of other works used or cited | | 525 |
| Notes | | 528 |
| Index | | 565 |

So Jacob was left alone, and there wrestled an angel with him until daybreak, who, when he saw he was not throwing him, struck his hip socket so that Jacob's thigh was dislocated . . . The angel said, 'Let me go for the day is breaking.' But Jacob replied, 'I will not let you go until you bless me' . . . The angel said, 'Your name will be Jacob no longer, but Israel, because you have striven with God and with men and have won' . . . And the angel blessed him there. Jacob named that place Peniel, for 'I saw God face to face and yet my life was preserved . . .'

*Genesis* 32, 24–31

## AUTHOR'S NOTE

Janet Frame agreed to cooperate with the writing of this book but expressed two preferences: that it not be a critical biography (an analysis of her writing); and that I do not quote verbatim from my interviews with her. I have complied with both requests. There was no question I put to her that she did not answer; and she made no attempt to dissuade me from publishing any information that my research uncovered. For all of which I thank her, and for permission to quote from her copyrighted material, published and unpublished.

Michael King

# *Prologue*

THE FRAME SISTERS THOUGHT OF THEMSELVES AS BRONTËS: BECAUSE they held, by right, 'silk purses' of words; and because their family was an anvil on which disasters fell. Not just the allotted portion of infant deaths, cancers and thromboses, but more than their share. One son stillborn. Another baby miscarried. The surviving son epileptic, a drunkard, and sometimes threatening. Two daughters dead of heart failure while swimming. One of the remaining daughters committed to mental hospitals for the best part of a decade. The other felled in young adulthood by a brain haemorrhage. And Uncle Bob who cut his own throat; Uncle Charlie who drank; cousin Robert who died in a motorcycle smash; and cousin Bill who shot his lover, his lover's parents and then himself.

One surviving daughter, the younger, would say that she spent her life dancing before a tide of doom that threatened to sweep her family to oblivion. The other, the writer, entered a territory which resembled the place where the dying spend their time before death. Those who return from there, she said, brought a point of view equal in its rapture and its chilling exposure to the neighbourhood of the gods and goddesses.

This is the story of the writer-sister, who persevered by making designs from her dreams and going out into the world 'with no luggage but memory and a pocketful of words'.

# CHAPTER ONE

# *Railway People*

'*T*HE PEOPLE ARE SCOTCH,' MARK TWAIN SAID OF DUNEDIN, NEW Zealand, in 1895. 'They stopped here on their way to heaven — thinking they had arrived.'[1] Twain's theology might have been suspect but his powers of observation were acute. Dunedin *was* celestially beautiful, lying at the head of a long narrow harbour. The pasture, groves of trees and dry stone walls on the surrounding hills hinted at an Arcadian version of Caledonia. And the city itself was Scottish in its appearance and in the ethnic character of most of its citizenry. Dunedin's street names, public buildings of brick and stone, church steeples, scattering of Queen Anne towers — all made it seem more like Edinburgh and Glasgow than any other New Zealand settlement. Its very name was the Gaelic version of Edinburgh. And in pride of place in the centre of town, a fine bronze statue of Robbie Burns overlooked the Octagon.

Janet Paterson Frame, born in Dunedin on 28 August 1924, was an heir to this character and to the traditions that came with it. She was named Janet after a Frame aunt who died in infancy; and Paterson from the family name of her Scottish grandmother. From the first, she was known by the very Scottish diminutive of Jean, contracted further by her immediate family to Nini. Her childhood was soaked in transplanted Scottish culture. When her mother spoke of Resurrection Day, Janet envisaged a heavenly kind of Sports Day, with a brass band playing 'The Invercargill March' and kilted pipers skirling 'The Road to the Isles'. Even the Second Coming, it seemed to her, would have a Scottish–New Zealand flavour.[2] The immediate history of her family explains how this eschatological vision developed.

Alexander Frame, Janet's father's father, was part of a chain migration that brought around 68,000 Scots to New Zealand, mostly to the southern parts of the country, in the nineteenth century. The first wave arrived in 1848 as part of the Free Church settlement of Otago — an attempt on the part of artisans, farmers, farm labourers and domestic servants to escape 'the gloom of Celtic twilight for the bright dawn of a new start in a new country', where organised British colonisation had been under way for less than a decade.[3] Specifically these largely Lowland Scots sought to escape the consequences of economic depression, poverty and religious controversy that characterised Scottish life in the 1840s. They sought also to plant a settlement where 'piety, rectitude and industry would feel at home, and where the inhabitants as a body would form a vigilant moral police'.[4]

The second group of Scottish immigrants followed in the 1860s to join the rush to the Otago goldfields and build on the foundations laid by their predecessors. Then the third and largest wave arrived in the 1870s as a result of the colonial government's drive to recruit more hard-working immigrants. They too gravitated to those parts of New Zealand already settled by their compatriots. And they included Alexander Frame, a stoker from Hamilton in the Clyde Valley, whose four older brothers had chosen to go to Canada and the United States. Alexander disembarked at Port Chalmers and was directed eighty miles to the north, to the coastal town of Oamaru, then burgeoning with a prosperity induced by wool and grain. Mary Paterson, who had begun work in a Paisley cotton mill at the age of eight but arrived in New Zealand as a domestic servant, followed him. She had come to New Zealand in 1874 on the maiden voyage of the *Mairi Bhan*. Her daughters believed that she had conceived a child en route for New Zealand and that the infant had died. True or not, she was unencumbered in May 1877 when she married Alexander Frame in Oamaru. He was twenty-three and literate; she twenty-one and uneducated.

Alexander established himself as a blacksmith and he and Mary had eight sons and four daughters, all born in Oamaru. In 1899, when the youngest were still infants, they shifted close to Port Chalmers where Mary, now able to read and write, acted as midwife. Port Chalmers was the deep water port for Dunedin; and Dunedin was the centre and dispersal point for the Scottish settlement of Otago. An explosion of wealth generated by the gold rushes of the 1860s had made it for a short time New Zealand's largest city and commercial capital. A grain boom in the late nineteenth century and the establishment in Dunedin of some of the country's major manufacturing and mercantile firms ensured that, as the gold bonanza waned, it remained a city of character and solidity.

The transplantation of Scottish names and influences had fanned out from Dunedin into the southern provinces of Otago and Southland, both of which would provide homes and work for Alexander and Mary Frame's children. In some instances, such as Strath Taieri and Glen Tiaki, the Scottish names combined with those of indigenous Maori. The stone walls around Otago Harbour and stone cottages in Central Otago were further indications of an attempt to transform an otherwise alien landscape into something that resembled rural Scotland. And the settlers chose to introduce trout and salmon for their food value rather than — as had occurred in the rest of the country

— game birds for sport. Caledonian Societies and pipe bands kept alive the trappings of Scottish culture, especially its music and dancing. Even 150 years after the beginnings of Scottish occupation, the cultural sediment was there still in the wintertime sport of curling and the burred sound of the Southland 'r'.

The New Zealand Frames were saturated in these early influences. They were part of a community of around 160,000 first-generation Scottish New Zealanders. Alexander and Mary relayed stories from the old country itself — though with the dourness characteristic of their people, they were not as communicative nor as chauvinistic as their fellow Gaels, the Irish, who were less numerous than Scots in the south. The Frame children, Janet's uncles and aunts, threw themselves with enthusiasm into competitions organised by the piping and dancing societies and frequently carried home trophies. And they listened to and recited the work of their own bards, the sometimes excruciating verses of immigrant poets determined to be the Burnses of the New Scotland:

> Though dear to my heart is Zealandia,
> For the home of my boyhood I yearn;
> I dream, amid sunshine and grandeur,
> Of a land that is misty and stern;
> From the land of the Moa and Maori
> My thoughts to old Scotia will turn;
> Thus the Heather is blent with the Kauri
> And the Thistle entwined with the Fern.[5]

George Samuel Frame, Janet's father, had been born in Oamaru in 1894, second-to-youngest in his family. In Dunedin he became, with his parents' encouragement, an accomplished piper. He would also fish South Island lakes and rivers for trout and salmon, able to do so because of the 'Queen's Chain'. This was an area twenty-two yards either side of most bodies of water to which access had been guaranteed in law by a Scottish New Zealand Minister of Lands, Jock McKenzie, who was determined to avoid the game regulations which made fishing and hunting in Scotland the preserve of the privileged. George's other favourite pastimes, unusual for a New Zealand man, included embroidery ('fancy work'), making rugs and working leather — activities which his family viewed as a continuation of the skills of the Flemish weavers from whom the Frames were said to descend through five hundred years' occupation of the Scottish Lowlands.[6]

By 1901 Alexander and Mary Frame had moved into the centre of Dunedin, possibly out of consideration for their younger children's education. George went to Albany Street School, only two blocks away from the family home in Hanover Street. He gained his proficiency certificate in the sixth standard and was selected for a group photograph of the school's 'Good Workers'. Then he sought casual work until he was old enough to learn a trade. His first job was to create sound effects, including galloping horses, for silent films in a Dunedin cinema.

Eventually, aged eighteen, George was able to join the railways, a government department for which his father had worked as a blacksmith in 1907. Railways offered a working lifetime of security in addition to a variety of benefits such as family travel concessions, accommodation in isolated communities, annual picnics and superannuation. As was customary at this time he started at the bottom, as a cleaner, with the opportunity to work his way through the ranks, with training and examinations, to echelons of better paid and more highly respected positions.

In May 1913 he was posted to Christchurch, and then to Taumarunui in the centre of the North Island, where he cleaned heavy black coal-powered locomotives. In 1914, the year the First World War broke out, he went to Wellington as an acting fireman. In May 1914 he returned to the South Island, to Picton, on the opposite side of Cook Strait.[7] There he became friendly with a fellow railways worker, a local named Billy Godfrey. And at Billy's home, in the idiom of the day, he 'met his fate' in the form of Billy's sister Lottie Clarice Godfrey, a beaming and buxom young woman two years his senior.

While the Frames descended from Scottish artisans, the Godfreys were largely English in origin and identified among their ancestors gentry and establishment figures: Anglican clergy, an Oxford don, an admiral, and a surgeon who made a fortune by concocting from opium, brandy and bitters what became the most successful painkiller of its day, 'Godfrey's Cordial'. This last was Dr John Godfrey, born in Oxford in 1799, who numbered the invalid poet Elizabeth Barrett among his well-to-do patients. One of his sons, also John, emigrated to New Zealand in 1850 and, known as 'the Duke', became a forceful local body politician who founded a provincial newspaper (the *Marlborough Express)* and owned a general store in the main street of Picton. His son Alfred, a blacksmith like Alexander Frame, was Lottie's father.[8] Alfred's wife, Jessie Joyce, was the stepdaughter of one of Cook Strait's most colourful characters, a ship's captain, pilot and former whaler named James 'Worser' Heberley, whose first wife and family had been Maori.★

While some families managed to better themselves through emigration to the colonies, the Godfreys' position — at least in the case of Lottie's branch of the family — had slipped. After raising nine children, Alfred Godfrey had few resources with which to equip his descendants. The nearest his daughter Lottie came to establishment figures was being employed by them as a domestic servant. She worked successively for a dentist, a magistrate, and — most memorably — for Mrs Mary Beauchamp, paternal grandmother of the writer

---

★ A misunderstanding of this relationship, and a misreading of Janet Frame's story 'The Lagoon' (Frame 1951, pp 7–11), in which the narrator has a Maori great-grandmother, has led some commentators to claim that Frame has Maori ancestry. She does not.

neighbour, Tommy Miles, was run over by an express train and died of horrific injuries.

In the course of delivering her earliest composition on the bank of the Mataura River, Janet came to another realisation that she would retain. It was not sufficient to have stories to tell, and an audience. One had also to be able to engage the audience with the wonder or the power or the humour of the tale. 'Mum,' she had to say on that debut occasion, 'Mum, Myrtle and [Geordie's] wiggling. Tell them to stop wiggling while I tell my 'tory.'[21]

It was at Glenham too that Janet experienced what she would remember as her first period of real unhappiness. George Frame was to go to Wyndham, fifteen kilometres to the north, in mid-1928, promoted to full engine driver. In the meantime there was an accommodation problem. The railway houses at Glenham were to be removed in preparation for the winding down and eventual closure of the Wyndham–Glenham line. The Frames would live for some weeks in a cluster of huts, placed on paddocks opposite the Glenham station. When a railways house became available at Edendale they would move there temporarily; and then on to Wyndham by the middle of 1928.[22]

Those weeks on the Glenham paddocks, battered by early winter storms off the Antarctic, were grim. The family lived in three 'railway red' huts. One served as a bedroom for Lottie and George and the baby; the second as a bedroom for the three older children; and a third, which was slightly larger, as a kitchen-living hut with a stove and a tin chimney. The lavatory or 'dumpy', Janet wrote later, 'was the usual enclosure about a deep hole, with a railway-red seat'.

> Our lighting was by candle and kerosene, and only the kitchen hut had a stove. The anticipated delights, intensified by Mother's ability to pluck poetic references from those many rooted in her mind, began to die with the first touch of the Southland blizzard. Tales of gypsy camps, or Arabs folding their tents, of Babes in the Wood, could scarcely defeat the bitter cold. It seemed to be always snowing, with the snow lying deep around the huts . . .
>
> I was miserable, locked away each night from Mum and Dad and unable to reach them except by going through the snow . . . We were all sick, with colds, and I began to suffer the pains in my legs that became part of my childhood. I was feverish and delirious, seeing insects crawling up and down the wall. The 'growing pains' and the fever were rheumatic fever. Everywhere was damp and cold, and the world was full of damp washing and nappies covered with green mess as if the baby, like a calf, had been eating grass.[23]

The very depths of discomfort, however, meant that the occasions of warmth and security were the more highly prized. They included Lottie playing her accordion and singing alongside the kitchen stove; and George 'striding up and down in the snow . . . [playing] his bagpipe tunes — "The Cock o' the North" or "The Flowers of the Forest" . . .'[24] And this recollection of their father outside in the dark piping them to sleep, in Glenham and later in Wyndham, became one of the most comforting memories that the Frame children would share and retain.

Eventually it was over. In the early weeks of June 1928 the Frames moved north to Edendale for a short stay in a house next to the railway station; and then to Wyndham, six kilometres to the east. There, less than a week after their arrival, the last child of the family, Phyllis Mary Eveline June, was born on the last day of the month. They would call her 'Chicks' and, as she grew up, June.

Wyndham is a rural township at the meeting of two Southland rivers, the Mataura and the Mimihau. It was established in the wake of the Crimean War, which it memorialised in its name (in honour of General Sir Charles Windham, but misspelt) and its roads. Balaclava Street was the main street. Ferry Street, where the Frames lived, formed a junction with Cardigan Road. If the nomenclature of Otago and Southland as a whole was a grid of Scottish allusions, individual townships emphasised the extent to which colonial New Zealand was sensitive to the fortunes of imperial Britain — as did the eagerness with which New Zealand troops had volunteered for service in the South African and First World Wars.

Wyndham had a population of just under seven hundred and served a dairy-farming district of several thousand more inhabitants. In addition to a railway station and a school it had shops, a post office, a courthouse, a picture theatre and a library. It had its own newspaper, the *Wyndham Farmer*. There was a racecourse at which crowds gathered in season and a pipe band which practised weekly. After Glenham, which had imprinted on Janet Frame her most vivid childhood impressions of 'sky, green paddocks, swamps, bulrushes, tussocks, snowgrass', Wyndham revealed that 'the world held more people than I had dreamed of . . .'[25]

The Frames lived in another railway house, at the railway end of Ferry Street on the edge of town. It was one of a row of near-identical properties with wooden houses at the front and vegetable gardens at the back, which adjoined the back gardens of the houses in the next street parallel. Again the family had a cow, Beauty, and a heifer calf, Pansy. And there was a fowlhouse with a dozen White Leghorn hens and a rooster.

'Wyndham,' Janet was to write later, 'was the time of cabbages in the garden, of pump water, of candles and kerosene lamps at night with "real" darkness and night shadows . . . Dad began painting pictures in oil on canvas and on velvet . . .[He] played football, breaking his ankle, which meant more time for painting the pictures. He played golf and dressed in plus fours . . . and went to the races . . . And still there were the picnics to remote beaches and rivers, travelling in the grey Lizzie Ford, stopping on the hot dusty roads while Dad fed water to the bubbling engine.' It was also the time when Lottie Frame began to publish verse weekly, in the *Wyndham Farmer*, and came to be known with pride as 'Lottie C. Frame, the local poet'.[26]

The Frame children were, in fact, immersed in their mother's poems — the ones that Lottie composed herself, generally of an 'uplifting' nature:

> Why be sad when autumn leaves
> Flutter to the ground
> When upon your garden beds
> Buds cannot be found?
> Fast asleep encased in brown
> Waiting to be born
> Dreams a dainty crocus
> Of the first spring morn[27]

and ones she had learned at school, especially those of the American New England poets Henry Wadsworth Longfellow and John Greenleaf Whittier, along with the classic ballads of English literature. Lottie also talked incessantly about the novels she loved, again largely American: Twain's *Tom Sawyer*, Harriet Beecher Stowe's *Uncle Tom's Cabin*. And characters from these stories — wicked Simon Legree, Eliza walking out on the ice — seemed to her children to spill out into real life and get mixed up with stories about the ancestors, the pioneers, Jack Frost, the Gypsies and Babes in the Wood. Janet, whose hair was red and frizzy, was called Topsy and learned to say, 'I'm the girl that never was born pras I grew up among the corn. Golly. Ain't I wicked!'[28]

The other book that the older children were now aware of was the *Bible*. On Sundays at Wyndham Lottie Frame, good Christadelphian, sat them round the large kitchen table where they 'pored over the red-letter *Bible*'. Lottie drew their attention to such Old Testament episodes as the Garden of Eden and the Flood. She sought meaning in present-day catastrophes by relating them to the revelations in the New Testament which prefigured the Second Coming of Christ and the Day of Judgement. And she explained that 'a poor man might come to the door and be refused food or even have the dogs "sooled" on to him, and lo! he would turn out to be an angel in disguise or even Christ himself. Mother warned us to be careful and not to laugh at people who we thought were strange or "funny" because they, too, might be angels in disguise [and] God still loved each one, no matter how poor or peculiar he might be.'[29]

This last story was especially apposite. A year after the Frames moved to Wyndham the Great Depression began to bite and New Zealand rural roads drew a growing procession of swaggers, itinerant unemployed men who went from farm to farm and door to door looking for sustenance, work or both. Lottie, whose husband would remain in work throughout the Depression, invariably gave them a cup of tea, something to eat and a box of food to take away. '[The] horror and fear in people's voices when they talked of them brought a feeling of doom, of loneliness,' Janet remembered, 'as if something were happening or about to happen that would belong not only to us, the Frames of Ferry Street, Wyndham, but also would be part of the street and the neighbours and other towns.'[30]

The onset of the Depression was part of a sequence of events that occurred while the Frames were at Wyndham which contributed to an erosion of Janet's early childhood expectation that life would deliver only good things. They left 'a certain wariness, a cynicism about the ways of people and of my family . . .'[31] One, a kind of private betrayal, occurred in the course of a family picnic. 'Playing by myself in the paddock, I saw a sheep staring at me, in a special way, with its head on one side and its face full of meaning. I ran excitedly to where Mum and Dad were drinking their billy tea. "A sheep looked at me," I said, feeling the occasion had been momentous . . . "How did the sheep look at you?" Dad asked. "With its head on one side." "Show us." Suddenly shy, with everyone staring, and sensing the ridicule, I refused; then, in a wave of (unconscious) generosity, unaware that I was creating an occasion that would be used for years to come, I said, "I'll show only Dad." I went to Dad, and shielding my face with my hand, I imitated the sheep's expression. Throughout my childhood Dad would say, "Show us how the sheep looked at you," and while the others giggled, I performed my "routine".'[32]

Then, on her first visit to the dentist, Janet was persuaded to 'smell the pretty pink towel' which in fact smelt acrid and put her to sleep. She awoke to the realisation that she had been deceived *and* had lost a tooth.[33]

In March 1929 George Frame, by this time earning two shillings and threepence farthing per hour, had his wages docked by a shilling an hour for three months. This was disciplinary action for driving a locomotive away from a station without waiting for a signal. Given that the penalty reduced his pay by almost half, it would have involved the whole family in hardship and stress. It may have been the reason that George sold the Ford, his golf clubs and his bagpipes at about this time.

For Janet, though, the most unpleasant experience occurred in February 1930, a week after she had joined her older sister and brother in the primary department of Wyndham District High School. The infant teacher, Miss Ethel Botting, exposed 'Jean' Frame as a thief after she had taken money from her father's trouser pocket and bought chewing gum for members of her class. In an exercise of the kind of sadism not uncommon in schools at that time, Janet was made to stand in front of the desks for almost a whole day until she confessed. Miss Botting then 'gave the news to the class and it spread quickly around the school that I was a thief . . . [I was] appalled by my future prospects.'[34]

Not long after this the family lost Paisley-born Grandma Frame, whom Lottie had been nursing. 'I believed that she had come from America,' Janet wrote later, 'that she had been a slave there, for she was big, with frizzy hair and dark skin, and sometimes when she sang about the cotton fields she would cry as if she were remembering her years as a slave.'[35] The black skin and the tears were symptoms of the illnesses that killed her, heart failure and senility. And prior to her death she had had to have both legs amputated.

When the old lady was 'laid out' in the front room, Janet recalled, Lottie asked the children if they would like to see her. 'The others said yes and went solemnly to look at the dead, while I hung back, afraid and always to regret that I did not see Grandma dead. When Myrtle came out of the room, I could see in her face the power of having looked at the dead. "What was Grandma like?" I asked her, unhappily aware of the low status of my second-hand experience and of my weakness at not being able to "look". Myrtle shrugged. "She looked all right, just like being asleep." For many years after that Myrtle was able to win many arguments with her triumphant "I saw Grandma dead".'[36] For many years, that is, until Myrtle herself was laid out in a front room and Janet, never learning, again declined to look on the face of the dead.

Less than a year later there was unexpected relief from an apparent continuity of negative experiences, especially from 'Jean' Frame's community-wide reputation as a thief. Her father was to be shifted. The railway people were on the move again. This time the destination was Oamaru in North Otago, the family's first New Zealand home and George Frame's birthplace. It would now be home for Janet and her siblings for the rest of their childhood and adolescence.

CHAPTER TWO

# *Kingdom by the Sea*

$O$AMARU, CHIEF TOWN OF NORTH OTAGO, SPRAWLS ALONG A NARROW alluvial plain. Its principal streets — Thames, Severn, Humber, Ouse, Tyne, Dee, Clyde, Tay — are named after English and Scottish rivers. To the west it is bordered by an amphitheatre of hills backdropped by the distant Southern Alps, to the east by the Pacific Ocean. It has no natural harbour, nor a sufficiently large river mouth to accommodate shipping. But a man-made breakwater running north from a natural headland, Cape Wanbrow, created an artificial port for the dispatch of the district's wool, grain and meat. And it was these commodities that made Oamaru prosperous in the 1870s and 1880s when the settlement — an entirely European creation despite its Maori name — was little more than a decade old.[1]

To reflect the wealth of the hinterland and express the optimism with which early Oamaru was infused, the town fathers raised a succession of mercantile and public buildings in classical and Renaissance styles. Almost all were built or finished with the region's creamy-white limestone that came to be called Oamaru stone.[2] One of the first and most imposing was the Bank of Otago, completed in 1871 and inspired by Edinburgh's Commercial Bank of Scotland.[3] The building itself was Italian palazzo, while the portico entrance was supported by six Corinthian columns. According to one commentator, it looked like 'a strayed Greek temple . . . Few things as impressive could have been found in the much larger settlements of the country further to the north, particularly if the observer ignored the fact that its depth was only half its frontal width.'[4]

Other monuments to prosperity and solidity followed: more banks, a customs building, harbour board offices, grain stores, insurance company premises, a courthouse, a post office, county council chambers and the Oamaru Athenaeum and Mechanics Institute, which followed the Victorian practice of associating education and the literary arts with the goddess Athene and her temple in Athens. By the turn of the twentieth century Oamaru was described as 'the best built and most mortgaged town in Australasia'.[5] The grandeur of its public buildings was said to give sensitive folk aspirations.

When the Frames arrived early in 1931, however, there was something faintly bogus about Oamaru's aspect. In neither a cultural nor a commercial sense had it become the 'Athens of the South', as Irish nationalist Michael Davitt had predicted.[6] Although coastal trading ships continued to use its port, the local grain industry had shrunk, and meat, wool and dairy products were now exported for the most part from Port Chalmers to the south or harbours to the north. The noble mercantile buildings down by the harbour retained the smell of grain and wool, but they were being abandoned gradually and grass grew between the cobblestones in Tyne Street. This led Janet Frame, when she walked there, to regard it as a ghost city, to shiver with a 'sense of yesterdays' and imagine that she was 'in London in the chapter of our history books that began "when grass grew in London streets"'.[7]

Oamaru as a whole survived, however, centred now on Thames Street, important for servicing the farming district of North Otago: a town of banks, stock and station agents, insurance companies, legal firms, a flour mill and a large woollen mill. But the scale and character of the Oamaru stone buildings now seemed, from Thames Street at least, excessive — as if the town were part of a much larger and more substantial community, a city, even. It did have its wealthy pockets, such as Reed Street, where many of the professional families lived, and the South Hill, site of some moneyed mansions. But it had more extensive precincts of modest houses, such as those in Eden Street, where the Frames would live in the company of other 'blue collar' families.

When the New Zealand rural economy was thriving, as it did for much of the 1920s, then Oamaru thrived and there was work and wages for all its citizens who wanted them. When the bottom fell out of the country's agricultural markets abroad, however, as it did in the late 1920s, then farmers stopped spending money and the businesses who catered for them were forced to retrench, lay off staff, and in some instances close. In February 1931 Oamaru had a high rate of unemployment; and so-called 'relief work' was poorly paid and available on alternate weeks only. As in Wyndham, a symptom of the times was the occasional appearance of vagrants, moving from door to door in search of paid chores, setting the dogs barking and reproaching the consciences of families whose breadwinners were still in work.

The Frames, of course, were one such family. George was now into his third decade as a railway employee and his second as an engine driver. His choice of career on grounds of security had been vindicated. Throughout the years of the Great Depression his salary increased, from two shillings and threepence farthing an hour in 1929, to two shillings and ninepence by 1936. But railways, forced like all government departments to curtail expenditure as national income fell, reduced working hours and overtime. So that even as George Frame's wages were increasing, his take-home pay was falling. And always there was the threat that if economic conditions deteriorated further, he might be laid off, as a percentage of his colleagues were between 1930 and 1933.

When the Frame grandparents had moved south to Port Chalmers thirty years before, their oldest surviving son, Alex, had remained in Oamaru. In January 1931, he was a taxi driver and lived with his wife, two daughters and one son, also Alex, in a comfortable home on the South Hill. George and his family stayed there several weeks until they found a modest house of suitable size to rent at 56 Eden Street. This was a late nineteenth century weatherboard bungalow, originally square with four rooms. By the time the Frames occupied it, three of those four initial rooms were bedrooms and one a sitting-room. At the rear of the house a kitchen, bathroom, scullery and back bedroom had been added; and there was a semi-detached washhouse and flush lavatory, the family's first.

Lottie and George took one front bedroom, Geordie the other. The four girls, top-and-tailing, shared one double-bed in the middle bedroom, opposite the sitting-room. Grandad Frame, widowed and now in fragile health, came to Oamaru with the family and occupied the back bedroom till he died there in September 1931. Then Geordie took it and the spare front room was reserved for guests or (at times of family bereavement) laid-out corpses.

The sitting-room, furnished with the King's sofa and chairs and the little-used Singer sewing machine, was reserved for special occasions: announcements by Lottie of triumphs and disasters (news of the calamitous Napier earthquake, for example, which occurred the week the family moved into Eden Street; and the outbreak of the Second World War some eight years later); and celebrations such as Christmas and New Year, the latter observed Scottish fashion with first-footing and lumps of coal. Most of the 'living', in fact, took place in the kitchen, which had a large kauri table, chairs, and a coal range that served to heat the room, keep water boiling for tea and cook meals. Here the family assembled to eat, drink, talk, do homework, and read before bedtime.

The house was badly maintained and from the time the family moved in the cousins on the South Hill regarded them as 'poor relations'.[8] The roof was rusty, the weatherboards rotting, some of the sash window cords broken and a few panes cracked. Cockroaches were in occupation under the scullery sink and slaters and earwigs emerged through cracks in the bare floorboards. The landlord was unwilling to spend money on renovations or repairs without raising the rent. However spartan, though, 56 Eden Street provided an affordable and secure arena for Frame family life and rites of passage for the next thirteen years.

The railway yards and locomotive sheds were about a mile away and George would cycle there each work day and sometimes at night. Myrtle, Geordie and Janet would walk to Oamaru North School, about two-thirds that distance from home. The feature that most impressed the family, though, was the novelty of moving from a town of 700 inhabitants to one of 7000. 'We've never been surrounded by houses before,' said Lottie Frame portentously as she looked up the rising length of Eden Street and its rows of dwellings; nor had they for the previous seven years — the whole of Janet's, Isabel's and June's lifetime to that point.[9]

Eden Street was scarcely 'urban', however. It bordered the edge of town and open spaces were close by. Behind the backyard, with its vegetable garden and fruit trees, was a 'bull paddock' and a creek; and behind those a grassed hill reserve with a zig-zag path, caves with fossilised shells and marine skeletons in the walls, remains of Maori ovens, and a seat on the summit donated by the Oamaru Beautifying Society. From that vantage point it was possible to hear 'the waves crashing over the breakwater [and see] Cape Wanbrow with its dark mass of pines and the ramble of buildings that were the Victoria Old People's Home, the town clock, the flour mill, the creek, the morgue, Thames Street, Reed Street, the Railway Station, the Engine Sheds, and far out the North Road by the Boys' High, the tall chimney of the woollen mills . . .'[10]

The Frame children explored every inch of their new environment, working their way outwards from the house, 'accumulating our treasure of new experiences', especially in the vicinity of the creek. 'We knew the plants on its banks and . . . the rocks, cockabullies, eels and the old weighted and shredded sacks of drowned kittens and cats. Each morning we set out foraging for experience and in the afternoon returned to share with one another, while our parents, apart from us now, went about their endless adult work.'[11]

Janet would remember that early time in Oamaru as an adventure.

I was now vividly aware of myself as a person on earth, feeling a kinship with other creatures and full of joy at the sights and sounds about me and drunk with the anticipation of play, where playing seemed endless, on and on after school until dark, when even then there were games to play in bed — physical games like 'trolly works' and 'fitting in', where each body curled into the other and all turned on command, or guessing games or imagining games, interpreting the masses of shape and colour in the bedroom curtains, or codes, hiding messages in the brass bed knobs. There were arguments and fights and plans for the future and impossible dreams of fame as dancers, violinists, pianists, artists.[12]

As a result of her attendance at Oamaru North School, where she was enrolled in standard one in February 1931, Janet found for the first time a friend outside the family with whom to share childhood experience and extend knowledge. Marjorie Firman, known as Poppy, was the same age and in the same class. She lived round the corner in Glen Street and they became friends walking to and from school. In Janet's adult recollection it was Poppy who passed on to her the rituals and folklore that children transmit to one another independent of the adult world: curing warts with the juice of ice plants; sucking honey from nasturtiums; linking fingers if they 'had the pip' with each other or said the same word at the same time; passing on the names of plants and flowers (shepherd's purse, fat hen, ragwort); communicating, in crude but accurate terms, the 'facts of life'. 'It seemed to me that Poppy knew everything.'[13]

Poppy Firman's most bountiful gift to the Frame children, however, was *Grimms' Fairy Tales* — not the book itself, which remained her property, 'returned and borrowed, again and again', but the stories, which Janet read to her sisters in an ecstasy of discovery and excitement. '[Suddenly] the world of living and the world of reading became linked in a way I had not noticed before . . . [We] were the Dancing Princesses — not twelve but four; and as I read I saw in my mind . . . orchards hung with silver and golden apples, boughs that spoke and sang and cried out, underground seas and rivers and splash splash through the dark caverns, then suddenly the lit palace and the ballroom. All the stories had a similar measure of delight . . . none of [the characters] were more nor less than we were for all the list of extraordinary gifts, miracles, transformations, cruelties, and the many long years of wandering and searching, full of hope and expectation. *Grimms' Fairy Tales* was everybody's story seen in a special way.'[14]

Books were scarce at this time at 56 Eden Street. Lottie Frame, Janet noted, came from a home full of books to one where there were few, kept on a shelf in the kitchen: twelve volumes of Oscar Wilde, which George had bought as part of a Wyndham auction lot that had included a chiming clock, a pair of hedge shears and a bagpipe record; the *Bible*; *Christendom Astray*, a Christadelphian manual; 'God's book' ('a luridly illustrated account of the creation and the prophets and the Latter Days'); and 'the doctor's book' ('an equally lurid account of the human body in sickness'). Somewhat later, after he had picked them out of the rubbish dump, Geordie Frame added Ernest Dowson's *Verses* and George MacDonald's *At the Back of the North Wind*.[15]

Janet's other sources of reading were the new comic cuts, which the Frame children were sometimes allowed to buy (her favourites being *My Favourite* and *Rainbow*); and the readers and journals available at Oamaru North School. It was in one of the school readers that she discovered the word 'island' and went on thinking of it as 'is-land', a metaphor for present time, even when the phenomenon of the silent letter was explained to her.[16] The *School Journals*, produced by the Department of Education and saturated in the kinds of values which governments and educationists of the day wanted to communicate to New Zealand children, dealt much in imperial themes (Robert Falcon Scott at the South Pole, Anzacs at Gallipoli) and stories about the British Royal Family. Among the few New Zealand stories was that of the Maori chief, Tamati Waka Nene, who persuaded many of his fellow chiefs to sign the Treaty of Waitangi with the British Crown in 1840. What struck Janet about this man was that, in addition to being 'a firm friend of the white people', his name Nene sounded like her own 'Nini', the diminutive of Jean by which she was still known at home.

By contrast, the *Journals'* poems were 'full of mystery and wonder'. John

Keats, Walter de la Mare, John Drinkwater and Christina Rossetti were the editors' first choices, followed by Alfred Noyes and John Masefield 'to give the rollicking touch'. Janet especially liked Keats's 'Meg Merrilees'. 'Gypsies, beggers, robbers, swaggers, slaves, thieves, all the outcast victims of misfortune who yet might be angels in disguise, had become part of my dreams and comprehension of the Outside World. I learned by heart "Old Meg she was a gypsy . . .", and again, sharing my discovery at home by reciting it to the family, I was urged again and again to repeat it, and . . . each time I came to the line, "And 'stead of supper she would stare/ Full hard against the moon", everyone would laugh . . . When I thought of Meg, I felt the sadness that came with the way the words went in the poem, the same way words went in songs about Glasgow and the sidewalks of New York and the streets of Dublin . . .'[17]

Sadness in song and literature seemed to mirror the sadnesses that punctuated family life. Grandpa Frame had died at Eden Street ten days after suffering a stroke. As he had clung to life precariously, he had asked for a piper to remind him of his childhood days back in the Clyde Valley. 'How the sadness of the pipes filled that small house,' a Frame cousin remembered. 'Janet then was a wee white frightened crying face in a doorway.'[18] When Grandpa was at last laid out in the front room, Janet again declined an opportunity to 'view the body'. But she did join expeditions to the family grave in Oamaru Cemetery and was surprised to find her grandmother's name on the headstone, and — even more astonishing — her own, Janet Frame, 'died 13 months, 22 days'. This was the aunt after whom she had been named but in whom, up to that time, she had never really believed. Another of George Frame's sisters, Aunty Maggie, came to stay at Eden Street in the throes of throat cancer. She too died and was committed to the family plot.

Early in 1932 the family discovered a more traumatic and enduring source of tension and grief. One night, not long after Janet had thrown a lump of coal at her brother and hit him on the head, Geordie, now aged nine, suffered an epileptic seizure. Neither parent knew how to cope with this frightening visitation. ' "A convulsion, a convulsion," Mum kept saying in her earthquake-and-tidal-wave voice.'[19] Later, as the fits recurred and the family knew what to do to make it less likely that Geordie would injure himself, the sense of horror and helplessness persisted. And for Janet, who feared that she may have caused this problem, the fits produced additional anxiety and guilt.[20]

There were at this time no effective drugs to mitigate or control the condition. Large doses of bromide, the sole recourse of the family's doctor, only increased Geordie's confusion and fear. '[Each] day at home there were episodes of violent rage when he attacked us or threw whatever was at hand to throw. There had usually been somewhere within the family to find a "place" however cramped; now there seemed to be [none] . . . Mother, resisting fiercely the advice of the doctor to put [Geordie] in an institution, nursed him while we girls tried to survive on our own.'[21] Epileptics were then defined as 'mental defectives' under mental health legislation. And what Lottie actually said as she rejected the doctor's advice was, 'No child of mine is going to Seacliff,' which was the Otago mental hospital. In the case of her son at least this ambition was realised. Geordie, deaf as well as epileptic, left school before he turned twelve and, in the recollection of his siblings, his mother 'devoted all her time to him'.[22]

As the Frames struggled to cope with this new set of circumstances and George Frame to find money to pay for mounting doctors' visits and hospital bills run up in Lottie's search for treatment for their distressed son, another explosion further fractured family relationships.

Myrtle and Janet had been up to the pine plantation on the reserve with Poppy Firman and her older brother Ted. There, among cut branches and pine needles, Ted and Myrtle, aged twelve, had attempted sexual intercourse, probably unsuccessfully. For Janet, this incident was of as much interest as everything else that occurred in the course of a normal day. 'Myrtle and Ted did it in the plannies this afternoon,' she announced at the dinner table that evening. 'Did what?' her father asked. 'Fucked of course,' said Janet, displaying some of the new vocabulary for which she was indebted to her friend Poppy. There was an instant of silence. Then George Frame crashed a fist on the table and made everything and everybody jump. Myrtle was thrashed with her father's belt and the other children fled outside. They were forbidden to have further contact with the Firman family. The Firmans, after some kind of parallel crisis, were forbidden to speak with the Frames. Janet had lost her only friend.[23]

> Anyone observing me during those days would have seen an anxious child full of twitches and tics, standing alone in the playground at school, wearing day after day the same hand-me-down tartan skirt that was almost stiff with constant wear, for it was all I had to wear: a freckle-faced, frizzy-haired little girl who was somehow 'dirty' because the lady doctor chose her with the other known 'dirty and poor' children for a special examination . . . I had tide marks of dirt behind my knees and on my inner arms, and when I saw them I felt a wave of shock . . . I had been sure I had washed thoroughly.[24]

At home, however, she played hopscotch and fantasy games with her younger sisters; and she became a closer friend and confidante of Myrtle, now in her 'proficiency' year at school and — since the incident with Ted Firman — getting increasingly into arguments with her father about boys, slacks, lipstick, dances, going downtown on Friday nights, chewing gum, and using slang (of which 'okay chief' was the source of current offence). Like her younger sisters, Myrtle had dreams of being an actress or a dancer, stimulated as much by her parts in school plays and Gilbert and Sullivan operettas as by her attendance at Saturday film matinees. Such ambitions were raised further when Myrtle, thanks to a 'radio aunt' who was a relative by marriage, was chosen to recite her favourite poem, de la Mare's 'The Prince of Sleep', on one of Dunedin's 4XD radio programmes.

The reality was that Myrtle's options were limited. Her father, frazzled by money worries and what seemed to him to be his eldest daughter's provocative behaviour, said she would have to work in the woollen mill since they could not afford to send her to secondary school.[25] However, towards the end of what was to be her final year at primary school, 1933, Myrtle collapsed on the sports field and was taken home. When she collapsed a second time several months later, the doctor who examined her told Lottie Frame that her daughter had a heart defect and could die at any time. Lottie, appalled, told Janet but said nothing to Myrtle.[26] Instead she was allowed to leave school and take up light housework for a Mrs McGimpsey, an Eden Street widow with two children who could afford domestic help.[27] Working in the woollen mill, it was thought, would be too strenuous. 'For a time we watched and waited, curiously and fearfully,' Janet recalled. '[But] Myrtle didn't stop breathing, and we soon forgot, for death was stillness, and Myrtle was full of movement and dancing, and a wireless star too.'[28]

By the standards of most of their neighbours, family life at 56 Eden Street was austere and chaotic. The Frames lacked sheets, pillowslips, pyjamas, carpets, a vacuum cleaner and a cabinet of fine chinaware. They bought mince, the cheapest form of meat, specked fruit and stale cakes. They did not throw children's birthday parties. Christmas presents were modest, and the most interesting of them sent by one of the childless aunts, George's sister Isabel (Aunty Isy). Another Frame aunt, Polly, made and sent the only new dresses the girls ever owned. More often they donned cast-offs or hand-me-downs that were worn to the point of disintegration. The house was usually untidy, strewn with unfolded laundry and piles of newspapers. In the earlier years of the Frames' occupation it was in danger of being overrun by dogs and fleas. One visitor reported, in a horrified tone, that she had called on 'Mrs Frame' one afternoon and found her 'sitting at the kitchen table scribbling poetry on an envelope, surrounded by dirty dishes and flies — well . . .'[29] This was not 'normal' behaviour in a New Zealand town in the 1930s where, even amid poverty, pretension and social ambition were rife, and women's domestic reputations were made or broken according to whether or not they scrubbed their front doorsteps.[30]

To outsiders too the Frame children seemed at times to be out of control. 'We were not civilised,' Janet was to write of the years she was at primary school. '[We] giggled at Sunday *Bible* readings [which Lottie then abandoned], we wolfed our food, stuck out our elbows, did not come when called at bedtime, refused to fetch a shovel of coal when asked to: we ran wild and pulled faces and said Bum and Fart and Fuck.'[31] Such behaviour and the neighbours' knowledge of it led some mothers to forbid their offspring to play with them and others to turn Frames away at the door. When Janet went home from school with Wendy Patterson, whose father managed the woollen mill, she was told to wait at the gate while Wendy consulted her mother. When she returned, she told Janet, 'My mother says you're to go home. I'm not allowed to play with you [because] you're dirty and your sister goes with boys.' Janet walked away and 'didn't cry until I got home'.[32]

Informal ostracism had the effect of making the three younger sisters in particular more dependent on their own company and games and — at times — still more boisterous. Geordie tended to be excluded from these activities because of his propensity for fits, and for cruelty (on one occasion he hanged a litter of kittens and Janet and Myrtle found them 'stiff on the end of little short ropes').[33] Until he began to find casual work in his early teens, he usually made his own entertainment by combing the Coquet Street rubbish dump for books, furniture and other oddments, some of which the girls employed as stage props. One of his finds was a set of dark red velvet curtains that his sisters used to convert the ramshackle summer-house in front of the house into a makeshift theatre. For Janet, Isabel and June, this was confident preparation 'for our lives as actresses and concert performers'.

Such imaginative self-reliance served only to give some neighbours a heightened sense of superiority. The Frame girls, one recalled, 'didn't fit into the pattern of New Zealand life [and] never made any attempt to. They were rowdy children forever clomping around the house on the bare floorboards.'[34] The most indignant of these observers summoned the council health inspector, a Mr Albert Crumb. '[He] arrived without warning and, standing fiercely in the middle of the bedroom, next to the full chamber pot with its mixed shades of amber, and pointing to the unmade bed and the general untidiness, threatened Mother that if we did not get rid of the dogs and if "those children" didn't do something to help around the house, he would send [them] to the *Welfare*.'[35] This intervention resulted in (for a time) a reduction in the number of household pets; and in more strenuous attempts by the Frame parents to persuade their feral children to become more biddable.

Given that George Frame, unlike many Oamaru wage earners, retained his job throughout the Depression, and that his income was higher than the country's average wage, opinions varied as to why the family seemed poor through those years. Both Frame and Godfrey relatives, at different times, accused Lottie of poor household management or — indeed — an absence of management, and commented on her inability to make clothes.[36] Her immediate family, however, were inclined to attribute the sparseness of money to the medical bills generated by Geordie's illness (there was no social security until the election of the Labour Government in 1935, and doctors', specialists' and hospital bills were a considerable burden); and to Lottie's inclination to give money away to down-and-outs who came to the door and whose needs always seemed more pressing than her own. 'Consider the lilies of the field,' she would say, drawing on her biblical conviction that, however reduced the family circumstances, God, rather than budgeting, would ensure their well-being. There was the fact too that it was invariably Lottie who took in the terminally ill relatives — the Frame grandparents, Aunty Maggie with her cancer — and not the members of the family who criticised her supposed improvidence. As for the absence of firm discipline, her children saw this as a consequence of her inability to say anything sharp. 'She could not reprimand her family,' Janet would write later. 'She was cruel to nothing . . .'[37]

What nobody in the family doubted was Lottie's devotion to duty. Her children viewed it subsequently as a form of slavery on their behalf and that of their father. Their overwhelming memory would be of 'Mother in a constant state of family immersion even to the material evidence of the wet patch in front of her dress where she leaned over the sink, washing dishes, or over the copper and washtub, or, kneeling, wiping the floor with oddly shaped floorcloths . . . or, to keep at bay the headache and tiredness of the hot summer, the vinegar-soaked rag she wrapped around her forehead: an immersion so deep that it achieved the opposite effect, making her seem to be seldom at home, in the present tense, or like an unreal person with her real self washed away'.[38]

That real self, however, when it indubitably *was* present, revealed the depths of Lottie's Christadelphian convictions. She viewed the natural world, for example, as numinous, expressive of divinity; she gave ordinary things an aura of mystery and magic. 'She had only to say of any commonplace object, "Look, kiddies, a stone" to fill that stone with a wonder as if it were a holy object. She was able to imbue every insect, blade of grass, flower, the dangers and grandeurs of weather and the seasons, with a memorable importance along with a kind of uncertainty and humility that led us to ponder and try to discover the heart of everything.'[39] And though her children were sometimes able to best her in argument, by cleverness or abuse, it brought them no satisfaction. '[When] she was not quite equal she would raise her chin as if she were trying to keep her head above water and a blush would appear on each cheek and a moistness that was not tears but a kind of helplessness came into her eyes . . . [And] then our clever victory made us unhappy . . .'[40]

George Frame, on the other hand, was inclined to 'dourness with a strong sense of formal behaviour'.[41] Like most husbands of his day he offered little help with domestic chores. He went out into the world to support the family financially by doing dirty and physically taxing work; he expected in exchange to be waited on by his wife at home, that she would have his clothes ready to wear, his boots polished, his dinner on the table, even the sugar in his tea. And on days when he had time off from work he would take it fishing — for blue cod from the Oamaru wharf, or for salmon out of the Waitaki, Rakaia or Rangitata Rivers. This brought food for the table; but it also gave him a periodic release from stress not available to Lottie.

When he *was* at home, George found it increasingly difficult to discipline his rambunctious children. He would be tired, particularly if he had worked night shifts. He was worn down by the continuous difficulty of stretching his income to cover all family needs, particularly Geordie's doctor and hospital bills. He even, on occasions, threatened bankruptcy and suicide. More often, he would kiss every five-pound note that went through his hands with the incantation, 'Now you see me, now you don't.'[42] His interventions in his children's lives tended to be swift, hot-tempered applications of the belt to their backsides when misbehaviour, argument or noise was judged to have gone 'too far'. And yet all his children had tender memories of the increasingly rare occasions when he sang sentimental songs or told jokes; and of a far more congenial parent when they were with him away from home, walking downtown, fishing at the wharf, participating in the annual railways picnic at Hampden, or sharing one of the family's camping holidays.

Condemnation of what was perceived as the family's 'batty ways' or lack of discipline was not universal.[43] Friends such as the Luxons at Ardgowan or the Walkers from Wyndham, who sometimes took family holidays with the Frames or had Myrtle to stay, and Mrs Violet Feathers, who owned the grocer's shop in Eden Street, admired Lottie's devoted sense of duty and the spiritedness and intelligence of the Frame girls. They were also compassionate in the face of the family's continuing money shortages. Mrs Feathers in particular allowed them to run up large accounts and never refused the family food on the basis of outstanding debt. She also took delight in giving the children treats — sometimes biscuits and confectionery, and always threepence a week to enable them to go to the movies on Saturday afternoons. On one occasion when Myrtle complained of not having anything suitable to wear to a dance, Mrs Feathers lent her one of her daughter's dresses.[44] Other neighbours such as the Robsons and Naylors befriended the girls individually and had them in periodically for tea and biscuits, or simply for conversation.

At Oamaru North School, however, in the wake of the broken friendship with Poppy Firman, Janet felt desolate. 'I longed for impossible presents, a doll's house, a sleeping doll, birthday parties, pretty dresses, button-up shoes, patent leather instead of the lace-up leather shoes with their heavy soles and heel and toe plates, hair that fell over my face so that I could brush it away . . . instead of frizzy red hair "up like a bush" with everybody remarking on it.'[45] Her red hair was a particular source of inconvenience and shame; and cause of some of her most frightened moments in summer when flies would get trapped there 'and panic and buzz and buzz as if they were in a spider's web'.[46]

In standard four, with Janet aged nine, the atmosphere at school at least changed dramatically for her. She was now in Reuben Eutycus ('Gussy') Dimick's class. A gifted and popular teacher, he made Janet, for the first and only time in her life, the 'teacher's pet'. Mr Dimick would 'sit me on his knee while he taught the class, and sometimes he would give me a small, special table in front of the class to share with his small son, who was known as a "mongol" and whom I helped with his lessons . . . Under [his] care I blossomed then both as a scholar and as an athlete, for Gussy believed that because every child had a special talent he, as a teacher, had to give everyone a chance to discover [it].'[47]

The year culminated in Janet's winning the school dux medal for 1934 and a year's subscription to the town library, still known as 'the Athenaeum'. This last enabled her to flood her near-bookless household with reading matter for each member of the family. 'My mother (excited at the thought of communicating with the characters and poems of her past) begged, "Bring home Charles Dickens, bring home Nathaniel Hawthorne, Henry Wadsworth Longfellow, John Greenleaf Whittier, Mark Twain (that is, kiddies, Samuel Clemens)".' Janet dutifully found such volumes and brought them home, with a 'William' book for Geordie and 'something about the sea' for her father.[48] This both satisfied and intensified what June Frame would remember as a state of 'print starvation' in the family. And when the Athenaeum subscription expired, its annual renewal became one of the few luxuries the Frames allowed themselves.

News of the dux medal also reminded relatives that the younger Frame girls might need more clothing if, as seemed likely, they were destined for further education. And so 'there arrived a parcel of assorted clothes from Aunty Polly and from Aunty Isy — "aunt smelling" clothes in "aunts' colours", brown, purple, maroon, dark blue, which we divided amongst ourselves'. None of these provided Janet with the school uniform she now needed for junior high school, an intermediate-level school attached to Waitaki Girls' High School. For this, Lottie bought 'on tick' some grey flannel from which she tried to make a tunic, 'which turned out as a disastrously sewn and shaped hybrid garment, neither tunic nor dress, with a curiously cutaway yoke that exposed most of the front of my bunched white blouse'.[49] Although she knew this garment was 'funny', Janet was not unduly bothered at the time. She was far too excited about the subjects she was to take at junior high: the French lessons, and — in particular — English: for she knew from Myrtle that a whole new world of English poetry was about to open up for her.

Poetry had become a consuming interest. Before Janet had finished standard four, Gussy Dimick had set the class the task of writing a poem for homework, which had to begin with the line, 'When the sun goes down and the night draws nigh . . .' Janet's was read to the class with the poet ensconced on the teacher's knee:

When the sun goes down and the night draws nigh
and the evening shadows tint the sky
when the birds fly homeward to their nest
then we know it is time for rest.
When rabbits to their burrows run
and children have finished their daily fun
when the tiny stars come out to peep
then we know it is time for sleep.[50]

She was not wholly satisfied with this first poem. She had an argument with Myrtle over the use of the phrase 'tint the sky' (Janet favoured 'touch', while Myrtle insisted that 'tint' was more 'poetic'); and she was dismayed that the class was able to predict the end of each line as it was read aloud. On the whole, though, her family regarded the poem and its reception as a triumph, and George Frame, because he was secretary of the local branch of the railway union, was able to bring home for his daughter a 'railway notebook' with marbled page edges so that she could write down and keep future compositions. 'How I would tremble, and whisk them away to secret places and immediately set to work to rule my index for the poems . . . Captain Scott, Sand, A Longing, The Pine Trees, My Rainbow . . .'[51]

The family interest in poetry remained continuous and strong. Lottie still wrote verse almost daily, published it in a variety of papers and journals (including the *Dairy Exporter*, and the *New Zealand Mercury*, whose tastes were decidedly Georgian), and recited it to her children.[52] She was paid small sums for some of her efforts and always hoped to win the *Mercury's* monthly prize of half a guinea for the 'best' poem. At the height of the Depression, in 1933, she also sold poems and songs door to door in Oamaru, following the footsteps of her 'angel-tramps'. Some of these compositions were printed on postcards, some simply handwritten. She collaborated for a time with a music teacher from Gore, James Jesse Stroud, to write songs that they subsequently sold to the music store Chas Begg & Co. Only lack of money stopped her copyrighting one of her songs that won an Australasian competition and — an even stronger ambition — publishing a book of poems.[53]

Encouraged by her mother's literary aspirations, her father's gift of notebooks and an emphasis on poetry and 'verse speaking' by a new form teacher, Miss Catherine Lindsay, Janet began to write poetry in earnest in 1936, her second year at junior high school. At this time she decided she would be a poet when she 'grew up'.[54] Her earliest efforts, she was to say later, were 'a mixture of conventional ideas about "poetic" vocabulary and the cowboy and prison songs recorded in my other notebooks and the contents of the small popular song books brought home by Myrtle and the songs sung by my parents and grandparents'.[55] One such effort, in four verses, concluded:

> A memory, half-forgotten day
> so full of spring sunshines
> told by the trees that gently sway
> and whispered by the pines.[56]

Sensing 'the birth of something she had mourned as lost from her own life', Lottie Frame now encouraged all her children to write poems and stories for publication in the *Otago Daily Times*, in a children's page dedicated to 'Dot's Little Folk' (which had been a feature of a sister publication, the *Otago Witness*, since 1889). Each of the Little Folk was given a pseudonym and every contribution published received a reply. Janet, appropriately enough given her colouring, became 'Amber Butterfly'. Myrtle was 'Good Queen Charlotte', Geordie 'Sergeant Dick' (he had wanted to be 'Sergeant Dan', but that name was taken), Isabel 'Apple Petal' and June 'Dancing Fairy'.

The girls' published letters to Dot told of sisterly outings in the paddocks behind Eden Street and the things they observed in the course of such walks (ants, migrating birds, mushrooms), family rituals at Christmas and New Year, the antics of household pets, and adventures that occurred on family camping trips to the banks of the Waitaki and Rakaia Rivers. These events often gave rise to verses which were published with the correspondence, such as this one from Janet:

> Oh mushroom, white upon the ground,
> How did you come to grow,
> Making not one tiny sound
> Within the earth below?
> Were you at the fairies' ball
> Clothed in snow-white sheen?
> How did you come to grow at all
> Upon the grasses green?[57]

While these early poems may suffer from 'rather precious subject matter and overlush imagery', they do show metrical control and a confidence remarkable for someone who was not yet a teenager.[58] And Janet's letters to Dot frequently had a didactic quality that showed her thinking analytically about the world around her, and about the poems she was studying in Miss Lindsay's class, and wanting to share and debate her views. It is not difficult to see why her parents and teachers came to believe that she was destined for a career as a teacher. This, for example, written when she had just turned twelve, reveals the extent to which she and her generation were conditioned by English poetry (indeed, apart from Katherine Mansfield, whom the Frame girls discounted because of their mother's association with her family and her ardent commendations, they knew of no New Zealand writers or writing).

Dear Dot, Does it ever occur to you that Nature is really wonderful in her ways? She has given us spring, green grass, and everything one appreciates. Poets are people who put their appreciations into rhyme. Some of them express their thoughts far more clearly than others. I think that William Wordsworth's 'Daffodils' and 'From Westminster Bridge' are different forms of Nature. One form is when Nature is happy and wishes to make everybody else so, such as with golden gorse glittering in the sunshine . . . Two is a scene when she is unhappy and tired of the bustle and noise of London. She shrouds the world in a grey mist, from out of which the dull, muffled sounds of machinery are heard. This is Nature's idea of showing that she is tired of her surroundings. All she needs to do is brighten up the world by making flowers and things of joy . . . Some of the other Little Folk may have different opinions. This may well do for a debate . . . Well, Dot, I think I shall close, with love to every Little Folk and yourself.[59]

Among the innocent tributes to dogs and cats and butterflies and birds that constituted the greater part of Dot's Page, eight-year-old June Frame made a startling announcement in 1937. 'Dear Dot, I am sorry to say that we lost our sister, Good Queen Charlotte, in March. We miss her so much. But we are going to see her when she wakes again . . . Love to the happy band and your dear self. Dancing Fairy (Oamaru).'[60]

The catastrophe had occurred at the end of a long hot summer. Janet completed junior high school with her proficiency certificate in December 1936 and came first in English and arithmetic and fourth in history and French. She had been accepted for a place at Oamaru's only secondary school for girls, Waitaki Girls' High School. Her parents, impressed by her continuing high place in her classes and her intelligent interest in the world about her, now took it for granted that their second daughter, like 'cousin Peg who emigrated to Canada', was headed for a career in teaching (though Janet's own secret ambition was still to be a poet).

'I dreaded returning to school,' she wrote of the summer of 1936/37, 'for I needed yet another uniform for the senior high, another tunic, dark grey serge, with a black felt hat and black beret for winter and a white panama hat for summer; grey flannel blouses and white cotton blouses as for the junior high, a white dress for the garden party at the end of the year and the school breakup in the Opera House; and a coloured girdle, the colour depending on which of the four Houses, named after the first four principals of Waitaki, we were ballotted into. Fortunately Aunty Polly had volunteered to sew my school tunic and, hoping that all would be well but dreading that it wouldn't, I waited for the parcel . . .'[61]

After day trips to Friendly Bay in the lee of the wharf and the Oamaru breakwater and to Caroline Bay in Timaru, the family took a camping holiday on the bank of the Rakaia River, where George fished for salmon and Lottie cooked, washed clothes, kept the billy boiling and wrote poems. The children, joined by their new Catholic friend from over the road, Marguerite Miller, 'explored, played, ate, boasting to Marguerite, yet submitting to her foreign power, speaking her language, playing her games . . . [How] we envied her mysterious life with priests and nuns and Confession and holy water'.[62] When they returned to Oamaru, school openings were delayed by an epidemic of polio, known as infantile paralysis. Janet began her secondary lessons by correspondence. There was a moment of fear when the photographs from the Rakaia holiday were developed and in one of them Myrtle appeared to be transparent. Omens of this sort always reminded Lottie of the doctor's warning about her oldest daughter's heart. But, despite the photograph, despite the warning, Myrtle bloomed and the moment passed.

On 5 March Janet was studying at the kitchen table and thinking about the books she would need for the coming school year. Myrtle asked her to come swimming with her at the town baths, but Janet declined and they quarrelled. Myrtle also quarrelled with her mother, who tried to talk her out of swimming, without quite saying why she was afraid. Myrtle was stubborn. She was a strong swimmer, a competent diver and a member of the Oamaru Swimming Club. She would swim when she felt like it. As her oldest sister struck out defiantly down the road, June heard her sing:

> And when I die
> Don't bury me at all,
> Just pickle my bones
> In alcohol . . .[63]

In the late afternoon a stranger came to the house and Lottie, thinking he was a salesman — he was *not* an angel, too well dressed — tried to close the door in his face. 'I'm a doctor, Mrs Frame,' the man said. 'I've come to tell you about your daughter Myrtle. She's been drowned. They've taken her body to the morgue.'[64] Swimming on her own at the baths, Myrtle had been seen to get into difficulties. She was brought to the surface by another girl, fifteen-year-old June Craddock, and dragged from the pool. Artificial respiration failed to revive her. It fell to Lottie Frame to identify the body at the town morgue. In her deposition to the coroner, she described her sixteen-year-old daughter as a 'well developed girl [who] looked older than she was'.[65]

As she tried to absorb the news that Myrtle was gone forever, Janet thought at first that she might be glad. '[There'd] be no more quarrels, crying, thrashings, with Dad trying to control her and angry with her and us listening frightened, pitying and crying too. Then the sad fact came home to me that there might be a prospect of peace, but the cost was the entire removal of Myrtle, not just for a holiday or next door or downtown or anywhere in the world, but off the face of the earth and out of the world . . . [My] teasing, pinching, thumping elder sister who knew more than I and who would some day have made music, boys, clothes, love, a mansion . . . [Her] removal was stressed when she didn't come home that night to do the things she ordinarily did, to finish what she had begun in the morning, bring in the shoes cleaned with white cleaner and left to dry on the washhouse windowsill in the sun.'[66]

Other events drove home the reality. For the first time the Frame children saw their father cry. After the inquest, which noted simply that she had drowned and did not investigate the condition of her heart, Myrtle's body was brought home and lay in an open coffin in the spare bedroom. When Lottie asked if they wanted to 'see Myrtle', Janet and June said no. 'We'll see her on Resurrection Day,' Lottie assured them, leaning heavily if desperately on the framework of her Christadelphian beliefs.[67] Her surviving daughters, envisaging a Resurrection Day of 'crowds, scanning of faces, the panic as centuries of people confront each other', were less confident.

After the funeral Janet began to explore the poetry book that, with Shakespeare's plays, would provide the basis for her early secondary school English studies: *Mount Helicon*. To her amazement she discovered that many of the poets 'knew about Myrtle's death and how strange it was without her . . . [In] each day there was a blankness, a Myrtle-missing part, and it was upon this blankness that the poets in *Mount Helicon* were writing the story of my feelings.' One was Walt Whitman, whose poem 'The Lost Mate' seemed to articulate everything that Janet was feeling. Another was Edgar Allan Poe's 'Annabel Lee':

> For the moon never beams without bringing me dreams
> Of the beautiful Annabel Lee;
> And the stars never rise but I see the bright eyes
> Of the beautiful Annabel Lee . . .
>
> I was a child and she was a child,
> In this kingdom by the sea:
> But we loved with a love that was more than love –
> I and my Annabel Lee . . . [68]

It was the words 'kingdom by the sea' that confirmed for Janet that the poet spoke to her directly. Without a doubt, Oamaru was 'the kingdom by the sea . . . Oamaru with its wild sea beyond the breakwater and the friendly bay safe within, with the sound of the sea in our ears day and night.'[69]

From that time, 'kingdom by the sea' was the phrase that characterised for Janet Frame her home town. It linked Oamaru to her memory of the loss of Myrtle, and it invested the town and with it the whole temporal world with the kinds of imaginative reverberations and consolations she would find in poetry. What she came to seek, she wrote later, was 'an imagination that would inhabit the world of fact, descend like a shining light upon the ordinary life of Eden Street, and not force me to exist in an "elsewhere". I wanted the light to shine upon the pigeons of Glen Street, the plum trees in our garden, the two japonica bushes (one red, one yellow), our pine plantations and gully, our summer house, our lives and our home, the world of Oamaru, the kingdom by the sea.'[70] It was the death of her sister Myrtle that helped create a need for this transformation; and it was the poetry she read in the wake of that death that pointed to a direction by which it might be accomplished.

CHAPTER THREE

# *Like Cousin Peg . . .*

𝓜ATTERS OF SCHOOLING IN OAMARU IN THE 1930S AND EARLY 1940S were dominated by two educationists who, in the eyes of their students and townsfolk, bestrode their respective domains like colossi: Jessie Banks Wilson, known as 'J.B.', headmistress of Waitaki Girls' High School; and Frank Milner, 'the Man', headmaster of Waitaki Boys' High School. Both had been appointed principals as outstanding young teachers. Both retained their positions for exceptionally long careers — three decades in the case of Miss Wilson, four in Frank Milner's. Although their schools were public ones established initially to cater for the secondary educational needs of Oamaru, each had a significant boarding establishment and reputations that attracted pupils from further afield.

Of the two, the boys' school was the better known, nationally and vocationally. But that was largely a reflection of the times: male alumni invariably went on to more visible public careers than women, the majority of whose lives were expected to be fully absorbed in the roles of wives and mothers and the tasks of domesticity. Waitaki Boys' High was viewed widely as a fertile training ground for scholars and for business and community leaders. Katherine Mansfield's brother Leslie Beauchamp had been a pupil. And two of its boarders from the 1920s, Charles Brasch and James Bertram, would figure later in Janet Frame's life, one as a patron and editor, the other as a literary critic and reviewer.

Nevertheless the girls' school contributed a small quota of scholars, teachers, librarians and health professionals to the national work force. J.B. Wilson and her senior staff, almost all of them well qualified spinsters,* were determined that young women of academic ability be encouraged to undertake secondary education. In the case of Janet Frame and her contemporaries, the introduction

---

* It was widely assumed by pupils that these women, including J.B. Wilson herself, had lost fiancés or 'intendeds' in the First World War. The fact was, however, that it was not acceptable for married women to teach at this time.

42

by the new Labour Government of free secondary places the year before these girls started high school removed one potential barrier, the cost, and eventually resulted in a higher percentage of women undertaking secondary courses. The brightest of these women at Waitaki Girls' High School were encouraged to move on to tertiary education, especially for teacher training, the most popular and attainable career for academically able women, and one for which the girls' high's own staff provided role models.

By the time Janet Frame enrolled in the academic or professional stream at Waitaki Girls' High School in January 1937, the family decision had been taken that she would become a teacher, 'like Cousin Peg who emigrated from Scotland to Canada'.[1] This choice of career was duly noted on her admission form. Money shortages at home continued to influence her choice of courses, however. Her father insisted that she take geography in preference to Latin, for example, because the textbooks were cheaper. And he warned her that if the economic recovery from the Depression faltered and times turned 'hard' again, she might have to switch to the commercial stream, which included book-keeping, shorthand and typing, or leave school altogether to contribute to the family income.

The teaching year did not begin until late March, when health authorities declared that the infantile paralysis epidemic was over. Janet took her place wearing a cobbled-together uniform that included the tunic which Aunty Polly had made far more satisfactorily than the one Lottie Frame had attempted two years earlier. This garment would have to survive six years of wear and tear and drastic adolescent bodily alterations. Aunty Polly's blazer, although well tailored, was the wrong colour and had to be reserved for home use. As before, Janet longed to 'fit in', to look like everybody else and be accepted as one of her peers.

While courses, books and teachers were all new to Janet, the school itself was not. The junior high which she had attended for the previous two years was on the same property as the senior school and shared its assemblies and sports facilities. So the magisterial Miss Wilson, 'big, with a head shaped like a bull and no neck to speak of', was already known to Janet by sight and by repute.[2] She had been characterised in a Frame family rhyme based on a popular poem about the *Titanic*:

> Out from the rooms at Waitaki
> Steamed on her maiden trip
> The magnificent J.B. Wilson,
> That mighty modern ship —
> Fifteen thousand tons of flesh
> Breasting the ocean waves [3]

Part of the culture of Waitaki Girls' High School was a strong competitive spirit. As Janet remembered it, 'if you were near the "top", as I, to my surprise, found myself, you lived in glory and privilege'. If you were among the rest, however, you suffered 'constant sarcasm from the teachers'.[4] Janet remained 'near the top' for almost all her years at secondary school, consistently coming first or second, sometimes third, in her chosen subjects. She was outstandingly proficient in English, French and mathematics. In all but her last term at school she was rated 'very good' for conduct, diligence and progress.[5] In Janet's second year Miss Wilson introduced speech contests, and Janet took the fourth form prize with an oration on — appropriately enough — Mungo Park, the Scottish explorer of Africa. She won books at each of the school's annual prizegivings: *Silas Marner, Emma, Boys and Girls Who Became Famous*, an illustrated volume on India, *The Oxford Book of Light Verse*, and complete works of Henry Wadsworth Longfellow and Rupert Brooke. After securing these prizes, Janet told a friend many years later, 'I would walk through the streets of our one-horse town with a glow in my heart, and a certainty that everyone was thinking, "There's Janet Frame of the clever Frame family, you know".'[6]

Such feelings were perhaps compensation for the fact that Janet felt she had no close friends at school over these years, and no suitors from the boys' high to make up for this absence. But she was part of a small group of scholars — Wendy Patterson, Marjorie Gray, Esme Miller, herself — which was often left to work on its own, especially in mathematics, ahead of the rest of the class. Wendy Patterson was the brightest and the one who most often pipped Janet for first placings. Her father was manager of the woollen mills and the family lived in a large house facing the school across Ouse Street. It was characteristic that Janet would remember that the Pattersons had a large doll's house on the back verandah.[7] But she noted also, with respect, that Wendy had read 'all the children's classics . . . and she knew the answers to questions that we thought obscure and unanswerable, such as quotes from poems we had not read or heard of. She was the girl to whom my father referred when he said to me, "Well, did you beat W today?"'[8] It is not difficult to imagine George Frame, engine driver, union secretary and avid member of the Labour Party, taking some satisfaction in his girl besting the daughter of the mill manager.

There was another body of girls within her class whom Janet would refer to as 'the Group', who were not among the top scholars. But by sheer force of personality, 'a combination of power and privilege', they were able to 'impose upon the rest of the class their taste in dress, manners, leisure activities, films, books, and their opinions on all topics . . . Their families were happier, funnier, more exciting than any others; and they all lived on the fabled South Hill. Even the teachers could not resist them, giving them regularly parts in class play-reading while we others watched and listened.'[9] Through her secondary school years and beyond them, Janet eyed the Group ambivalently — not sharing their values and preoccupations, but envious of the ease with which they appeared to live their lives and command attention and approval.[10]

At home in Eden Street some things had changed as a result of Myrtle's death. Lottie Frame seemed more tense, her voice 'high-pitched, in a permanent state of panic'.[11] Her husband displayed a fearfulness that was 'not in common with his usual forcefulness and dominance of the household'.[12] Much of the anger he had previously directed at Myrtle was now concentrated on Geordie, who was unable to find sustained employment — he was usually dismissed from casual work when employers discovered that he was epileptic — and he had discovered the delights of the town billiard parlour and the anaesthetising effect of alcohol. Confronted by frequent and noisy rows between father and son, Janet the scholar was allowed to retreat to the front room, 'where before only the dead and guests had slept', to study and complete school assignments, and to write letters to her French and Canadian penfriends, whom she had discovered through her membership of Dot's Little Folk.[13]

In a deliberate effort to lift family morale and recreate 'the good old days' at Wyndham, George Frame bought a house cow, a Jersey–Ayrshire cross named Scrapers. He obtained council permission to graze her, and subsequently a second cow, on the hill reserve behind Eden Street. Because of Geordie's ill-health and the youth of her sisters, it usually fell to Janet to carry out the daily milking. This was an added responsibility in the course of already full days and often left her school uniform dirty. But she grew to enjoy and value the time spent on the hillside with the animals. She enjoyed even more the walk to and from the hill in the company of Mac, the retired farm dog who was now the principal family pet, or Winkles the cat. Janet frequently sat on the top of the hill with either pet, stared down on her 'kingdom by the sea', and composed the poems she would later transfer into one of her railway notebooks.[14] Her one big argument with her mother over Christadelphian principles arose from that faith's insistence that 'animals have no place in the Kingdom of God'.[15]

After Janet's fourteenth birthday she became a contributor to Dot's Senior Page in the *Otago Daily Times*, and a little later had poems published in the children's section of the *Oamaru Mail* using a new *nom de plume*, 'Amera', a Maori-sounding near-anagram of Frame.[16] She entered a competition sponsored by the radio station 3YA and heard her winning poem broadcast; and she had other verse published in *Truth*, the *Dairy Exporter* and *Railways Magazine*. The *Railways Magazine* poem, for which she was paid one guinea, subsequently appeared in an anthology of work by New Zealand children edited by Tom Mills.[17]

By this time she was well on the way to being known as 'poetic and imaginative', she wrote subsequently. 'I have often wondered in which world I might have lived my "real" life had not the world of literature been given to me by my mother and by the school syllabus, and even by the death of Myrtle. It was my insistence on bringing this world home, rather than vanishing within it, that increased my desire to write, for how else could I anchor that world within this everyday world where I hadn't the slightest doubt that it belonged?' Such writing was also prompted, she noted, by a continuing need to have 'my place . . . [somewhere] undisturbed by outward pressures and expectations'.[18]

Her sisters too continued to write, poetry and imaginative prose. Janet thought Isabel's work the best, 'for she covered a wide range of experience unknown to her, set in other countries, too, where she had never been. June's was . . . the most poetic, for she used the "poetic" words, "dream", "misty", "stars lost", and so on, although her poems were vague, with few facts. My own poems, which usually had a satisfying ending, were in strict form, usually with the expected rhymes [but] lacking the vague otherworldliness which I admired in June's . . .'[19] All three sisters would attempt to write novels, but made little progress beyond titles — 'There Is Sweet Music', 'Go Shepherd', 'The Vision of the Dust' — and early chapters.[20] Once June had started junior high school, they intensified their intimacy by speaking French to one another at home, a 'secret' language that excluded their parents and their brother. Their shared rapport, and the inability of others to be part of it, led more than one teacher to exclaim in exasperation, 'You Frame girls, you think you are so different . . .' It also, in the opinion of one of her staff, led Miss Wilson, who disapproved of nonconformity and what she regarded as eccentricity, to treat the Frame sisters with more severity than she directed at other pupils.[21]

In one of Janet's 1937 prize books, *Boys and Girls Who Became Famous*, the sisters discovered the story of the Brontës and embraced it as their own.

> We felt close to the self-contained family with the 'wild' brother, the far-off parents going about their daily tasks, the Brontës with their moors, us with our hill and gully and pine plantations. They knew death in their family, as we had, and their lives were so much more tragic than [ours] that we could give them, thankfully, the sad feelings which sometimes overcame us, and giving our feelings to the Brontës was a much more satisfying exercise than offering them to Jeanette MacDonald and Nelson Eddy . . . Even my cherished cowboy songs and sad poems ('The dog at his master's grave') could not receive what we gave to the Brontës and what I now gave to the newly discovered [school] music ('Thou holy art in many hours of sadness') . . . I felt that life was very serious now. I thought sometimes, with curiosity and apprehension, about the state known as the future.[22]

In her mid-teens, about the time she began to menstruate and to feel 'imprisoned' in her increasingly ill-fitting school tunic, Janet's sense of apprehension grew. And, in preference to confiding in 'Emily' or 'Anne', her Brontë-sisters, Janet started to keep a diary addressed to the bearded ruler of an imaginary valley-world she called the Land of Ardenue. She began increasingly to dwell in this world 'whose characters were drawn from objects and people I met in my daily life, with occasional intrusion of characters from fiction'. Those characters included Hush, the Sea-Foam-Youth-Grown-Old, the Green Man, the Elfin Ran Boy, Wimere, Lovan, Arema Chale and Lanell. 'My home task of milking . . . enabled me to spend hours on the hills . . .

talking to and exchanging opinions with my characters while I persuaded the cows . . . to "let down" their milk.'[23]

One of the diaries from this time has survived. It provides a window into Janet's preoccupations, sensibilities and mood swings in the early 1940s:

Mr Ardenue, today was exquisite. Mac and I walked the hill in the evening, I absorbed in imagining a poem, Mac in his own dog-like pursuits . . . Somehow life is composed of cats and dogs and cows. Yet animals live once! Theirs is one life and one death! And we — stupid creatures some of us — are destined for immortality . . . I saw Mac staring at the sky and I felt sorrowful because I could not understand his soul. Goodnight.

§

Mr Ardenue, I want to write and write and imagine. I can imagine and imagine. God, kill me if I cannot write . . . I want to make something beautiful. I shall know it is beautiful as I know the stars and the night, and the moon and everything of the earth is beautiful. I shall not rest until I write something that affects me as the earth — her trees and stars affect me. Mr Ardenue, I am dead serious.

§

On Friday we read 'Ode on Intimations of Immortality' . . . I cried over it. Miss Macaulay saw. I can't help it. Whenever she reads poetry . . . a great sense of peace steals over me — peace, and sometimes other feelings. All the girls think I am mad . . . In future I shall be only physically present in this world — mentally & spiritually in other worlds . . . I wish I could see an angel. Goodnight.

§

Why need books have so much influence over me? I think I am too impressionable. Today I lived in dreams — I recited strange poetry to myself . . . If it were not for a feverish control I should at this very moment leap from my bed . . . and shout aloud to Eden Street — all the beautiful poetry I have read. I must do it. I must . . .

§

Today I walked out on Miss Macaulay. I was laughing. Everything seemed so funny . . . I imagined the wildest things. Katherine [Bradley] told me to stop . . . Then Miss Macaulay told me not to be silly. I am stupid. The slightest reproach I get at school I feel awful . . . I stared at the desk and my lips quivered frightfully. I stood up & walked from the room. I read Wordsworth's poetry to calm myself. Mr Ardenue . . . Why have I no self-control?

§

Tonight a mist like a blanket wraps the world. Dad is down on the wharf fishing. He wanted somebody to go with him. I would have gone, but I had no clean dress. Now — I think of him all alone on the wharf — staring into the mist with his very very blue eyes. Mr Ardenue, I think I am selfish.

§

I am a moral coward — irresolute and afraid to look life in the face . . . I must consider [real] things. There is a world at war. I think I shall go mad if [the] war continues because I cannot bear to think of people fighting and quarrelling . . . I can't realize a world exists . . . I can't realize reality.[24]

The Second World War had begun in September 1939, impinging on Janet 'in the midst of a concentration of characters from fiction and poetry, inhabitants of the Land of Ardenue . . . I had never felt so shocked . . . I had honestly believed that the days of war were over'.[25] They were not, of course, and the community of Oamaru, like other towns in the British Empire, was 'seized by a kind of madness, as if the Declaration of War were an exciting gift'.[26] Part of that 'madness' was the celebration of the country's centennial in 1940 — the anniversary of the annexation of New Zealand by the British Crown. Early in the year Janet, Isabel and June travelled with a Waitaki Girls' High School party to Wellington by ferry from Christchurch (their first venture to the North Island) to view the Centennial Exhibition, a chauvinist showcase for the country's industrial, material and social 'progress'. The Frame girls, however, who met Godfrey cousins for the first time in the capital city, spent most of the week avoiding the educational displays and running riot instead in the exhibition's fun fair precinct.

Back in Oamaru, young men were donning uniforms as they volunteered for war service. Troop trains passed through the town with increasing frequency. Concerts in the Opera House raised funds for 'patriotic purposes'. At home at Eden Street, George Frame commanded his children keep quiet during the radio bulletins of 'war news', just as he had required silence during the broadcasts of proceedings from Parliament. After the battles in Greece and Crete in 1941, local names began to appear in the casualty lists. A neighbour, Bluey Walsh, went missing in action. Myrtle's old boyfriend Vincent was killed. After the fall of Singapore and Pearl Harbor to the Japanese forces at the end of that year, an invasion of New Zealand seemed possible. Oamaru was 'blacked out' at night so as not to provide a coastal target. Bread, butter, meat, tea and sugar were rationed. Janet's father and brother 'joined up'.[27] George Frame, veteran of the Great War, went into the army's national reserve in 1940; Geordie, medically unfit for army service, into the Home Guard. For Janet, the last years at school became linked inextricably to war: the reading of casualty lists, the hymns, *Bible* readings and prayers for 'the fallen' at school assemblies; the blood-drenched rhetoric of Frank Milner's oratory in the course of joint school Scott Memorial Day services in the Hall of Memories at Waitaki Boys' High.[28]

In those years Janet continued to perform well academically and to win speech prizes. She passed her University Entrance examination in 1940 and in that same year was *proxime accessit* to the dux, her old rival Wendy Patterson (duxes were at that time selected from third-year classes, because the numbers fell away so drastically in the sixth-form years). She also became captain of the B basketball team and — the example of Myrtle's death never far from her mind — gained a certificate in lifesaving. In her last year at Waitaki Girls' High School, 1942, she was a prefect and captain of Gibson House. By this time her class had dwindled to the four scholars, all of whom were now preparing themselves for tertiary education. 'We were like young birds on the edge of a cliff; wings fluttering; the air . . . filled with rustlings and testings and chatterings.'[29]

In retrospect, though, Janet would regard that final school year as 'the cruellest I had known'. Her front teeth were now decaying, because Social Security did not pay for dental treatment beyond primary school and the family had insufficient money to pay for a visit to a dentist. She tried to cover her mouth with her hand as she talked, or to keep her upper lip lowered over the discoloured teeth. And her school tunic 'was now so tightly fitting that it pressed on all parts of my body; it was torn and patched and patched again, but obviously it was no use having a new one . . . Also, I knew that my homemade sanitary towels showed their bulk and the blood leaked through, and when I stood up in class, I'd glance furtively at the desk seat to see whether it was bloody . . . [No] one "formed twos" with me in assembly or physical education . . . My shame was extreme; I concluded that I stank.'[30]

Home life was no happier. 'Our parents had receded from our lives. We discussed school affairs with them, asked them for money for this and that, and either were given it or not. We were impatient with their ignorance of school subjects. Aware now that my mother had turned increasingly to poetry for shelter, as I was doing, I, with an unfeelingness based on misery of feeling, challenged the worth of some of her beloved poets, aware that my criticism left her flushed and unhappy while I felt savage joy at her distress.'[31] Geordie, relying more heavily on alcohol at this time and making his own 'home brew', was in 'a turmoil of adolescent confusion and depression at his sickness, having to bear Dad's continuing belief that "he could stop the fits if he wanted to" and Mother's urging, "Be strong" . . . Sometimes he was brought home after being found lying in the gutter outside the billiard room.'[32] One of the few people in Oamaru who took a genuine interest in Geordie at this time and tried to increase his self-esteem as a means of turning him away from alcohol was the local Church of Christ pastor, Garfield Todd, who, a decade later, would become prime minister of Southern Rhodesia. Isabel, who turned sixteen in 1942, was turning out to be 'fearless, adventurous, rebellious, a rule-breaker', as Myrtle had been. June was quiet and fey, and sometimes over-looked.[33] The domestic atmosphere on the whole was agitated.

Janet, feeling vulnerable about her appearance at school and still subject to unexpectedly strong waves of unresolved grief over Myrtle's death five years before, found it increasingly difficult to insulate herself from these tensions. She continued too to worry about 'the future', and about whether the teaching career that everybody took for granted she would follow was in fact what she wanted to do. As the year advanced, she slid towards some kind of breakdown. 'I am convinced that I shall commit suicide soon,' she confided to her diary. 'I could never bear a repetition of the agony I feel sometimes. Why . . . ? There is no bodily pain? I [just] want to cry and cry at the slightest sadness.' And later: 'I get fits of melancholy more frequently now. I will die. I will commit suicide. Why should I live? I hate myself.'[34]

This descent into a misery that she felt unable to relieve or divert, or even to speak about anywhere other than in her diary, resulted at the end of the year in the only poor examination results in her entire school career. After coming first in her class in English literature and grammar over the previous three years, she slipped to last. She was second-to-last in algebra. She did manage her customary first in French and a second in geometry; but her conduct, diligence and progress ratings all dropped from 'very good' to 'good'.[35]

What broke or at least interrupted a self-reinforcing cycle of depression was a dramatic change in circumstance and location. Her application for a place at Dunedin Teachers' Training College was accepted. Staff there were favourably impressed with all but her most recent school results; and with the fact that she was a cousin (albeit by marriage) of Iona Livingston, a daughter of one of Janet's Aunty Han's sisters. Iona, who had been a source of envy to the Frame girls because of her success in singing and dancing talent quests, was an outstandingly good student at teachers' college. Any relation of hers, the principal believed, would be a promising prospect.[36]

And so, with a monthly pay cheque of nine pounds three shillings and nine pence, Janet was to board with her Aunty Isy and Uncle George Renwick in a Victorian terraced cottage in Dunedin, undergo teacher training, and attend university lectures part-time. As a ritual act of separation from her 'old' life, she burned her notebooks of poems and all but one of her Ardenue diaries.[37]

The Dunedin to which Janet Frame returned in February 1943, eighteen and a half years after her birth there, was a city in conspicuous decline. The commercial and public buildings raised in the era of prosperity remained, but now seemed, at best, tarnished, at worst, shabby. There had been little in the way of recent downtown construction. Many of the mansions in the inner city had been abandoned by the wealthy and converted into offices or apartments. Carroll Street, where Janet would board with the Renwicks, was a working class area whose population was shifting to newer suburbs on the city's outer rim. It was known locally as the 'Syrian quarter' and was close to McLaggan Street, said to be the haunt of prostitutes and Chinese opium smokers. In the words of Janet's teachers' college principal, Mr Eric Partridge ('Party'), it was 'not a savoury area at all . . .'[38]

This was news to Janet. But she *was* disappointed in the house itself, 4 Garden Terrace, a lane off Carroll Street. Where she had imagined 'a place of light with a terraced garden looking down over the bays of the peninsula', what she got was a 'tiny room that looked out over brick walls [and] miles of buildings with tall chimneys'.[39] The Renwicks' brick cottage had 'a tiny scullery with a sink bench just inside the back door, a sitting-dining room, known as the "wee" room [and] the "best" sitting-room, just inside the front door. Upstairs [the] two bedrooms, both small. The bathroom was downstairs in the washhouse leading from the scullery.'[40]

Aunty Isy, Isabella Renwick, one of George Frame's two surviving sisters, worked in the Roslyn woollen mill. She presided over a spartan household and served frugal meals — made more frugal for Janet by a reckless declaration that she was vegetarian and ate very little (all part of establishing a soon-to-be-regretted reputation of being 'a lovely girl, no trouble at all'). Isy's husband, George, was a wool clerk who lay in bed upstairs, grey-pallored and dying slowly from lung cancer. The only other occupant was Billy the budgerigar, who could say 'Pretty boy, Billy' and 'Up the stairs to bed'. The whole establishment was redolent of the 'quiet desperation' of the ordinary. But the advantage for Janet was that she was to pay ten shillings a week board in a city where the going rate was closer to thirty shillings. Uncle George's two sisters lived next door. One of them, Aunty Molly, was the 'radio aunt' who had arranged the broadcast of Myrtle's poetry recital.

Janet began the year appehensive about the very idea of teaching. But what was the alternative, apart from her secret ambition to be a poet? She was fearful too of the challenges presented by a new life in a new institution, the Dunedin Teachers' Training College. The college was housed in one of the few new buildings in the city, in Union Street, adjacent to Otago University, providing an environment that Janet found pristine and clean to the point of sterility. Because of wartime conscription, there were nearly five times as many female students as male. The few men at college, Janet noted, were 'quickly claimed by the beautiful blonde women while the rest . . . survived by daydreaming of what might be and by concentrating admiration on the most handsome lecturers'.[41]

The two-year course she now faced would prepare her for teaching primary schoolchildren, aged from five to twelve, and would alternate classes at college with periods of supervised teaching in schools around Dunedin. Assuming she obtained satisfactory grades for these activities and associated examinations, she would then undertake a 'probationary' year of teaching, after which she would receive her professional qualification, a teacher's certificate. In February 1943 it seemed a lengthy process and a daunting one.

It came as a surprise to Janet to find that she enjoyed the first week at college, when all first-year students shared the newness and the strangeness. 'The gradual learning of the language, the attitudes, customs of behaviour and dress, produced in me a euphoria of belonging which was intensified and contradicted by my actual feeling of isolation.'[42] As the novelty evaporated, so did the euphoria. The college teaching programme was intensive and tightly timetabled. Students concentrated for most of each day on one field of study — music, say, art, crafts, homecraft, nature study, geography, history, English, or physical education — into which allied subjects were closely integrated. They had four three-week postings into local schools to observe and practise teaching (increased to five in the second year). Half the students, including Janet, enrolled in papers at Otago University, their fees paid by the college. Such additional study, in approved subjects, was considered to add to the student's qualifications for teaching. In practice, students from lower income families often went to teachers' college specifically to gain access to a university education. The best and the most ambitious of them were then able to launch themselves into careers as university teachers.

Janet's university subjects were English and French. Within weeks of the start of the teaching year, she found almost her whole life filled with the need to attend lectures, and to study and read: at college and university during the day, and in the cold scullery (where she ate alone) and bedroom at Garden Terrace at night.

In spite of meeting up with two contemporaries from Waitaki Girls' High School, Katherine Bradley and Rona Pinder, and starting a tentative friendship with an equally shy girl from Stewart Island, Sheila Traill, Janet took little part in college social life. She instinctively avoided the common-room and, at university, the cafeteria, noisy jostling places where most interaction occurred. Fellow students from this time remember her for her 'wild mop of frizzy red hair'; but also for her solitariness. The most common words associated with her behaviour were 'detached', 'shy', 'different', even 'forbidding'.[43] Her college record described her as 'highly intelligent', but 'lacking in social sense . . . [she] seems a lone friendless person always by herself'.[44]

Writing years later of that time, Janet Frame described her life and that of a handful of other timid students as 'frail, full of agonies of embarrassment and regret, of misunderstood communication and strong with the intense feeling of wonder at the torrent of ideas released by books, music, art, other people; it was a time of finding shelter among the mightily capitalled abstractions of

Love, Life, Time, Age, Youth, Imagination'.[45] Her only romance, she said, came from those old friends; literature and poetry. In the course of this year, with the encouragement of teachers' college staff, she was reading James Joyce and Virginia Woolf, and the poetry of W.H. Auden, George Barker, T.S. Eliot, Louis MacNeice and Laura Riding, and Dylan Thomas, 'the hero, then . . . of every student who read or wrote poetry'.[46]

She found most stimulation in the performances of her university English lecturers, Professor Herbert Ramsay and Gregor Cameron, and in their respective and resonant analyses of Shakespeare, and of *Beowulf, Piers Plowman* and Chaucer. Every line of *Measure for Measure* '[stirred] in me a host of ideas, crowding avenues of dreaming, lines of poems . . .'[47]

As she had done in other places, Janet looked for and found a place of her own: the Southern Cemetery which ran along the ridge at the top of Carroll Street. Here, among the 'old dead of Dunedin', she mentally pursued the dreams released by her lectures and reading, and she composed poems that were influenced by Gerard Manley Hopkins, Dylan Thomas and George Barker. One of these she wrote on the endpapers of a book on Giotto, her sixth form art prize from Waitaki Girls' High School.

> Giotto alone through
> serious red roofs
> and social gravity of smoke
> sees St Francis
> by the watered rock
>
> but here the passage of city bells
> is explored
> by no Giotto
> to the final resting water
>
> only limping he passes
> from the woman crying
> 'noli me tangere'
> to St Francis alone in the Octagon,
> under the sycamore trees
> given alas no pathetic honouring[48]

She also used the cracks and crevices of the cemetery to dispose of the soiled sanitary towels that she was too embarrassed to burn at Garden Terrace. And as she sat there, staring at the roofs of the city, thinking, dreaming, remembering, she ate Caramello chocolate as a distraction from loneliness and from the hunger that was a consequence of eating so sparingly at Aunty Isy's, where, locked into her role of 'lovely girl, no trouble at all', she could not bring herself to complain about the tiny meals and the cold.[49]

Family associations failed to provide alternative sources of support and comfort. Janet established no intimacy with the Renwicks. Indeed, she scarcely knew Uncle George, nor anything about him, other than the fact that he had been a clerk and had once lived at Middlemarch. In the company of her aunt she never even reached the point where they could talk about George's illness let alone anything as personal as feelings. She occasionally visited the uncle she regarded as her father's 'nicest' brother, Bob Frame, a baker, and his wife, Aunty Han, with whom she had once stayed briefly as a small child. They at least were prepared to 'feed her up' on cake and buns. But, again, because of the compliant role in which Janet had cast herself, there could be no discussion of 'problems'. And her Uncle Bob was a depressive who became 'sadder and sadder' and four years later would attempt to commit suicide by cutting his own throat — an action that filled Janet and other members of the family with horror.

Life was no more inviting in Oamaru. When Janet returned home periodically, it was to find that the hostility between her father and brother had, if anything, intensified. Her mother, as ever, refused to acknowledge the presence of real problems and looked for relief to the Second Coming of Christ. She also took refuge now in another dream which Janet found equally bizarre: that each of her daughters be given a white fox fur on her twenty-first birthday. Isabel and June were fully preoccupied with high school and with their own lives, from which Janet now felt excluded.[50] One of the few ways in which she impinged on them was by insisting that they start calling her by her real name, Janet, instead of Jean or Nini.[51]

Far from finding consolation in these visits to Eden Street, Janet was driven to behave in ways that widened rather than diminished the gap between her family and her new life. 'The ignorance of my parents infuriated me,' she wrote.

> They knew nothing of Sigmund Freud, of *The Golden Bough*, of T.S. Eliot . . . Overwhelmed with the flood of new knowledge I was bursting with information about the Mind, the Soul, the Child, both the Normal Child and the Young Delinquent, where I had only recently learned that there was such a creature as The Child. All were described, measured, labelled, expounded in detail to my bewildered parents . . . I explained theories as if they were my own. I had accepted opinions on the classification of people partly because I was dazzled by the new language and its powerful vocabulary. I could now say to members of my family, 'That's rationalisation, that's sublimation, you're really frustrated sexually, your super-ego tells you but your id disagrees.' Mother blushed when I said the word 'sexually'. Dad frowned, and said nothing except, 'So that's what you learn at University and Training College . . .'[52]

[All] my family were part of the shared 'we' which I knew to be lost. I tried to use 'we' when I talked of my life as a student, but I knew it was futile, that I was describing what 'they', the students, did, where they went, how they felt, what they said, and in order to survive I had to conceal my 'I', what I really felt, thought and dreamed about. I had moved from the first person plural to a shadowy 'I', almost a nothingness, like a no-woman's land.[53]

Back in Dunedin, George Renwick expired on the long weekend holiday in June 1943, when Janet was walking the Otago Peninsula with the Bradley sisters, Katherine and Nancy. The body went next door to his sisters for the obsequies. Janet felt that 'a long-lasting dispute about the possession of Uncle George had been resolved'. Aunty Isy said nothing to Janet about her husband's death beyond announcing it. 'She took little time off work, a day or two to tidy the house and wash or burn a bundle of bed linen. Sometimes her face and eyes had a dusky look, like that of grief when there are no tears being shed.'[54]

Despite sources of stress — perhaps *because* she was able to distance herself from them through work, reading and poetry and had so few social distractions — Janet's academic results at the end of that first year were good. At university she passed English I with an A grade and French I with a B. Her progress at teachers' college too was satisfactory and assessments of her 'sections' of classroom teaching included such comments as 'very good start made', 'pleasant manner' and 'enthusiastic, inspires response of class'. Only one school, Caversham, noted a perceived weaknesses by giving a 'fair' grading for class control, and 'very fair' as an overall assessment.[55]

Because of the country's war mobilisation, students were 'manpowered' to work in essential occupations over the summer of 1943/44. Janet was assigned raspberry picking on a farm at Miller's Flat in Central Otago. After a lifetime of hearing stories about the region from her relatives, most recently from Aunty Isy, Janet was at last to go 'up Central' herself. It was not the narrow ladder into a cloudy loft that she had imagined in her childhood. It was, if anything, something more miraculous: a vast lens of continental landscape in the centre of the South Island. Parts of it were dry and stony and Mediterranean-looking (good country for olives and grapes, though this would not be recognised for another fifty years); much of the rest, hills and plains, was coated in golden tussock. From the moment Janet saw them from the bus she fell in love with the hills, covered in their folds by their own shadow, 'with their changing shades of gold, and the sky born blue each morning with no trace of cloud, retiring in the evening to its depth of purple'.[56]

The work was taxing. The students picked raspberries by day in blazing sunshine and their faces, arms and legs flared with sunburn. At night they slept in corrugated iron sheds which retained the daytime heat. To escape both the discomfort and the claustrophobia of cramped socialising, Janet walked in the evenings, among matagouri ('a desert thorn bush') and snowgrass, 'golden silk like the strands of tussock which I used to think was named after "tussore silk" . . .'[57]

It was one such walk that took her to the bank of the mighty Clutha, the country's largest river, which carried the Gaelic name for the Clyde, in whose Scottish valley her Frame grandfather had been born. The Clutha River originated in high country snow, powered through gold-bearing gorges, 'through all its stages of fury and . . . now and then, peace, to its outfall in the sea, with its natural burden of water and motion and its display of colour, snow-green, blue, mud-brown, and borrowing rainbows from light . . . From my first sight of the river I felt it to be part of my life . . . I felt [it] was an ally, that it would speak for me.'[58]

The sight and sound of this river remained with her for the rest of her life. On one occasion she tossed a manuka stick into its flow and was thrilled and chilled to see it simply disappear, as if the black force of the water were a fiend that swallowed foreign objects without trace.[59] So strongly did this powerful current fascinate and attract her that her fruit-picking companions came upon her one night, prone on the edge of the river and in what they described as a 'trance-like' state. She was lifted and carried rigid to a vehicle, which returned her to the sleeping quarters.[60] Sixteen years later when she changed her name, she would choose that of the Gaelic Clutha to replace her Scottish family name.

When Janet returned to Oamaru in February 1944 for the tail-end of her holiday it was to find that, after fourteen years, the family had moved from Eden Street.[61] The landlord had sold the house. The new owner wished to occupy it with his bride. The Frames were reminded of the insecurity that was the price of not owning property. But they succeeded in turning a setback into an opportunity. George Frame joined a newly formed building society and within two months drew a ballot of three hundred pounds, enough for a deposit on a cheap property. The one the family chose, known as Willowglen, consisted of three rural and tree-strewn acres on the western outskirts of Oamaru, bordering the southern railway line. A poplar-lined drive led to a near-derelict cottage, which had almost the same number of rooms as 56 Eden Street but was considerably smaller. It was also colder, being set against a western hill and facing another to the east. The water tank was rusted, the kitchen floor collapsed down to bare earth and the rooms were coated in borer dust.

'Seeing the earth floor and the "nowhereness" of the interior,' Janet was to write, 'I felt depressed and lonely and I knew the Willowglen house would never be my home; it was too small, everyone was too close to everyone else; in the front bedroom you could hear the wireless from the kitchen as if you were in the kitchen. You could hear the arguments too, the raised voices, and the soft murmur of pleading that you knew to be, "Don't raise your voices to each other", from Mother.'[62] They made the best of it, even if it did seem at first that in joining the company of home owners, the family's standard of living had dropped still further. Isabel and June scrubbed the house thoroughly; father and son managed to put aside their differences long enough to repair the kitchen floor and install a new water system and septic tank; George established a routine of heaving 'spare' coal out of his locomotive where the railway line curved past the property, and picking it up when he came home; and Lottie, busy as ever in her new kitchen, looked down longingly towards the sunny flat below the house and declared that 'one of these days, in the cool of the evening', she would go and sit there among the pines.[63]

And Janet, though she never 'bonded' with the house, found the customary place of her own on the large property, by a creek. It was 'an old log [on which] I sat for hours watching the water, the ducks, the swamphens, and through the broken-down wire fence, the sheep nibbling the grass in the paddock of half swamp and half matagouri, *my matagouri.*'[64] As they had done at Wyndham and Eden Street, the Frames acquired a house cow, Bonnie, which had ample room to graze.

There was little time for Janet to digest these experiences or to explore her feelings about the new location. Within weeks she was on the train again, bound for Dunedin and her second and final year of teacher training. This time she was not alone, however. Her sister Isabel, her natural exuberance reinforced by a good performance the previous year at high school — she had topped her form in English and French and won prizes for speech and physical education — had decided to dispense with the sixth form. Rejecting an earlier ambition to be a doctor, she too planned to follow the revered example of Cousin Peg and become a teacher. She was seventeen. The family, proud that a second daughter was opting for an honoured profession, assumed that Janet would be pleased to have Isabel at teachers' college and at Aunty Isy's, where they would now share board. They believed she would act as a mentor to her younger sibling. The family was wrong.

CHAPTER FOUR

# *An Unravelling*

$\mathcal{J}$ANET, WHO HAD NOT EXPECTED ISABEL TO LEAVE SCHOOL UNTIL THE following year, was far from pleased that her sister was to share her life and career in Dunedin in 1944. 'I saw my own world falling apart,' she was to write. 'All my carefully cemented behaviour crumbling under the force of Isabel's unexpected weather.' While the sisters were friends, they were not close in temperament, outlook or experience. Isabel was bold and venturesome. It was she, for example, who instructed Janet and June in the 'ways of the world', that is, 'how to get a boyfriend, what to do when you had him and how to get rid of him when he outlived his usefulness . . . [Also] how to triumph over authority and its narrow-mindedness. Isabel was inclined to teach us by example.'[1]

The accuracy of Janet's forebodings were confirmed as soon as they arrived at Garden Terrace. Isabel was 'angrily incredulous' at the size of the bed and room they were to share, the coldness, the size of their meals, and the fact that they ate in the unheated scullery while Aunty Isy 'toasted her toes' in front of the fire in the dining room.[2] It took all Janet's powers of persuasion to prevent Isabel writing home at once and 'blowing the whistle'. Where else would they get board for ten shillings a week?

To her older sister's initial relief, Isabel's indignation was diluted by the distractions she embraced inside and outside teachers' college. Within weeks she had made friends, including a steady boyfriend; she went swimming almost daily; she discovered roller skating and, typically and rapidly, became an expert. Nothing could have emphasised the differences between the sisters more than this confident, headlong behaviour. Soon Janet had an additional set of anxieties. Isabel 'went wild with a wildness that was alarming only to my exaggerated sense of restraint . . . I saw my dream for her future fading and all her "education" wasted — why did she not study, why did she not seize the opportunity to read, learn?'[3]

Despite these differences, externalised in bitter fights at night for the bedclothes, the sisters did share what they would remember as 'episodes' at Garden Terrace. One was discovering that Aunty Isy had a drawer full of white knitted baby clothes wrapped in tissue, relics of an early infant death or a pregnancy that did not go to full term. This, they thought, might account for the eagerness, the hunger, almost, with which their childless Frame aunts had embraced their nieces as infants and showered them with presents.

The sisters' most celebrated escapade, however, was secretly devouring over a period of time all the chocolates that Isy Renwick had mounted on the picture rail in her 'front room'. These boxes, bound with satin ribbons and decorated with English and Scottish hunting scenes, were prizes Aunty Isy had won for Highland dancing. The sin of devouring the contents brought Janet and Isabel no joy. '[We] both felt distaste at what we were doing, eating Aunty Isy's cherished souvenirs: eating, eating . . .'[4] They re-wrapped and replaced the boxes on the picture rail, and believed they had got away with the misdemeanour undetected — until Isabel wrote home at the end of the second term, complaining about the conditions to which their aunt had subjected them.

Suddenly accusations and recriminations flew from all directions. Lottie Frame wrote an indignant letter to Isy, who replied to George, her brother, that Lottie had always been 'a bad manager'.[5] When Lottie protested, Isy disclosed that she knew about the disappearing chocolates and that she had been mistaken in her belief that Janet and Isabel were 'lovely girls'. In the storm of correspondence that followed, Janet wrote, George Renwick's sisters 'found disparaging things to say about the "awful Frames", how the children had always been out of control, running wild on the Oamaru hills, how the Frame home was like a pigsty, Mother didn't know the first thing about housekeeping . . . The result was that Isabel and I moved from Number Four Garden Terrace, I with shame and embarrassment and a sense of loss in being no longer thought of as a "lovely girl, no trouble at all", and Isabel with triumph because we had asserted our "rights".'[6]

The upheaval in effect accomplished the sisters' separation. Isabel moved to be with friends in a popular boarding house run by a Mrs Uren in Queen Street, Janet into the austere hostel Stuart House in Cumberland Street, where she had a cubicle in a dormitory-like room. 'If we saw each other at Training College, we said hello in an embarrassed way.'[7] Janet's embarrassment increased when the warden of the college, Joan Stevens,★ called her in to warn her that Isabel was making 'a guy of herself' by her behaviour and the outlandish nature of her clothes, in particular a skirt with a giraffe printed on it. The episode, Janet was to say later, illustrated 'the degree of conformity expected of us'.[8]

---

★ Subsequently to become a Professor of English at Victoria University, Wellington, and a reviewer and critic of Janet Frame's writing.

As she had done in her first year, Janet immersed herself in college work. She enjoyed especially the inspirational teaching of her art lecturer, Gordon Tovey. She took another university paper, English II, and continued to read widely and to write poetry. Her special places of peace, she recalled, were the English lectures, 'where I lived within Shakespeare and Old English, and the reference room of the Dunedin Public Library, where I read modern poetry, James Frazer, Jung and Freud'.[9] She also wrote a children's story, 'Keel and Kool', for Joan Stevens' literature class at teachers' college and was summoned to receive congratulations. The story showed imagination and promise, Miss Stevens told her, and she asked if Janet had considered 'taking up' writing for children (the 'Keel and Kool' published subsequently in Frame's first book was not the same story).[10]

In this year too Janet assembled the courage to submit two poems to the college magazine, *Te Rama*, 'Tunnel Beach' and 'Cat'. Both were products of her reading of Dylan Thomas and George Barker. The editor had no idea of their worth and consulted Joan Stevens. Miss Stevens in turn invited comments in the staff common-room, where opinion was divided between those who thought the poems 'brilliant' and those who suspected a spoof ('You don't think she's playing a joke on us?'). At last Miss Stevens announced that the poems were good, and the editor, in some relief, concurred.[11] Both were published over the initials K.K.A. (from the Greek tag *kalos kai agathos*, 'the beautiful and the good'); and one, 'Cat', won *Te Rama's* annual ten-shilling poetry prize:

> Deaf to the hammering window
> and the idiot boy's mewing,
> I leave the torn mice to flow
> in his vacant eyes
> and sit propped up by a fat thinking;
>
> but the will of the beating boy
> burgles my ear, creeps
> like a curled cat in my brain,
> purrs and sleeps
> and pads me from the house
> to the scratched clouds and the clawed moon . . .
>
> and the winds like torn mice
> flow through my vacant eyes.[12]

Even more controversial was Janet's major piece of written work for the college that year, a lengthy social studies assignment on 'The Growth of Cities'. 'The subject,' she wrote subsequently, 'excited me by its possibilities and repelled me by the prospect that I might have to record boring geographical and historical detail . . . In the end the text became a geographical and historical and social version of [Virginia Woolf's novel]. *The Waves*, with bizarre illus-trations cut from magazines, as I had [no] "flair" for drawing.'[13] Again, the assignment was passed around among staff; again, opinion was divided as to its merit. Dorothy Neal White, who had just joined the college as its first full-time librarian, recalled the lecturer responsible, Arthur 'Agony' Payne, saying, 'What do you *do* with something like this?' Neal White studied the pages, recognised that the metaphor-ridden text and illustrations embodied the principles that the assignment was designed to explore, and proposed that it be marked as highly as possible.[14] Mr Payne was not persuaded.

Work of this kind always presented a problem for examiners. Frame's special gift, which had already been noted at secondary school, was for producing the unexpected rather than the expected — an ability to look at subjects in an entirely fresh way. At high school, this had taken the form of 'focusing in places not glanced at by others, of deliberately turning away from the main view [or] looking at the general view [and] seeing an uncommon sight.'[15] At teachers' college and university she elaborated this characteristic 'originality' by often choosing to exemplify principles by parable and fable rather than by analysis. Because the form in which this work emerged was not always recognised or understood by those assessing it, opinions remained sharply divided between those who believed that she was exceptionally gifted and those who saw her as merely eccentric, or even backward.

Her grade at the end of this second year of teacher training, 63 out of 100, was a compromise between these extreme views. Her final assessment noted, ominously, 'An unusual type; brilliant scholar in languages and a highly intelligent person . . . but temperamentally something of a risk.'[16] Her uni-versity grade too was equivocal. She had scored 75 in one term's examination, 40 in the other. In contrast to her A grade in English the previous year, her 1944 result was a simple pass.[17]

In spite of such ambivalence, Janet finished the year bathed in a euphoria comparable to that with which she had begun her teacher training. She had completed her two mandatory college years despite aloneness and crippling self-doubt. She had gained another university subject towards a degree. As she stood on the stage at the Dunedin Town Hall in the college choir, she was 'full of tears at the momentous occasion, surrounded by singing voices, all in a sensation of being in an upper storey of the mind and heart, knowing a joy that I never wanted to end . . .'[18]

End it did, of course, in the forbidding and foreboding knowledge that she now faced a year's probationary teaching, assessment by a headmaster and a formal inspection of her classroom work before she would become profes-sionally qualified. Initially that reality was distanced by a summer holiday back at Willowglen, in which she explored the family acres, sat on her fallen birch log by the creek watching the pukekos, ducks and eels, and took walks through adjoining farms. Late in January 1945 Janet and her sister returned to Dunedin by train, Isabel to rejoin her congenial lodgings and undertake her second year of teacher training; Janet to board with a widow in Maori Hill, Mrs Elizabeth Wadsworth, and to teach a Standard Two class of eight- and nine-year-olds at Arthur Street School, the oldest continuously operating primary school in the country. She planned also to enroll for a course in experimental psychology at Otago University.[19]

For Janet, coming direct from the spartan features of Willowglen, Mrs Wadsworth's substantial and verandahed bungalow in Chamberlain Street, Maori Hill, was 'a place where "other people" lived; with carpets and wallpaper printed with roses, with plenty of furniture and knick-knacks, and upholstered sofas without a tear; and throughout the house, no sign of furniture stuffing or wooden floor or scrim behind the wallpaper. There was comfort with an air of concealment.'[20] Mrs Wadsworth spent most of each day at her married daughter's place in a neighbouring suburb and returned each evening full of stories about her grandchildren and her son-in-law, and about hours happily spent in joint expeditions and housework with her daughter.

Sometimes, 'for the sake of appearances', Janet would have an evening meal with her landlady. More often she ate in her own room, 'marking, preparing lessons and cutting out paper stars in different colours to reward the children's efforts; and studying my textbook of psychology; and writing and reading poems'.[21] She had been heartened by the appearance of her two poems in *Te Rama* the previous year, and by the award of the prize. But she sought no further opportunities for publication at this time: the writing was its own — and only — reward.

At Arthur Street School she appeared at first to be coping with the work, in spite of continuing reservations about whether she wanted to make a career in teaching. She was at ease in the company of her class of over thirty eight- and nine-year-olds and stimulated by the daily contact with them. She 'heard tables and reading and people of other lands, talked in a casual way about Robert Bruce and the Spider and King Alfred and the Cakes, and . . . spent all dinner-hour putting stars on neat work'.[22] She revelled especially in the children's art and in their poetry, for 'they wrote poetry and stories almost every day, and these, with the paintings, I pinned around the walls for everybody to enjoy'.[23]

Where she failed utterly was in her inability to participate in the corporate life of the school. Her cousin Iona Livingston and a teachers' college contemporary, Norma Mageur, were also on the staff at Arthur Street and valued it highly as a well-run school. They got on with each other, and with other staff; they simply never saw Janet and gained the impression that she was having trouble 'fitting in'.[24]

According to Janet's own recollection, 'my timidity among people, especially among those who might be asked to judge and comment on my performance as a teacher, led to my spending free time alone. Too timid to go to morning and afternoon tea with a room full of teachers, I made excuses about "having work to do in the classroom", aware that I was going against all the instructions about the need to mix in adult company, take part in social events and discussions with other teachers and parents, and that "morning tea in the teachers' room" was an almost sacred ritual.'[25]

The effort required daily to resist contact with other staff was considerable and one major source of stress in her life. The other, growing larger by the day, was her old fear of being judged and found wanting. She did develop a technique to keep the headmaster, Mr C.D. Gilling, at bay. She invented 'a serial story which I could continue whenever I heard the steps of authority approaching along the corridor, so that a visit by the headmaster to a class sitting rapt with attention . . . might "prove" my ability as a teacher'.[26] It was her hope that she could contrive a similar ploy when the dreaded inspector arrived. But as the year advanced she doubted her capacity to sustain this kind of pretence. She became progressively more apprehensive and depressed. 'I felt completed isolated,' she would write subsequently. 'I knew no one to confide in, to get advice from; and there was nowhere I could go.' If she 'failed' her inspection, as she was sure she would, what would become of her? 'What, *in all the world*, could I do to earn my living and still live as myself, as I knew myself to be. Temporary masks, I knew, had their place; everyone was wearing them, they were the human rage; but not masks cemented in place until the wearer could not breathe and was eventually suffocated.'[27]

Janet's major relief from this unhappiness, and one that was sufficiently invigorating to renew her stamina for teaching, was her university psychology lectures and laboratory sessions which she attended two evenings a week and on Saturday mornings. She was engaged by the subject itself, which offered a range of theories to explain the origins and vagaries of human behaviour; by the laboratory experiments; and especially by her principal teacher, a fresh-faced young graduate from Victoria University, 23-year-old junior lecturer John Money (whom she nicknamed 'Ash' after the fair-haired Ashley Wilkes, played by Leslie Howard, in the film *Gone with the Wind*).

Although former servicemen had begun to return to university by 1945, the war was not over and there was still a marked shortage of young men among both the university staff and students. Those who *were* there, especially staff, tended to be the subject of 'rumour, speculation and fantasy', especially if they were good-looking. John Money was not only good-looking; he was intelligent, forthright and charming.[28] 'Some of the women swooned over Ash,' Janet reported. She was one of them. When he chanced to smile at her, she said later, she was happy for days. When he failed to notice her, she was melancholic.[29]

Money's appeal for Janet was heightened by the fact that he was musical. He played the piano sufficiently well to have considered a career as a musician; the topic of his master's thesis had been 'Creative Endeavour in Musical Composition'; shortly after his arrival at Otago University at the beginning of 1945, he had instigated weekly lunchtime sessions in musical appreciation in the gramophone studio of the music department. Janet began to attend these sessions, rushing to and from Arthur Street in order to do so. One day when she arrived early she was transfixed to come upon Money playing the piano in the studio, 'up and down the keys in a flourish and swoop like a concert pianist, marshalling the notes together in a travelling force going somewhere'.[30] Later that same day Money played a record of Tchaikovsky's Fifth Symphony (the 'Pathétique'), the first sustained piece of classical music Janet had listened to. As a consequence of both experiences, the music room became another place where she felt at home.[31] Janet also began to attend lunchtime and evening concerts in the Dunedin Town Hall, often in the company of her former fellow teachers' college student, Sheila Traill, who was working out her probationary year at Ravensbourne School between Dunedin and Port Chalmers.

'I didn't know not to clap at the end of the first movement,' Traill wrote later. 'But Janet didn't clap at all, not even at the end. She just sat there in her own world, overwhelmed.' This behaviour, to Traill, seemed perfectly natural. What was less acceptable, in Traill's view, was the fact that Janet spoke of a developing 'passion' for John Money, whom she referred to as 'HCF' (for highest common factor: 'we dared not breathe the real names of the heroes we idealised'). More than that, the passion seemed to extend to the subject of psychology itself, which Traill was inclined to dismiss as 'a lot of nonsense'. Janet told her that she wanted to 'get to the bottom of the human mind' and — more alarmingly — to 'delve into abnormal psychology. She used to talk of "going mad" and what it would be like, just as she talked of how it would feel [in the words of the song] to "done get drunk".'[32]

In July 1945, everything that preoccupied Janet — her sense of isolation, the tension she experienced at school, her apprehension about the future, her 'pash' on John Money, her flirtation with the notion of 'going mad' — all combined to produce a crisis. A new lecturer recently discharged from the air force, Peter McKellar, took over the laboratory classes on Saturday mornings (temporarily as it turned out, but Janet did not know that at the time). This development, which appeared to erase her weekend contact with Money and hence her only source of pleasure and replenishment at that time of the week, coincided with a particularly unhappy week at school. She decided to activate another notion that until this time she had merely flirted with: she would attempt suicide.

On the evening of the same Saturday that Money was absent from the laboratory, her landlady was away for the weekend. Janet tidied her room, organised her possessions and, with the help of several glasses of water, swallowed a packet of aspirin. 'I lay down in bed to die, certain that I would die. My desperation was extreme.'[33] She did not die, however. She woke the next day, near noon, 'with a roaring in my ears and my nose bleeding. My first thought was not even a thought, it was a feeling of wonder and delight and thankfulness that I was alive. I staggered from my bed and looked at myself in the mirror; my face was a dusky red. I began to vomit again and again. At last my nose stopped bleeding but the roaring in my ears continued.'[34] Janet recovered sufficiently to face her landlady that evening and to return to school the following day, and generally to behave as if nothing extraordinary had occurred.

The following month was especially eventful. The war ended with the surrender of Japan on 14 August, Janet 'came of age' by turning twenty-one on 28 August, and, in the August holiday break between the second and third school terms, she wrote her first adult story for publication, 'University Entrance', which she sent to the *New Zealand Listener*. She also wrote an autobiographical assignment for John Money's course. This provided her with a means to hint at her distress and to discuss her difficulties, which until now she had kept resolutely to herself. And she would achieve these objectives by forming a more intimate association with Money than she had achieved up to this time.

John Money was well aware of Frame by August 1945. 'I already had a strong premonition of her literary capability because she didn't write up the psychology lab experiments in the routine way,' he recalled. 'Each one was done as a parable, with birds or other animals acting the role of the investigator, the experimenter and the observer. They were all brilliantly done, and she had the principles one hundred percent correct. Whereas other people I consulted would have failed her for not obeying instructions, I gave her an A-plus for understanding what the experiments were about.'[35]

Money set the autobiographical assignment in August 1945. Members of the class were to record the major and most influential events in their own lives. Frame's essay summarised her life to the end of her high school years. Then she added, as if in afterthought: 'Perhaps I should mention a recent attempt at suicide . . .' She described what had occurred the previous month and, 'to make the attempt more impressive', used the clinical term for aspirin — acetylsalicylic acid.[36]

Money, as Frame would have anticipated, called her to his office shortly after the beginning of the third term, supposedly to discuss the manner in which she had dealt with the assignment. In fact the confession of the suicide attempt had alarmed him, and his concern for her well-being went beyond his role as a lecturer in psychology. Earlier in the year, in the absence of any kind of student health service, Money and his colleague Peter McKellar had decided to advertise 'clinics', at which they would make themselves available to students to discuss problems of a psychological or vocational nature. Telling his mother in May 1945 about this additional responsibility, Money had written: 'I hope [we] will eventually get on to more interesting problems of personality maladjustment . . . [That] is quite a complicated business . . . one has to be very cautious not to make any mistakes.'[37] The student Money was about to counsel in September 1945 would provide precisely the kinds of problems that he would find interesting — and, for a 24-year-old psychologist with no clinical training or experience, challengingly and hazardously complicated.

Frame came to Money's office in the attic of one of the university's old ivy-covered professorial houses on 19 September. She told him that she had walked out of her classroom at Arthur Street the previous week 'as the inspector walked in'. This was in part a consequence of her deep fear of being judged; but it was related, she said, to the fact that she was even more unconfident than usual because Money had passed her in the street the previous day without recognising her. She said she had difficulty teaching because of 'bright ideas flitting through her mind . . . in the nature of metaphors which could be remembered for future use in writing'. Frame also told Money of her 'deep devotion to literature' and indicated it was in that direction that she would prefer to make a career. She had no wish to return to teaching, but had told her headmaster by telephone that she would produce a medical certificate to explain her sudden departure from school and continuing absence. Now she was additionally anxious about how to extricate herself when she had in fact no such certificate.[38]

To Frame's intense relief, John Money became fully engaged by her predicament and took control. He invited her back for further counselling sessions over the next two days, 'mainly an attempt to persuade her that she really wanted to live, that she wanted to create, and that she wanted to avoid the loneliness that she now imposed upon herself'. He then had telephone conversations with the Arthur Street headmaster, Mr Gilling, and the Education Board inspector, a Mr Hunter. Each told him that they were 'extremely perplexed' about what had occurred, but also 'very sympathetic'.[39]

On 24 September, Money escorted Frame to a meeting at Hunter's office. The inspector proposed that she complete her probationary year at Arthur Street, but that at the end of it he withhold her certificate on the ground that she was unhappy about teaching and therefore unsuited to it. This would enable Frame to leave the profession without penalty. In the meantime Hunter would speak to his friend, Donald Cameron, Mayor of Dunedin, about finding Frame an alternative job as a librarian, in recognition of her interest in literature. This proposed resolution, Money recorded, seemed 'generally satisfactory'.[40] While Frame was working out the year she would continue to have weekly counselling sessions with the psychology lecturer, or to see him more frequently if she felt she needed to.

While Frame was not overjoyed at the prospect of returning to the classroom, at least she could envisage an end to what had come to seem more like a penal sentence than a vocation. And she did now have the concentrated attention of the man with whom she was obsessed and guaranteed access to him on a regular basis. It is probable that already some of the so-called 'symptoms' that she discussed with him, such as the intensity of the ideas flashing through her mind and distracting her from teaching, were manufactured in order to enlarge and retain his interest. She was to confess to him eighteen months later that her contact with him had come about through 'scheming — I scheme more than you realise'.[41] But at the outset, Money had no inkling of this.

For two weeks the compromise arrangement appeared to work. Then, on 11 October, Money rang Arthur Street School and left a message to say that he was unable to see Frame as scheduled that afternoon, Friday, because he was leaving town early to go skiing for the weekend. He asked her to come the following Monday afternoon instead. At mid-morning Frame rang him from a public telephone box to say that she had walked out of school again and was calling to say goodbye to him. '[She] informed me that she was not going to see me again, ever. Nor was she going to see anybody else again, ever.'

Alarmed, Money consulted his head of department, Henry Ferguson, then rang the police. At his request a police car collected Frame from the vicinity of the telephone box and brought her to his office. 'I began an interview with her that lasted about one and a half hours. We got nowhere. She continually reasserted her need to die, and that there was no other escape.' Money, committed to his two days away, arranged for the police to collect Frame and to contact Isabel and her parents so that she would not be alone for the weekend. As a result George Frame came down from Oamaru.[42]

On the Monday, somewhat to Money's surprise, Frame turned up for her rescheduled appointment. Lying on the couch in his office, relaxed by what he called 'hypnotic chatter', she gave an explanation of what she believed had been going on. Money took notes:

> As I would know [Frame told him] all young people were likely to have infatuations . . . I had been the object of her pash since the beginning of the year . . . [Only] she, and possibly her sister and friend [Sheila Traill] knew about it. The person involved was rather a fairytale hero. If [he] smiled, Janet was happy for days, but if he did not look her way or was annoyed with her her misery was unbearable. In either case . . . her happiness was so intense or her misery so acute that she had to die. She could not live with such uncontrollable emotion. The first dramatic episode occurred [when Peter] took over the Sat. lab class . . . To no longer have me to teach her was unbearable . . . Next was the walking out of the room when the inspector arrived, occasioned really by the fact that I had passed her in the street the day previously without seeing her. Finally the phone call on Friday had been due to the misery of having had her appointment for that day cancelled.[43]

It took all of three hours to extract this story. When Frame left, after promising to return for another session in three days, Money wrote: 'We are now at the stage of having cleared . . . the debris away, and there is every possibility of building afresh. Much remains to be done, however . . . I think the crisis is past, now that so much pent-up emotion is got rid of.'[44] Money was mistaken. In the middle of that week he received a letter from Frame, written in what he had come to recognise from assignments as her 'parable' mode. It said, *inter alia*:

I am a snail. I was a happy snail at first. People tried to help me to poke my head out of my shell and wander (with my eyes on stalks) past rows and rows of beans and carrots and radishes. But I am easily frightened and it isn't always spring and the wind outside is very often a white whip-lash. So I am going back to the first place of my mind — my secret cabbage-patch world to feed alone on my private cabbage-leaves of fantasy; and even if the sky of my world is sometimes thick with thrushes I'll be a reticent snail and utter none of my secret snail-cries or thoughts to anybody. I am not returning to school. Snails are not teachers. I am leaving Dunedin as soon as I can for what T.S.Eliot would [call] 'a journey and such a long long journey'. I shall have my house on my back . . .[45]

The following Thursday Frame failed to keep her late afternoon appointment and again rang Money from a public telephone. His notes record:

After announcing her name she again . . . informed me of a renewed intention to die. [She] wanted no police sent after her. She was not going to be so naive about her death this time, but had planned it. She would not tell me where she was; and she was going straight away from there . . . to die . . . [She] was much more resolute and grimly determined, with no crying, but sometimes a deep swallow before the words flowed. I told her that I did not believe that she really would die; that she could look upon any hostile feelings towards me as quite in order . . . [Then] the penny ran out.

I rang Henry, feeling that before any major improvement came, Janet should receive some sort of convalescent guardianship. Then there was the risk that should her compulsion succeed, the Psych Dept's name would be black. As a result Peter and Henry and I went up to her boarding house, arriving at about 9.30. Everything was dark [the landlady was away in Wellington] and we could get no response for a long while. Then Janet appeared in night clothes. Henry announced himself. She screamed 'Oh' and slammed the door and ran away. Shortly she re-appeared and conversation was resumed . . .

She said there was nothing wrong with her, not even worry, which Henry suggested. Why were we concerned about her? At this point I took over . . . Wouldn't you be worried if someone rang you on two occasions saying that things were so bad that she would have to die? From this point on I had won, and it was just a matter of gentle suggestion and convincing that it would be a good thing for her to have a spell in hospital in order to pick up the threads and gain a new control over her emotions.

Her threatened suicide was not fantastic. Her shoes were muddy and wet, indicating the truth of her perfectly frank . . . statement that she had been out to the cliffs at St Clair, intending to throw herself into the sea . . . But she thought of something humorous about the camel with sore feet which prevented its getting to water which was not far off; and her own feet being sore, she decided not to continue the journey . . . I had previously discussed the matter with Dr Malcolm Brown of Seacliff, on the phone . . . so that there was no problem of admittance to the Public Hospital.[46]

And so at 10.30 pm on 18 October 1945, Janet Frame was committed to the Colquhoun Ward, which she later discovered was the psychiatric ward at Dunedin Public Hospital. It was only, she believed, for 'a few days' rest', and her initial reaction to that prospect was benign. 'I suddenly felt free of all worry, cared for. I could think of nothing more desirable than lying in bed sheltered and warm, away from teaching and trying to earn money, and even away from Mrs [Wadsworth] and her comfortable home; and away from my family and my worry over them; and from my increasing sense of isolation in a brave bright world of brave bright people; away from . . . being twenty-one and responsible; only not away from my decaying teeth.'[47]

Five days later John Money was reporting, after several visits, that Frame was 'getting on very well . . . She now talks perfectly normally to me, although she is very shy of the doctors and beats about the bush and talks rather stupidly with them. They . . . therefore settle themselves with the belief that she is on the way to being insane. I do so hope that they do not send her to Seacliff. I am working hard to get her in a frame of mind to be able to talk to them as easily as to me.'[48] Seacliff was the psychiatric hospital to the north of Dunedin, much feared among the general community in Otago for both its appearance ('grey stone, built like a castle')[49] and the fact that 'loonies' committed there were not infrequently incarcerated for life. Every family secretly feared the loss of a loved one through its grim portals. It was the institution that Lottie Frame had rejected so vigorously as a destination for her epileptic son.

Unbeknown to Frame, the 'few days' rest' that she had begun rather to enjoy was, as far as the health system was concerned, a period of observation to diagnose her mental state and decide where she should most appropriately be sent: 'home' to Oamaru, or 'up the line' to Seacliff; there was no third option. The speculation she had shared with Sheila Traill, about what it would be like to 'go mad' or be considered mad, was a game with far higher stakes and more drastic consequences than she could imagine. It would involve other people making decisions about how much control she would be allowed over her own life. But Frame had no idea what was at risk, and she behaved towards the hospital doctors as she had initially behaved in her counselling sessions with John Money.

As Money had observed, she now seemed relaxed and well in conversation with him, and pleased to be the object of his continuing attention. But when doctors attempted to interview her she became inhibited, elusive, sometimes overly dramatic, and subject to fits of nervous giggling. This behaviour, in conjunction with her suicide attempt and her interest in psychology, was subject to far more sinister interpretation than Frame could have known. The clinical notes from one of her interviews read:

> She lies in bed with her head buried in the bed clothes and grins foolishly when addressed. She is able to give a good account of her previous life . . . She admits having made an attempt at suicide by taking aspros . . . At this time, 'I fell in love with a man but he did not love me . . . [This] got me down.' She states that she does not like teaching . . . She has been attending lectures at Otago University and shows an *undue interest in psychology*. She is rather of the introvert type and finds mixing with others difficult. She plans leaving teaching and doing library work, showing no realisation of her present condition or of her future abilities.[50]

One interview, possibly that from which the above notes were taken, was by Dr Malcolm Brown, superintendent of Seacliff Hospital. He told John Money five days after Frame had entered Dunedin Hospital that 'he thought she would have to go out to Seacliff. His diagnosis is incipient schizophrenia. In her conversations with me all the schizophrenic symptoms [disappear], but they apparently reassert themselves when he interviews her, as he engenders fear and resistance.'[51] Frame was told nothing of this diagnosis nor, even, that transferral to Seacliff was under consideration. On the contrary, one of the nurses, Maitland Brown, told her confidently, 'You won't be going there . . . There's nothing wrong with you.'[52] And Frame, having just met and disliked a patient who *was* going to Seacliff, saw no reason to disagree.

John Money, who was at this time 'glistening with newly applied Freud', sought ways to help Frame and give her something constructive to do in hospital in addition to reading and resting.[53] He asked her to write down her dreams so that they could discuss their symbolism in the course of his visits to the ward. This was an attempt at an elementary form of psychoanalysis — a therapy with which Money was familiar through his reading, but of which hospital doctors in New Zealand at this time knew little; and what little they did know, they distrusted or dismissed. Frame was eager to cooperate and quickly produced a series of dreams which she would have known Money would find significant.

By 30 October it seemed that whatever crisis had seized Frame was now passed. Hospital staff announced that she could now go home to Oamaru and that, after a holiday there, she would be 'good as new'.[54] This was not what the patient had expected, however. *She* had assumed that, after her 'rest', she would be discharged to find a job in Dunedin, possibly in the library, and that she would be able to continue with her university studies and her writing. Frame wrote later:

Faced suddenly with the prospect of going home, I felt all the worries of the world returning, all the sadness of home and the everlasting toil of my parents and the weekly payments on the blankets and the new eiderdown from Calder Mackays, and the payments to the Starr-Bowkett Building Society or we'd be turned out of our house again; and the arguments at home, and Mother's eternal peacemaker intervention; and my decaying teeth . . . [When] I saw Mother standing there at the entrance to the ward, in her pitifully 'best' clothes, her navy costume and her navy straw hat with the bunch of artificial flowers at the brim; with a hint of fear in her eyes (for, after all, I had been in a 'mental' ward) and her face transparently trying to adopt the expression *All is well*, I knew that home was the last place I wanted to be. I screamed at Mother to go away. She left, murmuring her bewilderment, 'But she's such a happy person, she's always been such a happy person.'[55]

No one asked Frame why she had screamed at her mother, nor why the prospect of going home had caused her to panic. Instead she was forbidden further visitors (including Money) and all her books were removed, especially her psychology texts, which hospital staff were convinced were contributing to her illness. '[They] are accepting the popular fallacy that an interest in psychology and conversation about it is unhealthy,' Money noted glumly, 'and that this drives one mad.'[56] He sensed too that the ward doctors were now preventing him from seeing their patient, because of his insistence that it was therapeutic for Frame to talk about her difficulties. There would be no more therapy of this sort.

Events now moved swiftly and irrevocably. Frame was held incommunicado until Malcolm Brown was able to interview her again on 2 November. Having done so, he instigated committal proceedings under the Mental Defectives Act. Lottie Frame, as next of kin, was persuaded to sign an application to have her daughter admitted to Seacliff Mental Hospital. Two Dunedin general practitioners, Warren John Boyd and Eric Robin Harty, certified that in their view the patient was mentally defective and suicidal and required 'oversight, care or control for his [sic] own good, or in the public interest'.[57] A magistrate then signed the committal order and authorised a police constable to escort Janet Paterson Frame to Seacliff Hospital the following day.[58]

The trajectory that had previously lofted Frame, whether she wanted it or not, towards a career in teaching, had been arrested. Her life was now deflected with the same degree of momentum in an altogether different direction. And it would take her to some dark places.

CHAPTER FIVE

# Out of the Depths

$S$EACLIFF MENTAL HOSPITAL, AS ITS NAME SUGGESTS, LOOMED HIGH over the Pacific Ocean on a wild stretch of coast thirty kilometres north-east of Dunedin.* In keeping with Otago's predominant culture of origin, the hospital's architectural style was known as 'Scottish baronial'.[1] To non-residents, who feared both its patients and its staff, the turrets and mock battlements gave the building the appearance of a castle out of a Gothic novel or a horror movie.

Seacliff was, in fact, a Victorian lunatic asylum, with all the qualities that designation implies. It was vast — the largest public building in the country for fifty years from the time it opened in 1884. The main section was con-structed of stone and cement and was unheated. Some of the original sleeping accommodation for patients was in single cells, locked and shuttered at night; the rest in dormitories. A concrete exercise yard was surrounded by high walls. Even in 1886, when it was only two years old, the main building was described as 'inexpressibly dreary and dispiriting'.[2] Sixty years later little had changed for the better inside the hospital. In the absence of amenities which might be characterised as 'modern', the institution functioned in effect as a prison for most of the more than 1200 patients deemed to require custodial care. Treatment was limited to traditional work therapy, which for women patients meant sewing or cleaning duties, to electro-convulsive or insulin shock therapy, or to the operation known as prefrontal leucotomy, which severed many of the fibres connecting the front part of the cerebral cortex to the remainder of the brain and reduced some patients to a vegetative, albeit less anxious, condition.

---

* There was an inclination, in New Zealand as elsewhere, to give mental hospitals names that suggested rural estates or cheerful holiday resorts: Seacliff, Cherry Farm, Sunnyside, Avondale. Such names denied or masked what for some patients was a horror of having to live in such institutions.

If all these features were insufficient to terrify those threatened with incarceration in Seacliff, and their loved ones, there were conditions there that made life additionally unpleasant and unsafe. A continuing shortage of nursing and medical staff had been exacerbated through the war years to the point where, in the opinion of a 1943 Royal Commission, their numbers were insufficient to provide even the most basic care and supervision of patients.[3] Partly as a result of this, a fire that swept through one of the women's wards three years before Janet Frame's arrival had incinerated thirty-seven patients, the worst accident of its kind in the country's history to that time.

Further disasters were threatened by the fact that the hill on which the main building stood was gradually subsiding towards the sea. New cracks appeared almost weekly in the floors, walls and ceilings of the main building. Water supplies and sewerage lines were severed frequently by the slippage, causing unpleasant odours and sanitation problems and placing enormous strains on the minimal maintenance staff. And it was largely these structural problems that led to the progressive demolition of the hospital between 1937 and 1960, and the eventual removal of patients to other institutions, most notably to nearby Cherry Farm at Waikouaiti from 1957. For those who hated and feared the institution, this dismantling of Seacliff was analogous to the removal of a cancerous growth from the Otago landscape and body politic.

Critics of New Zealand's mental hospitals attributed Seacliff's multiple accidents and shortcomings to poor engineering and construction decisions, inadequate financial and human resources, and the inertia of a heavily bureaucratic health system that seemed unwilling to modernise methods of patient care and treatment. Otago Maori had another view of the origin of the hospital's problems, however. They believed that the authorities had courted physical and psychic disaster by building the hospital over a tribal burial ground. According to this interpretation, the structural collapses, the fire, and the general air of terror said to prevail in wards holding the most disturbed patients were all consequences of a failure to respect the ethos and the tapu of the location.[4]

Janet Frame arrived at Seacliff Hospital mid-morning on 3 November 1945, in the company of a police constable, two girls from borstal and a police matron. Her admission notes describe her as 'a well nourished young woman in good bodily health'. She was twenty-one years old, had frizzy red hair, stood five feet four inches in height and weighed nine stone six ounces. She bore 'no marks, scars or communicable diseases'. Because she was a committed mental patient, however, her every mannerism was noted in that light. 'This girl is most foolish and fatuous in her manner and conversation, grins foolishly when addressed and tends to inattention . . . Is quite unconcerned at being here and generally emotionally apathetic . . . [Adopts] a listening attitude but denies hallucinations.'[5]

To allow a period of observation, Frame was assigned to a women's ward and allocated domestic duties in the nurses' home. She was permitted to come and go between these places, and to wander further afield through the hospital buildings and spacious grounds. She chose to reveal little of her inner feelings to the overworked nurses and medical staff (hence the repeated comment in her notes, 'shows no concern at being here'); but they, forever busy and moving quickly, made no attempt to discuss her thoughts and feelings with her. In fact, her concern was considerable and she was profoundly shocked at much of what she saw — indeed, went out of her way to see.

> [I] peeped through the fence of a building called Simla, away up on the hill, where there were strange men in striped shirts and trousers and some without trousers, walking round and round in a paddock with the grass worn away; and [I saw] a paddock of women, too, wearing the dark blue striped clothes . . . [There] was a cart, like a rickshaw, that passed every day by the ward . . . full of coal and two men harnessed to the cart carried the coal, driven by one of the attendants . . . [I] peered into a room that stank of urine and was full of children lying in cots, strange children, some of them babies, making strange noises; their faces wet with tears and snot . . . I saw people with their eyes staring like the eyes of hurricanes surrounded by whirling unseen and unheard commotion contrasting strangely with the stillness.[6]

Still nobody informed Frame that she had been diagnosed as a chronic schizophrenic, though this term had entered her medical records at Dunedin Hospital. Because all discussion about her symptoms had ceased with the banishment of John Money — he was forbidden by medical staff to visit her at Seacliff — she remained unaware that she was in fact being observed closely and her behaviour interpreted and recorded in her medical notes. On 7 December, for example: 'Transferred to the Cottage [an open ward] today, her behaviour has been more stable of late . . . although still rather foolish. She has a detached mien and appears still to live in a phantasy . . . Writes extremely foolish letters.'[7]

Some of these letters were to her family, some to John Money and Sheila Traill (to whom she wrote, 'we are in a way kindred souls, n'est-ce pas?').[8] None that have survived seem especially 'foolish'. They simply display an understandable preoccupation with her own state of mind, in which nobody at the hospital gave her any indication that they were interested; and they express her customarily quirky view of the world — the 'difference' so often commented on by her teachers and lecturers — but unfamiliar to the hospital authorities, and apparently unwelcome. In one such letter, to her sister June, Frame described gorse as 'smelling like peanut butter'. A doctor who read this then withheld her outward letters for a time and told her mother that she had a 'disordered mind', quoting the peanut butter remark as incontrovertible evidence.[9]

To Money, after warning him that all her correspondence was read, she noted that 'in spite of the rather shocking conditions & meals, Seacliff life is interesting & Seacliff people most lovable . . . I am happy and extroverted with the patients but terrified of matrons, sub-matrons and doctors . . . I want to go home. Being good imposes an awful strain, and one becomes weary of smiling and singing and creating a happy impression so that the doctor will say, "You have recovered." '[10]

To Sheila Traill she quoted one of Money's letters to her, as an indication of how perceptive and helpful his advice to her had been. Money had written:

Many people suffer a loneliness of spirit which becomes so overwhelming that at last it forces its possessor to grasp violently at the nearest straw. This is a typical manifestation in our cultural pattern and produces a pattern of behaviour which is mostly called love, but which more truly can be called pathological love. It is a search for a redeemer rather than for a cooperator in the mutual enterprise of parenthood, which is the ultimate goal and rationality of true love. When such a person finds a possible redeemer he or she clings possessively for fear of letting such a fortunate looking chance escape.[11]

This was as close as anybody got at this time to understanding what was wrong with Frame — Frame the bereaved twin, who had grown up feeling that her family were outcasts and that she was 'different', who had lost her older sister when she was twelve and never properly grieved for that loss, who was awkward, unconfident and lacking in social skills in adolescence, and who in young adulthood took refuge in literature to compensate for timidity and loneliness. Her lack of socialisation made her less mature than most of her contemporaries, and she had indeed focussed a kind of pathological love on her handsome and charming psychology lecturer. When there seemed to be no prospect that her feelings would be reciprocated, she had been gripped by a form of hysteria that generated apparently psychotic symptoms. In the enforced isolation of Seacliff, Frame could perceive much of this and accept it. 'He's very frank, isn't he?' she wrote to Sheila Traill in reference to John Money. 'He is revising my ideas on love, but I think (as I nearly always think of him) that what he says is very true.'[12] Her future difficulties would result in part from an inability to retain this insight.

In the course of her six-week hospitalisation, however, it was the plight of patients in her own ward that most engaged Frame's attention and sympathies. As she had indicated to Money, in the company of people who were infinitely more damaged than she, her customary shyness and timidity seemed to evaporate. She became almost parental in her concern for them. She told Money about one woman who was obsessive about cleanliness. 'She would plunge her hands in hot soapy water and hold them under the surface. "Under, Janet?" she would question. And I would stand by serious and loving her very much. "Yes. Under." The highest tribute Miss X could pay to anyone was to invite the sharing of that "under" experience.'[13]

In another letter she attempted to convey the tumult of Seacliff life and the emotions she felt being part of it:

> Rise, ladies. Laundry, ladies. Sewing-room, ladies. Dayroom, ladies. Keys and locks, the nurses' uniform pink like the cherry-blossom, and the big deep pockets full of keys. Dayroom and park. Come and sit in the sun, I said to one woman, no no she cried, sun on the head'll make you mad.
>
> Oh and Gracie and Rosie and Big Lil and all of them. And the sad woman who thought she was living in a biscuit factory. Where's Mr Hudson [of Cadbury Fry Hudson], I want to speak to the manager this instant. And Ina who had been a music teacher. Music? Ina wets the bed and is struck for it and hauled across the floor. And the little brown-faced woman is slapped because when the door is opened she runs to get out. But we all do. They open a door and we run, What is it like Out? Out There? They kick her behind and push her and pull her . . .
>
> I do not forget what it is like to be made into an animal and see others trampled on and hurt and not understood. And why do the nurses shout? Hey you, get back in there. Hey Milly. Dear Milly you are my mother, you bathed me and fed me and warmed me when I was small, and when you got hot the sweat trickled down the hollow between your breasts and under your arms and I cuddled up to you and got warmer being close to you, warm and sticky and you tasted sweet . . . Hey you, Milly.
>
> Who walks among the loonies, kissing them and stroking their lousy hair? Dear J, where is the heart and the river?[14]

In her autobiography Frame said of this time that she had discovered 'a personal, geographical, even linguistic exclusiveness in this community of the insane, who yet had no legal or personal external identity — no clothes of their own to wear, no handbags, no purses, no possessions but a temporary bed to sleep in with a locker beside it, and a room to sit in and stare, called the dayroom. Many patients confined in other wards of Seacliff had no name, only a nickname, no past, no future, only an imprisoned Now, an eternal Is-Land without its accompanying horizons, foot or handhold, and even without its everchanging sky.'[15] So infused did Frame become with concern for the welfare of patients, and for their stories, that June Frame, visiting the hospital, became convinced that her sister had tricked her way in there so as to observe and write a book about human behaviour.[16]

There was no crisis in her own behaviour at Seacliff, however, no deterioration that would confirm the diagnostic label that had been attached at Dunedin Hospital. And yet she felt profoundly changed. 'I knew that I could not turn back to my usual life or forget what I saw . . . I felt as if my life were overturned by this sudden division of people into "ordinary" people in the street, and these "secret" people whom few had seen or talked to, but whom many spoke of with derision, laughter, fear.'[17]

Among those who shared the fear, of course, were members of her own family. And when she was released into their care on 21 December 1945, on probation, one of the doctors 'explained' her illness to Lottie Frame and warned the mother to be alert for any recurrence of symptoms.[18] 'I looked at my family and I knew that they did not know what I had seen,' Janet would write. '[And] I noticed that [their] behaviour had changed in subtle ways . . . Who knew what I might do; I was a loony, wasn't I? . . . It seemed as if, having been in hospital, I had, like a spider, woven about me numerous threads which invisibly reached all those who "knew" and bound them to a paralysis of fixed poses and expressions and feelings that made me unhappy and lonely but also gave me a recognition of the power of having spun the web and the powerlessness of those trapped within it.'[19]

After Frame had been back at Willowglen for a week or two, the family's apprehension diminished. Lottie Frame, as she was wont to do, began to deny everything. Janet was a happy person. There must have been some mistake. 'I found that everyone was pleased when I treated the matter as a joke, talking of amusing incidents at the "country estate", likening it to a hotel. I described the surroundings. "It's like a whole village," I said. "They have their own farm, their own cattle and pigs, and all the waste from foods goes into the pig tin. They have their vegetable garden, and their flowers, too. And the grounds are full of trees, and there's a magnolia tree near where the superintendent lives." It was easier to talk as if I were a child on holiday describing what I'd seen and what adventures I'd had.'[20]

Soon a real holiday was in prospect. The family decided that a change would 'do Janet good'. She was despatched by train with June to the care of Lottie's relatives in Picton in the Marlborough Sounds. Over two summer weeks they swam, picnicked, took launch trips, visited relatives and heard new versions of Godfrey family history. They returned to Oamaru with memories of 'steep green oppressive hills, their bushclad slopes rising as inescapably close as neighbours'.[21]

Janet also came home to some unpleasant surprises. While she had missed the 1945 end-of-year examination, she had been told by John Money that she would pass her psychology paper on the basis of the whole year's work. Instead she had failed. Had she neglected to fill in the appropriate forms? Then, when she attempted to withdraw money from her bank account, she was informed by an officer of the Public Trust that 'confiscation of my "property" was in my own interests as I was officially insane and would not have legal rights until my "probation" . . . ended, and only then if the doctor declared my sanity'.[22]

An even greater shock was reserved for her visit to the mental clinic at

Oamaru Hospital, where Seacliff Superintendent Malcolm Brown told her for the first time that she was suffering from schizophrenia. He gave her no explanation of the characteristics of the illness, acting as if she was incapable of comprehension. So she looked it up in one of her psychology textbooks to find it described as 'a gradual deterioration of mind, with no cure. Of mind and behaviour . . .' This revelation came at precisely the time that she had begun to feel 'cured' of whatever had been wrong with her. Now, she learned, she had a condition for which there was no cure. 'It seemed to spell my doom . . . [It] would lead me further and further away, and in the end not even my family would know me.'[23]

The need for a variety of decisions and practical arrangements kept even doom at bay, however. In 1946 June was to remain at high school for another year before starting university. Isabel was to take up her first teaching position at Windsor School, thirteen miles north-east of Oamaru. Janet had no wish to remain at home, where the tension between her father and her brother was still palpable. She decided to advertise for a 'live-in' job in Dunedin so that she could support herself, attend university and make a more concerted effort to write (although, as she told John Money in January 1946, she doubted if she would ever be able to show her work to anybody).[24] She had abandoned the idea of librarianship. That would have put her back in another 'institution' with layers of procedures, rules and supervisors that she did not feel adequate to face. Her advertisement brought a reply from Mrs T. Park of Playfair Street, Caversham. Mrs Park kept a guest house with half-a-dozen boarders and four elderly women. Janet was offered and accepted the position of 'housemaid-waitress-nurse' at fifteen shillings a week plus keep. Her afternoons would be free for writing and studying.[25]

Caversham in South Dunedin was 'a poor community where lives were spent in the eternal "toil", with the low-lying landscape reflecting those lives, as if effort and hope were here washed away in the recurring floods'. Frame had completed two of her teachers' college 'sections' in the district and noted 'the poverty, the rows of decaying houses washed biscuit-colour by time and the rains and the floods; and the pale children lank haired and damp looking, as if they emerged each day from the tide'.[26]

Frame's room at 63 Playfair Street was a converted linen cupboard, 'small, with shelves along one wall and a narrow bed against the other . . . The view from the one small window was "pure Caversham" — dreary grey stone buildings with a glimpse of the tall chimneys of Parkside, the home for the aged, resembling my idea of a nineteenth-century English workhouse.'[27]

Her duties, which occupied four hours each morning, were to 'prepare and serve breakfast, to clean the house, and to attend to the four elderly women who lived, bedridden, each in a corner bed, in the large front room. I washed them, helped to turn them or arrange the rubber ring beneath their gaunt bodies where the skin hung in folds like chicken skin with bumps where feathers might once have been. I rubbed methylated spirits on the bedsores, and powdered their bodies. I fed them, sometimes with the aid of a white china feeding-cup. I helped them use the wooden commode or arranged a bedpan beneath their drooping buttocks.'[28] To her surprise, Frame found that one of the women, Mrs McLennan, was the mother of Aunty Han, wife of her father's brother Bob Frame, and grandmother of Iona Livingston. Uncle Bob had by this time retired from the bakery and sold cigarettes, tobacco, horse-racing guides and lottery tickets in a kiosk on Dunedin's main street.

Also to her surprise, Frame discovered that she could cope easily with the work. 'I had gentleness and everlasting patience with the sick and the old. I enjoyed waiting on people, attending to their comfort, doing as they asked, bringing the food they ordered. I had no impatience, irritation, anger, to subdue: I seemed to be a "born" servant. The knowledge frightened me: I was behaving as my mother had done all the years I had known her, and I was enjoying my new role: I could erase myself completely and live only through the feelings of others.'[29]

Frame had told the Parks that she was a student engaged in private research. This explained her need to vanish into her tiny room as soon as her chores were finished, even to take her meals there, as she had done at Aunty Isy's and Mrs Wadsworth's. She did do some studying — she had enrolled in a philosophy paper, logic and ethics, at Otago University. But what she mainly did there, sitting on the bed, was read literature and write stories and poems.

The inspiration for her stories, she wrote later, came partly from reading the Californian writer William Saroyan and thinking, 'I can do that too.'[30] But now in this, her fourth year in Dunedin, she had begun to read the work of New Zealand writers. In Modern Books, a left-wing bookshop in Moray Place, Dunedin, Frame had bought three books published by the Caxton Press in Christchurch over the preceding year. One was a collection of precociously brilliant poems by an eighteen-year-old Dunedin writer, James Keir Baxter, called *Beyond the Palisade*. The second was *A Book of New Zealand Verse 1923–45* edited by the Christchurch poet and journalist Allen Curnow. And the third was an anthology of short stories collected by the Auckland fiction writer Frank Sargeson, called *Speaking for Ourselves*. All three were to have the effect of focussing Frame's imaginative vision back onto the country, and onto the specific places, in which she actually lived. The fact that they displayed the work of New Zealand writers, some of whom lived in Dunedin and Christchurch, the next city north, gave her an inkling that her own secret ambition to be a writer might yet be capable of fulfilment.

'As a child,' she wrote subsequently, 'I had looked on New Zealand literature as the province of my mother, and when I longed for my surroundings . . . to awaken to imaginative life, all I could do was populate them with characters and dreams from the poetic world of another hemisphere and with my own imaginings. There *was* such a creation as New Zealand literature; I chose to ignore it, and indeed was scarcely aware of it. Few people spoke of it, as if it were a shameful disease.'[31]

With the acquisition of the three Caxton books another world opened up for her. While she found the Baxter poems complex and 'intimidating', the force and the variety of work in the anthologies 'gave me hope for my own writing while wakening in me an awareness of New Zealand as a place of writers who understood how I had felt when I imported J.C. Squire to describe my beloved South Island rivers'.

> [Now] I could read in Allen Curnow's poems about Canterbury and the plains, about 'dust and distance', about our land having its share of time and not having to borrow from a northern Shakespearian wallet . . . And there was Denis Glover using the names of our own rivers and places, and even writing about the magpies, perfectly recording their cries on a misty autumn morning . . . [And] Charles Brasch confiding in the sea as I had confided, without words, in the Clutha, 'Speak for us, great sea.'★ The stories, too, overwhelmed me by the fact of their belonging. It was almost a feeling of having been an orphan who discovers that her parents are alive and living in the most desirable home . . .[32]

These writers, Sargeson, Curnow, Glover, Brasch and Baxter, and E.P. Dawson, who wrote the story in *Speaking for Ourselves* that most affected her, 'Maria' (about the influence of the New Zealand bush over an artist), each of them would eventually have roles to play in Frame's personal or professional life. Early in 1946, however, she was aware of them as a portent and part of 'the excitement of being in a land that was coming alive with its own writing, *speaking for itself*'.[33] There was, it seemed to her, a Great Awakening occurring in the imaginative life of her country.

The excitement generated by this realisation blended with the sense of discovery that six weeks in Seacliff had brought, and with the effect of interacting daily with the boarding house residents. Her experience was throwing up a myriad of ideas for characters and stories. 'While I fed the guests . . . they fed me from [the] invisible bowl of their feelings,' she wrote later.[34] At the time, she swallowed and digested great gulps of their actions and mannerisms. ' "No, I won't read the paper tonight, Annie, it's my eyes, just pass me the births deaths and marriages . . . Take out my curlers for me will you, there's a dear. I could swear that Dr Borrie wasn't married, but I may be wrong. I'll ask my niece, she knows Dr Marion White . . . Does she dear? I've heard she's good. You have to have an appointment" . . . Hell, the humanity, the wonderful humanity of people . . . I'm going to spend all my life studying and

---

★    Speak for us, great sea.
      Speak in the night, compelling
      The frozen heart to hear,
      The memoried to forget
      (from 'Great Sea' in *The Land and the People* 1939)

writing about [them],' she was to tell John Money, 'but the ordinary people mostly, who are in the dark.'[35]

In the course of her first month at Caversham her writerly ambitions were given further impetus by the publication of the story she had written the previous year for the *New Zealand Listener*, 'University Entrance'. This, her first piece of adult writing to appear in print, grew out of the anxiety she had felt in her schooldays whenever she had had to ask her father for money. It has recognisably autobiographical elements: the portraits of her mother and father, the 'pash' she had on Miss Macaulay (called Miss Heafy in the story), the depression she experienced leaving the world of literature at school and coming home to face more prosaic realities, and — above all — the constant anxiety about money. It adds up to a competently realised piece of fiction, however, with an axis that turns on her father's unexpected willingness to hand over the two guineas and the change of mood that this provokes in the narrator.[36]

Her reaction to the story's appearance in the magazine was ambivalent. The *Listener* was a national magazine published by the government-run New Zealand Broadcasting Service. It was, at this time, the most prestigious outlet for short fiction in the country. Frame was understandably relieved that the editor, Oliver Duff, had considered her work good enough for publication and paid two guineas for it. Once she had the issue in her hand, however, she experienced a reluctance to open it on the story, and — when she did — a sense of acute embarrassment. This was not an embarrassment about seeing her name on the page, for she had asked that she be identified simply as 'J.F.' It was a difficulty, almost a phobia, associated with seeing and accepting her own words in print. The experience was analogous to looking into a mirror and, Caliban-like, being frightened of what one might see there. Frame wanted to write; and she wanted to write well; and she wanted to be accepted as an author. But she was not at all sure that she wanted her work to appear in print, nor herself to be recognised as the writer of particular stories. This paradox, rarely encountered among the community of writers, would create problems for her as her career unfolded.

For Frame, and for Frame alone, there was an additional irritant about publication in the *Listener*. The magazine's artist, Russell Clark, had illustrated the story in a way that she felt was discordant with its content and (certainly) with the real-life circumstances that had spawned it. In the interior of the house in the drawing the windows had curtains, the table a cloth, the floor appeared to be carpeted. The schoolgirl-narrator, elegantly posed in a well-fitting uniform, faced a mother handling balls of wool on a tidy table-top and a father relaxed in a chair with a pipe. To Frame, this domestic idyll seemed far removed from the austerity implicit in the story and the disorder of 56 Eden Street.

The new stories Frame wrote in her Caversham linen cupboard in the course of 1946 were typed one- or two-fingered on a second-hand Barlock 3 typewriter, 'whose keys insisted upon performing an intricate mid-air dance before they deigned to touch the paper', and which she balanced on her knees because there was no room to put it anywhere else.[37] It was one of the first items she bought with her wages. The majority of the stories, like 'University Entrance', drew on childhood and family recollections; a smaller number grew out of more recent experience of adult life, including the spell in Seacliff and encounters with guests in the boarding house. Her life away from Playfair Street was given over to reading at the Dunedin Public Library, philosophy lectures in the evening at university, and — by early May — weekly 'talks' with John Money.

Money had never been far from Frame's thoughts since the series of events which had led to her hospitalisation the previous year. In spite of her social reticence, and in spite of the largely satisfactory regime of work, writing and study which she had established at Playfair Street, Frame was daily conscious of the fact that she had been diagnosed as schizophrenic, and that this illness, she believed, would slowly erode her capacities to think and to cope with the exigencies of living. Every time she felt odd, unwell or unhappy, she worried that it might be the inexorable advance of her schizophrenia, and this magnified and exacerbated the source of the worry. She was also lonely, despite occasional contact with the Bradley sisters and Sheila Traill — and lonely in particular for the company of the man who still interested and excited her more than any other.

Thus it was that late in April 1946 she wrote to John Money, told him that she was still unhappy, and suggested that he was the only person to whom she could bring herself to talk about her 'problems'. But was he, she wondered, prepared to see her again after all the drama she had generated the previous year?[38] Money replied by return mail. Of *course* he would talk with her again, he said. '[For] the psychologist there is no such thing as passing judgement and blame . . . Your past behaviour is past . . . I am quite convinced that the best thing you can do is to come and see me again . . . [The] more one knows about oneself the more one is a healthy personality; the real way to know the truth about oneself is to talk to someone else.'[39]

In May, Money and Frame resumed their relationship of clinical psychologist and patient. From Money's viewpoint, he was authorised to play this role as student counsellor (Frame being still, however tenuously, a student). There was far more than this inherent in their association, however. Money recognised Frame as a person of outstanding creative ability. He was interested in the extent to which Frame's diagnosed schizophrenia had some bearing on her creativity; and he had a genuine desire to help her remove some of the factors that might damage her self-esteem and well-being and impede her ability to write.[40] For her part, Frame believed that she was suffering from a degenerative mental disorder and that therapeutic sessions with Money might delay her expected deterioration and even halt it. She found that discussion with him helped clarify the nature and sources of her anxieties. And, of course, she still had an intense emotional attachment to him.

Their sessions proceeded by way of the kinds of conversations favoured in psychoanalysis. On the days when Frame found it difficult to talk (applying what Money described as 'elective mutism'), Money would ask her to describe her dreams and reflect on the meaning of symbols that appeared to arise from them. Soon she was writing down dreams as they occurred and bringing the scripts with her for discussion. When there were no dreams, or none remembered, Money would ask Frame to 'free associate' ideas from previous dreams, or from questions of his ('What do you remember about being five years old?'). They would then examine words, images, symbols or ideas that arose from her conscious and unconscious mind.[41]

Frame valued these sessions and — as she had done the previous year — came to look forward to them. She believed that they helped keep her illness at bay and wanted them to continue.[42] And so, in case the raw material from her 'real' life proved insufficiently significant or dramatic to retain Money's attention, she began to read case histories of schizophrenics in the Dunedin Public Library and to introduce the symptoms and symbols she found there into her discussions with the psychologist. 'I built up a considerable schizophrenic repertoire,' she wrote later. 'I'd lie on the couch while [he] took note of what I said and did, and suddenly I'd put a glazed look in my eye, as if I were in a dream, and begin to relate a fantasy as if I experienced it as a reality. I'd describe it in detail while [Money] listened, impressed, serious. Usually I incorporated . . . details of my reading.'[43] One of these fabrications was the appearance of 'fantasy people' who appeared to be threatening and evil and who, Frame reported to Money, sometimes turned up in her bedroom, in Money's room, and even on the tram when she was travelling to and from the centre of the city.

These inventions helped to persuade Money that the Seacliff diagnosis of Frame's schizophrenia, which he had initially doubted, was probably valid. He now devoted time to helping Frame come to terms with the illness. 'When I think of you,' he told her, 'I think of Van Gogh, of Hugo Wolf . . .' Frame, knowing little about either men, turned to books and discovered that the Dutch artist had shot himself in despair and the Austrian composer died in an asylum. She read too that Schumann had suffered a serious deterioration in mental health. 'All three were named as schizophrenic, with their artistic ability apparently the pearl of their schizophrenia. Great artists, visionaries . . . My place was set, then, at the terrible feast. I had no illusions about "greatness" but at least I could endow my work and . . . my life with the mark of my schizophrenia.'[44]

Frame's pretence also began to create further problems. 'I was playing a game, half in earnest, to win the attention of a likeable young man whose interest was psychology and art,' she said in her autobiography. '[Yet] I was growing increasingly fearful of the likeness between some of my true feelings and those thought of as belonging to sufferers from schizophrenia. I *was* very shy, within myself. I preferred to write, to explore the world of imagination rather than to mix with others.'[45] In addition, while the whole idea of being schizophrenic seemed unreal to Frame, she read that that very sense of unreality was a symptom of the illness.[46] The consequence was that far from becoming 'better' as the year and her course of therapy advanced, Frame convinced herself that she was indeed heading towards complete mental collapse. The anxiety raised by this expectation increased her unhappiness and the prevalence of symptoms which Money took to be schizophrenic indicators (such as her periodic inability to talk, and her panic if for any reason their sessions had to be rearranged).

One feature of the year and of their association that proved to be wholly fruitful, however, was Money's interest in Frame's writing. She told him in June that she was producing poetry and stories and that her *Listener* piece had been published three months earlier. She went further and said that her strong preference would be to be able to earn a living from writing rather than housework.[47] To Money, aware of her literary promise, this seemed a course worth encouraging. He already knew enough of Frame's character and reactions to approach the subject obliquely rather than head-on. Her stories and poems, he said, would help their discussions. Just as talking had the therapeutic value of making thoughts 'non-private', so did writing. He therefore asked to see some of her work for professional purposes. He also told her that delivery of stories and poems to him would mean that she could forget her occasionally expressed feeling of guilt about being unable to pay for the 'treatment' Money was prepared to give her. At this point, Frame told him that she was scared of other people reading what she had written, because they would then be placed in a position of passing judgement on her. Money persisted, nonetheless, as Frame seems to have hoped that he would, and she eventually obliged him.

On 28 June she brought with her the first short story she gave him. It was 'The Park', a narrator's perception of the behaviour of some of the more disturbed patients at Seacliff. Money filed it away and referred to it as 'a story with self reference [to] the mental hospital . . . an extremely good piece of literature'.[48] Over the next nine months (an appropriate period for gestation) she gave him copies — sole copies — of all but one of the stories that would make up her first published collection, *The Lagoon*. Some she handed to him; some she left behind when she walked out of his office; at least one she screwed up and threw at him. Money expressed praise for the stories and encouragement, which Frame later acknowledged gave her a degree of confidence in their worth. She also gave him poems, which she described as 'pure schizophrenia'.[49] Money retained both sets of manuscripts with the intention of eventually submitting them to a publisher on Frame's behalf.[50]

With her permission Money sent a single story, which she had given him in October, 'Alison Hendry', to the Dunedin poet Charles Brasch. Brasch, who had returned to New Zealand from England late in 1945, was a member of a wealthy Jewish merchant family which had lavishly endowed artistic and cultural activities in Dunedin. He announced in 1946 that he planned to bring out a serious literary quarterly the following year. It was to be called *Landfall*, would carry original poetry, fiction and essays of a high standard, and would be printed and published in Christchurch by Caxton Press, publishers of the three New Zealand books which had so impressed Frame. Brasch had discussed this venture with Money and was delighted to receive Frame's story, which he used in the second issue (June 1947).[51] Publication in *Landfall* would do little to promote Frame's profile as a writer, however, especially as she insisted on a *nom de plume*: Jan (for Janet) Godfrey (her mother's family name). The story was set in the Caversham boarding house and included some details from her real life, including a description of her room there and glimpses of her time at Arthur Street School, Dunedin Public Hospital and Seacliff.

Frame did not meet Brasch at this time, though Money gave him an account of her talent and recent history. But she did have a brief encounter with Dunedin's other major poet, James K. Baxter, whose first book had so intimidated her. And it was John Money who organised the meeting. Baxter, who turned twenty in 1946, was two years younger than Frame. After an indifferent year as a student at Otago University in 1944 he had taken a succession of manual jobs and was employed by the Burnside Freezing Works when Frame came into contact with him. When not at work he was spending his free time in public bars, drinking and talking; or at university, visiting friends among the staff and students. Money was one such friend, and he was highly impressed by Baxter's writing talent, erudition and 'intellectual maturity' (and agreed with a friend who said subsequently that meeting Baxter at that time was analogous to meeting the young Shakespeare).[52]

Money developed the notion that his two writers should meet and come to know each other. He believed they would find much of common interest to talk about, especially psychology, literature and the world of ideas; and he was hopeful that Frame would become less isolated and more socially confident if she could be persuaded to widen her unusually narrow range of acquaintances. It may also have occurred to him that a friendship between Baxter and Frame would drain some of the intensity out of her relationship with him.[53]

And so Money laid the foundations. He showed some of Frame's stories to Baxter, who expressed keen admiration; he lent Frame some of Baxter's recent poems (she had his book) and noted that her response was to weep. Then he set up a meeting, for 4 October 1946. He arranged for Baxter to be in his office at the time Frame arrived for her weekly appointment. Money had warned the poet 'that he might find the situation a little unusual'. It was. Frame walked into the office, then just as rapidly whirled around and began to walk out. Money urged her to wait, saying that Baxter was just completing typing a poem and would then leave. Frame sat down on Money's couch and managed to skew herself around so that she had her back to Money and Baxter. The poet, talking continuously as he typed, attempted to draw Frame into a conversation. But she, aware now of what was being attempted, declined to cooperate. Eventually Baxter left, surprised that he had been stymied, but recognising defeat.[54] The two writers did not see each other again for another twenty years, when they did become close friends.*

Another person whom Money was keen for Frame to meet, though solely on professional grounds, was a refugee from Hitler's Europe who had emigrated to New Zealand in 1939. Grete Christeller had trained as a psychoanalyst with Carl Jung in Zurich and planned to open a practice in Christchurch, once her qualifications were officially recognised. Money heard about her from some of the 'art-literature-music people who cohered around the Caxton Press'.[55] His primary reason for interesting her in Frame, and Frame in Christeller, was that he had decided in the latter part of 1946 to travel to the United States the following year to do postgraduate work in psychology. He was unwilling to leave New Zealand without making some provision for Frame to continue therapy and Christeller, possibly the only psychotherapist in the South Island, seemed the best qualified candidate to take over his troubled patient and keep her out of the hands of the hospital psychiatrists who, Money believed, had not been helpful to Frame.

Nor was Money sure, however, that *he* had helped her. The fact was that, after seven months in therapy, Frame seemed little better than she had been at the time their sessions began. She had abandoned university studies; she told Money that she still saw threatening hallucinatory figures; she was still at times mute, panicky and unhappy; she said she had renewed impulses to suicide. Her probation from Seacliff had ended with a visit to the hospital's Dunedin clinic in June 1946, when she was 'discharged unrecovered'.[56] Two months later, at the same time that the hospital pronounced her 'discharged recovered', Money concluded that Frame had 'totally regressed' into schizophrenia. Part of this apparent regression may have been Frame's response to the news that Money would be leaving for Pittsburgh the following July. That development fore-shadowed the collapse of what she had come to view as her secure schizophrenic world of 'little talks'; it raised the possibility that she would have to face her putative descent into mental disintegration without the man she had come to see as her guide and mentor. More than that, Money had become the closest friend she had ever had and the thought of a life without him appalled and frightened her.

Instead of their sessions winding down into a shared understanding that she would now be able to cope with her problems alone, Frame was producing alarming new symptoms right up to the final week of therapy. At the end of November she announced that she was suffering from tics and spasms which caused her so much embarrassment that she was unable to associate with other

---

* See p. 302. Money was also at this time counselling Jacqueline Sturm, a Maori student who would subsequently marry Baxter and, in the mid-1960s, become another close friend of Frame.

people or even to eat at the table at the boarding house. 'She told me that there are different tics for different occasions,' Money noted. '[One] is for home, there is another for people at close range . . . another for the meal table . . . I explained that these were attention attracting devices, that they were an indirect invitation for ridicule and punishment for guilt . . . Also that they are sexual: her real fear of people is because they are a sexual threat to her.'[57] Frame gave no sign of being persuaded by any of these explanations.

In an effort to reassure her and enlarge her vestigial feelings of self-reliance, Money told Frame that they had come a long way together on a voyage of exploration, even if they were only 'on the frontier of the promised land'. He said that when difficulties recurred she must remember the techniques he had shown her — relaxation exercises, free association, analysis of symbols — for dealing with them. Finally, if her own efforts at coping failed, she was to communicate with him. He would ensure that she had his future addresses.[58]

At what was supposed to be their final session, on 9 December 1946, Frame told Money that she was going home to Willowglen for the summer. Then she would find a job in Christchurch, where few people knew her and where she hoped to continue writing. She would also take up Christeller's invitation to visit her, possibly with a view to resuming the routine of 'little talks'. In the meantime, Money assured her, he would show her stories and poems to a neighbour of his mother's in Wellington, the poet Anton Vogt, who taught English at Wellington Teachers' Training College. He would be guided by Vogt's advice about approaching a publisher.[59] Money also asked Frame to continue to send him stories and she agreed to do so.[60]

Back in Oamaru, and specifically back on the parts of the Willowglen property where she enjoyed viewing the plants, birds and animals, she began what she would remember as a 'paradisal' summer. Sometimes, she noted, 'I was able to rescue a sheep from the swamp, and for this service the stock and station agent . . . paid me five pounds.'[61] In January 1947 she spent a fortnight in the far south, on Stewart Island, with her friends the Bradley sisters and Rona Pinder.

'I have thought so much about the sea,' she told John Money by letter on 18 January. 'If I lived near the water all my life I would grow silent until I did not care to speak at all, ever, for the speech of the sea would matter more than my speech. I feel that way about the bush too. I know now why so many people paint [it] over and over again.' On Stewart Island, she said, as usual on the rare occasions she found herself with a group of people, she had been 'on the outside looking in'. They had been joined there by several young men and everything became 'most interesting and thought-provoking. Although promiscuity and heavy drinking are not in my personal code, what other people choose to do is not my moral, but very much my aesthetic concern.'[62]

Meanwhile John Money had what he believed was good news for her. On Anton Vogt's advice, he had taken Frame's stories and poems to Denis Glover, the poet and printer who was one of the founding partners of Caxton Press in Christchurch. Glover wrote to Money on 24 January to say that the stories amounted to 'quite extraordinary writing. In fact I have not seen anything quite so unaffectedly natural and at the same time incisive for a long time . . . In spite of a heavy programme before us, so heavy that I scarcely know how we are to get through it, I would like to do something with these pieces . . . Please tell me more about the author.'[63]

After Money had supplied details of Frame's recent history, Glover made a firm decision that Caxton would publish the stories as a book. '[The] pieces stand together as a whole. It is going to call for some thought to get them in the best order, and to repunctuate very slightly for the sake of clarity . . . However it will be a good while before we can get round to doing anything . . . our path is daily strewn with broken promises.' He was far less confident about the value of the poems. 'These are brilliantly impressionistic, but very naive as verse, and might not go down without rather involved explanations.'[64]

Frame's response to this news was wary. The stories, she told Money, were 'yours to arrange in any way you like, except that my name must never be mentioned. Only whole things ought to have names.'[65] The exultation she had felt earlier in the summer was now being undercut by a renewal of foreboding about family fortunes. The tenth anniversary of Myrtle's death loomed in March 1947 and, as a consequence, Frame said, 'the idea of death is with me all the time'. In addition, 'my brother has been ill in hospital . . . and my father's nicest brother [Bob Frame] has tried to kill himself and is being taken to Seacliff'. But there *were* things to be thankful for. 'My sisters and I are whole. For the next three weeks I shall be looking after my father and brother while my mother and Isabel go for a holiday to Picton.'[66]

The holiday back to her home town, where she would stay with her oldest sister, May, was a gift to Lottie Frame from her grateful children, all of whom made a financial contribution. Isabel went for company, and to carry suitcases and make necessary arrangements. Since the birth of Myrtle twenty-seven years before, Lottie had never been anywhere without a family to cook, clean and care for. Hence, unlike her husband and her children, she had never had a 'proper holiday' in all that time. She was pleased about the family's gesture. 'We could see in her face the surfacing of former pleasure — Oh Waikawa Road, Oh Old Caps and down the pa, Oh the Sounds, and Port Underwood, Dieffenbach and the Pebble Path, remember the Pebble Path, kiddies, the storms and the shipwrecks. Oh the Pioneers . . .'[67]

As so many Frame family ventures seemed to do, it ended in disaster, a scarcely believable repetition of tragedy. Janet wrote to John Money on 24 February 1947: 'There are so many things I wanted to write in answer to your thought-provoking letter, but tonight I can think only of the overwhelming accident that has just happened in my family. My sister Isabel was drowned at Picton last Monday and buried here on Friday. "World is suddener than we fancy it" . . . I almost cannot bear to be thinking that tonight outside in the dark I have two drowned sisters, even colder than any live people.'[68]

Contrary to the rumour that immediately gripped Oamaru, Isabel had not committed suicide.[69] It transpired that she had had Myrtle's congenitally weak heart. Twice in the previous year she had collapsed: once while crawling under a farm gate, the second time in the Oamaru Baths, scene of Myrtle's accident. At the baths a doctor had been called who, after examining Isabel, said that the fainting fit had probably been brought on by sunbathing before she entered the water.[70] The Frame family refused to even consider the possibility that Isabel too might have a heart problem — she was, as Myrtle before her had been, loud, assertive and unmistakably present. On 17 February, the first day of the holiday, she had swum out into Picton Harbour, was seen to get into difficulties, and was brought to the shore dead. When Lottie Frame returned to Oamaru on the train with her daughter's body in a lead coffin, her surviving family found her 'bewildered, her eyes frightened, and her hair beneath the "picture hat" of straw had turned from brown-grey to white'.[71]

John Money, who had shown inexhaustible patience and sensitivity towards Janet over the previous sixteen months, now made what seemed to be a blunder. He overlooked the fact that, only months earlier, his patient had complained about the 'form letters' that well-meaning people had written to the Frames after Myrtle's death.[72] Money himself now wrote what Janet would judge to be another 'form letter': 'I am deeply grieved to hear of the shocking bereavement you and your family have sustained. Words are so inadequate; I can only offer you the little bit of human friendship and sympathy which is a fragment of help on such occasions. There is also the assurance that time is a kindly physician. Please convey my sentiments to the other members of your family.'[73]

Frame, exquisitely sensitive to the meanings and nuances of words, and overly sensitive to everything John Money wrote to or about her, made no allowance for the difficulties people experienced trying to respond to death. She described herself as stunned. Three decades later she remembered Money's letter for 'the shock of its language and my inability to accept the formal conventional expressions of sympathy and to accept John [Money] was so lacking in imaginative understanding that he could write such a letter'.[74] She sent two replies. One was wild and despairing and, again, raised the possibility of her suicide.[75] The other, written a day later, was measured and redolent of the sublime insights and language skills that her correspondent so admired and had tried to nurture.

'I think we are such sad small people,' the second letter said, 'standing, each alone in a circle, trying to forget that death and terror are near. But death comes, and terror comes, and then we join hands and the circle is really magic. We have the strength then to face terror and death, even to laugh and make fun of being alive, and after that even to make more music and writing and dancing. But always, deep down, we are small sad people standing humanly alone. Oh for the hands to be joined for ever and the magic circle never to be broken . . .'[76]

For the next seven years the qualities represented by these two letters, far-sightedness and myosis, dignity and despair, would war within her. And, for the most part, despair — and the fear that accompanied it — would be dominant.

CHAPTER SIX

# *Except through Storm*

*T*HE KNOWLEDGE THAT A FAMILY TRAGEDY HAD RECURRED, AGAINST ALL conceivable odds, overwhelmed Janet Frame in the months after Isabel's death. She no longer had any sense of which parts of her unhappiness and confusion arose from her illness, which were generated by the loss of her sister, and which were fabricated. She told John Money in March 1947 that she was going 'further and further away from the world. I cannot stop myself . . . I am not going to fight against [my] fantasy world any more. Everything is becoming stranger and more unreal.'[1] Eleven days later she was back in Dunedin, wanting — needing — to talk with the psychologist.

Money was alarmed at what he took to be a deterioration in his patient's mental health. He had therapeutic sessions with her over three days, and tried again to focus her attention and her ambition on things she might be able to accomplish. This was partly an attempt to convince her that she did indeed have a future and hence to wean her off the notion of suicide; and partly to persuade her that she needed to organise her life around attainable goals. He said to her that 'she had a very high chance of becoming one of the noted writers of the century . . . Alternatively, she had a chance of becoming a penetrating and successful psychologist. These direct appeals to vanity did seem to [help] . . .'[2]

The prospect of becoming a 'world famous writer' was not new, although in her more sober moments Frame ranked this ambition on a par with the Frame sisters' girlhood dreams of becoming film stars, dancers or handicapped musicians. The idea of becoming a psychologist, however, *was* new; and it appealed to her. She told Money that she was 'intensely interested' in people who were mentally ill. 'When I was in Seacliff I made up my mind that I would do all I could for such people. I write letters to some of my friends there and I send cigarettes and books sometimes, but when I stop to think of the hell they are in and how brave many of them are, I always know that I am not doing enough.'[3]

Back in Oamaru the following month her mind was still focussed on this subject when she wrote her first letter to a newspaper for publication, to the *Otago Daily Times*. It was provoked by criticisms of John Money's pacifist views made by one of the paper's elderly columnists, former cabinet minister William Downie Stewart. Frame, signing herself 'Madhatter', wrote that Stewart was guilty of jargon, misquotation and an inability to distinguish between widely based research and personal opinion. Money's original comments had been made in an address to the Peace Union on 'Psychological Aspects of Fighting and Pacifism'. In Frame's opinion, Stewart's comments lacked social awareness. 'May I remind [him] that 25 miles or so north of Dunedin is a world of horrors . . . that no adult with a sense of social responsibilty can afford to ignore.'[4] Meanwhile Frame told Sheila Traill that she was now thinking about taking a social science course with a view to becoming a 'social welfare psychologist'.[5]

By mid-May Money had finalised his plans to move to the United States. He informed Frame that he had been awarded a senior internship under Saul Rosenzweig at the Western State Psychiatric Institute in Pittsburgh and would leave New Zealand in August 1947. He continued to urge her to move to Christchurch and take up Christeller's offer of psychotherapy. Frame replied that she would go eventually; but for the time being she needed to remain at Willowglen because her parents and brother were 'lonely without Isabel, even lonelier than I am'.[6] Besides, she added later, she was now seeing 'a tremendous shape and meaning and clearness in everything . . . [My] father eating his tea, the *Oamaru Mail* propped up against the milk-jug, the low chair that is striped like a lizard, and the towel hanging on the back of the chair. Look, my father gobbles his pudding. I like to see life with its teeth out.'[7]

Thanks to Money's initiatives as unofficial literary agent, Frame's writing career now seemed to be taking shape and substance. Denis Glover wrote to him on 16 May to say that the typesetting of the book of stories was 'in hand'; and that he 'could not help making the Mansfield comparison all the time; and do you know, I think Miss Frame has her licked in lots of ways'.[8] June brought the promised appearance of her 'Alison Hendry' story in the second issue of *Landfall*.[9] Money reported that his artist friend Theo Schoon was 'wildly enthusiastic about it, [he] said it was one of the rare examples of true artistry he had come across in this Philistine country'.[10] Frame, however, far from expressing satisfaction, reacted in much the same way as she had to publication of her *Listener* story. She told Money that she 'hung her head in shame every time that she thought of it, that it was not meant to be a story, and that she would never be able to look at it in print'.[11]

In the middle of June she returned to Dunedin to take yet another 'positively last farewell' of her friend and psychologist. Once Money had viewed New Zealand from abroad, she told him, 'you will never want to come back . . . What a tiny land it will be, and what tiny people, and tiny ideas.'[12] Money saw the visit as one last opportunity to widen Frame's circle of personal and professional acquaintances. He arranged for *Landfall* editor Charles Brasch to be in his office when she arrived. But history repeated itself. As she had done in the case of the Baxter introduction, Frame 'turned her head to the wall . . . and remained so, refusing all attempts to [include her] in the conversation'.[13] Brasch, who was himself a reticent person, found this a trial and left after half an hour.

Writing to Money subsequently, Frame said by way of part-explanation, part-apology: 'I am a moron when people talk to me. My mind freezes. But sometimes when I am alone and peaceful, the sun comes out and a thaw sets in and the current of my mind flows, and I have ideas about things.'[14] Her major preoccupation, she said, was observing people. '[Intense] emotion seems to give me intensity of observation . . . I think you have given me a course in observation so that my passion for studying people is even deeper now . . . If I have tried to possess you . . . it has been the you which is a psychotherapist . . . I have needed to borrow some of your security. I would never possess you as a friend . . . It seems funny that I shall never see you again.'[15]

In August 1947, John Money headed across the Pacific in the passenger liner *Rangitiki* to a new life and new career in the United States.★ That same month Frame made her much-postponed move to Christchurch. After scanning situations vacant columns in one of the city's newspapers, she turned down the prospect of a job at the School of the Deaf because 'they wanted to know too much about me'.[16] Instead, fortified with references from the Caversham boarding house ('well spoken, polite to the guests at all times . . .'), she took a position as housemaid-waitress at the Occidental Hotel in Latimer Square, an establishment much patronised by the horse-racing fraternity.

Initially she enjoyed the hotel work as much as she had her chores at Caversham. She learned 'the language of horse racing, of trainers, breeders, buyers, owners, who were the main clientele, and I found the routine satisfying — serving meals on time and bar lunch at five in the evening, and seizing the opportunity to speak French to the French buyers, and feeling slightly superior when they asked why I, with "my education", worked as a waitress, and giving the usual reply because I was not yet able or ready to call myself a "writer", "I'm engaged in private research" '.[17]

The feeling of satisfaction did not last. Her decaying teeth, which had been hurting and embarrassing her since her last year at school, now became unbearably painful. 'There was no escape from them . . . my entire face throbbed. I snuggled under the bedclothes with a hot-water bottle pressed against my jaw.

---

★ After postgraduate work at Pittsburgh and Harvard, Money founded the Psychohormonal Research Unit at Johns Hopkins Hospital and University in Baltimore, and (later) the Gender Identity Clinic. By the 1960s he was one of the world's best known sexologists.

I knew I'd be forced to act very soon. I knew that the public hospital would fill or extract teeth free.'[18] The problem was that the trauma of her first visit to a dentist at Wyndham when she was four years old had created a phobia. She was unable to muster the courage to make an appointment for any kind of remedial work. And the only person to whom she confided this private horror was John Money, now 6000 miles away.[19]

Frame was also lonely in Christchurch. The thought that she knew nobody there, and in particular nobody who was aware that she had been in Seacliff, had initially seemed appealing. The reality, however, was dismal. She missed the possibility of weekend excursions with Sheila Traill or the Bradley sisters. She missed John Money. Her family were now beyond the reach of easy weekend visits. Even the unfamiliar landscape added to her sense of desolation. '[A] dreadful feeling of nothingness . . . was somehow intensified by the city itself,' she wrote later. '[The] endless flat straight streets, the sky without a horizon of hills, the distant horizon without sea. I felt as if I and the city were at the bottom of a huge well walled with sky, and who could climb the sky?'[20] Soon even the predictable routines of the hotel job were drained of satisfaction. 'I am beginning to wonder how on earth I got [into] this place,' she told Money by letter, 'washing dishes and tripping backwards and forwards with orders. It couldn't have been me that came here.'[21]

One potential source of company was the congenial crowd of writers and artists and musicians who reputedly — John Money had told her — gathered around the Caxton Press. And Caxton was publishing her book, making her, as it were, a member of the 'family'. Perhaps, she had thought, having a book gestating and growing in Christchurch would be like having 'a neighbour living nearby'.[22] Her extreme shyness left her unable to test this possibility. She did call on Denis Glover in September 1947. But the visit was over in record time. 'I called, said no I didn't smoke, and fled.'[23] It was not repeated. Glover fancied he had exposed Frame to rather much of his 'gruff quarterdeck manner'.[24] But that was not the source of her difficulty. 'I have got to learn,' she told Money, 'that I am alone for ever . . . I will never have anybody close to me. The rest of the world is miles away over desert and snowfield and sea. Nobody knows how far away I am from everything. Looking at living, for me, is like looking mentally through the wrong end of opera glasses.'[25]

Frame did at this time send a letter to James K. Baxter, whose company she had spurned when John Money had introduced them. Now she felt moved to tell him how much she admired his poetry, though she confessed herself 'scared at [being] so paper-bold' as to write to him. Poetry, she began, was in the memory.

> [And] to my mind there are two ways of remembering. You can walk a hundred years in time picking and pressing and saving the daffodils and buttercups and daisies . . . till you have a mind full, and then you can yawn and sit down to fondle your treasure. Look I am remembering,

you say. I am making poetry. But what a dead smell your flowers have and the daisies have all fallen to pieces, petal by petal.

[Or] you can remember another and true way. You can annihilate time if you have enough power in you, though you suffer terribly, it is like having your feet cut off because you want so much to dance. And then you can . . . dance up and down for ever and ever from beginning to end and end to beginning. And then look how wet and cool the flowers are for they are still growing and having summers and knowing what the rain is like, for ever . . . [The] more I read of your work the more I feel that you are remembering the real way, you are back with the first snows and the first spring, you are walking up and down there from end to beginning and beginning to end, making . . . How much clear world you have got, while we are bruised with water and looking.[26]

Frame asked Baxter to destroy this letter, which he did not. He replied to her, but she did not feel disposed to maintain a correspondence. Instead, the loneliness and the crescendo of anxiety over her teeth drove her in October 1947 to the home of Grete Christeller, the German Jungian psychoanalyst of Jewish descent recommended by John Money. She lived in a fashionable part of St Albans. '[When] she, a tall angular woman dressed in fawn and brown, opened the door, I, sensing the impossibility of being able to explain my plight . . . again turned on my "schizophrenia" at full flow; it had become [Frame thought] my only way of arousing interest in those whose help I believed that I needed.'[27]

Christeller could not have been more sympathetic nor more willing to help. As John Money had anticipated, she was deeply interested in literary and artistic things, and the fact that her new patient was gifted and well read gave her an additional reason to be attentive to Frame's problems and needs. Despite this commitment, however, the counselling sessions did not go well. Frame eventually confessed to Money that she found herself unable to talk with Christeller. 'I cannot free-associate. Even with you I have never been able to free-associate in speech. Now I cannot even in writing.'[28] There appeared to be two separate but related problems. Frame found herself unable to establish with her new therapist the kind of rapport that had enabled her, for the most part, to talk freely with Money and to manufacture her 'schizophrenic' symptoms; and, at times, the two women experienced problems fully understanding each other, apparently because of linguistic difficulties.[29]

There was one decisive thing that Grete Christeller *was* able to do, however. She arranged for Frame to have all her top teeth removed under anaesthetic at Christchurch Public Hospital. This operation was performed in December 1947. And she had an innovative suggestion to make about her patient's 'mental' or emotional problems. 'She thinks my mind is so much divided that only a physical shock will unite it,' Frame told Money. 'She has advised me to go to Sunnyside [Hospital] for some shock treatment . . . What are your thoughts about it?'[30] Cautiously, Money advised that she should not expect too much from the relatively newly introduced electroconvulsive therapy.[31]

Late in February 1948, accompanied by Grete Christeller, Frame went back to the Christchurch Public Hospital for an assessment of her mental health; and from there she was admitted as a voluntary patient to Sunnyside Mental Hospital. She was, again, desperately unhappy; and she had given up trying to distinguish which of her symptoms were real and which were fabricated in her efforts to preserve her 'schizophrenic identity'. Her letters to John Money at this time suggest that her state of mind was close to that of the fictional narrator in her later novel, *Faces in the Water*, who described entering 'a season of peril'.

> I was put in hospital because a great gap opened in the ice floe between myself and the other people whom I watched, with their world, drifting away through a violet-coloured sea where hammer-head sharks in tropical ease swam side by side with the seals and the polar bears. I was alone on the ice. A blizzard came and I grew numb and wanted to lie down and sleep and I would have done so had not the strangers arrived with scissors and cloth bags filled with lice and red-labelled bottles of poison, and other dangers . . . And the strangers, without speaking, put up circular calico tents and camped with me, surrounding me with their merchandize of peril.[32]

Sunnyside Hospital near Spreydon, on the outskirts of Christchurch, had been established a decade earlier than Seacliff and the first superintendent had been a grandfather of the writer Ngaio Marsh. Its grey 'Gothic-cement' main building was every bit as grim as Seacliff's 'castle'. At first, though, it did not seem to Frame to be as 'primitive' as her old Alma Mater, because of the kindness of nursing staff and the fact that she did not encounter the most seriously disturbed patients.[33]

Almost immediately her sympathies were again engaged by patients in the grip of unshakeable obsessions. One, an elderly woman, shuffled past her frequently, saying, 'Oh dear, what shall I do, I caused the world.'[34] Another refused to eat or dress because she believed that by doing so she would be stealing from others. This patient was tortured by a voice that said to her, over and over, 'Thief, thief, you're a thief.'[35] After her experience of therapy with John Money and Grete Christeller, Frame concluded rapidly that these disorders (and her own) were made more acute by the fact that the patients were not given an opportunity to talk about them. One doctor told her that the hospital disapproved of psychotherapy because 'it makes you talk too much and think too much about yourself'.[36]

What Sunnyside did believe in, for certain categories of patients suffering from depression or schizophrenia, was electroconvulsive therapy (ECT). This treatment had been introduced into New Zealand hospitals over the previous three years. It involved attaching electrodes to the scalp and passing an electric current through the brain of sufficient strength to cause convulsions and a short-term coma. At this time no anaesthetics or muscle relaxants were used in association with the treatment and patients were restrained manually to prevent injury. They were fully conscious up to the time the electric pulses took effect. They found it an exceedingly unpleasant experience. ECT also resulted in memory loss for immediately preceding events and, in the case of patients subject to multiple doses, in longer-term memory impairment. On days when ECT was to be administered the atmosphere in wards resembled that in prisons on a day of execution.[37]

Frame's experience of the procedure was traumatic. '[My] life was thrown out of focus. I could not remember. I was terrified.'[38] She had two 'courses' of ECT at Sunnyside, twice a week for a total of twelve weeks. In addition to memory loss, the treatment triggered nightmares. 'I dreamed waking and sleeping dreams more terrible than any I [had] dreamed before . . . [If] only I had been able to talk about some of the terror, I know I would not have so readily translated my feelings into action. It sounds silly, but my clothes haunted me . . . Everything tortures [me] and is on fire and is coloured.'[39] After one application of ECT, Frame 'smashed a window with my fist; I cannot remember why, maybe as an outlet for some strange feeling which had no other means of escaping.'[40] The letter in which Frame communicated all this to Money had to be smuggled out of the hospital, as she was convinced the Sunnyside 'censors' would not allow it to be posted.

So badly did Frame react to both the prospect and the aftermath of ECT that it became difficult to ascribe cause and effect to her subsequent behaviour. She believed that the treatment was making her more confused and disturbed; the doctors appeared to think that the appearance of such symptoms indicated a need for further ECT. The confusion was apparent in her correspondence with Money, and her handwriting became less legible. In one letter, characteristically undated, she notes: 'I had some verse from James Baxter recently and if my memory hadn't been so buggered with shocks . . . I could have quoted them.'[41] In another she has rallied sufficiently to say of Baxter, 'I am interested in the development of his work simply because he is all symbols now, so far down has he gone into the unconscious. More than that . . . he has reduced poetry to talking of birth and death.'[42]

After four months in Sunnyside Frame felt 'utterly alone . . . As in other mental hospitals, you were locked up, you did as you were told or else, and that was that. My shame at my toothlessness, my burning sense of loss and grief, my aloneness, and now, with [June] lost in marriage, I felt as if there were no place on earth for me. I wanted to leave Sunnyside, but where could I go? I grieved for everything lost — my career as a teacher, my past, my home, where I knew I could never stay more than a few weeks, my sisters, my friends, my teeth, that is, myself as a person . . . I had woven myself into a trap . . . All I had left was my desire to be a writer.'[43]

Frame determined to leave Sunnyside in the latter part of June 1948. She did so, according to her hospital records, 'against medical advice';[44] and she told Money that the doctor in charge of her case 'shook his head and stared seriously at me'. But, as she saw things, she had 'come up for a breath, out of the dark among worms and bugs and roots of dead and living trees'.[45] She fled back to Willowglen, that 'poky little doll's house', the only place she had any right to call home. As before, she was charmed by the trees, the paddocks, the birds and the animals; and dismayed by her mother's helplessness and her father's constant state of war with her brother. As before too, she found further refuge in reading and writing.

'Dostoevsky and Rilke are dear friends,' she told Money by letter in August 1948, 'though I do puzzle. When I read them I become more acutely alive . . . I do not live here with these people, yet I do.'[46] Frame had Grete Christeller to thank for her new awareness of the German lyric poet Rainer Maria Rilke. Christeller had lent her volumes of Rilke's poetry in translation, which led Frame to buy her own copy of *Sonnets to Orpheus*, in which the poet had attempted to discover 'a satisfactory spiritual position amid the decay of reality'.[47] Frame devoured the work greedily, recognising that its preoccupations were similar to her own, and that its expression was powerful and reverberative. She quoted to John Money:

> Be not afraid of suffering, render
> heaviness back to the earth again;
> mountains are heavy, and seas, and the tender
> trees that in childhood you set in their places
> have grown too heavy for you to sustain.
> Ah, but the breezes . . . Ah, but the spaces . . .[48]

Commenting on this stanza, she wrote: 'We are the children and we run about with worlds on our shoulders, little Atlases and not knowing, taking trees in our finger, saying stay there, tree, and the tree stays, even the giant fir and oak. Can one in childhood catch the other side of heaviness, seas flowing like light and mountains wavering delicate as shadows? . . . My friend, you see the struggle in me between body and mind.'[49]

Part of that struggle was externalised in Frame's ambivalence about the happiness of her surviving sister. In May 1948 June Frame had married Wilson Gordon, whom she had met the previous year at Otago University. He was a gentle man, twelve years her senior, who had been interned for four years during the war as a conscientious objector. For the first four months of their married life the Gordons rented rooms in North Dunedin, then shifted to Auckland in September. 'I do not confide in my sister now, though she confides in me,' Frame wrote to John Money in August. '[She] and Wilson are very happy and I love them very much. But when she takes his hand or touches him, something, a despair strikes me for I know that I will never be able to touch the man that I think of . . . I want the sun, somebody warm to touch and know, and make me feel that I am a wanted plant, not one of the lost seeds sprouting by mistake in a desert of ice and snow.'[50]

Nor was she unmindful of that other sister, lost the previous year. In July she had sent Money another story, 'Swans', to be added to the collection that Caxton would publish. It arose from the death of one of the Eden Street cats and an early family visit to the beach.[51] But like so many of the stories that would appear in her first book it was a suggestive exploration of innocence and experience, a juxtaposition of the timeless world of childhood with the adult world of time and death. In a subsequent letter to Money, in August 1948, Frame explained how 'Swans' came to be written:

> The last thing I ever want to be is literary. I write . . . because I am scared and haunted and lonely and in love and full of wonder . . . I am not thinking of what I shall say, in fact I do not remember how I manage to say anything. I remember being haunted, and very often the original haunting is scarcely recognisable in what has been written — unless of course you . . . have the clues. In ['Swans'], the original haunting does not appear on the surface at all. I had been feeling a bit lonely for Isabel, and I kept seeing her as a child, outside a country store and lost. I do not consciously remember her ever having been lost in that way, but the vivid imagery persisted. There was the store, you know country stores, the fly-dirt on the window and a dead fat blow-fly lying just inside, and the empty packets of food and the sham chocolates . . . And outside there was a little fair-haired girl crying because she was lost. Nobody in the street, and the grey telegraph poles eaten by borer. And the wind high-up, talking through the wires. I saw it vividly and I sat down and wrote, feeling sad because of Isabel's being lost, and my unconscious very kindly took us for a day at the beach, and sneaked in the sadness with the dead cat and the wrong sea, and the father away at work, not sharing and not knowing. And so on. That is how the story gets written. I am interested to see how . . . June's marriage will find its way on paper . . . I have been rather haunted, change and all that, and I am interested to see what kind of literary bread is baked when the haunting goes pop pop.[52]

'Swans', which Money forwarded to Glover at Caxton, was the last of the stories to be written for Frame's first book. Nearly two months later, instead of more stories, Frame had disturbing news for her expatriate friend. Even though her brother had moved, temporarily, to Australia, she was still finding life at Willowglen wearing. So for some weeks she had been sleeping away from the house, in a tent under pine trees on the property. From there she had visited the monthly mental clinic at Oamaru Hospital, which she had agreed to do at the time she left Sunnyside. She told Money what occurred early in October:

I was scared of course and didn't say much and got in a bit of a panic. This doctor has communicated with Sunnyside and they have decided that I should not be free, that I should have some further kind of treatment. The doctor has told my parents that my mental state is serious, that I am not well enough to be admitted to Seacliff as a voluntary boarder, and that my parents should commit me without delay . . . I don't care where I go or what happens to me for I am sane, I am terribly sane, so much so that it looks to other people like insanity . . . [So] they are taking me away to Seacliff. How strange . . . I do not feel that I shall lose any freedom there, for I have discovered that my freedom is within me and nothing can destroy it, and I remember Pierre in Tolstoy's *War and Peace*, how he was a prisoner and looked out of the window and laughed and laughed because the world was inside him, his own . . .[53]

It was dangerous to bandy about literary allusions in dealings with the mental hospital system. The following day, for the second time in her life, Frame was formally committed to Seacliff Hospital. And one of the general practitioners who signed the medical certificate noted gravely that 'she says she is a lot of people . . . One of the persons is Pierre.'[54] The other doctor identified her as a 'student' who was mentally ill because of 'competition and overwork for exams' — and this almost four years after she had sat her last examination. Such misunderstandings were possible because Frame did not cooperate with interrogation.[55] The second doctor went on to report that, when asked where she lived, the patient had replied, 'in the world'. When asked if this meant that she lived in China, she replied, 'at times'.[56] Lottie Frame was persuaded to sign the application for committal and declared that she did so 'on advice of medical authorities and of Dr McLachlan . . . so that she will have to remain in Mental Hospital to have treatment completed'.[57]

Frame arrived at Seacliff on the afternoon of 9 October. Admission notes state that she had been asked to return as a voluntary boarder but had been 'too mentally ill to appreciate her obligations . . . When questioned she repeated . . . "There's nothing to say, there's nothing to say" . . . She recognised the Hospital as Seacliff and admitted that she had previously been here . . . When asked about hallucinations patient replied, "I'll be silly if I tell you what I hear. You would not let me go home." When she finally talked freely, patient's conversation revealed the extent of her illness. "I am in all places and I am everywhere. I find every place interesting" . . . Patient is suffering from Schizophrenia and is in urgent need of treatment.'[58]

This time Frame was sent to Ward Four, which housed acute women patients. She was back in the monochrome world of hospital clothes and regimented routines of, 'rise, ladies', 'dayroom, ladies', 'dining room, ladies', 'lavatories, ladies'; and she was not allowed out of the ward for work therapy. Now all her days would be divided between the dormitory, the dayroom, the dining room and the treatment room. And the treatment, of which she was judged to be in 'urgent need', was to be a resumption of ECT. She was given daily shocks for the first fortnight, reducing to every two or three days for another month, then once or twice a week until mid-January 1949.

Lottie Frame, filled with anxiety, and perhaps too feeling some guilt, heard no news of Janet. And so, a fortnight after her daughter's admission, she wrote to Dr McLachlan, on whose pressing advice she had been persuaded to sign the committal application. The reply came from Malcolm Brown, still medical superintendent of Seacliff. 'Since admission Janet has had intensive electrical treatment . . . Her prospects of complete recovery are not good. In future would you please address any letters of enquiry to me, and not to individual members of my staff.'[59]

Frame was to spend four-and-a-half of the next six years in hospital. It was a period she would view later as the nadir of her life and she wrote of her 'feeling of panic simply at being locked up by those who reminded me constantly that I was "there for life" '.[60] The underlying cause of this sentence was not any continuing erratic or uncooperative behaviour on her part; it was the diagnosis of schizophrenia attached to her three years before and never queried subsequently. In her hospital notes, taken up and consulted by each doctor with whom she would have a clinical association, she was not simply a schizophrenic — she was now 'a known schizophrene of several [soon to be "many"] years standing'.[61] And schizophrenia, it was widely known, could not be cured. The most that could be hoped for was 'relief' or remission, and that was the purpose of the electroconvulsive therapy. There was never any expectation that Frame would again be well.

'As the years passed,' she wrote, 'and the diagnosis remained, with no one apparently questioning it even by formal interviewing or tests, I felt hope-lessness at my plight. I inhabited a territory of loneliness which I think resembles that place were the dying spend their time before death, and from where those who do return living to the world bring inevitably a unique point of view that is a nightmare, a treasure, and a lifelong possession; at times I think it must be the best view in the world, ranging even farther than the view from the mountains of love, equal in its rapture and chilling exposure, there in the neighbourhood of the ancient gods and goddesses.'[62]

That was very much a retrospective and a coming-to-terms-with judgement. Frame was unable to retain any such perspective while she remained in hospital. Her letters written to John Money at the time she was undergoing electro-convulsive and (later) insulin shock therapy are less agitated than those written from Willowglen. But they are also far more bland, and — unusually for Frame — banal. This was partly an expression of the numbing effect that ECT had on her mind and memory; and since any suggestion of 'genius' would have been attributed to the full force of her schizophrenia, it may also have been an attempt to convince medical staff, who read her letters, that she was 'well', able to behave like 'ordinary' people, and hence be eligible for discharge. Such banality might also have been an indication that she was becoming institutionalised.

One letter, written in November 1948, reads like a parody. Frame tells Money that she is deriving much pleasure from 'picture shows, cards, dances . . . The other night when we entertained ourselves with games I found myself with a few fellow-patients at a table in the Day Room sharing the excitement and vagaries of Snakes and Ladders.'[63] This from a person who only months before had derived her excitement from the insights of Dostoevsky and Rilke . . .

One source of continuing consolation, however, which she carried with her, alternatively clutched and concealed like a precious talisman, was *The Complete Works of William Shakespeare*, which June Gordon had given her in May 1948. It was confiscated when she was deemed to be 'refractory'; and then she would scheme for its return. Frame did not often *read* the book, but instead simply turned 'the tissue-thin pages, which somehow conveyed the words to me . . . I had absorbed the spirit of *The Tempest*. Even Prospero in his book-lined cell had suffered shipwreck and selfwreck; his island was unreachable except through storm.'[64]

In March 1949, when she was once more on probation, Frame took a more cynical view. 'I smiled and said very well thank you when the doctor came on his rounds, though when I left he told me he had never spoken to me and knew nothing about me . . . But if I told the truth they would have kept me there. If I had told them that . . . strange people . . . perch in my mind and drop their cloud-white droppings. Or said I could easily hang myself on a spider-web. Or said I am not real and am nothing, the sunbeam that is only a speck of dust.' The trouble was, she continued, 'I am two people and every day the division is more marked. The woman who smiles and speaks when spoken to . . . And [the one who] feels like a scaled fish under the water [among] secret weeds, where my mind . . . sees colour and listens to water moving and flowing . . . That is the only reality for me, my inside mind.'[65]

During this three-month probation she sent further poems to John Money, and a 3500-word story to Charles Brasch for *Landfall*. Her letter to Brasch showed her customary absence of conviction and convention. 'Mr Editor, a story. Crumbly and of poor grade. You probably won't want it. In that case burn it quickly or crush it into tiny pieces for Rat Darkness to sneak in and snuffle.'[66] Brasch neither accepted the story — he sent it on to Denis Glover — nor replied to Frame's letter.

Frame also wrote to Money at this time about a more substantial writing ambition. 'I have had a longing to write a sort of novel and trace the minds of people in and out of their mysterious weavings, and find what the whole of being has concealed . . . [But] hell, I have to come down to earth and sleep and eat and talk or at least answer when someone speaks to me, and all that interrupting and futile nonsense which breaks over any delicate web hung out quietly and peacefully to catch the overwhelming sun.'[67] There was no longer any mention by her of the putative book of stories which, more than two years after Caxton had accepted it, seemed no nearer publication.[68]

She had a further confession to make to Money. On the occasions that she was back in Oamaru, she said, she never visited old acquaintances, former fellow pupils or Waitaki Girls' High School teachers. 'I cannot . . . talk about myself. I cannot. Every month I have to go to the hospital and [see] one of the doctors from Seacliff . . . I have been able scarcely to say a word to them . . . I just go into a kind of dream, probably to escape the burden of their questioning. And my voice won't work. And if it did it would utter what they would think to be utter nonsense . . . I keep silent because, physically, I cannot speak. And last time it was worse because I acted like a child and ran away, and it was from Dr Brown too. They haven't whisked me back to their asylum [yet], they just fill in a form to say that I am "incapable of work".'[69]

Unaware that Frame herself was worried about such behaviour and reflective about its meaning, however, Malcolm Brown did have her recalled to Seacliff at the end of May 1949. The intensive course of electroconvulsive therapy was resumed and maintained until the end of December. There is no evidence that Frame was able to write letters, poems or stories over this period; nor was she permitted to bring her typewriter to hospital. Malcolm Brown wrote two letters in response to inquiries from Lottie Frame, assuring her that her daughter was 'thinking along more normal lines' and 'beginning to take an interest in things [and] doing some reading, needlework and helping about the ward'.[70]

In February 1950 Frame was released yet again on probation. As soon as she was reunited with her typewriter at Willowglen she reported to Money* on what she had seen as the resumption of a battle of tactics and wits:

> I tried hard to act in what the authorities consider 'the normal way'. I smiled when I waxed the floor. I said good morning when the doctor said good morning. I said yes certainly when I was asked to sweep and polish a long long corridor . . . [For] polishing is quite normal, and saying good morning and smiling with just the right degree of sanity — such behaviour is approved of and 'gets you out quickly' . . . In Seacliff I had to act like a tramp. I mean I wrapped my mind-belongings in a hanky on the end of a stick and slept on them, never daring to reveal them, or I

---

* This was Frame's last letter to Money for nearly three years. She learned in 1950 that he had married and subsequently 'no longer wrote the freely conversational letters' (*Autobiography*, p. 215). The correspondence resumed after the marriage ended late in 1952.

should still be polishing . . . I suppose all my life I shall be a tramp, spotted hanky and all. I don't care.[71]

But she *did* care. And now she followed what had become an established pattern of behaviour. Each time she was discharged from Seacliff she was longing to return to Oamaru. But, after two months at home, she was ready again to contemplate a return to hospital, indifferent to what would turn out to be its horrors. On 6 April 1950 she was found wandering the corridors of Oamaru Hospital and she asked for readmission to Seacliff. Two days later she was back in the mental hospital, where she resumed ECT for another five months. On 16 September, apparently happier (although, in effect, this meant simply less agitated), she was out again on probation.

This time, fully aware of the previous record of remission and relapse, Frame attempted to break the pattern by taking a job. She nursed a terminally ill woman in Oamaru, cleaned the house, prepared meals, and washed and ironed clothes for the invalid and her husband. But the household of 'grey people washed with sweat and tears' was too debilitatingly depressing and she left after a month.[72] On a whim she applied for a job in radio, which was advertising for women announcers with 'good vocal qualities, good educational background [and] a general and wide experience of life'. Frame had all these; but she was defeated by the prospect of having to fill in forms in triplicate and report to a radio station for an interview and audition.[73]

Instead, Frame decided to accept a long-standing invitation from her sister and brother-in-law to stay with them in Auckland. She was now convinced, and so was June Gordon, that to make significant progress and manage to stay out of hospital she needed to remove herself from the stresses and claustrophobia at Willowglen, which up to this time had seemed the only alternative to Seacliff. Frame, who had never been further north than Wellington, was also excited by the *idea* of Auckland. She longed to experience the northern climate, with all the differences of light, colour, weather and landscape that the word 'subtropical' implied. And she wanted to re-establish rapport with her sister and eliminate the guilt she had felt about their loss of intimacy since June's marriage to Wilson Gordon.[74]

. The stay with the Gordons, in Birkdale on Auckland's North Shore, lasted barely one month, however. 'They and their infant son enclosed one another while I stood awkwardly in the background,' Frame would write later. '[If] anyone called and looked my way, my shyness and self-consciousness, arising from my feeling of being nowhere, increased when my sister's friends asked, "How is she?" "Does she like being in Auckland?" I had become a third person, at home in Willowglen and now here in Auckland. Sometimes, as if I were my own obituary, people asked, "What was she?" . . . I could no longer bear the nothingness. I retreated to an inward state, that is, I put on a mask, while at the same time totally aware of everything. I, in my nothingness and nowhereness was asserting the nothingness and nowhereness of everything and everyone around me.'[75] This condition, identified by a well-meaning but uncomprehending doctor as 'catatonic', alarmed the Gordons and persuaded them to take Frame to the Auckland Mental Hospital at Avondale, where she was committed on 2 January 1951.

Just as Seacliff Hospital, in Otago usage, had been 'up' or 'down the line', in Auckland idiom Frame was now 'up the Wow' — the Avondale Mental Hospital stood on the bank of the Whau River, which drained into the upper reaches of the Waitemata Harbour. Like Seacliff and Sunnyside, it had been built in the nineteenth century and was modelled on large, prison-like Victorian asylums in England. If anything, conditions at Avondale were worse than those at Seacliff. More than one thousand patients were crammed into 'tumbledown and often insanitary conditions'.[76] Although the buildings were in the process of being renovated, the wards were unheated, the walls and ceilings covered with crumbling plaster. There was cracked linoleum on the floors. Acute staffing shortages meant that hospital routines were highly regulated: patients were 'managed' rather than treated.

On admission, Frame was described as suffering 'a very florid schizophrenic episode with pronounced aggressive trends and strongly expressed pre-occupations with death'.[77] Alarmingly, her height had risen three inches since her previous hospital admission — but this proved to be an error. 'She gave no response to questions and lay immobile in bed and resisted the taking of nourishment.'[78] Because of what her hospital notes describe as a 'strong resentment' of ECT, medical staff attempted to reduce the severity of her symptoms by the prolonged use of insulin shock therapy. This treatment produced comas and convulsions, accompanied by writhings and moanings, and was believed to have beneficial effects for schizophrenics.[79] It had no discernably beneficial effect on Frame, other than to leave her drowsy and 'mentally numb' in the immediate aftermath.

Frame believed in retrospect that she had been treated more harshly at Avondale than she had been at Seacliff or Sunnyside, even though the entire mental health service at this time was administered as if it were a single hospital. Her view was possibly a consequence of the fact that, once her earlier hospital records reached Auckland, she was identified as a 'schizophrenic of long standing' (six years now having passed since the initial diagnosis); and that hard-pressed medical and nursing staff paid little attention to individual patients with what were deemed to be chronic disorders. When Frame attempted to assert herself and secure some privileges (to retrieve her typewriter, for example, and to write), she was dismissed by staff as 'intractable'. And as the effects of insulin therapy intensified her confusion, she was consigned to Park House, a refractory ward where, as she wrote later, 'human beings became or were quickly transformed into living as animals'.[80]

This experience, in the early months of 1952, was the lowest point of all Frame's years in hospital. Once, in a moment of lucid optimism, she had assured John Money that, whatever happened to her, she knew that she had 'a final sanity, a kind of inviolable core from which in future I shall have to take my strength'.[81] It was in Avondale that she had to reach most deeply into herself and draw on that last vestige of stamina and hope. One night, sleepless in Park House amid the howls of the demented and the stench of urine, she came as close as she would ever come to losing belief in her own identity and hope that she had any kind of future. She rolled on her straw mattress to face the darkened wall and recited the Twenty-third Psalm:

> The Lord is my shepherd: I shall not want.
> He maketh me to lie down in green pastures:
> He leadeth me beside the still waters.
> Yea, though I walk through the valley of the shadow of death,
> I will fear no evil:
> For Thou art with me;
> Thy rod and Thy staff they comfort me.

Just to say the words was a source of comfort, as it always had been. But this time there was more than comfort. The following morning, as if in answer to a plea, Frame was moved back to Ward Seven, which she would always remember as 'an oasis with its park and willow tree and its friendly ward sister'.[82] She took this to be a sign that prayers *were* heard, and that somebody, something — one of her mother's angels? — was looking after her. She retained this conviction, and this memory, for the rest of her life.

If this advance had been unexpected, so was the sequel. When she was back in Ward Seven, thin, with sores and a discharging ear — infections picked up in Park House — a parcel arrived from Christchurch. The hospital's deputy-superintendent, who had an abiding interest in all things cultural, described the event in Frame's hospital notes for 4 March 1952. '[She] has just had a book of short stories, "The Lagoon & Other Stories", published by the Caxton Press, in which she displays good verbal ability & a keen perceptiveness of the finer shades of emotional experience in a childish & immature sort of way.'[83] Dr Geoffrey Blake-Palmer, who had already noted of this patient that, during periods of 'inaccessibility', she was prepared to speak with him in French, was intrigued and impressed.[84] And, though he was to leave Avondale that very month, he would not lose contact with his interestingly 'literary patient'. For, in succession to Malcolm Brown, he had been appointed superintendent of Seacliff Hospital.

# CHAPTER SEVEN

# Into the World

*D*ENIS GLOVER, WRESTLING WITH ALCOHOL, A DISINTEGRATING marriage and disagreements with his printing and publishing partners, had left Caxton Press in November 1951. The last job he did for his old firm was the printing of Janet Frame's stories. 'After all these years,' Glover told Money, they had lain like 'a dead dog across my conscience'.[1] The resulting volume was small in format, ran to 130 pages and looked both clean and delicate. In Frame's view, 'the appearance of the book was beautiful, with its pale blue design like links of stalks of wild grass'.[2]

There were some oddities, possibly symptoms of Glover's distractedness or his inability to supervise the final production. The title on the cover (*The Lagoon and other stories*) was different from that on the title page (*The Lagoon, Stories*). The given year of publication, 1951, was incorrect, although this indicated a delay in binding, for which Glover was not responsible. There was no jacket blurb about either the author or the stories, and no jacket photograph of the author. There was no sign of the requested dedication to John Money. The author's real name was used, though Frame did not now object to that.

When June and Wilson Gordon brought her six author's copies in to Avondale's Ward Seven, Frame, still in bed recovering from her Park House infections, 'spread them out on the white government counterpane embroidered with the New Zealand coat of arms: *Ake Ake, Onward, Onward* . . . I turned the pages, feeling the tiny grains within the paper. "What shall I do with them?" I asked.'[3] The Gordons explained that she should autograph the title pages and give copies to those who 'ought' to have one: her parents, of course, the Gordons themselves, and a couple for her; and perhaps one each for Drs John Money and Geoffrey Blake-Palmer? Frame immediately lent one to a patient in the ward and never saw it again. But she was gratified. She was now not only a writer, a published writer, but also an author: the evidence was tangible and indisputable.

The hospital authorities too were impressed. On 29 February they had declined to release Frame on probation. On 19 March 1952, however, a fortnight after Geoffrey Blake-Palmer had noted the arrival of *The Lagoon*, Frame was permitted to leave Avondale to fly to Christchurch and Oamaru with June Gordon and her (now) two young sons, Ian and Neil. Wilson Gordon, who was selling advertising calendars on commission, followed by car, working his way south. They would all stay at Willowglen. During the stopover in Christchurch, Frame's fragile pride in *The Lagoon* was shattered. Browsing through a copy of the Christchurch *Press*, she discovered the first review of her first book.

> [It] is produced with an elegance and care that the stories themselves scarcely deserve. This sort of thing has been done already by Frank Sargeson, and one wearies of his imitators. Nearly all the sketches are impressions of childhood, with little or no real point or narrative interest, written in a style that consists of simple statements endlessly joined by a chain of 'ands'. There is much use of the pronoun 'you', the dialogue is all run together into long paragraphs, and plenty of New Zealand slang and colloquialisms are thrown in to provide local colour. The fact that Janet Frame remembers her childhood with vivid intensity cannot redeem the style which, up to a point, is suitable for evoking material images of the New Zealand scene, but can convey no emotions other than the simplest and the most sentimental.[4]

The review, which was unsigned, ended with a quotation from the story 'Swans', which it ridiculed.

Authors' encounters with first reviews amount almost always, to them, to a rite of passage. If they continue to write, the nature and verdict of such notices can condition how they feel about the reviewing process for the remainder of their lives. Frame's reaction to this one, come upon so casually, was to experience 'painful humiliation and rejection [and] an immense torment of not knowing where to be — if I could not live within the world of books, then where could I survive?'[5] It was both characteristic and understandable that she would always remember it, word for word, and that she would remain apprehensive about all reviews from that time on.

Over a period of months, however, the consensus of reviewers was that *The Lagoon* signalled the arrival of a major new talent. The first notice to appear nationally, and one of the most influential, was Frank Sargeson's in the *New Zealand Listener*. Sargeson who, according to the *Press* reviewer, was the source of Frame's story models (and whose own first book had been disparaged by the very same newspaper), saw no evidence of imitation. Under the heading 'A New Light', he said that Frame's stories posed a momentous question.

Can people ever be said to be truly at home when they can never quite decide whether it mightn't be an advantage to be somewhere else? But in the meantime there is the brick bungalow to camp in — and beneath its tiles love grows timid and fearful, faith and hope eventually become pinned to the ticket in Tatts, the children develop the nervous tensions that may never be resolved in a lifetime, and the adults either sleep the mental sleep from which there is no awakening, or suffer the emotional strangulation that is slow but sure, and as deadly as death. It is . . . all there, all clearly rendered in language which, despite its simplicity of statement and rhythm, is the author's own special creation. From now on our literature is the richer, and the author, Janet Frame, becomes one more light to help diminish the vast region of darkness by which we are all surrounded.[6]

Dorothy Neal White, who had joined the staff of the Dunedin Teachers' Training College as librarian in Frame's second year there, reviewed the book for that city's public radio station, 4YA. Here, she said, is a collection of stories 'which will rank in New Zealand literature beside Katherine Mansfield's *Garden Party* and Frank Sargeson's *A Man and His Wife* . . . Janet Frame works within the tradition of the New Zealand short story — and she also extends that tradition . . . [She] weaves her prose from the thread and idiom of everyday speech [and] it is the sound rather than the sight of things New Zealand which is recorded . . . For Janet Frame [the] emotional peaks are the illuminating experiences of life — perhaps . . . the only moments when we live at all.' And, for Otago people, Neal White concluded, Frame's collection gave 'our experiences in these latitudes . . . "the sanctity of print" '.[7] Neal White followed this up with a letter to Frame in which she expressed congratulations and gratitude.[8]

The review in *Landfall* was written by Patricia Guest, whose sister Hillary Muir had been a contemporary of Frame's at teachers' college. It was not without qualification, but concluded that the stories were written 'unsentimentally, [though] with great compassion and understanding'. They provided an opportunity to 'put a wise ear to the keyhole of a mind more sensitive than one's own — an experience that induces respect and humility'. *The Lagoon* was 'a considerable achievement'; but, even more, it was 'a promise of future work of distinction'.[9] It is doubtful that any previous New Zealand book by a first-time author had attracted such widespread admiration.

The ripples, too, spread beyond reviews. Sargeson urged the book on Dan Davin at Clarendon Press in Oxford and persuaded him to include one story, 'The Day of the Sheep', in an anthology of New Zealand stories which Davin was selecting and introducing for Oxford University Press's World's Classics series.[10] 'It's a damn fine work,' Sargeson told Davin, 'and the poor girl is out of the Wow at last — I hope for good, though if it buggers her writing she might just as well have stayed in.'[11] Sargeson also recommended the book to fellow writers Maurice Duggan (who was in London in 1952), E.P. Dawson, Ruth Dallas and Dennis McEldowney.[12] Other writers-to-be and at least one future publisher would record being affected by *The Lagoon* at impressionable times in their lives.[13]

The book caused something of a minor sensation in Oamaru. Those who knew the Frames or who were part of the Waitaki Girls' High School network were astonished, and in some cases angered, that they could recognise the characters who had inspired some of the stories; and that some of these characters (Mrs Feathers, for example, and the teacher Miss Gibson) retained their 'real' names.[14] In spite of indignation expressed on her behalf, however, Janet Gibson pronounced herself 'pleased' with the story in which she featured, 'Miss Gibson and the lumber room'.[15] The book reportedly sold well in Oamaru, Christchurch and Dunedin and — although no sales figures survived — was printed by Caxton in a second edition in 1961.[16]

Meanwhile, in March 1952, Frame and the Gordons had reached Willowglen for the holiday that Janet subsequently described as 'an illuminating disaster'. George Frame had difficulty coping with the noise and disorder that two small boys brought into the house. And Janet felt excluded by the additional degree of intimacy which the shared role of motherhood now gave June and her mother. 'Always in our family there was the struggle between powerlessness and power, where closeness to people and the ability to prove that closeness became a symbol of most power [and] where each understands why the others must at times behave or speak with apparent glee at misfortune . . .'[17]

These accumulated tensions may have been the cause of Lottie Frame's heart attack one night in April. Janet referred to it as 'a night of the kind of violent change that always happens, and had appeared as a milestone in the landscape of our family'.[18] Lottie was rushed to Oamaru Hospital, sedated with morphine. George Frame's face showed 'complete loss and bewilderment'. Father and daughter cobbled together new domestic routines, but awkwardly. 'We were desperate to have her returned to us, returned whole without pain.'[19] Meanwhile Geordie Frame took to his bed after a series of seizures and expected to be looked after as an invalid.

Given past patterns, it was unsurprising that this crisis brought on another. Janet returned voluntarily to Seacliff on 9 May, telling the admitting doctor that the move was 'an escape mechanism from her inability to adjust herself to home life'.[20] Her 'treatment' was a repetition of what had occurred in Auckland. She was sent to Seacliff's equivalent of Park House, a ward for the most disturbed patients which was known as the Brick Building. 'I now had what was known as a "history", and ways of dealing with those with a "history" were stereotyped, without investigation . . . I was removed to the back ward

. . . where I became one of the forgotten people . . . It was [now] recognised that I was in hospital "for life" . . . [I felt a] sense of hopelessness as the months passed [in a] constant state of physical capture where I was at the mercy of those who made judgements and decisions without even talking at length to me or trying to know me or even submitting me to the standard tests . . . The state could be defined as forced submission to custodial capture.'[21]

Over the next nineteen months Frame was part of what she called 'a memorable family', a group of patients whose character and behaviour she would describe in detail in her second novel, *Faces in the Water*.[22] 'It was their sadness and courage and my desire to "speak" for them that enabled me to survive.'[23] She was helped also, she would say later, by the insight and care of nurses such as Buddy Doherty and Rosie Murray, both Tuhoe Maori from the Bay of Plenty; Gene Powell, who was Welsh and (inevitably) known as 'Taffy'; and Noreen Ramsay.[24] The attitude of those 'in charge', however, those who 'wrote the reports and influenced the treatment, was that of reprimand and punishment, with certain forms of medical treatment being threatened as punishment for failure to "co-operate" where "not co-operate" might mean a refusal to obey an order, say, to go to the doorless lavatories with six others and urinate in public while suffering verbal abuse by the nurse for being unwilling. "Too fussy are we? Well, Miss Educated, you'll learn a thing or two here." Dear Educated, Miss Educated: sadly, the fact of my having been to high school, training college and university struck a vein of vindictiveness . . .'[25]

Because of her extreme aversion to ECT, Frame was now treated largely with insulin therapy, as she had been at Avondale. But this time something worse was in store. In December 1952 she was informed by Cyril Burt, one of the young, overworked medical staff, that she had been selected for the dreaded 'prefrontal leucotomy' operation, known in the United States as 'lobotomy', which severed the fibres connecting the front part of the brain to the rest of the cerebral cortex. Dr Burt told her that 'it would be good for me, that, following it, I would be "out of hospital in no time" '. Frame heard this news with a 'swamping wave of horror . . . [Also] with a feeling that my erasure was being completed . . . [The] ward sister, suddenly interested that something was about to be "done" with me and to me, painted her picture of how it would be when it was all over. "We had one patient who was here for years until she had a leucotomy. And now she's selling hats in a hat shop. I saw her just the other day, selling hats, as normal as anyone. Wouldn't you like to be normal?" Everyone felt that it was better for me to be "normal" and not have fancy intellectual notions about being a writer, that it was better for me to be out of hospital, working at an ordinary occupation, mixing with others . . .'[26]

Frame was not convinced. There was only one person whose opinion she trusted on the matter. So she resumed her correspondence with John Money in order to express her fears about the operation, and to ask him, 'Shall I still be able to write, shall I still have the emotional urgency and need for writing?'[27]

Money replied from Johns Hopkins Hospital in Baltimore. '[The] very fact that you could ask me the question with such detachment is evidence that it would not do much for you. At this hospital it is generally felt that leucotomy has not lived up to expectations: they do not perform [it] here. So if you have any choice in the matter . . . I would say no.'[28]

At Seacliff, however, the scene was set. Lottie Frame, as next of kin, had been persuaded to sign a letter of consent ('I am quite sure you would not decline permission for [an] operation likely to benefit your daughter,' one doctor had written to her).[29] The letter said that 'Janet Paterson Frame, having failed to maintain a good level of response to the ordinary physical methods of treatment . . . is deemed to be a suitable subject for Prefrontal Leucotomy Operation to which I hereby give my consent . . . I understand to what extent this operation may offer a measure of relief and the minor element of risk involved.'[30]

It is unlikely that Mrs Frame understood any such thing. There was controversy within the medical profession about the efficacy and risks of leucotomies, and Geoffrey Blake-Palmer's predecessor as superintendent at Seacliff had believed that they achieved beneficial results 'only in a limited number of cases'.[31] The risks were that patients would be left vegetative, or that their depressions or obsessions intensified. There was an eventual consensus that the harmful effects outweighed likely benefits.[32] But this was a decade away. In December 1952, Janet Frame was on Seacliff Hospital's operation list.

It was Frame's writing, not John Money's postal intervention, that saved her. Lottie Frame's consent was signed on 20 December, Frame's plea to Money on 24 December. On 26 December, within days of the scheduled surgery, newspapers around the country carried a story headed, 'Writer Wins Prize for Prose': 'The New Zealand centre of the [writers' organisation] PEN announces that the Hubert Church Memorial award for prose has been won by Miss Janet Frame of Oamaru for her book "Lagoon and other stories".'[33] The prize, worth twenty-five pounds, was at that time the country's major literary award for prose (Frank Sargeson had won it the previous year). To those 'in the know', it represented a prestigious honour.[34]

One such initiate was hospital superintendent Geoffrey Blake-Palmer. He came into the dayroom of Frame's ward brandishing a copy of the Dunedin *Evening Star*. He told her about the award (she had never heard of it); and that, because of it, she would be taken off the operation list. 'I've decided that you should stay as you are. I don't want you changed.'[35] There would be no leucotomy for her; and she would be moved to a more open ward. This decision, combined with the attentions of John Stenhouse, a doctor recently arrived from Scotland, resulted in drastic changes in Frame's circumstances.

'I was [now] treated as a person of some worth, a human being, in spite of the misgivings and unwillingness of some members of the staff, who, like certain relatives when a child is given attention, warn the mother that the child is being "spoiled", spoke pessimistically and perhaps enviously of my being "made a fuss of".[36] This was no exaggeration. When Frame was again allowed the use of her typewriter, for example, her hospital notes record that 'various concessions have been made [and] she is rapidly becoming a "law unto herself" '.[37]

Relief at her own deliverance was undercut by the fact that a friend was not so fortunate. Audrey Scrivener, a fellow patient, was the daughter of Frame's teachers' college lecturer in nature study and agriculture, Len Scrivener. She had been committed to Seacliff in the belief that her asthma was psychosomatic in origin. At Seacliff her asthma worsened and she became severely depressed. She was scheduled for brain surgery at the same time as Frame; and she was not rescued by the award of a literary prize. Scrivener 'had her leucotomy and was returned to the hospital, where, among the group known as "the leucotomies", some attempt was made to continue, with personal attention, the process of "being made normal" . . . [They] were talked to, taken for walks, prettied with make-up and floral scarves covering their shaven heads. They were silent, docile; their eyes were large and dark and their faces pale, with damp skin. They were being "retrained", to "fit in" to the everyday world, always described as "outside" . . . In the whirlwind of work and the shortage of staff and the too-slow process of retraining, the leucotomies one by one became the casualties of withdrawn attention and interest; the false spring turned once again to winter.'[38]

When Frame eventually left Seacliff, Audrey Scrivener remained, and she was in and out of psychiatric hospitals for the rest of her life. Cruelly, the asthma which had been the initial cause of her illness was worse, not better, after the leucotomy. '[Although] she was formerly aware [of] and interested in things of the mind,' Frame wrote, 'now she sits and knits.'[39] Scrivener also now communicated, in speech and by letter, with a dogged, pedestrian determination. Frame, feeling a sense of guilt that she had escaped the operation while her friend had not, corresponded with Scrivener until her death in 1973. 'The legacy of her dehumanising change remains . . . with all who knew her,' Frame would say after that death. 'I have it with me always.'[40]

Over the next twelve months Frame progressed and regressed, as she had done in the course of previous hospital admissions. In the periods when she felt sufficiently confident and well to participate in occupational therapy she learned Russian weaving, and made a whitebait net for her father, a cradle for Dr Blake-Palmer and a scarf for Wilson Gordon, one of whose sisters was a fellow patient. There were other times when she felt confined, frustrated and angry and rebelled against hospital discipline.

On one of these latter occasions, when Frame had been placed 'in seclusion' for clambering onto a rooftop in January 1953, she was visited by Dorothy Neal White. 'I was crawling on the very bottom of living and never did I need a visitor so much,' Frame wrote later to Neal White. 'I remember that afternoon with delight, your talking about writing and *Anna Karenina* and Henry James; and Dr [Henry] Bennett being tactful and not appearing on guard . . . [After] you had gone they gave me a tomato . . . for tea. I made it last all the way to my room.'[41] Neal White herself left Frame a characteristic gift: a small photograph of Henry James's house in Rye, Sussex. Frame treasured this memento which became, like her *Collected Shakespeare*, a talisman to connect her with the world of the mind and the spirit beyond the confines of Seacliff Hospital.[42]

Frame was discharged on probation from Seacliff yet again on 29 November 1953. She returned to Willowglen, where her father had made shelves for her books in the front bedroom and her mother bought a new rose-coloured eiderdown. 'I don't want you ever to leave home again,' George Frame told his older surviving daughter.[43] Lottie Frame concurred. They spoke, Janet knew, out of real concern for her well-being; but also because 'it was the tradition for the single woman to remain with her ageing parents'.[44]

At first, despite her parents' worry that she might 'tax her brain', Frame applied herself to the business of writing. A succession of events had gently raised her confidence that she might, eventually, be able to live by herself and support herself by writing. There had been publication of *The Lagoon*, the generally favourable reviews, the award of the Hubert Church prize. Then, while she was still in hospital in 1953, she had been asked by Charles Brasch to sign a letter to Frank Sargeson, scheduled for publication in the March 1953 issue of *Landfall*. This commemorated the Auckland writer's fiftieth birthday and was a tribute unprecedented in New Zealand letters. Among other compliments, it noted that Sargeson had 'proved that a New Zealander could publish work true to his own country and of a high degree of artistry . . . You turned over new ground with great care and revealed that our manners and behaviour formed just as good a basis for enduring literature as those of any other country.'[45] These were accomplishments with which Frame's own ambitions were wholly in accord. The letter was signed by all the country's major writers of fiction, including Dan Davin (albeit an expatriate), Roderick Finlayson, A.P. Gaskell, John Reece Cole, Maurice Duggan, Phillip Wilson — and Janet Frame.

Eight months later, in November 1953, came publication of Oxford University Press's World's Classics edition of *New Zealand Short Stories*. Here Frame was grouped with (among others) Katherine Mansfield, Sargeson, Davin, Finlayson, Gaskell, Cole, Duggan, Wilson, Anton Vogt and Dennis McEldowney.[46] For the most part, good company. But here again the edge was taken off her pleasure by a single review, which appeared two and a half weeks after Frame had left Seacliff. Monte Holcroft, editor of the national journal *New Zealand Listener*, wrote that 'Janet Frame has won herself a sudden reputation which seems to justify [her] inclusion . . . It is easy to be impressed by her sensitive writing, but I notice with dismay that she uses in a modified way the stream of consciousness technique at least 15 years after it has been discarded elsewhere.'[47]

Despite this chastening note, Frame discovered William Faulkner and Franz Kafka in the Oamaru Library in December 1953 and 'began to write stories and poems and to think of a future without . . . fear that I would be seized and "treated" without being able to escape'.[48] She had an immediate success with a story, 'The Gravy Boat', which was not only accepted by radio's 4YC programme; she was also asked to read and record it in Dunedin. A *Listener* review of this performance, possibly by Dorothy Neal White, called it 'the best thing in the year's programmes . . . Its beauty and originality of imagery, its irony and its sadness were interwoven in a story that was itself interesting in its barest outlines. The full circle of local speech — heard, absorbed, written, read and thus heard again — gave the story overtones which involved the listener in his own experience. Janet Frame . . . has a voice of unusual charm, and her delighted savouring of the phrases, each one dropped and with reluctant irony, added the final measure of enjoyment to her narrative.'[49]

Frame spent the early months of 1954 drafting new work and attempting to live harmoniously with her mother and father. In April she told John Money that she had planned to leave Willowglen as soon as possible. '[But] my mother who was in hospital for the greater part of last year [still] needs my help. Her illness has had a . . . mellowing effect on the rest of the family.'[50]

A letter arrived from Charles Brasch asking permission to publish in *Landfall* one of her poems which John Money had given to Denis Glover seven years earlier.[51] Frame hesitated, re-read the poem when Brasch sent it to her, and then declined. 'It is too long ago and *Then;* it would have to have a Now attached . . . To make up for my saying No . . . I shall certainly send a bit of recent work — when I can bring myself to show it to anybody.'[52]

When, later in the year, she did send him new work, six poems and two stories ('Quick as Bream' and 'Gorse is not People'), Brasch rejected them. 'I'm afraid I don't much like the poems [and] the stories seem to me to be too painful to print . . . I'd rather wait till you have some more.'[53] He did, however, send Frame a book for review, *Take My Tip* by Terence Journet, from Pegasus Press in Christchurch (for whom Denis Glover had briefly gone to work after leaving Caxton). It was about horse-racing, a subject with which she was familiar from her days at the Occidental Hotel; in particular it offered advice on how to bet. Frame completed the review, and called the book 'fun to read, shall I say quite Gloverly fun?'[54] She did not appreciate that reviewers kept books and returned her copy to Brasch. The *Landfall* rejections were compensated for by the *Listener*'s acceptance of a story based on a tale her father had told her when they went fishing off the Oamaru wharf, 'Lolly-Legs', this time published under her own name; and two poems, 'The Waitresses' and 'The Liftman'.[55]

These last were written in Dunedin. Frame had moved there in mid-May, to take a live-in waitressing job at the Grand Hotel. She was forced to accept, she told John Money, that she would never be able to rehabilitate herself at Willowglen, 'where everything is always clouded and dark in a kind of dream. In some people's lives, after fires have burned, the smoke floats away, you can see it sailing up into the sky; in my family the smoke stays on the walls and blackens them; if you walk into the lives of my people you walk into a dark room.'[56]

The hotel, 'the Grand', had earned its name. It was built in 1883 on a commanding site in the centre of Dunedin to the plan of an Italian architect. It had external figureheads carved in stone, an Italian marble entrance, plaster ceilings modelled in London, and an ornamental glass dome. The Duke of Gloucester, staying there in 1935, had expressed amazement at finding himself, in the Antipodes, in surroundings of such 'refinement, luxury and sophistication'.[57] Frame, to be paid 'six pounds a week, all found', planned to support herself by waitressing and to continue writing in her attic room in the hotel.

> I wore a starched white smock, white shoes and a starched cap. I was given a 'station', or set of tables, to wait upon and I quickly learned the language and the behaviour that was expected of me. I learned the routine as well, from the attitude to adopt towards the head waitress, the manager and his wife . . . to the kitchen routine and the setting of tables, the special way to fold the serviettes into their rosette. I learned also to sense the excitement among my fellow waitresses when guests were leaving and there was the hope that a tip would be left under the plate. The regular guests, the good tippers, were known, and there was rivalry to have them seated at one's station . . . [It] was a congenial place to work. I enjoyed walking about the dining room in my uniform with the table napkin draped over my arm. I took pride in remembering the orders and stacking the plates . . .[58]

There were other things, too, to do in Dunedin, which Frame now thought of as 'one of my oldest acquaintances, perhaps my only acquaintance'.[59] Concerts (the Alma Trio) provided one option; dances another. Her fellow waitresses took charge of her choice of clothes, lipstick, perfume, hairstyle. 'Their chief desire . . . was to make me one of them.'[60] And Frame did want, at least at first, to be part of their tribe. She had nearly ten years of lost living to catch up on. 'When I was a child, I was always excited by the adventure of a *first time* . . . Now, I had missed so many experiences in ordinary living that my "firsts" [were] out of step with the "firsts" of others.'[61] So she did not tell her waitress companions that the dance they went to at the Dunedin Town Hall — where she did not, in fact, 'dance', because nobody asked her — was the first she had attended outside the grim parodies of such occasions organised in mental hospitals. Another 'first' was attendance at the Dunedin wedding of her cousin 'Big Bill' Frame, son of her father's brother Bill, for which Frame made a blue feather hat — and sold it afterwards for ten shillings.

In June, when the novelty of this new life was still fresh, she wrote to John Money: 'Living is terribly real. You know how you go to an art exhibition or look at a picture and someone beside you says of a Still Life With Grapes, "Look, they're so lifelike you could reach out and take one" . . . Well, living is like that, it is not rested, it has to be reached out for all the time and taken and tasted. Everything is so alive, even inanimate objects, the table in my room, the wall, my radiogram . . .'[62]

Browsing in Modern Books she re-met Charles Brasch, who invited her back to his home at 31 Royal Terrace for tea the following Thursday. The other waitresses, scenting matrimonial opportunities and impressed by the fact that Brasch was believed to be wealthy, counselled Frame on how to present herself ('Wear your jersey and skirt . . . [and] a brassiere').[63] Brasch, a man of exquisite taste and manners who was fifteen years her senior and lived alone, showed Frame into 'a large book-lined room where he served tea and seed cake while a white cat known as Whizz–Bang looked on'.

I told Mr Brasch that my mother had worked for old Mrs Beauchamp, Katherine Mansfield's grandmother, and for 'old Mr Fels', his own grandfather. 'She remembers you and your sister,' I said. Mr Brasch looked stern. I felt that he disliked personal reminiscences and references, but what else could I say? I knew so little. He began to talk of New Zealand literature. I remained silent. I thought, He must know where I have been for the past eight years. I suddenly felt like crying. I was awkward and there were crumbs of seed cake all over my plate and on the white carpet at my feet. Then, remembering the introduction to *Speaking for Ourselves*, I murmured one or two opinions on the stories, quoting directly from the text. 'I agree with you,' Mr Brasch said.

Our conversation died away. Mr Brasch poured more tea from an attractive pot with a wicker handle arched above it. 'I'm fond of this teapot,' he said, noticing my glance at it. 'I'd better be going,' I said . . . When Mr Brasch opened the door, he said in a startled voice, 'Oh, it's raining, and you haven't a coat. Would you like a coat?' 'No, thank you, I haven't far to go.'

When I returned to the Grand Hotel and my fellow workers asked about my visit, I said slyly, 'He offered me a coat.' They were impressed. 'You should have worn pearls, though,' they said.[64]

After several months Frame's enjoyment of both the city and the job began to pall. The parts of Dunedin that she had frequented previously, such as the university and the teachers' college, 'were no longer my world . . . [All] my former surroundings were like toy streets with toy buildings where the toy people had been replaced by new toy people, still talking and laughing about the old topics.'[65] There was also a peril that she had not reckoned on, running into Seacliff staff and patients — or former staff and patients — who knew who she was and her recent history. This, she found, undermined her confidence.

But it was the hotel kitchen that became the arena for the most unpleasant encounters.

The servings of dinner were different for men and women, with men given a larger portion, and, of chicken, the *leg* or *wing*, while women were served a smaller portion, and always *breast* of chicken, and thus when I came through the swing doors to call out my order I had to shout swiftly, *Chicken, a gent* or *Chicken, a lady. Beef, a gent. Beef, a lady.* My voice was soft, I was reluctant to shout, and I found the word gent distasteful. I therefore made my order, *Chicken, a man, beef, a man*, overturning all the tradition of the kitchen of the Grand Hotel . . . The second cook, a brusque bully, launched a teasing, angry attack on my language and refused to fill my orders unless I gave them in the traditional way, and, sensing my reluctance, she insisted that I repeat my order again and again. The giving of meal orders became a torment. One day I ran in tears from the servery . . . I wondered what I could do, where I could go. There was nowhere.[66]

Despite her hope — indeed, her belief — that she would never have to return to hospital, the effect of these bruising daily encounters eroded Frame's ability to cope with the 'outside' world. On 11 October 1954 she was given her discharge from Seacliff, having succeeded in staying out of hospital for almost a year — her second-longest period of remission since she had entered hospital nine years before.[67] But six weeks later, she visited Dr Blake-Palmer at the mental clinic at Dunedin Hospital and communicated a renewed sense of distress. He wrote: '[She] is again going through a period of acute internal stress out of which is emerging a considerable volume of morbid writings . . . [Most] of the discussion centred round the analogy of the kite and its string, and the fable of the kite that tried to get away and climb higher by breaking its string . . . I have since got in touch with the licencee of the Grand Hotel and suggested that [Janet] take a period of leave.'[68]

At the end of November, Frame was again home at Willowglen, from where she wrote to Charles Brasch on 9 December that she had become ill and been forced to leave the Grand Hotel.[69] Five days later she had herself readmitted to Seacliff Hospital as a voluntary boarder. On her application form she gave her occupation as waitress; her reason for seeking admission, she wrote in characteristically allusive and elusive terms, was

As I was walking on the stair
I met a thing that wasn't there
It wasn't there again today
I wish the thing would go away.[70]

Hospital authorities took this to be an admission of hallucinations, consistent with her schizophrenia. 'She is fully volitional [and] retains a surprising degree of insight,' her notes recorded. 'But [she] has become fearful and it is largely because of this fear and feelings of panic . . . that she seeks asylum.'[71]

This time, unlike the periods following previous hospital admissions, Frame made a steady recovery. She avoided ECT and insulin therapy and was simply prescribed a new anti-psychotic drug. Her hospital records chart rapid progress. 'Good rapport obtained . . . Clean and neat in appearance. Pleasant and cooperative . . . Is brighter, somewhat more outgoing . . . Plays basketball & mixes a lot with others . . . [She] has again started to write, having obtained her typewriter from home.' Finally: 'Discharged "relieved" ' . . . She proposes to return home . . . & carry on her literary activities.'[72] On 1 March 1955, Frame walked out of Seacliff Hospital for the last time and caught the north-bound train to Oamaru.

Her intention to return 'home' was stated only to facilitate her release from hospital. In fact she remained at Willowglen for the briefest time possible. Aware that family stresses had triggered previous relapses in her health, and oppressed by her parents' expectation that she would be the daughter who stayed with them and cared for them as they declined into ill-health and old age ('a final subtraction which I could not bear to face'),[73] Frame determined to break the pattern decisively. She would accept her sister and brother-in-law's invitation to return to Auckland.

Her efforts to obtain a sickness benefit on release from Seacliff, to allow her to write uninterruptedly, had been frustrated by Dr Blake-Palmer. He would never agree to that, he said. While he hoped that she would continue to write as a gifted amateur, it was even more important for her full recovery that she not risk losing 'the habit of working'.[74] That being the case, Frame determined, she would abandon waitressing 'to work as a housemaid only, where I could spend my time on my own with my own thoughts, moving from room to room, making beds, dusting, polishing, without the daily conflict with cooks'.[75]

And so it unfolded — or began to unfold. Frame bought her parents an electric blanket, 'to help them through the awful winter', then had a formal photographic portrait taken, 'a kind of reinstating of myself as a person'.[76] With the rest of her savings she bought her fares to Auckland. In mid-March she travelled by train to Christchurch, ferry to Wellington (where she stayed with her Uncle Vere and Aunty Polly Curtis) and train again to Auckland. '[Suddenly] there was "up north" again, the blue paradisal air and light.'[77] There too were June and Wilson Gordon and their three children (a daughter, Pamela,

had been born in August 1954). They were still on the North Shore of the
Waitemata Harbour but had moved to Northcote.

Within days of her arrival Frame had found a live-in job as a housemaid at
the TransTasman Hotel in the city. But it was not quite as she had expected.

[Unlike] the Grand Hotel . . . with its family atmosphere, there were
many rooms, many floors, a large staff and a sense of urgency about
every activity . . . People, unsmiling, spoke briskly, abruptly. I was given a
floor to myself and the usual duties of bedmaking, room dusting and
cleaning, cleaning of the corridors and bathrooms, with my own quarters
a tiny room upstairs in what was called the Gods . . . I soon discovered
that many of the guests on my floor were pilots and passengers (from the
early morning Pan American flights) who stayed in bed until late
afternoon, and it was on one of these afternoons when I was still
struggling with unmade beds and uncleaned rooms when I should long
ago have finished, that the housekeeper discovered me and threatened to
sack me if I could not work faster. I burst into tears and that evening I
left the TransTasman. I had survived only one week. Auckland was a real
city, a harsh city like those I had read about.[78]

Frame returned to Northcote, where the Gordons had just built a new home
on a bushclad slope above mangrove flats on the edge of the Waitemata
Harbour. For a week she devoted time to 'getting to know' June, Wilson and
their three children. Then, at the weekend, they went for a drive, supposedly
to 'see the sights' of Auckland's North Shore. It was in the course of that
outing that Frame met Frank Sargeson. And that meeting would deflect her
life onto yet another trajectory: this time, it would be one with which she
would find herself wholly in accord.

CHAPTER EIGHT

# Sorcerer's Apprentice

$\mathcal{A}$UCKLAND, JANET FRAME'S HOME FOR THE NEXT SIXTEEN MONTHS, seemed exotic to anybody conditioned by Otago and Southland. The city lay on an isthmus between two harbours. It was flat, but dotted with dormant volcanic cones, some of which were called mountains — a source of amusement to South Islanders accustomed to 'real' mountains. Among the features to impress Frame were the tropical vegetation, which included palm trees and hibiscus flowers, the heat and humidity, 'the everlasting sound of the cicadas and crickets, the bite of the mosquitoes . . . [and the] light alternating between harsh brilliance and paradisal cloud softness, like a storm oppressively, perpetually brewing'.[1]

Frank Sargeson, like June and Wilson Gordon, lived on the North Shore of Waitemata Harbour, facing Auckland city across a passage of water criss-crossed daily by ferries. His home was an asbestos cottage set in a quarter-acre tangle of hedges, vegetable garden and fruit trees. His street, Esmonde Road, ended at the mud and mangroves of the inner harbour. Sargeson had lived there for almost a quarter of a century, first in a one-roomed family bach and subsequently, from 1948, in the three-roomed cottage he occupied when Frame met him. Behind the cottage was an army hut, which Sargeson had previously let to friends and fellow writers.

After a conviction in 1929 for a homosexual act, Sargeson had turned his back on his first career as a solicitor, and on what he regarded as the materialist and bourgeois values of his Methodist parents. Living initially off journalism and the sale of home-grown fruit and vegetables, he had set out with monastic dedication to become his country's first full-time writer of fiction.* He had

---

* Katherine Mansfield, of course, had gone to England and Europe in the early years of the century and remained there.

found his own voice in a series of stories first published in a left-wing journal in 1935. From the late 1930s he was being published with some regularity in New Zealand, Australia, the United States and the United Kingdom. He had reached his widest audience during the years of the Second World War, when John Lehmann took five of his stories for *Penguin New Writing*, including the novella 'That Summer', which Frame had lent to fellow workers at the Occidental Hotel in Christchurch.

By 1955 Sargeson had had six books published, three in New Zealand, two in England and one in France. As the tribute printed in *Landfall* on his fiftieth birthday made clear, he was recognised by his peers as the foundation layer of a national literature — an exemplary role that had introduced his country's idiom into world literature in English and encouraged other New Zealanders, including Frame, to attempt to become writers. But Sargeson had done more than this. He was also an active mentor to would-be writers. The generation which followed him — A.P. Gaskell, Maurice Duggan, David Ballantyne, John Reece Cole, Greville Texidor — had all benefited from his interest and advice and publishing contacts. He was indeed, as the *Landfall* letter said, a symbol in his own lifetime.[2] And his Takapuna property, entered through a hole in an increasingly unruly hedge, was the centre of an Auckland artistic and literary circle and well on the way to being regarded as hallowed ground in New Zealand literary mythology.

Sargeson's interest in Frame was as strong as he had displayed for any New Zealand writer whose work he had admired — perhaps stronger, because of the circumstances in which she had begun to write and the belief in literary circles that she was a kind of untutored genius whose talent grew out of her 'madness'. Her vulnerability also interested him, because of his strong impulse to be of service to people who had been damaged by illness or injury or living, as he himself had been by his homosexuality and conviction for indecent assault. He had welcomed *The Lagoon* as 'one more light to help diminish the vast region of darkness by which we are all surrounded'.[3] He had urged the merits of Frame's stories on other writers such as Dan Davin, who had included Frame in the Oxford anthology. He had written to her in hospital, expressing appreciation of her writing.[4] And, when he was in Dunedin in July and August of 1953, he had attempted to meet Frame in Seacliff, only to be told by Charles Brasch that she was too ill to receive visitors (until her release from Avondale, he was unaware that she had also been hospitalised in Auckland).[5]

After he returned to Auckland from his visit to the South Island in 1953, Sargeson learned that Frame's sister, June Gordon, lived in Northcote, a suburb which adjoined Takapuna. He visited her in the course of one of his afternoon walks and told her that he would like to meet Janet and, if possible, to help her. If Frame should return to Auckland, Sargeson said, the Gordons must bring her to Esmonde Road. He would be happy for her to stay with him there, to write. June was grateful for this offer, because previous experience suggested that her sister might benefit from time away from the family. But she was also cautious, because to put a proposition of that kind to Janet, baldly, was to risk a negative response.[6]

By March 1955, however, Wilson Gordon had acquired a car. In the weekend that followed Frame's retreat from the TransTasman Hotel, it was a relatively easy matter to take her for a drive, 'to see the sights'; then, when they were in Takapuna, to suggest, apparently spontaneously, that they call in to say hello to Sargeson. And that was what occurred. As Frame recalled the occasion:

> Our visit was short. What could I say? I was self-conscious, the 'funny' sister being taken for a drive. Mr Sargeson, a bearded old man★ in a shabby grey shirt and grey pants tied with string, smiled kindly and asked how I was, and I said nothing. He had an army hut vacant in his garden, he said. I was welcome to live and work there. I neither accepted nor refused, I was so overcome by my 'mental' status, and by seeing in person the famous writer whose anthology of New Zealand writing, *Speaking for Ourselves*, was a treasured book; the famous writer for whose fiftieth birthday I had signed a letter of good wishes, not knowing him and knowing nothing of the other signatories . . .
>
> He suggested that I come to see him one day, by myself . . .
>
> 'Yes,' I said shyly.[7]

Sargeson reported this visit to Dennis McEldowney on 27 March 1955.[8] And Frame herself, as if fearing that her reticence would be mistaken for lack of interest or appreciation, wrote to Sargeson that same week: 'I thank you for your kind offer. I shall visit you one day soon; but send advance apologies for my inclination to silence rather than speech.'

Days later Frame walked to Takapuna from the Gordons' house, 'along the largely unformed road with paddocks of scrub and toetoe on either side, past swamps of mangroves — mangroves! — stands of native bush . . . I arrived at Number Fourteen Esmonde Road, walked through the gap in the high hedge and around to the . . . back door, brushing past washing hung between the lemon tree and the house. I knocked on the door.'

> Mr Sargeson was home. He opened the door and said, smiling nervously and speaking as if to a child, 'Come in, come in.'
>
> I walked into the main room while Mr Sargeson went behind the wooden counter and leaned on it.
>
> 'You've walked a long way?'
>
> 'About three miles.'
>
> 'Would you like to lie down on the bed?'
>
> Already apprehensive, I moved nearer the door and said primly, poised for flight, 'No, thank you.'

---

★ The 'old man' had just turned fifty-two; Frame was thirty at this time.

'Robin Hyde★ always used to lie down. She would come limping in here and fling herself down on the bed.'

'Oh?'

'Have you read her books?'

'I've heard of them,' I said. 'I know some of her poems . . .'

He then asked about [my] future work.

'I don't know,' I said guardedly.

'Have you thought about coming to live and work in the hut? You'd be free to write. It's no good your living in suburbia among the nappies and bourgeois life.'

I hadn't heard anyone say the word 'bourgeois' since history lessons on the French Revolution, and I wasn't sure if I knew its modern meaning.

'I have to find a job, though,' I said.

'Why? You're a writer.'

I smiled with wonder. 'Am I? They've refused to give me [a] sickness benefit.'

Mr Sargeson looked angry. 'After all those years in hospital? Look, I've a good friend, a doctor who's understanding and who will probably arrange a benefit for you while you work at your writing.'

'Really?'

I felt overwhelmed and shy, and protected. I accepted his offer of living and working in the hut, if he would allow me to pay him each week for my board. Although he objected at first, he finally agreed to one pound a week. His own income was low. The first flush of publication and attention given to his work was over and he had reached the stage when he most needed money, for his books were out of print.[9]

Sargeson, in fact, had entered a decade-long publication drought. At the time Frame arrived at his door he was working on the second of two plays he had written for the theatre. They would not be staged until 1961 and 1962; and he would not have another book published until his *Collected Stories* appeared in London in 1964.

In the first weekend in April 1955, the Gordons drove Frame back to Esmonde Road with her 'things' — the Remington typewriter and two suitcases of clothing and books. She carried them past Sargeson's door and into the hut, which stood ten yards behind the back of the cottage. Inside she found 'a bed, a built-in desk with a kerosene lamp, a rush mat on the floor, a small wardrobe with an old curtain strung in front, and a small window by the head of the bed. Mr Sargeson (I was not yet bold enough to call him Frank) had already arranged for a medical certificate and a benefit of three pounds a week, which was also

---

★ Pen name of Iris Wilkinson, another gifted writer who had spent time in mental hospitals and who had been a neighbour of Sargeson's in the 1930s.

the amount of his income. I thus had everything I desired and needed, as well as the regret of wondering why I had taken so many years to find it.'[10]

Frame accommodated herself at once to Sargeson's living and writing patterns. He, after all, was the mentor. They both woke early, Frame in part because of a habit inculcated in Seacliff, where the patients hastened to get up and dress in the mornings because there was no heating in the wards. She had to delay entering the cottage, however, because Sargeson liked to read in bed for an hour each morning — usually re-reading literary classics — before rising and dressing. Eventually, after 7.30 am, Frame came into the cottage with her chamberpot and washing and used the bathroom. Then they ate breakfast, sometimes together on either side of the wooden counter that separated the kitchen from Sargeson's bedroom/livingroom. Their customary meal was 'a yeast drink brewed overnight, home-made curds topped with honey, and bread and honey and tea . . .

'I was inclined to chatter,' Frame wrote later. 'Within the first week of my stay he drew attention to this. "You babble at breakfast," he said . . . [In] future I refrained from "babbling", but it was not until I had been writing regularly each day that I understood the importance to each of us of forming, holding, maintaining our inner world, and how it was renewed each day on waking, how it even remained during sleep, like an animal outside the door waiting to come in; and how its form and power were protected most by surrounding silence. My hurt at being called a "babbler" faded as I learned more of the life of a writer.'[11]

After breakfast Frame returned to the hut and Sargeson carried out household and gardening chores. Hearing him rustle through the plants around the hut as he watered, weeded and pruned, Frame would feel obliged to sound busy. So she typed again and again, 'The quick brown fox jumped over the lazy dog' and 'Now is the time for all good men to come to the aid of the party'. Hearing this, Sargeson felt admiration and sometimes depression at what he imagined was his guest's prolificacy. Only when the master had himself gone inside to write his mandatory four or five hundred words a day (after refining whatever he had written the previous day) could Frame also begin to write in earnest. There would be a gentle interruption at eleven o'clock for a cup of tea and a rye biscuit, which Sargeson passed through the door 'averting his gaze from the nakedness of my typed pages'.[12] And at one o'clock he served lunch in the cottage.

Frank would usually have a book in his hand or on the counter where we sat facing each other with our scrambled or poached egg or cheese and rye bread, and he'd read extracts aloud and discuss the writing while I listened, accepting, believing everything he said, full of wonder at his cleverness. I worshipped him and was in awe of him and with my now ingrained fear of authority or those 'in charge', I felt in need of his approval.[13]

In the afternoons they rested, napping or reading. At three there was another cup of tea and a biscuit. Then Sargeson would don his beret, throw his canvas bag over his shoulder and walk into Takapuna to shop for the evening meal, which was often shared with friends. This evening ritual of entertainment was one which Frame, absenting herself early, found at first difficult to endure; but she eventually accepted and enjoyed it as she came to know the visitors. Among those who came to drink Lemora citrus wine and eat Sargeson's superbly prepared meals were short story writer Maurice Duggan and his wife, Barbara, Barbara's school-teacher cousin, Una Platts, writer and librarian John Reece Cole and his wife, Christine, up from Wellington, historian Keith Sinclair and his poet friend Kendrick Smithyman, a would-be playwright John Graham, poet and student C.K. Stead and his wife, Kay, a librarian, who shared a flat overlooking Takapuna Beach, the music teacher Jess Whitworth (former wife of first *New Zealand Listener* editor Oliver Duff) and, later, the young Takapuna poet Kevin Ireland and artist Anthony Stones.

Of all these callers, it was the Steads, in their early twenties, to whom Frame grew to feel closest. But not immediately. In the course of early visits to Esmonde Road they were aware of her as 'a shadowy figure came into the room and listened silently and withdrew. But as the visits continued she was drawn into the conversation,' Karl Stead wrote subsequently. 'After a few weeks we were four friends, entirely relaxed together.' For six months that friendship was exercised in conversation about books, 'reminiscences, verbal games, jokes, gossip. We swam together and went for walks. Once the four of us went to a party . . . we'd been there I suppose ten minutes when Sargeson noticed that Janet was missing. She'd not been able to cope with so many people, and had run home.' On one of their swimming expeditions, Sargeson caught perfectly the exuberance of their escapades by crowning his head with a wreath of seaweed, putting a stick to his mouth, and performing a Pan-dance in the shallow water, 'lifting his knees high like a figure on an ancient urn . . .'[14]

For her part, Frame remembered the Steads as being in 'a golden glow of youth and love . . . [Both] became drawn with Frank into my web of worship. Their intelligence, their beauty, their love brought joy to Frank, who was often depressed by the general neglect of writers . . . The friendship with Karl and Kay filled my life, giving me at last a place in my own years . . .'[15] She recalled one evening in particular.

> [They] brought two records, A Little Night Music and Beethoven's Violin Concerto played by David Oistrakh . . . Frank said, 'We can play them on Janet's radiogram' . . . I can still see that room with the bare wallboard and the wooden floor which Frank oiled each Saturday morning with a mop soaked in linseed oil, . . . with the canvas chairs ('the most comfortable type') with their wooden arms, the room that already held all the characters from *War and Peace*, *Anna Karenina*, the stories of Tolstoy and Chekhov, from Proust, Flaubert, Olive Schreiner, Doris Lessing,

receiving now the music of Mozart and Beethoven while we listen. We play the record again. Karl and Frank begin to talk about Yeats. Karl reads 'Sailing to Byzantium', 'The Circus Animals' Desertion'. While I, bred on the 'old' Yeats, that is, the 'young' Yeats of 'Had I the heavens' embroidered cloths' and 'The Lake Isle of Innisfree', listen, bathed in the words and the music. I think that I recite, then, the poem I knew by heart, Dylan Thomas's 'After the Funeral', and we talk of the meaning of 'the strutting fern lay seeds on the black sill'. . . .[16]

This was the closest Frame had come to intimacy with people of like mind and spirit and literary inclination. The bliss of the four-way encounter was qualified, however, by a charged and indeterminate meeting that Frame and Stead had on their own. Among the many 'first' experiences that she was still to have, because of her time in hospital, was that of a sexual encounter with another person. In this area as in others her mentor, a novelist and playwright, was more than happy to create the circumstances in which action might plausibly occur.

Sargeson reported to Stead that Frame would welcome his opinion on poems she was writing. Stead, happy to oblige and not averse to hints of a dangerous adventure, went alone to the army hut. Nearly thirty years later he described, in fictionalised form, what followed.

Arriving at her door Curl Skidmore feels shy of her, and more so when he detects that she is shy of him. But he follows her directions and sits cross-legged opposite her while she makes tea . . . He is trying not to look at her knees. She has drawn up her skirt to make it easier to sit cross-legged, and sitting opposite her he is aware that her knees are neat and pale and that between them there is a dark space into which it would be improper to stare.

She is saying it's kind of him to come . . . She has so much enjoyed talking to him in the evenings . . . or not talking to him — it's much the same, doesn't he think? Communication and silent communication. But sometimes it's hard to get from one to the other . . . Curl sinks in on himself and his consciousness, wandering here and there, inside the hut, out through the half-open door, comes back always to that dark centre into which he doesn't look. Floating in him like a dream is the action of reaching gently forward into that darkness . . . The muscles of [his] arm are already under instruction, the hand, the fingers are in slow motion, the dreamaction is on the point of translating itself into the sphere of time and history, when the revolt occurs. Curl stands abruptly knocking the teapot on to the matting where it lies leaking a puddle of amber liquid. Cecelia falls silent . . . Curl, his voice rather louder than necessary, begins to talk about her poems . . .

He stops talking at last because he's getting no response. Cecelia has remained where she was, cross-legged on the floor. She sits very still and quite silent and when he allows himself a direct glance at her face he sees it set hard . . . It's not even anger he sees in it but something worse.

'Better go,' he mumbles, looking at his watch . . . He leaves her there and hurries away, and when Melior Fabro stops him along the path, his elbow nudging, his eyebrows going up and down like a blind, Curl Skidmore isn't able to do more than mumble incoherently that he's had tea thanks, and yes they've talked about her new poems, and maybe she isn't very well.

The sound of her door slamming makes them both start.[17]

On the more frequent evenings when Frame and Sargeson were alone they would play chess, which Sargeson taught Frame ('the queen always on her own colour, Janet');[18] or they would talk about books that they were reading, or re-reading, simultaneously. 'An accountant would say, "I must study those old columns of figures,"' Frame would write later. 'A writer re-reads the classics, sweeping away present trivia, renewing inspiration, and marvelling at the imperishable truth and beauty. Perhaps not *every* writer; but this was Frank's way . . . There is a freedom born from the acknowledgement of greatness in literature, as if one gave away what one desired to keep, and in giving, there is a new space cleared for growth, an onrush of a new season beneath a secret sun. Acknowledging any great work of art is like being in love; one walks on air; any decline, destruction, death are within, not in the beloved; it is a falling in love with immortality, a freedom, a flight in paradise. I cannot help remembering with love my days at Esmonde Road.'[19]

For Sargeson too, in spite of the inevitable interruptions to his routines involved in looking after a long-stay boarder, those first months of Frame's residence were companionable and deeply satisfying. He admired Frame's intelligence and intuitions and word-play; he enjoyed, as he almost always did, being of service to someone who seemed to need him (and over this same period he was looking after an elderly neighbour and two ailing aunts living on the edge of Takapuna Beach); and he liked nothing more than seeing a protégée flower, like one of his fruits or vegetables, under his watchful ministrations.

He told Dennis McEldowney in June 1955 that Frame was 'a neat athletic type with a Scottish fresh complexion and a fuzz of reddish hair . . . [A] most remarkable girl . . . and a very pure person in the best sense of the word . . . She manages to keep a balance between the spectres and something more solid by writing continuously. But she won't allow what she writes to be communicated to anyone.'[20] Here was a potential source of stress. Sargeson liked his protégés to discuss work with him; Frame, equally emphatically, preferred *not* to do this. On the one occasion she was persuaded to hand over a story, 'An Electric Blanket', for perusal and comment, she was devastated by Sargeson's criticism. 'He took the pages, scanned them, and read aloud, "Every morning she rose . . ." He looked sternly at me. "Rose? Went up to heaven . . . ? Why not say, simply, 'She got up'. *Never* use rose." I listened contritely, realising that "rose" was unforgivable. "The story is quite good of its kind," [he] said. I felt a surge of disappointment. I resolved not to show him more stories . . .'[21]

What was absorbing almost all of Frame's energy for work and pulling her to her typewriter each morning was a project she described to John Money in May 1955. 'I am writing . . . a long work which gets quite involved and exhausting, and I try to escape from it but cannot.' This 'long work' owed something, perhaps, to one she had contemplated writing in 1949, which would, ambitiously, 'trace the minds of people in and out of their mysterious weavings, and to find what the whole of being has concealed'.[22] At no stage in 1955 did Frame describe what she was writing as a 'novel'. But it *was* prose fiction; and it *was* to be long (64,000 words). Her own title for it was 'Talk of Treasure'.

> Pictures of great treasure in the midst of sadness and waste haunted me and I began to think, in fiction, of a childhood, home life, hospital life, using people known to me as a base for the main characters, and inventing minor characters. For Daphne [the central character] I chose a sensitive, poetic, frail person, who (I hoped) would give depth to inner worlds and perhaps a clearer, at least an individual, perception of outer worlds. The other characters, similarly fictional, were used to portray aspects of my 'message' — the excessively material outlook of 'Chicks', the confusion of Toby, the earthy make-up of Francie, and the toiling parents, the nearest characters to my own parents. The setting was W, a small town which the publisher later named *Waimaru* [a conflation of Waitaki and Oamaru] . . .
>
> Each day after breakfast I went to the hut to work . . . I had not, as Frank suggested, written a list of characters, but I had set out in my exercise book a few ideas and themes, and the names of the parts of the book which I saw as a whole before I began typing. In my exercise book I ruled lines to make a timetable with day, date, number of pages I hoped to write, number of pages written, and a space headed *Excuses*. Each day I marked the number of pages written, in red pencil.[23]

Because of her experience with 'An Electric Blanket', Frame resisted Sargeson's frequent blandishments to let him see the accumulating manuscript. She agreed, however, to read aloud to him the opening passage, an intensely poetic interior monologue in which the character Daphne, in a mental hospital, remembers the world outside. Sargeson liked it so much that he proposed that she send it as a poem to John Lehmann, who was now editor of *London Magazine*. This Frame did and — also at Sargeson's suggestion — she enclosed some additional poems. They chose 'Santie Cross' as the authorial *nom de plume*. And Sargeson enclosed a note which read, 'Santie Cross was born in Samoa. She is of mixed Polynesian and European parentage. She has lived for two years alone in a hut on an isolated island off the New Zealand coast. She is at present living in Auckland.'[24]

John Lehmann replied to Sargeson in late July. 'I read Santie Cross's [work] with great interest. There are really beautiful phrases in it, and she obviously feels a great deal: but I don't think it really comes off — she wants her spark to jump gaps that are too big for it — and I wouldn't care to publish it . . . Sorry about this. It was good of you to [send] it . . .'[25]

The following month, shortly before her thirty-first birthday, Frame finished what she still called 'Talk of Treasure'. Somewhat to Sargeson's chagrin, the whole book had taken her a little over four months to complete — a period in which her mentor had managed to write very little. Instead of sending it to a publisher, she bound the manuscript in tape and took it with her on the train as she headed south for a fortnight's stay in Oamaru.

The South Island, with its more strongly defined sense of season, was awakening to spring as Frame arrived at Willowglen; and fruit trees around her decaying family home 'showed buds fattening into blossom'.[26] Frame found the ambience depressing, however. '[The] sky seems more oppressive now,' she wrote to John Money, 'like a vast block of grey ice, with the people crawling about close to the leafless earth.'[27] Life at home was no less depressing. Her mother was thinner and more frail and gave every indication of being terminally ill. As usual, however, she was intent on denying that anything was wrong. George Frame, having his customary difficulty expressing emotion of any kind, reacted to his wife's illness by mocking her. Janet too felt helpless and found herself speaking to her mother sternly rather than compassionately. And when Janet baked one of her 'specialities', Lottie reacted immediately by baking one of *her* specialities. All the former cross-currents of competitiveness and tension persisted.

One thing Janet *was* able to do to please her mother: she read aloud carefully selected extracts from 'Talk of Treasure', the 'happy' bits. She omitted any reference to the death of the mother, who was in many respects based on Lottie. Her mother was pleased and proud and said faithfully, 'That's lovely.'[28] To please her father in turn, Janet went fishing with him off the Oamaru wharf and, as he talked about cod, she 'listened obediently, wonderingly, as if I was being taught by a great teacher, while, always aware of a life of writing, I stored the words at the back of my mind for future use'.[29]

As before, however, the difficulties and contradictory feelings became too much for her. As Frame boarded the northbound express train, sure that she would never again see her mother alive, she told her parents that she would never return to Willowglen. 'My words hurt, as I knew they would. I said goodbye and the train pulled out on its familiar track, and even as it began its *Kaitangata, Kaitangata, Kaitangata, Winton, Winton, Winton, Kakanui, Kakanui, Kakanui*, I knew there was no use escaping anywhere, from family or frost or land, the escape made impossible anyway because, as the daughter of a railway worker, I had to accept the possession of and by every inch of railway track in the country: an iron bond of mutual ownership. The train continued to say a new word, *Willowglen, Willowglen, Willowglen*, as we crossed the Canterbury Plains.'[30]

Back in Takapuna, Frame wrote her first will — intended, of course, to be her 'last' will and testament. Several factors precipitated this decision. Her spell at Willowglen had been redolent of intimations of mortality. She had also learned from June that, when their father died, Janet and Geordie would inherit the family property (because June was taken care of in her marriage to Wilson Gordon). The most pressing reason for putting her life 'in order', however, was that, with the manuscript completed, Frame was preparing to leave Esmonde Road. And Sargeson — fatigued by the business of looking after his guest at the same time as he was visiting and feeding his ailing aunts and nursing the elderly man next door, *and* struggling to write his play — was encouraging her to think of moving on. He persuaded her that a trip abroad would be the thing, what many other New Zealanders of Frame's generation were doing or planning to do (including the Steads who, in February 1956, were to leave New Zealand for New South Wales and then England).

Travel was believed to 'broaden the mind' ('who knows New Zealand who only New Zealand knows?' Sargeson said on more than one occasion).[31] It was also deemed to be enriching to experience life in European countries that valued matters of the mind and spirit more highly than did doggedly practical New Zealanders. And in some places it was possible to live far more cheaply than in New Zealand. One such place, recommended by friends of Sargeson who had just returned from Spain, was Ibiza in the Balearic Islands. This was not far from Barcelona, where Greville Texidor, another friend of Sargeson, now lived. Sargeson himself had travelled to England and Europe in 1927 and 1928 and attributed to that experience his decision to opt for the 'new world' and for a nationalist literary agenda. In addition to all this, Frame believed that unless she was able to leave New Zealand, there was a possibility that the same health authorities who had dispatched her to hospital previously might return her there, possibly permanently.

Because she had learned and enjoyed French at school, and been proficient in the subject, Frame's first move in the new plan was to write to the French legation in Wellington asking for information about bursaries available to New

Zealand students in France. Her second step was to compose her will, with Sargeson at her shoulder egging her on. It became both an exercise in elegiac writing and an attempt to entertain themselves by subverting the elegiac tone.

Assuming her inheritance of Willowglen, Frame left the property, 'rent-free, for a period not exceeding two years at a time, to any writer, young or old, who has no place to live in peace'. There was a condition, however. That writer would have to 'treat the earth and its vegetation as alive, and . . . leave the creek to flow, and not uproot the old trees, but plant new ones too'. The responsibility to provide income for the tenant was left to 'those interested people with money to spend . . . I also bequeath them the knowledge that . . . having cast their bread upon the waters, it will return to them in fresh and spiritually nourishing loaves; or, if they prefer it, [in] tasty popped-up toast, buttered and spread with beans and tomato sauce'.

She instructed that all her private letters be burned; and that any money in her possession be given to Frank Sargeson, 'an extraordinary and rare example of dedication and devotion to literature and its causes'. If he were dead, the money was to fund a literature prize to be administered by Dorothy Neal White, Pat Guest and Sargeson's friend E.P. Dawson. If they too were dead, then 'I leave it all to the Meat and Butter Board for the furtherance of export trade'. The document closed: 'I name my executor the Public Trustee, and leave my body to be placed unclothed, without funeral rites, in an unpolished coffin, and buried some place in New Zealand . . . where snow falls in August and the sea is heard.'[32]

As a kind of codicil, Frame then wrote to John Money, informing him of the will and of the provision that 'all letters I have written anywhere at any time be destroyed. If you ever hear of my death I should like you to . . . comply with my last wish.'[33]

Frame's third act of ordering her life was to contact Albion Wright of Pegasus Press in Christchurch, inform him of the existence of her manuscript, and ask if he would read it. 'If it were up to standard, maybe it could be published,' she wrote tentatively, 'though I understand publishing in New Zealand is in a bad way at present. Shall I send it to you?'[34] Wright replied by return mail and asked her to post it. With Sargeson's help, Frame parcelled up the 260-page document and dispatched it to Christchurch. Sargeson, ever sensitive to her well-being, prepared consoling words and a set of cautionary tales to cushion what he believed would be the inevitable rejection (he had not seen anything of the manuscript beyond the opening passage).

Instead, on 27 September 1955, Pegasus Press accepted 'Talk of Treasure' for publication. 'I think it an extraordinarily fine work and I would like to congratulate you on having written a story of such sustained power and interest,' Albion Wright wrote. 'I am quite sure you will not regret having sent it to us. You can rest assured your book will be produced by our press in a pleasing and attractive format.'[35] Frame *was* pleased; Sargeson was stunned. He splashed out on a bottle of Vat 69, which neither of them could afford, in celebration. Frame eventually signed a contract for her second book on 17 November 1955. Her career as a novelist was launched.

Pegasus Press had been established in 1947 by one of Denis Glover's old navy and sailing pals, Christchurch advertising agent Albion Wright. Wright, a handsome and urbane man, cut a dashing figure in person and in correspondence. His ambition was to print and publish quality books. After Caxton Press's florescence ended with Glover's departure in 1951, Wright persuaded him to work for Pegasus as a printer for a short period. He also succeeded, albeit briefly, in publishing work by some of the country's most admired poets who had previously been part of the Caxton stable (Allen Curnow, James K. Baxter and Glover himself among them). Frame had given little consideration to sending the manuscript of her second book to Caxton. She knew from her conversations with Sargeson that Caxton was now in trouble. She chose Pegasus because it seemed, in late 1955, the next-best alternative to Caxton.

With publication of the new book assured — though with details such as timing, quantity, price and title still to be settled (Albion Wright did not like 'Talk of Treasure') — life at Esmonde Road took on the character of a hiatus. Frame had produced the book that she went there to write; now she had been persuaded to travel; Sargeson wanted her to travel. But she was not yet in a position to begin to make the necessary arrangements. For one thing she had no money and needed to know whether she would get an advance on royalties which might allow her to book and pay for her passage out of the country (her letter to the French embassy had not turned up any bursaries or sources of money for which she might be eligible). For another, she had to know precisely when the book would be typeset so that she could be sure of being able to read and correct proofs. Resolution of these uncertainties depended on an application for a publication subsidy of three hundred pounds which Pegasus would make to the government-sponsored State Literary Fund in March 1956.

According to Frame's recollection of the latter part of 1955, 'Summer came too quickly. The heat persisted day and night. I slept with the door of the hut open, the entry and the window by my bed draped with muslin to keep out the mosquitoes from the mangrove swamp . . . [Being] thrust once again into the ordinary factual world, I grew restless, unable to work in the heat. I wrote poems, a few stories. I played chess in the evenings or again listened to the anecdotes and conversation of Frank and his friends, or he and I talked over the books we were reading, but we both knew there had been a subtle change of emotional gear, we were no longer on the same path, the honeymoon was over . . . Beginning, middle, end — how often we had talked of the fictional processes and how each could be expressed painlessly, invisibly.'[36]

Some of that 'post-novel' work, poems and stories, would be published over the following two years in the *New Zealand Listener, Landfall, Mate,* and the Department of Education's *School Journal.*[37] According to Sargeson, her two children's stories for the latter publication, for which she earned thirty pounds, were written in a twelve-hour burst.[38] 'I've been chagrined all morning to hear her typewriter going hell for leather while I've been tentatively pencilling six lines of dialogue.' She also wrote a rare review, of William Faulkner's *A Fable,* for *Parsons Packet,* the newsletter of Wellington bookseller Roy Parsons.[39]

Sargeson attempted to defuse the hothouse atmosphere developing at Esmonde Road by initiating walks with Frame around the North Shore. As they undertook these excursions, he would suggest apparently spontaneous visits to other writers in the neighbourhood — poet Allen Curnow and his family at Shoal Bay; Maurice and Barbara Duggan at Forrest Hill; the invalid writer Dennis McEldowney, up from Wellington and staying with an aunt at Bayswater. All these hosts were intensely interested in Sargeson's flame-haired visitor. All formed impressions of her character and mannerisms, conditioned by the sometimes overly dramatic groundwork laid by Sargeson before they called.

Maurice Duggan, for example, told Frame later that she had seemed 'on tip-toe for flight [fearing] that indecency of direct communication'.[40] He reported to Dan Davin that Frame was 'pleasant, but one cannot get through the thicket to where the composing princess sleeps'.[41] A month later, in October 1955, Dennis McEldowney's aunt asked Frame and Sargeson inside for afternoon tea and almost provoked a panic attack in her nervous and weak-hearted nephew. '[One] of the things Frank had told me about Janet was that after her long incarceration she could not bear the sensation of being shut in,' McEldowney wrote. 'An opening always had to be left, a way of escape. I had not told my aunt this . . . [She] sat on the window seat and drew the [tea] trolley across so that it entirely shut off the fourth side of the square bay. This was a moment of sheer horror for me. I wondered if Janet would jump out one of the side windows.' It was a scenario to which Frame was becoming accustomed: the 'normal' people watching to see if the 'mad' woman would do something erratic. In the event Frame simply 'drank her tea and continued alert to conversation'.[42]

Frame and Sargeson each received cheery correspondence from Lottie Frame in November. Janet's contained the usual family news (George Frame was fishing off the wharf; Geordie helping to rescue a bulldozer bogged in a swamp).[43] Sargeson's was to thank him for sending the family a box of lemons, grapefruit and Chinese gooseberries. Both letters gave optimistic prognoses of her health ('I am much better lately and hope to keep going for a long time yet').[44] Weeks later, on 2 December, June and Wilson Gordon arrived with news that Lottie had died that morning after suffering a stroke in the kitchen at Willowglen. Death had become 'a familiar visitor to our home', Frame told John Money. 'When we were children we had a custom of always leaving upon the table something for Santa Claus to eat and drink when he came to visit us. That, they said, would make him want to come over and over again. I think that in our lives we must have left many invisible meals for death, that he has come so often.'[45]

Frame was less equable than her correspondence would suggest, however. '[My] mixture of sadness and relief at Mother's death,' she would write later, 'was strengthened and sharpened by my familiar feeling of anger and depression at being treated as the "frail, mad" member of the family, who must be sheltered from unpleasant news. The well-meaning consideration of my family served to emphasise and increase my separation from them. I was jealous of my sister's first knowledge of the death, almost as if it were a treasured gift chosen to be given to her, then passed on, used and soiled, second-hand, to me. It was partly a reawakening of the former childhood rivalries in being first to know, to see, the first to embrace the cherished secret; in fact, the rivalry had never reawakened for it had never slept . . .'[46]

Her anguish increased when she told Sargeson the news and he, reflecting his relations with his own family, said that parents were better dead.

> That night in the privacy of the hut I wept, and the next morning, faced with Frank's scornful reproaches . . . I explained that I was weeping for Mother's life, not for her death. I regretted that with our parents' lives spent almost entirely in feeding, clothing, sheltering us, we had little time to know and be friends with them. My life had been spent watching, listening to my parents, trying to decipher their code, always searching for clues. They were the two trees between us and the wind, sea, snow; but that was in childhood. I felt that their death might expose us but it would also let the light in from all directions, and we would know the reality instead of the rumour of wind, sea, snow, and be able to perceive all moments of being.[47]

Frame and her sister did not go south again for the funeral. Instead, they spent a day together at the pictures in Auckland city; and, on behalf of the family, Janet answered the letters and telegrams of sympathy which had arrived at Willowglen. Her own mourning was carried on through poems, private poems:

> Burn the dirty clothes she died in,
> the sour stockings, the stained dress,
> the holey (holy) interlock
> she wore to greet the sad surprise
> the sad morning surprise of death.
> Put her costume on a hanger
> on the clothes-line for the wind
> to blow the shreds of sick disaster

into the trees or the next town.
Lay the death-sheets on the lawn
for dew and sun to bleach and clean.

I say that only fire and air
are kindly charities, so give
to them your pennyworth of grief
refusing earth and water who buried her body
her body, drowned her with too many tears.[48]

The betrayal she had felt when Sargeson seemed to have no sympathy for her sense of bereavement eventually melted. 'I overheard him say to Kathleen, our neighbour, "A mother's death is hardest to take. It's a sad time for Janet." Frank, too, had secret feelings to hide . . .'[49]

At year's end the bond between Sargeson and Frame was unbroken, though it had become stretched and frayed. With the diminution of initial excitement over publication of the new book, and with nothing definite arranged about her projected overseas travel, Frame began again to worry about her future. In particular she worried about the likely course of her illness, and the possibility that she might be recommitted to Seacliff never again to re-emerge. In the grip of such anxieties, she was unwilling or unable even to talk to her host and left explanatory and warning messages for him: '[Am] solitarily confining myself for the weekend. Have rung June to say I shan't be over there. If they call I'll commit murder. Shan't be having any meals. Thank you and my apologies. J.'[50]

At times Frame's feelings of alienation from her host were associated with what she called his 'vein of distrust, at times hatred, of women as a species . . . for I was a woman and he was speaking of my kind'.[51] At others, she became depressed by what seemed like eternally dependent status, and by the conviction that she was being tolerated and patronised. These latter feelings produced what she called a 'statement of place', which began with the announcement that 'in conversation I am bedevilled; in written expression an angel will visit'.

I am banished in a hut . . . I must go to the palace to receive my food three times each day, where a servant artistic, prudent, of culinary perfection, waits upon me and washes the dishes after we have eaten . . . It is urgent that I finish my meal quite quickly, for in conversation I am bedevilled, sometimes by a thrush who sits on the topmost twig of my head, repeating I-bore-you, I-bore-you, I-bore-you . . . [So] I leave the palace and the servant, and as soon as I walk out of the door I see the thrush lying dead at my feet, stoned by my angel. My angel waits on me when I am alone, writes for me, and tells me in my weeping, Don't go to the palace any more where the thrushes fly and sing and you sit in tattered clothes and are alone because of what the thrushes say . . .

The servant in the palace is . . . some kind of prince in his own right, who is visited on many occasions by other similar princes and princesses . . . [There] they sit of an afternoon or evening, talking and laughing about many things — including yet other princes and princesses . . . [The] servant imagined that I, too, was connected in some way with this royalty; that I would be as interesting and vital as all the princes and princesses that he had ever known and waited upon . . . Until the truth of me was discovered — What, a scullion, a mad woman with a thrush in the topmost twig of her head . . . [And] the servant nodded wisely. She is not, it is true, he said, our class of royalty. We must humour her, certainly; but not speak much to her; she has a thrush in her head. I try, myself, to get rid of her on every possible occasion — tactfully of course . . .

He does not know that my angel has dashed out the milk-white brain of every thrush in the world, as soon as I leave the doorstep of the palace . . . I admire them all, but I am not of them. I am a scullion with an oak leaf scratched over by the beak of a bird [and] my face is plain.

So, as my angel advises me, I intend to leave the hut of my banishing and the glittering towers of the castle, and go to the city, away from all the royalty where I do not belong because of my thrush . . . I shall there be my own servant, and prepare my own meal, and live my scullion's life, without being in the emptiness and loneliness of a grand palace. I will know people who are scullions like myself. They will talk to me and be friends with me; other times I shall be alone, packing oakleaves into rows and rows of empty acorns, to put in the earth, and see if they grow towards the sun.

All this my angel tells me. Next week I shall do as my angel bids.[52]

What she did was to apply for and obtain another job as a housemaid at the Masonic Hotel in Devonport. But, as with the TransTasman earlier in the year, the experiment was a disaster. The hotel turned out to be a 'sweatshop'. She could not work at the required pace and collapsed; and then returned to Esmonde Road.[53] In a letter to John Money, Frame reported that she and Sargeson would spend a quiet Christmas together. 'We have two large bottles of New Zealand wine — Lemora, to drink; we have buried the butter in the garden to stop it (the butter) from melting; we have also buried a couple of thousand silkworm eggs to stop them from hatching too soon — it was a fancy we had . . . Frank kept them when he was a child and I had never seen them before.'[54]

The silkworms represented a mutually sensitive attempt to bridge the troubled waters of their relationship. Frame had heard Sargeson speak of keeping them in what seemed to him like the 'golden age' of his childhood. When she saw a pet-shop in the city that sold caterpillars, she bought half-a-dozen and laid them that evening on the kitchen counter. 'He was delighted, with an immediate, not a recollective delight.' Then, 'he, in his turn, viewed the silkworms as a means of absorbing *my* attention while he and I planned my next move'.[55]

Sargeson provided a shoebox, Frame found a local source of mulberry leaves. Together they observed the cycle that unfolded: the caterpillars ate the leaves and spun themselves cocoons of silk; Sargeson removed the plaited silk and hung it on the wall, wrapping the naked grubs in cottonwool; the grubs became moths, emerged, mated with one another and produced eggs; and it was these eggs they buried in the garden, inside the shoebox. 'They'll stay there the winter and when the warm weather comes, I'll dig them up, they'll hatch, and the cycle will repeat itself,' Sargeson told Frame. She commented: 'The completeness, perfection and near-indestructibility of the cycle did not escape us.'[56]

Early in 1956, however, subterranean tensions ignited an explosion. At the Gordons on New Year's Day, Frame was given a package by her brother-in-law, who had received it in turn from Albion Wright when he, Wilson, had passed through Christchurch the previous month. It contained the poems John Money had collected with the *Lagoon* stories and sent to Caxton; and a letter from Denis Glover about Frame's novel. Glover was reading the manuscript of the novel as a member of the State Literary Fund. In the letter to Wright, he jokingly speculated that it was such an accomplished piece of work that it must be a collaboration between Frame and Sargeson. Frame was so furious at this suggestion that she burned the poems ('alarmed that [they] were apparently being shown to all and sundry')[57] and the offending letter. And she fired off a letter of her own to Glover: 'My lawyer in Oamaru has agreed to filing a claim against you for . . . libel. I have learned that you have declared . . . that my manuscript [is not] my own work entirely . . . [This] is an insult to me, to the person you have accused of collaboration, and to . . . everything I stand for . . . Please apologise or refute your statement, otherwise my lawyer will communicate with you directly.'[58]

This was all bluff. When Glover responded with a contrite letter, Frame's indignation evaporated and she apologised to *him*. 'I'm sorry I . . . invented the Fable of the Oamaru Lawyer. The only Oamaru lawyer I know is an elderly spinster who is very much your champion . . . so I should lose the case anyway.'[59] In response to Glover's query about the poems, Frame said that she had burned them, 'burying the ashes in the garden as nourishment for the sweet corn'.[60] When news of this conflagration spread, Sargeson, Glover and then Albion Wright feared that Frame might eventually destroy all her writing, including the new manuscript, which Wright had now decided to call, with

Frame's consent, *Owls Do Cry*. It was agreed that if parts of the story were to be queried in the course of editing and typesetting, then the manuscript itself must not be returned to the author.[61]

A subsequent near-crisis was precipitated late in February 1956 by Frame's eventual decision to take up Sargeson's suggestion that she apply to the State Literary Fund for two hundred and fifty pounds to enable her to undertake her travel overseas. The timing meant that this request would be considered at the same Literary Fund meeting that dealt with Pegasus's application for a subsidy of three hundred pounds to support publication of *Owls Do Cry*. Denis Glover, who as a friend of both Albion Wright and Sargeson was expected to steer both applications through the committee, was furious.

'Granted that a publisher's application & a writer's application are two different things,' he told Sargeson, 'I still see it as an unhappy conjunction, with somebody perhaps wanting to take both items together, to the detriment of them both.' To Albion Wright he wrote that 'Brother Frank is behind most of this: he is terrified that [Frame] will kill him or herself or go back inside . . . I just don't know how really mad she is, & Sargeson, not himself normal, is a fool in practical matters.'[62]

The problem that now presented itself was that, in order to strengthen Frame's case for her travel grant and make it more likely that she would move on, Sargeson had over-dramatised his guest's supposed mental difficulties. When Frame had arrived at Esmonde Road one year before, all that Sargeson knew was that she had been discharged from Seacliff after almost a decade in mental hospitals. Once Frame told him that she had been diagnosed as schizophrenic, Sargeson researched the illness in the Takapuna Public Library and became increasingly anxious about what he read.[63] He discovered that the disease was 'incurable' and progressively disabling. And having gleaned this information, like hospital authorities before him, he began to analyse all of Frame's behaviour in the context of the schizophrenia diagnosis.

'The aurally hallucinated receive commands which they must obey,' Sargeson reported to Glover. '[If] J received a command that she was to bump me off, she would have to obey.'[64] To Glover's objection that 'to subsidise genius is one thing, to subsidise lunacy another', Sargeson emphasised that the genius was real;[65] but went on to say that, like John Money, he viewed that quality as part of Frame's personal burden and mental problems.

She is undone by her brilliant intelligence combined with her frightening clarity of perception. If she was an intellectually mediocre zany scribbling away to amuse herself I should be sympathetic but only faintly interested. But she's so brilliantly acute she sees through every literary illusion until she becomes, paradoxically, the ultimate in blasphemy and heresy. She's a walking example of what happens when there are no gods to bear the burdens which human beings can't bear. She won't accept the illusions, and finds herself obliged to face up to emptiness and disorder. The problems the gods should be solving she attempts to solve herself. She's mad, as she must be — but the rest of us are blind if we don't see the limitations of love harmony order meaning and all the rest of it which she gets on to paper.[66]

To his friend E.P. Dawson Sargeson confided:

> I think I could have put up with the burden if Janet had been prepared to find three or four people about New Zealand to whom she could have gone for care and shelter in rotation (including myself, of course). But she has put up a most strange resistance to this suggestion. I am deeply attached to her — she is a brilliant and wonderful girl, but nobody on earth can be expected to put up with the strain all the time. In the last months I have felt over and over again I've been hanging by a hair over an abyss, but the thread hasn't broken yet . . .[67]

Eventually matters resolved themselves. The March meeting of the Literary Fund approved the Pegasus subsidy for *Owls Do Cry*, which allowed editing and typesetting to get under way. Frame's personal application was deferred until the following meeting, scheduled for May. In the meantime an Auckland-based member of the committee, retired secondary school principal Miss Agnes Loudon, was deputed to interview Frame and report on whether she was a suitable subject for a personal grant (the implication being that if she was indeed 'mad', the committee would not feel disposed to send her abroad). When the interview eventually took place at Miss Loudon's home in Parnell in April, Frame acquitted herself brilliantly. Miss Loudon subsequently told her committee that Frame was 'a thoroughly normal and healthy girl of highest intelligence, and knows [exactly] what she is doing'.[68] Which was good news, though it did rather puncture Sargeson's alarmist views about why the grant was necessary.

In May 1956, before the Literary Fund's verdict was known, Sargeson persuaded Frame to accept an invitation to stay with a woman who would become one of her closest friends. Elizabeth Pudsey Dawson, known to Sargeson as 'Peter' and to other acquaintances as Pudsey, lived in retirement in the Bay of Plenty. She was an upper-class English woman who had moved to New Zealand in 1925 to escape her family and what she saw as the expectations of her class. She was well educated (at Roedean School and Royal Holloway College in London), left-wing and lesbian. In New Zealand she had worked as a physiotherapist and published articles on nutrition and pacifism. She also wrote fiction, though without conspicuous success. The story of hers which Frame had so much admired in the Sargeson-edited volume *Speaking for Ourselves*, 'Maria', had been edited heavily by Sargeson to make it publishable. Its inclusion in the book had been a *quid pro quo* for the fact that Dawson had met the costs of publication from her private income, just as she had subsidised the printing of Sargeson's second book, *A Man and His Wife*, in 1940.

By 1956 Dawson was 62 years old and living off family money in a cottage at the small seaside village of Mount Maunganui. Since Frame had arrived at Esmonde Road, Sargeson had been encouraging Dawson to invite his guest to stay with her.[69] This was not simply a matter of giving himself a break from Frame's company. It was also part of his exploration of the possibility of a roster of people to look after Frame; and of what Frame referred to as Sargeson's propensity for dispensing people 'as if they were medicine and he were the doctor in charge of the case . . .'. "She'll like you," he said. "You'll be good for each other".'[70] And so it proved. In Dawson's phrase, the two women 'clicked'. On Frame's part, this may have had something to do with the fact that Lottie Frame had so recently died and Dawson was almost the same age. Conversation with her led Frame to wonder how she, Janet, would have related to her mother had they simply been 'two persons talking'.[71]

The relationship was not without a degree of strain, however, especially for the younger woman. Dawson wore 'grey flannel slacks, white cotton blouse like a school blouse, grey cardigan, and garberdine raincoat. Her shoes were black lace-up "sensible" winter shoes. She was eager and nervous, speaking in the English accent which we used to call "Oxford", heard in teachers, doctors and royalty, which therefore gave it an association with authority, a hint of admonishment . . . a permanent thread of *This is why it is so and it can't be helped* . . . [She] announced soon after our meeting that she always "said honestly what she thought".'[72] Although Frame too valued honesty, she was 'sometimes fearful of the sharpness, the hint of aggression with which it is so often expressed'. Peter Dawson's honesty came without the clothing of tact and she bristled with sharpness and, because of her personal history, a degree of paranoia.

She was generous, however, and went to considerable lengths to help Frame feel at home in her rather stark, wind-blown cottage by the sea (like Sargeson, Frame noted, Dawson had a dislike of 'frills and fripperies').[73] She cooked healthy meals and introduced her guest to books she had not read (*Alice in Wonderland*, *Through the Looking-Glass*, the works of Beatrix Potter, and the *Complete Sermons of John Donne*). Dawson introduced Frame also to her friends in the neighbourhood, including Michael Hodgkins, eccentric nephew of the painter Frances, and the Williamses, members of an 'established' family whose daughter in London was a friend of a well-known poet. Dawson, however, feared the loss of her own friends to the Williamses; and Frame, at that time in her life, 'could not quite imagine the importance of some of the territorial urgencies and restrictions of human friendship'.[74]

Late in May, while Frame was with Dawson, Denis Glover told Sargeson that the Literary Fund had not only approved Frame's application for a travel grant but had boosted it by a further fifty pounds. Sargeson at once sent a telegram to Mount Maunganui: 'Privately informed. Three hundred pounds granted. Congratulations.' Thus the prospect of overseas travel was transmuted from the realm of possibility to that of certainty. Once again Frame had a sense of 'being borne along on the wishes of others'.[75] But she was accustomed to that; and, despite her customary hesitations and fears, the objective in this instance was one that had, on the whole, come to appeal to her.

> I dreamed of seeing King's College Chapel, Cambridge. I wanted to roam the countryside of the Scholar-Gipsy, and that of the Hardy novels; to see, in Shakespeare country, the 'bank whereon the wild thyme grows'; and even to walk in Kew Gardens among the lilacs! . . . I longed also to wander in the *Euganean Hills*, . . . and to see
>
> The blue Mediterranean, where he lay,
> *Lulled by the coil of his crystalline streams* . . .[76]

She would now return to Auckland to book her passage and organise her 'affairs'. Before she left Mount Maunganui, however, her hostess gave her a present for the coming journey: a carefully folded pair of grey flannel slacks exactly the same as Dawson's own. Frame tried them on and they fitted. She could not bring herself to tell the older woman that she disliked both their shape and their colour.[77]

In Auckland events accelerated Frame's passage towards her 'almost visible future'.[78] With Sargeson's assistance she opened her first bank account, at the Takapuna branch of the Bank of New South Wales. Then she booked a berth in a six-berth cabin in the New Zealand Shipping Company's vessel *Ruahine*, which would sail from Wellington for Southampton at the end of July. It cost one hundred and twenty-five pounds. She applied for and received a passport and an income tax clearance certificate. And she had a smallpox vaccination, which left her ill for several days. Sargeson's music-teacher friend Jess Whitworth, 'eager, wise, literate, adventurous and soft-hearted', offered advice on how to travel simply and save money, and where to live cheaply in London.[79]

By 6 July Frame reported to Audrey Scrivener that the army hut was jammed with her cabin trunk, several suitcases, a haversack, and Sargeson's pumpkins. Trying to reduce the amount of clothing she would need to carry, 'I decided to make a warm lining for my coat, and use the lining as a dressing gown as well. I think it is only moderately successful.'[80] Sargeson, still the attentive godfather, persuaded Charles Brasch and E.P. Dawson to contribute money to the coming expedition, and Albion Wright sent a small advance on royalties for *Owls Do Cry*. After paying her fare, Frame still had around three hundred pounds to spend.

In the midst of these preparations the first galley proofs for *Owls Do Cry* arrived for correction and turned out to be 'a terrible balled-up job'.[81] Frame was obliged to set aside her reluctance to let Sargeson see the text and to accept his offer to read and correct the typeset material. He did so, and found it 'remarkably beautiful touching crazy, and (most remarkably of all) funny'.[82] He warned Albion Wright, however, that great care would have to be taken to ensure that the typesetter did not 'correct' what he described as 'the definitely Frame-ish bits, which are so important in creating the unique atmosphere she achieves'.[83] A further contribution to a sense of chaos was the news that, after nine years in the United States, John Money was returning to New Zealand for a visit and looking forward to seeing his former patient. Frame, no longer obsessed, was able to tell him levelly by letter that she would be in England by the time he arrived. She urged him, however, to pay a call on Sargeson.[84]

A month of frenetic activity took its toll on both residents of 14 Esmonde Road. When an especially stressful day reduced each of them to angry silence, Frame, feeling that Sargeson was attempting to do rather *too* much for her, rebelled. She delivered a note to the house. 'I may remind you that I am fully responsible for myself at all times; any communication that you ever made with anyone connected with me, I shall regard as what is called "cheek", but which to preserve the dignified tone of this letter, I shall call "impertinence".'[85]

Communication with her host resumed when she fell ill just days before she was to travel to Wellington, where she would be joined by her father, up from Oamaru to farewell her. Frame began to vomit when she tried to eat. Sargeson suspected, he told Dawson, that the symptoms were 'psychosomatic — she doesn't really want to go . . . [The] doctor I had to get was a stranger . . . [He] suspected from the setup and J's symptoms that she and I had been up to one of those back-street jobs.'[86] On a Sargesonian diet of soup and barley water, however, the patient recovered sufficiently to leave Auckland in time to board the *Ruahine* on 31 July — though she remained unwell.

Despite the drama of those final weeks and the mutual corrosion of nerves, Sargeson and Frame had established an intimacy and an affection which would endure for the rest of their respective lives. 'Christ knows whether she'll survive,' Sargeson wrote to Dan Davin after her departure, 'but Providence looks after its own, and [Janet] couldn't be so profoundly wise if she wasn't one of God's children specially in favour.'[87] And Frame would always look back on her sixteen months at Esmonde Road with love and gratitude, and say that Sargeson 'saved my life by affirming that I could spend my time writing', and by establishing the circumstances and discipline that enabled her to do so.[88]

When next they met seven years later, Sargeson would have published two more books and be even more the grand old man of New Zealand letters. Frame by that time would be the author of six volumes of fiction published and praised in the United Kingdom and the United States. And the balance of their relationship as mentor and protégée would shift accordingly.

CHAPTER NINE

# *Traveller's Joy?*

*J*ANET FRAME SAILED OUT OF WELLINGTON HARBOUR ON THE
passenger ship *Ruahine* on the still winter evening of 31 July 1956. According
to her passport, she stood five feet four inches, had blue eyes and auburn hair,
and displayed no visible peculiarities. At the wharf she had been farewelled by
her father, and by her Uncle Vere and Aunty Polly ('dressmaker to the world',
who had taken the trouble to remind her that her real place was at home, with
her but recently widowed father).[1] As the ship moved away from the wharf
the waterside workers' brass band played *Now Is the Hour*, the New Zealand
anthem of departure, and 'the music reached down like a long spoon inside
me and stirred and stirred . . . I felt like weeping with fear and delight'.[2]

Her travel plans had been worked out in detail by the well-meaning
Sargeson and his friends. She would arrive in London after the four-and-a-
half week cruise, stay in the Society of Friends Hostel in Euston Road, then
take a 'garden room' recommended by Jess Whitworth, behind a boarding
house near Clapham Common. After about six weeks there, as the London
weather grew colder, she would head for Ibiza in the Balearic Islands off the
coast of Spain, where two more of Sargeson's friends, the architect John
Goldwater and his wife, had said she could live pleasantly and cheaply. En
route for the island, at Barcelona, she would have the option of meeting another
Sargeson protégée, the writer Greville Texidor. Frame was simultaneously
grateful for and exasperated by these arrangements. 'I was again living the
submissive, passive role which in hospital had been forced upon me but which
my shy nature had accommodated with ease: at its best it is the role of the
queen bee surrounded by her attendants; at its worst it is that of the victim
without power or possession . . .'[3]

The *Ruahine* was one of the most modern of the New Zealand Shipping
Company's vessels, having been built only five years previously to replace
another of the same name which had been lost in the course of the Second

World War. Writing to Audrey Scrivener, Frame described it as 'smart, with posh writing room, lounges, library . . . and spacious cabins, even the six-berth one which I share with two other New Zealanders, a Norwegian woman [daughter of a famous author], and two English women'. There was also the luxury of 'having one's bed made, menus [and] one steward to each dining room table'.[4]

The gloss wore off rapidly. In the open sea the *Ruahine* pitched and rolled. The cabin was claustrophobically hot and throbbing and 'even the walls seemed to surge and sway'.[5] The influenza which Frame thought she had shaken off in Takapuna returned. After three days of continuing sickness she was lodged in the ship's hospital. 'I was unable to organise my defence against the awful diminishing of my human power where every move was a nauseating effort and the seconds, the minutes, the hours, the days became a mountain of oppressive time.'[6] The ship's doctor became so concerned at her inability to recover that he advised her never again to travel by sea.

Frame lay in the hospital for three weeks, amputated from the circulation of shipboard life, until the *Ruahine* reached the Panama Canal. Then she was able to make her way shakily on deck to watch 'the theatre of the Panamanian jungle with its basking crocodiles; the gaudy parrots flitting among the trees that leaned, burdened with blossoming vines, to touch the water'.[7] Days later, at Willemstad in Curaçao, she went ashore, her first footfall in a foreign country.

How clearly I understood the travellers' custom at the end of a long voyage of stopping to kiss the earth! In Willemstad, however, the immediate earth was concrete, and the smell was not of fresh grass but of oil from the refinery, yet the light was new, otherworldly above and upon the dull reds, browns, cream of the buildings, and the foliage glittered paintbox green with a poisonous brightness. I wandered alone through the streets . . . I sat in the Museum grounds watching unfamiliar lizards basking on unfamiliar stones, and birds that I'd never seen before or heard singing, flocking in the trees. Then I walked by the river and, noting the empty bottles and tins, I was aware of the 'other country' comparison — were not our rivers pure and swift, not sluggish and polluted? And the people walking by the river, how poor they seemed to be, and sickly, unlike the robust New Zealanders . . . [Faced] with Afro-Americans and Indians, I dismissed from my mind the comparison with teams of slaves. I said 'Hello' heartily, to show my lack of prejudice but I became alarmed when my greeting was followed by an attempt at conversation, for I had nothing to say. And here I was, travelling overseas to 'broaden my experience' and already undergoing the change forced on every new traveller and accomplished by examining not the place of arrival but the place of departure.[8]

For the final week of the voyage across the Atlantic, although she felt much better, Frame was permitted to remain in the relative luxury of the hospital. At night she took her bedding on deck and slept in the cool air under the stars. After thirty-two days at sea the *Ruahine* arrived at Southampton on 29 August, the day after her thirty-second birthday. With the other passengers she boarded the waiting train for Waterloo Station, London. And from there she took a taxi to the Friends Hostel in Euston Road, to which she had written from Auckland to reserve a room.

Because of the extent to which her journey had been discussed and planned, it was inconceivable to Frame that anything could go wrong. But all travellers, at some point, have to face an unravelling of arrangements as a result of letters gone astray, bookings doubled up or unannounced changes of schedule. Within an hour of her arrival in London, Frame was standing homeless on the grimy steps of the Friends Hostel, surrounded by two old suitcases, the green haversack Frank Sargeson had insisted she take (because he had travelled with one thirty years before), and a leather 'traveller's joy' handbag that had been her present from the Gordons. Her reservation letter had not arrived; there were no vacant rooms.

'I felt fleetingly at the back of my mind the perennial drama of the Arrival and its place in myth and fiction, and I again experienced the thrilling sense of being myself excavated as reality, the ore of the polished fiction. The journey, the arrival, the surprises and problems of arrival . . . For a moment the loss of the letter . . . seemed to be unimportant beside the fictional gift of the loss, as if within every event lay a reflection reached only through the imagination and its various servant languages, as if, like the shadows in Plato's cave, our lives and the world contain mirror cities revealed to us by our imagination, the Envoy.'[9] This intuition, suddenly and sharply apparent to her on a darkening autumn day in London, was not unlike the revelation that had come in the wake of Myrtle's death: that 'real' lives, and the world of dreams and mythology and literature, were intimately connected; and that the individual human imagination was the envoy that moved between those worlds.

Insight was all very well. Her immediate need, however, on a dreary day that seemed to her more like mid-winter than autumn, was for shelter. At the suggestion of the hostel receptionist she took another taxi, this time to the YWCA in Bloomsbury. There, she learned, she could share a room for two nights with a woman from Singapore. The respected but tawdry institution reminded her 'of a mental hospital without the noise, without the constant jingling of keys and the attempt to control the guests, although there were efforts to control in the sheet of rules pinned inside the doors of the bedrooms and bathrooms and lavatories that were in rows, institutional in appearance and smells . . . *Please leave the bath as you would wish others to find it.*'[10]

These undertones served only to make Frame marvel at the onset of a sense of liberty and independence which she had never felt in New Zealand, where she was always likely to encounter reminders of family, friends, or her time in hospitals — everything that is implied in the term 'personal history'. In London she had no 'personal history'; there was no one likely to recognise Janet Frame or know about her time in Seacliff or her family difficulties; and that experienced realisation was akin to the lifting of an enormous weight. She told Frank Sargeson that she had 'never felt more free . . . [How] I smile to myself as I look from this window on to Great Russell St, and try to pick from the passers-by the character from William Plomer's ballad "A Ticket for the Reading Room".'[11]

It seemed to Frame that almost everything she saw on those first days in London was charged with significance, and nothing more so than the city's underground railway, which she called 'that planned materialisation of a Kafka dream . . . where carriage doors are sinister and swiftly-closing; and the giant lifts of black lace and iron keep floating up and up . . . The Londoner says, "I'll take the Underground." He means, "I'll go down to my unconsciousness for a sixpenny racial nightmare . . ."' To John Money she wrote of 'buses like bright red sandwiches . . . and masked men with briefcases, yeast-bun hats and Freudian-sinister umbrellas'.[12]

She did not want to prolong observation of the caravanserai from an institution, however. And so, on the evening of her first night at 'the Y', she rang the telephone number that Jess Whitworth had provided for the 'garden room' in Clapham. An Irishman answered, told her that his name was Patrick Reilly, and that he had the authority to let rooms in the absence of the owners.[13] There was one available, as it happened, for one pound seven shillings and sixpence a week. She could move in at any time. Her 'down-under' accent, Mr Reilly said, proved that she was a genuine enquirer.[14]

The following day, 1 September 1956, Frame took a taxi to Cedars Road. Number Four was a three-storey Victorian brick house down the Clapham Common end. The street itself was broad and tree-lined and had been named after 'The Cedars', a house built early in the eighteenth century by a former partner of Samuel Pepys. By the late nineteenth century the thoroughfare was flanked with large terrace houses which, by the 1950s, had been grimed by the combined action of coal dust and smog. Patrick Reilly had taken time off work to greet Frame and settle her in her room. He carried her bags through a side gate and alongside a boundary wall which, behind the house, had four shacks against it in a row. They were set directly onto the earth, without piles or foundations. The 'garden' was a scruffy patch of grass with a clothes-line, an apple tree, a red currant plant and a line of gooseberry bushes.

Mr Reilly 'thrust the key into the lock of Number Three and with some urging and pushing he opened the door into a small damp-smelling room containing a narrow bed with some bedding, a curtained wardrobe, a chair, and on the rush-mat-covered floor a single electric plate connected to an electric meter, fed with shillings, just inside the door. There was one small square window by the door and one light suspended from the ceiling. A pile of assorted dishes and pots and pans stood on a box beside the electric ring. "I'll need a place for my typewriter," I said. "I'll fetch a table from the cellar . . . And I'll show you the bathroom and the geyser in the main house. Like a cup of tea?"'[15]

Patrick Reilly, who thus put himself out to make Frame welcome and — as far as possible — comfortable in this not untypical London boarding establishment, was a fogeyish forty-three years of age. He had been born in Westport in County Mayo, and told Frame that one of his cousins was a Catholic archbishop in Ireland. At the age of seven he had seen his mother struck and killed by lightning as he stood next to her in a field. Other members of the family had been arrested and imprisoned during 'The Troubles', and one of his sisters had had her fingers smashed in a door frame by the Black and Tans.[16] In London in 1956, Reilly worked as a bus driver and served on a church committee which was trying to rescue young Irish girls from prostitution. He was also, Frame would come to realise, intent on finding what he regarded as a suitable woman to marry. And in this quest his approach would be, in his own words, 'never to take your eye off the quarry'. Frame would, for a time, become that quarry; and Reilly, as a result, an obtrusive and eventually unwanted presence in her life.

In appearance, Frame would write later, Reilly was 'sturdily built, not tall, with greying hair, a large smooth pale face and brown well-spring eyes. His occasionally tightly pursed lips gave me a sign of a certain restriction of inward horizons . . . His step was agile and sure.' He was also 'a natural helper . . . dependable, self-satisfied, bigoted, lonely, religious, with an endearing [accent] . . . [He] was what my mother would have called "a gentleman".'[17]

In the course of carrying out what he saw as his responsibilities, and in an effort to keep Frame 'fancy free' and therefore eligible for marriage, Patrick Reilly would come to play a role in Frame's life not unlike those of the male authority figures she had encountered in hospitals; and to whose influence she remained vulnerable. They would tell her what to do and she would do it, though eventually with mounting resentment. In her post-hospital years she would find herself accepting the friendship of such people because of loneliness and the feeling that nothing better was on offer. In the case of Patrick Reilly, she would eventually be repelled by his dull, domineering narrow-mindedness.[18]

On that first day at Cedars Road, however, Frame accepted Reilly's offer of a cup of tea and a Peek Frean biscuit, and tried to absorb his instructions about the routines of the establishment and the dangers of the bathroom geyser and the 'blacks' who had moved into the neighbourhood. Listening to him, Frame was learning for the first time about 'the ritual of a way of living that was new to me, where people lived alone in one room of a large house of many rooms, each self-contained except for the shared bathroom and lavatory and the water tap above the basin on the landing where Patrick had filled the kettle for our tea. Already I had noticed two men with buckets fetching their supply of water either for washing or for drinking. "Women are not popular with landladies," Patrick explained. "They leave hair in the bathroom and are always washing clothes".'[19]

Frame was very soon shocked by the way her fellow tenants 'appeared to accept their dreary lives in gas-smelling rooms, their stained slop bucket and the "good" water bucket, their seldom-confessed loneliness that showed in the lingering way they clung to casual conversation as if words drifting by on stairs and in doorways must be snatched as a last hope'.[20] She, however, revelled in what felt like her first feelings of real freedom. She found even the mundane routines congenial. 'Each morning I crouched on the floor of the room waiting for the colour to surge into the electric plate to boil the kettle for washing and coffee, saving a shallow swill for rinsing the dishes, and then, following the example of a neighbouring tenant, I'd throw the dirty water into the gooseberry bushes that screened the rooms from the back lawn where the tenants from the main house hung their washing and on the rare fine afternoons sunned themselves in the company of the landlady's tortoise, it also trying to attract the smoke-filtered warmth of the now faraway sun.'[21]

To Sargeson she reported after four days that 'my angel has provided all, including very cold weather ideal for writing; my angel is now forgiven the dreadful days at sea'. With genuine independence, however, came new insights. 'This is [also] a letter of sympathy with you in your housekeeping. I never realised . . . Provisions, washing up; cooking; and everything is so dear, milk one and threepence a quart (inferior grade); I use margarine instead of butter; honey four shillings a pound; eggs six shillings a dozen . . . This is my city, but the money flows away from me.' Such prices, and the speed with which her meagre resources were evaporating, precipitated a realisation that she would have to find work if she was to have any money left by the time she reached Ibiza.[22]

First, though, she permitted herself some exploration of London, that 'beautiful grey city of smoke and rubbed stone'.[23] She made long bus journeys 'to places with haunting names — Ponders End, High Wycombe, Mortlake, Shepherds Bush, Swiss Cottage, each time arriving at a cluster of dreary-looking buildings set in a waste of concrete and brick and full of people who appeared to be pale, worried and smaller in build than most New Zealanders'.[24] She also visited Hampstead Heath and the neighbourhood where John Keats had lived. From the heath, 'the sky was grey, a mist hung over the city below, flocks of birds hurried through the sky in narrow formation as in a corridor, going somewhere towards the light; and the leaves trembled and tugged on the golden trees; and at the sight of the tall brown rushes growing at the edge of the pond I began to repeat to myself, naturally,

> "O what can ail thee, knight-at-arms,
> Alone and palely loitering?
> The sedge has wither'd from the lake,
> And no birds sing." "[25]

As she looked down on London from Hampstead Heath, Frame could sense 'the accumulation of artistic weavings, and feel that there could be a time when the carpet became a web or shroud and other times a warm blanket or shawl: the prospect for burial by entrapment or warmth was close'.

> How different it appeared to be in New Zealand where the place names and the landscape, the trees, the sea and the sky still echoed with their first voice while the earliest works of art uttered their response, in a primary dialogue with the Gods . . . I did not know whether to thank or curse John Keats and others for having planted their sedge, basil, woodbine and nodding violets, and arranged their perennial nightingales to sing in my mind. Misgivings . . . could not detract entirely from my first literary experience of London. That evening in my Garden Room I read and recited Keats and others . . . having followed the advice of Jess Whitworth and joined the local Clapham Library.[26]

In those early weeks at Cedars Road in September 1956, Frame also resumed writing. She bought copies of the journals and newspapers that published literary work (the *New Statesman*, the *Times Literary Supplement, John O'London's Weekly*, the *London Magazine, Poetry Review*). In them she found 'exciting new poetry and prose by writers from the West Indies, some written in literary English, others with a West Indian version of English but all charged with a morning vision of London and the United Kingdom. I was much influenced by the West Indian writers and, feeling inadequate in my New Zealand-ness . . . I wrote a group of poems from the point of view of a West Indian new arrival.'[27] One of these read, in part: 'The dancing woman wears amber beads/ and snip-snap the scissor cold/shortens the hem of summer.' Another:

> He came from a far country
> where they sit under lemon trees and ask
> riddles of giant vermilion cattle with white faces[28]

Repeating the experiment she had conducted the previous year with Frank Sargeson, Frame sent the poems to John Lehmann at the *London Magazine*, 'with a covering letter explaining my recent arrival from the West Indies. The poems were returned with the comment that they were "fresh, original" and the editor would like to see more of my work. The poems submitted did not quite come up to the standard of English required. I did realise that such literary pretences were a safeguard against the discovery by others that my "real" poetry was worthless. They were also a reflection then of a New Zealander's search for identity beyond her own country where being thought "more English than the English" was felt to be more insulting than praiseworthy. In a sense my literary lie was an escape from a national lie that left a colonial New Zealander overseas without any real identity.'[29]

In the same month that her London poems were rejected, one Frame had left with Charles Brasch in New Zealand was published in *Landfall*. It too had black/white overtones: 'The negro dark whitens/minstrels morning . . ./the sweet chariot hung low for to carry.'[30] Sargeson, commenting to E.P. Dawson on the quality of this verse, pointed to what he saw as the strength and weakness of Frame poems written around this time: 'It is very vivid,' he said, 'she writes such things in her head, and then transcribes them as fast as she can make her pen move or her typewriter type — hence the lack of working over, which might well clinch some of them as final and enduring works of art.'[31]

In London, there was another experience that underlay Frame's meditations on ethnicity. In one of her early letters to Sargeson from Cedars Road she reported that 'I have picked up with a negro law student and am beginning to understand more the "coloured" unhappiness, for I am "coloured" myself . . .'[32] The student was Clement Nweze, from Nigeria. Frame had fallen into conversation with him after they dismounted from the same bus. In what was, at the age of thirty-two, her first 'date' with a man, they had gone to the cinema at Leicester Square, then had sandwiches and coffee at a café. They enjoyed each other's company. 'We were both colonials with similar education — heavy doses of British Empire, English history, products, rivers, cities, kings — and literature. He too had been given lists of the good, the strong, the brave, with friends and enemies clearly, permanently identified . . . I was more favoured, however, in having my ancestors placed among the good, the strong, the brave, the friendly, in the position of the patronising disposers, the blessed givers.'[33]

Their rapport was broken, however, when Frame declined Nweze's invitation to 'come home and dance'. She felt threatened by the prospect of discarding inhibitions; he mistook her response for racism. They parted coldly. To impress upon Sargeson the supposed breadth and excitement of her life in London, and thus to emphasise her new independence, Frame gave a more dramatic account of what had occurred. 'His hands were too wicked and I did not want curly-headed piccaninnies bobbing up left and right. He was very naive and excitable and high spirited, and so serious, and the inside of his mouth was pink . . . But all that happened when I was first tasting my freedom to see what flavour it was . . .'[34]

Her second date, also an invitation to the cinema, came soon after her first. This time it was with an English physics teacher who lived in the main house at Cedars Road. This relationship too failed to flourish, though for different reasons. Frame found herself shocked by the teacher's lapses in grammar, and by his schoolboyish behaviour. 'I had certain notions of how different professions must be and . . . I believed that such experts as physicists, doctors, lawyers were beyond displaying childish traits . . . I found the behaviour of Jack, the physicist, almost incredible. I remembered the story of one of Tennyson's admirers who was shocked when Tennyson opened the conversation with a complaint about the price of coal.'[35]

Far more congenial was an evening Frame spent in a household of would-be writers and artists in Parliament Hill Fields, Crouch End, an address she had been given by Sargeson's friends the Goldwaters. 'I was impressed by [their] communal living, the freedom, the absence of demanding authority . . . Two of the girls were scholarship students at the Slade School of Art, while those without formal work while they pursued their chosen career earned money . . . as models in the art classes, and found much of their food by visiting the free sample areas of the Oxford Street and Knightsbridge stores . . .'[36]

The night Frame visited the group ate paella, which made her feel that she was back in Sargeson country.

> My new friends impressed me; they were gifted, intelligent, learned, more than I could ever hope to be, and, anxious to represent myself honestly in case there should be misapprehension, I [said] that my book had been published 'only in New Zealand', while the novel would be available 'only in New Zealand'.
>
> They asked for the name of my publisher.
>
> 'Caxton for the first,' I said, 'and Pegasus for the novel.'
>
> Their excitement about meeting a published author lessened as they admitted that already they had chosen their one and only publisher: Faber and Faber. Nothing less than Faber and Faber . . . 'There's Deutsch, of course . . . and Michael Joseph . . . and Calder . . .' Solemnly we raised our glasses of red wine in a toast to Faber and Faber, the supreme publishers of poetry.
>
> They talked late into the night while I listened with wonder to their hopes and dreams of exhibition, performance, publication . . .[37]

Frame stayed the night at Parliament Hill Fields and, on the way home the following day, lost the purse containing her money and her keys. Patrick Reilly replaced the keys, but lectured her on the company she had kept. 'They're not the type for you . . . They hang around and do no work. And their morals are no better than they should be.'[38] Frame commented: 'It seemed to me as if [he] had sprouted from a handful of New Zealand earth that had found its way into my green haversack and spilled into the garden at Cedars Road. Patrick Reilly had helped me. He was now trying to take charge of me. He had accepted, against his will, that I was leaving for Ibiza, but he was firm in his plans for me to return "fancy free" to London where I would find a decent job. "We can look to our future then," he said.'[39]

Early in October Frame booked and paid for her European travel for the following month: ferry to Dieppe, train to Paris, one night in a Parisian hotel, train to Barcelona, and ferry to Ibiza. Then, making use of her old New Zealand testimonials, she found a job for the remainder of the month as a housemaid/waitress at the Battersea Polytechnic Hostel, up the northern end of Cedars Road. There, from six o'clock in the morning until noon, she emptied ashes from fireplaces and cleaned and polished floors. In the evening she waited on tables at tea time. Her major source of interest and entertainment was listening to the rest of the household staff exchange stories about the Blitz over lunch.

> [Day] after day the women talked of the war, reliving horrors they . . . could only now describe . . . I [too] began to relive [it] as the Londoners had known it. The relics were evident: bombed sites not yet rebuilt, overgrown with grass and weeds and scattered with rubble; the former Underground station with its hundreds of entombed Londoners caught in an air raid; squares and streets where death and destruction had now been given a place and names. My interest in the storytellers of Battersea made more tolerable for me the early morning waking in the now cold damp Garden Room, the walk through damp fog to the hostel, the thankless task of emptying the ashes, and in the evening, the waiting at the High Table . . .[40]

The High Table for teaching staff, on a platform above the rest of the dining room, made Frame sharply conscious of the preservation of class in England. 'The hierarchy was respected: no one dared make a mistake in identifying rank or choosing the mode of address. I knew that in my past I'd witnessed similar behaviour in the mental hospitals where the doctors, matron and senior staff were regarded as gods; while I had looked thus on university lecturers and professors. At the hostel the fact that the surroundings were tailored to fit the superiority of some and the inferiority of others gave the system a permanence, locking everyone in place . . .'[41]

Back at Cedars Road, 'evening came earlier each day. It was no use pretending that summer was not over. The leaves rattled harshly brittle in the trees. The gooseberries had long been gathered and the bushes were bare. I returned to my Garden Room to study the maps for my coming journey to Europe. The lengthening, darkening days, the damp chill of early morning and evening, the comforting presence of the many buildings in London . . . seemed to paralyse my desire to travel into the European winter. Perhaps, I thought, Spain, the South, would be different . . . *Oh for a beaker full of the warm South* . . .'[42]

Most of Frame's last day of her first sojourn in London was spent in the company of David Kozubei, 'a slim dark young man with thin hunched shoulders and long arms'.[43] He was a poet of Polish–Jewish descent who lived in the Parliament Hill Fields flat of artists and writers. He had recently been in Scotland where, to his great joy, he had met the poet Hugh MacDiarmid. Together he and Frame tried without success to find a shop that sold a chess set. Then they went to Kozubei's parents' flat in Hampstead, where they talked about writers and writing and shared enthusiasms. Enjoying each other's company, they pledged to remain in communication.[44]

At the end of that day, the other man in her life, Patrick Reilly, took her out to dinner at a Clapham restaurant. 'Our conversation was dull. Patrick was lonely and ordinary with little trace of romance or excitement . . .' The next morning he took time off work to farewell Frame at Waterloo Station, where he handed over a going-away present of two cans of creamed rice. '"Keep in touch," he said. "And stay fancy free." His brown eyes were shining darker than usual, and I, softhearted, overcome by many goodbyes, felt tearful and sad to see him like another lost soul seemingly unaware of imprisonment or freedom.'[45]

By late afternoon of the following day, 31 October, after a journey by train, ferry, and train again, Frame was in Paris and Patrick Reilly forgotten.

# CHAPTER TEN

# In the Warm South

$\mathscr{T}$HE PLEASURE OF JANET FRAME'S FIRST VISIT TO PARIS WAS HEIGHTENED by her knowledge of French history and culture, a legacy of a good education at Waitaki Girls' High School. It was undercut, however, by the unexpected difficulties she experienced in making herself understood in French; and by the fact that, in her haste to get to Ibiza, she had allowed herself only one day and one night in the city. There was too the disappointment that she, child of a railway family, misunderstood the French arrangements for checked bags and, as a result, lost all her luggage other than her Traveller's Joy and a small carrier bag.

Retrospection dissolved this last regret, however. Following the advice of Frank Sargeson and his friend Jess Whitworth, *all* their advice, Frame had arrived in Paris with 'pots and pans, a Girl Guide set of cutlery, tin-opener, pocket knife, cooking stove fuelled with sticks of methylated spirits, and sleeping bag with sleeping sheet. I'd also accumulated many books, secondhand and new, during my time in London, with a *Teach Yourself Spanish Part One* and a *Teach Yourself Spanish Phrase Book*. These, and my huge hooded fawn jersey, exercise books, a rug ("all travellers have a rug"), a supply of clothing, packed into my now bulging suitcases, with my typewriter in the green haversack, made my luggage a wearisome burden.'[1]

She escaped this pile of impedimenta, and the effort required to move it and be vigilant about it, by going out to buy food (and then shedding tears over her inability to communicate with shopkeepers); and by getting lost in Les Halles, the city's vast vegetable market, 'tripping over [cabbages], sliding on cabbage leaves . . . unable to escape'.[2] She consoled herself by looking out her tiny hotel window on to the Bastille, reminding herself that here she was in Paris, and, by whispering 'loved passages of French prose and poetry', which now acquired a new relevance.[3]

The luggage mishap occurred at the close of her one whole day in the city.

Boarding the train for Spain, Frame handed in her bags at a counter marked 'Consigne', in the belief that she was 'consigning' them to Barcelona. When they failed to appear at the customs hall on the French–Spanish border, she discovered that what she had done instead was deposit them in the station's left luggage department. Her first reaction, as in the case of her 'lost' booking in London, was one of despair and then panic; her second, over the succeeding days, a growing sense of delight that she had been relieved of an encumbrance. The bags, she was assured by railway officials, could be sent for from Ibiza.

At Barcelona Frame was met at the station by Greville Texidor's daughter Cristina and her husband, the painter Keith Patterson. Texidor herself, a writer friend of Sargeson's with an exotic past — associations with artists such as Augustus John and Mark Gertler, winning an 'all-England' beauty contest, dancing in a Paris chorus-line, and touring America with a contortionist — was out of town.[4] The Pattersons took Frame to lunch at La Plaza Roma, where Frame was enveloped by a sense of 'being at home, in place at last . . . an abrupt removal of all tethering and bonds to a native land'.[5] This feeling intensified when, the following morning, she stepped off the overnight ferry at Ibiza, third-largest of the Balearic Islands, fifty miles from the east coast of Spain and just over one hundred from the coast of North Africa. Within days of arriving Frame had determined that, whatever she would do with the rest of her life, 'I am more than ever certain that I shall never return to New Zealand . . .'[6]

Ibiza, in November 1956, was a town of 12,000 people and 'capital' of the island of the same name. It was built on a chalk hill that rose amphitheatrically at the head of a large bay. It had been occupied successively by Phoenicians, Egyptians, Greeks, Romans, Carthaginians, Arabs and Catalans, all of whom had left an imprint on the island's architecture and culture, and on the genetic make-up of the inhabitants. Visitors from northern Europe or the Antipodes were struck by the 'intense light reflecting off the pale rocky earth and the whitewashed houses'.[7] There were no advertising hoardings, no motorised vehicles, and mules and carts proliferated on the roadways. Local women customarily dressed in black. Earlier in the century the landscape, the luminous quality of the atmosphere and the extraordinarily cheap cost of living had attracted a succession of artists and writers, among them the New Zealand painters Frances Hodgkins, Maud Burge and Douglas Glass. Artists living on the island in the 1950s included Jackson Pollock and Willem de Kooning.

Frame knew little of these associations at the time of her arrival. She had made Ibiza her destination simply because of the Goldwaters' recommendation that it was a place where modest financial resources could be stretched to support relatively lengthy and comfortable stays, especially outside the summer holiday season. There was virtually no cash economy on the island at this time and anyone with money — especially pounds, dollars, francs or marks — was wealthy by local standards. In winter it was possible to rent houses for next-to-nothing. Frame expected initially to stay there from four to six months.

The Pattersons had commended her to the care of a former English actor and now would-be poet, William Monk, who was travelling on the same ferry from Barcelona. He, showing no enthusiasm for his charge, gave Frame a motor scooter ride to a cheap hotel and left her there, having arranged in fluent Spanish that she would stay two nights. Unencumbered by luggage, Frame went out and bought a Catalan phrase book and some newspapers; then, using the phrase book, she purchased some bread, butter, cheese, an apple and a banana, and a cake of chocolate which turned out to be infested with insects. She was unable to read in her hotel room that night because the town's power supply was weak and intermittent. The shops, she noticed, were lit by candles.

The following morning she set out in search of a place to live:

> I walked towards the old city on the hill, along the narrow cobbled streets to the remains of the Roman wall with its stone figure of a Roman warrior at the entrance to the tunnel leading to the upper city. Walking carefully to avoid the piles of dog and human mess in every corner, I came into the daylight of the hill where I looked down on the harbour and the buildings across the harbour, perfectly mirrored in the clear tideless ocean. At the top of the hill I could see the other side of the island beyond the fields and olive groves to the transparent Mediterranean.
>
> I sat leaning against a grey rock that was massed like an accumulation of layers and layers of ancient olive leaves. I shared the solitude with a small herd of wild goats, and the silence with the distant sound of the fishing boats. The grey-leaved olive trees with their twisted branches and trunks turned in defence against the sea wind, and the white-grey stones like long-fallen snow that had refused to melt, on the red soil beneath the trees, drew from me a feeling of tenderness as if this land were mine and I had known it long ago. It was, of course, Shelley's world, and I *had* known it in poetry . . . I was happy just to *be* where I had always felt most at home — outside, under the sky, on a hilltop overlooking the ocean.[8]

Rousing herself from a reverie, Frame continued her walk and eventually came upon two middle-aged women 'in black shawls, stockings and shoes, bending to gather twigs and branches to heap into their large woven baskets, and again I recognised them because I had known them before — in paintings depicting the toil of peasants or as casual onlookers in the midst of a miracle, or in descriptions by Victor Hugo and Pierre Loti and Daudet . . . [They] furnished the landscape as if it were an interior long ago formed, decorated, occupied with no prospect of change.'[9] Referring to her phrase book, Frame wished the two women good day and explained that she was a New Zealand writer looking for somewhere to live and work. She stressed that she was not a tourist.

The women became excited and explained in a mixture of Spanish, French and sign language that the house of their *patron*, the director of the museum, was available for rent and that they would take her there. And so Francesca and Catalina (for so they introduced themselves) led her back through the cobbled streets to Ignacio Riquer.[10] El Patron was away from Ibiza and the house was in the care of his brother, Fermin. He, in his forties and slightly built, offered it to her for a rent of ten pesetas (about two shillings) a day. This was within the range recommended by the Goldwaters and Frame accepted.

The house had a spacious bedroom where she could both work and sleep, a kitchen with a wood range, and a lavatory at the end of the terrace. There was no bathroom. Other members of the owner's household would use the house from time to time including his son Jose, a law student at Valencia, Fermin, who practised the violin there in preparation for his evening performances in a café, and the widowed servants Catalina and Francesca, who lived next door but used the kitchen for preparing meals. Apart from these arrangements, Frame understood, she would be renting the whole house, including an upstairs floor which she did not investigate. She was pleased and proud to have so quickly found herself such satisfactory accommodation.

She wrote to American Express in Paris and asked them to collect and forward her luggage from the railway station. Fermin promised to look out for it and to let her know as soon as it arrived by sea from Barcelona. Then she went shopping for immediate needs — underwear, stockings, a skirt, jersey, nightgown and writing materials. One shopkeeper gave her, in change, a cluster of pre-1935 notes that were no longer legal tender. These chores accomplished, and this lesson learned, Frame sat down at the table in her room and began to hand-write verse, letters and, more tentatively, some short stories that would draw further on her experience of hospitals.

The room was 'large and airy with a niche window overlooking the harbour and the distant shore where the buildings lay like those of another city'. The letters she now wrote there were the kind travellers send 'from a new country where everything glistens with marvel . . . the light, the sky, the colour of the olive trees and of the buildings thumbed and worn like old stone pages, with none of the restlessness of New Zealand buildings, none of the sensed fear of sudden extinction by earthquake or volcano. These rose like opened books on a lectern of earth and were turned perhaps once in a hundred years, their certainty lying in their age and their openness. And crowning the marvel was the receptiveness of the tideless ocean admitting to its depths the entire world standing on its shores, creating a mirror city that I looked upon each day'[11] — a city that, in addition to being 'real', would become for her a powerful metaphor for the mytho-poetic world to which her imagination sought access through her poems and fiction; and which she would encapsulate in the title

Left: *George Samuel Frame, aged 18, in full pipe band regalia.* (Janet Frame)

Right: *Lottie Frame in the backyard at Wyndham, 1929: with June and Beauty.* (Janet Frame)

*Young Marrieds, Lottie and George Frame in 1922, with Myrtle and Geordie; on Lottie's sister's farm at Inchclutha.* (June Gordon)

Above: *Janet in her tartan skirt 'almost stiff with constant wear', with Myrtle, outside the Eden Street washhouse, 1932.* (Janet Frame)

Right: *The Frame children: Myrtle, Geordie, Janet, Isabel and June, Eden Street 1932.* (Janet Frame)

*Frame family camp at Rakaia, January 1937. Myrtle, finally allowed to wear slacks, fades out at the back; Marguerite Miller third from right.* (Janet Frame)

*Willowglen, 'that pokey little doll's house'.* (Janet Frame)

Right: *Otago University, Dunedin. Befitting the city's Scottish origins, the main building was modelled on Glasgow University.*
(Hocken Library)

Left: *John Money, junior lecturer in psychology, photographed by his friend Theo Schoon.*
(John Money)

Below: *Seacliff Mental Hospital, like a castle from a Gothic novel, a place of horror.*
(Alexander Turnbull Library)

Left: *Frame with the Gordons in Birkdale, 1950: 'They enclosed one another while I stood awkwardly in the background.'* (June Gordon)

Right: *After her final release from Seacliff, March 1955: 'A healthy young woman with obvious false teeth, a smirking smile and a Godfrey chin.'* (Janet Frame)

Left: *Frank Sargeson in the Esmonde Road cottage: foundation-layer of New Zealand literature and mentor extraordinaire.*
(Kevin Ireland)

*The desk inside the army hut, where Frame wrote* Owls Do Cry. (Barbara Duggan)

she gave thirty years later to her third volume of autobiography, *The Envoy from Mirror City*.

The letters went to members of her family, and to Frank Sargeson, John Money and Audrey Scrivener, to share her unexpected pleasure and to assure them of her safe arrival and well-being. 'I write to you from beside the Mediterranean Sea,' she told Money.[12]

> It is happy, peaceful [here] . . . Soon Francesca or Catalina will come to make my dinner. They will select pieces of *carbon* from the basket, and arrange them on the stove, and wave the straw fan to make the flames into a strong fire. And they will talk to me . . . [Catalina] is from Algiers and speaks French with me, also *espagnol*. Francesca, from Madrid, is little, old, sly and fierce . . . [Ibiza] smells with a mixture of olives, shellfish and donkeys; and honey stirred with dust and stored on high shelves . . . [There] are so many tiny snails everywhere, clinging to the trees and rocks and window sills and racing fast as centuries on walls of stones. And there is a [Roman] fort here did you know? And that the houses dazzle?[13]

To Sargeson she stressed that Ibiza was 'greatly to my liking . . . The night is without sound. The morning — cocks crow, children are smacked and cry, and then sing . . . Catalina has adopted me because in all her married (and unmarried) life she never had a daughter. Now she will even pick the bones . . . out of my fish if I let her; and at night she brings me a little tin full of warm ashes and embers so that I may "me chauffer".'[14] To a young woman who had lost her own mother less than a year before, as Frame had, such maternal attentions were a considerable comfort.

Apart from approaching William Monk at a café and being snubbed by him, Frame made no attempt to communicate with the English-speaking expatriate community in Ibiza. As a consequence, and of necessity, she told Sargeson, she was becoming 'quite *espagnol*'.[15] In addition to the tutoring and mentoring provided by the two widows, she had two further teachers. 'Fermin [who] comes in the morning to practise his violin . . . and in the afternoon to potter around cleaning his bicycle, or making little wooden carvings, or painting something or other; he also gives me very painstaking lectures in Spanish . . . [José] recites poetry to me. His favourite author is Tolstoy, his favourite book *War and Peace* . . . He knows more of Dickens than I do, Balzac, Dante, Flaubert etc . . . I asked him, Why did you not learn English at school? . . . And you, he said, why did you not learn Japanese . . . ?'[16]

One of the poets whose verse José recited, Miguel Costa Llobera, was almost a local, coming as he did from the island of Formentera, five miles south of Ibiza. In ancient times Ibiza and Formentera had been known as the Pityussae or pineclad islands, a reference to the trees that once covered them and became emblematic of their identity. Frame learned Llobera's poem 'El Pino de

Formentera' as a 'set piece . . . [a] focus for an Ibiza that I found to be so old, touched by the Moors and the Romans, and as young as childhood's blue-sky days'.[17]

However strong Frame's sense of well-being — and she was happier in Ibiza than she could remember being since childhood days in Oamaru — she was unable to exclude a note of anxiety from her letters to Sargeson. '[The] financial situation, whether good or bad, haunts me, with the thought of *el termino* — myself sitting crazily in a corner, mumbling an unpoetic pesetas, pesetas, pesetas. I need someone to take complete charge of my worldly affairs. Someone to operate me by radar, as it were. The situation is made worse . . . by the wait for my luggage, especially for my typewriter.'[18]

Sargeson, rarely of a mind to be reassured if panic was an option, became fixated by the loss of Frame's luggage and the dire effects he was convinced this would have on her finances and mental equilibrium. 'This is a great worry,' he confided to Dennis McEldowney, 'as I have to find some means of raising money for her in case she has to renew her clothing, & get hold of some typewriter.'[19] He wrote to a variety of would-be donors, including E.P. Dawson, the Steads in Australia, Dorothy Neal White in Dunedin, Albion Wright in Christchurch and Denis Glover in Wellington, using the supposed crisis as a lever to extract further contributions towards a 'Janet Frame fund'.[20] '[In] order to coax money out of the [Literary Fund] Committee,' he asked Glover, 'can you give me a line on what sort of story she should put up?'[21]

Glover would have none of this and exhibited a considerable degree of exasperation at Sargeson's continuing manoeuvres on Frame's behalf. 'It's a bad show indeed that Janet has lost her baggage (instead of her reason, as you feared),' he allowed. 'But I can't see that this entitles her to any more than the generous grant she has had. You surely realise that we have many other claims on this miserable sum, and with our meeting on Friday pretty well cleaned out the lot . . . I wouldn't support any proposal to give her more — not yet.'[22]

The putative crisis was at an end when Frame's luggage arrived in Ibiza the week before Christmas 1956. '[Like] all the bits of the self which have been left behind on this symbolic voyage,' she told Sargeson, 'it arrived shabby and worn, and nothing like what it had been — the new suitcase was battered; things broken, stale-smelling; so beware of leaving your mind in the left-luggage department; just see how your ideas will deteriorate. Fortunately my typewriter, by some miracle performed by my patron saint, who is St Augustine . . . is in A1 condition. And the price for all this [was] only, I repeat, only, fifteen pounds: eleven for my luggage to come from Paris to Ibiza, four for a new set of clothing . . .'[23]

In addition, gifts of 'Christmas monies' pushed financial anxieties further out of sight and mind: payments for a *Landfall* poem, and for a story in the *New Zealand Listener* ('I Got a Shoes', published in November 1956 but written the previous year at Esmonde Road);[24] five pounds from the Gordons; fifteen pounds by way of further advance from Pegasus Press, at Sargeson's instigation;

ten pounds from John Money; and a further twenty pounds from Sargeson's donors, which arrived in the New Year. From London, Patrick Reilly also offered money, and a holiday on the Isle of Wight when Frame returned to England. For Christmas, though, Reilly sent tins of corned beef and (appropriately enough) Irish stew.[25]

Ahead of the Pegasus money came a letter from Albion Wright explaining that although he had hoped to publish *Owls Do Cry* before Christmas, production difficulties had made this impossible. It would instead be the company's first book for 1957 and would appear in March. For Frame, this news served to make the whole idea of the book seem even more unreal than it had previously. '[It's] so far away and done with,' she told John Money.[26] Nonetheless she promised Money a copy, while warning him that 'it isn't a novel at all, though it's fiction'.[27]

The most important items in Frame's retrieved luggage were her typewriter, rug, and hotwater bottle, and the slacks from Peter Dawson — the temperature had dropped now, the house had no heating apart from the kitchen stove and the nights especially were cold. When she climbed gratefully into the slacks, Catalina and Francesca — who had told her previously that *pantalones* for women were the work of the devil — relented, and told her she looked chic.[28]

Reunited with her beloved typewriter, Frame abandoned stories and poems and set to work in earnest on a novel she had begun to write before she left Esmonde Road, tentatively titled 'Uncle Pylades'.[29] Early in January 1957 she told Sargeson that it was 'good to be doing something again, and to be muddled up with other people, fictional, not other people real'. She hoped to have the book finished by April, though it would need 'much revision'.[30] To Charles Brasch she wrote that she was 'very happy to be taking up my bed and walking; even though the paths lead always to the old unalterable home-town of the soul'.[31] And she told Albion Wright that, once the current manuscript was completed, she would again send it to him directly, 'with no one but yourself having read it . . . it will, I hope, have fewer signs of haste' than *Owls Do Cry*.[32] By the end of January she reported to Sargeson that, wrapped in her rug and nursing her filled hotwater bottle, she had typed 50,000 words of the new work.[33]

Thunderstorms [now] came crashing above the house. Lightning played vividly in the room, and winds wailed, cried, screamed as I'd never heard winds, reminding me of the ancient gods, creatures born of thunder, lightning, storm, raging up and down the window panes as if trying to get in, clawing the glass, mouthing it as if it were an instrument of music. Often, in the midst of the storm, I'd walk outside, up the street to the other side of the island and I'd sit on the grey rock among the battered silver-grey plants and trees, and I'd think that I had never felt so much at home. I rejoiced that I was alone on a Mediterranean island, speaking no English, with my Spanish welcomed as my English never had been, for my struggle to express my thoughts was attended by the kindness of those who were proud that I was trying to speak their language and who were eager to explain, suggest, help, and teach, whereas in speaking one's native language to others who also speak it one is alone, struggling to meet the expectations of the listener.[34]

These considerations pointed to apparent contradictions in Frame's ambitions and behaviour. As she wrote to a friend of John Money in January 1957, she wanted, as a writer and as a human being, 'to know people, and what they are doing, and how they are doing, and if they are sad or happy and why'.[35] At the same time, she told Money, she also felt that the only way she could communicate with people was through the written word. 'I can never give myself in other ways, neither in speech nor act. It is a lonely thought, set, it seems, irremovably in a stone truth.'[36]

Even as she wrote these words her behaviour in Ibiza seemed to belie them. Somewhat to her own surprise, and certainly to the surprise of those with whom she corresponded, her customary reticence seemed to be falling away in the face of people who spoke no English and had no reference points with which to locate her in the English-speaking world and therefore no detailed curiosity about who she was or where she came from. She was even sanguine about the kinds of encounters that might have been traumatic had they occurred in New Zealand or London. 'I do love the Ibizan people,' she said on more than one occasion. '[I had] a cross-purpose conversation with an elderly bearded gentleman I met on the hill during my afternoon wander. It wasn't till he began to unbutton that I realised he was offering to seduce me.'[37]

Speculating on the nature of this kind of experience in a letter to John Money, Frame said, 'I have not changed . . . yet I have been free from the oppressive fear that pursued me in New Zealand — the mental hospital shadow. Here, I feel, nobody knows my past.'[38] She took this theme further in a conversation with Money several years later, when she 'volunteered that it had been marvellous for her to be among foreigners . . . [Her] feeling of privacy and personal inviolacy had been secured. People's expectancies of her were reduced to the single one, namely that they had to refrain from [intimate] conversation . . . There was a rationale for being a person apart. People did not have to speculate that she was different . . .'[39]

That sense of inviolacy was challenged in the latter half of January 1957, however, and the living and writing routine that had been working so well was interrupted. El Patron admitted a second lodger into the house that Frame believed she had to herself. Worse, he was an English-speaker. Frame told Sargeson: 'I have an American artist living here, so that I've got to use my energy in keeping up appearances, and putting on defences, and I hate that, when I was so free with a language barrier to hide behind . . . I hate talking English again. Domestically we manage all right, for he's a good cook and we take turns at the meals.'[40]

The artist, a painter, was a Jewish New Yorker named Harvey Cohen. He too was taken aback to find another person living in the house; and he was far less comfortable than Frame about the intermittent company of Fermin, José and the two servants ('Who are those two old women wandering around prying into everything?'). Frame's sense of betrayal was sharpest when Cohen showed her his upstairs 'studio', the part of the house she had never investigated.

[It was] a large airy room with white stone walls, a skylight, and a door opening on to the roof with a panorama of the city, the fields, the ocean, and the mirror city. I felt suddenly disappointed in my restricting of my spirit of adventure — why had I never explored this upper storey of the house? . . . This revelation of the panorama from the rooftop when I had spent day after day huddled in a rug in my chair in my room, my typewriter on the table before me, my gaze when it strayed from the typewriter fixed only on the mirror city across the harbour, had the effect of an earthquake, shifting my balance, opening depths beneath me, distorting yet enlarging my simple view, as simple as the stare of the blinkered horse I had seen harnessed to circle the well hour after hour, to draw water. No doubt the water was pure and sweet, bearing little relation to the routine of the imprisoned agent working at the well, but I was not so sure that what had appeared on my typewriter was so fresh and sparkling.'[41]

The new presence in the house also required a new routine. Up early each day, as always, lighting the kitchen fire, Frame now 'set aside [Harvey's] shaving and washing water, and by the time he was out of bed I had breakfasted and begun work. For the evening meal he usually ate with friends at a café or stayed home and cooked his speciality, French onion soup, or shared what was now my speciality, paella with saffron . . . [Harvey] painted most of the day while I wrote and at times we'd have spontaneous or contrived meetings in the kitchen when he or I asked, "Quiere el fuego?"'[42]

And so, although Frame had lost the sense she had enjoyed previously of living in a contentedly self-contained world, the new arrangement was not disastrous. She still managed to write, Cohen painted, and he was a considerate companion, showing her his pictures, and being genuinely interested in Frame's work, offering, even, to put her in contact with London and New York publishers with whom he had had personal and professional associations.[43] Apart from their intermittent conversations and consultations and meals, they managed to lead separate lives.

But Frame now found that even this supposedly advantageous arrangement produced, in Cohen's absence, 'a nagging sense of loneliness and an unwilling-ness to return to my writing . . .' And when Cohen had a woman friend stay the night, and Frame heard them laughing and talking their way up the stairs to the studio, 'I felt the sudden unfriendly chill of being just myself and no one else: not dainty, but with legs that my sister had said were like footballer's legs, and wristbones that reminded me of railway sleepers.'[44]

The presence of Harvey Cohen that generated these feelings also brought the means by which she would relieve them. One evening early in February 1957 as she attempted to work, Frame heard men's laughter from the kitchen. On the pretext of fetching hot water she went to investigate and found Cohen there with an American friend, George Parlette. Parlette was a 30-year-old accountant, originally from Ohio but most recently living in Switzerland. He had left a wife and two children there and taken a labouring job on an oil pipeline that was being laid on the Spanish mainland. In the course of this work he had been injured, and come to Ibiza, where he had friends, to recuperate and to write (he was to tell Frame that he had ambitions of becoming a poet). The encounter in the kitchen may have been accidental, or it may have been contrived by Cohen so that Frame and Parlette would meet. Whatever the mechanics of the introduction, Parlette returned the following morning to invite Frame to accompany him on a walk. About a week later, with a kind of shy pride, Frame reported to Sargeson what had occurred.

> [At] the moment work is not going very well — I'm leaving it in my unconscious while I have some human experience . . . a love affair with a friend of Harvey. It's . . . illuminating to watch the gradual changing in feelings etc. We've got to the slightly jealous stage now, where he makes references to 'all the men you've known' and I refer to 'all your women'. We've also got to the stage of not suddenly going to bed in the middle of the day . . . The whole thing is very fascinating, and rather amusing really, for we have taken to going [for] long cycle rides around the island, to the amusement of other people, for it looks such a healthy occupation, a sort of sublimating boy-scout adolescent employment; but very enjoyable — miles and miles, and then we stop for wine, then return to the city at nightfall, then wine and dine, then go to his house, and go to bed, which occupation I like very much, it being more comforting than a hotwater bottle, for a hotwater bottle gets cold in the middle of the night, but a man stays warm at night, and in the morning is sometimes very hot.[45]

Such a letter was, in part, Frame announcing to Sargeson that she was at last catching up on the decade of pre-adult and young adult experience lost when she was in and out of mental hospitals. It was also a proclamation of a normality that she felt might have gone against the grain of her mentor's expectations for her. There were similar elements of mild exhibitionism in her letters about the affair to John Money. In *his* case, of course, there was an additional point to prove: Frame was establishing not only her normality, but the fact that she was decisively free of the obsessiveness which she had focussed on him ten years before. 'I went into the affair quite calmly,' she told him, 'under the spell of Spring in the Balearics, the almond trees, long walks and cycle rides in the hills and by the sea, and blissful days and nights in bed . . . a beautiful if adulterous experience, made possible by the fact that when we were together he became not himself and I became not myself . . .'[46]

Mindful of Money's earlier interest in Freud, Frame could not resist passing on to her old counsellor an account of a dream she had had in the course of the relationship:

I saw three figures . . . dressed in red velvet, walking about in the street. I thought, These three women are my mother, yet she is dead, so they can't be, yet I hear her talking. Eventually I persuaded myself that she *was* dead, and I felt very unhappy. I woke then to find my companion embracing me, and was much comforted . . .

[The] red velvet is significant for it concerns something my mother told me once about a party that she longed to be invited to . . . [When] the party was in progress, she sneaked past the window, and all she could see, all her share, was the red velvet tablecloth. Now every time my friend undressed me . . . I found myself saying to him, I wonder what my mother would say if she saw me now. So the ghost of my mother appeared triply and . . . powerfully to admonish me, and to blackmail me with her death, and to stand as a rival against me, by lavishly dressing in red velvet to proclaim her share . . . in a party she was not invited to.[47]

Frame was, understandably, self-consciously reflective about the relationship with Parlette as it occurred. She was, after all, thirty-two years old and undergoing her first sexual experience with a partner — an experience that most of her contemporaries, including her sisters, had had at a much earlier age.★ While it was unfolding, she concealed from Parlette the fact that she was a virgin (otherwise, how to explain it?); just as she withheld honest opinions about the callow, shallow verse, his own, that he recited or presented to her. Frame would have justified both decisions at the time, by the desire to ensure that the sexual encounter took place, so that she could taste and evaluate it, rather than snuffing out the possibility before it developed. She was frank in her admission to Money that the connection had been achieved because neither of them were being their honest selves; and she acknowledged, also to

---

★ Speaking twenty years later about what she viewed as a weakness of *Owls Do Cry*, Frame chose to say that, at the time she had written the book, 'I knew very little. I'd never been to bed with a man . . . [Although] one can do all these things in imagination, one learns a tremendous lot by living these things.' (*Janet Frame*, Endeavour Films, 1977.)

Money, that Parlette 'called himself a writer because he did not know what he was, and will perhaps never find out'.[48]

The whole experience, which had lasted little more than a fortnight, left her with a conviction that the major ingredient for any future relationship, in addition to compatibility, was absolute honesty ('pray for me,' she wrote to Sargeson, 'in all my deceits of the soul').[49] She was left also with a suspicion that she might be pregnant. 'My adulterous existence,' she told Sargeson at the end of February, when Parlette had left the island, 'leaves something quite beautiful behind . . . though not, I hope, something substantial enough to wail and wear nappies. I shall find out that detail later on . . . [Meanwhile] I have returned to my normal isolation.'[50]

Frame had budgeted to spend all her supplemented savings in Ibiza, barring thirty-five pounds which she reserved in her Berkeley Square bank account to support her eventual re-establishment in London.[51] By early March those savings were diminishing; so was her confidence in the value of 'Uncle Pylades'. 'I have written, say, about two hundred pages . . . which I now find to be unforgivably banal,' she reported to John Money. 'It's not showable for it's all muddled up, and I hate it so much that I have put the pages in a folder and refuse to look at them; I would like to scream.'[52]

She was also, now, voicing reservations about life in Ibiza for which, up to this time, she had only felt and expressed enthusiasm. '[It] is sheltered and calm and the frogs are chirruping now in the square ponds, by the windmills, and all the almond blossom has fallen. Yet I yearn for the ugliness of civilisation; for the masses of people disguised and going nowhere; the sinister furniture and buildings and the new cave-age paintings that are the hoardings in brilliant colours of people eating breakfast food.'[53] Much later, when she came to write her autobiography, Frame attributed part of this disenchantment to the fact that she had come to know people and be somewhat better known; and to the effects of her relationship with George Parlette. 'I was invaded by knowing others on the island, I was no longer alone, creator and preserver of my world, in harmony with other worlds because I could interpret them as I wished: I was tasting the sour and bitter of absence and lost pleasure, bound to a magnet of reality.'[54]

In four months in Ibiza, Frame had speculated about a range of future options: to spend time on the Spanish mainland, to return to Paris, to walk or cycle around Europe, to visit Berlin, or perhaps North Africa.[55] By mid-March, however, her choices had narrowed to two: to remain in Ibiza until her money ran out; or to go to some place where she could make it last longer. She chose the latter alternative, explaining to Sargeson that Harvey Cohen had a bank account in Andorra, 'which is a free money market, so that he gets for his dollars the full rate of exchange . . . I have written to [my] bank having what I shall need in Europe transferred to the Andorra bank . . . A pound inside Spain is exchanged for 109 pesetas. If I work through a free market bank I can get 150 . . .'[56] She was influenced too by the fact that if a pregnancy was confirmed, she did not want to have to address the problem in Ibiza, where word of her plight would eventually affect her relationships with those she knew. She decided, therefore, to move to Andorra to collect and spend her newly enhanced pesetas. She would leave Ibiza on 21 March 1957 to stay initially at Barcelona, where she would visit Greville Texidor and her husband. She might also, she hinted to Sargeson, enlist Texidor's help if she was indeed pregnant.[57]

After a stormy overnight ferry ride she arrived in Barcelona on 22 March and took a room in a small hotel. '[As] I walked into the hallway and smelled the pervading smell of olives and olive oil, I felt a wave of homesickness for Ibiza, Catalina, Francesca, Fermin, José, all my Ibicencan family and myself as the innocent *escritoria* with the quiet uncomplicated daily chores and the simple stack of typing paper and the communion with the Mirror City. And now it was [George Parlette] whose presence stayed, like a phantom. He was there beside me, around, within me. Hearing his laughter in the street I'd look out to see a stranger laughing and talking among strangers.'[58]

These feelings were not unconnected with the fact that it was in Barcelona that Frame confirmed her pregnancy. The knowledge plunged her into a state of depression and revived feelings of personal worthlessness. She felt again like killing herself, she told John Money. 'I kept thinking to myself, What on earth are you doing alive? . . . And I thought I would do it, but I didn't, I just wandered round and round Barcelona.'[59] The feeling of negativity leached out of her and penetrated everything around her.

I am not really a writer, and I will never again try to be one, or let people persuade me that I am one; I am just someone who is haunted, and I will write the hauntings, and that is all. And it is the people who haunt me, it is all the people in and out of the world; the long-ago people and the recent people; their faces and their voices and their fear; perhaps it is everything, even Franco on the stamps, with the flesh hanging under his chin, and twenty years ago because he was very handsome and romantic the young men did what he told them, and fought, and half the time didn't know what they were fighting for; but now his face has changed; he has a double chin; he is old; they come across his photo in their book of nostalgias, and they tear it up, because everything is different, and nothing happened as they thought.[60]

As an antidote to these feelings and fearful, perhaps, of where they might lead, Frame called on Greville Texidor and her husband and younger daughter Rosamond. The visit had the effect of turning her mind away from present anxieties. 'I liked them,' she told Sargeson, 'though I . . . did not mention my predicament to them. Greville says the only worthwhile things in New Zealand are Frank and the scenery.'[61] Texidor, reporting on the same meeting, noted that Frame had stayed eleven hours, 'quite a long visit, and seemed at ease. She talked to me about her life in New Zealand . . . and confided that she had a manuscript which was very heavy . . . So I said why not leave it with me? She thought that rather risky because somebody might look at it . . . [Eventually] she agreed to leave it in a sealed package to be sent to New Zealand.'[62]

The following morning, however, instead of depositing the manuscript with Texidor, Frame slipped a note under her door which thanked the family for their hospitality and said that she was leaving for Andorra. She had discovered that the only way to reach the principality at that time of the year was by taxi (the roads in the Pyrenees were still too clogged with snow to take buses); there was one leaving that morning, which she would be able to share with two other passengers. The fare was cheap.

'I could not believe,' she wrote later, 'that I, a New Zealander who never went anywhere by taxi, was travelling late that morning . . . through the villages of northern Spain, past the fields and ancient monasteries and the miles of red earth.' The villages seemed to grow 'like dark-red fruit and flowers . . . or like old wounds, still open in places, covered with congealed blood that beneath the brilliant blue sky were unrelieved by the usual benison of green'. As she had done in Barcelona, Frame could not help but think of 'the country's wounds opening up as in the Civil War and [of] my Ibicencan friends and Fermin pointing to the place of the executions beside the Stations of the Cross'.[63]

Once in Andorra, however, and specifically in Les Escaldes, where she left her taxi and sat on an upturned suitcase in the village square, she was high in the mountains, among heavy pines and snow. 'Ibicencan pines, those light infant green trees, have a special place in my mind,' she told Sargeson. '[But] I like the dark gloomy pines [here] that seem to make no concession to frivolity and immaturity, and make a low anguished, not a frivolous warm whisper, when the wind moves through them.'[64]

Frame found a room almost at once with an impoverished family who welcomed the income brought by an additional lodger. The household was made up of Miguel, an under-employed carpenter, his wife, Lola, and their two children, Antonio (six) and Xavier (four). To them Frame spoke Spanish. The other boarder, El Botti Mario, was an Italian from Milan, who had been imprisoned in France during the war and worked as a guide and smuggler of contraband goods during the winter; in autumn he picked grapes over the border, in the South of France. To him Frame spoke French. Her board was fifteen pesetas a day (when 137 pesetas represented one pound sterling).

'My room faces directly on to a mountain,' she wrote to Audrey Scrivener. 'At first, snow-covered, but the snow is gradually vanishing on the upper slopes; higher in the Pyrenees it seems to be always snowing . . . more like flour being spilt than the traditional old woman emptying feathers . . . In my mountain walks I stumble over violets, but their smell seems frozen inside them. The valley is full of trees, poplars and larches and pines . . . I do my washing in the communal washing trough . . . supplied with water from the hot mountain springs.' And, although she was getting more pesetas for her English pounds, 'life here is dearer than in Ibiza'.[65]

Frame's original intention was to wait out her pregnancy in Andorra and she began to knit baby clothes from French patterns. At the same time, she told Sargeson, she was taking quinine tablets and rushing 'like a terrier up and down the mountains, and [taking] immensely hot baths in the mineral pools'.[66] These measures achieved their melancholy purpose. One night when she was attempting to change a light bulb in her room, 'I became dizzy and sick and fell, and blood flowed . . . The blood was bulky. I collected it in a towel and flushed it down the lavatory, pulling the chain several times before it shredded (a quick horror-filled glance told me) and vanished . . . I did not realise until the baby was gone that I had accepted it and was preparing for it. I knew a feeling that was stronger than regret but not as intense as a bereavement, a no-woman's land of feeling where a marvellous sense of freedom sprang up beside hate for myself.'[67]

Telling Sargeson some of this by letter, Frame commented that 'fate is kind to me always, nearly always . . . I am not sure of my future plans which, because of diminishing finance (the old story) may include a move so revolutionary that I shan't mention it in the meantime . . . For now . . . I am Andorran, even with my hot bread and milk in the morning.'[68]

This news provoked in Sargeson another bout of impotent panic. Given the combined circumstances of the miscarriage, disappointment in her writing and declining funds, he assumed that the 'revolutionary move' was code for suicide.[69] Frame, however, was referring to the fact that her fellow lodger, El Botti, had attempted to make love to her and then, when repulsed, was sufficiently impressed by her virtue to propose marriage, all in the course of a (thus far) four-week relationship. She did, as she hinted to Sargeson, take the offer seriously. 'I was prepared to like this tall handsome man. I admired his fight against the Fascists . . . I sympathised with his suffering and torture in a concentration camp; the fact, however, that I could not accept his wearing of two-tone black and white shoes . . . is more a comment on me and the influence of my early life than upon [his] character . . . In my past and lost world, any man wearing two-tone shoes was a "spiv", a "lounge lizard", possibly a gangster.'[70]

There *were* more serious considerations, of course. How would English speakers (and her family) regard her if she were to become 'Mrs Botti'? Would she have to be, like her husband, a worker in the grape fields, a peasant? Would she become, like her mother before her, a full-time, housebound parent? What about the life of the mind and spirit? What about books? What of her own writing which, despite periodic lapses, she regarded as the most important feature of her life? What about a future in which she might never again be alone? And, most significant of all, what about the fact that she did not love El Botti? '[For] it was [George Parlette] who still occupied my thoughts and dreams. I realised also that because I'd had the years of my twenties removed from my life I was now behaving in some ways like a woman in her early twenties who had recently left school and home and was exploring for the first time the world of men, women, sex, love.'[71]

Frame did not accept the ring, formerly his grandmother's, that El Botti offered her. But nor did she reject it. 'He and the family therefore concluded that we were "engaged" and would be married in the church in Andorra . . . And so it happened that during the remainder of my stay . . . I found myself assuming my most accustomed role, that of the passive person whose life is being planned for her while she dare not, for fear of punishment or provocation, refuse.'[72]

So she simply ran away. Frame explained to El Botti that she had 'things to see to' in England; then bought a round-trip ticket to London, having first ensured that she would get a refund if she failed to use the return portion.* She undertook in reverse the journey she had made six months previously: Perpignan to Paris by train on 30 April; by further train to Dieppe; ferry to Dover; Dover to London by train.

There, at Waterloo Station, was her nemesis in the person of Patrick Reilly, ready to hear her story (or such of it as she was prepared to tell), to sympathise, and to say that he had warned her about the dangers of associating with artistic types.[73] He had changed lodgings to 37 Narbonne Avenue in Clapham Common South, and he had taken the liberty of accepting a room for her and paying the first week's rent. The landlady, Mrs Bagatti, liked to be called Ma and had a cat called Chummie.[74] In the circumstances, carrying as she did the ghosts of George Parlette, El Botti and a lost foetus, Frame was disposed to accept what Patrick Reilly had to offer, to be pleased, even, to see him — though the consequence was to enter yet another prison from which she would, in due course, be required again to flee.

---

* Frame's flight from Andorra inspired a scene in a short story in which her putative fiancé, searching for her, turns up at New Zealand House in London and is persuaded to dip a finger in a jar of Vegemite (see Bill Manhire, 'South Pacific' in *Songs of My Life*, Godwit, Auckland, 1996, pp. 151–2).

CHAPTER ELEVEN

# *Towards Sanctuary*

$\mathscr{T}$HE WEEK THAT JANET FRAME UNDERWENT HER MISCARRIAGE IN
Andorra, her first novel was published in New Zealand.[1] *Owls Do Cry* appeared
at last in a slightly sinister-looking jacket: a night-time view of a typical main
street in a New Zealand town, made more sinister by the fact that the title
'shuddered' against a star-lit sky.[2] The blurb announced the book's publication
as 'an outstanding literary event', and said that the author was 'already
distinguished for a book of brilliant short stories'. It alleged that
Frame had left New Zealand in 1946 and was 'at present living in the Balearic
Isles . . .'

Within New Zealand's tight literary circle, the novel was an immediate
sensation. Writers and readers were soon exchanging letters about its plot, its
themes, its 'meaning', and about the magnitude of its achievement. 'It's quite
amazing, frightening, and beautiful,' C.K. Stead wrote to Frank Sargeson.
'The sections dealing with Toby are terribly moving, and the satire against
[Chicks] quite devastating . . . [The] whole thing shows a surprising amount
of conscious artistry in construction, especially in tying everything up
imaginatively in the Epilogue.'[3]

Sargeson urged all his correspondents to read it, telling Wellington
bookseller Roy Parsons that 'the best parts of it [are] quite beyond anything
of the kind so far done here'.[4] A later crop of literary memoirs attested to the
wide number of New Zealand book people affected by the novel's appearance.
Publisher's editor Phoebe Meikle, for example, would write that she read *Owls
Do Cry* 'with exhilaration and tears . . . reading all night because I didn't put it
down until I had finished it'.[5] As a consequence of word-of-mouth recommendation, the book began moving rapidly out of bookshops, which tended
to order no more than one or two at a time, even before the publication of
reviews. An Oamaru retailer went so far as to draw attention to the novel by
placing it in the window with a display of mechanical owls.[6]

Published notices brought the merits and the unusual characteristics of the book to the attention of a wider audience. In a surprising display of unanimity, reviewers reached for such superlatives as 'the first important novel to emerge in this country', 'this New Zealand book [is] in world class', 'technically impressive by international standards'.[7] The Professor of English at the University of Canterbury, Winston Rhodes, said on National Radio that 'no New Zealand novel has impressed me as much'. He praised in particular 'the perceptiveness of the author, the quality of her writing, her capacity for finding the right tone, the vivid phrase [and] the suitable organisational structure for her experiences . . .'[8] An anonymous reviewer in the *Free Lance* concluded that 'Janet Frame is a genius. Her draught of words, of memories, is clean and pure, tinged with the blood of suffering and as cold as ice.'[9]

The reception was not without elements of controversy, however. Reviewing *Owls Do Cry* in the *New Zealand Listener*, regarded as the most influential publication in the country on account of its national circulation and the normally high standard of its literary contributions, David Hall called it 'the most interesting novel published by a New Zealander in the last few years'. But he went on to say that 'it is full of superb and triumphant realism, and at the same time it is a work of unbridled and richly endowed imagination. The two elements remain unresolved, fighting against each other from beginning to end.'[10]

One *Listener* reader who immediately challenged this assessment was Anton Vogt, the teachers' college English lecturer and poet from whom John Money had sought advice about the publication of Frame's stories. Vogt asserted that Frame's writing was 'strongly disciplined', and that the elements of imagination and realism within it 'fuse perfectly'. He concluded that *Owls Do Cry* was 'not only our finest work of fiction to date . . . but one of the finest novels written in English in this century'.[11] Another correspondent, historian and poet W.H. Oliver, took issue with both Hall and Vogt. The book was, he said, 'a good deal more mature and finished than Mr Hall would concede'; but also 'considerably less perfect than Mr Vogt, in another of his disastrous enthusiasms, would admit'. For Oliver, the novel's strongest features were 'energy, breadth, vehemence, a willingness to risk loss of decorum by letting out all the stops . . . a blessed lack of the decent reticences of contemporary New Zealand fiction'.[12]

Frame herself closed this published correspondence by proposing an 'audition', at which she would provide 'a juicy symbolic pie where the reviewers may gather to play at Little Jack Horner . . . [When] will my guests learn to *eat* the pie that is put in front of them, even if its patches of bad cooking make them suffer from indigestion?'[13] She chided W.H. Oliver for a reference to an 'oven-and-pikelet symbol', pointing out that pikelets could not be made in an oven. To John Money she confided that she had been amused by the 'ponderous discussion . . . people arguing about the meaning of it all as if the whole thing were a tremendous problem'.[14] She went on to say that New Zealanders who had sent her copies of reviews 'quite frighten me with their enthusiasm, so that I am glad I am not there just now, I would have to retreat'. She reacted affirmatively, however, to Money's characterisation of her as a spectator. 'You have the key there, to the whole thing . . . The trouble is I am too much of a spectator; everything is like a film that I am watching, and have no contact with.'[15]

Although he drew the ire of Frame's most loyal supporters (John Money called him 'a portentous fool and a shibbolethic nincompoop'),[16] David Hall had touched on what would come to be regarded as the most raw and controversial aspect of *Owls Do Cry*. What, in its story and plot, was documentary realism, and what were the inventions of a 'richly endowed imagination'? In other words, what in it was fact and what was fiction? C.K. Stead voiced a general preoccupation when he wrote: 'I can't help being curious about how much of it is based on her own life — did she really have a sister burned to death? And does she have a brother who takes fits? . . .[When] you know that some of the facts are autobiographical you can't help wondering about the rest . . .'[17]

Nowhere was this feeling stronger than in Oamaru, where people *did* know that parts in the book were autobiographical and parts were not. This provoked an odd conjunction of reactions in which Frame was criticised both for putting 'real' people in the book, and for getting it 'wrong' when she invented or fictionalised others. Most people who knew the Frame family and read the book could see a relationship between Oamaru and Waimaru; between Frame and her central character Daphne, who spent time in a mental hospital resembling Seacliff; between Myrtle and the fictional Francie; between Mrs McGimpsey, for whom Myrtle worked, and Mrs Mawhinney, who employed Francie; between Geordie and Toby, both of whom 'took fits'; between June Frame and Chicks (June had been called Chicks by the family); and between George and Lottie Frame and Mr and Mrs Withers. Indeed, June Gordon herself was hurt by the apparent parallels between her own life and that of the unsympathetically portrayed fictional Chicks.[18] Geordie Frame, however, seemed delighted to be identified as Toby Withers; and to discover that Willowglen came to be known, among some Oamaruvians, as 'Owls Still Cry'.[19]

Miss J.B. Wilson who had, on retirement as principal of Waitaki Girls' High School, married the mayor of Oamaru, J.C. Kirkness, was 'incensed' by the book. May Frame, one of Janet's South Hill cousins, reported that Mr Kirkness had been one of the first people in Oamaru to congratulate George Frame on his daughter's success when *Owls* appeared. 'However when JB and her husband *read* the book, [they] cut Uncle George and never spoke to him again.'[20]

To some extent, Janet Frame had anticipated this kind of response. Before she left New Zealand she had written to Sheila Traill, now Sheila Natusch, to say she was glad that she would be out of the country when *Owls Do Cry* was published. 'This will save having to face angry people who suppose they have been "put in" the book.'[21] She herself was not conscious of 'putting' real people into her fiction. She simply wrote, without thought to publication, and drew on the combined resources of her experience and imagination, without making a distinction between the two. Describing the process to a friend, she likened herself to a 'princess, shepherdess, waitress, putter-on of raincoat buttons in a factory . . . who chose rags from an old bundle, stitched them together, waved a wand, and found herself with a completely new dress . . . I *do* collect bundles of rags and I like to sew them together: I suppose I must accept the fact that I have no wand.'[22]

Frame would not need to face the minor controversy caused by alleged overlaps between fact and fiction in *Owls Do Cry* until she returned to New Zealand in 1963. In May 1957, what bothered her about the two copies that reached her, one of which she sent to John Money, was the fact that the jacket blurb described the work as a novel. '[Who], indeed, said it was a *novel*, when I seem to remember expressly mentioning that it was *not* a novel?' she asked Sargeson. 'The whole thing sickens me through and through.'[23] In a more level letter to her publisher, she repeated that she had never wanted the book to be described as a novel, because that provoked certain expectations which the book would not, could not, meet. She preferred the term 'an exploration', a fictional one.[24] To John Money, she confessed to a degree of vanity in her reaction to the whole business of publication and acclaim. 'I read the reviews [and] I think, perhaps, there's something in it after all, so I look at the book, but no, it bores me.'[25]

The most acute source of stress Frame had to face when she returned to England in May 1957 was not the consequences of the publication of *Owls Do Cry*, however; nor, even, the well-intentioned ministrations of Patrick Reilly. It was the unexpected presence in London of her brother, Geordie.

Geordie Frame, after briefly carrying out his threat to 'sell up and go to Australia' in the early 1950s, had thought the better of that option and returned to Oamaru to resume living with his parents. With the death of the mother who worshipped him and his relations with his father as acrimonious as ever, he decided early in 1957 to follow his sister abroad. He went first to Edinburgh, because of that city's historical association with Dunedin and the province of Otago. Then, after losing a job there, he moved to London in April 1957. When Janet re-established herself in Clapham in May, Geordie was working as a uniformed commissionaire outside a theatre in Piccadilly Circus and living in Rowton House in Camden Town, a home for down-and-outs.

He came to visit his sister in Clapham and brought to show her a sheaf of handwritten manuscript pages, unpunctuated and full of misspellings, on which he was writing the story of his life. Janet had gone overseas; he had gone overseas. Janet had written a book; he, Geordie, would also write a book. He had, after all, been published alongside Janet in the 'Dot's Little Folk' pages of the *Otago Daily Times*. Geordie wanted an opinion on the value of his manuscript, but his sister was unable to give it. The composition was like something written by a child.[26] Janet found this and subsequent visits by her brother a considerable trial. They brought back the whole atmosphere of life at Willowglen and vivid memories of the domestic conflict that had latterly made it difficult for her to live there. 'Mentally I'm having a hectic time . . . trying to avoid [him],' she wrote to Frank Sargeson. '[It's] just that he reminds me of New Zealand and all that I hated and wanted to escape from. Whenever he calls I am prostrate for a day or two afterwards.'[27]

Shortly afterwards Geordie moved to a house in Shepherd's Bush, where he shared a room with three or four rough Irish immigrants. With their help he found a labouring job on a building site. In August, to his sister's relief, he headed for the Continent: first to France, and then to Belgium, where he had a major seizure and was found unconscious. Belgian hospital authorities contacted the New Zealand High Commission in London about his plight, and the High Commission arranged for his repatriation on compassionate grounds. Geordie was brought back to London, and then shipped home to New Zealand. He was back in Oamaru by December 1957. Janet endured this saga with difficulty, made worse by the fact that she herself was unwell in the latter part of the year. She nonetheless admired the courage with which her brother had undertaken the whole adventure and, as she had done in adolescence, she identified closely with the sufferings and predicaments that he carried with him as a result of his disabilities. And she was to make sympathetic use of some of Geordie's experience in a book she would write before her own return to New Zealand: *The Edge of the Alphabet*, about 'that strange, incommunicable region of the mind walled by silence, noisy with dreams'.[28]

Frame's other source of anxiety in May 1957 was a chronic shortage of money. The house in Narbonne Avenue, Clapham South, offered far more comfortable conditions than the garden shed in Cedars Road and each room was equipped with a fireplace and gas ring and meters for electricity and gas. But it was also more expensive: one pound twelve shillings and sixpence a week. While she had received further payments for writing published in New Zealand — another *Landfall* poem and a story in the *School Journal* — these were insufficient to support her for more than a few weeks.[29]

And so, once again, Frame went job hunting. It was, she told Sargeson, a strain 'going from place to place . . . and trying to explain why I've got no diplomas etc. and no experience at my age. One man who was cross-eyed

gave me . . . a divided look and said sharply, "You won't do". Such commonplace blows to the ego, but they hurt.'[30] There was also, she told John Money,
the haunting spectre of 'the boss — as in the old days . . . at Arthur Street
School — the Boss and the Inspector'.[31] After failing to secure secretarial work
or a wardsmaid's position in a hospital, and retreating from a copywriting job
with a mail order firm in Brixton because it involved working with others,
Frame found a position in mid-May as an 'usherette' at the Regal Cinema in
Streatham.[32]

'Last week I saw *The Curse of Frankenstein* and *The Woman of Rome* eighteen
times,' Frame reported to Audrey Scrivener early in June. '[This] week we
have the inanities of a film made "with the full cooperaton of the U.S. Navy"
. . . Anchors Aweigh all day and in my sleep.'[33] For Frame the writer, however,
the compensation of the job was the character and experience of her fellow
workers, who included 'an ex-night club hostess, and another woman who
. . . is off to Holloway for a few years . . . [When] I mentioned this to the
horrible rice man who lives downstairs and is very moral . . . he [repeated]
that I would be "dragged down to their level". I was furious . . .'[34]

Finding cinema work 'tiring and depressing', Frame left the job after only
four weeks and took advantage of Patrick Reilly's absence on holiday to return
to writing. She would survive in the meantime, she told Sargeson, on twenty
pounds from Peter Dawson and a further contribution from John Money. She
was 'itching to get back to the cheap Continental regions but cannot stand the
hot weather; have to wait until autumn, by which time I [hope to] have finished
something else in the literary line'.[35]

The 'something else' Frame proposed was a revived version of 'Uncle
Pylades'. She reported to John Money that, in 'New Zealand language', what
she had written in Ibiza was 'a curtain raiser, and the Shield Match will happen
quite soon, if I can breathe and am not suddenly followed up by inside pursuers
. . .'[36] One possible way of helping to sustain her writing career, of course, was
to find further publication outlets and consequent income from her stories
and from *Owls Do Cry*. Money had undertaken to retype and submit the five
stories she had written in Ibiza to the literary agents Curtis Brown in New
York, with whom he had had some previous association through his former
wife.[37] And Frank Sargeson had sent copies of *Owls Do Cry* to his friend
William Plomer, who was chief reader for Jonathan Cape in London, and to a
New York publisher, Sussman and Sugar, recommended by Harvey Cohen.
Cohen also suggested Frame write to his friend, the West Indian novelist
George Lamming, who published with Michael Joseph in London. The only
one of these who replied was Plomer, who wrote to Sargeson on 21 May:

> I have read *Owls Do Cry* with a kind of fascination. It is so real and so
> sad, like the sadness of the moon & of the night sky above the mountains
> and housetops in the picture on the jacket . . . The family is made rather
> painfully real, & the use of surface detail, so minute and exact, serves to

bring out somehow the whole atmosphere in which they live. I particularly liked Chicks' diary . . . I find the book very feminine, and the work of a caged spirit, and I am glad to have had the chance of reading it. But I am sorry to say that the feeling at 30 Bedford Square is that it is not a book which would have good prospects in this country . . . I suppose the reason is that it doesn't appeal enough to common appetites & is not sensational, topical, sexy . . .[38]

Sargeson conveyed this to Frame as diplomatically as possible; but, understandably, she was hurt by the verdict. '[You] tried to disguise from me the fact that Plomer etc. thought my work was bad, by saying it wasn't sexy or topical. Of course I shan't take any notice of that, and I am not going to entitle my next work *Conversation with My Lover*.'[39] Instead, having little confidence that Pegasus would even seek let alone succeed in securing foreign editions of *Owls Do Cry*, Frame made the sensible decision to look for an agent in London to carry out this task on her behalf. From the *Artists' and Writers'Yearbook*, she chose as candidates Curtis Brown and A.M. Heath Ltd.[40] The reason why the second of these had caught her eye was that it handled the work of e.e. cummings, 'and therefore, I reasoned, must be willing to deal with experimental writing, that is, sacrifice money for faith in a writer'.[41] Curtis Brown sent a cold form letter in reply; A.M. Heath a personal one, inviting Frame to visit their office in 35 Dover Street. Frame accepted the invitation and went to Soho to meet the company's principal, Patience Ross.

At this time, July 1957, Frame had no idea how apt would be her choice of A.M. Heath. It is unlikely that any other literary agent in London would have become more interested in her work than Patience Ross.[42] Ross, who was then fifty-three, had been working for A.M. Heath for thirty-one years. She was a lesbian who lived with a long-time partner. This circumstance, along with the fact that she was a lifelong sufferer from depression and obtained psychiatric help for this illness, meant that she viewed herself as someone who lived on society's margin; partly as a consequence of this, she would become deeply sympathetic to the themes and characters of Frame's fiction.[43]

What surprised Frame when she entered Patience Ross's office, however, was not unexpected sympathy, but 'the general air of disorderliness . . . manuscripts everywhere, some piled on the floor, some on shelves, newly published books with the gloss still on their jackets displayed on stands and upon the walls, in cases, on bookshelves; photos of authors, many authors, men and women, all unknown to me'. She was welcomed by Ross, wearing 'black and grey with grey short hair, grey eyes, and a kindly manner'.

[Ross] reached into a large handbag crammed with books and drew out the copy of *Owls Do Cry* that she had been reading. She had been impressed by it, she said, although she did not suppose it would be of popular interest. If I agreed to allow them to be my agents they would begin submitting the book to English publishers and, through their agent in the United States, to American publishers, although I must bear in mind that publishers preferred to handle manuscripts and not books already published in another country. Did I realise, she asked, that under my contract with Pegasus Press they would be entitled to fifty percent of all my earnings from overseas? The prospect of royalties being so distant I merely smiled with an air of 'who cares?'[44]

A few more years down the authorial track she would care very much about this subtraction from her income; but not in July 1957. To Sargeson, Frame reported that 'my work clicks in a slight way with [Ross] . . .' A.M. Heath, she said, had particular hopes that *Owls Do Cry* might appeal to the American market; and she told Sargeson that, in addition to e.e. cummings, the company represented Eudora Welty and Mary McCarthy. Sargeson was properly impressed; but it was to be a long while before this initiative bore fruit.[45]

It was shortly after visiting Patience Ross that Frame made her first trip out of London and through the English and Welsh countryside. She travelled by train to Cardiff to stay a weekend with Gene Beach, a former Seacliff nurse who, as 'Taffy' Powell, had treated patients with care and compassion. Beach, assuming that Frame would never have been sufficiently well to leave hospital, had written to her care of Seacliff; and Seacliff had forwarded the letter to Frame's father, who in turn sent it on to Ibiza. In that letter, Beach had apologised for the harsh treatment inflicted on Frame and other patients in the 'back ward', and expressed the hope that she was now 'out of a single room and allowed into the park on fine days', Frame recounted to Sargeson. 'She also told me much about the hospital which, if made public, would not prove very happy for Blake-Palmer, poor whiskered gent.'[46]

In July 1957 Frame accepted an invitation to visit Cardiff, and she enjoyed a weekend there with Beach and her husband and small son. Beach was 'terrified that I would have changed', Frame told Sargeson, 'and so relieved to find that I hadn't. [Of] course I *have* . . . but this is the basis of tragedy and time and the underground stream.'[47] Although Frame's own recollections of 'Taffy' at Seacliff were wholly genial ones, she found the former nurse troubled about the impersonal and even brutal manner which the mental hospital system in New Zealand had required staff to act with patients. What surprised her about Frame's visit was the fact her former charge had survived that treatment with her humanity and sense of humour intact.[48]

After Wales, the next trip Frame planned was a return to southern Europe after the worst of the summer heat had subsided. She was drawn back there, she told John Money, because, in addition to climatic and financial advantages, 'people have suffered there, and the trees are dark against the mountains. There is a darkness there that I must seek, and it is in the poverty and illiteracy that I lived among, where summer means work, and winter means no work and being inside and the children crying for *la calle*, and the big pot of water being mixed with flour to make it like some kind of soup and fill the empty places.'[49] This was an ambition that, in an immediate sense, would remain unfulfilled. Instead of relocating herself on the Continent in the latter part of 1957, Frame would spend the autumn and the coming winter back in a mental hospital. She would not have an opportunity to return to a Mediterranean country for a further seventeen years.

The first steps on Frame's path to the Maudsley Hospital in Denmark Hill, London, were taken in Ibiza in February 1957, when John Money sent her a course of the anti-psychotic drug chlorpromazine.[50] He did this because he deduced from her letters that she was still subject to depressive and hallucinatory episodes, and because he was concerned that, in a foreign country, she might be unable to seek or obtain medical help if she needed it.

Money still believed at this time, as did Frame herself, that she was a chronic schizophrenic; and in the United States drugs such as the one he prescribed had been found to reduce some of the symptoms of schizophrenia. His belief was strengthened when Frame told him of her sense of distress in Barcelona where, she said, she had felt as if she were 'dog-paddling out of a dream-sea'.[51] This provoked a repetition of the misunderstanding that had occurred a decade earlier: Frame was using a metaphor to describe how she felt; Money thought she was describing an hallucinatory experience. In his view, this experience might presage a new round of psychotic episodes which he believed had plagued her in the mid-1940s. The consequences of such episodes recurring while she was in Spain or Andorra could be dangerous, even fatal. Money therefore proposed that she take the tablets he sent to relieve her symptoms; and that, when she reached London, she visit the Maudsley Hospital, which had a worldwide reputation for enlightened treatment of psychiatric patients. He offered to put her in touch with a psychiatrist there, Dr Michael Shepherd.[52]

By July 1957 Frame was unhappy in London. Despite the fact that she had jettisoned paid employment to concentrate on writing, that writing was not going well. She again felt ambivalent about the whole process and its culmination in publication. She told Sargeson that she was 'exhausted after all this Owling' and that, when she received a letter from Pegasus Press, she burst into tears, even though it contained good news (that *Owls Do Cry* had sold over nine hundred copies of its thousand-copy edition in two months). '[If] I were in New Zealand now I would go straight to the Pegasus Press and kill Albion Wright for having published my book. It would be a violent death for him too, let me tell you. And anyone who had read the thing would suffer second or third degree assault . . . I'm rather afraid to consider my future.'[53]

To John Money several weeks later, she described her state of mind as 'pretty bad . . . On several occasions I have got ready for a final over-dose of something, and then have set about tidying my room and destroying my papers; but all has been in such a mess that I couldn't be bothered killing myself; not that night anyway. The feeble excuse [masks] the deeper excuse, I imagine . . . [It] has happened so often; the old dream and muddle and wandering; the very near and the very far; . . . the way people change their size and shape, even faces change and their voices; it's like Dante's *Inferno*.'[54] What had also been revealed before, of course, was this capacity to describe her state of confusion with complete clarity and accuracy, a faculty that was not consistent with the presence of serious mental illness.

Whatever was ailing her now, Frame was of a more activist disposition than she had been in New Zealand. In Ibiza she had been, for the most part, happy and productive; in London she was not. She wanted to find out why this should be so. She determined that the most useful thing she could do was to take up Money's suggestion that she seek help at the Maudsley Hospital. 'I do not much like the idea of saying much about myself and my inside mind,' she told him, 'for fear I may be thought not quite responsible for my actions . . . I would feel, though, a little easier if I had myself more on my side, to keep the balance, so myself would not be able to surprise and frighten me with so many dark obsessions and commands. I don't want to change myself, only to have command in my own house, and the right of shutting or opening the door on the darkness. You know that I live almost completely in a fantasy world, that though I may walk fearfully in it, I never want to leave it, only not to be exhausted there, to death.'[55]

Referring to what she saw as her current predicament, she emphasised in a later letter: 'I do not want to become placid, only a *little more* placid, so that each day is not such an exhaustion of wasted emotion . . . To me the need to write and the act of writing are worth more than any opinions of what I write. You understand that if I change myself, I fear that perhaps I may no longer *need* to write; yet such has been my recent confusion and exhaustion that I am not *able* to write.'[56] And such was her sense of urgency that she rang and made an appointment at the Maudsley before she had heard back from John Money, and before he had had an opportunity to compose a letter of referral. Frame walked from Clapham South to Denmark Hill to see Michael Shepherd on the afternoon of 22 July.

'Because of my rather timid condition,' she reported to Money the next day, 'I panicked during an interview with a woman who had a face like a dungbeetle (How many in your family? What is your work? Usherette? Waitress? You change jobs rather frequently, don't you?) . . . [By] the time I arrived at Dr Shepherd I wasn't in a state to conduct a very rational conversation . . . I spent the time trying to hide the answers to any questions he asked — I mean about having been in mental hospitals . . . I left because it was all too much; I cannot talk to people. He suggested that . . . it may be better for me to try again and call in a few weeks' time. Forgive all this . . . The visit to the hospital brought back all the fear and terror of imprisonment, and the realisation that, with all due respect to Dr Donne, each man *is* an island "entire to itself", and *send* to know for whom the bell tolls — it *tolls not for thee*.'[57]

Given that Frame had accepted his advice and appeared to want to develop an association with the Maudsley, John Money now wrote what was in effect his promised letter of referral to Michael Shepherd, outlining her personal history and his view of both her difficulties as a patient and her talent as an artist.

Miss Frame has evidenced a remarkable ability to express herself [to me] with complete lucidity and insight in writing, even at times when she has found it impossible to open her mouth and say a word vocally . . . It is unique in my experience to find such a split between written lucidity and oral muteness, a muteness that becomes sheer panic on many occasions when Miss Frame has to enter into conversation, especially with strangers . . . [She] is very highly thought of by many of the dominant figures in New Zealand letters. I am quite willing to make the statement that she is, like Vincent Van Gogh and Hugo Wolf, a genius, endowed with the assets as well as the liabilities of schizophrenic cognition. Sometimes the liabilities become almost too much for her to tolerate.

I sense that you will comprehend deftly what will best help her . . . [She] will be greatly helped by a trial period of treatment with the new drugs, under such supervision as is deemed necessary, even before she finds a way of breaking the ice and getting into fluent communication with you. Even though she may not have the resource to do much talking with you, I am sure that it will help her immensely to know that she has a person and a place to turn to . . . I feel a strong enough sense of responsibility toward her that I do not want her to be in total isolation and anonymity. I want her to have the safety of a good doctor.[58]

The week John Money dispatched this letter to London, Michael Shepherd wrote to him and to Seacliff Hospital in New Zealand, requesting details of Frame's previous illnesses and treatments. 'She was obviously in two minds whether to discuss her history and symptoms [with me],' he told Money, 'and in the end provided me with a few scrappy details and a promise to write out the remainder, though she refused to guarantee its accuracy.'[59]

Not knowing precisely what Money had written to Michael Shepherd, only that the letter had been sent, Frame was filled suddenly with a sense of doom at the thought that her 'personal history' in New Zealand, fraught with all its deceptions, misunderstandings and complications, was about to envelop her again in London. One of the reasons she had left New Zealand was to escape such a possibility. Year by year, she wrote later, she had become buried beneath a weight of nothingness heaped upon her.[60] Now, it seemed, that nothingness was about to overtake her again and suffocate what she had envisaged as a fresh and hopeful beginning with new medical advisors. She wrote to Money on 12 August:

> [Your communication] gives me the feeling that everyone I know seems to be conspiring to give information about me — incriminating information. I think that even you have betrayed me now, for just because information was given to you years ago in Otago, it is now no less confidential; distance in time is no excuse for divulging anything I have ever told you . . . I feel that you are all in conspiracy against me, you are all sneering at me, laughing at me because I don't quite measure up to the accepted normal; I am a nuisance wherever I go and have to be got rid of; it would be a kindly act if I killed myself . . .
>
> What I may do is cut myself off completely from everyone I know; treat my past life as forgotten: wander away somewhere and begin a new life, wholly new, as a different person, under a new name . . . [For] those who now know me and know of me, die. Ah, it is the age-old fantasy of all harassed people . . . [It] is an easy matter for me to finish all communication with people in New Zealand. It is quite easy for me to finish communication with anyone I know in Great Britain. I shall of course have to cease any communication with you . . . [You must] burn this letter immediately after you have read it, as I hope you have destroyed all communications I have ever sent to you.[61]

Despite these threats, which Money had the good sense to recognise as a symptom of her current distress, Frame kept her next appointment at the hospital on 19 August. There, according to her patient notes, she was judged to be 'beset by strong suicidal impulses, heightened hallucinatory experiences, and progressive inability to think and communicate verbally . . . Hospitalisation was recommended . . . and she accepted.'[62] Thus, two-and-a-half years after her final discharge from Seacliff, Frame became a voluntary patient at the Maudsley Hospital; and this, her first admission, would keep her there for the next six months.

CHAPTER TWELVE

# A Home in the Maudsley

*T*HE MAUDSLEY HOSPITAL IN DENMARK HILL WAS AN EDWARDIAN-style brick building whose grim appearance was mitigated slightly by cosmetic additions designed to give it a Georgian character: a concrete portico at the main entrance and miniature porticos projecting from the downstairs windows. For one accustomed to the graceful stone colonnades of Oamaru, however, the façade was ineffective as a disguise. The building was clearly an institution, a medical institution, with all the connotations that carried for Janet Frame of authority figures and incarceration. Given that she had left her own country in part because she feared permanent confinement in just such a place, it took a considerable effort of will to walk through the front doors.

The appearance belied what went on inside those doors, however, and that was why Frame had been persuaded to make the effort. In the 1950s, the Maudsley was widely known as an oasis of good psychiatric practice in what was, generally, an impoverished sector of medicine. It had won this reputation partly because of the circumstances of its establishment. The hospital was named after Henry Maudsley, a distinguished turn-of-the-century psychiatrist, who had bequeathed money for its planning and construction. Maudsley had envisaged a mental hospital that was more than simply a custodial institution. This one would have an outpatients' department, unusual at the time of its conception, would accept voluntary patients, and would actively treat people in the early stages of breakdown to make it less likely that they would become chronic patients.

Because the building went up in the early years of the First World War, it was used initially to treat the victims of shell-shock and did not begin to function fully as a mental hospital until 1923. From that time on, however, the London County Council gave it favoured treatment over its other hospitals and ensured that it was well funded. The specialist departments advocated by Henry Maudsley were developed; and the hospital as a whole was run by highly qualified medical and nursing staff. Throughout the 1920s and 1930s the Maudsley's professional reputation grew as the finest mental hospital in the United Kingdom and one of the best in the world. After the Second World War it was amalgamated with the Bethlem Royal Hospital (whose early existence had given rise to the expression 'bedlam') and taken over by the National Health Service, which continued to fund it generously. Aubrey Lewis, a formidable Australian, was appointed professor of psychiatry, a consequence of the Maudsley being also a teaching hospital for the University of London, and he oversaw the practice of appointing high-calibre staff. It was because of this history, and in particular his professional respect for Aubrey Lewis and the senior lecturer Michael Shepherd, that John Money had recommended Frame approach the Maudsley if she felt in need of medical assistance.

Frame's retrospective view of her admission there in August 1957 was that, as she had done in the past, she exaggerated her symptoms of distress so as to engage the interest and sympathy of the medical staff who interviewed her, especially Dr Michael Shepherd.[1] She would write subsequently that she wanted 'to discover by objective means whether I had ever suffered from schizophrenia'. With Dr Shepherd's recommendation that she enter the hospital voluntarily, 'my plan had succeeded. I would now have my questions answered.'[2] So she would; but neither the diagnosis nor the cure would be instantaneous.

Following her placement in Ward One, the women's admission ward, Frame's first discovery about the Maudsley was that it differed greatly from the hospitals she knew in New Zealand. 'Nowhere in my own country would I find the kindness and care offered [here],' she told John Money within weeks of admission. 'There is an old-world gentleness that our brash young land will take a long time to acquire . . . So, having recovered from my initial fear, I am more settled, and I hope and pray . . . that I shall not have to spend my life . . . running on quicksand . . . Certainly procedure here is very thorough. For the first time in my life I have had an electroencephalogram . . .'[3] This test, which measured brain wave function, produced a reading that turned out to be 'more normal than normal'.[4] To Sargeson, Frame spoke of 'softly-spoken staff, individual doctors, a pampering place . . . [And] I can leave when I wish . . . there is no compulsion.'[5] A third letter of commendation went off to Peter Dawson, to whom Frame reported that she had her typewriter with her and was 'able to use it in my small room (which is not locked) . . . I have been having a wonderful time painting and experimenting with colours . . . I [also] have a few Penguin poets with me, and am reading Keats, Hardy, Arnold etc . . . I can appreciate what they say more than ever I could, now actually having experienced darkling thrushes; alas, I cannot yet report a nightingale.'[6]

Such enthusiasm might have prompted her correspondents to ask why she had thought it necessary to enter hospital. What Frame was voicing, however, was the wonder and pleasure she felt at encountering the Maudsley's remarkable staff-patient ratio: one nurse to every five patients, and her own personal doctor. This meant that she was being spoken to frequently and considerately, and listened to, as an individual human being. The Maudsley approach to psychiatry was that it was about the mind in distress, and that being in hospital could have no therapeutic value unless medical staff listened to, and reflected on, what patients had to tell them.

> [In] New Zealand hospitals the nurses spent their time on domestic chores, cleaning, distribution of meals, etc., with moments between spent in conversation amongst themselves. At Maudsley, the domestic work was being done by maids employed for the purpose, the nurses were free to perform their nursing duties . . . [Nursing] was treated and practised as an art and science, with skills that could be developed and perfected through communication with the [patients] . . . I [had] moved from extreme, almost disastrous poverty of communication to an unbelievable luxury, where I was actually asked to offer my thoughts and feelings; where it was taken for granted that I did have thoughts and feelings . . . [This] helped to give the patients a sense of being, and of being *somewhere*.[7]

The same feeling of gratitude accompanied Frame's discovery that she had been assigned her own doctor who would initially talk with her every day, and subsequently three or four times a week. This gave him an opportunity 'to know me. Not solely through the observations, inferences, judgements of others, but through my own words, however inarticulate . . . I was able to have my say.'[8]

The doctor to whom she 'had her say' was Alan D. Miller, a young American graduate posted to the Maudsley that year to begin specialisation in psychiatry. When Frame met him in August 1957 he was 'a burly man who was feeling the cold of the English winter, and so appeared to be wearing many layers of clothes, increasing his bulk. He worried about his weight. He often ate chocolate bars during our interviews. For recreation he played the viola and was proud to correspond once a year with Pablo Casals. He had brought his wife, his children and his American Ford station wagon for his year at the Maudsley . . . Dr Miller talked freely about himself and his feelings and opinions in contrast to the serious sober Englishmen who stared, frowned, half-smiled, and uttered only "M-m, I see." I was grateful to have as my doctor someone who was not afraid to acknowledge and voice the awful thought that he belonged, after all, to the human race, that there was nothing he could do about it, and pretending to be a god could never change it.'[9]

To John Money, who had recommended to Michael Shepherd that Frame be given an opportunity to try new medication, Frame reported that Dr Miller 'rejects the thought of tranquillising me, but admits that I cannot live untranquillised — hence his provision of a new skin, plastic or otherwise. The *how* of it is the problem.'[10]

The 'how' was to be a smorgasbord of Maudsley treatments: most importantly, the 'supportive and re-educational' talks with Alan Miller, to help her understand the nature and consequences of her thinking and behaviour; some occupational therapy (painting and, if she felt like it, writing — though she found writing other than correspondence difficult, even in such benign surroundings); and what the hospital referred to as 'the support, safety and understanding' provided by the nursing and ward staff. Her hospital notes record that, over six months, her episodes of withdrawal and depression recurred; but they became briefer and less frequent.[11]

The major item of progress, at least in the patient's view, was a considered opinion that she was not and never had been schizophrenic — that the initial diagnosis made in the psychiatric ward of Dunedin Hospital in October 1945, twelve years earlier, which had pursued her and conditioned the observations of her behaviour and mannerisms by medical and nursing staff in three New Zealand hospitals, was wrong.

'You've never suffered from schizophrenia,' Alan Miller eventually told her. 'Schizophrenia is a terrible illness.'[12] More formally, the results of the tests, observations and interviews to which she had been subjected in the course of treatment were coordinated by Michael Shepherd and formally reviewed by the hospital's full panel of psychiatrists, chaired by Aubrey Lewis. On 18 October 1957 Frame found herself 'summoned to the interview room where the medical team sat at a long table with Sir Aubrey . . . at the head. The team had already had its meeting and formed its conclusions, and after a few minutes' conversation with me, Sir Aubrey gave the verdict. I had never suffered from schizophrenia, he said. I should never have been admitted to a mental hospital. Any problems I now experienced were mostly a direct result of my stay in hospital. I smiled. "Thank you," I said shyly, formally, as if I had won a prize.'[13]

Any sense of relief Frame felt upon hearing this verdict was all too soon replaced by the anxiety that grew up around the next question: if she was not schizophrenic, what was she? What was the nature of the disorder — for it had to be seen as a disorder — that caused her periodic bouts of confusion, fear and unhappiness?

[I] had suddenly been stripped of a garment I had worn for twelve or thirteen years — my schizophrenia. I remembered how wonderingly, fearfully I had tried to pronounce the word when I first learned of the diagnosis, how I had searched for it in psychology books and medical dictionaries, and how . . . I had accepted it, how in the midst of the agony and terror of the acceptance I found the unexpected warmth, comfort, protection: how I had longed to be rid of the opinion but was unwilling to part with it. And even when I did not wear it openly I always had it by for emergency, to put on quickly, for shelter from the cruel world. And now it was gone . . . banished officially by experts: I could never again turn to it for help.

The loss was great . . . Schizophrenia, as a psychosis, had been an accomplishment, removing ordinary responsibility from the sufferer. I was bereaved. I was ashamed. How could I ask for help directly when there was 'nothing wrong with me'? . . . The official plunder of my self-esteem was eased by the attitude of the staff at the hospital. As Professor Lewis had said, I did need help to free myself from the consequences of my long stay in hospital; in the meantime I would remain in the Maudsley while my interviews with Dr Miller continued.[14]

The hospital's formal diagnosis at the time of her discharge said she had 'a pathological personality with schizoid and depressive features, and difficulties in ordering perceptions and controlling behaviour'.[15] In an attempt to prepare her for imminent release, and because she was a writer, she was given a job in December 1957 assisting the hospital's medical librarian. According to her hospital notes, 'her work was unreliable but at least she had made a . . . sustained effort'.[16] From there she was moved to the 'brain museum', where Michael Shepherd arranged for her to catalogue medical papers. 'The brain museum! Blissfully alone, I spent many days sorting through medical journals in the company of glass display cases filled with preserved, labelled tumours and brains.' She wrote a poem about one of these specimens. It ended:

> In formalin
> my prestige grows fat. I survive
> as Dobson's tumour, nineteen fifty-five.[17]

Unlike Seacliff, there was no censorship of mail at the Maudsley. Consequently there were times when the outside world broke through the hospital's protective membrane. Albion Wright wrote to say that the entire edition of *Owls Do Cry* had sold out and that he would not, and then that he would, print a new edition.[18] What he would prefer, he said, was to receive and publish an entirely new manuscript. Frame's response was that pressure to deliver a new book made it impossible for her to part with typescripts.[19] What this meant was that she remained convinced that 'Uncle Pylades' was of an insufficiently high standard for publication and she did not have anything else ready. Letters from Sargeson reported that, *inter alia*, another of her stories had been published in New Zealand in the new literary journal *Mate*, edited by one of his young protégés, Kevin Ireland.[20] She told Sargeson that without the need to spend money on items other than toiletries and fruit, and with the odd payment and donation still finding their way to her, her savings of around fifty pounds remained static instead of decreasing.[21]

The most unpleasant intrusion she had to face was a stream of relentless visits from Patrick Reilly, who was storing her cases in Clapham and delivering mail as it arrived there for her. He also brought with him his puritanism and censoriousness, telling her — among much else that was unwelcome — that he was disgusted by her *Encyclopaedia of Sex*: 'No one should know so much about their body . . . This book goes into the rubbish can tonight.'²² With the encouragement and cooperation of Dr Miller, Frame summoned the willpower to tell Reilly that 'it would be better if he no longer came to see me. I was soon to leave for America, I said, where I had friends.'²³

Real friends were also turned away on at least two occasions. Karl and Kay Stead were now living in Bristol, where Karl was writing his doctoral thesis on modernist poetry. They had not seen Frame since they had left New Zealand for Armidale in New South Wales nearly two years before. At Sargeson's urging, they came to the Maudsley in December 1957, with instructions to report back on Frame's health and, if possible, to extract manuscript material from her which might be made the basis for raising further funds for her from Pegasus or from the Literary Fund. Sargeson remained convinced that any work Frame refused to give up was the product of genius and would be eminently publishable. '[Anyone] who can make a successful raid on the mountain of typescript she has somewhere would be assured of gratitude from posterity,' he told the Steads.²⁴ On the day that they tried to visit, however, 19 December 1957, they were told that they would have to come back on Boxing Day at 2 pm, and this they were unable to do.

The following month, in response to an encouraging note from Frame, they tried again and Karl reported to Sargeson what occurred:

> We called on Saturday but she got frightened and of course couldn't see us. I talked to the nurse who said that . . . she gives notice every so often that she is going to leave. However as she hasn't anywhere specific to go the Drs always talk her out of it. She sometimes packs her bags and even sets off, but then comes back the same day . . .
>
> I rang on Sunday morning & the sister said J would see us. I went in first by myself, and she had got into bed and put on sun glasses to hide behind. However she soon got used to talking to us, and I couldn't see any sign that her mental state was worse than . . . at your place . . .
>
> She . . . said that speaking Spanish almost all the time [had] made her respect English much more when she came to write . . . and that it improved her writing and made her much more conscious of how she was using the language . . . (She was reading a book on semantics when I arrived!) . . . The Ibiza novel is 'locked away'. . . and the more pressure she feels from NZ to produce it the less inclined she is to do anything with it . . . [She] feels that everyone is waiting for her to publish something more & this makes it almost impossible . . .
>
> She seems very vague about her future — no clear idea at all of what she will do . . . [But] she said quite definitely that she would leave the hospital soon.²⁵

'She is an uncomfortable symbol for the mind to assimilate,' Stead continued just over a month later, 'very gay, not in the least sentimental, her criticism of everything exceptionally sharp and objective, detached, and her hair standing out straight all round her head (no doubt electrified by what is below its roots) . . . [She] is just as frighteningly sane as ever.'[26] As for what was wrong with her, the Steads agreed with Alan Miller's metaphor: Frame lacked 'one layer of protective skin; and . . . it was a lack which had been made worse by her incarceration at a time when young people need to be out in the world learning social skills and defences'.[27]

For her part, Frame told Sargeson that Kay Stead looked like 'a little gipsy with a red and white spotted handkerchief on her head, and Karl's forehead is transparent . . . They are homesick for Takapuna and the life there and the evenings in Esmonde Road; they want it to be all as it was before. Oh the tragedy of little gipsies and poets . . .'[28]

Despite a pattern of progress and regression, progress dominated and Frame was judged well enough in January 1958 to be allowed day leave from the hospital in order to find new accommodation, well away from the blighting surveillance of Patrick Reilly. Once released she would be eligible for National Assistance until she was sufficiently settled to 'hold down a job'. She was disappointed, she said later, that nobody suggested that she simply take National Assistance as a means of supporting her writing; and that her outpatient visits to Alan Miller would come to an end with his return to the United States in June 1958.[29]

Frame found and arranged to rent a dark and damp basement flat in Fortess Road (which she read as 'Fortress' Road) in Kentish Town. Her establishment there was assisted by a cheque of seventy-five pounds from Pegasus, who also confirmed that they were proceeding with a second edition of 2000 copies of *Owls Do Cry* in April.[30] With this security in prospect, she was discharged from hospital on 12 February, with the recommendation that she continue to talk with Alan Miller, in weekly sessions.

The Kentish Town flat that Frame had chosen on impulse, because it was cheap, lay below a three-storey Victorian terrace house in a grimy, traffic-laden street. She told an alarmed Sargeson about its 'bedbugs, non-human, one blanket . . . [a] sink that was blocked, [a] bath that wouldn't bath, [a] lock that wouldn't lock . . . At the foot of the bed, arranged for the head-in-the-oven dramatics, stood an antique gas stove, with splayed feet like George the Fourth . . . I thought that any moment it would up and dance a duet . . . I yet forgave my landlady and my landlord (he spat and one eye was closed), for they were musical, and their daughter played in the Halle Orchestra.'

Conditions deteriorated further, however, and Frame's capacity for forgiveness was stretched. 'The building was cold, without heating, and when one day the electricity was cut off because the landlord had not paid the bill, I discovered, exploring, that the other tenants were poor, overcrowded, depressed by the damp, cold and dark and by the bedbugs. I spoke to a woman upstairs, at street level; her baby lay asleep in bed while the woman sat by the bed with scores of dolls' heads heaped beside her, laboriously painting the eyes in the blank faces. And now there was no light for her to work by.'[31]

The impossibility of trying to write in a darkened basement drove Frame out to look for alternative accommodation. Directly across the street, at 20 Fortess Road, she found a room to let in a second-floor flat above a shop. It was occupied already by three other women: a teacher, a librarian and an office worker. Frame's room was small and looked out onto a brick wall. She shared the bathroom and kitchen with the other tenants. She told John Money that there were Italian children next door, whose chattering was audible, and that the landlord lived upstairs. The latter 'listens, listens, in case someone is sneaking a sixpenny bath free, or switching on what should be switched off, or leaving things where the typewritten notice warns Please Remove . . . [He] has an electric meter for a heart; it is common in London.'[32]

The flat was quiet when the other women were out at work, however, and Frame resumed writing, initially verse. Such work, she told Albion Wright, was 'for private consumption only'. And, because Sargeson had spoken to Wright about 'Uncle Pylades', she closed the door firmly on any possibility that that manuscript might be her next published novel. 'It is not satisfactory enough for publication.'[33] She received without comment the news that another of her *School Journal* stories written at Esmonde Road had been published in New Zealand.[34]

New prose writing did not go well. Frame seemed to have 'lost all power of communicating . . . I am cut off: [perhaps] I did not pay the communication bill.'[35] To distract herself from this period of apparent stagnation, she took walks on nearby Hampstead Heath, where 'the willows and birches are budding [and] tiny whitish mother-of-pearl clouds are floating up beyond the smoky haze'.[36]

In March 1958 Frame re-established contact with her poet acquaintance David Kozubei; and he introduced her to an artist friend of his named Lionel, who had just returned from twelve years in the United States.

[They] formed the habit of 'dropping in' to the flat in the early morning on their way to town, that is, to their haunts in Soho where they usually met other unemployed poets and painters and sat and talked in the French café . . . [Feeling] reluctant to face the Kentish Town brick wall, I'd go with them [and] we met an assortment of people whose ambition was to write or paint or compose, and I felt at home with them, yet saddened by their everlasting dreaming, their talking about what they hoped to produce when they knew clearly (as I knew) that while they talked and dreamed, their work stayed untouched in the loneliness of their bedsitters or their poky gas-reeking flats with share bathroom share kitchen share everything . . . Through [David and Lionel] I met many of the 'outsiders' of Soho . . . I visited sleazy clubs, becoming a member for the evening to gain admission. I met prostitutes, male and female, and I listened to their stories, gaping impolitely as I cherished my growing 'experience of life' . . .[37]

While it was David Kozubei to whom Frame initially had felt drawn, this time round it was Lionel who claimed her as his 'girl'.

I was agreeable but lukewarm, refusing to put myself again in danger of another pregnancy but willing to be comforted and to comfort, naked body to naked body. When [Lionel] began arriving at the flat at half-past eight in the morning on too many mornings, [Mildred] expressed her disapproval, Jane also did not think I should entertain a man so early in the morning. Only Gloria, in the end room and apart from the others, because she too had 'entertained men', understood, and she and I, like two sisters, had many confiding talks.[38]

While Frame attempted to write and disguised her discontent with expeditions to the cafés and clubs of Soho, and to inner-city art galleries, her agents, official and unofficial, remained at work on her behalf. Dan Davin of Clarendon Press in Oxford, novelist, story writer and friend of Sargeson's, wrote to her at Sargeson's suggestion and proposed that they meet.[39] Frame, intimidated by this unofficial high commissioner for New Zealand culture, failed to reply. In the United States John Money sent the stories of Frame's he was holding to the New York literary agency Brandt and Brandt, only to be told that they already knew of her work via Patience Ross, and were enthusiastic about Frame's prospects. '[We] truly feel that the lady has considerable talent,' Carl Brandt wrote in April 1958.[40] Brandt was unable to place the stories with American magazines, however. And A.M. Heath, despite numerous approaches, had been unable to find a British publisher for *Owls Do Cry*, though Gollancz had shown serious interest. Brandt and Brandt began circulating the novel among American publishing houses.[41]

Concerned that the book might eventually appear in London, and still flirting with her own notion of 'disappearing', Frame took one decisive course of action at a time otherwise characterised by a paralysis of will. On 22 May 1958, she informed Sargeson and Money, she had changed her name by deed poll to Janet Clutha.[42] She took this step, she would say later, to preserve her anonymity in the event that books might appear in London under her own name, or stories or reviews about them in newspapers. So while some authors *wrote* under a *nom de plume*, Frame's choice was to live under an alias and continue to write and publish under her own name.

The full new name she had selected was Nene Janet Paterson Clutha: Nene because of her admiration for the Maori chief Tamati Waka Nene, and the fact that she had been called 'Nini' as a child; Paterson, her Scottish grandmother's surname, had previously been her second name; and Clutha was a tribute to the river that had so impressed her on her fruit-picking summer in Central Otago in 1944, as well as being the Gaelic name for the Clyde, in whose valley her father's parents had been born. News of the name change led Karl Stead to write to her, tongue in cheek: 'You are indeed fed by the cold snows and flow deeper and more powerful than any other among the hot rocks. I am still ambling in green pastures.' He signed this note 'Karl Waikato'.★[43]

In an effort to shake off the lethargy she complained about at this time, Frame began to teach herself Latin and Greek, neither of which she had studied at school or university. 'A refuge into these languages,' she told John Money, 'is welcome and restful and rather less dangerous than refuge solely into a fantasy world.'[44] She also answered an advertisement from a middle-aged Scottish translator of plays, who wanted a live-in secretary. The man, who was also a 'recovering' alcoholic, 'wined and dined me at his house and told me my duties,' Frame explained to Audrey Scrivener. '[The] job was mine, but I got cold feet, and I knew [it] would mostly consist of "looking after" him, and I'm not prepared to go "looking after" any man, so I unhooked the telephone.' But, by way of compensation, he had taken her to a production of Chekhov's *Three Sisters*, performed in Russian by the visiting Moscow Art Theatre. She was moved by the play, despite the language barrier, and told Sargeson that its beauty lay in its being 'an uncompleted circle — from illusion to disillusion [to] the unwritten third part — the final illusion.'[45]

Throughout this period Frame continued her weekly sessions with Alan Miller at the Maudsley's outpatient clinic and found that they helped her to cope with anxieties. But she grew increasingly worried as the time for his departure neared. When he introduced her to the man who would replace him as 'her' psychiatrist, Dr Michael Pare, 'I felt my heart sinking as I heard the crisp English accent contrasting . . . with Dr Miller's rich cheerful voice with its accent that I had known for years, in Hollywood films.'[46]

Shortly before he left London, Alan Miller gave John Money an account of Frame's progress, trying to establish (as Money himself had done a decade earlier) that he was leaving his patient in better health than he had originally found her. He reported that Frame appeared to be coping with her new living arrangements 'far better than she or we expected. She . . . has not neglected herself physically, visits with friends, reads widely of course, and . . . is much less frequently overcome by feelings of impending doom or obsessed with ideas of destruction. However, she is writing only sporadically and has made no substantial efforts to find salaried employment.'[47]

---

★ Almost two decades later the critic Patrick Evans would write: 'The name [Frame] was born with connotes rigidity and fixity; to take the name of a river is to opt for fluidity, adaptability, and elusiveness.' (Evans 1977, p. 55.) The Waikato is the longest river in the North Island of New Zealand.

With Miller's departure in June, and the growth of a conviction that she now had no one to 'tell my story to', Frame's fragile sense of well-being drained away.'I felt completely alone in the world, in a grey world . . . I found ludicrous the idea that I would ever be able to communicate with a doctor who during our first interview, with a well-meant cheerfulness and a desire to prove perhaps his wide range of interests, talked of the coming world heavyweight championship and asked me if I thought Floyd Patterson would win. Other remarks he made were just as remote from what I felt to be the centre of concern. Knowing the ways of psychiatrists I was ready to suppose that his approach was planned, scientific . . . but my feelings were that everything he said was out of tune.'[48]

Her letters to Sargeson and Money were now redolent with the familiar signs of distress. 'I think I shall not do any more writing; which is a strange thing to say when I have so much that moves me to write; yet I seem to be living in a nothingness; I feel like a stagnant pond giving habitation to a few inflating frogs and the same old weeds . . .'[49] And, in August 1958: 'I cannot and don't want to write. I can't face myself any more, or people either.'[50]

As she had been before, Frame was sucked into a descending spiral of anxiety and confusion. The fact that she now knew she was not schizophrenic was no immediate help. A question remained unresolved: if *that* was not what was wrong with her, what was? Dr Pare decided to take a step that Alan Miller thought was unnecessary: he prescribed drugs that he thought might help to relieve her anxiety.'I don't know what [the tablets] are,' Frame told John Money, 'for though he is the man-who-sees he is not necessarily the man-who-tells.'[51]

Over the weeks that followed, Frame's unhappiness increased and her letter-writing stopped. Towards the end of August, Pare suggested that she ought to have herself admitted to Friern Barnet Hospital in North London, within the local body zone in which she now lived. This was an unfortunate development. Friern Barnet, built in 1850 and known originally as Colney Hatch, had a reputation for being the most forbidding looking and dysfunctional mental hospital in the country.* Frame took a bus there, clutching her referral from Dr Pare. But she froze when she saw the tall grey stone building, 'menacing, like an old workhouse or prison. A feeling of terror came over me.' Instead of gaining admission, she got on another bus and returned home.[52]

What Frame had wanted at this point, and what Dr Pare had failed to understand that she wanted, was not admission to a hospital: she wanted, specifically, admission to the Maudsley Hospital, in whose confines, and among whose staff, she had previously felt safe at a time of intense anxiety. One night the following week, as she walked along the bank of the Thames, her anxiety turned to panic. She rang the Maudsley from a public telephone near Waterloo Bridge and announced that she was going 'into the river'. The duty doctor

---

* Ironically in 1998 Friern Barnet, renamed 'Princess Park Manor', was converted into 'luxury apartments set in thirty acres of park land'.

kept her talking until the call could be traced and the police sent to collect her. Frame described to Sargeson what followed:

> [I] was given an illuminating insight . . . into methods of police procedure and of moronic sergeants and hefty lesbian WPCs . . . [They] kept pressing me for a statement . . . in a small room with three taps dripping . . . Finally I was removed to a grim hospital from where I was rescued by [Dr Shepherd] . . . It was very good of him to take me in . . . for according to zones, I should be in a strange tower-like place . . . I'm an awful fool really, having allowed so much material to accumulate in my head without saving my sanity by writing it down.[53]

Frame had been taken to the Southwark police station, and from there to St Francis Hospital, which had an emergency observation ward for psychiatric patients. This was a little more than a mile from the Maudsley. Although, as Frame said, she should have been sent to Friern Barnet, from which she had recoiled the previous week, Michael Shepherd arranged for her to return to the Maudsley, for which she was profoundly grateful. She was admitted as a voluntary patient for a second time on 4 September 1958.

If Frame had been fortunate to establish an association with the Maudsley Hospital in 1957, she was now doubly lucky in being assigned, not Dr Pare, with whom she had been unable to establish rapport, but Dr Robert Hugh Cawley, a trainee psychiatrist her own age (thirty-four).

Robert Cawley was from Birmingham, where he had taken an undergraduate degree in zoology, becoming especially interested in genetics and ecology, and then a doctorate in medical statistics. He was also passionate about music and had edited the student newspaper at Birmingham University and a literary magazine. His entry into medicine was relatively late because of long periods of illness in adolescence — he was initially rejected as a medical student because of a supposed lack of stamina. A result of his background, as Frame noted later, was that Cawley had a wider view over a range of studies, disciplines and personal experience than might be expected of a junior registrar.[54] Like Alan Miller, and unlike some others of his colleagues, his qualifications in medicine and psychiatry were extensions of the man, not starting and ending points. As a consequence of this, Frame found that she could talk with him.

Not immediately, however. Cawley recalled how he was summoned to Ward One and placed in one of the hospital's confined consulting rooms with 'this slim woman of average height who had striking curly reddish hair and a soft, sometimes barely audible voice'.[55] He began to put to her a set of standard questions designed to reveal the patient's 'mental state'. Frame seemed at first reluctant to talk. But, as Cawley worked his way through the list, she thawed. He asked, for example, the name of the Queen, something every sane person in the British Isles was expected to know in 1958. Frame responded by saying that was a parochial question: Britain was not the only country to have a queen. 'Right,' said Cawley, 'what other country has a queen?' 'The Netherlands.' 'What's her name?' 'Juliana.' 'What's her mother's name?' 'Wilhelmina.' The sparring continued as Cawley put forward another series of questions to test concentration. 'Can you take seven from one hundred?' 'No, that would be stealing.' 'Well, then, *subtract* seven from one hundred.' 'That would be ninety-three.' 'Can you go on subtracting?' 'Not with impunity.'[56]

In those first conversations with Frame, Cawley concluded that she was 'rather anxious and unhappy. She was a bit perplexed, and not always able to express her thoughts and feelings in anything more than brief sentences or phrases.'[57] But when he attempted to apply such techniques of psychiatric treatment as were available to him, it seemed that 'an instrument of clinical investigation was meeting some powerful resistance from a force which could perhaps challenge and debunk much of what I believed I knew . . . [As] I proceeded, the patient became rather dogged, more alert, more confident. Her eyes brightened.'[58] The woman he had at first found quiet, nervous and enigmatic now had eye contact with her doctor. Each was engaged by the other. And the engagement intensified over the succeeding weeks and months of their discussions.

Frame had guessed, correctly, that Cawley was a shy man. Like Drs Pare and Shepherd, 'he spoke with an English accent that chilled me when I first heard it in the distance but in his presence it could not frighten me for he was not aggressive, his manner was excessively polite, his smile kindly as if these were more a protection for himself than a gift for me. I felt that he was a clever, uncertain man, whose sole triumph in our interviews was the accuracy of his recording the content. Sometimes he had a cold; he sniffed, he took out a large white handkerchief like a conjuror's aid, and blew his nose. He wore black-rimmed spectacles, magnifying, I thought, much of what he saw; and his shoes were black, well polished. He dressed as for a day in the office.'[59]

Robert Cawley agreed with Michael Shepherd that Frame was again in need of the healing processes that the Maudsley had to offer. And so she was absorbed back into the environment that she had found so helpful at the time of her first admission, giving her respite from apprehension, support during periods of depression, exposure to the 'therapeutic community' of nursing and ward staff, and — most importantly — access to Dr Cawley several times a week. For Frame, those sessions with her doctor became 'an accounting process, an examination of my emotional, personal, and even financial budget with a view to balancing all so that I could survive in spite of the bankruptcy imposed during my long [previous stays] in hospital, and my existence since then on unreal notions of myself'.[60]

Cawley noted subsequently that, in addition to their conversations (he declined to use the term psychotherapy), their communication with each other included 'devising and breaking verbal codes', and the writing of 'many brief but endlessly fascinating notes, letters and poems'.[61] He came to believe that

Frame's periodic use of alphabetical codes, mirror-writing and even algebraic formulae reflected her simultaneous wish and reluctance to communicate. It was often easier for her to say things obliquely. At one point she even prepared a report on herself as if written by a relative, assuring him that this person, Janet Frame, was deserving of a decent chance in life and that she, as next-of-kin, would vouch for her.[62]

Cawley also became increasingly aware that Frame, with her considerable intelligence and her erudition in literary matters, could often become bored by and unresponsive to the conventional techniques of psychotherapy. Indeed, there were occasions when she recognised, disparaged, and set out to subvert such techniques. He was therefore happy to accept the games and the puzzles she proposed as a means of sustaining her engagement and communication with him. He even, on one occasion, accepted her challenge to a game of chess, but did not repeat this experiment because she beat him soundly. He also proposed that the hospital occupational therapist find more demanding activities for her than making baskets, stools or lampshades, and this woman responded by providing Frame with the materials and equipment to make French lace, as she had done at one time in Seacliff.

A further advantage that Cawley had over some of Frame's former psychiatrists was that, on the whole, he recognised her literary allusions and did not mistake them — as at least two previous doctors had done — for symptoms of insanity. And he appreciated that his patient's gift for apt metaphors and vivid imagery to evoke subtle nuances of perception and behaviour were not psychotic or hallucinatory, as medical officers in New Zealand hospitals had supposed.[63]

Improvements in Frame's condition were, as before, incremental rather than sudden or dramatic. In November 1958, two months after admission, she told John Money that she was 'three-quarters down a well. I must either be drawn up empty-handed or sink to the bottom where the treasure lies: it remains a mechanical problem to get myself out again, with the added weight of gold, rubies, and uncut diamonds. I am being given some tablets to protect me from too much fear when things and people and places become so vivid that they threaten and pursue me. It is valuable to be haunted, certainly, but I prefer the haunting which I can watch at a safe distance, and control; not the kind which causes panic and disorder.'[64]

Hospital routines were occasionally punctuated by the appearance of visitors. Her flatmates came from Kentish Town, and she formed a closer relationship with one of them, Mildred Surry, the librarian. Motherly Jess Whitworth, on holiday in England from Takapuna, turned up several times in the weeks following Frame's admission. The younger woman found her 'a dear person' and was left with 'very happy memories of her company'.[65] Rita Mander, wife of Frame's Oamaru dentist, called in several times and accompanied her on outings into the city. And the Steads continued to visit from Bristol.[66] As before, Frame was moved to see the young poet and his wife and, in their company, she was reminded sharply of New Zealand. '[Karl] talked in such a rich New Zealand accent of mountains and creeks and snow, snow, snow. I think I myself have tied in my heart a remembrance-knot of snow-grass. My mind has gone up-country among avalanches, glaciers [and] grazing sheep.'[67]

Karl Stead, still concerned about Frame's health and pressured by Sargeson for authoritative news, wrote to Robert Cawley with Frame's consent to inquire about her condition and progress. Cawley told him, as he was to tell Frame, that she was certainly not suffering from schizophrenia. In his opinion she was undergoing 'an identity crisis or an existential dilemma'. Cawley subsequently elaborated on this description: 'She was a highly intelligent, sensitive, and artistically creative person with desires and abilities for verbal expression of ideas and associations . . . Her long periods in hospital had been occasioned, and prolonged, by what could be regarded as the negative side of her exquisite sensitiveness. She had become overwhelmed by a world in which harshness and cruelty, indifference and loneliness, appeared to threaten the splendours of the human spirit — splendours of which her deep awareness was itself searchingly painful.'[68]

News from home, of positive and negative varieties, came sometimes in surprising guises. Geoffrey Blake-Palmer, for example, wrote from Seacliff Hospital, congratulating her on her success and inviting her to apply for the New Zealand Literary Fund's new scholarship in letters (valued at five hundred pounds).[69] Sargeson reported that the Literary Fund had given her an unsolicited one hundred pound 'award for achievement' for *Owls Do Cry*.[70] This provoked an impulse in Frame to return to New Zealand as soon as she left hospital, and she wrote to Sargeson asking if one of the 'anonymous donors' (principally Charles Brasch and E.P. Dawson) might be able to raise the cost of a fare.[71] Then, just as suddenly, the news that her brother had been to Christchurch to discuss with Albion Wright the publication of *his* putative book, and that Geordie was, at the age of forty, actively seeking a wife, reminded her of what seemed like Byzantine complications in the life of her family and diminished the appeal of a return journey.[72] In one of his letters Geordie signed himself 'Toby — that's what everybody calls me'.[73] For Frame, this was a surprising and chilling example of life imitating art and confirming connections she would rather were not made.

Over a period of nine months in hospital, Frame's confidence alternately flowed and ebbed. On 1 December 1958 she told Peter Dawson that 'the

Persephone in me is emerging from the Plutonic darkness — in contrast to the northern winter scene outside . . . I feel so much the sense of oncoming doom after the mere simulation of death which the southern winters give; but I'm true to the south, like Swinburne's swallows.'[74]

A fortnight later, however, she reported 'a slight setback . . . [I] have been moved to a ward where the patients are rather more disturbed. [But] I have to compare it more than favourably with similar wards in NZ hospitals — there are ten patients occupying six rooms and a four-bedded dormitory. I am lucky enough to be in a room which rather resembles a garage at night when I shut the double doors to keep out the light. It is small wonder that last night I dreamed I was a motor-car and my sleep was the heavy wheels grinding sand into a concrete road.'[75]

On this occasion and others she had been placed on 'suicide caution', which meant that staff believed there was a possibility, however slight, that she might attempt to take her own life. While these episodes persisted, Frame remained under close surveillance. They were never continuous, nor of lengthy duration, however. At the most they lasted two or three days. Much more often, Cawley was to note, medical and nursing staff found her an immensely likeable person and there was frequently laughter associated with their interaction with her.[76]

Cawley found, in his own conversations, that Frame was usually unwilling to discuss her previous medical 'history' in a conventionally therapeutic way (exploring the feelings that consideration of past events or relationships brought to the surface). She *was* learning to cope with matters as they occurred in the present. But what seemed to distress her most was the fact that she could not see that she had a future; and it was this apparent absence of a specific and predictable way ahead in her life that made her anxious and contributed to periodic impulses towards suicide. It also impelled her, with some frequency, to give the seventy-two hours' notice required of a voluntary patient who wished to leave hospital; and then to withdraw the notice as the time for departure drew near.[77] It was this question of the future, therefore, that Cawley judged to be the major feature of her outlook and behaviour that they needed to work on together in their discussions. And it was in this area that he made progress with his patient on a scale that exceeded the results of any previous treatment.

Frame herself would say subsequently that Cawley eventually convinced her that 'I was myself, I was an adult, I need not explain myself to others. The "you should" days were over, he said . . . [It] was time to begin again.' Cawley was also convinced, and managed to convince Frame, that 'I genuinely needed to write, that it was a way of life for me, and that the best practical help for me was to arrange a National Assistance weekly payment and for me to find accommodation near the hospital so that we might continue our talks. It was his opinion also that as I was obviously suffering the effects of my long stay in hospital in New Zealand, I should write my story of that time to give me a clearer view of my future. In his response to the lifelong urging of others to me that I should "get out and mix", Dr Cawley was clear: his prescription for my ideal life was that I should live alone and write while resisting, if I wished this, the demands of others to "join in".[78]

By June 1959 Frame felt able to act on this prescription with some confidence. She had begun to write again, in earnest, in her 'small private room which looks out upon [the] red-brick mortuary with its meat-safe windows'. What she was writing, at Cawley's urging, was a narrative account of her years in Seacliff, Sunnyside and Avondale Hospitals. On 4 June she was able to report to Sargeson:

> I am leaving the hospital on June 12th to go to a room in this area, for I have to [continue to] attend as an outpatient . . . I am going to write like hell, though I'm somewhat muddled at times . . . I'm sure that what I'm writing is utter nonsense, indeed it *is* nonsense, but my doctor has assured me — in a nice hypnotic session — that I must stop deciding what is and is not nonsense — that I must throw away [that] label.[79]

One week later, as she told Audrey Scrivener, relishing the poetry of the names, Frame 'picked up my baggage and struggled out of the door of the Maudsley and up Denmark Hill, along Champion Grove (past Ruskin Park), up Grove Lane to Dog Kennel Hill and along Grove Hill Road to my furnished room, share kitchen, electricity included, thirty shillings a week plus two shillings for gas'. That room was on the first floor of a gabled terrace house and had 'five windows . . . which look out on the street, so that I sit, with the curtains drawn, and peep out at the passers-by'.[80]

This address, 39 Grove Hill Road, Camberwell — a suburb in which John Ruskin, Robert Browning and Felix Mendelssohn had at one time lived — would be her home for the next three years, a longer period than she had lived anywhere other than in the family homes in Oamaru. Here, only twenty minutes' walk from the Maudsley, with weekly encouragement from Dr Cawley, she would revive her vocation as an author and see her orphaned first novel find new publishers. Indeed, unbeknown to Frame, the New York publisher George Braziller had agreed to take *Owls Do Cry* on 10 May 1959, breaking what had been up to that point a log-jam of unsuccessful submissions to publishers on both sides of the Atlantic.[81] The momentum of her career as a writer, which had commenced under the nurturing of Frank Sargeson, was resumed under the patronage of another mentor whom readers would encounter on the dedication pages of seven future books as RHC. That career would not stall again for another three decades.

CHAPTER THIRTEEN

# A Career Resumed

BY THE TIME *OWLS DO CRY* REACHED THE MANHATTAN OFFICE OF the publisher George Braziller in May 1959, the book had already been rejected by about twenty larger and better-known American publishing houses. As the literary agent Carl Brandt had told John Money the previous year, most of them preferred to deal in manuscripts that had not been published elsewhere. Most had also been put off by what they regarded as the novel's unconventional structure; and by the fact that the author was a New Zealander, whose country and its doings held little interest for the majority of American readers.

George Braziller's perspective was different, however. Braziller was a forty-three-year-old New Yorker whose Russian–Jewish parents had emigrated to the United States from Minsk before the First World War. He was open-minded, good-hearted, and, in an effort to distinguish his imprint from his larger competitors, determined to publish innovative fiction. He had launched his own publishing company only four years earlier, after having founded and managed two successful book clubs; and he had begun to publish in English examples of what critics were calling the 'nouveau roman' — novels by such French writers as Jean-Paul Sartre, Nathalie Sarraute and Claude Simon, which challenged what had previously been regarded as the accepted and acceptable forms of fiction. He was consequently more open to what might be seen as the less conventional features of *Owls Do Cry*.

Years later he recalled what happened when Brandt and Brandt sent a copy of the novel to his office:

> The book was a bit banged up, as though it had gone through a laundry cycle. I knew nothing about the author. I looked at the flap and read . . . 'This novel about a New Zealand family is by an author already distinguished for a book of brilliant short stories. The publishers believe that *Owls Do Cry* will prove an outstanding literary event.' I thought,

200

I've heard that before, put the book down, and didn't think much more about it.

As I was leaving the office a few nights later, I noticed that someone had put the book in a box that contained papers and books we were planning to give away. I decided to take another look at it, and so brought the book home. I read it in one sitting, never once putting it down. The flap copy was right. The book was one of the most original pieces of writing that I had read in years. I immediately decided that we would publish it . . . Janet's form was less consciously new [than that of Braziller's French authors], but . . . equally striking and powerful for its authenticity.[1]

News of this decision in the month it was made, which would buy rights for the novel in the United States and Canada and generate an advance of two hundred and fifty American dollars, would have encouraged Frame's decision to leave hospital and return to a career in writing. But nobody told her. John Money and her agents believed that she was still in the Maudsley and hence, it was assumed, not well enough to make decisions about her career or even to take an interest in the further publication of her books. Three months would elapse before she was informed.

Braziller made his decision in consultation with Carl Brandt. Brandt told John Money and Patience Ross.[2] And even Patience Ross, when she began her negotiations with Pegasus Press (who held rights to the book both within and outside New Zealand), wondered in August 1958 whether Frame's consent should be sought. 'Ought we to get in touch with her through the hospital?'[3] she asked Albion Wright. None of them knew that Frame had left the Maudsley almost two months earlier. And they did not know because Frame, now engaged in settling into Grove Hill Road and writing what would become her second published novel, had not thought to tell them. The fact that two years had now elapsed since her visit to Patience Ross meant that Frame had dismissed from her mind any thought that *Owls Do Cry* might find another publisher.

The terrace house at 39 Grove Hill Road was owned by Richard and Doris Parry, who lived there with their daughter, Ursula, and another boarder, a middle-aged Londoner named Peggy Rawlings, who worked at an electrical appliance factory and was away early in the day and home late.[4] Frame's first-floor accommodation was next to the Parrys' bedroom, with a small kitchen (shared with Peggy) and a bathroom and lavatory on the same floor shared with the whole household. The room itself had 'a large mirrored wardrobe, a dressing table, a large dining table covered with a green and white checked oilcloth [on which] I spent most of my time writing at one end, eating at the other; two chairs, one a fat armchair with outsize padded arms and floral covering, an old stretcher bed dipping in the middle beneath a mattress full of hard unevenly distributed parcels of kapok. There was a disused fireplace and a small kerosene heater.'[5]

Doris Parry was alarmed at first that Frame would be 'home all day'. In her mind ideal tenants were those like Peggy Rawlings, who went off to work on weekdays and were often away at weekends too. 'I explained that I was writing a book. "Oh, a journalist," Mr [Parry] said with some deference. "More of a book writer." "We'll say you're a journalist," he said.'[6]

Richard Parry, whom Frame referred to in letters as 'big Daddy', was about forty. He was 'sleek, with a coat buttoned to show his continuing sleekness, with a small moustache and a plausible manner suited to his work as a [radio and] television salesman, but reminiscent for me of my idea of a con-man'. His wife, in her mid-thirties, who had inherited the house from an aunt, was 'small, dark, businesslike, the part-owner with her sister of a hairdressing salon "down the Green"'. Their daughter, Ursula, 'practised the piano each afternoon in the room beneath me [and] was at that serious stage of English life known as the "eleven-plus" year, with an examination looming, followed by her "streaming" into grammar, comprehensive or high school' (she eventually graduated to a grammar school). Her parents hoped she would become what they insisted on believing that Frame was, a 'clever journalist'.[7]

To Frank Sargeson, Frame characterised her new situation as the heart of middle-class suburbia. The Parrys' paper of choice, she noted, was the *Daily Telegraph*. 'Car: Anglia, green . . . Children: one (ballet, piano). Holidays: seaside caravan on site at Bognor Regis. Sunday newspaper: *News of the World*, *Daily Express*. Hobbies: redecorating, television, car-cleaning on Sundays . . . Up and down the street as far as I can see, people are lovingly tending their cars, cleaning, polishing, stroking the haunches and brows of the sleek multi-coloured idols . . .'[8]

At night, she went on, '[I] look out of the windows like the aunt in Proust. It is profitable . . . when one can see into people's living rooms and bedrooms and . . . the dark front rooms with their televisions flickering like stars as the cowboys race across the screen and the shots ring out; believe me Frank it is like war in the evenings in Grove Hill Road.'[9] It was especially like war inside Number 39, with the noise of the upstairs lodger's television coming through Frame's ceiling and the commotion of the Parrys' set rising through the floor. She experimented with earplugs, then turned up the volume on her radio to disguise the cacophony with the sound of music.

Not only was Frame *not* the working journalist that the Parrys imagined her to be, she was not even earning money from her writing in her early months at Camberwell. Having qualified for National Assistance, which required applicants to produce a medical certificate that they were unable to work and had less than six hundred pounds in the bank, Frame received three pounds seventeen shillings a week. She initially concealed from the Parrys the source of this income, however. She explained to Sargeson how the system worked. The inspector 'calls once every two months, and I sneak him upstairs to my room, and look suitably dotty . . . [He] hurries away with his briefcase, and in a couple of days I get a book of cheques through the post. It wouldn't be so easy if I didn't have the backing of the Maudsley, and didn't mention casually that I go to the hospital twice a week.'[10]

This income, and outgoings of around three pounds ten shillings a week (including thirty shillings for her room), enabled Frame to resume work on the manuscript she had begun to write in the Maudsley, at Robert Cawley's suggestion. It had become

> the story of my experiences in hospitals in New Zealand, recording faithfully every happening and the patients and staff I had known, but borrowing from what I had observed among the patients to build a more credibly 'mad' character, Istina Mavet, the narrator. Also, planning a subdued rather than a sensational record, I omitted much, aiming more for credibility than a challenge to me by those who might disbelieve my record . . .
>
> I kept to the routine I began when I was in living in Frank Sargeson's hut in Takapuna. I also continued the method I had adopted of buying a new school exercise book, carefully writing my name in the space provided on the cover, with the word 'Novel' in a juvenile, laborious hand beside the *subject*, then ruling various columns to record timetable, progress, with spaces for *Excuses*, now called *Wasted Days* as I did not need to identify the known excuses to myself. I had already made, in my mind, an entire book from which I chose chapter headings to remind me of the whole. There was more enthusiasm than usual in my working: each week had an impartial observer in Dr Cawley to talk to and complain to and tell of my progress.[11]

Early in October 1959 Frame heard from both Patience Ross and John Money that *Owls Do Cry* was to be published in the United States; and three months later that Nannen-Verlag in Hamburg would publish a German edition of the book in 1961 and were interested in a German translation of *The Lagoon*.[12] She was more ambivalent than jubilant at the news about the novel. 'Since I wrote the book,' she told Money, 'I have realised more and more how much it is ill-written and shoddy and lacking in everything a good book should be; I have partly escaped from the shame of it by changing my name; in fact it is a child I disown; and if ever I write anything again, it will be because I am so dissatisfied with the moulting owls, half-awake, suffering all sorts of nutritional deficiencies, trying to speak doom with such feeble cries.'[13]

There was also the curiosity that nobody had, at that point, asked for Frame's permission to publish new editions of *Owls Do Cry*. 'As I had "signed away" to Pegasus Press in New Zealand most of the rights of the book, the contracts would be the affair of Pegasus, not myself.'[14] And, indeed, the negotiations were completed among the literary agents, the new publishers and Pegasus. Payments of advance royalties to Frame as author shrank drastically before they reached her: A.M. Heath and Brandt and Brandt shared ten percent as the agency commission; in the United States one-third of Frame's earnings there was deducted as an alien or non-resident tax; then she was obliged to share half of what was left with Pegasus. The result was that Frame collected seventy-five pounds on what had been an Amercian advance of $US300; and on this she was obliged to pay her British income tax. She gave retrospective approval to these arrangements, despite complications and disadvantages; and she told John Money that she had done this via Dr Cawley, 'for the agents [initially] communicated with him'.[15] A.M. Heath and Brandt and Brandt had done this on Money's advice, since neither office was certain about Frame's state of mind or ability to make business decisions.

After the closure of the American deal, however, and assurances from Cawley about Frame's health, Patience Ross wrote and asked her to 'send publicity details and a photograph' to Carl Brandt in New York. This prompted Frame to tell Money that she was 'quite at a loss; and when I am [further] asked to "call and tell us about your writing plans" I feel quite sick . . . I live here having no contact with anybody, because I'm so scared of everybody; I hardly dare go into the street on some days. And then to be asked to "call and discuss" my greatest shame with Patience Ross! Why, it is too much . . . I still have the habit of bursting into tears and running away from people; it's a rather worn-out habit when one has recently turned thirty-five.'[16]

There *were* variations in Frame's strictly imposed morning and afternoon writing regime. Every two months she went to North London to visit the librarian friend, Mildred Surry, with whom she had lived in Kentish Town. On Wednesdays she was obliged to vacate the house in favour of 'a small dumpy woman who wears a yellow coat and is called Daisy [who] comes to clean the premises. I walk around Camberwell . . . and into the South London Art Gallery, which has a series of changing exhibitions, mostly of local and provincial painters and sculptors.'[17]

Some afternoons she went to the cinema (to see the film of Neville Shute's book *On the Beach*, for example; and to the National Film Theatre to see some of Jean Cocteau's work).

At half-past four I'd leave . . . noticing as the lights came on that many others in the audience had discovered a place to keep warm and to hide on a dreary afternoon — poor Londoners, middle-aged men alone, young women with babies who cried and cried until the audience began to murmur and the usher to shine a torch on the offender; West Indian immigrants, men and women; most were alone and, suddenly illuminated, they looked like plants set the required distance from one another in some unkempt allotment by the railway line.[18]

Other afternoons she went to the Dulwich Library; or to the Portrait Gallery, the Museum of Musical Instruments, the Victoria and Albert Museum. She would have liked to go to live concerts and theatre, but felt that she could not afford such luxuries (also, she confided to Sargeson, on the rare occasions she saw plays she was visited 'by the almost overwhelming impulse to join in and call out my own part').[19] Back at Grove Hill Road in the evenings she read, watched a little television (her landlord had installed a faulty set in her room), or — more often — listened to music on the radio to insulate herself from other noises in the household, or to such spoken features as *My Word*.

Late in September 1959 she made use of the Parrys' caravan at Bognor Regis for what she called a few days by the 'sewer-drunken sea-weed smoking sea; among derelict people and poodles and shut funhouses. My God! I felt I needed a change of voice in my ear, and I could not go to Inverness or John o' Groats or the Orkneys; so English voices had their way, but the sea spoke, beneath its tameness and its foamless bald head, with a little more passion and honesty. And the old ladies forked their chocolate cake; and the old men ate fudge. The birds cried Defeat Defeat Spit-on-it Spit-on-it.'[20] For Frame visits to the seaside now involved 'playing about in the water' — but not swimming. The deaths of her sisters by drowning had left her with 'a kind of horror and a sense of doom . . . when I go into the water'.[21]

Soon after the Bognor visit she had tea with the poet Jon Silkin, who was a boyfriend of one of Frame's Maudsley nurses and had asked if they might meet. They spent a pleasant hour together and, to commemorate the encounter, Silkin wrote Frame a poem.[22]

For a good part of the time, however, Frame was not even conscious of the fact that she was living in London — though 'I realise where I am when I cross Westminster Bridge, or stand beside the giant sloth in the Natural History Museum — he is a friend of mine, I go to him and his prehistoric companions and sit with them when I am depressed and would like to get rid of all human beings from the earth and return to the time before speech and words and complexities . . .'[23]

This was hyperbole, of course. Frame was now committed more than ever to survival in the real world, albeit on her own terms. And her most visible sign of commitment was her twice-weekly 'conversations' at the Maudsley with R.H. Cawley, which usually took place at five o'clock in the evening when his other work for the day was completed. At these sessions she discussed her routines and writing progress and, throughout the latter part of 1959 and early months of 1960, she brought along chapters of her 'work in progress'. She also talked about life at 39 Grove Hill Road and the sources of irritation there, especially the noise created by traffic, neighbours and other members of the household. She spoke too of her current feelings about herself and about the small number of other people with whom she interacted, including Cawley himself. And she expressed some anxieties focussed on politics (there was a general election in Britain in 1959), and on the threat of nuclear war, which was sometimes a cause of nightmares.[24]

Invariably, Frame found these encounters with Cawley supportive and helpful. She looked forward to them more than to any other regular feature of her life. '[He acts] as friend-priest-husband-father without the inconvenience (to him) of assuming the actual relationship,' she told Audrey Scrivener. 'He looks like a wasp, and he wears discreet dark suits and drives a black car and shudders with horror at the thought of driving a car of any other colour but black. He is B.Sc., M.D., Ph.D., D.P.M, and usually has his room cluttered with computers and books on statistics and letters from the Medical Research Council, and notes from colleagues beginning, "Dear Bob". You see, I am studying him just as much as he is studying me . . .'[25] To Frank Sargeson she added that Cawley had 'the manners of an angel'.[26] She could not have paid him a higher compliment: he was the anchor that allowed her to remain moored in an otherwise turbulent world.

For a brief period, in September 1960, Frame was seen by another psychiatrist while Cawley was on holiday. This man, Michael Dixon, turned out to be 'a very erudite Oxford scholar, a student of Greek, Latin, Philosophy etc. before he took up medicine'. He was also George Orwell's brother-in-law. Dixon offered Frame the option of psychoanalysis, but she refused, preferring the less formal conversations she enjoyed with Cawley, which confirmed her increasingly confident grip on life and the value of what she was writing. Cawley was able also, on occasion, to provide logistic assistance, such as lending her an office 'puncher' to make holes in her manuscript pages so that they could be threaded together. This was done 'in great secrecy, because it had to be returned without anyone knowing it was gone'.[27]

Back at Grove Hill Road Frame had by now confessed tearfully to Doris Parry that she was on National Assistance. Her landlady offered a confidence in exchange: Richard, her husband, was alcoholic, and most nights of the week fell through the front door when he arrived home — an occurrence that Frame had witnessed on more than one occasion. The landlord had also been affected by alcohol the night he had come into her room to replace the tube on her television, then seized her and kissed her. 'Just a token,' he had said. 'Just a token.'[28] Frame and Doris Parry did not speak again of their 'broken secrets. Instead we sealed them with a new formality until it might be necessary to break them and inspect the contents and sweep away more tears in a process similar to a periodical airing and storing of bed linen that lay too long against our skin.'[29]

Early in April 1960, before the appearance of the American edition of *Owls Do Cry*, Frame completed the manuscript of what would become her third book, which she referred to at first as 'Landscapes with Loonies', or 'Lunatic Landscapes'.[30] It was, as Bob Cawley had proposed, an account of some of her experiences as a mental patient in Seacliff ('Cliffhaven' in the manuscript) and Avondale ('Treecroft'). The story was told, however, from the point of view of a fictional narrator, Istina Mavet, whose names linked the Serbo–Croat word for truth with the Hebrew word for death.[31] Only some features of this narrator's life were based on Frame's own experience and rather more on Audrey Scrivener's. Many of the other characters, however, were recognisably drawn from 'real' doctors (Geoffrey Blake-Palmer appeared as 'Dr Portman', for example, George Emery as 'Dr Howell'), 'real' nurses (Grace Knox was 'Sister Bridge', C.M.J. Wylie 'Matron Glass') and 'real' patients. Cawley's first reaction to the whole manuscript, Frame recalled later, was to say, 'It's not brilliant, but it will do.' Then, observing her disappointment, he added his usual and overly modest disclaimer: 'You know I'm not a literary chap.'[32]

In search of an alternative response, Frame sent the manuscript to John Money in Baltimore with a note that read: 'Dear John, An autobiographical sketch of a few years in hospital.'[33] In the letter that followed, she told Money that this text was 'most private and not meant for publication: it is simply an almost truthful account of a few past experiences, and not entirely truthful because so many more dramatic things happened that if I had included them the whole account would have seemed invented. For things seem to fall into place in my life as if it were a work of fiction and not, which I doubt anyway, a real act of living.'[34]

In subsequent letters she suggested 'The Faces in the Water' as a title, and said that the purpose of writing it had been 'to get rid of painful memories — or at least come face to face with them'. On reflection, she had decided that she *would* like to see it published 'if a few revelations . . . would help to get [hospitals] improved and perhaps help to change the public attitude to mental illness . . . Old buildings can be pulled down and new ones put up almost overnight but it is harder to deal with the invisible structures, the medieval castles of suspicion and fear . . . I do have a sense of responsibility in this matter for — who knows — I might have been still wandering around the yard of Ward Two and being told that there was no hope for me for the rest of my life.'[35] Nonetheless she worried about the effects of publication in her own country. 'I still have a superstitious kind of fear of being surprised and whisked away to NZ and put in hospital, and a memory of what the woman I mentioned as Sister Bridge said to me: "If ever you write about me and print it I'll get my revenge if I have to travel to the ends of the earth".'[36]

With John Money's strong encouragement, Frame sent copies of the manuscript that would eventually become *Faces in the Water* to Patience Ross in London and Albion Wright in Christchurch. Money sent his copy to Carl Brandt in New York. Because Pegasus had a contractual first option on Frame's next book after *Owls Do Cry*, and ownership of rights outside New Zealand as well as in that market, no firm commitments could be made to publish in the United States or the United Kingdom ahead of Albion Wright's decision.

In June 1960, as she waited for verdicts on the future of *Faces in the Water*, Frame received advances for the imminent American edition of *Owls Do Cry* and for the German one, *Wenn Eulen Schrein*, which would appear later in the year. The total payment came to a little over three hundred pounds.[37] Braziller's edition, reprinted from film of the Pegasus one, reached American bookshops in July and reviews began to appear the same month. One of the first, by C. Hartley Grattan in the *New York Times Book Review*, speculated that Frame had been influenced by the Brontës, William Faulkner and Carson McCullers.

The theme of *Owls Do Cry* is simple if rather gothic. It is a study of the disintegration of a poor family, the members of which are in one way or another intellectually handicapped. The plot entails violent death, temporary insanity, suicide and consignment to institutional care. The manner is 'contemporary poetic', the style imagistic, always cleverly, occasionally brilliantly, employed . . . One is rather more apt to be impressed by the manner than the matter, and there is little doubt in my mind that it is the manner that chiefly supports the opinion that *Owls Do Cry* is a proof of New Zealand's literary maturity.[38]

Florence Bullock in the *New York Herald Tribune* noted that, while the book appeared to be set in New Zealand, it was located more significantly in the human heart:

What makes *Owls Do Cry* more . . . than a mere case history of a not too unusual family of ill-adjusted, unfortunate incompetents who keep alive by hanging on by their fingernails to the fringes of our whirling and ruthless modern world? Two things: the compassion of their narrator, and her poet's temperament. With her passion for the particular truth that is hers, she portrays life as difficult, painful almost beyond endurance for these underprivileged few . . . Yet everything she touches in *Owls Do Cry* glows with the inner light of her human awareness — a cool flame that neither cauterises nor heals but in some mystic way purifies, substituting an essential beauty for superficial pain and squalor.[39]

An anonymous reviewer in the *New Yorker* referred to Frame as 'a very sharp judge of character . . . with a real narrative gift', but called *Owls Do Cry* 'a tantalising mess'.[40] Dorothy Parker in *Esquire* said the novel was 'compact of tragedies [and] almost excruciatingly difficult in its writing, and yet you can never stop reading it'.[41] A highly favourable review written for *Time* magazine, which Carl Brandt was shown in July, was for some reason withdrawn.[42] Those that *were* published pleased George Braziller, though Frame was to earn only a little more from the edition beyond her initial advance. This pattern of good reviews followed by relatively poor sales in the United States was to be repeated in the case of subsequent books, and Frame's agents attributed it in part to Braziller's unwillingness or inability to promote his titles effectively.

John Money, Carl Brandt and Braziller all conspired to show the author only those notices of *Owls Do Cry* that were unreservedly favourable. Frame herself told Money that she would like to have a copy of the *New York Times* one, 'to use as a sop to my landlady and the [others] in the house to whom I have said vaguely that I "write things" and felt even as I answered that they did not believe me'.[43] Later, after sighting the *New York Herald Tribune* notice, she said she was more interested in the accompanying photograph 'in which I have acquired the patched splattered look of the criminal and the dead'.[44]

Oddly, it was the appearance of the American edition of *Owls Do Cry* that led to its acceptance by a British publisher. A.M. Heath had had no success in trying to place it in London, although one company, Hutchinson, had come close to taking it early in 1960.[45] George Braziller in New York, however, was evangelically pleased about the 'discovery' of his New Zealand author and issued a press release extolling what he saw as her strengths. 'Her writing is closely akin to that of the best of our contemporary American story tellers,' he said. 'Her novel is touched at all points by a beauty of vision which is nothing less than poetry. She uses her vivid impressionistic style like a precise instrument to achieve virtuoso effects.'[46]

Braziller carried this enthusiasm into his conversations with other publishers in the latter half of 1960. One such colleague, visiting New York to scout for new titles and authors, was Mark Goulden, owner and managing director of the London-based publishing house W.H. Allen. In Braziller's view, Goulden was a 'trade' rather than a 'literary' publisher: his background had been in journalism and he was at one time the youngest editor of a daily newspaper in the United Kingdom (the *Hull Daily Mail*, when he was 21). But Goulden did have literary interests. As editor of the *Sunday Referee* in 1933 he had been one of the first to recognise the extraordinary poetic talent of the young Dylan Thomas; and in 1958 he had accepted and published Alan Sillitoe's best-selling first book, *Saturday Night and Sunday Morning*.

In the course of a lengthy and wide-ranging discussion, Braziller told Goulden about Janet Frame and urged him to read *Owls Do Cry*. The English publisher took a copy of the novel back to London and asked his stepson Jeffrey Simmons, the most 'literary' member of the firm, to read it and evaluate it. Simmons, especially interested because he had an aunt permanently confined in an English mental hospital, did so and recommended publication. Mark Goulden accepted this advice and began negotiations with A.M. Heath early in November 1960.[47] With Frame's consent an agreement was reached on 8 December and a contract with Pegasus signed on 21 December. Frame would share a seventy-five pound advance (less agency fees and taxation) with Pegasus. The book would appear in London in July 1961.

A month after this agreement to publish *Owls Do Cry*, Brandt and Brandt finalised a contract with Braziller for an American edition of *Faces in the Water*. That same month, January 1961, Pegasus Press agreed to publish *Faces* in New Zealand in association with W.H. Allen in London, who would print 2100 copies with the Pegasus imprint for the New Zealand market. The formal agreement with W.H. Allen to publish the new book in England was signed in March 1961. With all these editions in prospect, including the German version of *Owls Do Cry*, and with news that *The Lagoon* was to be reprinted by Caxton in New Zealand in 1961 and brought out in a German edition by Nannen-Verlag, it seemed to such close observers as John Money, Frank Sargeson and Bob Cawley that Frame's career as a writer had at last taken on a momentum of its own and from this point would require less active intervention on their part.

It seemed so to Frame too. Looking back on what had been by far her most productive writing year, she told E.P. Dawson in January 1961 that she was indebted to her and Frank Sargeson for 'books, pipis and sea', and for their respective financial contributions; and, more immediately, to National Assistance, which had relieved her of previous anxieties about income. She reserved her strongest expressions of gratitude, however, for 'the kindness and understanding which I have received from the people at the Maudsley Hospital' and in particular for R.H. Cawley.[48]

The sense of momentum was also reflected in the fact that Frame had begun a third novel within weeks of completing *Faces in the Water* in April 1960. This, the manuscript that would become *The Edge of the Alphabet*, was the first of her books that she referred to from the outset as a novel, rather than 'an exploration' (as she had initially called *Owls Do Cry*) or 'a series of sketches or episodes' (*Faces in the Water*).[49] In the new book she would draw from the troubled experience of her brother, Geordie, calling the character based on him — as she had done in *Owls* — 'Toby Withers'; and from her knowledge of Patrick Reilly, whose character drawn from him would be identified as 'Pat Keenan'.

Progress on this work was not continuous, however. In July 1960 she told John Money that she had been 'sidetracked down a blind alley of verse, where I seem always to love to linger and never want to emerge to face the traffic of crossroad sentences and green and red and amber lights of reason and pedestrian obligations . . .'[50] Two months later she had accumulated over 280 typed pages of the novel, yet felt there was still much that had to be written. Despite her initial optimism about publication, it was turning out to be 'very private stuff . . . [Perhaps] I have had enough of offering work for publication. I still think the ideal, for me, is the printing of one or two copies which are then distributed among friends — not this wholesale impersonal spate of volumes.'[51] This was, however, no more than the by now customary attack of cold feet that always overtook her when she came close to the completion of a manuscript.

In that same letter to John Money she noted that 'the weather has been creeping into my writing as surely as the fog creeps through the window in the morning . . . My only true relationship is with the weather.'[52] And, a week later, to E.P. Dawson: 'I find English winter and its approach very stimulating, there is such a looming of death and decay, a wonderful procession of darkness; and at night when I have to turn on the light and draw the curtains at six o'clock, I am faced entirely with myself, and there is no escape, I cannot look out of the window . . . and watch the people passing. I have just got to face myself alone.'[53]

Part of facing herself alone involved, inevitably, reflecting on the plight of members of her family back in New Zealand. And while she had long since decided that keeping away from Willowglen and the tension between her father and her brother was a necessary element in her own path to well-being, she could not avoid feelings of anxiety about their welfare. Her father, now aged sixty-four, had taken a retirement job as night watchman at the Oamaru woollen mill. Although, according to Geordie Frame, he now had a 'girlfriend', he still asked his older daughter in letters, sometimes piteously, if she was not ready to come home. The implication was that she would make the return journey in order to care for him.[54]

Even more worrying, June Gordon's five-year-old daughter, Pamela, had had to have surgery in March 1960 to correct a congenital heart defect, something that the family now believed may have been responsible for the premature deaths of Myrtle and Isabel. The operating team included a surgeon named John Williams, who was a friend of E.P. Dawson and whom Frame would eventually meet in London. Pamela Gordon survived the operation and subsequently showed no effects of either the initial condition or the surgery.[55]

Meanwhile Geordie Frame was living with his alcoholic uncle, Charlie Frame, back on the Willowglen property but in a house separate from the old family home. The manuscript of his book had been rejected by Pegasus; Albion Wright, Frank Sargeson told June Gordon, had simply laughed at it.[56] Geordie was confident, from his days as Sergeant Dick, contributor with Myrtle, Janet, Isabel and June to 'Dot's Little Folk's' page in the *Otago Daily Times*, that there was nothing wrong with his writing. It had to be his spelling, he told anyone who would listen: only his inability to spell conventionally prevented him from being a writer like his sister.

After a series of bizarre jobs, which had included demolition work and drilling for oil on the outskirts of Oamaru, Geordie too had found employment at the Oamaru woollen mill. In April 1960, the month Janet finished *Faces in the Water*, he had been involved in a traffic accident on the day of his thirty-eighth birthday. He was returning home after visiting Lottie Frame's sister Grace Hislop in Kaikoura. Driving into Oamaru he swerved his truck to avoid running over a black cat. A car which had been attempting to overtake him crashed into the back of the truck and propelled a variety of timber and machinery into the cabin. Both vehicles were written off. Geordie had to spend the next six months in Oamaru Hospital recovering from fractured vertebrae and an injured hip. Consideration of his plight, and of his previous difficulties coping with the combined effects of epilepsy, deafness and alcohol may have prompted Frame to build her next novel around some of his experiences and escapades. 'The edge of the alphabet' was a potent metaphor for the incommunicable world in which her brother lived; and it was no coincidence that Toby Withers, the central character, dreams of writing a book.

Frame had also resumed contact with the man who provided a model for one of the other characters in *The Edge of the Alphabet*. Patrick Reilly, under the impression that Frame had gone to the United States three years earlier and then returned to London, wrote to her care of the Bank of New South Wales.[57] He said that he too had been back in London for 'some time' after working in New York; and that there had been 'many changes' in his life. He hoped to be able to see her again. And Frame, despite the ambivalence she had always felt about the man — an ambivalence that had frequently veered towards active dislike — agreed to see him. She was lonely; he was there. They resumed their meetings and joint expeditions to cafés, parks and cinemas. And he began to come for tea on Saturday evenings.

[I would] look out of the window to see Patrick, faithful Patrick, still with his jaunty walk and his bumptious air, coming down the road past the hostel for the blind, past the house next door where the Italian and Polish families lived, to the [Parrys']; and always he'd be carrying his Woolworths paper bag with the string handle: packed with food. I felt like a child at Christmas as he set the bottles and jars and packets on the table . . .

There was always an assortment of Peek Frean's biscuits, Irish bacon and butter, a Hovis loaf, tinned creamed rice or white grapes: Patrick's channel of communication was food. He brought me notebooks, too, as my father had done when I was a child, from his workplace. His resemblance to my father, particularly when his lips pursed with disapproval, was uncanny and caused me to wonder about myself and my life. Dr Miller had said frankly that he thought my father was a bully; he had a similar opinion of Patrick Reilly. My life had been erased, almost, by expert bullying while I played the role of victim that like any other repeated role resists a change.

Patrick became the provider, the companion. He gave no sign of wanting to touch or kiss me; if he accidentally touched me he said, 'Excuse me, I'm sorry.' I depended on him yet I found him repugnant; I felt no sexual desire for him. I liked him best when he talked of the leprechauns and the Irish language, and we shared a love of weather, of sky and sea and green, and as we had done in my early days in London, we walked in Ruskin Park or on Clapham Common where he now had a single council flat on the ground floor.[58]

They planned to spend Christmas Day, 1960, together. But Reilly's failure to keep a pre-Christmas engagement aroused in Frame old feelings of rejection, and she sent the Irishman an angry message. He replied: 'When I read your card I decided it would be better if I did not see you . . . When Christmas is over write to me again and let me know when to call on you . . . I am spending the day completely alone now.'[59]

Frame too was alone at Christmas — the Parrys and her fellow boarder were with relatives — but she considered that a better option than risking further misunderstandings and emotional tumult in association with Patrick Reilly. 'You are right in your surmise of me living a hermit's life,' she told Audrey Scrivener, 'but it is better for me not to be too much among people and though it seems . . . a lonely kind of life, it is through living in this way that I have kept out of hospital . . . [The] bustle of everyday living's far too stimulating and depressing and confusing . . . [When] people say, as they do, "Why don't you go out and mix?" — as if I were a pudding . . . I don't bother any more to give my excuses.'[60]

She had finished drafting the manuscript that would become *The Edge of the Alphabet* and stowed it out of sight for several months, to postpone corrections and rewriting. She explained to Sargeson that she was now 'resting between engagements'.[61] As she had done before, she looked for consolation and renewal from the sense of season she experienced so strongly in England, and in particular from that old friend, the weather:

All New Year's Day it snowed heavily and I put on my raincoat over my coat and my snow-boots, and took my umbrella and walked out in the snow. There were few people about and no division of pavement and street and the traffic was almost stopped. I walked into Brockwell Park and stayed there, in a blizzard, and it was like Antarctica with darkness coming swiftly and the mist mingling with the flying snow, and then the street lamps began to shine and it seemed like moonlight. It was wonderful . . .[62]

# CHAPTER FOURTEEN

# On the Rock of Her Self

*F*RAME REMAINED AT GROVE HILL ROAD THROUGHOUT 1961 AND MOST of the first half of 1962. The pattern she had imposed on her life over the previous eighteen months — the settled accommodation, the twice-weekly visits to the Maudsley, the strictly observed writing routine, periodic contact with friends — enabled her to continue to live and function productively. Seeds were sown and duly came to fruition.

She eventually sent the finished manuscript of *The Edge of the Alphabet* to John Money in Baltimore in March 1961, and he opened discussions with Brandt and Brandt and A.M. Heath about its placement.[1] In February she got down to work on a set of ideas for short stories which she had been accumulating while she wrote *Faces in the Water* and *Edge*; she had completed thirty-nine stories by the end of April, when she handed them to Bob Cawley. Late in May she began work on what would become her fourth published novel, *Scented Gardens for the Blind*, a story with three narrators who are eventually revealed as three personalities of a single character.[2]

In May 1961, in response to Audrey Scrivener's frequent complaint that, while Frame took the time to write to her, she did not reveal enough about herself, Frame described her daily routine at Grove Hill Road:

I get up at half-past six in the morning and sneak out to the kitchen and make myself a cup of coffee and eat an orange, bringing them back to my room. Then I make my bed, dress, tidy my room a little, by which time it is about half-past seven; and then I go to the kitchen where I have my real breakfast of a cup of coffee and an apple. I used to have a newspaper delivered (on my doctor's instructions!). But I found that reading it interfered with my work for the morning so I stopped its delivery. At eight o'clock . . . I turn on the radio and hear the weather forecast and the news. Then if I am working I begin work for the day, sitting down at my table and my typewriter. At about half-past ten or eleven o'clock I have a break, go out and perhaps buy a *Guardian*, do some shopping, food etc., then come home, work again till lunch, when I read my paper, listen to the one o'clock news, and then begin work again . . . till half-past four when I make myself my tea, which consists *always* of two pieces of toast, one with jam, the other with cheese, a cup of coffee and an apple . . . Of course all the time the outward things are happening I am having my inward dreams . . .[3]

And, of course, it was the 'inward dreams' that nourished the daily writing.

As before, there were periodic interruptions to the routine. Jess Whitworth arrived from New Zealand on 10 April and, feeling daughterly and concerned, Frame met her off the boat-train at Waterloo Station. She found 'an amazing woman — seventy-seven and on her third trip alone from New Zealand . . . I was not afraid to meet her [again],' she told John Money, 'because she is so elderly and has closed many of the reception centres of her being in that wonderful way which elderly people acquire.' Whitworth rented a room from a woman in Balham with whom she had stayed previously, and she and Frame made several excursions to concerts at the Albert Hall, museums and galleries, and went to 'smoky dirty noisy Oxford St . . . to see the Indian film, *The World of Apu*'.[4] They also visited Cambridge together one weekend, to look at university colleges; and, on another, Canterbury Cathedral.

In the second week in May, Frame mounted an expedition of her own that would take her further away from London than she had travelled since her trip to Ibiza four-and-a-half years earlier. 'I am going to walk in the Lake District with my pack on my back,' she told Frank Sargeson, 'and camp beside mountain streams and pluck a few lesser celandines; happily it is not yet time for tourists to haunt Dove Cottage, though maybe it is haunted all the time . . . I [shall] walk myself into forgetfulness and listen to the nightingale in May, and peer into Derwent Water, Buttermere, Rydal Water.'[5] The very thought of such a holiday brought an ecstasy of anticipation. The experience itself came close to meeting expectations.

Frame had not attempted to live under canvas since her days at Willowglen in the late 1940s. To better meet the challenge, she borrowed a library book called *Camping: Know the Game*. Despite this preparation, she spent only one night in the tent, at Seathwaite in the Borrowdale Valley, in what she told Audrey Scrivener was 'the wettest place in England . . . You should have seen me crawling out . . . and trying to make myself a cup of coffee with water in which sheep had paddled.'[6]

The next day, 'with my too heavy pack I fell off a bus and collapsed in the street'. She climbed back on and took the bus to the end of the Langdale Valley, then 'walked as far as my pack would let me, stopped at a tiny farmhouse, and found a bed for the rest of the week . . . I walked all day, cooking my meals on the fells, sitting high up and alone with the ravens, looking down on the tarns and lakes; listening to curlew, cuckoo, pied wagtail, meadow pipit — and English thrush. I walked over Wrynose Pass into the Duddon Valley, to see Wordsworth's "infant Duddon".[7] Sargeson told his correspondents that Frame had been astonished at the lack of space in the Wordsworth's cottage at Grassmere — 'what poor Dorothy must have suffered with William cuckolding her with his wife, only a few inches away on the other side of a thin partition'.[8]

The thing that most impressed Frame about the district, she said, was the quality of the darkness — 'an absolute black which makes no concessions to objects by providing them . . . with a faint token shadow or outline so that when morning comes they may with more confidence adopt their pose of substance'. She spoke too of walking along a road with an elderly shepherd. 'He talked to me, and every word he said . . . was careful and precious, like white butter: I mean that his thoughts had been hoarded inside him, like cattle kept inside in winter, and when they, like the cattle, were let outside in the sun, they gave bare valuable produce . . .'[9]

Frame undertook another trip out of London in the first week in August, travelling an even greater distance. This time she went with Jess Whitworth by bus to Glasgow, where they stayed in the YWCA (but were thrown out after one night because they complained that an advertised supper was not complimentary); and Edinburgh, where they checked into a hotel. Whitworth was a good companion, knowledgeable about Scottish history, literature and painting (like so many people born in Otago, including the Frames, her antecedents were Scottish). Frame felt fortunate to be with such a guide in the country of her father's ancestors. In the course of the week, the older woman became confused and disoriented and it was apparent that she was suffering from some kind of memory loss associated with age. It took some effort and tact on Frame's part to prevent the excursion collapsing in disarray. Whitworth's eventual return to New Zealand, early in September, came as a relief to the younger woman.[10]

In July 1961, when *Owls Do Cry* was at last published in London by W.H. Allen nearly five years after Frame had written it, she experienced for the first time a 'publication day' for one of her books.

I wasn't sure of the English routine, although since I'd been in London I had read avidly in the newspapers of theatre first nights, art gallery private viewings, launching of books at an author's or publisher's party, with the newspapers the next day proclaiming . . . 'A hit, a palpable hit', or perhaps burying the latest works of art . . . The newspapers presented a world of vicarious excitement where authors, painters, sculptors, playwrights, especially if they were sons or daughters of lords or had some other unusual distinguishing feature . . . were wined, dined, romanced, gossiped about. What if . . .? I dreamed briefly . . . I [wondered] how I would feel on publication day when I opened the newspaper and there were the headlines. *New Author of Fine Novel* . . .

On publication day I took the bus to Westminster, bought newspapers at the Westminster Station, took them to the lavatory in the subway, and began to read, as I thought, of my *publication*. I searched the book pages. I could find nothing. I think there was one . . . with a small note at the bottom of a 'continued' column, about a novel of poverty in New Zealand . . . I don't think it gave an opinion.[11]

There was, in fact, a clutch of reviews published over the following days and weeks in the weekly papers and journals. As in America, most were favourable; those that were not were baffled.

Dan Davin's review in the *Times Literary Supplement* likened Frame's achievement to that of Virginia Woolf. 'The whole structure of the book [is] strongly reminiscent of *The Waves* . . . [The] comparison is valid and the compliment is deserved . . . Miss Frame writes so well . . . and so compassionately that she has made an extremely good and moving book [with] many virtues, and they are perfectly clear.'[12] Richard Mayne in the *New Statesman* made his comparisons with Katherine Mansfield, but noted that *Owls Do Cry* had 'a raw edge and a controlled bitterness much sharper than the mere sting of Katherine Mansfield's stories . . . Miss Frame's writing has a suppleness, an informality, an ability to shift with the blur of thought and feeling, and a consequent power in the big scenes, that are far removed from the conscious precision of even the best of Katherine Mansfield.'[13]

In the *Sunday Telegraph*, Colin Wilson identified the influences on Frame as 'Faulkner, *The Sound and the Fury*, with a dash of Dylan Thomas'. He believed that the novel showed 'more of promise than achievement: but its imaginative delicacy makes it likely that Miss Frame is going to have some important things to say soon'.[14] William Cooper in the *Sunday Times* found much of the text 'a poetic, rather dotty stream of consciousness, whose texture is too thin to support the violent events that occur'. But he conceded that the book succeeded, 'in that one cannot read about the people in it without being moved to pity'.[15]

There is no hint of Frame's reaction to these reviews in her surviving correspondence, nor even evidence that she read them, other than that in the *TLS*. She said subsequently that the sometimes contradictory nature of their diagnoses and conclusions was good reason for an author not to take them seriously. Instead, she would make a conscious effort 'to smooth my feelings about all reviews, to allow myself to believe neither the praise nor the adverse criticism, become neither overjoyed nor depressed, and if possible not to read reviews unless it was obvious that the writers had read the book and not just the blurb and a few biographical notes . . . that referred to "insanity" '.[16] It was to shield herself from association with such notices that she had changed her name to Clutha three years previously. One unexpected result of favourable reviews, however, was that they provoked correspondence from other agents and publishers asking if they might represent her or publish her.[17]

Frame seemed far more anxious about an impending visit to London by John Money in July and August of 1961 than she was about the appearance of reviews. Money was coming to England to visit his sister and her family who were living there temporarily. It was exactly fourteen years since he and Frame had last seen each other, and the circumstances of their original association had been fraught with difficulties and complications. Money, ever the optimist, expected and hoped that they could meet as old friends. Frame was by no means so sure that they ought to. She remained grateful for Money's continued interest in her welfare and for his willingness to go on acting as an unofficial agent for her writing; she even admitted, at times, to enjoying their correspondence. But meeting? 'Correspondence is all very well,' she told Audrey Scrivener, 'but I should not really like to see him in person.'[18]

To Money, Frame excused herself. '[Though] I should like to see you, I'm afraid I had better not.'[19] She confided to Bob Cawley that her image of Money was of 'a conceited young man, flashily dressed, rather arrogant'.[20] But just over a month later she changed her mind and wrote again to Money to tell him so. 'I am much more mature than ever I was in my Otago days — besides, I now wear dark glasses when meeting people. Also my intense human curiosity will not rest until I have observed the results of the transactions you have made with Change, what bargains he has offered you, how much you have had to pay for the privilege of travelling in Time. Time and Change obsess me these days.'[21] In the same letter she said she would allow him to read her new collection of stories and to take them away with him.

In the event, Money visited Frame at Camberwell twice, in July and August, and he took her out to dinner on the South Bank of the Thames. In her report to Bob Cawley, she said her friend had come 'with flowers, a briefcase and a look of apprehension'. But he was, she emphasised, 'a much nicer man' than she remembered.[22]

Money recorded in detail his own impressions of the visits. He described the houses in Grove Hill Road as 'ugly old buildings, row houses . . . built around 1875'. Frame's first floor room was 'clean and tidy, though really very dowdy'. Once inside the room, with Frame, he was conscious of 'a hasty preoccupation with covering and tidying papers on and near the typewriter . . . as though I had surprised a lady at her toilet. There were various apologetic expressions explanatory of this tidying up, and then Janet put on, briefly, her dark glasses . . . It was now that my hostess began the little ritual of saying: I don't know you, do I? I don't really know you. I mean I know who you are, but I don't really *know* you.' Despite these preliminaries, Money found it 'remarkable how quickly we settled down into mutually interested conversation, quite at ease with one another . . . I was very much impressed by this contrast between the initial panic-button effect and the happy camaraderie of our talk.'

There was a copy of the *Times Literary Supplement* on the table with its highly favourable review of *Owls Do Cry*. 'It was [only] with a shy reluctance that Janet managed to acquaint me with the existence of this review and show it to me. Patience Ross had told her about it, she said, apologising for her vanity in buying the paper to see it. She had thought of clipping it to send to her father in New Zealand, or her sister, knowing that they would be proud and pleased. But no. She couldn't bring herself to do it . . . She couldn't even summon courage enough to send [it] to Frank Sargeson, who probably would not otherwise see it . . . [She] gave it to me when I asked.'

Frame also gave Money carbon copies of the thirty-nine short stories recently completed, and told him of a letter she had received that day from Patience Ross proposing that some of the stories be sold by Brandt and Brandt and A.M. Heath to American and British magazines. 'The issue arose of changes to please editors . . . She had been rehearsing all morning . . . how to reply. The trouble is, Janet said, that having completed and retyped a piece of writing, she is through with it. Forever. She wants to have nothing more to do with it. To have to reopen the manuscript and work on it again would in all likelihood lead her to burn it . . . to destroy it as the worthless thing it already seems to her.'

She went on to tell Money that the original purpose of her writing would be destroyed by modifications to make manuscripts saleable. The stories were written as works of art, and 'whether they sold or not for good prices was irrelevant'. Money then suggested that she be 'uncompromising about those writings that are essential to her artistic integrity, while offering to her agent . . . a certain type of writing with good financial possibilities . . . Janet thought she might entertain this. She had followed the [same] method once in Auckland when advised that she could earn well by writing children's stories for School Publications.'

Reflecting on this conversation, Money noted that his friend had 'a level of aspiration that constantly elevates so that nothing, once completed, can measure up . . . That is why the good artist is forever discontented, forever self-critical. It is also why the artist's decision to suppress or destroy work can be bizarre . . . Her standards are at variance with those of the rest of the world, and it is the world's job to rescue what it can.' And, though Money still felt at times as if, in prising Frame's work free of its author, he was having to cajole secrets from a reluctant child, he concluded that the new Janet Clutha had 'a lot more artistic self-assurance than Janet Frame . . . She did find herself an agent and does submit her manuscripts . . . and does agree to their publication.'[23]

Back in the United States on 28 August, Money told Carl Brandt that his encounters with Frame had 'turned out remarkably well, with no panic reaction

. . . Janet was better than I have ever known her.' He reported also that he had brought with him the copy of the manuscript of stories and suggested that at least some of them be sent to *Landfall* in New Zealand, so that Frame could continue to be a visible literary presence there.[24]

Brandt replied that he was immensely grateful for the report on Frame's 'health and state of mind. I cannot tell you how difficult and frustrating it is for us to feel so totally out of touch with an author.' He told Money too that he already had the A.M. Heath copy of the stories, and that he wanted to submit them to American magazines ahead of those in New Zealand or the United Kingdom. '[Since] they do pay so much more than magazines in other countries, they do have the right to first publication.'[25] Less than a month later he was able to report that he had sold two of the stories, 'Prizes' and 'The Reservoir', both based recognisably on childhood experiences in Oamaru, to the *New Yorker;* and soon afterwards he sold a third, 'The Red-Currant Bush', to *Mademoiselle.*[26]

That month, September 1962, Frame completed *Scented Gardens for the Blind.*[27] With publication of her second and third novels still to come, and the collection of stories awaiting evaluation, she was placing her agents and publishers in a position analogous to that of an airport with planes coming in at a faster rate than traffic controllers can accommodate. The queue was reduced almost immediately, however, by the simultaneous publication of *Faces in the Water* in New Zealand and the United States in that same month.

Strangely, although the structure and narrative of this new book would attract more universal praise than those of *Owls Do Cry*, the New Zealand Literary Fund turned down an application for a grant to reduce the retail price of Pegasus's New Zealand edition of 2000 copies. 'I do not feel that Janet Frame has full literary control of her material, or that she has shaped it into anything of great value,' the fund secretary wrote to Albion Wright, transmitting the views of his advisory committee. '[The] final result is no more than the personal jottings of one who has been through a dreadful experience without transcending it or transmuting its impact into art.' Wright had the grace not to communicate this verdict to Frame.[28]

Such responses assumed that the novel was no more than an unprocessed documentary work. Indeed, anticipating and hoping to forestall this very reaction, Frame had been careful to change the names of all characters and locations in the book to fictitious ones, including, at the last moment, Park House, which was at Avondale, to 'Park Lodge'; and she had asked the publishers to place a disclaimer at the beginning of the novel, which read: 'Although this book is written in documentary form it is a work of fiction. None of the characters, including Istina Mavet, portrays a living person.'[29]★

---

★ At the same time, however, Frame had asked that the final paragraph in the manuscript, which would have further distanced the book's narrator from the author, be removed. It read: 'Note: Some time after writing this account of her life in hospital Istina Mavet committed suicide.'

On the whole, New Zealand reviewers accepted the disclaimer and assessed the work as one of imaginative writing. Several quoted with approval, as an example of the flavour of the prose, the passage from which the book's title was derived:

[Someone] who walking at night along the banks of a stream catches a glimpse in the water of a white face or a moving limb and turns quickly away, refusing to help or to search for help. We all see faces in the water. We smother our memory of them, even our belief in their reality, and become calm people of the world; or we can neither forget nor help them.[30]

The first review to appear, and one of the most influential, was broadcast on National Radio's books programme. It was by Arnold Wall who, in a subsequent career, would become senior editor of New Zealand's largest publishing company, A.H. and A.W. Reed. It concluded:

There is much [here] that is horrifying to any humane person . . . but there is little that is harsh or strident about *Faces in the Water*. It even has its own humour, muted by place and circumstance. Terrible as it is, there is also a beauty about it, a beauty that is a result of its authenticity and a humanity that prompts the question — are these faces in the water merely faces to be quickly forgotten, or faces to be remembered because they, too, are the faces of living, suffering human beings?[31]

Similar notes were struck in other New Zealand notices. Paul Day, writing in *Landfall*, said that *Faces* offered 'a perceptive comment on the tragedy of the sensitive and afraid in a conforming society. Miss Frame shows the hospital as a totalitarian microcosm — a society in which everything is supposedly done for the individual's benefit; where terror reigns, and humanity is forgotten by a ruling class whom power has utterly corrupted. In opposition to this corporate image she narrates the pilgrimage of the individual, through the circles of an inferno that culminates in the refractory ward . . . In defining the terms of a world of individual martyrdom with such haunting power, Miss Frame has written a novel that will endure.'[32]

David Hall in the *New Zealand Listener*, who had damned Frame's first novel with the faintest of praise, did much the same with *Faces*, though he insisted it was 'a more disciplined work than *Owls Do Cry*: it does not fall apart, like that disorderly book, into its component themes . . . [It is] much more workman-like.'[33] He was also a member of the Literary Fund advisory committee which had refused the book a grant. Such overlapping of roles was inevitable in a country with New Zealand's population (fewer than 2.5 million people in 1961).

A minority of New Zealand reviewers voiced what one called 'an uneasy suspicion that some of the characters might have an existence outside the pages of *Faces in the Water*'.[34] At least one of those who read the book in manuscript believed that this was the case and warned Pegasus of possible legal consequences.[35] There were none, and Seacliff Hospital, as a consequence of its widely acknowledged structural and administrative shortcomings, was in the process of being shut down at the very time that the book was published (though parts of it remained open until 1972).

The appearance of *Faces in the Water* nonetheless provoked consternation among some of the hospital's senior staff and former senior staff who, even in their darkest moments, had never envisaged that a former patient might write an account of her treatment, especially one who had been for a time in a ward for refractory patients. These doctors and nurses had little difficulty recognising some of their own words, actions and mannerisms in the novel, and those of their colleagues. While the book was subsequently prescribed as required reading for medical, nursing and occupational therapy staff in training, especially for those who planned to specialise in psychiatric medicine in New Zealand, it was never commended or highly regarded by those who felt that they had been caricatured in its pages.[36] One practitioner went so far as to claim, privately, that in writing of her treatment, Frame had breached the accepted contract of doctor–patient confidentiality.[37]

Health professionals who accepted the validity of the book's implicit criticisms of New Zealand psychiatric services, however, applauded both its appearance and the shock effect it had on former members of the Seacliff hierarchy, including Dr Geoffrey Blake-Palmer, who by 1961 was director of mental health in the country's Department of Health.[38] One senior administrator at the hospital in Frame's time there said subsequently that, after reading *Faces*, he felt guilty that a woman with such gifts and sensibilities had been required at one point to provide morning and afternoon tea for the staff.[39]

Reaction among those who read the book in Oamaru tended to be as literal and as parochial as the responses there had been to *Owls Do Cry*.[40] Geordie Frame reported to his sister that everyone he knew was reading the book and trying 'to puzzle out who is who in it'.[41] Even more alarmingly, he claimed that some of the events depicted fictionally in *Owls* were coming to pass: he himself was now living in a house built over the old rubbish tip; and a woman he said he wanted to marry had instead married a local social security agent. This appeared to suggest to him that anything in *Faces in the Water* that was fictional would also 'come true'.[42]

Even as educated a woman as Frame's former English teacher, Janet Gibson (she of 'Miss Gibson and the lumber room' fame), who admired her former pupil and was proud of her achievements, wrote to a friend: 'It's extraordinary Jean's books are put on such a high pedestal by critics — no doubt her writing is clever, but the subject matter is so sordid . . . [Can] she write a book that is not subjective and not about her family and herself? . . . It is interesting to read that she has changed her name to Janet Clutha. At least the first name is a good one!'[43] This last comment was provoked by a review of the American edition of *Faces* in *Time*, which had appeared shortly after New Zealand publication. While it may have caused Miss Gibson's eyebrows to rise, it had the effect of making some other Oamaruvians decide that the book must have merit if it was noticed by an international magazine. An acquaintance from school days wrote to convey this information and to send consequent congratulations.[44]

Despite elements of controversy — perhaps, even, because of them — *Faces in the Water* sold rapidly in New Zealand. Within a month of publication Pegasus was making arrangements with W.H. Allen to import a second printing of the novel.[45] In addition Albion Wright was also in communication with Spanish, Italian, Finnish and Dutch publishers over foreign language rights for *Owls Do Cry*, and with a French publisher for rights to *Faces*.[46] At the same time the German edition of *Owls*, *Wenn Eulen Schrein*, arrived at Pegasus's Christchurch office with the news that it had been acclaimed by the journal *Die Zeit* as a work of 'great, very great literature'.[47]

Frame, pleased about all these developments, and still withholding from Pegasus the manuscripts of *The Edge of the Alphabet* and *Scented Gardens for the Blind*, had her second meeting with Patience Ross and asked that A.M. Heath handle contract negotiations with her New Zealand publisher for all future books. In particular she wanted Pegasus's rights restricted to New Zealand and Australia, so that she would not continue to lose half of all her earnings from the British and North American sales to the New Zealand company.[48] The need for such a provision was glaringly apparent in a royalty statement for August 1961: of a payment of $US146.90 for sales of *Owls Do Cry* in the United States and Canada, Frame received only fourteen pounds six shillings once tax, agency and Pegasus's deductions had been made.[49] And, to make an unfavourable arrangement even more disadvantageous, Frame was discovering that Pegasus did not send out royalty statements and cheques as a matter of course: Albion Wright released money to her — including money earned from British and American sales of her books — only as a consequence of pestering letters.[50] Now that her books were at last generating income, Frame longed for a degree of regularity in her business arrangements, especially in regard to payments. Patience Ross convinced her that this was most likely to be achieved by allowing her agents to deal directly with her publishers.

Meanwhile *Faces in the Water* appeared also in the United States in September 1961. There, of course, it was not subject to speculation about local considerations that preoccupied some New Zealand readers and reviewers. Carl Brandt reported to John Money that the book was being published there with considerably more optimism about reception and sales than had accompanied *Owls Do Cry*.[51] As in the case of *Owls*, the notices were encouraging. *Time*, in a review that this time was carried over into print, said that the novel was 'especially brilliant in its description of what happens inside the patient's mind'. Frame, it went on, 'writes with a cool eye, a detached sympathy, and a warm but unsloppy love of sane and insane alike'. Thus far, so good. But the review concluded: 'Author Frame has herself been in and out of mental hospitals as a voluntary patient. Shy and wary of publicity, she has recently changed her name to Janet Clutha (after a New Zealand river).'[52]

Robert Pick in the *New York Times* affirmed that 'Miss Frame's talent as a novelist carries her beyond her own narrator's memories. She [brings] to life the precariousness of Istina's existence as an allegory of the insecurity of human relations at large. She is a very gifted writer.'[53] In the *Atlantic Monthly*, Charles Rolo credited Frame with 'a poet's imagination, and her prose has beauty, precision, a surging momentum, and the quality of constant surprise . . . [An] extremely fine book.'[54] Other compliments came from *Life, Harper's Magazine*, and Dorothy Parker in *Esquire*.[55]

The concluding comments in *Time* represented everything that Frame feared and abhorred about publicity associated with book publication. As Sheila Natusch pointed out, unnecessarily, the review made reference to her 'retiring nature' in one breath and revealed her pseudonym in the next. 'I was very distressed by the reference to my private life and to my name,' Frame told John Money. 'When I read that I had been "in and out of mental hospitals" I realised that my distress would not have been so severe had I read that I had "suffered for many years from polio" . . . It was almost as if I had read that I had been convicted of crime & had served my sentence . . . [The] language was in poor taste also, cheaply emotive . . .'[56]

This reaction was a portent of problems to come. The biographical information had been supplied to *Time* in good faith by either an employee of Brandt and Brandt, or of Braziller. When news media wanted to draw attention to a book by highlighting unusual facts about a writer's life, the inclination of publishers and agents, seeking to promote sales of their authors' books, was to cooperate. In the case of Frame, however, this strategy was unappreciated by the author and unsanctioned. She believed that the attention of the reader and reviewer ought to be limited to the text that the writer chose to release for publication. She did not want her career dogged by constant reference to her time in psychiatric hospitals, with its implication that she had been — and possibly still was — mentally ill. Nor would she countenance the even more newsworthy corollary of this scenario: that she was a 'mad genius' whose creativity was a product of insanity. She rejected it because it was simply untrue; and because it camouflaged the real nature of whatever talent she had.

The same month that Frame complained to John Money about the content of the review in *Time*, she took renewed consolation in the approach of her favourite season. 'I really feel it is the first day of nipped fingers and nose and fog,' she wrote to Peter Dawson. 'I can feel the cold breeze sneaking under the door and through the windows . . . I like the sense of preparing for battle; and though it is morbid of me, I like the public appearances of death, for in winter there are so many funerals . . . One can go deep and deep in winter: into oneself and into meanings.'[57]

Frame concluded this letter by saying that she saw no people now other than Bob Cawley, had 'no visitors, and lead a very solitary life'. Which was partially true: she had at last persuaded Patrick Reilly to cease his weekend visits, though he continued to send her letters requesting further meetings.[58] She had resumed occasional meetings with her poet friend David Kozubei, however; and she was seeing rather more of Mildred Surry, the librarian with whom she had shared lodgings in Kentish Town. In November 1961 Frame accompanied Surry to her parents' home in Bury, Sussex. 'For the first time,' she told John Money, 'I spent the weekend in an English household . . . in an old-fashioned cottage in a tiny village in Sussex, near the downs. And by Sunday evening my knees were wobbly with the effects of cider! The cottage was filled with books, and each evening I lay in bed reading the Letters of William Cowper, and sometimes I thought I was home . . . Yet I had so much dreaded the weekend . . .'[59]

The following month Mildred introduced Frame to another quintessentially English experience: she took her to the reading room of the British Museum Library in Bloomsbury, where Frank Sargeson had begun his writing career thirty-four years earlier. 'She was very good, explaining things to me in whispers, warding off officials, making me feel at home at my desk for the evening (N14), and though I could not pluck up the courage to make an application for a book, I watched while she filled in [hers], submitted it, and waited at the desk for the book to arrive . . . I know that I shall keep in mind as long as I am capable . . . the shape of the Reading Room, the colour of the books, and the sound of turning pages.'[60]

In December 1961, almost to her astonishment, Frame found that she had accumulated sufficient income to go off National Assistance.[61] She had banked two hundred pounds worth of advances for *Faces in the Water* and earnings from *Owls Do Cry*; and, even after tax and commission deductions, she received two hundred and fifty pounds for the stories bought by the *New Yorker*. *Faces in the Water* was to be published by W.H. Allen in January 1962; and in March 1962 she would sign contracts with Braziller and W.H. Allen for *The Edge of the Alphabet*, and with Pegasus for the same book in July. Explaining some of this to Peter Dawson, Frame said that she wanted now to try to live for one year on three hundred pounds of her savings, and would no longer need contributions of the kind that Dawson had been sending.[62] She had the option of returning to National Assistance, she said, 'should things get desperate'.[63]

The following month, January 1962, brought the surprising news that Dawson, who had lived in New Zealand since 1925, planned to return to England in the coming year. She was now sixty-seven, most of her New

Zealand friends other than Frank Sargeson had died; she felt that her adopted country held diminishing interest for her. She had three sisters and a brother still alive in England; and she decided to relocate herself before she was too frail to make the journey. Dawson was also — though she did not tell Janet this — influenced by the fact that Frame was in England and showed every sign of wanting to remain there. Dawson envisaged some kind of house-sharing arrangement that might eventually include her writer friend, and she had already decided to make provision for Frame in her will.[64] Initially, however, Dawson simply told Frame that she planned to live out her final years in England.

This prospect, Frame responded, was 'a mingled sad and happy surprise' — sad because Dawson would no longer be at Mount Maunganui, where the writer had fond memories of staying and to where she had hoped to make return visits; and happy because the older woman was so clearly excited about returning to her native soil. 'You have made your decision . . . with its new experiences and linking of old ones,' Frame wrote, 'and you will be able to carry to this hemisphere, where you were born, your store of past experience . . . What a cross-fertilisation of hemispheres!' In a footnote that may not have been entirely welcome to Dawson Frame added: 'I look on your journey with a personal interest, because in the years to come, if H-bombs have not exploded and the earth and men are still here, maybe I shall be making the same kind of journey back to New Zealand.'[65]

The major event affecting Frame in January 1962, however, was the English publication of *Faces in the Water*. 'Again I bought newspapers to discover what "they" were saying . . . and I was startled to find my photo on the book page of the Sunday papers and relieved that I had changed my surname.'[66] One such paper with her photograph was the *Observer*; and the review that accompanied it, by John Mortimer, was redolent of high praise:

> [The novel] has an atmosphere of old, mad and drooping women; an aura of urine and carbolic and discarded sanitary towels . . . Miss Frame is very good on the satisfaction of being totally mad, the pleasure of food throwing and the wild Hogarthian revels of the deeply disturbed, which are unknown on the grey borderland of sanity . . . And yet the book is lyrical, touching and deeply entertaining.[67]

Dan Davin's review in the *Times Literary Supplement* called Frame 'an original writer, giving us new eyes for the familiar, a new language for the tragedy and joy of the humble and ordinary world, and a new sympathy for the desperate insulated worlds of the insane . . . Miss Frame is the most remarkable New Zealand writer since Katherine Mansfield and Frank Sargeson.'[68] Francis Hope in the *Spectator* said that Frame wrote 'with a sad, sensibility-ridden beauty in the tone and tradition of an older generation of women novelists: Rosamond Lehmann, Elizabeth Bowen, even Virginia Woolf . . .'[69] And Stella Frank in the *Sunday Times* was similarly complimentary: 'Miss Frame writes beautiful, exciting prose and her large canvas is skilfully organised.'[70]

Inevitably, some reviewers voiced reservations. Patrick Crutwell in the *Guardian* found the first-person narrative 'impossible: could someone who had been what this narrator has been remember and describe it as she does?'[71] And both Elizabeth Jennings in the *Listener* and the anonymous reviewer in *The Times* argued that the novel was not a success. Such varieties of opinion, Frame said later, and the conflicting advice she would get from agents and publishers, reminded her that 'a writer must stand on the rock of her self and her judgement or be swept away by the tide or sink in the quaking earth: there must be an inviolate place where the choices and decisions, however imperfect, are the writer's own, where the decision must be as individual and solitary as birth or death. What was the use of my having survived as a person if I could not maintain my own judgement? Only then could I have the confidence to try to shape a novel or story or poem the way I desired and needed it to be, with both the imperfections and felicities bearing my own signature.'[72]

To Frank Sargeson she wrote that the whole experience of being in a country when a book was published there had been 'appalling . . . [It] doesn't matter whether it's the effect of failure or success; it strengthens my belief that writers should not be published until they are dead.'[73] Sargeson, who was at that time unable to find a publisher for his most recent novel, *Memoirs of a Peon*, would in fact have welcomed such an appalling experience. But in the case of *Faces in the Water*, there had been an additional horror for Frame to face:

> Some horrible *Woman's Mirror* wanted to serialise the book, using real photographs taken in Paris [to accompany extracts from the novel published in *Réalités* magazine]. I should have got about twenty pounds for it when . . . agents had taken their share, and though the money would have been very convenient, I felt it was not worth the worry the whole thing would have caused, both to myself and to people with relatives or friends who are ill. I think it would have been the last straw for my sanity if I were forced to pass placards in the street which said . . . 'I was among the mad' by JF. Fortunately I refused the whole thing.[74]

Such proposals, from agents or publishers, made Frame cringe and led her to joke to Sargeson that she had retained her integrity if not her virginity.[75] Nevertheless she was now getting on well with her English agent Patience Ross who, she said, 'had a high reputation for integrity, judgement, literacy [and] literary knowledge', in spite of having joined A.M. Heath thirty-six years before as a typist.[76] After their second meeting, Frame told John Money, she had found Ross 'very likeable, entirely unpretentious'. Now, in February 1962, sensing that Frame had been bruised by the publication process, Ross offered her the use of the holiday cottage at Mevagissey in Cornwall that she shared with her partner, Louise Porter.[77] Frame would not need to pay rent or fuel costs. Her only outgoings, other than having still to pay rent at Camberwell, would be for food.

Frame accepted the offer with gratitude. The noise at Grove Hill Road was at this time driving her close to distraction. Before setting out for Cornwall in March 1962, however, Frame submitted to a portrait session, organised by W.H. Allen, with the American photographer Jerry Bauer, well known for his photographs of writers; and she began a new piece of writing, which she called her 'snow obsession'. It had begun, she told Money, in 'the memory of the first of January snowfall [which] stays with me so vividly . . . I began it and would have finished it if I hadn't had televisions through the wall every evening . . . It is depressing when the impulse to write is upon one and one cannot carry it out in the evenings or the weekends. I prefer day and night writing for first drafts.'[78]

She recovered the desired conditions when she reached Cornwall at the end of the first week in March — although she walked, literally, into a storm. 'The day I arrived [there] was a tide of seventeen feet, with a gale blowing . . . I looked out of the window and watched the sea breaking over the roofs of the cottages and flowing in the street. I walked in the gale a mile or so along the coast where the storm was even more fierce, and I saw the roof of one cottage carried away. The damage was very heavy all along the coast and in Penzance over two hundred people had their homes destroyed. And now it is late afternoon and the sea is lying calm and snug and wandering in a dazed slow-motion manner in and out of the rocks and around the corner of the sea-wall into the harbour; such innocence.'[79]

The cottage was luxurious alongside what now seemed to be the spartan conditions at Grove Hill Road. 'The water is constantly hot, which is such a change from the niggardly London supply and the grudging twice-weekly bath . . . There are pop-up toasters and day-and-night fires and bathroom wall heaters, and they have left out their portable radio for me . . . I am over-whelmed by the kindness.' Most blessed of all, however, Frame was 'drunk with the sea . . . just outside my window . . . It is utterly blissfully peaceful without being surrounded by television noises. I do think that when I return to London I shall have to look for a quieter place, as the summer is coming soon and all the windows will be opened, and the noise . . .'[80]

Frame walked each day, bought fresh bread at the village bakery, drank the local milk, 'thick and creamy'. But for most of the daylight hours she worked, reducing the manuscript of her 'Snowman Snowman' fable, which had been inspired by observation of winter life around Grove Hill Road, from seventy to thirty thousand words. 'I shall send it to you,' she promised Money, 'also I shall send you the first draft if you promise never to read it for it is just written roughly and half the sentences are interspersed with remarks like . . . by god improve, who do you think you are trying to write — and so on . . . The version I typed after that . . . is much cleaner and no threatening remarks from the writer to herself! But please don't ever read the first draft . . . I shall also send a copy of *Scented Gardens for the Blind* which I finished when you were over here last year . . . I did show it to Patience Ross two days ago, by post.'[81]

To Frank Sargeson Frame wrote on 2 April that she was spending the afternoons 'wandering around the cliffs gazing at the Silurian rocks, the curlews, gulls, ravens; and picking primroses, ladywhites, balm and lesser celandines. I wander for miles on the country roads and don't meet a soul, and every time I glance at the horizon I half expect to see the Southern Alps . . . Oh how I dread the return to Camberwell.'[82]

Two weeks later, when Frame was back in London, Patience Ross summarised for her the publishing programme which her agents had arranged with publishers for the coming year. Braziller and W.H. Allen would publish *The Edge of the Alphabet* in September and November 1962 respectively; Pegasus in February 1963.[83] Carl Brandt was keen for Braziller to then bring out a volume of her new stories in 'spring' 1963, to be followed by *Scented Gardens for the Blind* in 1964. W.H. Allen, however, would publish *Scented Gardens* in mid-1963. In addition, Pegasus had sold French, Italian, Dutch and Spanish rights for *Faces in the Water*. All these commitments brought immediately available income of more than four hundred pounds, with further staggered advances to follow.[84]

This programme showed what Frame had been able to achieve professionally in just under three years of living at Grove Hill Road: the writing of three novels and what would eventually be published as two volumes of 'stories and sketches' and 'fables and fantasies'.[85] Now, because of restrictions imposed on the household by Richard Parry's taking a night-time telephonist's job, which required him to sleep during the day ('no typing or flushing of the lavatory, please');[86] and the continuing volume of television noise in the evenings and weekends, Frame was determined to find new lodgings. She told John Money that, as she had feared, Camberwell had been rendered unbearable by the tranquillity of Cornwall.

I have been looking around ever since for somewhere quiet. I hope that I have found it at last. A fifteenth century thatched cottage in East Suffolk, two miles from the nearest village. Mod. cons. but no electric light — heating by calor gas. An 'Ideal' boiler for heating water . . . I shall pay thirty-five shillings a week (not including lighting, heating, cooking) and in return I am expected to keep the place aired and clean, to look after an aged bitch, to fetch the gardener when the lawn wants cutting.

The owners use the place for holidays and occasional weekends, and I can stay on . . . (I have half of the house for my own use) or can stay in their London flat. They are two women, one a former Australian — employees of the Moorfield's Eye Hospital. I think the arrangement ought to work very well . . . There were many applications for the caretaking and I felt very flattered when I heard they had chosen me. I shall probably come to London about once a month or six weeks to see my doctor at Maudsley.[87]

When she was made aware of how much income was imminent, Frame added, she had an impulse to return to New Zealand, 'to wind up my affairs there'. Then she realised she would not have quite enough money to guarantee her return journey to England. '[But] I really must go some time before I die, which is always going to be tomorrow; death, as you know, is my constant preoccupation.'[88] Instead, though, she moved on 18 May 1962 to the cottage at Braiseworth, near Eye, in East Suffolk.

CHAPTER FIFTEEN

# A Roots Crisis

*F*RAME'S NEW HOME STOOD IN A QUARTER ACRE OF LAWN AND GARDEN among the fields of East Suffolk, two miles from the village of Eye.[1] The owners were there to 'receive' her when she arrived and to instruct her in the ways of the house and her duties as caretaker.

They had prepared a bedroom upstairs below the sloping roof, with a dormer window and dark exposed beams and a view over the fields . . . and the ninety-foot lilac hedge just beginning to bud. Downstairs they had thoughtfully cleared the top of the old sewing machine and arranged a likely place for me to work where, as they said, I could gaze out of the window 'for inspiration', at the ninety-foot lilac hedge. They kept noting its length and describing how it would appear in flower . . . They'd installed hot water, with the Raeburn stove, a flush lavatory, and a bath. Coll, with her special feeling for roses, had planted the rose garden while Will had cleared the paths and repaired the front gate and searched until she found the heavy oak door to replace the too modern glass-panelled door with its frosted picture of a stag beside a mountain. East Suffolk had been the most wonderful discovery of their lives.[2]

The trouble would be, as Frame discovered, that *their* dream was not her dream. Just over a month after establishing herself, Frame was complaining to John Money that, with walking the dog twice a day, weeding the flower garden and putting in a vegetable garden, and having to travel the two miles to the village on an old bicycle for food and mail, there was insufficient time and energy left for writing. 'It would not be so bad if the owners didn't visit every now and again, and if they were not so bald-lawn, house-clean-proud, mark-on-the-wall conscious.'[3]

Even when Frame was on her own with the dog, problems occurred. In

231

July, when she applied weed-killer to the nettles alongside the garden, the
wind carried the spray on to her tomatoes, cabbages and turnips and killed
them. The dog, Betty, went on heat and Frame had to 'keep applying Anti-
Mate to her nether regions, and the cottage stinks of Anti-Mate, enough to
put off any intruder who appears in order to rape me!'[4] And at night, Frame
was surprised to discover that 'for the first time in my life I was living alone in
a house and I was afraid'.[5]

On the rare occasions that she managed to get to the sewing machine desk,
looking out on the fields, she experienced an odd and unexpected sense of
disconnectedness — 'a sensation of falseness, of surface-skimming . . . the
feeling, perhaps, when after writing a letter and sealing it and writing the
address on the envelope one might find that the stamp won't hold, that there's
nothing to glue it to the envelope and no matter how hard one tries, the
stamp keeps coming unstuck . . .'[6]

As the weeks and then months went by, difficulties seemed to multiply.
'The dog follows me everywhere,' Frame eventually exclaimed to John Money.
'I can't make a move without [her] making the same move, it's uncanny . . .
[even] to the lavatory and into the bathroom . . . I came here for isolation and
I've never been so crowded in my life.'[7] And the visiting owners became out
and out ogres. '[Their] first remark on entering is — we'll have to get into the
garden look at those weeds; we must clean up these windows; just look at the
nettles, how high they've grown! And so on . . . [There is] the usual
misunderstanding that people who work at home do not work at all and are
therefore free to carry out all kinds of domestic duties.'[8]

By contrast, Frame looked forward increasingly to the days when she had
her appointments with Bob Cawley in London. 'I woke early, cycled two miles
to the nearest railway station, Mellis, left my bike with the stationmaster, and
caught the train from Norwich . . . Approaching London, I felt the excitement
of coming home, the train gathering speed, the countryside left behind for the
brick oceans, the dirty city, the squalid warehouses and factories of East London
— ah the delight! — and Liverpool Street Station, just in time to step out to
the marching tunes played over the loudspeaker and encouraging the ten
o'clock city workers at a brisk pace.'

Then I'd make my way to Camberwell, to see Dr Cawley . . . And after
we'd had our talk I'd just have time perhaps to browse in Charing Cross
Road or the Strand before I caught the one-thirty train to Ipswich, and
then the bus to Braiseworth. I'd arrive home to be welcomed by [Betty],
and feeling tired and wondering why I was living in the country when it
was the city that attracted me, and wondering where my writing day
had gone . . . I wanted to return [to London] where I was happy to be
alone in the crowd, surrounded and maintained by the immensity of
people.[9]

She persisted for four-and-a-half months, however, and there *were* consolations. Occasionally she did get some writing done, some verse and work on a projected new novel, 'Letter to a Sculptor', a spin-off from the abandoned 'Uncle Pylades'. Such days were all the more precious for being rare. Once she took a whole day off all chores just to reread Longfellow's poems. '[It] makes me weep to think that writers go so much in and out of fashion, and so few people care about the musty red-bound books on the bottom shelves of the libraries . . . I'd ban the publication of more books until we've learned to read and respect those already written.'[10]

And, digging in the garden one day, 'I found a piece of stone which seemed to have been shaped by human hands. I found several which seemed to be tools, and . . . what I imagine is a ring worn by a Roman woman . . . It is possible that I have unearthed a few antiquities . . . [The] old Roman road which is the present Ipswich–Norwich road is at the end of the lane.'[11] The ring turned out to be of the variety that held up curtains; and the cottage owners reprimanded her for digging ground beyond the designated garden.[12]

Despite her inability to establish a continuous writing routine, and despite the fact that she would complete no more new work for publication before she left England the following year, Frame's career seemed to continue on its own momentum. A.M. Heath wrote to say that they had at last sold one of her stories, 'Royal Icing', to a magazine in Britain, *Harper's Bazaar*, for thirty guineas.[13] A highly complimentary letter arrived from Robert Hemenway of *The New Yorker*, telling her how much he admired 'The Reservoir', which the magazine was to publish in January 1963.[14] And in July 1962, Frame signed her first agreement with Pegasus (for *The Edge of the Alphabet*) that would restrict their publisher's licence to New Zealand and Australia.[15] At about the same time Frame asked that her share of money for foreign sales of earlier work be paid to her directly from Europe and the United States rather than being sent to New Zealand first and then remitted back to her in England with con-sequent exchange rate losses and delays.[16]

There were further surprises. Peter Dawson, now in England, sent a letter announcing that she would soon be living in a 'tiny cottage' at Itteringham Common in Norfolk, the county immediately north of Suffolk; and that, as soon as she was settled, she hoped Frame would come and stay with her.[17] June Gordon wrote from New Zealand with news that she had sent a manu-script of her own to Pegasus, for a potential volume of poetry; and that Pamela Gordon had so completely recovered from heart surgery that she had passed her grade one ballet examination with honours. What June did not tell Frame, however, was that their brother, Geordie, had been arrested. This latter episode had begun with a dispute between Geordie and his father over who would be hosting June on a visit to Oamaru. He had threatened to shoot his sister and then himself.[18] George Frame had called the police, who had disarmed and arrested Geordie. In the subsequent court case he was convicted, fined and placed on probation for being in possession of unregistered firearms and presenting a loaded firearm at another person. The charges — and the consequences — could have been far more serious.

Perhaps the most surprising letter of all, however, came from W.H. Allen. Frame had never met her English publisher Mark Goulden, though she had visited the company office and spoken with her editor there, Goulden's stepson Jeffrey Simmons. Now, early in August 1962, Goulden himself wrote and asked her to come to London 'to exchange views . . . about your future writing plans'. He had a proposition he wished to put to her; if she would make the journey, the company would meet her expenses.[19]

Frame went to London the following week and arrived at 43 Essex Street, off the Strand, far too early for her appointment. She was forced to loiter in the neighbourhood until it was time to be ushered into the presence of her publisher.

Mark Goulden's office was suitably booklined with windows facing the street; a thick carpet, and a large desk where Mark Goulden sat while I sat in the deep easy chair and thought, so this is my English publisher. I thought he looked like a bookie or a 'spiv', a small grey-haired wiry man with a 'weathered' face. A gambler–publisher. His voice was rich, musical, his eyes quick, lively. He said that although my books had excellent reviews, they did not sell: he was hoping that some day I would write a 'bestseller'.

He then began to reminisce while I listened fascinated as he referred to [a] controversy over who had 'discovered' Dylan Thomas, and the recent published statement by Edith Sitwell supporting Mark Goulden's claim that *he* had discovered Dylan Thomas. . . I listened enthralled by his charm and his power as a raconteur. He was evidently a joyful man, delighting in himself and others.[20]

Not as joyful on this occasion as Frame believed, however. Goulden has left his own account of the meeting, and of what prompted his talkativeness:

[We] faced each other across my desk. What I perceived was a plumpish, rosy-cheeked, demure young woman, indifferently dressed, and bearing unmistakably that scrubbed, carbolic look which is the hallmark of people who have lived in institutions . . . [It] turned out to be as trying a half hour as I can ever recall. I opened the conversation gambit as brightly as possible but after ten minutes, I realised this was decidedly a one-way dialogue — my visitor hadn't uttered a word or batted an eyelid. Nor did she break her silence during the next ten minutes, by which time I had completely run out of conversational steam . . .

Unable to endure this ordeal by silence any longer, I am afraid I blew my top. 'Look here, Miss Frame,' I almost shouted, 'I've been talking to you for nearly half an hour and you haven't said a damned word. If you're not interested in what I'm trying to say about you and your work, please don't waste any more of my time,' with which admonition I moved towards the door.

But suddenly she unfroze and smiled. 'I have heard every word you have said,' she announced in a firm voice that had distinct Colonial overtones. 'And,' she continued, 'I agree and accept all your excellent advice.' With that the whole ambience changed. Here, it soon emerged, was a woman who was not only a gifted novelist but an articulate speaker with a perfect delivery. I rang for the coffee and sandwiches and from thereon we chatted amiably during which I got the drift of her own astonishing life story.[21]

The respective accounts of author and publisher agree that Goulden then made Frame an offer. 'I would install her in a furnished flat for which the company would pay all expenses, and there she could get on with her writing, unworried by financial or any other obligations. One condition I imposed: as she had already written novels dealing with mental disturbance, she must now concentrate on an entirely different theme.'[22]

It was not quite this straightforward. As Goulden explained in a letter to Albion Wright on 21 August, the cost of putting Frame up in the manner to which she was not accustomed would be about six hundred and fifty-five pounds a year. 'It is my suggestion that George Braziller . . . and we should bear five hundred pounds of this cost and that you, as her New Zealand publisher, should contribute the balance of one hundred and fifty-five pounds. All these payments would be in the nature of loans to be deducted in due course from the royalty earnings on Miss Frame's work. Naturally, each of the publishers concerned would have an option on the future work of Miss Frame covering a period of five years so that the outlay could be amortised over a period without undue strain on the author's earnings.'[23]

Pegasus Press agreed to contribute up to one hundred pounds; and George Braziller accepted an agreement to take Frame's next four books — *Scented Gardens for the Blind*, two books of stories and a subsequent novel, which would turn out to be *The Adaptable Man* — for an advance of $US3000, part of which would go towards the payment of the lease arranged by Mark Goulden, and the rest paid out in staggered instalments over two years. But not everybody associated with Frame was enthusiastic about Goulden's Svengali-like manipulations. Patience Ross thought the idea that Frame would write a 'cheerful book' if she lived in a 'cheerful place' simply idiotic; and George Braziller believed that Frame was being 'set up' in the flat so as to become Mark Goulden's mistress.[24] Carl Brandt told John Money that Goulden had even suggested that Frame's psychiatric care, particularly her visits to Bob Cawley, was responsible for what he regarded as her morbid state of mind.[25]

Frame, however, knowing nothing of these contrary currents of opinion among her professional advisers, reported to Frank Sargeson on 25 August that the previous fortnight had been a series of 'whirlwind episodes': the visit to London, the suggestion of the apartment, her agreement to accept 'a certain amount of publicity' to promote her books, then the finding by Mark Goulden's wife, Jane, of a suitable apartment to lease.[26] After another trip to London to inspect the property, which was in Brechin Place, South Kensington, an L-shaped road to the south and west of Hereford Square, Frame accepted the proposition.

'It is a charming little . . . basement flat,' she told John Money, 'but very light, with a double bedroom, a bathroom and w.c., a sitting-room, and a kitchen and a little entrance hall where the . . . two telephones are — one for outside calls and one for answering the door. The place has hot water (a miracle in England) and all such conveniences . . . [It] appears luxurious to me because it is so long since I lived where hot water, baths and a lavatory [are] not shared with four floors of people.' The one-year lease would be paid by W.H. Allen, and 'I shall be paying as much for electricity and telephone as I normally pay in rent'.[27]

She would move in on 24 October, after leaving East Suffolk on 29 September and spending the intervening weeks with Peter Dawson in Norfolk. Now that she *was* abandoning the cottage, Frame characteristically found grounds for regret. 'I shall be sorry to leave the countryside, particularly now when it's going into rehearsal for Death and the script says Ominous Silence above Cornfields, Migrating Birds Gather, Rats Venture in the Dwelling-House, Pipes Prepare to Freeze.'[28]

In fact the three weeks with Peter Dawson postponed the need to grieve for the loss of a country landscape. Norfolk, Frame told Audrey Scrivener, was abundantly and fruitfully rural. 'There was a massive harvest . . . stacks and stacks of beautiful hay and straw and sugar beet; and the grazing cattle look fat and happy, so do the pigs.'[29] Dawson's semi-detached house, Flint Cottage, was one-half of a double unit whose exterior walls were plastered and inset with local stone. It stood in fields and was partially surrounded by an ample flower and vegetable garden. The only drawback was a poultry farm over the road, owned by a family named Fowell, which smelled and was the cause of noisy trucks coming and going several times a day.

The two women got on well together, rekindling the relationship they had established at Mount Maunganui with its mother–daughter overtones. They talked easily of literary matters and felt a blessed absence of any need to 'explain' themselves to each other.[30] Frame helped Dawson unpack and settle into the cottage; and then they visited the older woman's sisters at Great Yarmouth and Winterton. From Winterton they cycled up through the Broads, following the Bure, to Aylsham and on to Itteringham Common.

Here too was a further surprise. George Braziller, Frame's American publisher, sent a telegram to say that he was coming to visit and arrived at the cottage one evening bearing a bunch of flowers. He had been keen to meet Frame and, while visiting London, tracked her whereabouts through W.H. Allen and A.M. Heath. Then he took a train to Norwich and a taxi to Itteringham. While Frame, burdened with stereotypic views of a New York businessman, took refuge in the kitchen, Dawson talked with Braziller and found him gentlemanly attentive and charming. At last Frame emerged and was introduced. She and Dawson subsequently disagreed over whether Braziller said, 'I love this kind of night' or, 'it's a lover's kind of night'; whichever it was, Frame allowed herself to be taken out to dinner.[31]

In the taxi, Braziller revealed himself to be an incurable romantic. As they drove past a malodorous pig farm and Frame told him what it was and prepared to commiserate, the American, brought up in the Bronx and a long-time resident of Manhattan, took a deep breath and said, 'I just love that smell'. They both wrestled with shyness until they had drunk wine with dinner at a Norwich restaurant, when their inhibitions fell away and they talked easily. Then they walked through the old part of town where ancient stone buildings glistened with nocturnal damp, before Braziller returned her safely to Flint Cottage.

His subsequent letter to Frame was as exultant as that of a man in love. 'I have gone over in my mind a dozen times my visit to you . . . The contents of *your* letter had me reeling for two days — the perception, the humour, the strength . . . Remember you have a standing invitation to come to America at any time, and could I hear from you whenever you felt like writing.'[32] Frame told Dawson that the more she thought about the encounter, the more she warmed to Braziller. 'I suppose his visit has taken on the quality of a dream; it will be in my mind always [mixed] with Flint Cottage, the pigs, the sugar beet [and] the blackberries.' The two were staunch friends from this time; and Braziller reinforced in his sense of mission to bring Frame to American readers.

Frame arrived at the Kensington flat in the last week in October 1962 to be greeted by a huge bowl of live flowers — ten varieties — as a house-warming gift from the Gouldens. She was appreciative, but could not help thinking of the cost. She told John Money that she expected to settle in quickly, 'and soon I shall be working again, for the atmosphere is most congenial — very private, quiet, without landlady [or] lodger worries, but of course with the usual existence worries, which make it necessary to write . . . But I can get up when I like and go to bed when I like.'[33] She soon discovered she was now 'somebody'. 'A miracle seemed to occur in libraries, museums, shops as soon as I gave my address: I was treated with kindness, I was offered credit; and could they call me a taxi? The tendency to questioning and suspicion by the keepers of Camberwell had vanished.'[34]

One of her immediate 'existence worries' concerned Bob Cawley. Her Maudsley doctor, who she now discovered had been living in Kensington no more than one hundred yards from her new address, had been appointed to a senior lectureship in psychiatry at the University of Birmingham. She would be able to continue consultations with him, for he would commute to London several times a month; but not with the same frequency. 'He was an enormous stabilising influence when I was seeing him twice a week,' Frame told Peter Dawson, 'and I could get on with my work.' She hoped that the new dispensation 'will be enough to settle me into some kind of calm; otherwise I really shall have to "end our acquaintance" . . . It [has been] such a perfect relationship — the advantages of a friend without the turmoil of being too close. Here's hoping . . .'[35]

Another source of immediate anxiety was that Mark Goulden had set up an appointment for the *Guardian* to interview Frame — about her work in general (this was a quid pro quo for the provision of the flat); and about *The Edge of the Alphabet*, which had been published in the United States in September and was appearing in the United Kingdom in November 1962. As with all such encounters Frame dreaded the meeting and what she expected would be some kind of interrogation.

In the event she enjoyed it. Geoffrey Moorhouse was then thirty years old and chief feature writer for the *Guardian*. He had lived and worked in New Zealand and married a woman from Christchurch. Frame found him 'awfully nice and intellectual and intelligent and handsome . . . and he has invited me to stay with them [in Stockport] whenever I feel like it'.[36] Moorhouse would remember 'a short woman with frizzy hair, painfully shy and very quietly spoken, who smiled a lot to fill in pauses between speech, which could be quite disconcerting . . .'[37]

In his feature, headlined 'Out of New Zealand', he made reference to recent novels by Sylvia Ashton-Warner, Noel Hilliard and Ian Cross.[38] Then he went on to say that no literary development had been more exciting than the arrival of Janet Frame. 'She has already been compared freely to Katherine Mansfield . . . But in technique, range of experience, and sense of direction they are so completely unlike each other that any attempt at comparison here is futile.' Frame, he said, had been concerned to interpret the state of Outsiders and to identify with them in a way that Mansfield had never done.

Frame also differed from other New Zealand writers, Moorhouse continued, by not straining 'to identify herself with her locality. The self-conscious writers' atmospheric props — clapboard houses with red tin roofs, kowhai and manuka always someplace in the background, are missing . . . Janet Frame is a refugee from a personal condition which could have occurred in Wellington, West Bromwich or Washington.' And her two most recent books 'are terrible statements of a human situation which shed more light on dark corners than a whole sheaf of social surveys'.[39]

None of which Frame took issue with. She had more difficulty, though, with a review of *The Edge of the Alphabet* which appeared in *Time* magazine in late October and which, she told Peter Dawson, 'some oaf sent me'.[40] This declared that the book's title had a 'properly demented ring . . . because novelist Frame, in both fact and fiction, has spent some time in asylums'. It went on to say that the narrative 'occasionally bogs down in unintelligibility [and] often seems tainted by abnormal morbidity'. As in her earlier books, however, Frame 'writes with power and makes the dismal fumblings of her creatures seem touching'.[41] Other notices expressed similar views, including that by William Wiegard in the *New York Times Book Review* which said that Frame was 'possessed by death, madness, loneliness and pain';[42] and one by William Smith in *Commonweal*, which characterised the book as 'so profoundly melancholy that it was painful to read [and] is not for the suggestible'.[43]

Critical reception of the British edition was on the whole more favourable and the book was 'specially recommended' there by the Book Society prior to publication. As on previous occasions, Dan Davin in the *Times Literary Supplement* voiced the highest praise. 'The narrative is beautifully economical and told in a mixture of realism and fantasy, through interior monologue and flights of brilliant description.'[44] Neal Ascherson in the *New Statesman* wrote that *Edge's* 'main characters are those whom the world considers a bit half-baked and embarrassing [but] Frame does not treat them sentimentally, and the experience of their slow undramatic defeat is moving'.[45] Several reviewers unwittingly commented on characters that had some relationship to 'real' people: Toby (Geordie Frame) with his commissionaire's work and street-sweeping job and determination to write a book; the bus driver Pat Keenan (Patrick Reilly), obsessed with fears about 'foreigners and blacks' and too troubled by his relationship with the Blessed Virgin to get married; the landlady Ma Crane (Ma Bagatti in Clapham Common South); and the cinema manager Mr Beanman (Mr Holman of the Regal in Streatham).

The *TLS* review concluded with two observations that had not been made elsewhere: 'Miss Frame tends to take out her resentments on those who can find their way about easily in our urban world'; and '[she] is now, we must assume, an expatriate. In this novel she has successfully fused her experience of two worlds and made them one.'[46] This last comment, at least in respect of her own life, was premature: but it raised issues to which she would be giving increasing thought in the coming year.

Unexpectedly, given Geoffrey Moorhouse's words of praise for her work, the *Guardian* review described *The Edge of the Alphabet* as 'unreadable in the worst sense'.[47] Concerned that Frame might be made dejected by this comment, Moorhouse sent her a note of commiseration and reminded her that James Joyce and William Faulkner were both 'not understood' when their books first appeared. By way of consolation he invited her to spend Christmas with him and his family in Stockport. Frame declined, but promised to visit in the New Year.[48]

There were other distractions that inhibited Frame from getting down to 'serious' work in November 1962. She had Mildred Surry to dinner to show off her new accommodation. A fire in a next-door flat was responsible for the death of an elderly baroness; another neighbour, 'around the corner', shot his former fiancée and her father; and a distraught woman spent a whole night weeping outside one of Frame's street windows.[49] Then she accepted an invitation to visit a New Zealand woman, who was a former journalist, and her Scandinavian art dealer husband in their 'sumptuous (Picassos, Braques, Chagalls on their walls) Mayfair flat. They are intelligent, interesting people, although I thought the woman was slightly predatory — the result of life in Fleet Street . . . I was dumb and scared but bold enough to say No to an invitation to dinner . . . for these things can only be taken in small doses.' Repeating this story to John Money, and emphasising how exhausted she had been by this encounter, she exclaimed: 'My God, doesn't one pay for *everything!*'[50]

The consequence of what seemed like a stream of interruptions, the shock of discovering that she owed the British inland revenue service five years of unpaid taxes, and her initial inability to see Bob Cawley with any degree of regularity (he had succumbed to jaundice several weeks after moving to Birmingham) — all these factors contributed to a familiar but dreaded tide of anxiety and depression. And on 1 December 1962, three-and-a-half years after her discharge from hospital, Frame was again admitted to the Maudsley as a voluntary patient.

What had contributed to the rising sense of panic, she told Peter Dawson, was the fact that when she told hospital staff that she had an appointment with Dr Cawley the following Monday, they had viewed this as a symptom of insanity and assured her that Cawley no longer worked there.[51] He duly turned up, however, and confirmed her admission on the ground that she needed a period in which to calm down.[52] She remained there for three weeks and was discharged on 21 December, since she and her doctor thought it inadvisable to be in hospital over Christmas — 'hospital celebrations can be rather depressing, having the opposite effect of their intention'.[53] Instead, she spent Christmas in the flat on her own, 'eating bread and cheese, drinking coffee and turning the clock back three hundred years by reading Samuel Pepys, to find out how things were going with him. . .'[54]

The tax arrears were sorted out by an accountant recommended by the Society of Authors ('an elderly white-haired lavender and lace lady,' Frame told Peter Dawson).[55] She had earned so little over the period and could claim deductions for work-related expenses, so that the money owing was able to be paid from her relatively healthy savings account (in effect, the money she had put aside from the sale of her two stories to *The New Yorker*).

In the excessive cold that followed New Year 1963, Frame, wrapped in a shawl, with a hotwater bottle under a rug over her knees, began work in earnest on a new manuscript which would become *The Adaptable Man*. This had its genesis in a visit the previous year to a dentist in Camberwell.

> His consulting room looked so old and everything was frayed, and the tap was dripping in the little bowl, and it looked very sad . . . There were two things he said. He went over to the window and drew the curtain aside (it was spring) and said, 'What wouldn't I give to be in Sussex today.' He said it with such longing. And when somebody called downstairs, he said, 'Rinse whilst I'm gone' . . . It seemed like something out of the past. And so I wrote about a dentist . . . I wrote the book around him as I imagined him . . . [I] quite enjoy imagining lives for people whom I see only once or twice and don't know.[56]

The narrative of this book would also be saturated in her East Suffolk experience, its village of Little Burgelstatham owing a good deal to Frame's contact with Eye, near Braiseworth.

That same month, January, Frame read a manuscript that had been sent to her by Lady Constance Malleson, daughter of the fifth Earl of Annesley, who was better known as the actress Colette O'Niel and longtime mistress of Bertrand Russell. Her first letter to Frame, written in November 1962, had arrived the week before she returned to the Maudsley and around the same time as correspondence from two former mental hospital patients who had read and identified closely with experiences described in *Faces in the Water*.[57] Lady Constance was *not* an ex-patient. But she had known a woman named Joan Sturges, who had been committed to an English hospital in 1933 and underwent a leucotomy in the early 1950s. She had died in 1954, but left a manuscript of a novel which thinly fictionalised her hospital experience in much the same way as Frame had done in *Faces*.

'She had a good brain, a good education, and she was not entirely without money,' Malleson said of Joan Sturges in the course of describing the manuscript and the circumstances of its composition. '[Also] an extremely good sense of humour, and her skill was not only for writing but also for drawing, weaving, and crafts of several kind; nevertheless she had a terrible life and suffered deeply. Her nature was a poet's, but she also had a downright honesty which the world finds so difficult to put up with . . . Please will you say a curt yes or no as to whether you might ever be interested in making something of all this material? The financial profits would be entirely your own.'[58]

This, of course, was not the kind of project for which Frame's publishers were putting her up in a South Kensington flat; indeed it was the very kind of book with which Mark Goulden wished her to have nothing more to do. But nor was Constance Malleson's appeal the kind that Frame could easily resist. She wrote back to Lady Constance to say that she had been affected by her letter, 'because it recounts a story that is only too sadly familiar. If there is a work of literary or artistic value I think there is perhaps a moral duty to have it arranged and submitted for publication . . . [These] writings could be of tremendous help to others — to people who are suffering or have suffered in this way, and to those who are trying to help them.'[59] She asked to see the manuscript, and she read it in the New Year. On 27 January 1964 she wrote back to Lady Constance:

> I have been deeply moved by ['Trespassers on Earth'] . . . because I know from experience the truth of her descriptions both of the conditions that have prevailed in mental hospitals, and of the feelings of the bewildered patients . . . a tragic international language which gave those who learned it an extension of the vocabulary of suffering — at too high a price . . . [Much] of the writing is on the level of poetry; the characters, even the minor ones, are vividly and accurately observed; the landscape has a special place as one of the minor characters . . . I cannot tell you how much I have valued the privilege of sharing part of this woman's life-story . . . I should like to see the book published.[60]

Frame's interest in the manuscript was heightened by the fact that Joan Sturges, like Audrey Scrivener, had had the dreaded brain operation, with some of the same consequences. Further, her case had been taken up in the 1930s by a campaign for mental health reform led by Constance Malleson, Bertrand Russell, Havelock Ellis and H.G. Wells. The American writer Kay Boyle had encouraged Sturges to write. And Lady Constance's sister, Mabel Annesley, a famous wood engraver, had lived out the final years of her life in Takaka, at the northern end of the South Island of New Zealand.

When Lady Constance replied to Frame's letter she asked if, in view of the writer's favourable response to the manuscript, she would 'tighten it up, add an introduction of your own and persuade your publisher to take [it]?' In addition, she offered Frame her cottage in Lavenham, Suffolk, rent-free, from May to October. 'It's rather shabby, rather crumbling [but has] PLENTY of books.'[61] Frame agreed to edit the manuscript; but said she was currently busy on her own book, which she hoped to finish in the summer. 'I shan't be free until July to write an introduction and type the work [but] once I begin I shall have it done quite quickly.' She declined the offer of the cottage — not on the ground that she had recently had such a cottage; but because the lease on the South Kensington flat would run till October. And she rejected the idea that she should take any income from the resulting book. 'I'd be happier if any profits were used to help those still suffering as Joan suffered.'[62]

Another who wrote to Frame at this time as a result of reading her books, in this instance *Owls Do Cry* and *The Edge of the Alphabet*, was the Australian novelist Patrick White. He told his American publisher Ben Huebsch of Viking Press in February 1963 that *Owls Do Cry* 'makes me feel I have always been a couple of steps out from where I wanted to get in my own writing'. Ironically, in view of Geordie Frame's firearm conviction the previous year and his association with Toby Withers of *Edge*, White went on to say that the Withers family revealed a characteristic 'despair and confusion under the simple, uncomplicated New Zealand surface. I shouldn't be surprised if any New Zealander took a gun to his neighbour. Guns are to New Zealanders what axes are to Poles.'[63] The following month White told his friends Geoffrey and Ninette Dutton that he had also read *Edge* and had been 'knocked sideways. [Frame] strikes me as really doing something that nobody else has done.' Her time in mental hospitals, he said, 'has probably given her just that extra insight to burrow further than any of us'.[64]

White's letter to Frame, also written after he had read *The Edge of the Alphabet*, appears not to have survived. But she referred to it in her correspondence that year, telling Constance Malleson that it was 'so wonderful and unselfish, particularly from one writer to another, that I've not been able to answer it'. For his part, White told a correspondent two decades later that he did not write fan letters, 'except once to that great writer Janet Frame from whom, rightly, I didn't receive an answer'.[65] Frame *did* reply, but not until 22 years had elapsed and White had won the Nobel Prize for Literature.[66]

Early in February Frame made the postponed visit by train to Lancashire to stay a weekend with Geoffrey Moorhouse (whose own first book, *The Other England*, would appear later in the year), his wife, Janet, and their two children. She told Peter Dawson that they were 'a marvellous family . . . how drab my flat seems after their Spartan house toppling with things that really *matter* — books, books, books; serenity; gentleness; she is a NZ girl, former secondary teacher . . . [He] an expert on New Zealand affairs and New Zealand is his passion . . . Their two little children are beautiful, just like little Borrowers.'[67] Before she left Stockport, Geoffrey Moorhouse asked Frame to join the family on their summer holiday in the north-west of Scotland which, he said, was 'just like the West Coast of New Zealand'.[68]

To Frame's surprise, this taste of family life, with its strong flavour of New Zealand, provoked what she told John Money was a 'roots crisis':

[To] spend a weekend having repeated, strong, undiluted doses of New Zealand has almost put me off my balance. I sit here . . . dreaming of snowgrass and snowberries and tussock . . . of the Southern Alps, and of rivers — where's the Rakaia, the Waitaki, the Maheno? Good God, I've kept asking myself, what am I doing on this side of the world? If I don't get back to New Zealand I'll die, or, which is equivalent to death, my writing will get worse and worse . . .

I have gone to the Shipping Companies for brochures, worked out costs etc. I do this one day. The next day I remember that a doctor advised me never again to travel by sea . . . I remember [too] that the sight of what is left of my family might be too much to bear; I remember that I haven't enough money to visit New Zealand, stay for six months, return here and keep myself for at least a year before I settle to work again. I've even thought of applying for one of those New Zealand scholarships in letters, but I don't know if I would be eligible or worthy . . .[69]

Astonishingly, the very morning she posted this letter Frame received one from the New Zealand Literary Fund inviting her to apply for assistance for future writing projects.[70] She did so at once, and received a further communication telling her that her letter would be treated as an application for the fund's annual scholarship in letters, worth one thousand pounds; but if that was unsuccessful it would be treated as an application for an ordinary grant to writers, worth two hundred and fifty to three hundred pounds.[71]

She also went to a travel agent in Haymarket and booked and paid a deposit on a sea passage to New Zealand in January 1964, opting for a single cabin with bathroom facilities which, while more expensive, would enable her to cope better with the expected onslaught of seasickness. At the same time she made tentative reservations for a return trip to England in September or October 1964.[72] 'I care very much for the NZ scene,' she told Constance Malleson, 'but human gentleness means more to me than glaciers, and I've found gentleness here.'[73]

If she needed further evidence of an apparent telepathy at work in all this activity, it came in mid-March 1963 with the news that the remnants of her family, of whom she had been thinking so concernedly since her visit to the Moorhouses, were wrestling with yet another series of crises. During the last week in January, Geordie Frame had arrived unannounced to stay at the Gordons' house in Northcote, Auckland. He was suffering from untreated head injuries caused by falling off and then being kicked by a horse. Not long afterwards June Gordon, severely strained by the effect of the appearance of her brother so soon after the firearms incident, collapsed with a brain haemorrhage. She was only thirty-four years old. Then Geordie too collapsed, and also had to be rushed to hospital by ambulance. For a period brother and sister both lay in separate wards in Auckland Hospital. June was in a coma and was at first not expected to recover. Even when she regained consciousness after a week, Wilson Gordon was told that it was possible that she could remain in a vegetative state.[74]

For the next six weeks, Frame told John Money, her sister had been 'out of her mind'; but then she continued to recover slowly, until eventually there were no visible after-effects. 'Of course the affair revived my memories of the tragedies affecting my other sisters, and brought the anxiety that perhaps her illness may recur, as it is rather unusual in one so young. I began to worry about my . . . visit to NZ early next year — whether the excitement may upset her again, whether I may find her to be "herself" . . . ; and to be more and more aware that she is the only one left in the family with whom I have some means of communication, and with whom I may share memories.'[75]

She was now more than ever worried too about the plight of her brother. 'I cursed my mother (though what else could she have done?) for devoting her whole life to my brother. Since she died he has become gradually more ill, depressed, reckless, violent; and now the alcoholic that he was when I was in my teens . . . The Frames have this intense creative urge, which very easily becomes destructive — he has no outlet for himself.'[76]

The 'roots crisis' and bad news from home had brought Frame's work on *The Adaptable Man* to a halt. She estimated that this novel was about 'half-finished' by mid-March.[77] Now, drenched in the preoccupations triggered by the weekend with the Moorhouses, she began to write something altogether different: a short novel she called 'Towards Another Summer', on the theme of migration. In it she quoted and extrapolated on the poem of Charles Brasch that begins

> Always, in these islands, meeting and parting
> Shake us, making tremulous the salt-rimmed air

and ends:

> Everywhere in light and calm the murmuring
> Shadow of departure; distance looks our way;
> And none knows where he will lie down at night.[78]

This piece of work, which Frame finished in May, was never offered for publication. Later she would call it 'embarrassingly personal'. It was put away with other unpublished — and, she believed, unpublishable — manuscripts.

There was further dismaying news from New Zealand. Copies of *The Edge of the Alphabet*, printed in England, had been shipped there too late for the Christmas market, so its release was held over until March 1963.[79] This seemed to be yet another reach of the arm of coincidence: it meant that the book based so closely on Geordie Frame's personal history and difficulties appeared in New Zealand within weeks of his hospitalisation and his sister's stroke.

The book's reception there was less comprehending and less complimentary than responses to the earlier novels. Even David Hall, one of the few reviewers who had not been enthusiastic about *Owls* and *Faces*, now announced that they were superior in accomplishment to this latest offering. 'The prodigal displays of "writing" cannot altogether compensate for the book's emptiness. It has not the spontaneity of its first predecessor, or the art of the second,' he wrote in the *Listener*.[80] And Thomas Crawford in *Landfall* said that the novel's 'wisdom appears pretentious, and the compassion too often like condescension:

a sad falling off from *Owls Do Cry'*. He believed, nonetheless, that the book's virtues outweighed the flaws. 'When [Frame] keeps her eye on the object, she can do better than the realists. She is also a wonderful craftsman — mistress of pedal and keyboard, princess of the arpeggios and cadenzas of prose; and she has a nice sense of humour.'[81]

By the end of March 1963 Frame had made another decision about her future: when she returned to England from her New Zealand visit in 1964, she would live with Peter Dawson in Norfolk. Dawson had proposed this, and Frame warmed to the idea. She had already told the older woman that the quality of her life in England had improved immeasurably since Dawson's return, that it was 'wonderful to have someone in this country whom I really *know'*.[82] Up to this time, the balance of advantage had rested with her decision to remain in England; but the decision retained a quality of hollowness by virtue of the absence of close friendship and a place of her own in which to live. She treasured the letters she received from friends outside England, Frame told Dawson, because she had such little firsthand communication with people inside the country.[83] Now Dawson, with her palpable concern for Frame's well-being, her bookishness and her shared reference points derived from both England and New Zealand, had filled the remaining vacuum. And for Dawson herself, the notion of intensifying companionship with Frame and having somebody trustworthy close by as she aged — these had been among the factors considered in her decision to return to England.

After a visit to Flint Cottage which clinched the arrangement, Frame wrote to Dawson from Brechin Place:

> I am 'impossible to live with' for any length of time; by that I mean that there are days when I prefer to be entirely by myself . . . I am [also] rather timid about practical matters such as pouring coffee making tea etc. in the presence of another person . . . I think the answer to this problem would be a caravan . . . in your back garden . . . Then we could both have the advantanges of aloneness and of company, going on expeditions etc., having someone to talk to and share ideas with. I could help with the garden & other things & if any visitors came to you I shouldn't be in the way . . . [If] you get tired of my being in your garden I can always tow myself away . . . [How] I look forward to a simpler life. The flat is oppressive, too many levels above necessity.[84]

There was a need, nonetheless, to propitiate her current benefactors. In the middle of April Frame accepted an invitation to afternoon tea in Mayfair with Jane Goulden, who had made the arrangements for the lease of her flat. The fellow guests were Alan Sillitoe and his wife, the poet Ruth Fainlight. Sillitoe, in the wake of his novel *Saturday Night and Sunday Morning* (1958) and his collection of stories *The Loneliness of the Long Distance Runner* (1959) was W.H. Allen's star author. It was Ruth Fainlight, however, who had requested the gathering. She had read Frame's first three novels, admired them, and was still (she said many years later) 'naive enough to want to meet their author'.[85] Mrs Goulden provided an occasion on which such a meeting could take place. 'As usual,' Frame reported to Peter Dawson, 'things went wrong. I was caught in the rain & arrived soaking wet while everyone else was so *dry*.' She was also red-faced and full-bladdered.

I took the lift to the top floor, rang the bell, and was admitted by Mrs Goulden, tall, dark, regal (with a remarkable resemblance, I thought, to the Queen of Spades in the film I had lately seen, *The Manchurian Candidate*). She wore black and had an air of having lived inside her skin as if it were a house, polished, prepared daily, with herself as the mistress in total possession. She was not an immediate person; there was a porch, an entrance hall where one waited to be received. She introduced me to Alan and Ruth Sillitoe . . .

[There] was consternation that my clothes and shoes were saturated. Mrs Goulden took me to a bedroom where she found dry clothes and shoes for me to wear while mine dried, and so I began my visit wearing a tight-fitting dress and black evening shoes with gold borders, peep toes and two-inch heels.

Presently Mrs Goulden rang a silver bell and a servant, a darkhaired buxom woman named Columba, appeared with the afternoon tea and when she had left the room, Mrs Goulden explained that Columba had been brought from Portugal and spoke little English. This caused excitement between the Sillitoes . . . who had been living in Morocco and had brought a servant home with them, they said, but when they arrived in England, they discovered they had purchased and paid for her as if she were a slave . . . I listened, quietly amazed, while Mrs Goulden and the Sillitoes ranged from the servant problem to the *au pair* and back to the servant problem; there in the Mayfair apartment with its Persian rugs, Turkish cats, exquisite paintings, dark knobbly furniture.

I had little to say. I smiled a lot and said, 'Yes, yes.' My evening shoes were pinching. And when the time came to leave and I changed into my dry clothes and shoes, Mrs Goulden parcelled up the black dress and evening shoes. 'You're welcome to keep them,' she said.[86]

The Sillitoes' view of this occasion was, understandably, rather different. Ruth Fainlight recalled that Mrs Goulden's sitting room was 'as alien to me as it was to J.F.'

I found it impossible to engage Janet in any conversation about her books [or] literature in general . . . I felt awkward enough myself. In that situation, my first impression of her was of a surly and truculent individual. Nor did I have the necessary social skill and self-confidence to divert the direction of Mrs Goulden's amiable chatter . . . I have to feel sorry for Mrs Goulden also, being presented with two such awkward young women. She had kindly set up this meeting, and cannot be held responsible for its total lack of success . . . J.F. had obviously decided immediately that I was exactly the same kind of person as Mrs Goulden, and despised us equally.[87]

Throughout April and May 1963 Frame continued work on 'Towards Another Summer'; and, as occasional relief from this, on editing and re-typing Joan Sturges's novel 'Trespassers on Earth'. She had been so busy, she told Constance Malleson, that 'my typewriter is wearing out; the keys have become quite vicious — they are biting into the paper [and] I have tiny stencilled o's and a's and n's lying on my table'.[88] Parts of the Sturges manuscript were in poor condition because, as Constance Malleson explained, a water pipe had burst over it the previous winter and the resulting flood had frozen both the manuscript and the books that surrounded it. The papers had had to be chipped out and thawed.[89] Frame finished this job in mid-May, and then showed the new typescript to Patience Ross, who believed it was publishable. But the agent worried that, even with Joan Sturges's name attached, the fact that it might be published with an introduction by Frame would lead people to believe that it was in fact another Frame novel about insanity.[90]

Planning for her eventual re-establishment in Norfolk, Frame began to inquire about bicycle and caravan prices, and about such fixtures as heaters and cookers. 'I've gone a bit crazy, you know,' she told Dawson. 'This caravan is working out to be pricey, and I'm appalled by the fact that I can afford it.'[91] Indeed she could, and she bought a small model, which was delivered to Itteringham Common in mid-June, when Frame was again visiting. The two women then spent weeks debating by letter exactly where on the property the caravan should sit, and at what angle to the cottage. Frame also began to pack up books and papers into suitcases and a trunk for eventual delivery to Dawson for safekeeping. She had far too many possessions of this kind, she said, 'chiefly because the complications of noisy London induce a kind of frenzy that makes it difficult to think'.[92] Letters were in a different category, however, because 'they are communications to me from other people . . . My regret is that when I'm an old lady living in my witch-cottage in Suffolk (if I'm not a suicide buried in unhallowed ground in South London) I shan't have any love letters to turn over and enjoy: it's a loss to me that no one has ever written

"My Darling" . . . the only man who has ever placed a ring on my finger is one who did not know how to read or write!'[93]

Over this period Frame was focussing her attention increasingly on Norfolk rather than London. Since buying the caravan, she told John Money, 'I've felt much more settled, as I now have a permanent address in this country . . . [If] I do visit NZ early next year it's terribly important for me . . . to have made my home here, for then I'll avoid all kinds of worries about having nowhere to live, nowhere to return to.'[94] And her letters to Dawson betrayed a mounting sense of anticipation. 'I aim to make Norwich my place of interest. Norwich Library, University of East Anglia, any drama it puts on . . . Blickling Hall and Anne Boleyn's presence, and the old churches, and the cold east wind . . . And there's always the possibility that the Am. publisher may visit!'[95]

The American publisher did visit again — but in London, not Norfolk. First Frame went out to dinner with Marsha Braziller, George's wife, when she was in London on her own in May; and then with George himself the following month when he was in transit from Rome to New York. They discussed her stories, which Braziller was to publish in August in a boxed set of two volumes, the production of which he was overseeing with great care;[96] and he was relieved to confirm that his author had not become, as he had feared, Mark Goulden's mistress.[97]

Frame continued to see Bob Cawley when he was down from Birmingham about once a fortnight — though some weeks he was unable to keep their appointments. One Monday in May he arrived in London 'with a cracked jaw, stitches in his chin and in both arms', Frame told Dawson. Her valued doctor had 'fallen off a bicycle . . . on a lonely traffic-free road'.

I, being myself and anxious to know who binds his wounds, was told, 'Sometimes I do, sometimes it is done for me.' A pause. 'I ask the sister of the ward to do it.' He's probably lying for my sake; if he said, 'My loving wife does,' I'm sure I'd be cured of him for ever . . . [We've] moved into an easy relationship where we just talk and laugh — though maybe that's just his skill. On the other hand [Barry Gurland] is dreadfully serious and probing, intent on asking how I feel, and I never know . . .'[98]

A month later, returning to the subject of Cawley, Frame added:

I don't know anything about his private life. I *think* . . . that he is not married, though I know he admires pretty women . . . [He] is the rather lonely sort of personality which blossoms . . . in the midst of hospital life. I know he loves it. He's . . . very modest, rather shy, and hospital is just the place for him — surrounded by pretty nurses and sisters (*all* nurses and sisters are *always* pretty), in company with them, yet never forced to come too close . . . And then there's the devotion which his patients . . . feel for him . . . But you know me when I get on to *that* topic . . . How right you were to put him in his proper setting, 'hospital life' — I think he would die if he were forced to leave it.[99]

It was not Cawley who died and disrupted the slow pattern of events by which Frame was organising her disengagement from London, however. It was another member of her family. But first, there was the publication of further books to be endured.

Throughout July 1963 Frame showed even more apprehension than usual as publication day in England approached for *Scented Gardens for the Blind*. She knew it would be a potentially difficult book for readers and reviewers to deal with. The theme, she explained to a puzzled Albion Wright, was 'implicit in the title . . . [It] is the refusal of life to be destroyed and a fantasy of what may flourish when not only one sense but a whole world is in danger of being destroyed.'[100] That threatened destruction was the potential effect of the hydrogen bomb, whose capacity for annihilation had worried her and disturbed her sleep in the course of her years in London.

After a bruising pre-publication encounter with a journalist from the *Daily Express*, Frame decided to hide at Peter Dawson's cottage on publication day itself. Such occasions, she told Constance Malleson, were lonely rather than celebratory ones. '[For] I don't make a practice of "telling" people . . . [When] the time arrives, the realisation is brought home to me that even after six or seven years in this country the only people I know closely enough to tell are my two stalwarts [Cawley and Dawson]. It's one of the times when I wish I'd been more brave . . . and moved towards people instead of always away from them.'[101]

When reviews did appear, they were largely as uncomprehending as the author had feared. As on previous occasions, however, there was respectful admiration in the *Times Literary Supplement* from Dan Davin, who described the characters and their significance:

> Edward Glace, who pursues his obsession and avocation of genealogy in England; Vera, his wife, whom he has left in New Zealand; and their daughter Erlene, who after leaving school has suddenly become dumb . . . Edward eventually returns to New Zealand and all hopes are centred upon Erlene's speaking when she sees him again. But she and we are robbed of this release. Instead we are given to understand in a final chapter that the whole novel is a fantasy in the mind of Vera Glace . . . a spinster who was struck dumb at the age of thirty and has remained in hospital uncured for another thirty years . . .
>
> Perhaps Miss Frame wishes to indicate that not only are art and our

fictions the product of our fantasy, but even the reality we take for granted is scarcely better grounded . . .

[There] is no mistaking the power of Miss Frame's imagination and the anguish of her concern for suffering and beauty. The collision between her sensibility and the reality it encounters creates a world which it is a memorable experience to enter though one it would be a martyrdom to inhabit.[102]

*The Times* review tempered praise with qualifications: 'Miss Janet Frame's book is a very good book. She manipulates her three central characters and her three peripheral characters with a delicacy and elan which deny the clumsiness of their conception.'[103] The rest, however, were predominantly negative. '[The] style throughout is liable to slide into affectation [and] quivering plangencies . . . The ending [is deplorable], a Golding-like trick which up-ends everything' (*New Statesman*);[104] 'as exasperating a novel as I've come across . . . tiresome and pretentious to a degree which makes it unreadable' (*Sunday Times*);[105] 'the resonance of the [questions] is diminished by the tricksiness of the structure' (*Observer*).[106]

'It seems that I've had very bad reviews,' Frame reported to Dawson when she returned to London. According to Constance Malleson, 'the *Sunday Times* let themselves go with ill-will, as if . . . they were paying off old scores. The scores, if any, would be with the publishers, for I know nothing of the *Sunday Times*, except that they dismissed my *Owls* as "dotty". It is perhaps some consolation to know that the reviewers seem very upset that *SG* is not a "conventional novel" . . . It makes me wonder at the source of their anger.'[107]

*Scented Gardens* was published in New Zealand the following month and provoked a largely puzzled response. Owen Leeming in *Landfall*, while allowing that it was 'an interesting example of a Semantic Novel', castigated the author for 'indulgent lapses into sheer meaninglessness' and insisted that 'greater rigour is essential to her if she is to attain real greatness'.[108] As if to prove that he must always swim against the tide, the most emphatic compliments came this time from David Hall in the *New Zealand Listener*. He called *Scented Gardens* 'a startling event in a career already surprising' because Frame had apparently abandoned realism 'for an excursion of the imagination'. He called the end of the novel 'brilliant', and said that the book as a whole 'demonstrates conclusively Janet Frame's firm control of her material'.[109]

In the United States, *Scented Gardens for the Blind* was withheld for another year to permit the publication in August 1963 of the two volumes of stories, *The Reservoir* and *Snowman Snowman*, which Frame had written at Camberwell. These drew a mixed reception. *Time* was scathing:

It is a fairly good rule of thumb to avoid books that come in cardboard slipcases . . . [The] contents of a slipcase either have calcified into the classic condition or are so fragile that they need an especially strong container to keep them from crumbling. Most of Janet Frame's stories, sketches and fables in these two prettily boxed booklets fit the second case . . . [They] deal with failure, loneliness, quiet despair, and the rubble-filled borderland betwen sanity and madness.

The same review misidentified the long fable, 'Snowman Snowman', as the 'long, long thoughts' of a snowman 'melting in the front yard of a middle-class New Zealand family'. And the stories as a whole, it alleged, represented 'not a dark night of the soul but a sun-filled afternoon with curtains blowing drowsily at the window, a stack of clean paper on the desk, a typewriter at hand, and nothing to say'.[110]

Other publications made distinctions between the two volumes, most seeing the 'stories' of *The Reservoir* as more successful in conception and execution than the 'fables and fantasies' of *Snowman Snowman*. David Dempsey in *New York Times Book Review* said the stories revealed that 'the Welfare State has lighted up the dark places of the soul without filling the emptiness. People die without having really lived, and those who make a try at life are usually disappointed . . . [Or] people pursue a dream and then, when it is within reach, are afraid to grasp it.'

Dempsey went on to note that 'death fascinates Miss Frame. Almost a third of the stories include the word in the final paragraph, where it is usually capitalised.' In the second volume too death had 'the last word in a third of the fables and appears in one of them no less than nineteen times'. He characterised the fables as 'personal statements by an enormously gifted writer' and the fantasies as 'science fiction with a conscience'. Unlike most other reviewers, he admired 'Snowman Snowman' as 'a dialogue between an existentialist snowman and a Platonic "Perpetual Snowflake" . . . [It] is free from Miss Frame's customary morbidity, and . . . it dares to elevate the fundamental questions of Being and Reality to the level of poetic contemplation.'[111]

With *Scented Gardens for the Blind* and the stories published in July and August 1963, Frame's agents and publishers had now brought into print all the work she had decided was ready for publication since she arrived in England in 1956. Frame was not consciously aware of the symmetry of these events, however; nor did the reviews published in the United States and New Zealand in August register any impression on her. Her preoccupations by now were elsewhere.

During the second week of that month Peter Dawson and her sister Rachel were staying at Brechin Place, sleeping in the bedroom while Frame used a folding bed half in and out of the hall cupboard. She returned home late one morning from Lords, where the three women had been watching cricket, to find a letter from June Gordon. This informed her that their father had collapsed on the road near Willowglen while he was cycling to work at the woollen mill. The following day, 3 August, he had died in the course of an x-ray at Oamaru Hospital. The cause of death was undiagnosed haemorrhaging from a stomach ulcer. He was 69.[112]

When they got back to the flat, her two elderly guests were sympathetic to Frame's plight, but unable to help her. All they could do was reminisce about their own father, a distant, kindly clergyman who had visited them occasionally in the nursery.[113] Instead, Frame mourned her father in letters to her sister, and to John Money in Baltimore. 'I'm grieving for [him], and for the other members of my family who died,' she told Money on 11 August. 'I'm missing very much the interesting, consoling accompaniments and rituals of death — the family tradition of letters, telegrams, the current of excitement, almost pleasure, flowing beneath the grief; the opportunity to review the assembled family, the aunts, uncles, cousins etc. I miss all this terribly much; instead I'm here in London with only a brief letter from my sister.'[114]

Another letter reached her soon after, from a lawyer in Oamaru, telling her that she and Geordie Frame were now 'joint owners of Willowglen and that I had been left all the contents of the house, and would I be returning to New Zealand as I was sole executor of my father's estate'.[115]

Frame wrote again to John Money:

I'm [now] trying to visit New Zealand earlier than I planned . . . for I do so want to see Willowglen before strangers come to live in it, and that will be quite soon, for my brother whose hate against my father has intensified since last year . . . has been waiting to 'sell out' [and] go to live in Australia. He has grown very bitter about my references to Toby, who, he thinks, is himself, and certainly there is an element of his life in the Toby I have written about; though my brother is far more intelligent . . . He has been stricken with a terrible unhappiness and jealousy, almost to the point of insanity, which has not been helped by his having had two accidents to his head . . . So you see, NZ life, as far as my family is concerned, has continued its tradition of being like a William Faulkner novel.[116]

Events now accelerated with the momentum of urgency. Frame arranged for the transport of her effects (four suitcases, one trunk, one haversack, one bedside table, one typist's chair, one hundred books) to Itteringham Common. To her dismay, Peter Dawson began to hint that the storage of all these chattels at Flint Cottage might not after all be convenient, undermining the feeling Frame had developed about having a home base there.[117] She rebooked her passage to New Zealand, securing a single cabin on the Shaw Savill liner *Corinthic*, leaving England on 12 September (and arriving in Auckland on 14 October). Then she wrote to Constance Malleson, promising to complete her introduction for 'Trespassers on Earth' 'before or during' the sea voyage (it turned out to be after);[118] and to A.M. Heath and W.H. Allen, undertaking to complete *The Adaptable Man* in New Zealand.[119] A.M. Heath managed to generate two hundred and twenty-three pounds in advances, to help finance the coming trip. Frame also went to the Maudsley for a final session with Bob Cawley, who wondered if perhaps Frame was not too dependent on their consultations to risk a severance;[120] but who, when it was apparent that she was determined to travel to New Zealand, reminded her that she should live as *she* wished, and not as others would have her do.[121]

Then Frame wrote to friends in New Zealand — Frank Sargeson, Audrey Scrivener — advising them of her new arrival date;[122] and to her sister, who replied, 'I'm so thrilled about your coming I'm almost walking on air.'[123] To Constance Malleson, Frame speculated that 'my return to New Zealand will be difficult, as there is now no member of my family strong enough to share experience and memories with: my sister and brother are both in poor health. And there is no home there now. All the same I have many people's thoughts to sustain me, and once the few family affairs resulting from my father's death are dealt with, I shall make my visit entirely a writing pilgrimage.'[124] She retained her intention to return to England the following year, telling John Money that she would fly back in March 1964; or, if she won the Literary Fund's scholarship in letters, in August or September. En route, she said, she would visit New York to take up George Braziller's invitation to stay with his family.[125]

And so, on 12 September 1963, Patience Ross 'farewelled me at Victoria Station, and when the train arrived at the East London docks there was [Mildred Surry] who had taken an extended lunch hour to say goodbye. We had afternoon tea on board ship. I thanked her. She returned to work. And as the engines started and the last farewells were made, and the ship began to move down the Thames, I looked about me at the sober, subdued passengers. There had been no band playing, no streamers. Some of the passengers had the air of being about to sail to their doom; many, no doubt were immigrants who had said last goodbyes and would never return; faces showed anxiety rather than anticipation, a certainty of a journey away from rather than a journey towards.'[126] It was a feeling Frame shared.

# CHAPTER SIXTEEN

# *Return of the Prodigal*

$\mathcal{T}$HE JOURNEY HOME TO NEW ZEALAND WAS NOT NEARLY SO GRUELLING as the voyage out. Frame told John Money that she had labelled all her available courage 'Wanted on Board'.[1] But, to her surprise, she 'found her sea legs' for the Atlantic crossing. It helped to have a deck cabin to herself, with a fresh breeze blowing constantly through the door and window. It helped too to have a consort, 'a nuclear physicist who was escaping from England while escape was possible, before the arms race triggered . . . you know'.[2]

The physicist was thirty-two-year-old Allan Phillips, 'a mild, shy, pale young man'. Formerly a research worker at the atomic energy establishment at Harwell, he was en route for New Zealand to take up a lectureship in physics at Victoria University in Wellington. He had moral and humanitarian reservations about atomic research and had attended meetings of the Society of Friends. He was also — and this was what most interested Frame when she met him — a great-nephew of the 'poet of the road' W.H. Davies. 'He brought me food from the dining room [and] became my attendant and companion throughout the voyage,' Frame wrote later. 'He was curious about the nature of the world, and I was an eager listener . . . [He] brought news of life on board ship and of the world of science.'[3]

Frame and Phillips went ashore together at the *Corinthic's* only ports of call, Willemstad at Curaçao on 23 September, where they walked beyond the town and through outlying villages; and Cristobal on 25 September. Once the ship was through the Panama Canal and into the Pacific, Frame's sea legs deserted her and she became as sick as she had been for most of the first voyage. 'I should never have been so optimistic,' she told Peter Dawson. 'The staff . . . were very kind to me [but] I shan't return by sea.'[4] Allan Phillips too was kind, continuing to bring her food and the distraction of conversation. Frame considered that 'his presence on board, through luck, coincidence or mysterious providence, had enabled me to survive'.[5] She did not manage to work on either her introduction to the Joan Sturges manuscript or *The Adaptable Man*: prior to Panama the weather had been too hot; and through the Pacific she was too ill.

After passing Henderson and Pitcairn Islands on 5 October, the *Corinthic* sailed into the Hauraki Gulf on 14 October 1963, 'past the bays with their unexpectedly colourful houses like rows of boiled sweets . . . set against the vivid green grass . . . and the darker green where stands of native bush remained. I'd forgotten about the confectionery housepaint and the drowning depths of the blue sky, not distant, but at hand, at head, a shared sky.'[6]

Janet Frame's major dread associated with her return to New Zealand was that family tensions might cause her to relapse into anxiety and depression; and that such an episode could result in her recommittal to a mental hospital. She had no idea to what extent the Maudsley verdict that she was not schizophrenic would influence New Zealand doctors, who had decided previously that she was. Hence her fear that, if she was returned to hospital, she might never re-emerge.[7] Frank Sargeson's parallel worry was that Frame could only be kept well and functioning as a writer by being looked after by a series of sympathetic friends (it was unthinkable, he now believed, that any one person could endure the emotional stress that he had undergone prior to her departure for Europe).[8]

Neither of these scenarios took sufficient account of the progress Frame had made towards well-being ('being well') as a result of her treatment in the Maudsley and continuing association with R.H. Cawley; and both proved to be without foundation. The Janet Frame who arrived back in New Zealand in October 1963 was not the highly vulnerable and largely unknown woman who had left the country seven years earlier.

The most dramatic evidence of her change of status was that the press arrived to interview her even before she disembarked. '[A] dam of opinion and speculation burst over me . . . I came home to find that I was looked on, variously, as famous, rich, a woman of the world, sane, insane, inevitably different from the shy unknown who had departed. Had I not lived and worked *overseas*? Had not my books been noticed *overseas*? Why, I was asked . . . should I want to return to New Zealand?'[9]

These kinds of questions were provoked in part by the publication in New Zealand earlier in the year of newspaper stories organised by Mark Goulden in London. One of these had referred to Frame as 'perhaps the finest writer that New Zealand has yet produced'; another anticipated that she would return to New Zealand in the course of the year 'to write a further novel with a Dominion background'.[10] Both stories, and another that appeared in *Northland Magazine* in July 1963, made it sound as if, in addition to fame, Frame had the resources and the inclination to travel the world at will.

Now journalists quizzed her about her intentions. The story that appeared in the following day's *New Zealand Herald* informed readers that she had intended completing her fifth novel 'aboard ship', but had been unable to do so. 'Perhaps her best known work is the novel *Faces in the Water*, which centres around New Zealand mental institutions. But Miss Frame said . . . she had finished with this theme. "I think I've said all I have to say on that" . . . She is now in New Zealand for an indefinite period. "I've missed it, you know. After all, it is my native country."'[11] She coped with this encounter. But it dismayed her that, even before she set foot on that native country, she had been publicly associated yet again with mental hospitals.

The Gordons were at the wharf to embrace her joyfully and give Frame a sense that she had indeed 'come home'. They drove her across the new coathanger-shaped bridge over the Waitemata Harbour to Northcote. And where they had once been 'surrounded by bush with tall kauris, there were now rows of houses and acres of concrete', a consequence of the mushrooming development which had followed the opening of the harbour bridge in 1959.[12] Frame told Peter Dawson that 'Wilson has bought a tiny caravan . . . where I've my bed, wardrobe and a desk. I can thus escape whenever I wish. There is electricity in the van — somehow arranged by my young nephew [Ian], who is a whizz at this sort of thing . . . He has [also] put an instrument for measuring wind velocity on top of the van.'[13]

Letters, telegrams and telephone calls of greeting rained down on Northcote from, among others, Albion Wright ('Waimaru welcomes you'), her cousin May Williamson (one of her Uncle Alex Frame's daughters), Sheila Natusch, and former Seacliff nurse Buddy Doherty. There were invitations to lecture to the Auckland branch of the Workers Educational Association ('you have [such] a lovely speaking voice') and address the Oamaru Jaycees and their wives. There were requests for further interviews from *Woman's Weekly* magazine and the radio station 1YA, who had engaged Auckland poet and teacher Kendrick Smithyman to record a conversation with her.[14] Frame politely declined all such requests. Her sister June deflected others, including an invitation to speak to the local epilepsy association and another, initiated by Geoffrey Blake-Palmer, for Frame to inspect Avondale Hospital to admire alleged reforms achieved since he had become director of the mental health division of the country's Department of Health.[15]

While eschewing public engagements, Frame did visit Jess Whitworth and Frank Sargeson in her first week back in Northcote. Whitworth, she told Peter Dawson, was bed-ridden, 'looking very frail and tired as if all that tremendous energy by which we remember her so well has at last come to an end . . . There is also a calmness about her . . . I feel as if she may not live very long now . . . Dear Jess.'[16]

The visit to Sargeson was potentially more fraught, because of their strong feelings for each other, the stress that had warped their relations in the final months of Frame's sojourn at Esmonde Road in 1956, and the fact that in the intervening years she had had six books published and Sargeson none. Each was tentative in their preambles to reunion. 'I'll be coming, wearing my dark glasses, to visit you one afternoon when you're free, though . . . I know that writers are *never* free and friends are idiots to suppose that they are,' Frame had written to her mentor in August.[17] Sargeson in turn had discouraged her plan to return to New Zealand with 'gloomy ruminations'; and then offered an invitation that he seemed to think would be refused. '[I] will of course be very glad to see you [but] you must please yourself entirely . . . I imagine strains once you land will be very frequent and severe.'[18]

Frame *did* visit him, of course. Her first consideration as she walked from Northcote to Takapuna was how much the landscape had changed in seven years. '[The] end of Frank's road, once secluded with mangroves, swamp, sea, had been extended, the swamp filled in, the land reclaimed . . . Frank's bach had been almost surrounded by "units" built upon what was now expensive "real estate". I felt sad as I bent forward to clear the ever-growing hedge with the honeysuckle as its sweet parasite, and trod the path that was now set with concrete paving stones, like stepping stones from one world to another.'[19]

Frame entered the cottage and found that, despite the traffic that now sped down Esmonde Road towards the harbour bridge, the enclosing vegetation deadened the sound. Inside, the house remained 'a haven of peace and books — I feel as if so many years of quiet thought and dedicated work have almost embedded themselves in the walls — as if the walls were lined with thoughts'.[20] Sargeson came in behind her and Frame 'sensed that he was as apprehensive as I about our meeting . . . I could see his nervousness, but when we saw each other we knew we . . . were recognisable to each other . . . The tension eased. Frank, preparing a cup of tea behind the counter, said hurriedly, "You know, I'm not jealous. I'm not jealous."'[21]

The very fact that he said it, and said it twice, was an indication that he *was* in some measure jealous. In the time that Frame had consolidated her career, Sargeson's had stalled. He was by now sixty years old and into almost his fourth year of seeking a publisher for his picaresque novel *Memoirs of a Peon*. These circumstances had caused him to feel chafed when Frame had complained by letter of all the vicissitudes and difficulties associated with being published. They were vicissitudes that Sargeson would have preferred to have had rather than not have. This set of circumstances would change, however. Although he had no premonition of it in October 1963, Sargeson was about to enter his most productive period as a writer. In the coming decade 1964 to 1974, he would have nine books published and become 'a professional writer in the most exact sense of the word'.[22] And this would ease and finally erase any feelings of envy he felt about the progress of his protégée.

There was one ritual to be endured at Sargeson's. Frank had had to destroy the army hut, which had fallen into dereliction and been overrun by rats. He assumed Frame would be distressed by this news.

I was touched by [his] everlasting concern, and I felt ashamed of my lack of feeling for the hut. We went down the overgrown garden [and] came to the heap of rubble that had been the hut where I lived and wrote . . . [Now] it was hidden by grass and wild-seeded sweetcorn. I could see the burnt circle of earth where I used to destroy all but the last version of manuscripts. I felt no regret, although careful of Frank's feelings and expectations, I sighed. 'Well, it's sad,' I said, and felt sad then, but I knew that although I had lost the hut when I left Takapuna, I had kept within myself the memory of the time I spent there, knowing it was one of the most cherished times of my life: the material vanishing now was nothing.[23]

When Sargeson asked her where she would live, and offered her a bed in his now-enlarged cottage, Frame reminded him about her application for the scholarship in letters. After her visit to Oamaru, she said, she would find a room on the North Shore in which to read and write. Meantime there was the caravan at the Gordons.[24] Although he never said so to Frame, Sargeson was relieved by this news, as he was by her apparently robust state of health. He reserved his expressions of deliverance, however, for his correspondence.[25]

Frame's next obligation was to travel to Oamaru, to carry out the tasks that had precipitated her return to New Zealand. These were to tidy up the loose ends of her father's estate, of which she was executor; to see Willowglen in the state it had been left at her father's death; and to decide whether she wanted to live and work there herself, to share it with her brother, or to dispose of her interest altogether. June Gordon was encouraging her to sell, because of the likelihood that Geordie Frame would expect her to assume sole responsibility for the paying of rates and the financing of maintenance.[26] Indeed, no sooner had Frame arrived in Auckland than her brother was demanding payment for work he had supposedly done on the property before their father died, and which he expected Frame to pay, even though they were now joint owners. He had the unshakeable notion that the 'half' of the property where Willowglen stood was his sister's, and that the 'other half', where he had moved a house on to the lower part of the section and stored his junk and scrap metal, was his.[27]

Frame went to Oamaru alone, because June could not face the risk of being confronted again by their brother. She travelled by train, ferry, and train again, arriving on 31 October. She had booked a cabin at the town motor camp, and was spotted there by an *Oamaru Mail* reporter as she returned from the dairy with supplies of food. Again, she discovered, she was news. The journalist 'hoped I would give him first chance to talk to me as the provincial paper was also looking for me . . . He'd been sent to find the New Zealand author who was now jewelled with *overseas*, to gaze on her and share the jewels; and I, in my paste and glitter, felt embarrassed.'[28] She submitted to an interview nonetheless, and had her photograph taken in the 'Oriental Garden' section of the Oamaru Public Gardens.

The story appeared in the paper the following day:

> Miss Janet Frame said she had returned after ten years overseas [*sic*], and might return to Oamaru to complete her latest book, *The Adaptable Man*. Miss Frame already has ideas for another book which she would like to write in Oamaru. Asked if the book would have a local setting, [she] declined to answer. 'I lose all enthusiasm in my writing after reading about ideas in the Press,' she stated. 'I generally talk trivialities and do my serious thinking when I'm writing,' she added.
>
> Janet Frame didn't know how long she would stay in New Zealand . . . 'I have more friends in other lands. Although New Zealand is beautiful [that] does not mean it provides the right environment for writing,' she added . . . [When] writing she did not look at the view, but into her heart. 'I like to be alone, not necessarily away from people, so long as they do not speak to me or bother me' . . .
>
> [She] wrote [poetry] mainly for her own enjoyment. 'I care more for poetry than prose,' she said, 'but I'm not very good at it, I'm afraid' . . . [She] and her two sisters, the late Isabel and June, had their poems, written in their schooldays, published in the *Mail Minor* . . . 'I keep my eyes open in daily life and see things and meet people who interest me and make me want to write. I am very fond of seeing the scene behind the scene,' she added.
>
> Efforts were made to get Janet Frame to talk about herself; but this quietly spoken woman refused to be drawn.[29]

The day of the interview was the same day that Frame visited the lawyer to sign papers relating to her father's estate. She also collected the key to Willowglen and returned to the old family home for the first time in eight years. That return was 'softened by the green of the leafy trees, and the sight of the once slender pines trees "down on the flat" [which] were now a dark forest . . . and by the sound of the distant roar of the surf pounding at the breakwater on the shore'.

> The driveway of Willowglen was overgrown with cocksfoot and littered with rusting parts of old cars, old stoves, and remains of a dray. The shed where the pictures and heavier furniture had been stored after the move away from Eden Street was collapsed upon itself, open to the sky, with picture frames and table-legs still angled among the ruins. The cowbyre, the fowlhouse, the old pigsty overgrown with hemlock, the apple shed

were all gradually falling apart, boards hanging, swinging to and fro as if the months and years had passed with such violence as to rip them apart like useless limbs. A wild black cat, perhaps one of Siggy's families, lurked in the hawthorn hedge.

Frame walked through the sagging porch and into the house:

The old iron boot-last was still there [and] Dad's fishing bag, as I remembered it . . . fishy stink and scabbed inside with old dried fish scales; and there were his thigh gumboots for wading in the shingle beds of the Waitaki, Rakaia, Rangitata . . . [Inside], my father's pyjamas hung over a chair. His long cream-coloured Mosgiel underpants with a faint brown stain at the crotch lay on the floor; even his last cup of tea sat in its saucer, a swill of tea in the bottom of the cup, making an old brown ridge against the china. The latest — two-and-a-half-months-old — newspaper folded to present the crossword half filled in with the stub of the ink pencil beside it, lay by the cup of tea. There were ashes in the kitchen range with the ashpan half drawn out ready for emptying, while above on the brass rack, neatly folded pyjamas lay ready for the night . . .
I built a fire down on the flat to burn the rubbish collected in the house — old papers, receipts going back many years. I read everything before I burned or saved it. I burned family letters. I saved documents that I thought might be wanted by my sister and brother or myself, [and what] might be looked on as keepsakes . . .[30]

The 'keepsakes' so saved included her prize books from Waitaki Girls' High School, her father's 'book' of fishing flies, his bagpipe chanter, his paintings, and a bedcover sown by George Frame from blazer material from throughout the country. 'Each object was alive with its yesterdays. I wanted to embrace them . . . I looked regretfully at those I [was] forced to leave behind.'[31]
The things left behind became the subject of guerilla warfare on the part of Geordie Frame. He bombarded his sister with letters, claiming that all the rubbish left on the property was on 'her' half, and she would have to return to remove it, or pay him to pay someone else to remove it. He, meanwhile, was threatening once again to 'sell up' and move to Australia. Early in 1964 the tone of his letters changed, however, and he announced that he was in love with a twenty-three-year-old woman named Zelda Chalmers (he was forty-two). They would marry in November 1964; and Frame eventually decided to gift her half-share of Willowglen to her brother — partly to halt the flow of manic and complaining letters, and partly to acknowledge that his life had been filled with misfortune, for which little of the blame was his own. It had become obvious to her by this time that Geordie had expected one or both of his sisters to step into their dead mother's role and take care of him for the rest of his (and their) life.[32] Frustration of this expectation had probably been the

cause of his attempt to take June hostage the previous year. It was equally
obvious that his longing for sibling maternalism would never be realised, and
his eventual comprehension of this had further embittered Geordie. His best
prospect for some relief from his multiple sufferings and resentments, his sisters
came to believe, lay in his proposed marriage.

In the course of her week in Oamaru Frame was contacted by her old English
teacher, Janet Gibson, who invited her to afternoon tea with another former
teacher, Catherine Lindsay. Frame went, and Miss Gibson was relieved to be
able to report that she was 'just like any other old girl'. Miss Gibson told
another former pupil, Jean Smith, that Frame chattered 'about this and that
and spoke very nicely about Waitaki Girls' High School and her teachers and
how much she owes to them. She said little about herself and then only when
answering a direct question. She is still difficult to "get at". In her books she is
an entirely different person. We didn't see that side of her at all.'[33] Miss Gibson
went on to say that J.B. Kirkness, the former headmistress of the college, had
also wanted to come to tea. But Miss Gibson felt that that would have made
the occasion too 'difficult'; and, given JB's likely recollection of her appearance
in *Owls Do Cry* as a neckless bull, that was a fair assumption.

After tea, Miss Gibson took Frame for a drive around Oamaru, to view the
once familiar landmarks of her 'kingdom by the sea' — the schools, the
Oamaru stone buildings, the town baths, Takaro Park, the boat harbour and
the breakwater. In the course of this excursion the retired teacher confessed
that she had read all of Frame's books. 'Oh, we won't discuss *them*, Miss Gibson,'
was all the former pupil would say. And Miss Gibson, who had been hoping
for a literary conversation, was disappointed.[34]

With the Willowglen house cleared and the bedclothes washed and dried,
Frame slept there for a night in the middle room. 'I was wakened by the wind
in the many trees, by the silence, by the searchlight glare of the midnight
express train as it turned the corner past the Gardens towards the railway
crossing. The trees heaved and rocked in the rising wind; moreporks and the
little "German" owls called from the macrocarpa. And in the morning I was
wakened by the gurgling gargling magpies. I decided I would not stay at
Willowglen. I would walk into town that morning to book my return passage
to Auckland . . . I would leave Oamaru.'[35]

And so she did, heading first south to Dunedin, where she renewed her
acquaintance with the former teacher's college librarian and now city children's
librarian, Dorothy Neal White, who had visited her in Seacliff and reviewed
*The Lagoon* with such enthusiasm for radio. Neal White invited Frame to dinner
with the family in their stately Victorian home in Littlebourne Road, City
Rise. There the writer met Dorothy's husband, Dick White, who owned

Newbold's, the largest antiquarian bookshop in the city, and their two daughters, Kerry, aged eighteen, and Vicky, fourteen. Rarely had Frame felt so much at ease in a family. She came to regard Neal White as 'the most verbally literary woman in New Zealand'; but she also enjoyed the company and conversation of her husband, and of the girls, who were lively and precociously well read. She loved the whole evening, Frame told Neal White in a letter of thanks, but especially 'our conversation about rivers'.[36]

In Dunedin too Frame went to see *Landfall* editor Charles Brasch who, in the wake of correspondence with Sargeson, was exploring with the Minister and Department of Internal Affairs the possibility of organising a 'civil list' pension for her. There was a precedent: previous governments had authorised similar arrangements for Frank Sargeson and a small number of other writers including the poet Eileen Duggan, understood to be a lady of 'retiring and delicate character', a description that could have been applied with equal validity to Frame.[37] The problem was that the previous pensions pre-dated the establishment of the New Zealand Literary Fund. Civil servants and politicians would not be easily convinced that there was a justification for special assistance to writers outside the operation of the fund. If Frame was to have any chance of qualifying for such assistance, Brasch advised, it was likely that she would have to remain in New Zealand.[38]

Frame was grateful for these efforts made on her behalf. She told Brasch that the only reason she had been able to return to writing in England was because the Maudsley doctors had arranged for her to be paid National Assistance. She was not eligible for such support in New Zealand, and she did not think she could return to the 'nightmare' of working in hotels. 'A pension,' she wrote to him later, 'would be a huge relief.' Brasch asked her to send him a detailed account of her income and expenditure over the previous years, as a basis for establishing her needs and a reasonable degree of financial support.

In that same conversation Brasch invited Frame to contribute to an autobiographical series he was planning for *Landfall*, initially called 'How I began. . .' He hoped for an essay of around three thousand words on the origins of Frame's life as a writer. In response to a question from Frame about how other writers might best be protected from the contractual bind in which Pegasus had trapped her, absorbing half her income from book sales outside New Zealand, Brasch advised her to tell Albion Wright that such a condition was unfair, and that it differed from arrangements offered by other publishers.[39]

Despite the remembered disaster of her visit to Denis Glover at Caxton Press sixteen years earlier, Frame did summon the courage to breast Albion Wright in his lair, a Victorian cottage housing Pegasus Press at 14 Oxford Terrace, when she passed through Christchurch the following week. It was the first face-to-face meeting between author and publisher in all the eight years of their professional association. Wright, who was delighted by the encounter, photographed Frame for the firm's gallery of author portraits; and he reported to A.M. Heath that she looked 'fit and well . . .[She] told me that she intends "to write more and publish less". By which I take it [that] she wants to be more selective and deliberate about what work she offers for publication. She was not altogether happy about the publication of the [Braziller edition], because some of the stories and sketches . . . were far from what she calls "finished art".[40]

Expressing regret for the loss of Frame's poems, which he had returned to her via Wilson Gordon in 1955, Wright offered to bring out a volume of her verse in 1965, if Frame would assemble old and new work for him in the coming year. He also proposed publication of a single volume of her stories if — as seemed likely — the American double-volumed edition proved too expensive to import and sell in New Zealand. Frame undertook to consider both proposals.[41]

In the excess of bonhomie that the visit generated, Frame could not bring herself to press Wright on what she regarded as the shortcomings of Pegasus's contracts and system — or lack of a system — of payments. She did report to Charles Brasch that she had raised the matter of overseas earnings, and that Wright had said that in future he would leave this question open to negotiation with authors.[42] She did not query his persistently irregular payment of royalties, possibly because Wright had a cheque ready for her from additional New Zealand sales of *Owls Do Cry* and *The Edge of the Alphabet*. Frame also learned that W.H. Allen in London had still not made a decision on whether to publish the stories and fables; and that A.M. Heath did not intend to press them to do so until they could at the same time offer the publisher the manuscript of *The Adaptable Man*.[43] Almost two years would elapse before these arrangements could be finalised.

The same week that Frame returned to the Gordons in Auckland, the Literary Fund announced that she had been awarded the scholarship in letters, worth one thousand pounds, for 1964. The Minister of Internal Affairs, Sir Leon Götz, said that Frame was 'among the leaders in a movement that had raised the New Zealand novel to a new peak of achievement'. The minister's grasp of the topic was rendered suspect by the fact that, confusing her new name with a non-existent place, he described her as 'Miss Janet Frame of Clutha'.[44]

The effect of this news was that Frame now abandoned any intention of returning to England in the early months of 1964. She told Peter Dawson that she was 'honoured and humbled, but I don't know whether or not I'm pleased . . . [One] thousand pounds will enable me to stay (more or less oblige me to stay) until late '64, but by Holy Holy I'm homesick for the northern hemisphere! At the same time I'm bursting with gratitude for the sun, the sea, the pohutukawas, and I want to stay in NZ permanently . . . You're the only one I know who has undergone this ambivalence, with a heart really in each hand . . . [I think] that my home is in the northern hemisphere, but this is the land I want to write about.'[45]

# CHAPTER SEVENTEEN

# Exiled at Home

*T*HE AWARD OF THE SCHOLARSHIP IN LETTERS GAVE JANET FRAME A means — and an obligation — to stay in New Zealand for at least twelve months from November 1963. The first new tasks she set herself when she returned to Auckland from the South Island in mid-November, therefore, were to find more permanent accommodation, on her own, than that offered by her sister and brother-in-law; and to supply Charles Brasch with detailed information on her income and expenditure, in the hope that his prospective pension would provide her with income beyond the coming year.

The minimum amount of money she could live on, Frame estimated, was six hundred and sixty New Zealand pounds per year; to live 'comfortably', she would need nine hundred and five pounds. In the previous twenty-four months she had earned a little over one thousand pounds a year, but those were exceptional years, she noted. 'The burst of prosperity that came with *Faces in the Water* was depressing and confusing. I would be happy to give up any possible further excess royalties in return for a small regular income.'[1] It was predictability she wanted, not poverty interspersed with windfalls.

While she was working on these calculations she found a small basement flat in Northcote, not far from the Gordons, with a panoramic view of the Waitemata Harbour. But after only a few weeks' occupation she discovered that it was cold, infested with silverfish and earwigs, and admitted noise — radio programmes from the upstairs tenants, a Scottish couple. She then tried a 'sleep-out' on the bush-clad northern fringe of the city, but was constantly under attack there from sandflies and mosquitoes. Eventually, in January 1964, Frame was able to rent the upper floor of a house in Devonport, an Edwardian-looking seaside settlement facing downtown Auckland from the North Shore of Waitemata Harbour. Frame told John Money that the husband and son of the owner, Mrs Edna McCormick, were away until the end of the year, and that her quarters were 'comfortable and convenient and quiet . . . with two pounds five a week (including electricity and hot water) to pay'.² This was fifteen shillings cheaper than the basement flat.

Before she got down to work in earnest she continued to visit Frank Sargeson, who was troubled by gradual loss of sight in one eye and the prospect of similar degeneration in the other. On 13 December she had dinner with Sargeson and the writer Dennis McEldowney, whom she had met in 1955 when he was visiting Auckland from Wellington. McEldowney now lived in Dunedin, and had had the second of two operations to correct a congenital deformity of the heart and coronary arteries. He was now leading a near-normal life and had been able, at the age of thirty-seven, to enter the work force for the first time. In his diary for 13 December 1963 he noted that Frame was 'still very quiet; still charming. She talks (it was mostly on neutral subjects like the growing of olives and the architecture of Dunedin) rather breathlessly, in little gasps.' McEldowney also noted that Sargeson had just heard that his collected stories were to appear the following year and that an English publisher, MacGibbon and Kee, was at last showing interest in his orphaned novel, *Memoirs of a Peon* (they would publish it in London in 1965).³

Frame was also spending occasional days with Audrey Scrivener, with whom she had kept in contact by correspondence while she was in England. Scrivener, in the periods when she was out of hospital, was now living with her parents in the same Takapuna street as Frank Sargeson. But, despite good intentions, Frame found her encounters with her lobotomised friend stressful. Scrivener's obsessive behaviour took the form of constant complaining about her own plight and sniping critically at her parents and at Frame. When she was returned to Avondale Hospital in January 1964, Frame was unable to accede to her requests, and to those from Audrey's parents, that she should visit her old friend there. The senior Scriveners seemed to believe that, because Frame had managed to extricate herself from the mental hospital system, she ought to be able to contrive a 'cure' and release for their daughter, if only she spent sufficient time with her.⁴

John Money visited New Zealand from Baltimore in December and January. On Christmas Eve 1963 he had a two-hour stopover at Auckland's Whenuapai Airport before flying on to Wellington. The Gordons drove Frame there to meet him. Money noted that June's recovery from her stroke had been 'little short of miraculous'; and he observed that she seemed to be 'a pretty sturdy specimen of New Zealand's wife and motherhood, with more than the typical suburbanite's alertness and keenness for community cultural affairs, especially . . . drama'.⁵

In the course of his second visit on 10 January, Money joined Frame in the city and took her to the Auckland City Art Gallery. There they met and spoke with Colin McCahon, who was keeper of the gallery, but also well on the way to his eventual reputation as the most original and most important of New Zealand's modern painters. After this encounter, in which Money and McCahon did most of the talking, Money and Frame shared a restaurant meal and then retired to her Northcote flat, where Money stayed the night in what he termed a 'Platonic role'. As he had been in London more than two years earlier, Money was 'tremendously impressed at how well Janet is, psychiatrically speaking'.[6]

And so she was. Bob Cawley was writing regular 'reassurance letters' from Birmingham (his secretary, Frame told Peter Dawson, put a blank aerogram on his desk each Friday to remind him).[7] And, at Cawley's suggestion, Frame had begun occasional sessions with an Auckland psychiatrist, Roger Culpan, who had worked at the Maudsley for three-and-a-half years and whose initials, auspiciously, were RHC.[8] In a letter that referred Frame to Culpan, Cawley had stressed that the Maudsley investigations had found no evidence that Frame was schizophrenic. The hospital's view was that 'she is a highly intelligent and highly sensitive person, with tremendous over-awareness of the nuances of daily personal experience; she continually feels very threatened by any sort of personal contact, is acutely aware of her isolation, and has a dread of being known . . . I should be very grateful if you could help by giving her some understanding and support, and by ensuring that she does not get admitted to hospital through lack of any person with whom she can communicate.'[9]

Culpan, who had seen Frame when he was on the staff at Avondale in 1951, pronounced himself happy to see her, indeed 'fascinated' to do so. They had their first 'discussion' on New Year's Eve when, for the first half-hour, Frame 'performed rather like a startled rabbit speaking unintelligibly in whispers'.[10] After that, however, she relaxed and told Culpan that she was finding it difficult to tolerate 'the insensitive and materialistic attitudes of people she encountered'. This session and the ones that followed were not conspicuously successful, in that Frame and Culpan never established the kind of rapport that allowed her to talk easily. And, after the free care provided by the National Health Service at the Maudsley, Frame was outraged to find that patients were expected to pay for the same service in New Zealand. The cost of her visits over a year would equate with 'five *Oxford Dictionaries*, four sets of *Everyman Encyclopaedias*, eight sundresses, one typewriter plus ribbon plus stationery supplies for three novels . . . [Psychiatric] services seem not to have advanced in this country (as Dr Blake-Palmer, in a recent letter to me, has claimed . . . ), if help can be given only to those who can pay.'[11] They compromised. Culpan was happy for Frame to pay five shillings a time in lieu of the normal two-guinea fee (indeed, he was prepared to waive the fee altogether); and Frame continued to find it helpful to have somewhere to go when she needed to voice and deal with her anxieties as they occurred.

Her need for such an opportunity was emphasised in January 1964 when Frame read Owen Leeming's largely unfavourable review of *Scented Gardens for the Blind* in *Landfall*. This alleged that she had 'a decided weakness for metaphor. Everything must be seen in terms of something else.'[12] Her distress at this comment prompted her to write one of her rare responses to a review, to Charles Brasch:

To me, [this] was as depressing as if someone had told me I'd better stop writing. I can understand a statement that I've a weakness for *weak* metaphor — but isn't the need to compare, to perceive relationships, the essence of all art? . . . Leeming's objection is a philosophical one, to the definition of one thing in terms of another; or he's expressing the hope for a pure literary style which I . . . am not equipped to find. I'm afraid I breathe metaphors . . . it is the obsession with images which prompts me to write. I know the path to good prose isn't necessarily tangled with metaphors; it can be clearer, more serviceable, more beautiful if the wayside is bare; it can have a dignity and a strength which no images blossoming in the hedgerows can provide. I don't think I'm equipped to operate the verbal DDT. I can aim to be more disciplined, less indulgent with my images, but they *are* the basis of my life and my need to write, and they all have meaning.[13]

It was not until she was established in the Devonport house in mid-January that Frame resumed writing. The first piece of work she completed there was the 'How I began' essay for *Landfall*. She posted it to Charles Brasch on 29 January 1964. Her accompanying letter said that it was 'so bound up with my personal life that I have to include the overworked autobiographical details. The script has little depth. Some day I'd like to write from "within" instead of from "without".'[14] Despite the author's customary reservations, Brasch said he was delighted with the essay. 'I'll be lucky to get other pieces in this series which can stand beside it without looking pretty dim,' he wrote in reply.[15]

This 'Beginnings' essay (as the series came to be called when Brasch began to publish it in December 1964) was to become the source of future unease for Frame. Until she published her first volume of memoirs nearly twenty years later, it would be her only major piece of autobiographical writing in print. Hence, for the better part of two decades, it would be ransacked by critics and journalists for the scarce items of biographical data it provided. The comments she made there about the Gothic quality of her family life ('a background of poverty, drunkenness, attempted murder and near-madness') and the supposed relationship of her writing to her hospitalisation ('I knew . . . that unless I devoted my time wholly to making designs from my dreams, . . . I should spend the remainder of my life in hospital')[16] — these were conditioned by Charles Brasch's efforts to secure her a pension and his intimation that her case would be strengthened if the essay established that her background was exceptionally disadvantageous and that she needed to be able to sustain her writing career if she was not to be a permanent drain on the public purse as a hospital inmate.

In later years Frame was to regret the use that others made of material in this essay, to hypothesise about which members of her family might be drunkards, murderers and lunatics, and to support the 'insane writer' scenario — that of the genius whose inspiration and perception arose from her madness. Such speculations would plague and depress her, the more so since she herself had provided the grounds for the conjecture. In 1964, however, she was prepared to trust Charles Brasch's judgement that an exposition of this kind would strengthen her case for a pension; and the pension seemed to offer her only long-term hope of sufficient financial security to be able to carry on writing.

No sooner was the 'Beginnings' essay despatched than Frame was plunged into a Gilbertian situation that drove all other considerations from her mind and appeared to indicate that even short-term financial security was illusory. On 27 January the Department of Internal Affairs had posted her the scholarship in letters cheque for one thousand pounds, to be drawn on the Government's own consolidated account. Frame received it on 30 January. When she tried to cash the cheque, however, and then simply to deposit it, she could not find a bank that would accept it. Various reasons were given: she no longer had a current bank account in New Zealand; she had no employer to vouch for her; she had no recent local address where she had lived for longer than three months; her passport was in the name of Janet Clutha whereas the cheque was made out to Janet Frame. Frank Sargeson told one of his correspondents that the Auckland Savings Bank had no confidence in Frame's *bona fides* and was convinced that the cheque was some kind of 'lunatic hoax'.[17]

It took several weeks of worry, fruitless interviews with bank officials, correspondence with Wellington, and, finally, a letter from the lawyer in Oamaru who had filed the documents relating to her father's estate, before the Bank of New South Wales accepted her as a new customer, opened an account for her and processed the cheque.[18]

In the midst of this crisis a letter arrived from Norfolk formally asking Frame if she would agree to be Peter Dawson's executor and chief beneficiary under *her* will. Acceptance would mean that the younger woman inherited Flint Cottage, the section on which it stood, and all Dawson's personal belongings apart from books, which would be bequeathed elsewhere. These would be hers to own, to let or to sell; and if she sold them the proceeds were to be 'absolutely' hers.[19] Dawson had been making these arrangements on the assumption that Frame would return to England to live, and there was an implication that inheritance of the estate would be compensation for Frame's living alongside Dawson in the latter's old age (in 1964 she was in her seventieth year). But Dawson recognised the possibility that their joint occupation of the Norfolk property was now less likely than it had seemed the previous year; and emphasised that Frame was to inherit the estate no matter where she lived.

Frame replied by return post that she was greatly moved by her elderly friend's offer, and that she would accept it. 'The idea of living in Flint Cottage, if I survive more years, makes me want to weep . . . I'd not really known how fond I've grown of it . . . [Of course it] may be too sad to face if you are not living — I had some experience of the strength of ghosts when I was down at my old home.'[20]

A week later, on 9 February 1964, Frame was back in touch with Dawson — and with Bob Cawley and John Money — with news of a serious nature which might have some bearing on Dawson's plans: 'I've suspected cancer of the breast & go into hospital next week for an operation, after which I'll have to make future plans which do or do not include further operations and prolonged treatment.'[21] Ten days later, the operation over, she told Money the full story.

I've been in a most fantastic state of suspense and anti-climax. The woman specialist whom I consulted said that she believed I had a disease which had turned into cancer at an early stage. She sent me immediately to a surgeon who examined me [and] said he thought there was little urgency . . . [He arranged] a mammography . . . The results showed a tumour . . . The surgeon arranged immediately to operate, the operation was performed, and a few days ago I learned . . . that a tumour which he called an adenoma was removed from my breast [and] that it had no trace of malignancy . . . [No] further surgery was needed. I shan't, therefore, be entirely left-breastless, though [some] has been removed . . . I leave it to you to imagine the mental story of the past three weeks . . . [22]

To Peter Dawson, Frame wrote that Bob Cawley had been 'marvellous, even at this distance; he said that should I need another operation he could arrange for me to go either into his hospital in Birmingham or into a London hospital . . . I wanted to be in UK to see my friends before I either died or set out on a prolonged period of illness.'[23] Cawley, voicing concern in his doctorly way, had come as close as he ever had to expressing a personal feeling towards her: '[Be] assured that you are in receipt of all support and friendship and whatever understanding humans are capable of from this side of the world.'[24]

With that crisis resolved, Frame faced another. The family members previously absent from the Devonport house had returned, and it was no longer a suitable place for her in which to live and work. '[They] are trying to take me over as a member of the family, and I'm looking for somewhere to be alone, completely alone, while not entirely away from the sight of people . . . I've been able to get a little work done, though not one quarter of what I want to do.'[25]

She thought at first that she had found an ideal base, a cottage in Milford, a small community just north of Takapuna where the writer Robin Hyde had lived more than two decades earlier. But in mid-April she sighted an advertisement for what seemed to be an even more desirable location: a bach on Waiheke Island, a sub-tropical outpost of Auckland that lay on the Hauraki

Gulf only ten miles east of the city and twenty-five minutes' ride by hydrofoil. The cottage belonged to an Auckland family, the Greens, who used it for summer holidays and let it in other parts of the year to protect the property from burglary and vandalism.

Frame and June Gordon travelled to the island to inspect the bach, and another that was occupied temporarily by the author James McNeish. Like Frame, he was a New Zealander who had just returned from seven years in Europe; like her, too, he had lived part of that time on the shore of the Mediterranean (in Sicily); and like her, he had sought a quiet location in order to complete a book which he had begun to write on the other side of the world.[26] In April 1964, however, they had never heard of each other. McNeish invited the sisters inside, and discovered that he and Frame shared the notion that Auckland houses looked like confectionery. 'Like boiled sweets,' he said. Frame laughed and repeated the expression. 'Like boiled *lollies*,' June Gordon, immune to English idiom, corrected them.[27]

Frame moved into the Greens' bach soon afterwards and discovered another coincidence. The previous owner had been Rebie Rowlandson, a distinguished scholar of music and literature who had taught Frank Sargeson English at Hamilton High School during the years of the First World War. Miss Rowlandson had died in the house and Frame found there a paperback edition of one of Sargeson's early books, *A Man and His Wife*, which he had inscribed for his old teacher in the early 1940s, and a 'music diary'.[28] Frame would soon make some use of Rowlandson's story, and of the Waiheke cottage, in the novel *A State of Siege*.

The Greens' bach was on the northern side of Waiheke, on what was then an extension of Ocean View Road, near the small settlement of Oneroa.[29] As the name suggested, it had a fine view down a tree-clad valley to the waters of the Hauraki Gulf and the circular volcanic island of Little Barrier. It was on tank water and had primitive sanitation facilities, a reminder for Frame of her childhood years in Southland. 'We still dig and bury and wait for water out of the sky,' she told Peter Dawson with some satisfaction. Most importantly, the location was, at first, quiet. 'I'm going to stay here for the winter months,' Frame told John Money early in May 1964. '[Motor] mower noises are few, and traffic is slight . . . I'm really savouring the tastes, smells, sights, sounds (even the sounds!) of New Zealand. The sight of a lone cabbage tree still seems to tear my heart away from me, and . . . toitoi growing on the side of the road and sea beyond makes me want to sit down and weep.'[30] It was the kind of land and seascape whose absence she had mourned in the course of her years in England.

Frame now applied herself to an intensive writing routine for the first time since she had returned to New Zealand six months earlier and, in her own estimation, she was satisfactorily productive for the first eight weeks on Waiheke. In late April she had been 'startled and honoured' to receive a commission from the *Times Literary Supplement* to produce a two-and-a-half-thousand-word article on how she had been influenced by literature. Publication would coincide with the World Book Fair in London in June. Frame wrote the piece early in May and called it 'Memory and a Pocketful of Words'. Perhaps more than anything else on which she worked at this time, it reveals her unsurpassed capacity to burrow deep into truth and human consciousness with the twin spades of language and metaphor.

The essay divides the world of literature into 'cities' (of tragedy, of fire, of firesides, of biography and autobiography); and makes reference to makeshift boom towns and shanty towns and the 'journalistic New Town'. Then she writes of the gateways through which readers may enter these cities, such as those of nursery nonsense and humour, 'received by owls, pussycats and Alice'; and of doom, 'where the United Kingdom was portrayed as a land of storms, tidal waves, lonely moors, misty highlands, the ghosts of star-crossed lovers, the murdered and the drowned . . . [Even] at night when most of the city of tragedy is quiet one can hear the inner explosions of Shakespeare's unattended works as new layers of meaning are cast spontaneously from their context.'

I came to this city as reader about the time . . . when lilac bloomed in Paumanok and the 'fifth-month grass' was growing, when Helen died on Kirkconnell Lea, and Whitefoot, Lightfoot, Jetty roamed the sands of Lincolnshire. At the same time . . . there was lilac in bloom in our New Zealand back garden, there was death in the mountains and in the bush, while I, an Antipodean milkmaid (two cows to milk before and after school) brought not 'Whitefoot, Lightfoot, Jetty from the milking shed' but Bluey and Pansy from the cowbyre, to spend the night on the Oamaru reserve.

At another time, she continued, she would go to 'the city of firesides among the essayists, diarists, letter-writers, and putting on my Antipodean Woolworth's slippers, I'd sit listening to Goldsmith, Lamb, Hazlitt, Pepys, Cowper . . . Or I may visit the novelists of domestic and social life . . . whose detailed observation and precise language are a delight and a revelation . . . They lick the surface of everything as if they are feeding upon it; objects and people accumulate within their alert minds like the ball of fur inside a Persian cat.'

It may be well for a reader to enter the world of literature, to stay there, going from favourite city to favourite city, taking a full share of the good things; it is not well for a writer. To visit the land — yes; again and again; but not to stay, not to set up house within a favourite gateway where the view of the 'world' provided by Dostoevsky, Tolstoy, Shakespeare, may combine to give a lifetime of spectator pleasure. A writer must go alone through the gateway entered or arrived at, out into the other 'world', with no luggage but memory and a pocketful of words, some of which may be like shells crumbled to sand before the oncoming waves, while others may turn out to be jewels — turquoises — that time has shown to be the teeth of the dead mastodons.[31]

By mid-May, Frame was also close to completing *The Adaptable Man*, but — suffering her usual second-thoughts — put the manuscript away before deciding whether to send it to A.M. Heath (it was to be eight months before she looked at it again).[32] She sent a carbon copy of what she had written to Bob Cawley, however; and he eventually wrote back to express strong approval.[33] She then wrote a talk for the YC radio stations (which broadcast classical music and 'quality' features) about the experience of returning to New Zealand. Called 'This Desirable Property', it echoed the themes of travelling and returning that had been the focus of her unpublished novella 'Towards Another Summer'.

> [At] the moment of birth every human being is an exile — or at the moment of consciousness of the first thought we are exile and home comer, we make both landfall and departure; there is nothing remarkable in our journeys unless it is that human beings . . . celebrate their movements in works of art . . .
>
> We need . . . to remember that we are human, to forget our preoccupation with distances between continent and continent, the measurement of physical miles, and remember the unbearable closeness of one human being to his neighbour. Unless we have the courage to use our inherited human riches to name name name things . . . invisible in our land, . . . to raise a few more rich fat dreams and poems and get a fair price for them, we'll be spiritually hungry and poor; we may not even survive.[34]

Frame took the hydrofoil ferry to Auckland to record the talk, and it was broadcast in mid-June. Her former English teacher Janet Gibson heard it in Oamaru, and told her correspondents that Frame had 'a pleasant speaking voice, though perhaps it got a bit monotonous at times . . . [Her] language was almost poetical.'[35] The following month it was printed as a feature in the *New Zealand Listener*.[36]

Also in mid-June, Charles Brasch received four poems from Frame for *Landfall*, and accepted three of them for the September 1964 issue.[37] One of these, 'Scott's Horse', was about one of her few encounters with a Waiheke neighbour (on the whole she had avoided contact with the locals and found even the manner of the Oneroa postmistress unpleasant). 'On Sunday a small boy kept knocking at my door, asking if I had seen Scott's horse. "I'm not allowed to ride it," he said. "I want to ride it. It's the last day of the school holidays." When he finally believed that I had not seen Scott's horse he went away. I saw him take the change from my milk bottle . . .'[38]

In his letter acknowledging receipt of the poems, Brasch had news of the pension campaign. There was a new Minister of Internal Affairs, David Seath, and he was prepared to 'investigate' the proposal. '[This] means chiefly searching for precedent, ways and means and the rest . . . I hope they won't give you much trouble. He wrote that it would take time . . .'[39]

Time was something Frame had. Tranquillity, though, was a rarer commodity. The ubiquitous problem of noise had invaded her island fastness. She had succeeded in outdistancing suburban motor-mowers, which she had begun to think of as voracious grazing animals. But an imminent housing subdivision above Oneroa had brought bulldozers, to squash scrub and level hillocks and gulleys, and to extend the island's roads. Frame told Frank Sargeson in June that she was having to write 'between the barking of dogs and bulldozers' — but added that there were still a sufficient number of quiet hours during the day and night in which to work.[40] The difficulties, however, produced a verse which she later shared with correspondents:

> We are the front-end loaders
> we are the movers of earth
> wheel-deep in drainage odours
> assisting at bungalow's birth
> we are the grim foreboders
> of a world without trees or mirth.[41]

Throughout the rest of June, and in July and August, Frame worked on her 'Waiheke novel', about a retired school teacher not unlike Rebie Rowlandson who retires to a white cottage by the sea on an 'idyllic island' not unlike Waiheke. As always, however, the core of this novel, which she would call *A State of Siege*, was about the interior landscapes of the human psyche and heart. Working steadily on this manuscript for three months, she had it 'almost finished' by September 1963.[42]

Meanwhile the noise from road and construction work was increasing in frequency and volume, and circular saws now added to the orchestra of cacophony. Then a series of 'unfortunate incidents' shattered whatever charm the island had initially held for Frame and created a sense of menace, which found its way into the current manuscript and created something analogous to the 'state of siege' experienced by her fictional character, Malfred Signal. It began with 'a scare in the middle of the night when prowlers threw a brick through my window . . . [Then] a narrow escape from death on the hydrofoil: it moved away from the wharf without untying, with the result that the bollard was wrenched from the wharfside, flung through the window of the hydrofoil . . . and catapulted straight at me, smashing through the wall, returning, encircling my head, scratching only my arm, and landing at my feet . . . Finally, [another] house I'd looked at to rent was burned to the ground — again by part of the violent element on the island [which] has been called, among other flattering names, the "Skid Row of the South Pacific".'[43]

These setbacks were compensated for to some extent by the unfolding of rather better news. *Scented Gardens for the Blind* appeared in the United States in August and — although it attracted fewer reviews there than earlier novels — a proportion of them, passed on to her by Brandt and Brandt and John Money, were highly complimentary. Stanley Edgar Hyman in the *New Leader* called it 'a brilliant and overwhelming *tour de force* . . . the most remarkable novel I have read in a long time'. It was distinguished, he said, by 'intellectual complexity, ornate and figurative language [and] intense moral seriousness'.[44] This was precisely the kind of review of which she had daydreamed when *Owls Do Cry* and *Faces in the Water* were published in London. Most other reviews, however, were critical of what they saw as the novel's 'trick' ending.[45]

The New Zealand branch of the writer's organisation PEN, to which she had just been elected a member, sent a letter to say that she had won the Hubert Church Award, worth one hundred pounds, for the local edition of *Scented Gardens*, which recognised this novel as 'the best prose work published by a New Zealander' in 1963. Frame could not help but remember the previous occasion when she had won the award, in December 1952, when she was in the dayroom of Seacliff Hospital and Geoffrey Blake-Palmer walked in to congratulate her and tell her that she had been taken off the leucotomy list.[46]

More surprisingly, she received a letter from Howard Gotlieb of the Boston University Library. This informed her that 'it is our intention to collect the papers of outstanding literary figures, house and curate these materials under optimal archival conditions, and attract to us scholars in the field of con-temporary literature . . . A Janet Frame Collection would certainly be a distinguished nucleus around which this University could build a great literary centre.'[47]

The letter was a classic example of what writers came to call 'the Boston Lure'. Mr Gotlieb was offering flattery in place of money to build up his library's literary archive; and, for Frame, there was considerable irony in the suggestion that her papers should be housed 'in optimum conditions', when she herself, a living writer, was now without accommodation, optimum or otherwise.[48]

For, at the beginning of September 1964 she had abandoned Waiheke and returned to the Gordons' caravan in Northcote. That same week another set of circumstances that had been worrying her over the previous month reached a point of crisis. One of her stories in the Braziller volume *The Reservoir*, 'The Triumph of Poetry', was about a promising poet who is gradually seduced by academic advancement and conformist living and loses his poetic gift. When she had begun writing it three-and-a-half years earlier in Camberwell, she had initially had in mind the example of Gregor Cameron, her English lecturer at Otago Universty, who appeared to have sacrificed a writing life in favour of one as a scholar and teacher. As she composed the story, however, she drew increasingly on recollections of the only poet she had actually known up to that time.

Thus the fictional poet *manqué* of the story had a biography that overlapped in many respects with that of Karl Stead: a bright young man from a non-professional family who was good at athletics, went to university, published poems in small magazines, married a young woman who worked in the university library and lived in a tiny flat close to a beach not unlike that at Takapuna. The wife became pregnant before it was convenient for the couple to have children. And so, at some legal and medical risk, they obtained an abortion in Freeman's Bay, Auckland. Then, as the poet lost touch with his talent, he began to go bald prematurely.

Karl Stead had advanced up the academic promotion ladder since Frame had last seen him in London in 1959. By 1964, aged thirty-one, he was already an associate professor of English at the University of Auckland. He showed no sign of losing his flair for poetry, however — or, for that matter, for any other kind of writing (*Kenyon Review* had just accepted one of his short stories, 'A Fitting Tribute', based partly on encounters with the Australian *enfant terrible* Barry Humphries.[49]) But it was inevitable that some of the few New Zealand readers who managed to obtain a copy of *The Reservoir* would assume that the whole story was derived from the Steads' life, particularly if they knew that Karl and Kay Stead had been closely associated with Frame; and, given this interpretation, the story appeared to reflect Karl Stead in an unsympathetic light and to reveal information to which Frame could only have been privy on a confidential basis.

It was an angry Frank Sargeson who drew Frame's attention to the potential problem. And it was he who wrote to Karl Stead about it. 'This business that Janet has been up to is a very odd matter indeed. It seems obvious that recognisable portraits in the book are either of people one likes or people one dislikes, and the presentation accords . . . Well, well, one of course just doesn't eat at people's tables and then do this sort of thing — unless you are apparently Roy Campbell [or] Janet Frame . . .'[50]

Frame became increasingly distressed as she realised and then worried about the likely implications of the story as Sargeson defined them. Unaware that he had already alerted Stead to the existence and nature of 'The Triumph of Poetry', she decided on what she believed would be a pre-emptive strike. When Sargeson accompanied her to dinner at the Steads' home in suburban Parnell, to give her an opportunity to apologise for the gaffe, she said nothing about it. Instead she left with her hosts a boxed set of the two Braziller volumes. An enclosed undated note suggested that her first inclination had been to post the books. 'I'm sending you these. I hope you'll forgive them . . . Excuse pretentious home for these books.'[51]

In the following days she realised that her actions to that point amounted to something short of an explanation. So she wrote to Karl Stead on 5 September:

Recently when I heard from Frank that you might be sending to USA for a copy of my stories I decided to give you and Kay my only copy because I did not want you to read the last story without having been warned by me and without having known that I asked forgiveness from you and Kay for what might seem — and be — an unkind intrusion into your life . . . [I] hope that you will believe me when I say that I would never deliberately hurt anyone, particularly anyone I'm fond of. The poet and his wife in this story are not meant to represent you and Kay . . .

The 'poet' is based on my English lecturer at Otago University . . . He was going bald, he was getting old, his lectures were not delivered with assurance or brilliance. I told myself he was this way because he was writing poetry in his head, because he had always wanted to be a poet but worldly affairs . . . had intruded and he never realised his ambition. Still, from time to time, to keep 'in trim', he wrote a few verses. Poor old 'Gregor', as we called him.

[For] certain details of his I've drawn from the only poet I've ever known and talked to — Karl Waikato . . . I apologise [therefore] for indiscretions that may seem to identify you . . . I want you and Kay to understand that I've never felt any malice towards you, that the poet of the story is a certain elderly Scotsman who is now living in Dunedin, dividing his time between his garden and Shakespeare . . . I only hope [this matter] hasn't distressed you as much as it has distressed me.[52]

The Steads, who had not read the story until Frame presented them with the volumes, *were* distressed by it, and puzzled. 'It seemed,' Karl Stead would write later, 'like a curse . . . a malediction.'[53] He replied to Frame's letter: 'It's difficult to know what to say . . . I had hoped I wouldn't have to say anything. It had its effect, and still has, despite your letter. I hope it won't be published in New Zealand.'[54] Frame's response to this was 'a single sentence, blazing with anger', which Stead threw into the wastepaper basket.

Frame stood by her explanation. She *had* written the story at the end of a severe London winter, at a time when she was seeing few people, none of them New Zealanders. New Zealand and its people seemed a long way away. She had no literary mentor at hand to raise the possibility of non-literary consequences of her fiction, and to discuss them with her; and Bob Cawley and John Money who did see the stories would have been unaware of connections between the fictional characters and people Frame actually knew.

On the other hand, the Steads felt that the story had so many elements taken from their lives that Frame's protestations about Gregor Cameron were unconvincing. They noted her acknowledgement that the story may have been 'tinged . . . with feminine jealousies and hopes'.[55] When Frame and Karl Stead eventually met again almost two years later in Dunedin, 'The Triumph of Poetry' was not mentioned, and their relationship was resumed. But the incident cast a shadow over their friendship and had a possible consequence in a novel that Stead would publish twenty years after the affair.

In mid-September, while Frame was wrestling with her conscience over the relationship between fiction and actuality, she received a further shock. The species of tumour which had been removed from her left breast now appeared in her right one, and necessitated further surgery. 'It seems that the affair stems from my brief one and only pregnancy some years ago when I fell under the spell of the almond blossom,' she told John Money. The result was that she could now 'wear topless dresses with equanimity'.[56]

Despite a determination to make jokes of this kind, Frame experienced a period of intense anxiety until the new growth was removed and confirmed to be benign. As she came out of the anaesthetic, June Gordon was waiting by her bed at Auckland's Mater Hospital with two items of mail. One was a card from John Money, wishing her well and inviting her to visit Baltimore to convalesce at his expense. The second was a telegram from the University of Otago in Dunedin asking if she would accept the Robert Burns Fellowship for 1965.

Frame had not sought the writer's fellowship, but the university had been dissatisfied with the calibre of the applicants who had applied. The selection committee, which included Dorothy Neal White, had resolved to write to Frame to offer her the position, which carried with it an office in the English Department, a salary of fifteen hundred pounds, a promise to find suitable accommodation, and the freedom to write as and when she liked.[57] After minimal consideration, Frame decided that each proposition made the other feasible, and she accepted both; in doing so, she would resolve the dilemma about where to settle. She would carry on to England from the United States, she told Charles Brasch on 7 October, to 'fix my affairs there [and] collect my books'; then she would return to New Zealand in late December to live and work, basing herself from the beginning of 1965 in Dunedin, her first home town.[58]

As always when Frame had made a decision after a long period of vacillation, she now acted swiftly. She booked a flight leaving Auckland on 15 October for Fiji and San Francisco. Then she would fly to New York, visit Baltimore, then on to London, arriving there in late October. She cabled these plans, including the intention to accept the Burns Fellowship, to Bob Cawley in Birmingham, and he replied, succinctly but reassuringly, 'Excellent idea.'[59] In devising this itinerary Frame had been persuaded by John Money's insistence that jet travel had shrunk the world by making it possible to travel from one side of the globe to the other in the course of a weekend.[60] Intellectually she acknowledged the convenience and the value of this possibility, especially for one who was dogged by seasickness; but she was nonetheless fearful of flying, having travelled by air only once before, when she and her sister flew from Auckland to Christchurch in March 1952. Frame's worst expectations seemed about to be realised when her plane, landing at Nadi Airport on 17 October, suddenly filled with steam. 'I thought it was curtains for everybody,' she reported to Audrey Scrivener. But the aircraft touched down safely and nobody else showed concern.[61]

Her stopover in San Francisco encompassed a day and a night. To her surprise, Frame felt immediately safe there and wandered about the city confidently on foot. It seemed to her in retrospect that she had been prepared for the experience by the fact that so many of the writers whose work her mother had read and recited were American (Longfellow, Whittier, Poe, Twain, Harriet Beecher Stowe) — 'I'd lived there before . . . in American poetry.'[62] And there was the feeling of being in 'Movieland'.[63]

These feelings were even stronger when she arrived on the east coast on 18 October. John Money was waiting to greet her in New York and was surprised at how confident she seemed as a traveller among travellers. Their meeting, he wrote, was 'completely undemonstrative'. Then Money took her for a Sunday morning drive around Manhattan, to 'see the sights' (Central Park, Fifth Avenue, Wall Street, the Empire State Building), and to visit an artist friend of his, Lowell Nesbitt. Money, remembering his attempts to introduce Frame to Charles Brasch and James K. Baxter, recorded his pleasure at how unrestrained the meeting was between Nesbitt and Frame. 'She said afterwards that she liked [the] experience of hearing an artist talk about his aims and his work.'[64] After this encounter they drove south on the turnpike through New Jersey and into Maryland. 'The colours of the fall were spectacularly and unbelievably beautiful.'

Frame spent the next three days with Money in his recently acquired home in East Baltimore. His career had advanced spectacularly since he had left New Zealand in 1947. He had done postgraduate work in psychology at the University of Pittsburgh and then taken his doctorate at Harvard in 1952. He then moved to Johns Hopkins University in Baltimore and established the Psychohormonal Research Unit there, becoming the world's first pediatric clinical psychoendocrinologist. His pioneering research centred on birth defects of the sex organs and therapies to deal with resulting physical and psychological problems, especially in children. By October 1964 he was an associate professor of medical psychology and pediatrics at Johns Hopkins and widely respected for his work in his chosen sector of sexology.

He was not, however, wealthy. Frank Sargeson, misunderstanding the nature of Money's eminence, told Karl Stead that the sexologist was paying all Frame's expenses and had bought and renovated an old house on the Baltimore waterfront, where he 'entertains some of the city's negro population'.[65] This was incorrect. Money was not even on salary from Johns Hopkins for most of his career. He was obliged to apply for research grants, and his income was seldom guaranteed. The house he had bought, a former corner store in East Madison Street, was in a seedy district of 'row houses' in East Baltimore, within walking distance of his office. Frame was slightly apprehensive to find herself transported to the 'poor quarter' of the city and one that had one of the highest crime rates in the United States. But these same conditions gave her a *frisson* of excitement, almost enjoyment, that she was 'living in the midst of the human condition' — a feeling that was virtually absent from her places of residence in New Zealand.[66] It was intensified by the fact that one of her mother's heroes, Edgar Allan Poe, had collapsed in the streets of Baltimore and died shortly afterwards in hospital. She explored some of the city on foot while Money was at work, visiting galleries and walking through slums; and in the evenings they called on Money's friends, including a jewellery maker, Billy Hadaway, and a black family, the Beasleys.[67]

Frame had intended to leave for London after her three days in Baltimore. But when she rang her publisher George Braziller, he was made desolate by the information that she was so close to New York but planned to fly on without seeing him. He invited her back to New York to spend a week there at his expense, staying in the Hotel Gramercy Park in Lexington Avenue. Frame was too moved by Braziller's warmth and affection to refuse, and she returned to the city by bus.

To Frame's embarrassment, Braziller took her on a tour of the very landmarks which she had seen with John Money the previous weekend. Such was his enthusiasm — 'Look! Your first view of New York!' — that she could not bring herself to tell him that she was on the circuit for the second time. In the course of the week she had lunch with her American agent Carl Brandt and got quietly drunk on dry martinis, which she ordered recklessly, unaware of their effect until she tried to stand up. Brandt, to her surprise, was young (twenty-nine), attentive and urbane. She went to the theatre twice (Saul Bellow's *Last Analysis* and Dürrenmatt's *The Physicists*), to some of the art museums, and to the United Nations building. George Braziller also took her to a restaurant atop a skyscraper where she met James Thurber's widow and friends of Mary McCarthy.[68]

One morning she simply wandered the streets of Manhattan alone trying out the automat machines which dispensed food and drink. 'I behaved like a child,' she said later, 'reminded of my first visit to a big city, Wellington, when we went with the school to see the Centennial Exhibition in 1940 [and] spent the time in the fun fair, riding the ghost train. Similarly, there was nothing sophisticated about my enjoyment of New York.'[69] To Audrey Scrivener she wrote that the city was potentially a violent place — 'callous, if you like, but the buildings are exciting and I've fallen in love with skyscrapers, also with red maple trees and little dogwood trees and pancakes with maple syrup, and central heating'.[70]

By the time she came to leave the United States, flying out of Boston at the end of October, she was hooked on American society and culture to an extent she had not anticipated.'Well man I miss the scene in the States and Baltimore,' she wrote to John Money from London. 'I done thought of it often with pleasure. I done been too much recovering from it all to get in trouble with anyone. Man have I blistered my feet walkin' on smokin' memries with words growin' green between the weeds they are.'[71] She was determined to return, eventually.

In London Frame based herself at Chesham House, a cheap hotel near Victoria Station, and at the YWCA in Great Russell Street (partly as a penance for what she regarded as the extravagance of her New York hotel). As she told Money, she spent most of her seven weeks there recovering from travel — the jet flights had exhausted her — and seeing few people other than Bob Cawley at the Maudsley, Patience Ross at A.M. Heath and Mildred Surry. She had a full medical examination, arranged by the Maudsley. But the physician who performed it refused to give her any kind of prognosis about the breast tumours. She was found to be mildly anaemic, however, which accounted at least in part for her exhaustion, and was prescribed iron tablets.

She spent a couple of weeks with Peter Dawson in Norfolk. They organised joint expeditions into the countryside and neighbouring towns, though cold weather restricted both their inclination and opportunities to travel far from Flint Cottage. Frame repacked the suitcases, trunk and boxes of books which Dawson had been storing for her, in preparation for their eventual return to New Zealand. In doing so she was acknowledging the likelihood that she would not now return to England to live. On 23 December she flew out of London, and returned to New Zealand via New York, San Francisco, Honolulu and Nadi. She was back in Auckland on 27 December.

At the Gordons in Northcote, where she would stay until her departure for Dunedin, she found mail from Charles Brasch, requesting further details of her income and expenditure;[72] and a letter from the registrar of Otago University, announcing that he had found her a furnished and self-contained flat less than one block from the English Department. 'The owner, Miss I.G. White, lives in an [adjoining] flat. She is a quiet, retiring lady and a gentlewoman in the true sense . . . a daughter of a former Professor of Education.'[73] Indeed, Miss White's father, David Renfrew White, had at one time been regarded as the most prominent educationist in the country on the basis of having been, at various times, foundation professor of education at the university, principal of the teachers' training college and first secretary of the primary teachers' union, the New Zealand Educational Institute.

What the registrar did not say, for he did not know, was that Miss White was also John Money's former landlady, and that in taking her upstairs flat, Frame would find herself sleeping in the very bed that Money had occupied over the period that she was obsessed with him.

Frame farewelled the Gordons and headed south by train on 12 January. She stayed two days in Wellington and spent them both in the company of Allan Phillips, the physicist she had met on board the *Corinthic*. Phillips, she told Sargeson, 'took me to the university stage two darkroom and asked if I wanted to see his — detonator . . . I [did], and quite startling it was too . . . [Then] we cooked meals over the Bunsen burner and he showed me his latest experiments with PETN . . . an explosive more powerful than TNT. Interesting but scary.'[74] On the second day they visited Sheila and Gilbert Natusch at their home on a windswept hillside overlooking Owhiro Bay and Cook Strait. Phillips escorted her to the Christchurch ferry that evening. After the overnight crossing and a further train trip from Christchurch, Frame arrived in Dunedin on the morning of 16 January 1965, to be met by Dorothy Neal White and her husband, who drove her with her luggage to Miss White's flat in St David Street.

There the following morning, upstairs from his old landlady, Frame wrote the first letter of her Burns Fellowship stint to John Money. 'Sunday morning. Quiet. Dunedin church bells . . . What thin long-faced houses face me from near the Town Belt . . . I think I could live the life I [have] now for the rest of my days — somewhere to write, the library a stone's throw away, a hermit's life that yet includes acceptance somewhere, a belonging . . . [It] has all the shelter that I need.' Her new situation was, she concluded, just like being in a mental hospital: but with a key, and without the horror.[75]

# CHAPTER EIGHTEEN

# Dunedin and the Messrs Burns

$\mathcal{T}$HE ROBERT BURNS FELLOWSHIP AT THE UNIVERSITY OF OTAGO WAS the only writer's fellowship on offer in New Zealand universities in the 1960s; and, apart from the Literary Fund's scholarship in letters, the only one in the country. It was endowed in 1958 by a group of Dunedin citizens with a gift to the university of shares to the value of twenty-six thousand pounds. Those donors requested anonymity, but in later years it became known that they were Charles Brasch and his cousins Esmond, Mary and Dora de Beer, all of them descendants of an extended family of Jewish merchants who had made a fortune in the prosperous years that accompanied and followed the Otago gold rush. Shrewd commercial and investment decisions in later years had enlarged the family's wealth, and Brasch and the de Beers were among a very small number of New Zealanders able both to live off their private means and to endow artistic and cultural institutions (members of the same family also made substantial donations to Dunedin's museum and art gallery; and Brasch and the de Beers would later establish music and painting fellowships at the university).

The purpose of the 1958 endowment was to promote imaginative writing and its association with Otago University. And, while the donors may have been Jewish, the occasion for establishing the writer's fellowship was rooted in Dunedin's Scottish heritage: to commemorate the bicentenary of the birth of the Ayrshire poet Robert Burns and the contribution members of his family had made to the settlement of Otago.

The importance to a Scottish colony of the bard, whose statue had presided over the Octagon in the centre of the city since 1887, needs no explanation. Robert Burns was read and revered throughout Otago and 'Burns Night' suppers had long been a feature of the province's calendar of Caledonian festivities along with the Highland games, Scottish country dancing, pipe band competitions and Hogmanay celebrations that had so engaged Janet Frame's father and uncles and aunts. What was less well known outside Dunedin was that the poet's nephew Thomas Burns, son of Robert's brother Gilbert, had been one of the two principal leaders of the Otago settlement.

Thomas Burns, a stern, puritanical and humourless Free Church minister, had been appointed chaplain to the Otago settlers even before they left Scotland in 1847. In Dunedin he emerged as undisputed leader of the local Presbyterian Church, first moderator of its synod and, in 1869, foundation chancellor of the University of Otago which, when it opened its doors to students two years later, was the first university in the country.

Filial piety towards the Burnses was, perhaps, a reflection of the Scottish respect for education which the Otago settlers had brought with them and communicated to their immediate descendants. But reverence for both men was also symptomatic of contradictory notes in the character of Dunedin in the 1960s. Thomas Burns reflected the Calvinist ethic which had dominated the public face of the city, especially through the sermons and pronouncements of a succession of city fathers, from the mid-nineteenth century. Robbie Burns, especially the satiric Burns of 'Holy Willie's Prayer' and the bawdy Burns of *The Merry Muses*, could be said to be emblematic of more anarchic and artistic elements in Dunedin. These were present in a small community of writers and artists and theatrical people; and in the student body, which had produced writers and activists of its own and at times thrown up leaders of a more disputatious and nonconformist nature than its counterparts elsewhere in the country.[1]

The two elements had been visible in *Strait Is the Gate*, a play written by the fourth Burns Fellow, the Marxist poet R.A.K. Mason, in 1962. This told the story of a Dunedin student who 'sinned for love', became pregnant, and was refused entry to her local Presbyterian church. At Heaven's gate, however, it was the unyielding minister who was turned away, while the sinner was welcomed. Despite an unusually active local drama scene, Mason was at first unable to persuade anyone in Dunedin to produce the play, though this may have been a consequence of its enormous cast, all of whom were required to deliver verse dialogue in a Scottish accent.[2]

Another writer who had embodied, but was unable to reconcile, the legacies of the two Burnses was the Dunedin poet James Keir Baxter, whom Frame had met in John Money's office in 1946. Baxter descended from Gaelic-speaking Highlanders on his father's side; and his maternal grandfather, John Macmillan Brown, a Lowland Scot, had been a foundation professor at Canterbury University College. Baxter's own early student years in Dunedin in the mid-1940s had been squandered in a haze of sexual and alcoholic experimentation. But Baxter, conditioned by the Calvinist heritage of his ancestors, was unable to enjoy the fruits of his libidinous or alcoholic propensities, and much of his early poetry had the character of a dialectic exchange between his conscience and his poetic self:

*Per ardua ad astra*: blind
Inscription from a catacomb.
*Lost, one original heart and mind*
Between the pub and the lecture-room.[3]

Baxter had lived away from Dunedin since 1947. But he was to return in 1966, as Frame's successor as Burns Fellow, to resume his interrogation of the Thomas Burns legacy with the sensibility and the language of the poet's.

Janet Frame had links into both Dunedin traditions. She was well acquainted with the city's Calvinist character from her days at Aunty Isy Renwick's and Mrs Wadsworth's; and from her observation of the *mores* and behaviour of senior staff at the teachers' training college and Arthur Street School. Soon after returning in January 1965, she wrote a poem that addressed that dimension of the city's life, 'Sunday Afternoon at Two O'Clock'. It said, in part:

> Having been to church the people are good, quiet
> with sober drops at the end of their cold Presbyterian noses,
> with polite old-fashioned sentences like Pass the Cruet,
> and, later, attentive glorying in each other's roses.[4]

Frame also knew of the city's writerly connections. She was at this time in awe of Charles Brasch and of the journal *Landfall*, which, with the help of poet Ruth Dallas, he edited from an office above the University Bookshop in Great King Street. She had re-established her acquaintance, soon to become a friendship, with the librarian Dorothy Neal White and had enormous respect for her erudition. She had been introduced to Baxter and been, initially, intimidated by the precocity of his early poetry. She knew that her first publisher, Denis Glover, had grown up in Dunedin under the vigilant gaze of a sternly Presbyterian grandmother. And she had met Sargeson's friend Dennis McEldowney, whose company she had shared in Oxford University Press's 1953 volume *New Zealand Short Stories* and whose first book had been published in London in 1957; his second was nearing completion at the time she returned to the city.[5] And she admired the line of her predecessors in the Burns Fellowship — Ian Cross, R.A.K. Mason, and the three Maurices, Duggan, Shadbolt and Gee, all of whom had visited Sargeson at Esmonde Road around the time that Frame lived there and featured in his letters to her while she was in England.

These associations were ones which Frame viewed as enriching the city of her birth. In company with the stories that linked her family to Dunedin from the time her Frame grandparents had moved there in the early 1900s, her own happy occasions there with such relations as Aunty Han and Uncle Bob Frame and such friends as Sheila Traill — all these memories served to diminish the recollection that Dunedin had also been the arena for some of the least happy episodes in her life, particularly her time at Arthur Street School and her initial breakdown.

The city's Scottish features too had additional resonance for her since she had visited Glasgow and Edinburgh with Jess Whitworth in 1961. She now recognised how much of Dunedin's appearance — the stone public buildings, especially the older parts of the university, the church steeples, the Queen Anne towers — was reminiscent of the cities and culture of origin. And she was attracted by the fact that Dunedin's climate was more like that which she had experienced in Britain: it was, she said, the one place in New Zealand where one experienced 'vivid seasons', and where the extremes would be those of cold rather than the enervating heat and humidity which had often sapped her energy and her will to work in Auckland.[6] She now looked forward to the kind of climate in which 'one can work twelve months in the year'.[7]

In January 1965, therefore, Janet Frame was excited and optimistic about her immediate prospects. She did not expect to be happy in Dunedin, she wrote to Constance Malleson; but she had every hope of being creative there.[8] A fortnight later her ambitions had advanced. Now she was 'blissful and workful', she told John Money, and expected to remain so.

When Frame took up the Burns Fellowship her corporate host, the university's English Department, was housed in Leith Street, where her father's family had lived in 1912. The building had been the home of the first professor of medicine. Frame's study was in a small upstairs room that had originally been a children's bedroom. It looked into the branches of a redwood tree and Frame found it conducive to writing. 'I like it,' she told Frank Sargeson, 'I like knowing that in the other rooms everyone is thinking . . . high thoughts about Milton or Shakespeare . . .' She also liked 'swank notepaper, and . . . a magnificent almost too hot to handle new typewriter . . . with a big desk and (alas) a man-sized chair . . . I'm having a wonderful, lonely time with my work, and no one is bothering me. I've met the [eight] members of the department, said hello, and that's that.'[9]

The person to whom she would be nominally responsible was Alan Horsman, professor of English, a gentle-mannered and attentive man who was on leave when Frame arrived in Dunedin. Because of her long-established fear of authority figures, Frame confided to Sargeson, she planned to post a note on her door when he returned: 'Horsman pass by'.[10] The acting head of department was Margaret Dalziel, a commanding and sharply intelligent woman possessed of what Frame recognised as a 'voice of authority'. She was, however, immensely kind to Frame from the outset and said how pleased she was that the fellowship had, after five years, been awarded to a woman. Frame appreciated Dr Dalziel's kindness but was, at first, intimidated by her complete absence of self-doubt on any issue. The other staff members who interested her from the outset were Gregor Cameron, whom she had so admired when she was a student and who was now nearing retirement; and a young tutor recently arrived from England, Raymond Ward, who had had poems published in *Landfall* and was, Frame told Sargeson, 'an interesting fellow (just as I am an interesting Fellow)'.[11] She went to visit her old English professor, Herbert Ramsay, who had become reclusive after his retirement and the death of his wife.

She was pleased too with Miss Ida White's upstairs flat in St David Street, which had a kitchen, bathroom, bedroom and small sitting room, and seemed luxurious after the kinds of accommodation she had had to endure in England. It was also quiet (though this would change when students arrived back in the city); and it had a view. 'Looking from my window I can see the university, the main building, the Water of Leith flowing quite swiftly . . . beds of bright geraniums, a dark wine-coloured cherry tree; and above the sky is clean clear blue.'[12] Conveniently, it was no more than a five-minute walk from her office.

Dunedin being Dunedin, there was always the possibility of reminders of unpleasant events. Frame joked about this by referring to her arrival in the city as 'the classic theme of return to the scene of the crime', or — invoking her time as a waitress at the Grand Hotel — 'the triumph of the little serving-maid . . . who is invited to the castle'.[13] There was nothing triumphant, though, about seeing in the street the doctor who had been responsible for the applications of ECT at Seacliff. And when Miss White had a visitor who recommended that she read *Faces in the Water*, the landlady did so and thereafter, Frame reported, 'has become rather anxious in her gaze towards me'.[14]

'I have had certain frightening experiences,' Frame wrote to John Money on 6 February, 'with my past rising up to meet me, and myself living on two levels of time . . . [When] I began teaching I could not go to the staffroom for morning tea . . . and I was given to believe that my not attending was a major crime . . . The other day when [Dr Dalziel] popped her kindly head in the door to tell me that they had coffee at eleven each morning, I felt my blood and my innards draining away through my body, through my feet and into the floor. There was and is no compulsion to attend . . . But the compulsion has become my own [and] I hate to be beaten by fear.'[15]

The course of February brought news that the writer Greville Texidor, who had entertained her briefly in Barcelona, had taken her own life in Australia, where she had been living since 1962. In the same month two of Frame's uncles, her mother's and father's eldest brothers, also died. But there was a graver shock pending. On 13 February she picked up the *Otago Daily Times* to read, in the lead story on the front page, that her cousin Bill Frame, son of her Uncle Bill and Aunty Dolly, had shot his lover in Christchurch, killed her parents, then turned the rifle on himself.[16] He was thirty-two years old and left a pregnant wife and two children in the Dunedin suburb of Green Island.

The shock was perhaps greater than it might otherwise have been had somebody else carried out these killings: because Bill, 'Big Bill', tall, handsome, intelligent, had been a member of the family whom they had expected to do exceptionally well in life. He had studied accountancy, and won early fame throughout Otago as a star bowler in the provincial cricket team (in his debut, against Canterbury in 1955, he had taken five wickets for forty-nine runs in the opposition's first innings and five for fifty-six in the second). Janet had gone to his wedding in 1952, the only one she had attended in her life to that point. Subsequently she had sometimes taken rides in his car when she worked at the Grand Hotel. She had liked his confident and easy-going manner.

'Four wickets, including his own, was a fair display of bowling, don't you think?' Frame asked John Money. 'I write facetiously, [for] it was a terrible shock to see the Frame Doom once more on the prowl . . . [If] you read chapter fifteen of *Scented Gardens for the Blind* you will find a view of his old St Kilda home, and of his mother. Poor Bill! They did not even put his death notice in the paper.'[17] Various family members came to Dunedin for the funeral, including her brother, and his wife, who turned out to be pregnant (the baby was expected in October, Frame told Sargeson, 'Labour Day, I presume').[18] She made her own gesture of mourning through a poem, 'Big Bill'.

> Big Bill, Big Bill, High School Boy, Accountant,
> Cricket star, hero of Plunket Shield Play,
> thirteen years ago I went to your wedding
> at St Kilda on a cold dark winter's day.
>
> What happened between then and now, Big Bill,
> to bring madness, murder, suicide your way,
> riding with us in triple nightmare to your funeral
> at St Kilda on this cold dark winter's day?[19]

The combined effect of these setbacks, especially the horror of the family tragedy, had an effect on Frame. It drove her to seek an appointment with Wallace Ironside, professor of psychiatry at the university, who had been recommended to her by Roger Culpan in Auckland. She was not ill, she emphasised to Professor Ironside, just seeking someone with whom she could talk from time to time. She would also welcome having some sleeping tablets for occasional use.[20] Ironside, a Scot by birth, was understanding and happy to oblige. Frame spoke with him periodically for the doses of reassurance Bob Cawley had been able to provide, until, three years later, he left Dunedin to take up a post at Monash University in Melbourne.

Early in March the English Department shifted to the new university library building, where Frame discovered that her office was now alongside that of Margaret Dalziel. The walls were thin temporary partitions that would be removed when the first floor assumed its library function; consequently the rooms were far from sound-proof. '[I] hear from all around me people dropping Christian names,' Frame wrote to Sheila Natusch.[21] 'But Bert, surely you think . . . but Alf . . . but Minnie . . . It's like a ship [and] the rooms have numbers like cabins.'[22] This enforced intimacy was not wholly disadvantageous. Frame could hear Margaret Dalziel conducting tutorials through the wall and, she told Sargeson, they were 'compulsively interesting . . . I get mixed up with *Paradise Lost* and the Stygian Pools.' As the rest of the year advanced, however, Frame increasingly took to writing in the flat in the mornings, because the noise entering her office had become intrusively distracting at that time of day. '[We] knew that she was among us,' Alan Horsman would say later, 'but only, like ultra-violet light, imperceptibly.'[23]

On 19 March the student newspaper *Critic* ran a report of an interview with the Burns Fellow written by Laurie Bryant, a student friend of Dorothy Neal White's daughters. It identified Frame as the country's 'greatest living author'; and asked her response to a suggestion that she should lecture on *Owls Do Cry*, which was prescribed reading in a first-year English course. The response was not favourable. '[The book] has a special meaning for me, and while I could explain the theme and underlying currents and simplify the characters . . . I feel there is nothing better than reading, criticising and interpreting a book for oneself. My explanations . . . would detract from this.'

Frame went on to say that she did not mind discussion of her writing style, 'but I rather object when people say I keep on writing about outsiders and people on the borders, about the "world abnormal". I insist I am writing about normal people within a little boundary.' And as if that was not sufficiently provocative, she added, when asked about the possibility of setting new novels in New Zealand: 'This is almost a foreign land to me now. I have never really lived here as an adult.'[24]

Up to the end of April, the only people with whom Frame had socialised in Dunedin were Dorothy Neal White and her family, and Charles Brasch. Dorothy and Vicky had come to dinner at the flat for what Frame claimed was the first occasion she had acted as a hostess.[25] In the course of the evening Frame had let slip that she had written some poems in an invented language. Dorothy and Vicky were 'stereophonic' in their insistence that she should read one and, after a show of reluctance, Frame did so. Vicky White recalled:

It was all very onomatopoeic, not a discernible word of English. When she finished I said, 'Oh, I know what that is all about.' And Mother looked nervous, as if I was about to embarrass them or say something that would offend Janet. I said, 'This is a poem about trolls, evil trolls, and they mine and forge metal underground, and they're going to use this metal in a menacing way above the ground. And Janet said, 'You're absolutely right. It's a poem about the Battle of Britain. The Germans coming to bomb England.'[26]

Charles Brasch had her to afternoon tea and dinner at his house in Heriot Row where, initially, Frame 'nearly died of inferiority and disapproval; he always has that effect on me'. Subsequently, however, she wrote to Sargeson that Brasch had been 'a gracious host, most kind and gentle'.[27] And to Peter Dawson: 'Seeing him from time to time, one [begins to find] him more approachable. I think he is a shy man.'[28] She also went to local drama productions, sometimes in Brasch's company, sometimes by herself. In these early months of the year the plays she saw included *Richard III*, *Antigone* and Lorca's *Blood Wedding*.

To Frame's dismay, Brasch's news of the pension campaign did not sound promising. He told her that 'the minister has said . . . try the Social Security Department for a medical benefit. Which means that JF is not worthy of [a literary pension], only of being declared a lunatic . . . I don't think I can accept [this], as it would bring so much loss of confidence and continued need for the presentation of certificates.'[29]

On 7 May Frame was invited to dinner at Margaret Dalziel's, and discovered that her fellow guests were Charles Brasch (there was a danger, Frame told Sargeson, that she and Brasch were now being viewed as 'a couple'),[30] Professor Alan Horsman and his wife, Dorothea, writer Dennis McEldowney, and the vice-chancellor, Dr Arthur Beacham, a Welshman. According to McEldowney, 'Janet . . . scarcely said a word except to murmur a bit when the Vice-Chancellor wanted her to do a *Lucky Jim* about Otago. She didn't think it was quite . . . "What kind of writer are you?" he wanted to know.'[31] Frame told McEldowney afterwards that she had enjoyed the evening but had been over-whelmed by the number of people there.[32]

McEldowney followed this up by asking Frame to dinner with him and his widowed mother the following month, when the only other guest was the poet Ruth Dallas. 'Janet and Ruth talked shop, about the choice of words,' McEldowney noted. 'Janet is worried because she finds she has a small vocabulary; Ruth deliberately uses a small vocabulary . . . Ruth said she always felt sad when she read a completely worthless manuscript [for *Landfall*] because of the work that had gone into it. Janet said, "I know, I'm having that experience now."' They confessed to one another their favourite comic strips. Frame's was Dr Kildare.[33] Afterwards, she told Sargeson that she found McEldowney 'so civilised. His long period of disability has been a sort of aristocratic Leisure, put to the best possible use . . . Ruth Dallas,' she went on, 'is very gentle, contained . . . She nursed her mother for over twenty years . . . [Such] an experience would bring serenity or insanity.'[34] Along with Neal White and Brasch, Dallas and McEldowney would become her closest friends in Dunedin.

The day after the McEldowney's dinner, on 23 June 1965, Frame came down with mumps. The women from the English Department rallied round mag-nificently, she told Sargeson, bringing her hot soup and other nutritious meals; the men stayed away, alarmed, Frame thought, by the prospect of damage to their testicles.[35] She spent most of the next two weeks in bed, rereading Thomas

Hardy's *Tess of the D'Urbervilles* (and giving into 'much sobbing. A wonderful book, glaring with faults, but so strong, clear, tragic');[36] and reading for the first time a novel written by an earlier Burns Fellow, Maurice Shadbolt's *Among the Cinders*. Of this last, she told Sargeson that, with the final one hundred pages omitted, it would make a very good children's book.[37]

Despite interruptions associated with changing office, losing some evenings to social events and contracting mumps, Frame declared herself 'amazed at having done so much work [and] so quickly'.[38] In the first four months of the fellowship she had 'tidied up' *The Adaptable Man* and dispatched copies to A.M. Heath, completed *A State of Siege*, and written one hundred thousand words of a new novel, which would become *The Rainbirds* and which, she told her correspondents tentatively, she thought was better than *The Adaptable Man*.[39] Patience Ross told her that *AM* had been read with 'real enthusiasm' at Heath's, a comment that had not been made about her previous manuscripts. And W.H. Allen came up with the largest advance she had ever received, two hundred and fifty pounds sterling (her Braziller advance had already been paid under the four-book deal signed in 1962). This novel would be published in the United States in August 1965, and in the United Kingdom and New Zealand in November.

With the help of Margaret Dalziel's rigorous editorial eye, Frame made a selection of work to reduce Braziller's two-volume edition of her stories to a single volume for the United Kingdom and New Zealand markets. They dropped six from *Snowman Snowman*, including the long title story which Frame hoped might be republished separately, with illustrations; and two from *The Reservoir*. The resulting new volume, *The Reservoir and other stories*, would be published by W.H. Allen in March 1966, and by Pegasus in May of that year.

Frame began to work on new stories in the second half of the year. The first of these, 'The Bath', arose from a visit to the now frail widow of her favourite uncle, Bob Frame. Aunty Han had become trapped in her bath one day and would have died from exposure had it not been for a fortuitous visit from a neighbour. Frame was 'haunted' by this tale and worked it into a story which she sent to *Landfall*.[40] It was published in the September 1965 issue. She also continued to write verse, and sent a batch of poems to Charles Brasch in the middle of the year. He kept one, 'The Clock Tower', as a future candidate for publication and returned the rest, which Frame stockpiled for a volume of poetry that Albion Wright had been keen to publish ever since she burned her first potential collection in 1956. Frame now told Wright that he would have to wait until she had a sufficient quantity of work in which she had confidence — 'or until I die'.[41]

She had a further confrontation wth Pegasus Press, though not about her poems. Having engineered agreements for her most recent books that enabled her to earn the full author's royalty of ten percent in the United States and the United Kingdom, she now discovered that Pegasus was taking half her New

Zealand earnings from *Faces in the Water*, on the ground that it had been printed in England by W.H. Allen and exported to New Zealand. 'I hope that this . . . is in ignorance rather than in deception,' Frame wrote sternly to Albion Wright. '[It] is important to me for I haven't even a place to live, and . . . there is nothing else that I can apply for after this year.'[42] Wright apologised and restored to her the misappropriated income.[43]

As the second half of her fellowship year advanced, Frame became increasingly anxious about prospects for the following year and beyond. There was still no sign of the proposed pension. It seemed to her that the options were to apply for a second year tenure of the Burns, which was allowable under the regulations but had not been done previously; to return to the Gordons' caravan in Northcote; or to get herself, somehow, back to England. 'The direct disadvantage [of Auckland] is the unavoidable contact with the family, and the old mental hospital feeling that one is an "extra" in the world,' she confided to Sargeson. '[And] the suburban wilderness of Northcote seems barren after the dour tough south with its big-roomed old houses (old cold houses), and its areas of bush and sea and countryside and seagulls . . . I do like [this] small-town gossipy place very much; I can well see a modern equivalent of Jane Austen's Bath or Lyme . . . [And] the "rightness" is helped by the fact that the Professor of Psychological Medicine [Wallace Ironside] has been very good in making me feel safer . . .'[44]

There was one other possibility, but it seemed to be surrounded by longer odds than the pension proposal. John Money had discovered that Boston University, which had sought to acquire Frame's papers, was planning to establish a writer-in-residence scheme. He shrewdly suggested to Howard Gotlieb that the institution was more likely to secure Frame's manuscripts and correspondence if it was able to offer her such a position. Gotlieb agreed, and undertook to explore this possibility. When Money put this proposition to Frame she was enthusiastic. The prospect of a year in the United States was highly appealing, she told Peter Dawson. But it was unlikely that any firm offer would be made for another year or eighteen months.

With all these factors in mind, Frame decided to apply for another year on the fellowship. '[I've been] told that it might come about quite easily,' she reported to John Money in August, 'as long as someone like James Baxter doesn't apply.'[45] Baxter, by now thirty-nine years old and working as a postman in Wellington, was not only widely regarded as the brightest star in the New Zealand literary firmament; he was a product of Dunedin, whose parents and married brother still lived in the district. He also had a wife and two children to support, and had never previously enjoyed the benefits of a literary fellowship.

While she awaited the result of her application, other circumstances combined to generate a degree of gloom. Frame learned that Constance Malleson had had a stroke and lost the use of her left limbs; and, before that occurred, her cottage in Sussex was flooded and her entire library destroyed. She was returning to Ireland, to be looked after by her nephew, Earl Annesley. 'I'm rather sad to think that I shall probably never meet her now, and never see her cottage,' Frame told Sargeson.[46] And there was no news from A.M. Heath of publishing interest in the Joan Sturges manuscript.

In the wake of this news she heard from Bob Cawley, after a long silence, that he had suffered a heart attack while holidaying in Devon. Frame described herself as 'devastated' by this development; but reported to Sargeson that Cawley himself made light of the episode. 'He asks will I lighten the darkness of his stay in bed by . . . sending him something to read! . . . I have written to him reminding him of the nurse who made the patient without disturbing the bed.'[47] Frame was also worried, she told Peter Dawson, by not knowing whether Cawley had a devoted and encouraging wife at his bedside.[48] He did not; but he made a slow recovery and was back at work again by the end of the year.

Throughout this period too Frame was distressed by her awareness of the war in Vietnam. In May 1965 the New Zealand Government had agreed to send an artillery unit there to support the country's American and Australian allies; and the first group of these gunners was despatched in July. The decision was a controversial one. Hardline anti-communists felt the country's contribution was insufficient; while those opposed to any participation in the conflict began a protest campaign that would be carried on over the next six years. Frame said to John Money that the spectacle of New Zealand's involvement in the war was 'too terrible to think of. I read in the press of the "air of anticipation and excitement" among the young men chosen . . . [It] is sickening.'[49]

As a partial antidote to such considerations, Frame accepted invitations to Sunday lunches at Dorothy Neal White's and stayed on in front of the living room fireplace to talk with the family. According to Neal White, these conversations were 'more intensely exciting than her books, which were like good recordings compared with the live performance'. Their talk was 'very swift, backwards and forwards, gold flecks in the air, like sparks'. To Neal White's daughters, Frame seemed 'very chatty, very lovely. She reflected a version of us back to ourselves that we really appreciated.'[50] On one such Sunday, 8 August 1965, Frame brought with her discarded manuscript pages and fed them into an incinerator in which Neal White was burning leaves. Vicky White remembered 'the flames roaring up and Janet red in the face and her hair red, and my mother red in the face, and they were cackling: they looked like Macbeth's witches with one missing'.[51]

In August too Frame was distracted and comforted by her first visit in thirty-five years to the communities in Southland where the family lived in her childhood: Glenham, Edendale and Wyndham. Glenham had disappeared but for the country store, Presbyterian church and school. Edendale had grown and the family's railway house removed to allow an expansion of the station. But Wyndham, where she started school, was largely unchanged.

[The] railway line has been disconnected and the place has not become industrialised. Our house was there — with a crowd of Maori children playing on the lawn and, I declare, *our* cabbages in the garden . . . I felt enormous pleasure that children, rather unkempt, ragged, full of life and laughter and tears, should be living there, carrying on the tradition . . . [The] storekeeper and the grocer have stayed and grown older . . . [The first] has the same stern face that looked into mine when I was five and tried to buy some sweets with Egyptian coins . . . Southland is very beautiful and lovely . . . [Ruth Dallas] too has the feeling that it resembles an idea of Russia, the steppes, tundra. And I saw my first hawk for years.[52]

Two poems, 'Wyndham' and 'The Place', arose out of the Southland pilgrimage and expressed some of the sediment of memories it had stirred:

Stones do not move here;
people sleep while
the cows make milk
the sheep make wool

and in the empty
railway houses
no Dad sits each morning
on the satin-smooth
dunny seat.[53]

And:

I do not remember these things
— they remember me,
not as a child or woman but as their last excuse
to stay, not wholly to die.[54]

August 1965 brought, again, the season of publication with its attendant anxieties and indignities. *The Adaptable Man*, the novel that explored ways in which humankind might adapt to the 'modern age', and which had grown out of her visit to a Camberwell dentist and her soujourn at Braiseworth in East Suffolk, was published in the United States. The first review that Frame and most other readers saw was that carried in *Time* on 6 August. This introduced the characters, beginning with the Reverend Ainsley Maude, vicar of the Church of England:

Tuberculous and gently tormented, he is a man with no gift for life in his own century, at ease only in his dreams of Anglo-Saxon times. In order to recuperate from his malaise, he leaves his London parish for a quiet East Suffolk village. There he lives with his brother, a dentist, who also dislikes everything modern; his brother's wife, a disappointed woman who digs in her garden as if she had lost something there; their son Alwyn, amoral, educated, cheerfully modern; and Alwyn's fiancée, Jenny, who has no characteristic except marriageability.

*Time's* evaluation of the writing was complimentary. The review spoke of sentences so good 'that they strike a hush in the mind'. But it went on to say, 'the novel's perfect parts do not cohere; there is no novel . . . It becomes a series of aimless events and objectless soliloquies. Although no one seems insane, the tensions of madness, which have preoccupied the author in her earlier writing, are injected in a mechanical and unconvincing way . . . Novelist Frame . . . is too fine a writer to puff up emptiness in such a way.' Reflecting this conclusion, the heading over the review said, 'Emptiness Puffed Up'.[55]

As Frame told Sargeson, she gave way to vanity and read the piece, and was consequently suffering from 'the usual battering of the ego'.[56] The same day she wrote this she ran into the McEldowneys at the museum, and McEldowney recorded that 'she was determined not to be upset [by the review] and *was* upset . . . concerned that they had missed what she was intending, yet thought that their opinion was what she had been feeling about the book. Familiar reactions!'[57] Frame told John Money that even when *Time* had praised her work in the past, they had always been 'low in their tone. I think the only reason they review me is that they think of me as "a madwoman".'[58]

There was an especially interesting feature of the *Time* review that Frame could not resist pointing out to Money. The accompanying photograph of the author, taken by a Christchurch photo-journalist on commission for Pegasus, showed two buildings in the background. One was Miss White's house, where Money had lived twenty years before; the other was the professorial house on campus where he had had his office, and where Frame used to visit him for counselling.[59]

After that poor start, the tone of the American reviews lifted and the consensus was far more positive than the verdict favoured by *Time*. Carl Brandt went so far as to tell John Money that the notices had been 'far, far better, more extensive, and more "selling"' than those for the earlier books'.[60] The *New York Times Book Review*, for example, said the novel was about the urge of people and things 'to assume the right shapes for the twentieth century. Each of her characters would like to become the human equivalent of a television antenna or a three-day deodorant or a really good museum piece. Under Miss Frame's curse they become instead crystal radios, one-day deodorants, museum rejects.' The review concluded:

Miss Frame is undoubtedly the real thing. Her prose is haunting and she can use it to lay a spooky atmosphere over anything she chooses, from a stamp album to a row of teeth. Occasionally she wrestles a metaphor too fiercely and winds up in a snarl of arms and legs, but few writers have ever used so many of them so successfully . . . [She] has done what every writer strives to do: find and perfect a form that fits over her ideas and dreams like a skullcap.[61]

In England, where the book appeared in October 1965, the reviews were deferential rather than complimentary. William Plomer, writing to Sargeson, summed them up by saying that Frame's view of life 'is made to sound rather beyond the reviewers' understanding, but not beyond their respect'.[62] This was certainly the tone in *The Times, The Times Literary Supplement, New Statesman* and *Listener* reviews. In the last of these Jocelyn Brooke concluded that 'Frame is inclined to be occasionally obscure, but she does seem . . . to have got clean away from the general rut of contemporary fiction, which is something to be grateful for . . . [An] impressive and disturbing book.'[63]

Respect too, interspersed with superlatives, permeated the New Zealand reviews which followed publication of *The Adaptable Man* there in November. The *Press* in Christchurch said that the achievement of the book was to reveal Frame to be 'the finest novelist we have had'. The *Hawke's Bay Herald Tribune* spoke of 'genius'. Even David Hall in the *New Zealand Listener* was moved to call the novel 'easily her cleverest book so far . . . What [it] lacks in incandescence of mood, it retrieves in its order, balance and firm intellectual grip.' Hall also believed that the novel was Frame's 'wittiest', though not all its humour was apparent to readers (such as the fact that the Italian farm worker murdered by the novel's 'adaptable man', Alwyn Maude, was called Botti Julio and was a faithful representation of the author's fiancé in Andorra). By shifting her attention to East Suffolk, Hall declared, Frame was making 'a conscious attempt to exorcise her "Waimanu" origins [and] to stand outside them'.[64]

The soberest New Zealand review was that by academic and poet Michael Joseph in *Landfall*. Sobriety did not imply disfavour, however. Joseph considered that *The Adaptable Man* marked 'an outward movement away from the private worlds of her earlier novels', and that its 'patterning of ideas, and even more of the images associated with them, saves the book from being invertebrate'. His conclusion was that 'Miss Frame's special virtue [is] to be our most discerning as well as our most literate novelist'.[65]

If David Hall had, at last, become an aficionado of Janet Frame's novels, so had Frank Sargeson. In *The Adaptable Man* he found for the first time a sustained piece of writing from his former protégée which he could praise without reservation. It erased the doubts which he had formerly expressed about her work and her state of mind, particularly those which had arisen out of publication of 'The Triumph of Poetry'. 'I love it,' he told Peter Dawson, 'the power of her mind, its range, and the way she *creates* — a connection with the world one daily experiences of just exactly the right tenuousness. A brilliant girl, and . . . so human and marvellous as a person.'[66] From this time on, apart from expressing intermittent and minor irritations, he had fewer serious doubts about the range and power of Frame's potential and achievement.

August 1965 was also the month in which Frame moved into what would be her third office in the course of the year. This one was on the south side of the library building, facing Albany Street, where her father had attended school sixty years before. 'I get the traffic noises but I don't mind them,' she told Frank Sargeson. 'It's human voices that . . . drown my concentration.'[67] There she resumed the routine of writing at the university in the mornings, and spent the last three months of the fellowship working on stories and poems ('as in the old days', as she reminded John Money, thinking of her time at Caversham).[68] She planned thirty-five stories for a new collection, and to take 'more care over them than I did over the [previously] hastily published ones'.

She had a mild tussle with Karl Stead, who wanted to include one of her early stories, 'The Reservoir', in the second Oxford University Press world classic edition of *New Zealand Short Stories*, which he was editing. Stead told Sargeson that he presumed Frame was 'punishing me for her misdemeanour';[69] but Frame maintained that she did not 'want to be represented by a "child" story, and [if they are] the best I've done, then I'd rather not be represented at all'.[70] Eventually, after diplomatic intervention by Sargeson and the publisher's editor, she relented and the story duly appeared in the collection the following year.[71]

Throughout this period she maintained a more active social life than she had led at any other time. She continued to attend concerts and plays with Charles Brasch, Ruth Dallas, Dennis McEldowney and Dorothy Neal White and Vicky White. She went to dinner with Brasch at the Grand Hotel and was served by waitresses in the very dining room where she had waited on tables twelve years earlier. With Ruth Dallas at the Horsmans' one night, she burst into tears when Dorothea Horsman looked at her penetratingly and said, 'I know what you've been up to.'[72] Despite this uncharacteristic lapse back into reticence, Frame assured Bob Cawley that 'for the first time in my life I am moving among people [preferably] never more than four . . . in the group. It's my working life that I find exhausting.'[73]

Family circumstances again generated anxiety. Her brother's wife gave birth in late September, to a daughter they called Zarene Rose. But within two weeks Zelda Frame was in Cherry Farm mental hospital, having suffered a breakdown. The baby had to be cared for in Oamaru Hospital because of Geordie's inability to cope with the care of a young child.[74] This was the beginning of another long and troubled chapter in Frame family history to which Janet would apply the label 'William Faulknerish'. That same month another of Lottie Frame's brothers died; and Uncle Charlie Frame, the last surviving brother of Janet's father, was admitted to Dunedin Hospital with lung cancer.

'I've never [really] known him,' Frame wrote to John Money about this uncle, 'he's been drunk most of his life . . . [But] I've been visiting him because I can't bear to think of [him] unvisited . . . I find he knows the works of Dickens thoroughly . . . My ghoulish mind quite enjoys entering, every few days, a world where death is known to be close . . . and where it stalks in the male version of the Belle Dame Sans Merci, along the corridors. I don't think I have ever seen so many walking corpses.'[75]

In the second week in October Frame heard the result of her application for an extension of her Burns Fellowship. As she had half-anticipated, half-feared, the fellow for 1966 was to be James K. Baxter. She bore neither the poet nor the university any grudge over this appointment, for she recognised its merit. But, to assuage any disappointment she might have felt, the university was able to offer her, from surplus funds in the Burns investment account, a grant of one thousand pounds to 'complete the work that you already have in hand'; and she was welcome to remain at the university as a 'guest' for a second year.[76] 'So Baxter and I shall be [together],' Frame wrote to John Money. '[It's] going to be a rich place — I think especially of Baxter's "mythological" ways . . . I'll also feel less upset about my own retiring ways with someone as eloquent as [him] around to . . . lecture now and again.'[77]

The ostensible purpose of Frame's grant, which — because it was not a salary — was offered to her free of tax, was to complete the book of stories on which she was already embarked and to begin work on a new novel.[78] Because she would receive it in two lump sums of five hundred dollars, she was able to combine the first instalment with the money she had saved through the year and pay a deposit on a cheap Dunedin house that would cost her only twelve hundred pounds. 'It's ridiculous, I suppose, to want to settle anywhere but in one's grave,' Frame had written to Sargeson in September. 'But . . . I'm getting too old to carry suitcases of books from station to station . . . [I need] a centre of gravity that I can live in and return to should I have the good fortune to venture abroad again in future years . . . [And] experience tells me it is better to be in or around the city.'[79]

The house she settled upon was a dilapidated late nineteenth century workman's cottage in Opoho, high above Dunedin's North-East Valley. Up there, Frame would write, an 'immense sky sprawled above the hills, with every cloud going somewhere in a trail of white or black smoke, pursued by storm and wind and sun'.[80] The original house had had four rooms, of which Frame would use one as a study, one as the living room and two as bedrooms. The built-on lean-to out the back contained the kitchen, bathroom and toilet. 'I wish you could see it,' she told Peter Dawson in a state of high excitement. 'In imagination I am [already] sitting at my window writing, not bothered by landladies, not caring whether it is or is not in the middle of the night. It is also quiet, very close to the [Botanical] Garden and the trees.'[81] It was also in the very road, Evans Street, in which June and Wilson Gordon had lived immediately after their marriage.

Frame had no furniture, nor a great deal of surplus cash with which to purchase any. But friends rallied round and made contributions. Ruth Dallas, who had found the Opoho house for her, gave her two beds and took her to Brown's, dealers in cheap furniture, to buy further chattels. Charles Brasch offered a floor rug. Raymond Ward, the English tutor whose book of poems was about to be published by Caxton, and his wife, Joyce, donated other items, including a parson's 'prayer chair'.[82] Dennis McEldowney and his mother had her to dinner in the week of the move, so that she would have one less meal to worry about.[83] The whole experience impelled Frame to exclaim to Peter Dawson that 'Dunedin, more than any place I have lived in . . . is rich in rewarding and kind people'.[84] And the person uppermost in her mind as she wrote this was Ruth Dallas, whom Frame described gratefully as a friend 'of rare serenity'.[85]

Frame took possession of 61 Evans Street on 2 November 1965 and one of the first people to see her *in situ* was Dennis McEldowney. He described the house as 'small, wooden, almost on the street in front but falling away behind, a round bow window, bits of damp, very active borer, lovely view and sun in the bathroom and kitchen, yet cosy enough . . . We sat on the steep wooden back steps in the sun, ate strawberries and cream, talked of borer and dentists, and of how she sees people seldom but — for that reason she believes — enters into them intensely.'[86]

That was not always the impression others had. Ruth Dallas, pleased about the warmth and trust that had grown between Frame and herself, noted nonetheless that they 'did not talk about literature, but about everyday lives . . . Our friendship did not progress past the delicacy of the early stages, where one must not approach too closely . . . But who could fail to love such a gentle and shy person who passed no judgement of any kind on other people?'[87]

This mirrored McEldowney's experience. He too felt close to Frame, especially when they talked of experiences they had shared that were uncommon in the population at large ('anticipation fever' was one such common denominator — an agitation when waiting for a visitor or an outing that drove everything else from the mind and eventually generated a fear, which also sharpened perception). But McEldowney too felt a wall of reserve around Frame. 'I can [hardly] ask who is RHC, to whom she dedicates all her books, & when & why she changed her legal name to Clutha,' he confided to his diary.[88]

As the year drew to an end and Frame prepared to travel north in mid-December so as to spend Christmas and New Year with the Gordons, she put aside the stories and poems on which she had been working to tackle three 'loose-end' tasks. One was to write the long-postponed introduction for the

Joan Sturges manuscript 'Trespassers on Earth', which she then sent off to Constance Malleson and A.M. Heath. Another was to do some research in the Hocken Library for Frank Sargeson, who was writing an imaginary 'dialogue' between Samuel Butler, who had lived in the South Island high country between 1859 and 1864, and William Yate, a nineteenth century missionary who had been dismissed from his post in New Zealand following accusations of homosexual behaviour.[89] Her third job was to report on her tenure of the Burns Fellowship.

In the last of these, she described her year as 'rewarding and productive . . . I may have complained about the noise, and I still complain about it, but the conditions have been such that I have been able to write.' She summarised the work she had done on *The Adaptable Man* and *A State of Siege* (which would be accepted for publication the following month), and described her completion of *The Rainbirds*. In addition, she said, she had written 'about one-third of a book of stories and about sixty poems'. She thanked Professor Horsman and the English Department staff for their hospitality; and she quoted Edmund Gosse on the advantages of working for the Board of Trade in late nineteenth-century London: 'an assured income, a state of comparative isolation, quiet, and unlimited stationery'. These features, she concluded, with the possible exception of quiet, were the very ones offered and most highly valued in the Burns Fellowship.[90]

There were consequences of the fellowship she did not mention, however, for she did not fully recognise them at the time; even if she *had*, a university report was not necessarily the most appropriate forum in which to voice them. In giving her a means of staying in New Zealand beyond her intended sojourn of one year in 1964, in connecting her with a small band of people who were supportive of her professional and personal lives, and, finally, in providing her with the resources to buy a house and property that were her own and nobody else's — by making all these things possible, the Burns Fellowship precipitated the decision that she would remain a New Zealand writer living in New Zealand in preference to being an expatriate one living abroad. And while she would, from time to time, reassess the wisdom of that decision, she would never revoke it.

# CHAPTER NINETEEN

# Home and Away

*F*RAME WAS BACK IN DUNEDIN BY MID-JANUARY 1966. THE SUMMER BREAK in Auckland had not been a happy one. She had been stricken with a lingering virus, and this had made her more than usually susceptible to the city's heat and humidity, and to the inevitably noisy activities of her nephews and niece (now aged fifteen, thirteen and eleven). In addition, Frame felt, there had been a new and palpable tension between her sister and herself.

[For] the first time in my life I went [there] as one who has a home of her own, with no longer the expressed or implied need to be 'taken in' [by] the Gordon family, to be 'cared for' by the kindly sister and her husband and family as an act of charity to a poor incapable sister. I think this was almost more than my sister could bear. By finding for myself a place to live I had annihilated her role in my life. I also had invaded her territory . . . I found it all most distressing. In a way also, just as she lost me as someone to be cared for, I lost her as someone to care for me and 'take me in'. Quite a depressing phase.[1]

It is probable that this view of her position had more to do with the virus and the depression it engendered than with June Gordon's behaviour which, as always, had been generous; and Frame carried that depression back to Dunedin. While she was pleased and relieved to be back in her own home ('the silence is so wonderful it is like velvet'),[2] the gloom persisted, and was not helped by the fact that the Evans Street house was cold and damp when she returned. One of the penalties of ownership was that there was no landlord or landlady whom she could call on to rectify these kinds of problems or to blame for them. They were part of the 'meaning and consequence of possession'.[3]

The result of accumulated tensions was a familiar one. '[The] course I am taking now is the only one left for me,' she wrote to Bob Cawley on 24 January.

'I am withdrawing from people and the world and I am growing successful at it, for it is becoming more and more difficult to communicate . . . even to hold a simple conversation. Aunt Ada Gloom. Yes.'[4] A week later, on Wallace Ironside's advice, Frame checked herself into the Dunedin Public Hospital's psychiatric unit at Wakari and stayed there for three weeks.

'You can imagine how frightened I was,' she told Cawley afterwards, mindful of the catastrophic consequences of her previous stay in that hospital's psychiatric ward in 1945. '[But] I need not have been . . . for all the time I was there no one spoke an unkind word to me, and no one gave me an order. The unit is most uptodate in its treatment . . . [Or] should I say enlightened? . . . [The] mixing of the male and the female patients relieved the tensions in the ward, and also diminished the demand that female patients often make to "see the doctor" — when what they want is to see a *man*.' She had entered the hospital, she added, because things had become 'too much for me'. And she emerged on 21 February 1966 feeling 'a lot more cheerful'.[5]

Almost immediately Frame was thrown together again with people; and whereas her mood the previous month had been one of withdrawal, she had now regained her appetite for moderate socialising. She attended a party at the Horsmans' on 26 February to welcome the new fellows, James K. Baxter (Burns) and Michael Illingworth, holder of the university's inaugural Frances Hodgkins Fellowship for artists. In Baxter, Frame found a 'kindred spirit' whose poetic sensibilities made him an 'intense creature' and a 'tortured soul . . . His conversation is a compelling poetic monologue . . . I am impressed that he is not afraid.'[6] Neither was Frame, and this time she did not flee from contact with her voluble colleague, as she had done two decades earlier. Of Illingworth, a thirty-three-year-old English immigrant, she said that his work was 'very good [and] he promises too to be a refreshing fly . . . in the academic ointment'.[7]

It was the Baxters, however, who became particular friends as the year advanced. Even before the Horsmans' party Frame had reintroduced herself to Jim Baxter at the university and found him to be 'a most colourful character, though his poetry is marred by the fact that he is . . . inclined to act rather than to feel'.[8] Baxter's wife, Jacquie, Frame remembered from the year they had overlapped as university students at Otago, 1945, when, as Jacqueline Sturm, she had been one of only two Maori women on campus. In 1966 they met in the street shortly after Frame had come out of hospital, recognised each other, then had a cup of tea together at the two-storey brick university house in which the Baxters were staying in Cumberland Street. Unusually for Frame, she felt an immediate rapport with the poet's wife, who was a poet and fiction writer herself and would have a story published that very year, 1966, alongside one of Frame's in the second Oxford University Press series of *New Zealand Short Stories*.[9] Writing admiringly of her to Peter Dawson, Frame noted that 'when Jacquie speaks it's as if the whole world is hushed'.[10]

Finding Frame's company agreeable, both Baxters set out to include her in family occasions with their children, Hilary, aged sixteen, and John, thirteen.

*On the broken steps of the army hut in Sargeson's garden, 1955.* (Janet Frame)

*Ibiza in the Balearics as a 'mirror city'.* (Gil Hanly)

Left: *At Willemstad,
Curacao, en route for Europe,
first footfall in a foreign
country.* (Janet Frame)

Above: *Maudsley Hospital, Denmark Hill, 1950s: an oasis of good practice in an impoverished sector of medicine.* (R.H. Cawley)

Below: *Psychiatrist Robert Cawley, who persuaded Frame to meet her own expectations rather than those of others.* (R.H. Cawley)

Above: *Mark Goulden, the 'gambler-publisher', and his wife Jane, who had 'a remarkable resemblance to the Queen of Spades'.* (Jeffrey Simmons)

Bottom left: *Albion Wright, owner of Pegasus Press, Frame's New Zealand publisher for fourteen years.* (Pegasus Press) Bottom right: *George Braziller, first publisher outside New Zealand to generate an evangelical enthusiasm for Frame's writing.* (George Braziller)

Above: *Frame on the Victoria Embankment, alongside the Thames, in February 1962; a publicity photograph taken by Jerry Bauer for W. H. Allen.* (Canterbury Museum)

Below: *E. P. Dawson (at right) outside Flint Cottage, Itteringham Common, with her neighbours, the Lubbocks.* (Janet Frame)

*Frame with her niece
Pamela and the caravan in
which she worked and slept
at the Gordons', Northcote,
October 1963.* (Janet Frame)

*Local girl makes good:
photographed for the
Oamaru Mail in the public
gardens, 'where she spent
many happy hours in her
childhood'.* (Oamaru Mail)

Below: *The front door of
61 Evans Street, Opoho, the
house Frame was able to
buy with Burns Fellowship
money.* (Janet Frame)

Right: *Frame with poet
James K. Baxter,
Dunedin, 1966.*
(John Money)

Below: *Jacquie Baxter
at Evans Street: 'When
she speaks it is as if the
whole world is hushed.'*
(Janet Frame)

*At Charles Brasch's crib on Otago Peninsula, May 1966: Frame 'behind the safety of
dark glasses, Charles clinging fruitily to a verandah post and Karl Stead looking like a
Viennese doctor'.* (Ruth Dallas)

Frame joined them for evening meals, outings to the movies and weekend visits to Jim Baxter's parents at Brighton, a river-mouth community on the coast south of Dunedin. This elderly couple, Archibald and Millicent Baxter, retired farmers, were considerable characters in their own right. Archie had resisted conscription in the course of the First World War and been shipped to the battlefront in France and tortured for his obduracy. Millicent was a daughter of one of Canterbury University's foundation professors, John Macmillan Brown, and had undertaken postgraduate study at Cambridge University in the years before women were awarded degrees there. Both senior Baxters had been prominent for more than forty years in the New Zealand peace movement. Frame was slightly in awe of them, but touched by their kindness and gratified to have opportunities to participate in the life of their extended family. Jim Baxter, she told Peter Dawson, was close to his parents, but somewhat haunted by them: he seemed to have 'taken on himself the burdens and the lightnesses of their journeyings'.[11]

The hills around Dunedin provided Frame and the younger Baxters with another source of weekend activity. They took to walking them together, Frame told Sargeson, 'in rain sun and mist'.[12] After one such excursion, Jim Baxter and Frame each wrote poems arising from their recollections of the afternoon. His was titled 'The Cattle Shed':

> Do you remember that afternoon in winter
> When we left the town of bones behind us, and walked on
> Up the Leith Valley road? All of us
> Were wet as shags! Your coat and hair wet.
> Branches unloaded rain on us. The creek
> Was talking all along the gully
> About whatever suits a water spirit,
>
> And we climbed further up to a cattle shed,
> Crossing the soaking clumps of cocksfoot grass
> With wet shoes. We sat down
> Among the rusted harnesses,
> And ate our bread and sausage,
>
> And you spoke of Andorra — how those churches
> Are built like barns out of the valley rock —
> Being ourselves in such a place; as if, Janet,
> To have been born were enough, as I incline
> To think it is. You and Jacquie
> Made water on the dung-black floor
>
> Before we left. I remember it as a barn
> Made out of rock; a womb; a stopping-place.[13]

Frame's matching poem, 'The Reply', said in part:

> I remember our joy at being in [that] place. There was nowhere
> to sit or stand. The cattle before us
> had made no provision for our comfort, not
> aware perhaps that our thinking bulk
> churns with ideas and feelings and transformations
> other than flesh into beef and grass into milk.
> Or are we so different?
>
> Yes, Jacquie and I squatted on the floor; we made
> the living hieroglyph that John will tell you about
> if you don't already know: the gesture that portrays birth.
> For the memories of women and cattle sheds are enduring;
> how the strangers were given warning, No Admittance.
> Keep Out. No Vacancy.
>
> Yes, I remember that afternoon in winter,
> but I remember chiefly how the cold and wet became
> more cold and wet than we could bear, and like exiles
> we talked of home, of how to get there,
> of how in the evening we'd sit around the manuka fire;
> you hurried on ahead to make the dream come true.[14]

That particular day, 26 March 1966, was not quite winter; but seemed like it, because of Dunedin's propensity to revert rapidly to cold temperatures at almost any time of the year other than high summer. For Frame and the Baxters, the day ended, not with the evening at the fireside for which they longed, but with a dinner party at the Horsmans' for a visiting Danish professor whom Frame described as being 'led, lowing gently, to be milked of expert opinion on the New Zealand cultural scene'.[15] By exchanging poems and recollections of such events, Frame shared the Baxters' ambivalent, even subversive, feelings about having to alternate 'being themselves' with being distinguished writers and fellows invited into the more formal world of dining with academics and literati. They also enjoyed swapping mildly risqué squibs about the character of the city that was hosting them:

> It's no surprighs
> to find Dunedin has no thighs
> that all is cold loin of mutton
> beneath the belly button.[16]

Hilary Baxter was of an age where she preferred to be away from home as much as possible in an effort to establish a life independent of the family. John

Baxter was not, however. Frame formed an especially close relationship with him at a time when, in his early teens, he was feeling rebellious and intolerant of the kinds of compromises that adults make in order to be able to live and socialise with one another. What he valued most about Frame, he said later, was that she would listen to him in a non-judgemental way and take his opinions seriously — the very same qualities appreciated by Dorothy Neal White's daughters. John Baxter shared poems with her, and pieces of artwork — paintings and plasticine sculptures — that other people seemed to find difficult to live with.[17] Frame, astonished at John's knowledge of ancient civilisations, acquired not from school but through his own reading, told Peter Dawson that she was 'grateful that it is the privilege of single women to get to know the children of others in a way that their parents are unable to. It is aunthood plus . . .'[18]

Frame's view of the Baxters, written after she had had them to dinner early in June and spent the evening playing chess with John, was that she found them 'the most congenial family I have known, where congenial is far from genial; they are intense, sensitive, tragic, but I find there is a rare communication between us. I shall miss them when [the] year's term of fellowship is up.'[19]

Time spent with the Baxters was time not spent with Dorothy Neal White and her family who seemed, the adults at least, considerably more restrained in comparison with the Baxters' unbuttoned informality. And so she drew closer to one family rather at the expense of the other. But she continued to visit the Whites and to join Dorothy and Vicky for occasional outings, especially concerts. And when Dick White closed his bookshop and retired in August 1966, Frame sent a telegram of lamentation and good wishes.[20] His retirement, however, was to be of short duration and memorable largely for ill-health.

Another household Frame visited was that of her cousin by marriage, Iona Livingston. Iona had left her teaching position at Arthur Street School in 1948 to marry a university lecturer in economics, John Williams. They had lived abroad for twelve years, in Ghana and the United Kingdom. By 1966 they were back in Dunedin and John Williams was professor of economics. They had two children and lived on Signal Hill, not far from Frame's house in Opoho. Although she found her cousin an intimidating figure, Frame also recognised Iona's kindness and she did have a meal with the family on at least one occasion.

She continued to see and to enjoy occasional outings with Charles Brasch and Ruth Dallas. And she and Dennis McEldowney developed a custom that he would come to lunch from his job as Knox College librarian most Wednesdays. This arrangement continued until McEldowney left Dunedin in November 1966 to become editor of publications at the University of Auckland (a position eventually transmuted into managing editor of Auckland University Press).

In May 1966 Frame attended a literary seminar at the university organised by a student, Kevin Cunningham. At this event, Jim Baxter and Karl Stead read poems and talked about poetry. Stead, Frame reported to Sargeson, was 'magnificently lucid, illuminating. It was wonderful to see him again and to hear his prose and poetry.'[21] After the formalities Frame joined Brasch, Stead and Ruth Dallas for an afternoon at Brasch's bach at Broad Bay on the Otago Peninsula. There was no mention of the falling-out over 'The Triumph of Poetry' and no visible sign of what Brasch, briefed by Sargeson, speculated might be a 'cool breath' between the two writers. Stead would write later: 'I have a photograph of the three of us outside Charles's cottage . . .Janet sitting, smiling straight at the camera from behind the safety screen of dark glasses; Charles clinging fruitily to a verandah post and smiling down at her; me leaning back against another post, pencil thin and formal, with a goatee beard, looking like a Viennese doctor . . .'[22]

Another writer visiting Dunedin at about this time was Phillip Wilson, a Sargeson protégé who had worked for the *New Zealand Listener* and been writing short stories since the 1940s. By 1966 he had had one volume of stories published and three novels and, privy to Sargeson's yarns about Frame, was keen to make her acquaintance. He rang her and then called on her one night after a family wedding at Mosgiel. She, recognising in him a delicacy and a fragility not unlike her own, made him welcome despite the lateness of the hour.[23] They remained loosely in touch after Wilson returned to Wellington and, from 1975 moved to Auckland.

The exercise of friendships and attendance at events and occasions which arose from them were an antidote to the depression which had troubled Frame early in the year. They also cut into time and concentration which she might, in other circumstances, have committed to writing. A consequence was that she was slower finishing the new group of stories than she had anticipated; and even as she did work on them, she was conscious of a new novel 'flowing through me like water over stones. I may be able to walk from shore to shore; I may drown or break a bone.'[24] One of the stories, 'Winter Garden', which would eventually be published in the *New Yorker*, was sparked by her autumnal observation of a solitary neighbour at work in his garden, which included a rowan tree.[25] In April she sent three new stories to Charles Brasch to consider for publication: 'Reminders', 'Back to the Oil Pipe-Line', based in part on her encounter with George Parlette in Ibiza, and 'A Boy's Will', which arose from her stay at the Gordons the previous summer and was focussed on an adolescent not unlike her nephew Neil. Brasch returned the first two and accepted the third for the December 1966 issue of *Landfall*, the last he would edit before his retirement.[26]

Meanwhile Patience Ross informed her that the English *Sunday Telegraph* had accepted an earlier *Landfall* story, 'The Bath'; and that *Harper's Bazaar* had taken another of the new ones, 'In Alco Hall', a 'Waimaru' story based on Myrtle's friendship with a 'fast' woman of whom her father and the neighbours had disapproved.[27] Best news of all was that *Harper's Bazaar* would pay three hundred American dollars for their story. At the request of an editorial committee member, Frame also sent a poem, 'A Timely Monologue', to the Christchurch socialist journal *Monthly Review*, which published it in May.[28]

Frame reported to Professor Alan Horsman that she had completed the new collection of stories by May 1966, but was in no hurry to submit it anywhere because 'I'm ahead of myself in publication of my work' (the completed novels *A State of Siege* and *The Rainbirds* were still to appear; she had not yet submitted the latter to her agents). And one story, 'The Problems of the Newly Born', she continued to 'take up as a piece of embroidery'. She now planned to begin work on a new novel, which she initially called 'The Mill Belongs to Sandy'. She also told Professor Horsman that she would spend the remainder of the year working at home, in preference to her university office. '[Now] I "know" members of the English Department, I do not find, as I did last year, a natural barrier of isolation. I must create my own barrier, and this, I've found increasingly, I can best do at home.'[29]

The single volume *The Reservoir and other stories*, a compression of the two Braziller story volumes, appeared in the United Kingdom in March 1966 and in New Zealand in May. *A State of Siege* was published by Braziller in the United States in July and sold to W.H. Allen in June and to Pegasus in July. In August, A.M. Heath sold New Zealand and Australian paperback rights for *Owls Do Cry* to Sun Books in Melbourne, which seemed a good idea at the time but dissuaded Pegasus doing a third hardback printing for the New Zealand market and had the eventual effect of making the novel difficult to obtain in New Zealand.

English reviews for *The Reservoir* ran the now customary gamut. High praise in the *Guardian* (which Frame described as 'the best review I've ever had') was countered by unconvincing ridicule in the *New Statesman* ('Miss Frame goes in for Katherine Mansfield whimsy'). Her usual champion, the *Times Literary Supplement*, was more emphatically critical than previously (a 'tremulous affair', an 'uneven selection', 'gauchely naive').[30] New Zealand reviews were more welcoming. David Hall in the *Listener*, consolidating his changed position as a Frame supporter, spoke of 'the successful metaphors of the poetic style so much at her command'. But, a trifle more ambiguously, he declared that 'prose is a veil through which [Frame's] imaginaton shines with a light which can blind the fainthearted and the faithful alike'.[31] James Bertram in *Landfall* wrote that Frame 'cannot put words on a page without generating the kind of magnetic attraction that seizes and locks the reader's sensibility . . . For the patterned words, and all the talent and courage behind them, we can only be grateful.'[32]

Reactions to the American publication of *A State of Siege* were muted, with Frame going so far as to tell Sargeson that the book had 'been ignored, which is just as well'.[33] This was not quite so, though some of the higher profile journals, such as *Time*, omitted to review it. Millicent Bell summarised the story in the *New York Times Book Review*:

[The] desire to see truly is . . . the compelling force that drives a retired art teacher to leave her southern New Zealand birthplace for an island in the sub-tropical north. Malfred Signal hopes to be alone with nature and the 'room two inches behind the eyes' — free of the dominating presences of her family, free of the long habit of attaching 'correct' shadows to coal scuttles, milk pitchers and other humdrum objects. She . . . moves into her beach cottage and —? Well, what happens is not clearly evident in the bright outer air of the sunny island.

It is somewhere within our heroine that one stormy night . . . the drama of her existence seems to stage itself. She hears (or dreams?) a midnight-to-dawn pounding on her door. And while she wakes and sleeps and gets on the disconnected telephone to neighbour, priest, police and doctor, the phantasms of her past rise within her, and those she has loved or hated seek entrance into her present life. When morning comes she is dead, her intruders repelled, though a stone, perhaps proof of some outer reality, has been cast through the window and is found clutched in her cold grasp. What has happened?

Bell was not quite sure what to make of all this. Frame's style, she wrote, 'tends to dissolve in mere obscurity. Her poetic voice croons and haunts, she summons wraiths upon the dark heath, but the night passes without revelation. And yet, her fragmented visions are true nightmares, raising authentic goose-pimples upon the skin.'[34]

Charles Poore in the *New York Times* daily edition was less impressed. He quoted Wilfred Sheed to the effect that Frame was a 'witch-novelist' who stirred her plot under a full moon and had access to dark powers. While this formula had potential interest, he felt it had been used mechanically in *A State of Siege*, which he called 'a hardly enthralling display of psychedelic adventure'. He was even less impressed by what he called the 'modernity' of Malfred Signal's New Zealand island. 'Teenagers go around with transistors poulticed to their ears. Hydrofoils ply the waters. When Malfred swats a bug, her weapon is the *Listener*.' He viewed these features of Waiheke Island life as an unconvincing contrivance on Frame's part to imply that faraway New Zealand was part of the world's cultural mainstream — unaware, perhaps, that the magazine title applied to the local journal, not the London one.[35]

One unexpected consequence of being reviewed in American and British papers and journals was that some readers concluded that Frame was better established and far more prosperous than she was, and sought favours accordingly. The National Jewish Hospital in Denver, for example, wrote to her in July with the announcement that its librarian had selected *A State of Siege* as 'an excellent addition to our collection of fine books for the use of our adult patients . . . Since our budget is limited, it is our hope that you will donate a copy of your book [and] we would like you to autograph it.'[36] With its mixture of flattery and pleas of insolvency, this was a variation on the 'Boston lure'. Another correspondent, from Hungary, asked that she send him a complete set of all her published work so that he could write 'a long survey on the development of contemporary novel in your country . . . [At] the same time a complete and up-to-date bibliography of your work would also be welcomed.'[37] Most requests of this kind went unanswered.

The same month that *A State of Siege* appeared in the United States, Frame accepted an invitation to dine at the home of Otago University's director of adult education, David Hall. Hall was the man who had thus far reviewed all her novels for the *New Zealand Listener*. To allay what she assumed would be her embarrassment at listening to someone speak about her writing, she arrived with wool and spent most of the evening knitting a scarf.[38] She *was* embarrassed, but not by discussion of her own work. To her surprise, Hall turned his considerable critical powers on the absent James K. Baxter, and accused him of mounting 'a religious gravy train'. The wool Frame knitted as she listened to this diatribe was left over from one of the pullovers Jacquie Baxter had knitted for her husband.

Days later came unwelcome news that the 'family doom' was once more on the prowl. Frame picked up her copy of the *Otago Daily Times* to read that her brother's daughter, Zarene Rose Frame, to whom she had written a poem the previous year, had died in her sleep aged ten months.[*] The baby was in foster care, having been removed from Geordie and Zelda Frame's charge on the ground that they were unfit to look after her. Dennis McEldowney reported on 29 July that Janet was 'very upset . . . It was such a Frame thing to happen, she said, but [when] she said to Jacquie Baxter, "Why couldn't it happen to someone else for a change" . . . [Jacquie] said, "It does." '[39]

For Frame, the highlight of August 1966 was a three-day visit by John Money, in Dunedin to participate in a symposium on homosexuality. He stayed at Evans Street 'like Miss Gee, "with the bedclothes right up to his neck",' Frame told Sargeson. 'He need not have worried.' They also had a meal at the Baxters, of muttonbird, a southern New Zealand — and Maori — delicacy; and visited their mutual landlady, Miss Ida White, who was now markedly

---

[*] Geordie Frame too wrote a poem about the death of his daughter:

> On yon hill where the cold wind blows
> Lies my darling Zarene Rose.
> The Welfare said they'd take care of you.
> It wasn't very often.
> They took you away in a cradle
> But brought you back in a coffin. (*Oamaru Mail*, 28/12/87)

more frail than she had been when Frame was in her flat. For days after Money left Frame was able to detect an aroma of Old Spice aftershave, which was still a novelty in New Zealand.[40]

The following month she had further house guests, and ones she found more of a trial. The bereaved Geordie Frame and his wife, Zelda, came to stay — for three days and three nights 'and too long . . . They sat on the sofa and cuddled and ate chocolates . . . [Then] they got into the bath together . . . Both weigh fifteen stone . . . Hippos bathing.'[41] Frame was at first pleased that they seemed happy after the baby's death; and then wondered if they were callous. And she found the whole experience too disruptive and exhausting to risk a recurrence. So she got rid of one of the two spare beds so that in future she could say truthfully that she could only accommodate one guest at a time.[42]

In September too Charles Brasch stepped down as editor of *Landfall* , twenty years after establishing the journal. With a circulation of some fifteen hundred copies by the mid-1960s it was not an economic proposition and had been able to survive and to pay contributors only because of continuous support from the New Zealand Literary Fund. But its influence was out of all proportion to the size of its readership and its ability — or inability — to generate cash. It had become, as Brasch intended, the country's leading literary journal; it had persisted where others had continually arisen and failed; and its standards of editorial taste and discretion, while ridiculed in some quarters as being élitist, were unquestionably and consistently high. Between 1947 and 1966, most new New Zealand writers of poetry and fiction cut their teeth on and in *Landfall*; and the Sargeson generation found there its first journal publication outlet that managed to maintain regular publication. All contributors benefitted at some time from Brasch's skills as an editor and mentor.

To mark Brasch's departure, and to thank him for his editorial contribution to New Zealand letters, Frank Sargeson organised a 'round robin' of signatures to appear in the last issue of the journal for which Brasch was responsible. It was headed, 'This page is to surprise and honour Charles Brasch,' and it was signed by Sargeson, Frame, Ruth Dallas, C.K. Stead, Allen Curnow, Denis Glover, Dennis McEldowney, and all the major writers, reviewers and artists of the initial *Landfall* era. Frame said to Sargeson that the gesture, which did succeed in surprising Brasch, was 'a masterpiece of good taste . . .'[43]

Caxton Press would continue to publish *Landfall*, and the new editor, Robin Dudding, a teacher and former founder and editor of a smaller literary journal, *Mate*, was to work from Caxton's office in Christchurch. Consequently Brasch shut down the *Landfall* office which he and Ruth Dallas had run above the University Bookshop. Frame was a beneficiary of the closure. 'You [should] see my swanky office,' she wrote to John Money in October 1966. 'I [now] use the front room . . . to work in as it stays cool all day . . . though the sun comes in in the early morning. It is also the quietest room . . . Charles offered me [his] desk, a filing cabinet, and an armchair. So now I sit behind the historic Landfall Desk, and it's marvellous to be able to spread papers . . . [It] has four big drawers with locks.' It also had eight legs, and Frame had to cut each of them down several inches so that she could work comfortably on the desk's leather-covered surface. On this surface, she told John Money, 'I've started a new book which I hope to finish (first draft) before Christmas.'[44]

This was 'The Mill Belongs to Sandy', which she described as another 'Dunedin novel'. The first Dunedin novel, *The Rainbirds*, written in her Burns year, she had sent to A.M. Heath and Brandt and Brandt only the previous month. Patience Ross told her on 23 September that in it 'you have come much farther to meet the reader so that Godfrey's story will be "understanded of the people", and this should help to enlarge the public for your work . . . You have made me *see* Dunedin in *The Rainbirds* — and I feel as though I've been living next door to the family.' She added that everyone at Braziller was enthusiastic about the manuscript.[45]

The following month Frame sold half-a-dozen stories from *The Lagoon* to the New Zealand Broadcasting Corporation, and they offered to increase the fee if she would read them herself, which she — who had twenty years before aspired to a job in radio — could not resist. This small windfall, the fee from *Harper's Bazaar*, advances for *The Rainbirds*, and five hundred pounds of her grant from the university still to come, meant that Frame's financial position towards the close of 1966 was strong. She told Alan Horsman that, if she likened her mind to a sheep farm, 'I could say that financial security has set free the home paddock where the best grazing is, but has not removed the need to let the flock wander out of sight in the dangerous places — snow, swamps, rivers, cliffs.'[46]

And she set yet another book in motion when she posted one hundred and sixty poems (out of an accumulation of around three hundred) to George Braziller on 10 November. They were accompanied by the usual deprecating letter, as if Frame wanted to forestall Braziller's rejection of the collection by first rejecting it herself. 'Re-reading [the poems] with detachment I pronounce them pusillanimously pastoral, gently Georgian, and not at all the sort of verses I dream of writing. They are technically poor, also with jiggety-jig instead of concealed rhythm . . . but I'm improving . . . All but a few (say, twenty) have been written in the past two years.'[47] Which meant that all but a few had been written in Dunedin. Frame suggested calling the collection *The Pocket Mirror* — 'because writing them as I do, in odd moments, is really a kind of sneaking out of a pocket mirror to check up on appearances and reflections'.[48]

Braziller did not reject the poems: he had not rejected any work Frame offered him for publication. And he suggested that he bring them out in April or May of 1967. He also suggested, after consulting John Money, that Frame come to the United States so as to be there at the time of publication. 'We will, of course, reimburse you for your ticket when you arrive.'[49]

This invitation, and the prospect it presented of seeing again friends in the United Kingdom as well as John Money and the Brazillers in the United States, and further experience of America, released in Frame a surge of exaltation.

'I'm *so* excited,' she told Money, 'quite mad with delight and feel I owe you many many thanks and Geo B also for his quite incomprehensible generosity.'[50] To Bob Cawley she wrote that it was 'impossible for me to think of coming to the northern hemi without a visit also to the UK . . . Do give me some advice on how not to be in a cold panic when I fly.'[51] Her feelings of anticipation intensified when Money said she could use his Baltimore house as a base (he would be away for part of the first half of 1967); and that he would arrange some foundation support to contribute to her expenses, and, possibly, some story and poetry readings to generate further income.[52]

Frame's only source of regret about the coming adventure was that, if she spent most of 1967 away from Dunedin, she would lose touch with the Baxters. Jim Baxter's application for a second year on the Burns Fellowship had been successful, so the family would remain in the city for at least another twelve months. Once that period was over, however, they would be obliged to return to their home in Wellington. It was some consolation for Frame, therefore, that she was asked to dinner with the family on Christmas Day 1966, in Jim and Jacquie's university house. The grandparents were there, Jim's brother Terence and his wife, Lenore, and children, and Jim, Jacquie, Hilary and John. Writing to John Money, Frame described the gathering as 'historic' and said that the family had 'helped me tremendously just by being themselves and accepting me as myself: an act of acceptance that is rare in my life'.[53]

She decided to let her house while she was away, to cover the expense of rates and insurance. Then she changed her mind — because the university accommodation service recommended that she charge more than she thought was reasonable; and because the first group of prospective tenants wanted her to install a refrigerator and a washing machine, both of which she lacked.[54]

Frame bought a round-the-world air ticket and planned to begin the trip from Christchurch on 18 January 1967 (which meant she would have to be back in New Zealand within twelve months of that date). From there she would fly to Auckland, spend a month with the Gordons, then fly to Mexico on 20 February, and on to Baltimore two days later. She planned to base herself at John Money's house for about six weeks, then move to New York at whatever time was convenient for George Braziller. Then, in the northern hemisphere autumn, she would visit England on the way home, to stay with Peter Dawson and to see Bob Cawley, Patience Ross and Mildred Surry. She aimed to be home by the end of the year.

Three days before she left Dunedin, Dick White died. Frame could not bring herself to attend the funeral. But the day it took place, 16 January, she came to the house to support Dorothy, Vicky and Kerry when they had people there after the service. She felt immensely dejected at their (and her) loss. The following day Dorothy and the Baxters saw her off at the Dunedin Railway Station for her trip to Christchurch, Auckland and the world.

The month in Auckland seemed to pass rapidly, though the city was hotter and wetter than Frame remembered — it seemed to be undergoing a tropical monsoon season rather than a sub-tropical summer. She visited Jess Whitworth, still alive, but more fragile and confused than ever; and saw Audrey Scrivener at her parents' home in Esmonde Road. She had several meals with Frank Sargeson, including one on 28 January with the additional company of Dennis McEldowney, who was now deeply immersed in his publication work for Auckland University. Sargeson teased her about the nature of the books she was likely to encounter as 'bedside reading' in John Money's house; and speculated that, while he liked and admired Karl Stead, he felt that he had been handicapped by reading an insufficient quantity of bad literature in his childhood.[55]

The following week Frame had dinner with McEldowney at his new flat. They met in the city, looked at paintings in a gallery, then caught a bus to Remuera. On the bus, however, both writers were overcome by heat and humidity, and Frame by motion sickness as well. 'We did not have a very auspicious beginning,' McEldowney wrote in his diary, 'what with the heat, the crowd, the bucketing [rain], the excitement. Janet began to feel faint.' They got off the bus at Newmarket and tried to find a taxi for the remainder of the journey. When the queues proved to be too long, and the taxis too few, they reverted to a bus and this time arrived in Remuera without further incident.

At the flat, where McEldowney was, for the first time in his life, living on his own, Frame 'seemed quite herself . . . [She] has concluded she does not like Auckland. One thing that distresses her is that it is such a holiday town . . . "and I am a puritan".' She told McEldowney that she had already been at the Gordons' 'too long, & although she still has the American trip ahead, she's homesick for Dunedin. The first time she has been homesick . . . for it is the first time she's had a home she wanted to return to.'[56]

# CHAPTER TWENTY

# Utopia Discovered and Postponed

*D*ESPITE HER UNCERTAIN ABILITY TO NEGOTIATE THE CITY BY BUS, Frame left Auckland by plane on 20 February 1967 and flew to Mexico via Tahiti. The trip was a 'long nightmare' of turbulence and discomfort.[1] What should have been two days of recuperation in Mexico City was sabotaged by an attack of altitude sickness and she spent the time in bed. It was not until she reached Baltimore on 23 February that she felt she was beginning to recover from the first leg of the journey.

John Money greeted her with the news that he had secured for her a grant of two hundred and fifty dollars from the Henry Foundation, a private trust established by the wealthy father of one of his former students. The purpose of the money was to enable Frame to 'collect materials and impressions for a U.S. novel'. If she was deemed to have made sufficient progress on this objective, there was the prospect of another grant, and the possibility of the loan of an apartment in New York.[2] Money also reported that Frame's American agent, Carl Brandt, was investigating the availability of fellowships that might provide additional support for her to work in America.

Money had a further surprise. On her first night in Baltimore he took Frame to dinner at the home of the writer John Dos Passos, author of the much admired *USA* trilogy of novels. 'I spent the evening (in dark glasses) listening to every word Dos Passos said and trying to remember everything he revealed about himself,' she wrote to Sargeson. 'I suppose my attitude was one of hero-worship . . . what Karl Stead . . . referred to as "a Scotsman's gaze at his porridge".' Dos Passos told her that he was reading 'an eleventh century account of the Lisbon rebellion with footnotes in Latin; also *Barnaby Rudge*'.[3]

She woke at four o'clock the following morning in Money's spare bedroom to see snow whirling against the window and hear 'the howling of the wind and of what sounded like wolves . . . but they were dogs making long lonely howls'. At daybreak she took a quick walk outside 'to get my bearings — and how surprised I am to find that even with the temperature below freezing it feels no colder than Dunedin except that here, if the wind blows in your face, you cannot breathe for the cold of it'.[4]

Frame overlapped with Money for just over a week before the sexologist set off for a tour of Australia and New Zealand, leaving Frame at work in his basement with a typewriter, an ample supply of Johns Hopkins paper, and an unexpected companion named Ed Brown, who had just been appointed lecturer in history and economics at Copplin State College.[5] 'I'm glad of the company,' Frame told Peter Dawson, 'to ward off the gangsters . . . That is no exaggeration. America's a tough place, and this part of Baltimore is very tough: each night and day there are several beatings and shootings, and last night the shot was about thirty yards away. I find it hard to get used to the fact that I can't go out into the street as soon as night falls; and I can't get used to the screaming sirens — police, fire, ambulance — rushing every moment to an emergency.'[6] When Ed Brown was out during the day, Frame added, she barricaded herself in the house.

A week later, writing to Dorothy Neal White, Frame said she had become convinced that 'the only way to travel is to stay in one place. I'm getting quite absorbed in the constitutional affairs of the state. Maryland has just abolished the death penalty, has repealed a three-hundred-year-old law which forbade inter-racial marriages, has decided to appoint an ombudsman . . . and has introduced a bill to appoint a State Poet Laureate . . . I've also attended a performance of Beethoven's Ninth Symphony by the Baltimore Symphony Orchestra and the Maryland State College Choir.'[7]

Frame tried to work on the novel in progress but found herself too restless to settle to a concentrated routine of writing; what she was best able to do, she told Sargeson, was 'gather impressions. Last evening one of the medical students took me to a lecture on the modern European novel . . . I was not terribly impressed by the lecturer's ideas and style, but I enjoyed his sense of humour . . . And the young student generously said to me, taking it for granted that I have a driving licence . . . "You can have my car all day if you like, to drive yourself around and see the sights."' For all the size of the city and of the state of Maryland, however, Frame remained more impressed by the literacy of New Zealand.'I have yet to find a bookshop in Baltimore . . . There's a small medical bookshop down by the hospital, and it stocks a shelf of classics, and I found a big shop full of paperbacks, but no poetry among them, [only] "best sellers".'[8]

In mid-April Frame moved to New York and checked into the YWCA. She lasted one night. In a repeat of her experience in Glasgow with Jess Whitworth, she was asked to leave, this time because she tapped on the walls of her room in an effort to persuade other tenants to turn down the volume on their radios. The desk clerk already had doubts about her *bona fides* because the name on her traveller's cheques (Clutha) did not match the name in which her booking had been made (Frame). She was rescued the following night by George Braziller, who had her to dinner with the French novelist Nathalie

Sarraute (whom he also published in America) and found her temporary accommodation.

That evening with the Brazillers at Washington Square on 15 April was 'so wonderful', Frame told Peter Dawson. '[The] *most* wonderful part was when I somehow found myself next to the Writer . . . and talked with her about the problems of writing.' The practitioners of the *nouveau roman* had argued that the traditional novel created an illusion of order and significance that was not matched by reality. Having reached the same position by instinct rather than argument, Frame was excited by the opportunity to talk through its implications with one of the leading writers of the genre. 'I drank every word she said . . . I dared to make a comment on her book *The Planetarium* and pursued a metaphor of the stars . . . [She] said, "That's exactly what I meant . . . It's so gratifying to find someone who understands what one is trying to say." '⁹ Reassuringly for Frame, Sarraute, who was sixty-five, looked like a replica of Peter Dawson at the same age.

Braziller arranged for her to stay for a week in the apartment of one of his staff who was on holiday. While she was there she began to explore and to enjoy the city as much as she had done on her previous visit. 'I love the tall buildings . . . with the windows lighted at night as far as the sky, like squares and oblongs cut into mountains,' she wrote to Peter Dawson.¹⁰ 'I don't feel a bit homesick here as I did/do . . . in Baltimore. And the art is so wonderful. And it's fun getting to know the people at . . . Braziller's.'¹¹ Her publisher's office was now in what Frame described as a 'luxurious' suite at Number One Park Avenue.

Over the next week and the three that followed — when she stayed on a special weekly rate at the George Washington Hotel near Gramercy Park — the impressions came 'thick and fast'.¹² Frame visited 'galleries and galleries' and saw a major exhibition of Aubrey Beardsley's work. She viewed W.C. Field films for the first time. She visited Central Park Zoo, and was especially engaged by 'the elk, the yak and the buffalo, that bears himself as if he were the last buffalo on earth'. This thought produced the germ of an idea that would, over the next two years, develop into the 'American novel' which Money had assured the Henry Foundation that Frame would write. She took part in a massive Peace Parade from Central Park to the United Nations Plaza, and was gratified that George and Marsha Braziller had been there too, though there had been far too many people there for her to locate them.¹³ With a gaggle of 'famous authors' she attended a cocktail party at which everyone stood up 'to talk and pee . . . [When] one is poised for flight, this helps. The trapped sitting-down dinner party is the horror.'¹⁴

Frame also took the opportunity to visit her old London publisher Mark Goulden, who now worked in New York for Doubleday, the American company which had bought W.H. Allen in 1961. Goulden and his wife, Jane, were 'extraordinary people', Frame told Money. 'She is remarkably like a puppet with no one to jerk the strings. He is plastic.'¹⁵ Plastic or not, Goulden remained an admirer of her novels, and he was able to tell her that *A State of Siege* had been published that month in London by W.H. Allen, and that Allen had also bought an edition of *The Pocket Mirror*, which they planned to publish early in 1968. The American edition of the poems was now scheduled for July 1967.

News of further publication of the poems, in which Frame had had such little faith, was welcome. But the volume had been the subject of some controversy among her publishers. Frame had posted the manuscript directly to George Braziller. He had made a copy and sent it on to A.M. Heath, who then offered it to Jeffrey Simmons at W.H. Allen. Simmons agreed to publish it, but only to 'keep faith with a good author . . . I doubt whether anybody will make any profit.'[16] Pegasus, who had been the first publisher to ask Frame for poems, knew nothing about *The Pocket Mirror* manuscript until Jeffrey Simmons offered the company 750 copies as a run-on from the British edition. Wright accepted the offer, but was offended that he had not been sent the manuscript at the outset, and that, because of the agreements now made in the United States and the United Kingdom, he would not be able to typeset and print the book in New Zealand.[17]

The best news of her New York stay, indeed, of her entire trip, was that her American agent Carl Brandt had been able to arrange a residency for Frame, at short notice, at the Yaddo artists' and writers' colony. She could stay there for virtually all of May 1967, and there was a possibility that she would be able to return in October and November. These stays would cost her nothing more than her bus fares to and from upstate New York.

Yaddo is an estate of 550 acres of woods and lakes near Saratoga Springs. It had belonged to the wealthy Trask family who, having lost all four of their children through illness, bequeathed it as a working place for creative people. It opened in this role in 1926 under the directorship of Elizabeth Ames who, when Frame first went there forty years later, was still in charge.

'The mansion . . . and the three small houses are part of a corporation which invites writers, painters and composers to spend up to two months here, free, while they work,' Frame told Peter Dawson on 14 May. 'I am here for the whole of May . . . [You] have a bedroom, bathroom, studio provided, and of course all meals, with lunch made up early in the day so that you can take it to your studio and have all day free of interruptions. The only things not provided are your working materials . . . Also there is a wonderful library, a music room, and . . . acres of woods, lakes, lawns and gardens . . . [Most] of the writers of today in the US have spent some time here — Truman Capote, Delmore Schwartz, Carson McCullers, Eudora Welty, and so on . . .'[18]

After a flash of fear when she sighted the huge Mansion House (it looked, she said later, like a mental hospital), Frame settled quickly and comfortably into the Yaddo routine.[19] Her room was on the ground floor of West House, one of the smaller accommodation buildings. She attended the communal breakfasts and dinners, and worked contentedly through the day in her studio on the novel in progress. In the afternoons she walked around the lake where, in mid-May, she had 'my first glimpse of a hummingbird, like a huge dragonfly . . . I sat on a fallen log and watched it dancing in and out of the bushes. Being in the woods seems to make one extra alert . . . [I] hope that the snakes come out of hibernation before I leave.'[20]

Slowly, tentatively, she met and spoke with her fellow residents: novelist Robert Stone, poet Ann Stanford, Frederick Bock (former editor of *Poetry Chicago*), painters Lucia Vernarelli and Norman Daly, and journalist and fiction writer John Phillips Marquand jnr, who wrote under the name John Phillips and was son of the well-known novelist of manners John P. Marquand. For Frame, living and working and (in the evenings) interacting with these people gave Yaddo its special character and value. 'It was a rich experience for me to feel for the first time in my life that I was among my own kind,' she said later. 'I [found] it exciting to be in a community where imagination and acute perception were the rule, and where one didn't have to explain oneself . . . the right working conditions during the day and, if one wanted company, the right company in the evening.'[21]

One of the first people with whom she shared that company was the painter Lucia Vernarelli, who invited Frame back to her studio to 'turn on'. Frame, who had never smoked marijuana, did so apprehensively — she was curious to see what would happen. Initially the drug seemed to have no discernible effect on her. But early the following morning, about ten hours later, she had an 'out of body' experience in which she seemed to float in the air. This frightened her, and she never repeated the experiment.[22]

The fellow colonist with whom she formed an especially close rapport, however, was John Marquand, who was one year her senior and, like her, had not been to Yaddo previously. A descendant of the old colonial aristocracy of Newburyport, Massachusetts, Marquand was 'tall and slim and somewhat stooped, had sandy hair and bright blue eyes, and . . . dressed casually in tweed jackets . . . He had a keen mind and a wicked sense of humor.'[23] He had also attracted attention by arriving at Yaddo in a blue Ford Mustang convertible car. He and Frame sat next to each other at the briefing for new residents; and, in Peter Dawson's phrase, they 'clicked'. They shared a sardonic view of the proceedings and a similar sense of the ridiculous. They continued to meet and talk daily.

After attending New England church schools and Harvard University, Marquand had served in the American army towards the end of the Second World War and in the course of that service had visited Andorra. He then returned to Harvard, worked for four years for *Cosmopolitan* magazine, and published his first novel, *The Second Happiest Day*, in 1953 under the name John Phillips. This book was praised as an ironic chronicle of his generation and his

WASP-ish class. He spent much of the 1950s living in Europe, working as a journalist and short story writer and mixing with such luminaries as George Plimpton, James Baldwin and Jacqueline Bouvier, whom he courted in France before her marriage to John F. Kennedy.

John Marquand's great burden, however, was his father and his name. John Phillips Marquand senior, who died in 1960, had been a best-selling author who managed to achieve wealth and popularity (especially for his pre-war *Saturday Evening Post* stories featuring a Japanese detective, Mr Moto) and a degree of critical acclaim (a Pulitzer Prize, for example, for his 1937 novel *The Late George Apley*). John P. Marquand junior wanted to be a writer; but he wanted to accomplish this outside the shadow of his domineering father. So he used his forenames as a *nom de plume*; and, after reviewers had detected similarities between his first novel and his father's *oeuvre*, he tried to write in a manner as unlike Marquand senior as possible. One consequence of this was that his putative second novel was never completed (though he would publish a memoir, *Dear Parrot*, in 1980). Instead, he won his reputation among his peers for his journalism and short stories, and for his geniality — his friend Jules Feiffer said he had one of the most 'discerning and entertaining minds of our time';[24] and he was published in such journals as *Esquire*, *Paris Review*, *Harpers* and *Commentary*.

By the time Marquand met Janet Frame in May 1967 he had been married for twelve years to the editor Susanna Coward, and they lived with their young son, James, in a New York apartment formerly owned by the actress Ethel Barrymore. They spent part of each year at their summer home in Martha's Vineyard and, in concert with other families, rented an island in the Caribbean for Christmas vacations.

It was the Marquands' summer routine that became relevant to Frame's prospects. When John Marquand learned that she hoped to stay longer in New York, and that the accommodation hinted at by the Henry Foundation had not materialised (though the foundation gave her a further $250), he offered Frame the use of the roomy apartment in West 57th Street, rent-free. 'How tantalising it all is,' Frame told John Money. 'I wish now that I *had* let my home in Dunedin, then I would feel more like staying longer; but I think it is just as well to have something to remind me that I live in NZ — the longer I stay away the harder it will be to return.'[25]

Marquand's offer was the first of many kindnesses that he and his wife would offer Frame in the coming years. These would arise partly from their feeling that she was a major talent who needed nurturing and protection; and partly from the considerable enjoyment they experienced in her company. John Marquand would come to the conclusion that Frame was a genius; and he was evangelical in urging the merits of her stories and novels on his friends and professional associates.[26] For her part, Frame was charmed at the outset by Marquand's good looks and easy, courteous manner. But she came to admire his work too once she had had the opportunity to read his novel and his stories. 'He is a very powerful writer with deep sensibility,' she told Peter Dawson, 'a much better [one] than his father, but he has the problems of being the son of a famous father.'[27] And to John Money she wrote: 'I checked proofs for a story John had written and I read another . . . there's no question of his literary power.'[28]

Without fully comprehending the complexities of John Marquand's genealogical connections to the rich and famous (his stepmother's sister was married to John D. Rockefeller III, for example, and Buckminster Fuller was a cousin), Frame was especially intrigued to discover that her mother's Curzon ancestors had been friends of *her* mother's favourite New England poet, John Greenleaf Whittier; and that the literary agent Carol Brandt had been the long-time mistress of Marquand senior, and Carol Brandt was the mother of Carl Brandt, Frame's agent. Such a tight mesh of associations made the American literary world, at least on the east coast, seem unexpectedly close, even incestuous.

Frame left Yaddo at the end of May 1967, full of praise for its emotionally supportive environment and for the 'incidental riches' she had found there.[29] She now had a specific and clearly defined notion of a writer's Utopia. In four weeks she had made 'considerable progress' on the new novel, which would eventually emerge as *Intensive Care*; and she confirmed with Elizabeth Ames that she would return in October and November, between visiting England and returning to New Zealand at the end of the year.

She accompanied John Marquand back to New York, where he introduced his new friend to his wife, Sue, and showed her the apartment in West 57th Street. The latter, Frame noted later, had 'Rosettis on the wall, ancient fine furniture and [on] the pipe rack "contentment in the bowl of the pipe"';[30] there were fifty bottles of wine on the wine rack. It was also, she added approvingly, 'almost next door' to the Museum of Modern Art.[31] Sue Marquand, who was working for the publisher Random House, was initially guarded about the visitor who had been sprung on her, assuming that she was — or wanted to be — her husband's mistress. After an hour of conversation, however, she melted. There was nothing even vaguely threatening about Frame's mien and mannerisms; she readily agreed that Frame should have the apartment the following month.[32]

Frame then returned to Baltimore to 'see out the month' with some impatience. She accompanied John Money on a visit to Buffalo on Lake Erie in the northwest of New York state, where he was to see the father of one of his students. While there, she joined a party of American tourists to cross the border into Canada and view Niagara Falls (illegally, for she was a non-American who was not carrying her passport). Asked by a border official where she was born, she said 'New York', in what she hoped was a plausible accent. As she sat in the tearooms overlooking the famous falls, one of the women in the group she had joined opened her purse to display a small nickel-plated revolver. When Frame asked what it was for, the woman said she planned to shoot her husband.[33]

Money returned to Baltimore on his own and Frame carried on by plane to Chicago, where she spent three days seeing the sights ('Lake Michigan is beautiful')[34] and visiting museums and galleries. After her return to Baltimore, she made day trips to Washington and Philadelphia. It was in the Philadelphia Natural History Museum that she witnessed the lesson in snake-handling that became the subject for the story 'You Are Now Entering the Human Heart', which was subsequently published in the *New Yorker*.[35]

On 10 July Frame took up residence in the Marquands' apartment. She did not, initially, have it to herself. Sue Marquand was there, because she needed to make periodic appearances at the Random House office over the summer. 'She and I have complete privacy,' Frame told John Money, 'as the apartment is long with rooms opening off its long corridor . . . [There is] a nursery suite at one end [and] another suite at the other, with the kitchen and diningroom and breakfast room in between. There are two bathrooms. I'm in the nursery suite but I hadn't the heart to move into the little boy's room and so am sleeping in the nursemaid's room, which has an adjoining bathroom . . . I can lock myself in here all day and not be bothered or bother. I'm a bit scared [but] I love being in New York.'[36]

Over the next six weeks Frame wrote further chapters of her enlarging novel. She also began work on a children's story, *Mona Minim and the Smell of the Sun*, which grew out of her fascination with the social organisation and life cycle of ants and a tale about an imaginary ant, Mona, which she had shared in Northcote with her niece Pamela (like most South Islanders, she had been unprepared for the lengths that Auckland households had to go to prevent kitchen and food areas being overrun by ants).

She was not at work continuously, however. She met the novelist and short story writer Hortense Calisher, who lived upstairs in the same apartment building and was a friend of the Marquands. They exchanged greetings but did not converse. 'I admired her fiction, but I did not want to invade her shyness or reticence,' Calisher was to remember.[37] They would meet again when Calisher's husband was for a time executive director at Yaddo. The Brazillers had her for a weekend at their summer house at the Hamptons on Long Island, where Frame was astonished to discover that her publisher was 'a golf fiend'.[38] The most exotic weekend, however, was one she spent with the Marquands at Martha's Vineyard, the island resort off New Bedford.

'The place is paradisal,' she told John Money, 'including a studio for John away from the house, with boat with an outboard motor moored at the doorway and the Atlantic across the inlet . . . [There] are no neighbours, no made road, but all modern conveniences . . . I had some fascinating talks with

Sue — we get on very well [and] I listened dutifully while James showed me all his treasures.'[39] She was particularly engaged by James Marquand, 'a tiny boy of six', who had a Scottish nanny and was therefore developing a Scottish accent. '[He] reminds me perilously of one of the children out of — is it *Jude* or *Tess*?' Frame asked Peter Dawson.[40] 'I could have stayed longer at the Vineyard but I was trapped unhappily in undercurrents all weekend . . . People here seem to live so much on edge . . . I'll never again make fun of the Americans for going to psychiatrists . . . because they need to, desperately.' She pronounced herself 'overwhelmed' by the generosity and kindness of both adult Marquands.[41]

In the course of July 1967 *A State of Siege* was published in New Zealand and *The Pocket Mirror* in Washington, where the State Department organised a launch for the book, attended by the poet James Dickey. Apart from this function, Frame was not called upon to make any public appearances or to participate in promotion for the poems, for which she was grateful (although she did agree to an interview with a single American journalist).[42] The consensus of such few American reviews as appeared was that the poems had been written hurriedly and thrown together without conspicuous evidence of reflection or revision. A later assessment of them in *Contemporary Poets*, published in New York, echoed this verdict. While conceding that Frame was immensely talented and endlessly inventive, it went on to say:

[Her] natural mode of thinking is not abstract but in images. So her poems are mostly 'thoughts', 'ideas', put down in the form of free verse. Their weakness is often that they are neither fish nor fowl — too abstract for the images to seem solid, hard, irreducible reality; and not rigorous enough to seem more than whimsical when considered as ideas. They are also a kind of verbal conjuring, the images conjured into being as an illustration of her thought rather than convincingly confronted in nature. Thus Miss Frame has primacy over Nature, which seems the wrong way about.[43]

This was also an acute description of the manner in which Frame used metaphor in her prose fiction. It was odd to her that a process that was sometimes identified as a weakness in her novels — that she was being overly poetic — should now also be identified as a weakness of her poetry. More sympathetic reviews would follow New Zealand publication of the book in March 1968.

Frame did not initially sight reviews of *The Pocket Mirror*. And she told Peter Dawson that she dared not look in any of the New York bookshops to see if they stocked the volume. But, accidentally, she 'saw some in the window of a religious bookshop, and it occurred to me that the blue and white cover looks chastely religious [and] good beside statues of Mary or the Bibles . . .'[44]

Frame left New York on 21 August 1967 and returned to Baltimore for a week before flying out to London on her forty-third birthday. There she checked into the YWCA for a week, had lunch with a visiting Charles Brasch at the beginning of September and caught up on Dunedin news, and met a New Zealand friend of Peter Dawson's, John Williams, who was working on heart research in the physiology department of University College at London University.

John Williams came to collect her from the YWCA in Great Russell Street on 6 September, saying that he had always wanted to meet her. He was an oddball character, a brilliant researcher with degrees from Victoria, Otago and Sydney Universities, and a profound interest in music and literature. Williams had met Peter Dawson through their joint membership of the New Zealand Peace Union and had often stayed with her at Mount Maunganui. He was awkward in manner and shy among people he did not know well. He also had a reputation among his friends of being erratic.[45] Among those he did know were John Money, who was teaching at Otago when Williams was a student there; and the Gordons in Northcote, from the time he had participated in Pamela Gordon's corrective heart surgery in 1962. Since then he had worked at the Mayo Clinic in Rochester, Minnesota, and he had joined London University in 1965.

In September 1967, Williams offered to take Frame back to his new flat in Dukes Road, St Pancras, to show her how he had redecorated it. Frame felt unwell that evening, but nonetheless accompanied Williams, since he indicated that the flat was roomy and might be a suitable base for her to stay when she was visiting London. He recommended that she take aspirin for a headache that grew worse in the course of the evening. Back at the YWCA the following morning Frame was very ill, and vomiting. She hoped to be able to spend the day in bed. But the maid who came to service the room told her that was against the rules and that she would have to see a doctor. Frame did so, and he sent her to Middlesex Hospital with what was at first thought to be appendicitis, then (because of her sister's history) a brain haemorrhage; but, after a range of tests, turned out to be viral meningitis. She would have to remain in hospital for the next six weeks and would thus see her English stay and then her return trip to America evaporate in a haze of dizziness, headaches and fatigue. She had little energy or concentration for reading over this period; but she did manage to write some letters.

'The word meningitis . . . still wakens childhood bogies,' she told Dorothy Neal White on 17 September. '[With] the physician and medical students discussing the case unreservedly (but in low tones) around my bed, I imagined the direst of fates . . . [When] the consultant gazed into my eyes and asked earnestly, "Can you see me? Are you quite sure?" I was already arranging myself for a course in braille with a guide dog especially imported to Dunedin.'[46] This prospect was made to seem more real when Frame discovered that a handicapped woman working on one of the hospital desks had lost most of her sight as a consequence of meningitis. To Constance Malleson she wrote that, in such an environment, 'I was forced into thinking more than I wanted to . . . about pain; most often one is faced with contemplating the alloy; here it was the pure product.'[47] She was agog with astonishment when two women patients in her ward who 'died' were resuscitated.

Much of what she saw in hospital seemed to present possibilities for use in fiction; and she was soon contemplating extending and recasting 'The Mill Belongs to Sandy' with the inclusion of hospital scenes. As an antidote to monotony, she also considered composition of a detective novel. 'I have in mind . . . the young house surgeon,' she wrote to Bob Cawley, 'who, not being able to decide whether to be a private detective or a doctor, chose medicine with detecting as a hobby: the two professions are indeed complementary. I have not yet chosen the victim . . . but I do feel the x-ray basement is swarming with opportunities for bumping off Russian/Chinese diplomats.'[48]

One of the few books she tried to read, slowly, was Gustave Flaubert's *Madame Bovary* and, she told Cawley, 'I've had the extra relish of comparing Charles Bovary's life with that of the modern doctor . . . in a modern hospital':

Charles rode through the country lanes in rain and snow. He ate omelettes at farmhouse tables, thrust his arm into damp beds, had his face splashed when he let blood, listened to death rattles, examined dirty chamber-pots and rolled up a deal of dirty linen.[49]

There were visits from John Williams, Patience Ross and Mildred Surry (who, Frame now decided, more resembled a policewoman than a librarian). And Bob Cawley arranged for one of the former Maudsley nurses to see her. But it was Williams' visits she enjoyed most with his talk of music and literature; and, because of the rapport they established, he suggested to Frame that she convalesce at his flat after her discharge from hospital on 20 October. After considering the cost and inconvenience of a rest home for professional women in Sussex, suggested by Patience Ross, Frame decided to accept John Williams's invitation.

On 26 October, Frame wrote to John Money that she had had to cancel her proposed second visit to Yaddo, 'though I almost weep at the thought . . . [What] a gloomy ending to a wonderful year.'[50] She was still suffering from fatigue, intermittent dizziness and difficulty in reading. '[My] cell count indicates that some of the virus is still in my brain . . . [but] it should go away gradually if I loll around keeping busy doing nothing.'[51] A bus trip or a two hundred yard walk still exhausted her, she said. She would not be well enough to fly out of London until 10 December; and doctors were advising her to delay the final and longest leg of her journey to New Zealand, which she was supposed to take before her ticket expired on 19 January 1968.

Frame told Audrey Scrivener that John Williams's flat in Dukes Road stood 'beside St Pancras Church & around the corner from a house once occupied by W.B.Yeats'.[52] On Sundays she was able to hear a plenitude of church bells — but having so many in earshot meant that she was aware of a discordant lack of coordination. She described the flat as 'big [and] roomy, on three floors: a kitchen & sittingroom; a bathroom & his bedroom; & upstairs two small rooms, one of which I'm using as a bedroom. [John] has been very kind . . . [but] I rarely see him except for an occasional evening cup of coffee.'[53] In fact she and Williams did manage to see something of each other; and a degree of intimacy developed. A little later Frame was acknowledging that she 'enjoyed his company immensely, and admired him greatly . . . [He] gets top marks from me for "livability-with".' She would certainly consider staying with him on future visits to London. And she went on to say that she was increasingly grateful to Frank Sargeson for introducing her to Dawson, who in turn introduced her to Williams, 'and so on and so on into richer paths . . . [My] debt to Frank S increases every year, in a positive way . . .'[54]

In the days before she left England, Frame attempted a few expeditions, to test and (she hoped) increase her stamina: to the gallery at the Courtauld Institute, to the theatre (Ibsen's *Ghosts*, featuring Peggy Ashcroft), and to Bob Cawley's consulting room at the Maudsley. At this last, in addition to their customary 'conversation', she had a full physical examination (a 'chaste' one, Frame assured Peter Dawson).[55] Cawley was of the opinion that she should not attempt the full trip back to New Zealand for a further six weeks to two months.

She *was* able to return to the United States on 10 December, however, and hunkered down once more in Baltimore, to continue recuperation and consider her next moves. John Money had gone to New Zealand, where his mother had died in November, and Frame had the house to herself for three weeks. '[Not] a pleasant prospect in some respects,' she told Peter Dawson on 17 December, 'but in others quite enjoyable. The house is now well barricaded with bars on all windows & chains & locks on both back & front doors — what a bizarre pretence of being civilised! Also I have a tear-gas gun [which] might be helpful if I were attacked.'[56] A fortnight later she reported to Sargeson that a neighbour had been attacked over Christmas. The intruder had 'tied up the woman, legs and feet, robbed her, raped her, and left her strangled. My turn will come . . .'[57] Her proximity to such crimes continued to thrill and appal her.

A letter arrived from Patience Ross to say that A.M. Heath were delighted to read her ant story, *Mona Minim and the Smell of the Sun* — 'it is so fresh and full of fun and poetry, and so utterly original'. The agency was close to an agreement with both W.H. Allen and Braziller for this book. Ross was also keen to get both publishers committed to *The Rainbirds*, but lacked a copy of the manuscript.[58] Publication details for both books would be finalised in the coming months.

Before he left the country, John Money had used the full weight of his university and hospital designations to persuade Pan Am to agree formally to a postponement of Frame's return to New Zealand without financial penalty to her. Her intention was to remain in Baltimore until early February, then fly home. Towards the end of the first week in January 1968, however, the Marquands contacted her from the Bahamas and insisted that she fly to them, at their expense, to continue her convalescence in warmth and sunshine (by this time it was snowing in Baltimore and the temperature had dropped to eight degrees Fahrenheit).

Writing to the Gordons on 8 January, Frame was full of excitement at the prospect of this unexpected adventure:

> It is half past eight in the morning and I've been up since half past six and made my bed and tidied my room and put out the trash can and packed my suitcases for my visit to the Bahamas on Thursday. You'll laugh when I say I've made myself a bathing suit. They are so dear to buy and they are out of season at the Veterans . . . After [the Bahamas], a week here to clear up and post excess luggage, and maybe a weekend in New York, then back to New Zealand. I'm feeling so much better, having had time on my own, though I admit that every sound in the night scared me and I kept my tear-gas gun handy and memorised the police telephone number.[59]

The following week she flew from Baltimore to Miami, and from Miami to Nassau on the island of New Providence. John Marquand collected her from the wharf for the four mile trip to Salt Cay, an island owned by the estate of the Chicago *Tribune* cartoonist John T. McCutcheon, where the Marquands spent most Christmases. The launch trip ended just as Frame was reaching for a bag in which to be sick.

'It is more than I dreamed it would be,' Frame told John Money on 22 January, 'a private island with no other inhabitants.' She described the Great House with its high terrace overlooking the sea on one side and its sheltered vine-covered terrace on the other, with ships' lanterns swinging over a long wooden table. There were two guest houses and servants' quarters. After that, 'nothing but about five square miles of coconut groves & beaches & hibiscus trees. Some of the other vegetation is very much like the New Zealand bush.' She was perpetually hungry, however. 'Meals are at 8, 1, & 6.30 with nothing in between . . . [Have] you ever been famished on a coral island with hundreds of ripe coconuts lying on the ground & no machete to break them open?'[60]

In the course of her first week on Salt Cay, which the family called Treasure Island, John Marquand, James and another couple staying as house guests set off on a chartered yacht for a fishing trip and tour of other islands in the group.

> I was invited but I said no thanks, so Sue & I and Nanny are here by ourselves for three or four days. The seas have been very rough & the

weather made cold by the trade winds — I mean cold enough for sweaters to be worn & for me to look for an eiderdown to put on my feet . . . There was a party last night — just us & the servants & their relatives & I made a hit with my playing of the drums . . . [And now] I'm lounging alone on one of the many beaches, under the pine trees & coconut palms.[61]

Frame remained on Salt Cay until the Marquands left with her on 31 January. It had been a perfect finale to her year abroad and some kind of compensation for the opportunities lost as a consequence of the meningitis. She returned to Baltimore feeling pampered, rested and stronger, and enormously grateful to the Marquands for their continuing solicitousness.

After two-and-a-half weeks at John Money's, to recuperate further and organise her departure, and a visit to New York to say goodbye to the Brazillers, Frame flew to Los Angeles on 19 February. En route, she told Money, 'I almost wept — a combination of fear & sadness at leaving.' The aircraft's heating–air conditioning unit failed and passengers spent the journey 'freezing to the tune of . . . Beethoven's *Moonlight Sonata*'.[62] There was fog at Los Angeles and the plane circled for two-and-a-half hours before landing at another airport forty miles east of the city. From there passengers were bussed to their hotels, arriving in the early hours of the morning. Frame spent the following day with Ann Stanford, the poet she had met at Yaddo; and the day after, they went to Disneyland, where Stanford's husband worked as a designer and took them 'behind the scenes'. Then she flew back to New Zealand via Honolulu and Tahiti, crotcheting a long multicoloured scarf ('my suffering scarf') to take her mind off the journey.

She arrived in Auckland in the last week in February 1968, one year, one month and one week after leaving it, and in time to catch the end of the city's hottest summer in thirty-seven years. She went straight to bed in the Gordons' caravan for another week, an acknowledgement that she was still 'with virus', and listened to the cicadas and crickets singing 'day and night'.[63] She stayed in Northcote into the second week in March, 'moving only between caravan and house and back', and visiting no one other than Frank Sargeson, who reported that she looked ill and was cagey about future work.[64]

Waiting to greet Frame was the New Zealand edition of *The Pocket Mirror*, an additional printing of the W.H. Allen edition. Any pleasure she might have taken in this new book was undercut at once by the high number of misprints and editing errors. 'There's one poem about a turkey,' she told Albion Wright in indignation. 'The whole meaning . . . depends on the particular cry which a turkey makes. Can you imagine my shame and perplexity when I read that someone . . . has decided that I'm writing about a *turnkey!*' To add to her dejection, June Gordon went into hospital for a hysterectomy.[65]

In mid-March Frame returned to Dunedin where, she reported to John Money, she was still weak on her legs. 'My walking seems to be getting worse instead of better . . . my legs feel disconnected from my body.' And her home city, after New York, London and Baltimore, seemed all too like a cemetery — '[it] is embalmed in sweet-smells with perpetual arrangements made to view the corpse'.[66] Her first visit to Dorothy Neal White's was a miserable affair: Dick White dead, Kerry married and gone from the family home, only Dorothy and Vicky in residence. When Dorothy expressed her disappointment at the 'failure' of the occasion, Vicky pointed out that, for Frame, who had last been there on the day of her father's funeral, the return visit was the equivalent of the day after the funeral.[67]

The first job Frame set herself as she eased into a work programme was to prepare new copies of *The Rainbirds* for Braziller and W.H. Allen. 'I was so appalled by it that I decided to rewrite it,' she wrote to John Money on 29 March. 'It's a dreary task, as you know . . . to type, first, four hundred pages, then another four hundred with carbons.'[68] Dreariness turned to gloom when Geordie Frame arrived uninvited with a torrent of complaints about his marriage. '[He] lives in and brings the past with him,' Frame reported. '[His] wife . . . is pregnant again after having a miscarriage following some violence on my brother's part; she writes pathetically about his . . . constant threats; it's all sad and I don't want to get involved with any of it . . . I've written and asked him not to visit me again.'[69]

Geordie's appearance on top of the lingering effects of the meningitis led to an intensification of depression and another crisis in confidence. Frame checked herself in again to the psychiatric unit at Wakari just before Easter. While she was there, the tail of a tropical cyclone swept down the country causing unprecedented damage. It sank the passenger vessel *Wahine* in Wellington Harbour with the loss of fifty-one lives, flooded those parts of Dunedin that were close to the river Leith, and caused the entire evacuation of Wyndham, the family's old home town in Southland. It was, Frame wrote to Peter Dawson, as if 'the land and the sea [were] speaking for us, when we rather presumptuously say so much for and about the land'.[70]

While the country reeled from this trauma, news came of riots in Baltimore and elsewhere in the United States following the assassination of Martin Luther King. John Money found himself in the midst of 'neighbours fire-bombed, police shooting and death in the streets'[71] — the same streets that Frame had been walking with a *frisson* of excitement two months earlier. This prompted her to write, with apologies to Robert Browning:

O to be in Baltimore now that April's there,
for whoever wakes in Baltimore finds some morning unaware
that the strongest lock on the five-lock door
has been smashed (as so many times before)
and the sweat of fear is on everyone's brow
— in Baltimore now.[72]

Any regrets she had had about not being able to stay on in the United States were cancelled by the horror of what seemed to her to be the setting off of 'one huge fire bomb'.[73] When she emerged from hospital towards the end of April 1968, her memories of the fleshpots of North America, especially the collegiality and congeniality of Yaddo, were not forgotten. But nostalgic consideration of them, and the making of plans to return, were for the time being postponed.

# Cherishing America

$S$OME PLEASANT SURPRISES AWAITED FRAME'S RETURN TO DUNEDIN in March 1968, and they eventually punctured the gloom that initially surrounded her. One was the news that Ruth Dallas had been appointed Burns Fellow for the year. Another was the fact that the Baxters were still there. Jim had secured a job in the local Catholic education office and — though he would soon tire of it — it kept the family in the city until the end of the year.

A further source of pleasure arrived in the form of a *New Zealand Listener* review of *The Pocket Mirror*, which turned out to be one of the most favourable she had ever attracted. J.C. Reid, professor of English at Auckland University, said that the volume revealed 'beyond doubt that Frame is a true poet; any future consideration of her achievement must take into account the poetic personality revealed here . . . The sensibility informing the poems is tinged with melancholy — death and mutability loom large — but there are moments of whimsy, sardonic comment, capricious humour. And the work is suffused with an intense sensuousness . . . [The] strength of these poems,' the review concluded, 'lies in their imagery, their intellectual subtlety, their strong yet controlled feeling, their powerful sensuous response to the world seen anew.'[1]

This notice went some way towards reducing a feeling she had expressed of being an 'interloper' among 'real poets'. It came in the same month as a royalty statement from Pegasus containing the good news that, in the six months since publication, *A State of Siege* had sold 1297 copies and earned her $292 (the country had converted to decimal currency while she was abroad in 1967).[2] These figures appeared to indicate that local sales of her books were returning to the level they had set at the time *Owls Do Cry* and *Faces in the Water* were published. Alas, this turned out to be an illusion. A month later came an acknowledgement of error. An order of 400 copies from the country's largest book-selling chain, Whitcombe and Tombs, had been entered twice on Pegasus's stock cards. Consequently the total sold was a more conventional

897 copies, not 1297. '[We] have overpaid you the sum of $80.99. We shall debit this amount against the next payment.'[3]

Frame was incensed and wrote one of the few intemperate letters she ever sent a publisher. 'Can't you forget it for once?' she asked Albion Wright on 29 April. 'You've made small steady sums from *Owls Do Cry* and *Faces in the Water* on the basis of a contract which the Society of Authors was horrified to read . . . I don't think that a mistake in the accounts department, especially in my favour, should be looked up with such care. I've already put the original royalty in my income tax return . . . I can't face receiving a reduced advance if you decide to take the children's book and the (so-called) novel. I think I'd rather try someone else.'[4]

Albion Wright replied in contrite terms, and said that any deductions would come solely from future sales of *A State of Siege*. But he took Frame up on something else she had mentioned. He was dismayed that she wanted to change the title of *The Rainbirds* to *Yellow Flowers in the Antipodean Room*. The new title, he said, 'does not fill the requirements of a good [one], which should be easy to remember and to ask for, and be readily quotable'.[5] To which Frame replied that these were the least of her considerations when she was writing. 'And just as well. I've learned not to listen to advice about my work; and publication or no-publication does not worry me greatly . . . [Posthumous] publication is one of the few forms of literary decency left.'[6] The trouble with posthumous publication, of course, was that it did not generate income for the living writer; and the living writer needed income to be able to go on writing.

W.H. Allen also held out against *Yellow Flowers*, and did so on the ground that they had already prepared the jacket for the book and that it featured birds; Frame pronounced herself 'too exhausted to argue'.[7] In fact, like Albion Wright, they simply did not like the new title and considered it uncommercial. George Braziller, however, as usual, gave priority to his author's wishes and duly published the Dunedin novel the following year as *Yellow Flowers in the Antipodean Room*; the W.H. Allen and Pegasus titles would remain *The Rainbirds*, thus creating a source of confusion for future bibliographers and critics.

Albion Wright was at pains to point out to Frame that book sales had fallen off in New Zealand through the 1960s — ostensibly because of the new competition from television, which had only become available in that decade, and the depressed state of the country's economy.[8] Despite these factors, Frame's income prospects for the coming year looked good, partly because her book and story sales were not locked exclusively into the small New Zealand market. The second half of her 1967 grant from the University of Otago had been deposited in her bank account at the beginning of 1968; she still had monies paid to her as advances on *A State of Siege* and *The Pocket Mirror*; and further advances were imminent for *Yellow Flowers* and *Mona Minim* from the United States and for *The Rainbirds* from the United Kingdom, and probably from New Zealand (W.H. Allen and Pegasus decided not to take *Mona Minim*). Her American advance for *Yellow Flowers*, fifteen hundred dollars, would be — apart from her four-book deal with Braziller in 1962 — the largest she had received. 'He is, in effect . . . keeping me,' Frame said to John Money of her American publisher. 'The sales of all the books are abysmally few, and the advance [for] the past three or four has not been made up, yet he continues to publish me.'[9] Her gratitude for this, and for the fact that Braziller had taken her on in 1959 when nobody else was interested, meant that she remained loyal to him — even when, in the following year, her agents urged her to move to an American publisher who would promote sales of her books more energetically than Braziller had done.

In May 1968, however, Frame told Sargeson that she had sufficient funds imminent or in hand to enable her to go on writing for another 'couple of years'.[10] What she *was* writing, however, or trying to write, was not going well. She had returned to the manuscript of *Intensive Care*, the novel that had grown out of 'The Mill Belongs to Sandy', and she told Bob Cawley early in July 1968 that she was writing 'automatically — I've never done this before; and I've no idea what it's about'. Perhaps, she suggested, 'I had too many experiences in the northern hemisphere and all are fermenting froth only, and will have to mature before I can quaff them.' She added that she would much rather continue to write poems, and say the kinds of things she wanted to say obliquely. 'I feel that one can discover so much by looking away rather than by paying attention to.'[11] To John Money, she said that she found herself too much 'cherishing American memories'.[12]

Beyond the usual business of trying to write, and dreaming of America, 'I lead a very quiet life indeed. I see the Baxters about once a week, and I talk on the telephone to Ruth Dallas . . . I sometimes go to the children's library to say hello to Dorothy White . . . and occasionally I see Charles Brasch hurrying along the street . . . [The] rest of the time I stay at home trying to work and enjoying my privacy.'[13]

The Baxters, she said, were 'so awhirl with family affairs that it's like trying to stop a merrygoround to introduce [new topics] into their life . . . Hilary is pregnant among other things . . . but it is talked about openly among the family and that is good.'[14] Frame had also been shown a collection of stories Jacquie Baxter had written, 'and I feel that if they're not published, there is something missing from our "literary scene" . . . She's a fine skilled sensitive writer, full of gifts.'[15] The stories were eventually published as a collection; but not until 1983.[16]

The 1968 winter in Dunedin was an especially punishing one, and Frame's cottage lacked insulation. 'I decided to live in one room only,' she told Audrey Scrivener in August, 'which meant putting on an overcoat and balaclava every time I went to the kitchen or the lavatory or indeed anywhere else in the house . . . My heart is frozen to my side and won't beat. The fire is frozen in the hearth. My brain is frozen in my head.'[17]

In the midst of lamentations about climate and her imaginative 'cherishing' of America, a telephone call from Martha's Vineyard exploded into her life on

5 August 1968 like a *deus ex machina*. 'Sue, asking will I come to [Salt Cay] for Christmas . . . fare paid . . . I really can't think very coherently because it seems to my narrow provincial mind an awful waste to go "all that way" just for a few weeks . . . [Pack] a little bag with insect lotion and sunclothes, get on a plane, go, arrive, enjoy myself, repack my little bag and fly home without casting eyes west to US or north to UK . . . I'm not really ready for another "fling" . . . I may say postpone it until the following Christmas, but the world might have ended and private islands in the Bahamas will almost certainly be in the past [tense].'[18]

After weeks of vacillation, only intensified by the arrival on 21 August of a cheque from the Marquands for her fare (large enough, Frame said, to support her writing at home for almost two years),[19] she decided to accept the offer. She would, she told Peter Dawson, 'make a year of it'. She now planned to let her house to students, visit the United States and the United Kingdom, and — if accepted — take another residency at Yaddo and try to kick-start the stalled novel.[20] If she was unable to return to Yaddo, Carl Brandt told her, he would investigate the possibility of a place at the MacDowell Colony in New Hampshire. John Money undertook to approach the Henry Foundation for further assistance.

There was now an additional reason why she decided to initiate these moves. Faced with the likelihood that Britain would join the European Economic Community and reduce its market for New Zealand agricultural exports, the country had become intensely preoccupied with matters of economics and trade and the search for new markets. Newspaper stories and parliamentary debates returned continually to these topics. For the present, Frame told John Money in early October, 'I'm tired of New Zealand and its talk of overseas exchange and trade and sheep sheep sheep; when people individually are nice, as I think most New Zealanders are, what makes them so frightful collectively?'[21]

Something of this same feeling leached into a letter she wrote for publication in the *Otago Daily Times*, criticising a Health Department decision to build a large institution for handicapped children at Templeton, near Christchurch:

No large orphanages or homes for children are being built except, surprisingly, in New Zealand. Perhaps it is not so surprising to us: we are used to dealing with hundreds of sheep in paddocks; one might suppose that sick lambs brought into a warm home receive better treatment than children in a large institution.

Our country with its small population has an unequalled opportunity to practise being human instead of identifying itself always with its larger population of sheep and aspiring to Sheepity and Sheephood rather than to humanity.[22]

Elaborating on the theme, she told Bob Cawley that New Zealanders had 'privileges or rights which only the wealthiest in the overpopulated nations can afford — privacy, a vast area of "unspoiled" natural [scenery], accessible silence . . . beaches, sun, and so on. And so far I doubt if we've done much to earn [it]; all we've done is gloat over it, as I'm doing now . . . We're a selfish people.'[23] And she wrote to Peter Dawson: 'I do miss the consciousness of poverty and suffering . . . [because] here it's so easy to go to sleep.'[24]

Such considerations did not sit easily with her acceptance of the Marquands' invitation to stay in a millionaires' playground; but her ticket to Salt Cay was also a ticket to New York, Baltimore and London, where she would experience those features of human life — poverty, discomfort, crime, marginalisation — that both alarmed her and energised her; and it was a passport too back to Yaddo, where she believed she would be treated with care and support as a writer, get more work done, and complete a sequence of development begun but interrupted in the previous year.

John Money was again in and out of Dunedin in late September 1968, turning up the morning after Hilary Baxter's labour, which had been so prolonged and difficult that her parents had serious worries about the survival of mother and child. No sooner was it over than Jim Baxter and Frame had to rush to the airport to meet the visitor; and hours later they sat down to a promised meal of muttonbird and crayfish at the Baxters', with Money oblivious to the drama that had preceded his arrival.[25] Hilary and her daughter, Stephanie, did survive, and Stephanie became a loved member of the Baxter family. 'I, as an observer, am enjoying the human drama and rather envy the baby and its long self-absorbed kind of sleep,' Frame told Money afterwards.[26]

Throughout October and November 1968 Frame's prospects and plans for the following year unfolded as she had hoped they would. Yaddo accepted her as a resident from mid-February 1969 to mid-April. Henry Granoff wrote to say that the Henry Foundation would support her with a grant of one thousand American dollars, with an additional amount to be set aside for 1970.[27] *The Rainbirds* was published in the United Kingdom in October and was generally well reviewed, and A.M. Heath retained her advance for this book for her to spend in England in the four to six months she planned to be there after she left Yaddo. The *New Yorker* accepted her story set in the Philadelphia science museum, 'You Are Now Entering the Human Heart', and agreed to make payment to her when she was in the United States.[28]

In Dunedin, Frame arranged to let her house for eight dollars a week to a student couple who would marry in December. 'Her mother, a paper-hanger and interior decorator, has offered to do some of the papering free,' Frame told John Money on 19 November. 'I'm not mad on paper, but it's good to get the place spruced a bit . . . The house is beginning to show all its aches and pains much like people when they get to eighty-six.'[29] Dorothy Neal White agreed to keep an eye on both house and tenants while Frame was away.

On 4 December Frame flew to Auckland to stay with the Gordons for a fortnight; then on 18 December boarded an international flight for Mexico City via Tahiti. She flew from Mexico to Miami on 21 December, and on to Nassau the same day. There she took a taxi to the wharf, where John Marquand collected her for the launch trip to Salt Cay. The flights had not bothered her this time; and the transference from one hemisphere to another, and from one *world* to another in such a short time had seemed miraculous, she told John Money.[30] She was as enchanted by the island and the living arrangements as she had been on her first visit; and she spent Christmas with just the Marquands and the staff, who included Josephas, the caretaker and manager, whom Frame referred to as 'a wonderful man and a wonderful sailor'.

Do you know the 'dry rages' . . . that sweep over these seas, when there is no evidence of storm in the sky, and no wind? It's like the Clear Air turbulence a plane meets. I've seen Josephas calmly steering, his foot on the tiller, while the huge waves, rising suddenly, threatened to drown us all . . . At breakfast the banana birds and hermit crabs come on to the verandah . . . There are scorpions, too, and a legendary giant iguana which I set out to search for . . .[31]

After Christmas the establishment became considerably more lively with the arrival of guests from New York and Boston, among them Marquand and Sedgwick relatives, Jason Epstein of Random House and his wife, Barbara, one of the founding editors of the *New York Review of Books*, and the novelist William Styron, who had won a Pulitzer Prize that year for *The Confessions of Nat Turner*. Frame retreated to the boatshed to sleep, took long walks on the beaches and joined the enlarged party in the main house to eat and observe. As always, she was at her happiest listening to witty and articulate people without feeling compelled to participate in conversations. On one occasion the other women were in the kitchen while their husbands were discussing erections.[32] Ever attentive, John Marquand reminded them that Frame was present; her chameleon qualities made it easy for others to overlook her.

One evening she sat in on the men's poker school but withdrew when she realised how serious they were and how much money was changing hands. Instead she joined seven-year-old James Marquand and the Styron and Epstein children at their games, intrigued that even on a coral island they played at being mothers and fathers in New York. And, recalling the days of her own performances with her sisters, she was delighted that each child had an act — singing, tap-dancing, comic monologues — and was keen to perform it: 'Ya wanna hear my routine?'

The most dramatic events were triggered by John Marquand's half-brother,

Elon. He had a manic episode, in the course of which he hired a launch and sped round and round the island. He was eventually restrained, sedated and delivered to a Bahamas hospital, which turned out to be more in the nature of a gaol, and a primitive one at that. Further difficulties arose from the fact that all the wealthy people present had chequebooks but no cash and were not recognised by the authorities as 'people of prestige'. Eventually Sally Sedgwick, John's aunt, a Cabot by birth, managed to persuade authorities that she was creditworthy.[33]

On 8 January 1969 Frame flew to Baltimore. She found John Money's neighbourhood more blighted than ever by the ruins of shops and buildings gutted in the riots and fires sparked by Martin Luther King's murder the previous spring. Frame also found Money dejected about the unbridgeable gulf between blacks and whites in the city and the conditions which had underlain the riots. But he was determined to remain there, continuing to research and teach at Johns Hopkins and fiercely attached to his home in East Madison Street. Money had by now filled the street window of the house with tropical plants which, viewed from the footpath, gave it the appearance of an aquarium. The room immediately behind was jammed with his collection of Australian Aboriginal and African wood sculptures and masks. It looked like a voodoo parlour, a factor which might have discouraged would-be vandals and burglars. 'The house has a characteristic smell,' Frame noted. '[It's] the smell of absence; nobody spends the day . . . here and I suppose all the objects have their special kind of breath and sweat with no human smell to mask it . . . [For] the most part he spends his time in his hospital office trying to solve other people's sex problems.'[34] Money customarily remained at work until the early hours of the morning. Over three weeks Frame took full advantage of his absence to rest, read and write in his basement.

Early in February Frame moved on to New York where George Braziller had made an apartment available to her in Manhattan for a fortnight. She did little there, she told Frank Sargeson, 'occasionally wandering around, but chiefly having my old cheese-on-toast and apple and imitation milk . . . in my instant coffee'.[35] She had some bad news. 'Marsha (George's wife) has cancer . . . If I had any regrets about coming here I haven't now as I would never have seen her alive again, otherwise. She buried her sister with cancer [when] I was last here.'[36]

The *good* news was that her Burns Fellowship novel, *Yellow Flowers in the Antipodean Room*, was published in the United States on 3 February. A witty and scathing portrait of Dunedin in the 1960s, it recounts the death of thirty-year-old British immigrant Godfrey Rainbird after a traffic accident. His wife prepares for life as a widow, his children adjust to being orphaned, his sister arrives from England for the funeral, an elaborate coffin is prepared. Then, thirty-six hours after his 'death', Rainbird wakes from a deep coma. But his resurrection is not welcomed. He loses his job and is resented by his family and shunned by society. He disintegrates to the point where he decides to complete his *mortem interruptam*.

This was the first time Frame's presence in the United States had coincided with publication of one of her novels (and the children's story, *Mona Minim and the Smell of the Sun*, was to follow a month later). As usual, she declined to endure press interviews or other kinds of promotional activity. As usual too, she dreaded the appearance of reviews which, inevitably, were mixed. John Leonard in the *New York Times* greeted the novel as 'a cold, haunted, brilliant book — a moon in the night's imagination'. He noted that it was not in fact about death but about perception. 'She meditates upon the disrelation between inner and outer landscapes, mental and physical colours, cruelty and the withdrawal from cruelty, the experience of chaos, of inexplicable evils, of broken perceptions and intuitions of dismay and splinters of demonic force. Her children, Godfrey's children, are the casualties of a terrible innocence, an inability to cope and to justify that bleak knowledge inadvertently conferred by happenstance.'[37]

Joyce Carol Oates in the *New York Times Book Review*, on the other hand, saw Frame as preoccupied with the mysteries of madness and death, and accused her of being unable 'to create a fable strong enough to bear the weight of her thematic obsessions'.[38] *Time* allowed that Frame had developed 'a tidy reputation as a wild necromancer', but called the new book 'little more than a tepid and distended mood piece'. It did, however, praise 'an interlude of exuberant Joycean punning' which occurs when Godfrey is unable to stop turning words inside out. The 'Drol's Pryer', for example: 'Our afther which rat in heaven; hollowed be thy mane; they dingkum come; thy will be done on thear as it is in heaven; give us this day our daily dread and frogview us pour press-stares as we frogview those who press-stare against us.'[39]

Rather more heartening, because it meant publication and income without concomitant criticism, was news that Carl Brandt had succeeded in placing some of the stories she had handed over to him the previous year. *The New Yorker*, having previously accepted 'You Are Now Entering the Human Heart', now also published 'Winter Garden'. And *Harper's Bazaar* took 'Birds of the Air', a story based on Grandmother Godfrey's visit to the Frames in Oamaru and not republished in subsequent story collections.[40]

By 19 February Frame was installed again at the Yaddo colony in Saratoga Springs for what would prove to be her longest stay there, four months. Elizabeth Ames, still executive director after forty years and now aged eighty-seven, put her in the ground floor rooms in West House that she had so much liked on her first visit. The Mansion, being too costly to heat in winter, was closed.

As she had hoped she would be able to do, Frame plunged straight into the reorganisation and extension of 'The Mill Belongs to Sandy' that would transform it into *Intensive Care*. For this purpose she drew to some extent on the family story about her father falling in love with a nurse in the course of the First World War and her own stay in hospital in London the previous year. She estimated that she had written one quarter of the new material in the first ten days, helped by the fact that in the early weeks she tried to avoid contact with her fellow interns, writers Alan Lelchuk and Philip Roth (whose third novel, *Portnoy's Complaint*, had just been published and was attracting controversy on account of its frank depictions of masturbation), cartoonist and playwright Jules Feiffer, and two women artists.

Soon, however, Frame was reporting that she felt close affinity to Lelchuk, a thirty-year-old academic and critic who was at that time working on his first novel, *American Mischief*. '[We] play chess and go for midnight walks in the snow,' she told John Money. 'He's a lusty young blood with lots of women — trust me to be original; but . . . *also* a brilliant chap.'[41] For his part, Lelchuk was to remember 'her frizzy hair wild, her cheeks ruddy, her sturdy handsome figure . . . [and] her high clear voice, with her hometown accent . . . I tried to draw her out, and she responded always as though she were waiting to talk.'[42] The two verged but did not quite embark on an affair. Frame made jokes to her correspondents about the 'older woman–younger man syndrome' (there was a fourteen-year age gap).[43] Lelchuk felt an attraction that 'grew on me quietly . . . she had a wildness about her, on display for example in the evening ping-pong games . . . [and] of course her wild imagination — a Brontë sister resting up in Yaddo . . . [Yet] she usually was quite restrained, keeping that side of her private . . . I liked her for it . . . I loved her too.'[44]

Increasingly other guests too began to claim and entertain Frame. 'I have never heard anything so brilliant as the impromptu drama the other evening with Philip Roth and Jules Feiffer acting life in New York and the dangers of answering the doorbell.'[45] She enjoyed a deepening rapport with Roth, who confessed that he too ate his packed lunch early in the day and was hungry by noon.[46] Soon they were exchanging fantastical and bawdy notes, of which one from Roth reads: 'Dear Mrs Breast, It has come to my attention that you have not only failed to pay your rent on the nest we have provided for you, but that you sit down there all day twittering your little ass off. Between the twittering and the chirping, the other little birds are having one hell of a time getting their eggs laid. They are a flock of very pissed-off birds, Mrs Breast, and if I were you I'd watch my tail. Yours, Simon Legree.'[47]

Frank Sargeson, cynical about the notion of writers' colonies and more than a little jealous of the company his protégée was keeping, wrote a letter disparaging Yaddo.★ Frame replied with a spirited defence of both the purpose

---

★ Referring to *Portnoy's Complaint*, Sargeson, writing to his poet and publisher friend William Plomer, appeared to break his own admonition to others about not confusing authors with their fictional narrators. When Frame returned to New Zealand, he said, 'I shall particularly want from her information about whether she had to clean up [Roth's] mess from all over the lavatory whenever she was next in the queue.' (FS to WP, 26/12/69, ATL 432/187.)

and the achievement of the place. 'The people who come [here] are professional writers, and they don't get their books from Yaddo, they bring them, inside their heads, *to* Yaddo; all Yaddo provides is the retreat — quiet, food . . . shelter — while the books are written . . . Yaddo has saved many an artist from breakdown . . . Eudora Welty, Carson McCullers, Sylvia Plath, all came here to work. Eudora Welty, I'm told, was so timid that she would not come to dinner for three weeks . . . In a world where people don't really care what happens to artists, a spell at Yaddo has helped some to regain confidence in themselves, for here, by order of the Yaddo Corporation, everyone is *cared* for.'[48] She wrote passionately, because she was speaking out of her own experience. She could have added that, in her case, Yaddo was bringing access to literary friendships and enriching cultural associations in the United States which might otherwise have eluded her.

By mid-April the snow was gone and 'the layers of leaves in the woods are warm and dry', Frame was telling Peter Dawson, conscious of the older woman's interest in the natural world, but also expressing her own delight in the strong sense of seasons which America gave her. '[All] the creatures are coming out of hibernation. The chipmunks are "out", and the black king snake is waking . . . and the swallows will return this week . . . [All] the birds, including the outsize U.S. robins, are building and making a merry din dawn and evening. The days are warm, the skies are blue and the pine trees . . . sparkle in the sun. Leaves are slowly budding.'[49]

Warmer weather allowed some changes in routine. In the first week in May Frame travelled to New York. She stayed with the Marquands on West 57th Street and told John Money by letter that, when she was able to live under the same roof with John and Sue, their common intimacy quickly returned.[50] She also visited Carl Brandt and George Braziller. That same week *Mona Minim* was published and immediately drew a glowing review in the children's book supplement of the *New York Times Book Review* (six months later that same publication would list it as one of the ten best children's books of the year).[51]

*Mona Minim and the Smell of the Sun* is a personalised story about the life cycle of ants. It grew from Frame's childhood observations of insects and her discussions about house ants with Pamela Gordon; she dedicated the book to both Pamela and James Marquand. It is possible to read the story in two ways: as a tale for children which anthropomorphises and explains ant behaviour; and as a fable about shedding illusions and reaching maturity. The text was leavened by Frame's love of language and detail and sense of humour. And this first edition had charmingly intricate drawings by Robin Jacques.

By June 1969, new guests were arriving at Yaddo as Frame prepared to leave. One, a composer, wanted to make an opera of *Mona Minim*.[52] Another, Hyde Solomon, painted her portrait. And the biographer and critic James Mellow handed her a letter warmly appreciative of *Scented Gardens*, which he had borrowed from the library. He praised the way in which language 'becomes, in a sense, the protagonist of the book. I'm sorry to say I hadn't known of your work before I came to Yaddo . . . [It] is now one of the good experiences of the place.'[53]

Bathed in the colony's support, buoyed by such compliments, with her new novel drafted and several new poems completed, Frame left Yaddo on 22 June. She spent several more days in the Marquands' New York apartment while they were at Martha's Vineyard. Then she headed to Baltimore for a week with John Money. On 3 July she flew to England for two-and-a-half months. She was booked to return to the United States in mid-September, to join the MacDowell Colony of writers, artists and musicians in New Hampshire.

In the English summer Frame divided her time between John Williams's flat in London and Peter Dawson's cottage at Norfolk. At Norfolk she helped the ageing Dawson pick gooseberries, raspberries and blackcurrants and did some of the heavier household chores such as washing. She also met Dawson's neighbours, poet George Barker (whose work she had imitated in her student writing days and who had been published in *Penguin New Writing* over the same period as Frank Sargeson), his wife, Elspeth, and their three young children. Dawson told Sargeson that Barker, who had previously shown no interest in New Zealand writers, now thought Frame was 'smashing'; and Elspeth considered her 'the most powerful woman writer in English today'.[54] Frame herself described Dawson and the Barkers as 'all sharpening their intellectual claws on one another' and she was not entirely comfortable in the atmosphere this generated.[55]

Back in London she visited Bob Cawley at the Maudsley and watched on television as Neil Armstrong stepped onto the moon on 20 July. But there were complications. John Williams's flat was now packed with a visiting New Zealand family who had just arrived from Nigeria where the husband, Peter McKenzie, was a lecturer in religious studies at the University of Ibadan. To make matters worse they all had influenza and the wife, Renate, was bedridden. Frame had to buy a camp stretcher and had nowhere to work during the day. In the midst of this chaos, Williams proposed to her ('Why don't we formalise our relationship?').[56] Frame, who had not anticipated this possibility and did not welcome it, gave no answer and fled back to Norfolk — which was tantamount to a refusal.

She returned to London on 7 August, by which time the McKenzies had departed. So, apparently, had John Williams. Frame guessed that her host had gone on a planned tour of Greece and she used the space and peace to rewrite and type the novel she had drafted at Yaddo. It turned out that Williams had vanished, however, and Frame never heard from him again. There were confirmed sightings of him in Europe over the next decade, and he renewed his New Zealand passport in Geneva in September 1979.[57] But for all practical purposes he disappeared. His worried brother and sister in New Zealand asked Interpol to locate him, which that agency was unable to do. The fact that Williams had been working on classified medical research at the Mayo Clinic (for NASA, on the effects of weightlessness on blood presure and cardiac function) added fuel to conspiracy theories about what might have happened to him.

None of this was known to Frame in August 1969. She simply got on with her work. The only thing that distracted her was the discovery in one of Williams's *Landfalls* that John Money had written to that journal to draw attention to her financial insecurity and to the iniquitous regulations that apparently obliged her to pay full taxes in both the United States and New Zealand. He also emphasised 'how essential it is that a writer of Janet Frame's world-renowned calibre be kept full-time at her profession. Otherwise we all lose too much.' This was the kind of public airing of her affairs that Frame abhorred. 'I wasn't too pleased that you wrote it,' she reprimanded him by letter, 'in fact I was mad; but I suppose you meant well . . .'[58]

At the end of August she was back in Norfolk and stayed on for Dawson's seventy-fifth birthday on 5 September; Elspeth Barker made a cake and the children decorated it with flowers. George Barker gave his neighbour a briefcase, ostensibly to help Dawson keep track of her increasingly voluminous and disorganised papers. Frame and Dawson also spent an evening with the Barkers at which the adults sat at the hosts' enormous table and entertained one another by reciting poetry from memory, Frame opting for Hopkins's 'Felix Randal'. By chance there was another Frame visiting, a singer named Robert who, like her, had a grandmother named Paterson who came from Paisley. He told her that the Frames were descended from Flemish weavers who had crossed to the Scottish Lowlands in the fourteenth century, and that the name was originally Flamand.[59]

There was one further distraction before Frame left England on 15 September. The night before her flight the police came to the door of John Williams's flat and told her that they had been chasing a man who had robbed a nearby hotel. He had tried to escape across roofs but had fallen into Williams's back garden and was lying there injured. Policemen retrieved him and carried him through the house on a stretcher and out the front door. To Frame he looked impoverished and frightened, exactly the kind of person who could have been one of her mother's 'angels in disguise'.[60] The incident seemed ominous and intensified her eagerness to return to the United States.

En route for MacDowell Frame spent a couple of hectic mid-September days in New York. She had become increasingly perplexed and upset by how little money her books were earning in the United States. Even apart from low sales, A.M. Heath and Brandt and Brandt both deducted agency commissions; and the US Inland Revenue Service took one-third of those earnings. What little income dribbled back to Frame then attracted New Zealand tax. She estimated that the American authorities owed her around $US3000, given that they should have been taxing her at a rate of only ten percent.

Carl Brandt sent her to an attorney who advised that there *was* a reciprocal tax agreement between the United States and New Zealand, but that authors' royalties were specifically excluded from it. The only way round the problem was to give American rights to a British publisher, so that American royalties could be paid into Britain without tax, and then remitted to Frame from there. Armed with this potential solution, and with advice from Carl Brandt that Braziller had not served her well by virtue of his lack of promotion of her books, Frame met her American publisher for breakfast to tell him that she wanted to be released from further contractual obligations to him. George Braziller's eyes filled with tears and he said that publishing her had meant more to him than any other aspect of his career.[61] What is more, he continued, he would publish *anything* she submitted to him. Frame felt herself overcome by grief and shame, and she withdrew her request. The moment passed, and George Braziller remained her American publisher; and the American tax problem stayed unresolved.

On 18 September 1969 Frame arrived at MacDowell near Peterborough, New Hampshire. This colony had been established sixty years before by the pianist Marian Nevins MacDowell in memory of her husband, composer Edward Alexander MacDowell. It provided a creative base for writers, artists and musicians, and gave rather more encouragement to the latter groups than Yaddo. Here too Frame's room and board would be paid for by an endowed fellowship so she had to find money for personal items and incidental expenses only.

Confronted by the discomfort of new faces and a new institution, Frame scarcely spoke to anybody for the first few days and left the dining room rapidly after communal dinners.[62] In her own way, however, she was settling in. She told John Money that the 400-acre property was 'very pleasant. Each studio is at least a quarter to half a mile from the others and all are deep in the woods. [Mine] has a large room and a small one with a lavatory and wash-basin and a porch with wood stored. The fireplace is at least ten feet wide [and] as I write I have a fire blazing . . . There are squirrels, bobcats, foxes, racoons, woodchucks, chipmunks and black bears . . . [Something] large and heavy (a man perhaps?) tried to get in . . . in the middle of the night . . . I have been warned not to leave food out as [bears] become angry if they can't find it and will smash their way in.'[63]

Largely eschewing social contact, Frame quickly established a work routine.

In two months she was to write some verse and two new stories and to begin the first draft of what she called her 'U.S. novel' (it would become *Daughter Buffalo*).[64] From mid-October, however, her letters were making increasing mention of one fellow colonist. 'There's a painter who's a marvellous pianist and he plays in the evenings and I swoon over him . . . He is wonderful company and I suspect that like most people I give my heart to he is "one of the boys". I'm still romantic enough to want to spend the rest of my life with someone who can play Beethoven sonatas to me . . . [Actually] my heart goes either to "one of the boys" or to those charming philanderers with a woman in every port.'[65]

The painter was William Theophilus Brown (Bill), a fifty-year-old artist from California. He was indeed 'one of the boys' and lived with fellow artist Paul Wonner near Santa Barbara. Both were part of the group identified by critics as the Bay Area Figurative Painters. Brown had attracted national attention in 1956 when *Life* magazine published a spread of three of his football paintings done in abstract expressionist mode. He was also, as Frame had discovered, an accomplished pianist who had majored in music at college. The Savidge Library at MacDowell had an especially fine Steinway, on which Brown took to playing Beethoven and Schubert sonatas in the evenings.

By late October Frame was part of a group of four who gathered early for dinner each night at what they called the 'baby table'. Other members were Brown, his novelist friend Josephine Carson, and a black woman writer, originally from Philadelphia but now living in New York, Elnora Coleman, who was writing her autobiography. The point of their association was to avoid conscientiously the 'significant' or 'serious' conversations that occurred at other tables. The baby group would joke and pun their way through dinner, then — when Brown was not heading for the piano — retire to one of their studios to drink rosehip tea, play scrabble or anagrams, or compose salty limericks about fellow colonists.* Frame, Brown recalled, would invent the most outrageous words in the course of all three activities.[66]

Brown had other associations that interested Frame. He was a friend of Christopher Isherwood and Igor Stravinsky and, in the course of his time at MacDowell, travelled from New Hampshire to New York and back to witness Stravinsky's will. Like John Marquand, his ancestors had connections with the New England aristocracy: his great-grandfather, also Theophilus Brown, had been a tailor in Worcester, Massachusetts, and a friend of Henry David Thoreau. Brown had inherited some Thoreau manuscripts. Another friend, the poet

---

* Let one example suffice:

The pecker of Harrison Kinney
was so excessively skinny
that like a Greek statue
his balls stared back at you
with little eyes, nosey and chinny.

and feminist May Sarton, lived at Nelson, New Hampshire, not far from MacDowell.

Early in November, Brown invited Sarton to Hancock near Peterborough for a meal, to meet Frame. As usual when she encountered new people, Frame spent most of the evening listening to others talk. She was engaged especially by Sarton's stories of Leonard and Virginia Woolf, the Huxleys, and other members of the Bloomsbury set that the older woman had known more than thirty years before. At one point, though, Sarton and Jo Carson were discussing fan mail. Sarton turned to Frame and asked whether she received any. 'I did get a letter from Patrick White,' the New Zealander said in her most tentative voice. When Sarton had recovered her composure she said, 'What? All I get is letters from women in basements in Ohio with rats nibbling at their feet.' She then asked if Frame had replied to White's letter. No, Frame said, she had not. 'But you must, you must,' said Sarton. [67]

By the time Brown was ready to leave MacDowell in mid-November, nine days ahead of Frame's departure, she announced that she was 'hooked on him, you know, really hooked . . .'[68] She told Peter Dawson that she had 'given up on all my cold inaccessible men . . . I'm on the warm side of life from now on.'[69] The 'baby group' drove to Boston on 15 November in Brown's car. They had lunch at an oyster house, spent the afternoon at the Museum of Fine Art, dined at a Greek restaurant, then slept the night in sexually segregated rooms at Boston's combined YM/YWCA. The following morning the women delivered Brown to a plane for the west coast and drove back to New Hampshire, where the car was to be collected by Brown's niece. The next day Frame wrote him the first of what was to be a lengthy series of daily letters:

> The day in Boston was strange and sad and vivid, from the drive in sunlight and clean air and the arrival over Mystic Bridge . . . to the bizarre farewell in the lounge of the YWCA. In my mind it is a lived piece of fiction or film. I can see you in your black coat and black cap standing larger than life like a monument against the clear blue sky, as if I had been a child gazing upward; Elnora like a figure from a painting in her bright strong colours and dark face; Jo with a kind of pearl-coloured vivacity; I, squirrel-bulky in my coat, clutching [your] sweater as a child away from home clutches its favourite toy; the smiling man with the briefcase; the city benevolent because we were there. And all day was a journey with the four of us performing some kind of ritual dance, person to person to person to person, a long long journey to say au revoir; it would have been impossible to say goodbye . . .
>
> Well, it was a dream. Was it a dream?[70]

In Brown's absence all immediate interest Frame had had in MacDowell drained away. The three women, however, remained in close and supportive contact ('we had one of those confessional chats that women have when they're taking off their make-up and fixing their hair, their glass eyes, their false teeth').[71] All she could think of now was enduring the coming month. In mid-December she would fly to California to spend a week with Brown and his partner.

She served out the time at John Money's in Baltimore like a prisoner awaiting release. She played records of pieces Brown had performed at MacDowell, following Money's sheet music as she listened; she dreamed; and she sent long letters to California.'I find that the day passes without my doing much work yet I can't account for the hours. John . . . usually goes off to his work at half-past eight and has been coming home at quarter-past one in the morning and though I need not stay up, I do, because there's a heavy iron bar I put against the door . . . [This] is a wild neighbourhood with bottles being smashed around outside and a few street fights. I wish you and Jack Daniels would walk in now to say hello. I wonder how your work is going. I'm wearing your sweater to shreds . . .'[72]

Frame flew to Los Angeles in the second week of December and Brown collected her from the airport. En route for Montecito, near Santa Barbara, they stopped for tea at the home of Christopher Isherwood and his artist partner, Don Bachardy, in Santa Monica. As Brown and Isherwood talked, Frame, mildly in awe in the presence of one of the gods, listened. Brown soon realised that Frame did not need to be entertained with outings of this kind, however; she simply wanted to be with him and Wonner. Isherwood returned the visit later in the week and brought English poet Stephen Spender with him. This did interest Frame; but Spender 'earmarked or otherwise marked a handsome young guest' and disappeared for the afternoon.[73] On this occasion Bachardy sketched a portrait of Frame.

The rest of the week in Santa Barbara passed in a haze of contentment. To her immense relief, Frame liked Brown's partner, Paul Wonner, and felt that he was accepting of her presence in his and Brown's lives. She liked their cat, Ned, who would become a character in their subsequent correspondence. They ate and drank on the patio, walked on the seashore, and in the forested hills behind the suburbs where they spotted hundreds of butterflies moving south for the winter, and listened to music.[74] Frame and Brown also began to translate together Rainer Maria Rilke's French poetry (previously she had read only the translations of Rilke's German poems, to which she had been introduced more than twenty years earlier by Grete Christeller). And they looked at and talked about both men's paintings. Frame especially admired a picture of Brown's — a circle of naked men on a hilltop — and he gave it to her.

B and I went to Malibu and stayed a night there, intending to spend the next day in Los Angeles, but the weather was so wonderful that we just turned around and came back to Santa Barbara, to laze again in the sun. We simply played around and laughed a lot . . . I can easily see how [Bill] has come close to some of the great people of this age, including

Stravinsky [and] Paul Hindemith, for his musical gifts are extraordinary
. . . I've never heard anyone play so much *music* instead of mere notes
. . . [His] paintings [are] full of poetry and colour and motion and
harmony.[75]

An immediate result of the friendship with Brown was that Frame became
more actively interested in art and music and noted things in both media that
she had not been consciously aware of previously. The use of pause and silence
in music, for example; and the way that light fell on paintings, making them a
collaboration between painter and the natural conditions. 'I like the way you
treat people and their environment as equals,' she told Brown, 'as beings with
no barriers between them.' Such work, she said, was 'full of the bliss of being
in a world where rock, tree [and] sky spring from the same source and are
untroubled by trying to separate themselves . . . [There is] a suggestion that
plants, rocks, deserts were in the world first and have the right to change man
more than he has the right to change them.'[76]

Another consequence of Frame's association with Brown was that it led to
a friendship by correspondence with May Sarton. After the joint dinner at
Hancock, Sarton had sent Frame a copy of her book *Plant Dreaming Deep*,
about her life in an old farmhouse on thirty-six acres of land near Nelson in
New Hampshire. Back in Baltimore in the weeks before Christmas 1969 Frame
told Sarton by letter: 'Your book is so wise and just. It is like a poem in that it
*names* and makes alive every stick, stone, creature, season, silence, sound, feeling
that belongs, invited or uninvited, to the story of the house, or perhaps it is
these that are the host, with the house and its story as the guest. To me, [it] is a
wise generous story of hospitality in many forms.'[77]

Later, responding to Sarton's expressions of admiration for her own books,
Frame noted: 'I can't receive praise — I can just watch it arrive [and] know
I'm pleased that the offspring is bathed a while in the light of a reader's
perception.' She added that her guardian angel had been especially attentive to
her in New Hampshire, and that getting to know Bill Brown had been 'the
chief experience of my life'.[78]

Frame tried to keep depression at bay in Baltimore by reliving her time
'out West'. She complained to Brown that 'the East seems oxygen-starved and
murky after California with [its] blue skies and the butterflies and the beautiful
Ned with his fur like feathers. Wherever you live, I think it is naturally a place
of many blessings just because you are there.'[79] She told Peter Dawson that
Brown 'has taught me a lot about myself, for I recognise in him the male
counterpart of what I am, although he shares his life with a man as I would
never share mine with a woman. In that, I suppose, I am outside both sexes.'[80]

Another consequence of the time with Brown and Wonner, Frame said,
was that she had come 'more and more to reaffirm my faith in . . . the quiet
life: books, music, a garden. Anything else is direct poverty of spirit . . . John
Money's world is not mine and we are far apart in interests . . . and

understandings.'[81] She spent Christmas at Baltimore, nonetheless, alone with her one concession to festivity, a cheesecake. '[Every] few hours I hacked at it until it gradually diminished.'[82] She got through the festive season by looking forward to her return to California in March; and, more immediately, by anticipating her reinstatement as a resident at Yaddo early in the New Year. 'I shall be able to walk outside in the woods in the snow, and I expect that my new novel will be filled with snow. I am comforted and enclosed by my preliminary vision and I shall try desperately to keep it whole while I reach out to find the words . . . I know from experience its depressing fragility.'[83]

Back at Yaddo on 5 January 1970, however, Frame found that there had been changes; and they were not to her liking. Octogenarian director Elizabeth Ames had been persuaded to retire. The new directors, Granville Hicks and his wife, Dorothy, were insisting that colonists meet with them for pre-dinner cocktails and post-dinner coffee and conversation. Dinnertime discussion alone was difficult enough for Frame, although she reported to Brown that she had managed to make one of her startling interventions. Everybody at the table was talking about difficulties with cars and household appliances, and how shoddy and expensive was the work of repairmen. Asked for an opinion, Frame allowed that, 'I once spent a whole day putting in a ball-cock.' This produced such a chorus of 'Whats' and 'What-did-she-says' that she blushed and took refuge again in silence.[84]

Frame soon had favourites among the new intake of fellow colonists. Two were the (to her) avuncular critic Alfred Kazin and his wife, Ann, who were there at separate times. Another was the literary and philosophic writer Kenneth Burke who, among many books, had written a fine translation of Thomas Mann's *Death in Venice*. 'He sleeps in the room above me,' Frame told Brown. '[He's] an insomniac [with] a preference for listening to allnight radio. He has a sly sense of humour, an unusually humble appraisal of his work and a voice that's inclined to explode . . . His mind at 75 is agile, full of unusual & exciting analogies; he moves in a rich landscape of ideas.'[85]

Only weeks after meeting Burke, Frame did something she was normally reluctant to do: she handed over some unpublished work, three new poems, for Burke's appraisal. '[He] read them so carefully and wrote a detailed two-page note which in itself reads like a poem . . . "[The] closing two lines are good emotional bookkeeping. As long as we have to live, that's the best we can ask for, as regards the past". . .'[86] When the *New Yorker* published Frame's story 'Winter Garden', about an elderly man patiently visiting a dying spouse, Burke brought *her* a poem, about his recently deceased wife. Frame's opinion of Granville Hicks was not improved by the fact that he treated her with more consideration after the appearance of the story.

The major fruit of this period at Yaddo for Frame was the production of ten new poems and the rewriting and organisation of sixty-five written previously, all of which she despatched to George Braziller for a new collection (subsequently she changed her mind and withdrew them). She told Brown that this excursion into verse had been a necessary preliminary, 'as it always is', for getting to know the characters in the new novel. That book, however, remained 'out of reach like a tame chickadee that's decided it won't settle on my hand after all although it can't resist the sunflower seeds. It goes over my mind . . . & becomes grimmer & grimmer & more like a hawk . . .'[87]

Meanwhile she had news that her earlier collection of poems, *The Pocket Mirror*, had won the New Zealand Literary Fund's award for achievement, worth two hundred dollars.[88] She posted a copy to Bill Brown, lamenting that it was 'full of misprints. Also it lacks dignity and beauty — I want to write a dignified and beautiful poem; my tone [always] lapses into banality, I tend to leave the dark places where the poems are best made and loiter around in the stereotypes and trivialities.'[89]

No sooner had she sent off the new collection to Braziller than she sprained a wrist and found she could not type, giving her further grounds for delaying a start on the new novel. This accident, combined with the greater air of formality imposed by the Hickses, diminished her enjoyment of the colony. Yaddo was now a concentration camp where one could neither concentrate nor camp, she told Brown with a degree of exaggeration. 'I haven't laughed — real laughter — for ages and ages. . . . [Everyone] is determined not to spill a clue of irrationality or disorder, and one is reminded all the time that one is a Writer, and Artist.'[90] She concluded that her reaction was in part 'my own constitutional dislike of the presence of institutional authority', a reminder, perhaps, of hospital days.[91]

Because of this combination of difficulties Frame left Yaddo earlier than scheduled and headed for New York by bus with Alfred Kazin on 11 February 1970. They were met by Ann Kazin, who had returned home earlier, and all three were joined by the Kazins' fourteen-year-old daughter for a family dinner at their apartment in West End Avenue. Frame reported that it was one of the rare occasions on which she drank too much alcohol. 'Another martini to celebrate being out of Yaddo, then wine at dinner, then chocolate liqueur, and I'm afraid I still have the hangover. I was glad to see the Kazins in "real life" because at Yaddo Ann was very too-brilliant and witty, and Alfred seemed shyly disapproving, but in their home they were warm and happy . . .'[92] Frame was intrigued, however, to witness a family discussion on the placement of an elderly relative in which nobody suggested 'taking him in', as Lottie Frame had done with her in-laws; the only options canvassed were those of retirement or nursing homes.

For the next week Frame based herself at Elnora Coleman's apartment, also in West End Avenue but about twenty blocks from the Kazins. On one day she went north to Springfield, New Hampshire, to join Jo Carson and her husband, Mark. They then drove together to MacDowell, where Coleman was again in residence completing her autobiography, which Frame found 'very moving in its detailed record of the indifference & insensitivity shown by otherwise "nice" people'.[93] She spent the night in Coleman's MacDowell studio, then returned to New York the following day. There she made further fruitless attempts to sort out tax problems and visited the Marquands. All the while she worried about returning to New Zealand; and specifically about whether the relationship with Bill Brown and the feelings it generated would make life there more difficult or less so.[94]

'[I've] been trying to imagine what [it] will be like,' she told Brown. 'I'm going to miss you terribly . . . there'll be a kind of loss around as there is now and as there used to be at MacDowell when B was absent . . . I see myself in my little house and am cheered by the thought that I like my study and it's a good place to work and the changing light is magnificent to watch . . . I love my solitude and my books . . . and I'll have to get some kind of music . . . I live there chiefly by the sky and the light. My contact with people will be pretty meagre. The chief problem will be to get my necessary supply of laughter: Dunedin is a prim place and my friends there are on the sedate side.'[95]

There was only one thing about which she felt certain. '[I] am dying to see the blue skies of California . . . I see myself on the patio hogging *that* chair while humming birds hum near by . . .'[96] She had to spend a further week in Baltimore, however, where John Money had arranged for her to have her periodic cancer check at Johns Hopkins. It was clear. On 4 March she flew to Los Angeles for a final three-week stay before her return to New Zealand.

Again the time spent with these new friends constituted the nearest thing she had experienced to an idyll. It was extraordinary, Frame told Peter Dawson, to be with 'one's other self'. She and Brown had carried on translating Rilke together and had discovered the quatrains that she was to make such telling use of in her autobioigraphy fifteen years later, and which matched her mother's Christadelphian belief in the presence of angels ('Stay still, if the angel/at your table suddenly decides;/gently smooth those few wrinkles/in the cloth beneath your bread').[97] All three of them had meditated before meals (Brown and Wonner were Buddhists). They had continued to listen to music and to discuss art. She loved both men, Frame told Dawson: Wonner 'figuratively' and Brown 'literally'.[98] To Sargeson she wrote that 'one can deplore . . . almost everything happening in America except that apparent ability — or freedom — of people to live the kind of moral life they chose'.[99] She saw no sign of such freedom in New Zealand in general nor in Dunedin in particular.

With these considerations weighing on her, Frame returned to New Zealand late in March 1970, determined to find some way to arrange a long period of residence in the United States.

CHAPTER TWENTY-TWO

# Lonely for Her Own Kind

*I*N AUCKLAND THE GORDONS HAD ONCE AGAIN HIRED A CARAVAN FOR Frame to sleep and work in for the week she spent there before flying south. As usual she found her sister's family life 'hectic', but relished the time spent individually with her now near-adult niece and nephews.

> After their first day's shyness & strangeness (& mine too) the young people are eager to show me their accomplishments and treasures . . . [Ian] switches on his homemade stereo equipment to play pop songs . . . & Neil tries to explain computers and remarks . . . that there is little or no scope for creativity in what he is doing . . . Pamela, the youngest, fifteen, is a Latin and French scholar with long blonde hair.[1]

Frame visited Jess Whitworth, who no longer recognised her and whose 'life in senility [is] restricted marvellously to music, especially Mozart' (she would die two years later).[2] Frank Sargeson, who had just turned sixty-seven, informed her that she was to be a beneficiary in his will. 'He told me several bawdy stories and read to me from his latest work [a novella called *Man of England Now*] . . . He is writing more fluently than at any time in his life and enjoying an Indian summer.'[3] Both encounters made her think of 'how I love the continuity of life and death and how the past eats up the present and the present the future, and I like the way that death, seen from a distance, fits into the pattern'.[4]

The presence (or at least the possibility) of death had brought one of the Marquands' friends to the city. Phillippe de Rothschild, owner of the Chateau Mouton Rothschild vineyard, had accompanied his American wife to Auckland for heart surgery at Greenlane Hospital. There she had experienced cardiac arrest on 25 February, but recovered after resuscitation. The baron stayed on in Auckland throughout the period of his wife's convalescence and was

350

sometimes seen cavorting 'naked around the swimming pools of the city's socialites'.[5] Frame did not so see him; but she spoke with him on the telephone and he gave her up-to-date news of their mutual friends.

On her way south Frame stayed two nights with the Baxters, who had returned to their home in the Wellington suburb of Ngaio at the end of 1968 and whose family life was now considerably altered. Jim had gone north to Jerusalem, a small Maori community on the bank of the Whanganui River, where he planned to set up a haven for people damaged by drugs and other corrosive encounters with modern life. Jacquie had returned to work, as a library assistant in charge of the New Zealand Room at the Wellington Public Library. She was enjoying the job, though she had at first been suspicious of the motives of her employers — 'appointing her, a Maori . . . as a show-piece in the capital city full of overseas diplomats etc.' By contrast, Wellington's museum 'makes her weep because her race is dealt with in the past tense'.[6] Granddaughter Stephanie lived at home with her, and Hilary and John came and went and shared the running of the household. When Frame arrived, they had all just returned from a hui (a Maori gathering) 'upcountry', which led Frame to exclaim that she felt ashamed for knowing so little about Maori language and culture.[7]

She reached Dunedin on 1 April. 'When the plane landed . . . I felt I had come to a lonely wilderness and yet I was happy to see the sheep and cows and horses and all the green hills and the trees. My tenants left my house in good condition, with vegetables still in the garden — fat cabbages and spinach and rhubarb, but they have cut down the beautiful young Australian fir tree . . .'[8]

The tenants had also, in order to use the front room as a bedroom, removed the *Landfall* desk. But to move it they had had to slice it in half so as to be able to get it out the door. They had done this roughly, sawing through the leatherette and wooden top from either side in cuts that did not quite meet in the middle. Then they stored both halves in the basement. Dorothy Neal White, now Dorothy Ballantyne (she had married a Dunedin doctor in Frame's absence), broke the news to her gravely, and Frame tried to take it seriously, so as not to offend her friend. With the help of Dorothy and her husband she retrieved the divided monster from beneath the house, propped the two halves together, and continued to use it as a workplace on account of its overwhelming and undiminished virtue: the size of its surface. Later, it became the subject of a commemorative poem:

You refuse to stay tidy, you get stuck and you wobble on your cut legs
The edges of the wound around your middle
will never quite meet again; you are unbalanced, overweight . . .

Eight-legged, a kind of spider secreting, outpouring your daily web,
a mad, crooked, crippled piece of furniture,

bathing in golden literary history,
in spite of all, you go with me, *Landfall* desk, kept,
endured, burrowed in by the blossoming alphabet
in spite of all, in my shifting life, you go with me . . .'[9]

'When Dorothy and Robert were in my sittingroom yesterday,' Frame reported to Bill Brown, 'Dick's ghost was there too, I'm sure . . . Dorothy is . . . brilliant, witty, with allusive literary conversation — she can produce a quote from everyone who's ever written, to put her point across: consequently she's rather exhausting. Her [new] husband is a quiet thoughtful type, inclined, I imagine, to be in amused retreat much of the time.'[10]

As for her other Dunedin friends, after Frame's recent experiences in America they seemed on the 'sedate' side. Ruth Dallas led 'a very retired life . . . with her niece, about fifteen minutes' walk from [here] . . . She has leanings to Buddhism and speaks Japanese . . . and lives entirely for her garden, poetry, music and art. She exudes such purity that whenever I visit her I feel positively . . . unclean.'

Charles Brasch she now described as 'a pure earnest bachelor in his early sixties, also a poet, a scholar . . . Until his mid-fifties he led a shattering lonely life . . . but suddenly people were saying they had seen him smile . . . About once in six or seven weeks C invites me to dinner and after a suitable interval I invite him to my place.' Much as she valued these two relationships, she told Brown, with the Baxters gone from the city, her chief concern was 'where to get my necessary supply of laughter'. It would certainly not be from Aunty Han Frame, whom she now visited in a resthome. '[She] likes me to go because I look like her husband . . . [She] has led a barren kind of life and now she is old the barrenness shows.'[11]

In a fit of depression Frame told Bob Cawley, from whom she seldom concealed her mood changes, that 'I'm happy to be alone . . . but I'm not happy to be half-alive simply because this is the way people here seem to live.' The major source of distress now was her inability to see Bill Brown (though she was still writing to him frequently). It was compounded by the absence of her Dunedin psychiatrist, Wallace Ironside, who had abandoned Otago in favour of Monash University in Melbourne. Consequently there was now no one in Dunedin with whom she could discuss her private fears and disappointments. '[He] gave me the name of a psychiatrist [but] I have not consulted this man and don't intend to. It is much simpler to be by oneself and know that one will either die or live, accepting both in the appropriate mood.'[12]

A further source of disappointment in the early months of 1970 was that Charles Brasch had still not succeeded in securing for her a civil list pension, though he continued to hope that this might eventually be achieved. In the meantime, he suggested, 'various people' who admired Frame's work wanted to offer her $720 a year (sixty dollars a month) from their own resources. 'I hope you'd be willing to accept this in a quite impersonal way. It would have to be an entirely confidential arrangement.'[13] Frame was more comfortable with the pension proposal than she was about the offer of private support which, despite Brasch's mention of 'various people', was most likely to come from his own means. Accepting such an arrangement might bind her more closely to Dunedin at the very time that she was less certain that she wanted to live there. In the event, both proposals remained in limbo throughout 1970.

One of the reasons she did not activate the offer of private support was that her own resources were adequate to support her through the coming year; her anxieties focussed, as they usually did, on future rather than immediate prospects. She still had savings; there was an advance from Braziller for *Intensive Care*, accepted in December 1969 for publication in the United States; and a cheque for $206.69 from Pegasus awaiting her when she returned from America. *Intensive Care* would appear in the United States in May 1970. W.H. Allen took considerably longer to make up their mind, eventually publishing the book in September 1971; while New Zealand publication would be delayed even further by Frame's decision to change her local publisher. Meanwhile she began to focus attention on her new novel, the 'American' one, and reported in May 1970 that ideas for it were 'swirling around like a current'.[14]

*Intensive Care* was Frame's first novel since *Faces in the Water* that was not dedicated to 'RHC'. This time, in what could be seen as an arrival at a new plateau of self-reliance or — at the very least — a transference of primary dependence, a carefully worded statement offered the book 'to Sue Marquand and Bill Brown for the possible and the impossible greeting and parting'.[15] Acknowledgements were made also to Yaddo, MacDowell and the Henry Foundation, each of which had supported her through part of the writing of the novel, which was written in a combination of poetry and prose narrative and divided into three parts.

In the first section, Tom Livingstone, a First World War veteran with clear links to George Frame (he also works as a furnace operator and has an undiagnosed ulcer), returns to England from New Zealand in search of the nurse with whom he had fallen in love during the war. His brother Leonard, a bibulous bachelor, is in some respects a recreation of Uncle Charlie Frame. In the middle section the Livingstone descendants set about ruining their lives; one of Tom's grandsons, Colin, murders his lover and his lover's parents, as Bill Frame had done. In the final section, in the wake of another more destructive world war, what survives as human society in New Zealand is organised to kill off those identified by computer as defective or unpromising. This third part of the book is narrated by an administrator of the Human Delineation Act, with certain resemblances to Frame's Dunedin bank manager, and by an autistic girl named Milly Galbraith, a simpleton with the unwitting capacity to tell the truth.

Thanks to the international circulation of *Time*, Frame was reading her first review of *Intensive Care* before she had seen copies of the book itself. On this occasion, the magazine neither praised nor condemned the work but suggested that, in Frame's view, history was 'a hereditary malignancy that engulfs the present and dooms the future to madness, loneliness and death . . . Madness and violence are seen as the tragic lengths individuals and societies will resort to in order to prevent the obliteration of their identities or collective memories.'[16]

John Leonard in the *New York Times* was more forthright about the achievement and value of the novel. He called it 'a superb meditation on the dreams that distinguish us from stones ("Livingstone . . .")', and spoke of 'the spell Miss Frame casts on the reader in her extraordinary novels. This is one of the best of them.'[17] Another strongly favourable review, by Granville Hicks late of Yaddo, appeared in the *Chicago Sun-Times Book Week* ('in the organisation of her prose, the depth and originality of her figures of speech and the breathtaking force of her descriptions, she establishes a place for herself among the best of contemporary novelists').[18] Julian Moynahan in the *New York Times Book Review*, however, said that the novel was 'sprawling and invertebrate, overwritten . . . in a vein of capricious prose-poetry and actual poetry, indifferent to problems of construction and coherence [and] simplistic and even careless in respect [of] moral issues'.[19] John Money, ever the loyal consort, wrote to Moynahan that his review was 'living testimony to the minor league status of Rutgers University [where he taught] and to your own fifth grade status as a literary hack'.

Answering a query from Bill Brown about the effect of negative reviews, Frame said that she never cried over them. 'I just get a cold feeling of hopelessness and a desire to remove myself to the furthest corner of myself and never emerge again. And it's almost as bad with good reviews, when I feel my head swelling and get the idea that I'm good and that everybody knows it.'[20] In the case of *Intensive Care*, as with previous books, her consciousness of 'bad' reviews was to some extent erased by letters of appreciation from readers. Charles Brasch, for example, wrote to tell her that the novel was 'probably the most powerful of all your books [and] an incisive satire on New Zealand, a warning one would like to think will be taken to heart'.[21]

At the same time that American reviews of *Intensive Care* were being published, the *New Zealand Listener* carried the text of a talk which had been broadcast on radio by Joan Stevens, now associate professor of English at Victoria University, but long before Frame's English lecturer at teachers' college. Titled 'The Art of Janet Frame', it attempted to define 'the central feature of her work, the different quality of her vision'.

[Frame] sees life as a terrifying brilliance from which most of us must hide. We learn the tricks of the eye, seek the shadows, mask the truth with linguistic deceptions, and for mutual support conform to accepted patterns. But, says Janet Frame, she herself has been unable to obliterate the clarity of her first perceptions. She has never learnt to accept things as they seem; she hasn't modified her childish vision or put away childish things. She's not, to use one of her own titles, 'An Adaptable Woman' . . .

Each of her novels is a symbolic structure designed 'to undeceive the sight', to show us the world we knew first, but have forgotten, the world where things are not subject to the tricks of the eye . . . In [this structure], every slightest thing sets vibrating the whole circle of meaning. 'Multiple Insight' is the happy term [used] to decribe this gift. Significance is absolute in the smallest item. And over the whole picture, there is no artificially imposed 'sense of proportion' . . .

Who else is like her? I am reminded of Virginia Woolf, Iris Murdoch, William Faulkner, Muriel Spark, but I believe that her quality is better suggested by a comparison with a painter like Hieronymus Bosch, whose extraordinary vision encompassed the natural and the supernatural at once, picturing them together in a fantastic 'total clamour of fore-ground'.[22]

The same month that this talk was published, May 1970, Frame herself was interviewed for radio — and paid for the interview — on the subject of artists' and writers' colonies in the United States. She told Bill Brown that there was considerable local interest in the topic; and that Phillip Wilson was keen to go to a place like Yaddo, 'because he finds, as I do, that in New Zealand the loneliness outweighs the benefits of the aloneness'.[23] On air, Frame said that working at Yaddo and MacDowell had been 'a rich experience for me, to feel for the first time in my life that I was among my own kind'. Asked about the violence of American society, however, she observed that in 'the cities or anywhere near the main highways you find yourself almost licensed to be paranoiac. You tend to be suspicious of every stranger [and] a connoisseur of locks and keys.'

Invited to comment on criticism of her work, Frame referred to the problem of being identified with her fictional narrators. 'If you're an actress and play Lady Macbeth, no one is going to assume that you yourself are ruthless, ambitious . . . But if you are a writer and write about a character — which is a kind of acting — many people assume that the character's beliefs and way of life are your own.'

Finally, she was asked about Joan Stevens' opinion that she saw life as a terrifying brilliance from which most people needed to hide. 'I'm not sure that I see life at all,' Frame ventured. 'What I do see is life within. I suppose you could call it the imagination. I'm rather unconscious of things around me . . . I've a kind of arrangement with a part of myself which is given the menial task of absorbing things . . . I don't know what these things are until I see them in an imaginative light — which is a bright light, without shade — a kind of inward sun.'[24] This latter expression, 'inward sun', was to provide the title of two future books about Frame and her writing.

The problem of the 'loneliness outweighing the benefits of aloneness' was one Frame felt especially acutely by the middle of 1970. 'I miss the warmth of my faraway friends,' she told May Sarton in June. '[And] I am homesick for darkness and burial in snow; I want to do away with the ever open-eyed sin and light . . .'[25] These feelings were both relieved and exacerbated by her correspondence with Bill Brown. She spent a good deal of her time thinking about him; and almost as much writing to him, still several times a week. In this correspondence, Frame told Bob Cawley, they had created a world 'full of private fantasies and language, based initially on the [French] poems Rilke wrote . . . and extending now to cover [his] life and my life.'[26] The letters were 'full of fun things' and she enjoyed both writing and receiving them.[27] But the not inconsiderable time allocated to this task was time that would formerly have been devoted to her work; and the more she fantasised about life with Brown and Paul Wonner, the more the notion of living with them in California, as they had lived in the course of her two brief stays there, appealed to her. 'I found their world so natural and warm after the constrained life in New Zealand,' she said to Sargeson.[28] And to Brown: 'I am just lonely for my own kind who care for the poetry of existence.'[29]

That loneliness was not assuaged by the kinds of interruptions that would have constituted adventures had she been travelling, but which, at home, were simply intrusions. Early in July 1970 she told Brown that she was being pursued by a young French woman 'who sounded very twittery and fluttery over the phone. It [seems] incredible and crazy . . . but she is here from the University of Toulouse . . . and is completing a thesis for Professor Du Pont [*sic*] . . . on Janet Frame in her New Zealand setting!!! Natural habitat, I suppose. I've invited her [here] because I've been rather annoyed that she's been paying visits to people who know me.'[30]

This was but the first of many such attempts to interview her about her life and her work in a manner that she could only view as an invasion of privacy. She simply could not understand why people who were interested in her *writing* had also to be interested in her *life*, and in particular want to relate the one to the other. As far as she was concerned, her writing was what she chose, not always wholeheartedly, to send out into the world to be read; the rest was her business; or, at the most, family business. The last thing she wanted was people raking over the ashes of her time in mental hospitals or her sometimes difficult relations with her family.

The French student's supervisor, Professor Victor Dupont of the Faculté des Lettres et Sciences at Toulouse University, had himself visited New Zealand the previous year in search of information and insights about Frame's writing. He had been desolate to discover that she was in England at that time and therefore unable to be approached for interview. Instead, he had spoken to people such as June Gordon and Charles Brasch, a process that left Frame feeling decidedly uncomfortable. In the course of a quaintly worded letter written at that time, Dupont had assured Frame that 'I am myself extremely shy, except in my intercourse with students'.[31] Frame had not wished to meet him in 1969; nor in 1974, when Dupont would actively pursue her in France.

In the course of this same month, July 1970, contrary pressures and inclinations became too much for Frame and some kind of emotional dam burst within her. Geordie Frame, who had heard her speak about Yaddo and MacDowell on radio, wrote her a letter 'full of viciousness and vague threats'.[32] This was followed by 'unhappy letters from unhappy people, asking advice and detailing their mental miseries . . . I don't think it is good to be reminded about a past which I . . . don't think of when I leave the country.'[33]

Her solution was drastic. 'I am going to live in California with my friends,' she informed Bob Cawley, 'as soon as they get a new house back in the hills with room for me. The regular small income I thought I would get when I came home has not happened — chiefly because I do have enough for a couple of years if I stay where I am . . . My two [American] friends . . . are trying to work out something for me so that I'll be able to leave here and live with them. We all get on very well together and love one another and the "permissive society" is greatly to be commended.'[34]

This decision taken, Frame made others while she was carried along on a tide of determination. She dismissed her agents A.M. Heath and Brandt and Brandt, because of the commissions they deducted from her income and 'because I keep getting enormous bills for books they buy to offer all around the world for films etc . . . Also I've been paying agents' income tax . . . So I've finished with them.' She decided also, by the narrowest of margins, to remain with Braziller and W.H. Allen, because 'at least they want to publish most things I write'.[35] But she asked Allen to sever her connection with Pegasus, largely on the ground that they paid her royalties only when she begged for them; but also as an expression of the bitterness she still felt for the fact that they had absorbed half of her potential income from *Owls Do Cry* and *Faces in the Water*, her highest selling books; and would have continued this arrangement with subsequent books had it not been for the intervention of A.M. Heath. She instructed Allen to offer *Intensive Care* and future novels to another New Zealand publisher.[36] While the bases for these decisions are all understandable, the person who was most unfairly served by them was Patience Ross, who had laboured on Frame's behalf well beyond the call of duty or the earning of commission, and was distressed by the author's decision to cut herself free.

Frame's next objective was to obtain an immigrant visa for the United States (as distinct from her previous visitor's visas) which would allow her to live and work there if she could come to a satisfactory arrangement with Brown and

Wonner. The American Embassy in Wellington advised her what applications she would need to make and warned her that there was an 'indefinite' waiting period for the granting of such visas.[37] Frame filed the necessary documents, including testimonials to her literary achievement and good character from John Money and Charles Neider, the writer and critic who had been one of her fellow-colonists at MacDowell ('in my opinion she would do us an honor to reside among us');[38] and a citation from the Mark Twain Society declaring her 'a Daughter of Mark Twain'. Then she waited; and as she waited she worried about the fact that she had been asked to declare whether or not she had been mentally ill or suffered from a mental illness.

'I don't consider I have ever been mentally ill and of course am not now,' she wrote to Bob Cawley on 7 August. 'If I was ever mentally ill then I still am. I'm the same inside my mind as I have ever been, except that I know more and understand more . . . [However] I don't feel I can ignore the question . . . the warnings about concealing facts are dire . . . The effect on me of the thought, merely, of being refused entry to the US is also dire . . . I dare not approach any of the hospitals or superintendents in this country . . . who were my doctors when I was in hospital [here] . . . I am afraid of their power. And I would incur their displeasure.'[39] Cawley undertook to provide documentation, if asked, that as far as the Maudsley Hospital was concerned, Frame was not and never had been mentally ill.[40]

Another worry which now took hold was the thought that perhaps she needed the companionship of Brown and Wonner more than they needed hers. 'I don't think they're missing me as much as I'm missing them, as they have many friends . . . [But] I know that [Bill] has a special loneliness that was helped while I was there. Our affections are a kind of narcissism . . . yet [Paul] says that he and I [too] are twin personalities . . . They are both saintly men, and life with them is happy for me — quiet, governed by routine and work, with plenty of fun between and during . . . I live in a world of fantasy [and] it is good fortune for me to know [people] who live in a similar world.'[41]

That same month, August 1970, Frame spent time with the one friend in New Zealand whom she felt came closest to sharing that world. Jacquie Baxter, needing a break from both a demanding job and domestic responsibilities came and stayed a week at Evans Street. Frame, of course, was far more accustomed to the role of guest than that of host. 'God,' she asked John Money, 'how did you ever put up with me? I didn't realise having a guest, even one like Jacquie, one of the nicest, could be such a strain.'[42] Within days of Jacquie's return to Wellington she had to turn round and fly back to Dunedin when her father-in-law, Archibald Baxter, died on 10 August. Frame did not attend the funeral. Ruth Dallas told her: 'Funerals are for men.'[43]

In September the Marquands began to figure again in Frame's American calculations. Sue Marquand, who responded to Frame's correspondence by telephone rather than by letter, rang to offer her a fare to the United States, a monthly allowance, and the use of her recently deceased father's apartment on

East 53rd Street in New York. She also said, Frame reported to John Money, that 'if I wanted to remain in the USA it "could be managed". I didn't ask her how . . .'[44] Frame turned down the fare, because Brown and Wonner had undertaken to pay this; but she accepted the offer of the allowance and the apartment, which she described to Money as a 'little cosy place . . . His books are still there, lining the walls of the little sittingroom. There's a double bedroom, bathroom, and kitchen as well.'[45]

Frame had no further books or stories published in 1970. In November, however, Dunedin's Globe Theatre, established and run by a husband-and-wife team, Patric and Rosalie Carey, put on a two-week season of a dramatised version of her novel *A State of Siege*. The adaptation was done by Rosalie Carey, who also played the role of Malfred Signal. Frame attended the dress rehearsal 'in the back row . . . hunched up in a greatgrey tweed overcoat'.[46] But she stayed away from the public performances. She pronounced herself 'a little happier' with Dunedin as a result of seeing the play and what the Careys had made of it, though she thought Rosalie's Malfred 'a neurotic sexual virgin' who would elicit 'contempt rather than pity'.[47] The *New Zealand Listener's* Dunedin drama critic, Philip Smithells, called the production 'a major literary and theatrical event' and 'an acting triumph for Mrs Carey [who] played Malfred with great skill, especially in her graduated control — an imperceptible crescendo — of emotional intensity'.

The question of whether the Malfred in the play is the same as in the book must, of course, be asked. This adaptation was good theatre, well staged, well acted. One might have expected lines from a novel to be too 'literary' for the stage, but it is clear that much of Janet Frame's language is acceptable in the theatre. In a sense this version was Frame de-Freudianised.[48]

The following year, when Frame was again in the United States, the play was filmed for television, again featuring Rosalie Carey as Malfred. This production too drew favourable reviews.

Frame left Dunedin on 4 December 1970 having arranged, again, to let her house. She flew to Wellington to spend two nights with the Baxters, then on to Auckland on 6 December. This time she stayed not in a caravan at the Gordons' but in the bedroom of her nephew Neil, who was in Wellington attending a computer course (and preparing to get married). She had timed her visit so as to attend June Gordon's graduation from Kindergarten College. 'The setup — the audience, the clothes Doris Day style [were] all part of a world I don't inhabit and don't care to,' she told Bill Brown, 'a sad sort of world, everyone a little tired, uttering the old clichés. The only worthwhile aspect, for me, was the triumph it gave my sister and her family, and the admiration I and they feel for her courage and perseverance.'⁴⁹ Her immigrant's visa had not arrived at the American consulate and Frame was now told that it might take as long as a year to be processed. Meanwhile she would be permitted to travel on a visitor's visa, and the authorities would notify her about the other when she was in the United States.

In the New Year Frame returned to Wellington by train to spend a further week with the Baxters, because Jim was visiting home from his Whanganui River commune and its 'floor-beds and eel diet'. In Ngaio, Frame said, she observed Baxter 'being himself & living his philosophy but also catching up on civilisation by watching TV & having an occasional bath & reciting a lot of poetry & enjoying the attention of his little granddaughter . . . Though his heart is wrapped up in his Jerusalem project even he seems to need to have one foot, if not in materialism, then in the home comforts of shelter, privacy, warmth, light; and to need the strength of his wife's presence.'⁵⁰

Back in Auckland Frame received a hurt letter from Albion Wright, her New Zealand publisher for the previous fourteen years, who had just heard from W.H. Allen that his star author wished to end her association with Pegasus. 'I am unaware of any reason for [this decision] . . . If you believe that we have made money from the sale of your books we are sorry to disillusion you, or anyone else who may be interested in the figures. Confronted with these, I cannot imagine another publisher rushing in to share our losses.'⁵¹ In fact the largest New Zealand publisher, A.H. and A.W. Reed, approached by Allen on Frame's behalf, added her to their list for the time being and agreed to publish *Intensive Care* in January 1972. This was entirely a result of the respect in which Frame was held by the company's senior editor, Arnold Wall. Eschewing an emotional response towards Albion Wright, Frame told him that 'my main reason for wishing to change is that you have not kept to the contract . . . in which you promise to give me a twice-yearly statement. For the past few years I've had to ask you . . . I know that I'm not an asset to a publisher [as] you imply.'⁵² Wright appears not to have debated the matter. He had never understood that his inability to supply Frame with regular statements and payments had been the source of considerable anxiety for her, particularly when she was living in England.

As Frame prepared to leave Auckland, the Gordons were engaged in preparations for the wedding of their son Neil. '[Mostly] I'm enjoying it,' she told John Money, 'except when people (as they do in New Zealand) start patronising me & sympathising with my single state. God, for the permissive US, where you can settle down with a sheep or a cow & not be looked at askance.'⁵³ On 28 January 1971 she flew out of Auckland for that 'permissive' country. Like Captain Oates, she expected to be gone for some time.

Frame spent most of February 1971 in Montecito with Bill Brown and Paul Wonner. As she had been on previous visits, she was deeply content there. 'I had a very happy peaceful time,' she told Frank Sargeson, 'lounging around; much music; looking at paintings . . . [An] earthquake happened while I was there — a very severe shock [which] almost shook us from our beds. No damage, though . . .'[54] The bad news was that Brown and Wonner's dealer, Felix Landau, was having to close his galleries in Los Angeles and New York to allow the division of matrimonial property that followed his divorce. As the press noted at the time, Landau had been able to secure good prices for his artists' work because his client list read like a Hollywood *Who's Who:* Jack Lemmon, Billy Wilder, Julie Andrews, and so on.[55]

There was further bad news in New York when Frame arrived there late in February. Sue Marquand's father's apartment was no longer available. Frame slept one night on the Marquands' sofa (while John went out with William Styron); then spent the rest of the week at the Marquands' nanny's *pied à terre* on the Midtown East Side, 'among all the funeral parlours. Nanny's room was filled with bowls of artificial flowers. I found it so complicating to unlock and lock three door-locks to get outside to the bathroom that I held on for days and days.'[56]

With the Marquands' help Frame found another apartment, on East 74th Street, between Second and Third Avenues. Sue Marquand arranged a lease (until September 1971) and deposited $3000 in Frame's bank account for six months' living expenses. Frame moved in during the first week in March. '[It] is a fairly large room with a bathroom and a small kitchen, with one ordinary bed and one convertible bed,' she told Brown. '[Again] I spend five minutes outside my door fiddling with the locks [and] when I'm in I spend as much time locking myself in . . . New York is a wilder town even than when I was here last.'[57]

As if to emphasise this, Sue Marquand was mugged in the street the week Frame settled into the apartment. '[A] man . . . approached her in broad daylight and said softly, How much money do you have? He then struck her. She gave him ten dollars whereupon he struck her again and threw her to the ground. All this in full view of passersby.' While Frame found this kind of episode horrifying, she was simultaneously fascinated and excited by 'the variety of people, faces, clothes, bodies, attitudes, miseries, delights'.[58]

Frame's intention had been to live and work in the apartment for at least a year, interspersing this spell with trips to Baltimore, California and Yaddo. She lasted only three months, however. She discovered almost immediately that the walls were too thin, and most of each day she was subjected to the sound of neighbours' conversations (in particular a loud German woman who seemed to speak to her husband all day of every day), toilets flushing and radios blaring. In a desperate effort to block these sounds, she bought a 'white-noise' machine; it was only moderately successful. Then, in April, her benefactress became seriously ill when the rest of the family was on holiday and had to be taken to hospital. 'She was very sick and only her stepmother and I knew, and until this week we've been going to see her every day,' Frame told Sargeson. 'I may have to cut short my stay in this expensive shabby apartment, but I don't think she [is] in a fit state to consider these things.'[59]

When Sue Marquand was well enough to discuss such arrangements, Frame discovered that she was on the point of leaving her husband, which news — on top of Sue's illness and the degree of noise in the apartment — seemed to promise 'battalions of misfortune'. Frame decided, with her friend's approval, to quit the apartment, retreat to John Money's house in Baltimore for two weeks, then return to New York to move into the Marquands' apartment, rent-free, on 15 June.

All this unfolded without hitch and, in Money's absence, his basement in East Baltimore was peaceful and conducive to uninterrupted writing, in contrast to the turmoil Frame had experienced in New York. There were, of course, the usual kinds of distractions *outside* the house: the bank across the road was robbed and a child was beaten to death as he got off a bus a couple of blocks away.[60] And there was a new source of disruption that began to disturb Frame's routine inside. Money had recently acquired another piece of African sculpture. 'He arrived in a coffin from Kenya and he's carved from a complete part of a tree — a large head, body, large penis, his right hand holding a spear.' Word of the acquisition had passed around the neighbourhood, and children kept coming to the door and asking to see the 'boogie man with the big ding-ding'.[61] Frame eventually disconnected the doorbell.

Early in June 1971 Bill Brown, who had business in Boston, came to stay a couple of days at East Madison Street. 'Details of the visit are censored,'[62] Frame told Sargeson. To Brown, she wrote that she 'hate[d] it here now you are gone . . . I sit here sadly fingering my Spill and Spell game and wish you were here to help me shake out the letters to make a new word.'[63] She undertook to return to California by the middle of August.

Back in New York in mid-June Frame found Sue Marquand again in hospital, this time in West 76th Street, an institution that also had a psychiatric unit. 'Yesterday when I was leaving,' Frame told Brown on 16 June, 'one of the attendants asked me where I was going and when I told her she said, "You're a patient, aren't you?" Fortunately someone said, "No, she's a visitor." Shudder shudder.'[64] Marquand was weak and being fed intravenously. The only salutory feature of the situation, according to Frame, was now that a statement of her intentions had been made, her new partner, a senior official in the Central Intelligence Agency, was able to visit her 'without deception'.[65]

Panicking about her prospects for being able to remain in New York, and feeling that it was unfair to rely on Sue Marquand for continuing support, Frame looked for alternative sources of income and accommodation. She answered an advertisement in the *Village Voice*: an apartment to let, with reduced rent for a writer. 'I phoned and made an appointment and arrived at the seedy office of a seedy-looking lawyer on the upper West Side. The apartment (which wasn't attractive — it was new and noisy) would be let to me if I agreed to write detective novels while this chap provided the plots. He had a dream of being another Erle Stanley Gardner with a Perry Mason detective. I just went . . . for the adventure of it, as . . . adventure is free (very) in New York.'[66]

In the event Frame was able to remain in the Marquands' apartment until mid-August. Sue was released from hospital in July, but only came home because Frame was there to look after her. When she felt well enough, she left 'for the country'.[67] Frame managed to get a little more work done on the 'American' novel before flying to Los Angeles on 16 August. She told John Money that she would be on the west coast until 9 September, then hoped to return to Baltimore to finish the book. She had tried to arrange time at Yaddo but the colony was fully booked until early the following year.

On 20 August, after only four days with Brown and Wonner in Santa Barbara, Frame wrote to tell John Money that she was returning early: first to New York, then back to Baltimore. 'It is heavenly here and I'm enjoying every minute but I feel I should leave . . . it's unrealistic to stay.'[68] To Frank Sargeson she reported more baldly that 'I closed down my love-life, finished my relationship with my dear friends . . . made a clean break which is (of course) always a dirty break. I'll be in touch with them occasionally.'[69]

What had happened was that, after Brown's weekend with Frame in Baltimore, he and Wonner had concluded that they were unable to offer her the degree of intimacy for which she hoped. 'Its inescapable conclusion [was] more than I could handle,' Brown said later.[70] While Frame, back on the east coast, wrote to both men:'I couldn't stay with you any longer because I was so lonely at night, not being able to snuggle up to you both occasionally. I've already trained for death in that direction. Anyway, I'm sorry that I embarrassed you by anything I said, say, did, do, imply or desire.' The Grand Passion was over. It was replaced by a brotherly-sisterly relationship among the three and what Frame now described as 'a penfriend's love'.[71]

In New York, where she slept in the Marquands' near-empty apartment (which they had now decided to vacate), she was subject to further shocks. Sue Marquand was back in hospital. And, when Frame rang Elnora Coleman, her friend from MacDowell, to investigate the possibility of staying in her apartment as she had done in 1969, the person who answered told her that Coleman was dead. She had committed suicide on 8 August.

Almost reeling now from the effect of too many emotional blows in too short a space of time, Frame retreated to John Money's at Baltimore, hoping to rediscover sanctuary, equilibrium and an opportunity to complete her novel. To her relief Money was away again, this time in Australia. 'This month alone [September] will be very profitable, I hope,' she told Brown and Wonner. 'I shall be making decisions about whether I've lived long enough or can or want to continue. I hope you keep in touch with me during this time . . . I won't embarrass either of you by getting too personal . . .'[72]

It was as well that she did not, at this time and in this mood, see some of the harsher reviews of *Intensive Care* which appeared in England in September 1971. Robert Nye in the *Guardian*, for example, complained that the book was 'ruined by over-writing . . . [The] prose, overburdened by a sense of the difficulty of what it is attempting, descends . . . to the condition of bad verse.'[73] The effect of such comments would be balanced, however, by another glowing review in the *Times Literary Supplement* from Dan Davin, who said that *Intensive Care's* 'urgent theme, reiterating the importance and uniqueness of each solitary being, gives this novel considerable stature'.[74]

All sense of despondency in Frame's correspondence was pushed aside by a jubilant announcement in late September that a cancellation at Yaddo would allow her to rejoin the writers' and artists' colony in October.[75] Like the news of her first literary award which saved her from a leucotomy, the proclamation of her return to Yaddo had the character of cavalry arriving at the rescue. Brown, Wonner, Sargeson and Money had all been worrying at a distance about whether combined stresses on Frame might produce another breakdown. Sargeson went so far as to organise a transfer of funds to the United States, through the Gordons, because he believed that Frame's reference in letters to Coleman's suicide was a veiled warning of the proximity of her own.

In fact Frame's letters from Yaddo in October and November 1971 were redolent of relief and satisfaction. 'I'd forgotten how much work one can do when all the ordinary chores of cleaning, shopping, cooking are taken away; and how much space is left in one's head for just ideas about work.' She added that the company, seven in all — writers, painters and one composer — was dull; and that was good, because it ensured that relationships did not distract her from the primary business of writing. The young composer, 'who seems out of place with his clean-cut American boy hairstyle [when] the other men all have long hair', endeared himself to Frame by offering her piano lessons; she accepted. She also played an occasional game of pool with other male residents.[76]

Frame was pleasantly surprised to find that the new director was Curtis Harnack, husband of writer Hortense Calisher, both of whom she had met in 1967 in the Marquands' apartment building. They were, Frame said, relaxed, warmly welcoming, and even offered her *their* New York apartment, which was always vacant in the summer.[77] Yaddo itself was not in such good shape as it had been, however. Frame reported that a severe tax regime, introduced in 1969, had gutted the corporation of much of its income from endowed property and dividends. This reduced money available to spend on the number and comfort of residents and on maintenance.[78]

Frame wrote and typed steadily for the first months and was able to report on 18 November that she had finished the first draft of the new novel, which she would call *Daughter Buffalo*. 'I rewrote it completely, deleting much of the character . . . which might have borne resemblance to the life of Frank Sargeson. I've demoted Turnlung to an accountant turned writer, which Frank never was.' (Sargeson was a solicitor-turned-writer.) This same letter contained further good news, which had been relayed to her from New Zealand by Charles Brasch. '[The] Government has granted me an annuity of one thousand dollars [per year]. This is confidential. It's enough to live on . . . with my slight royalties contributing extras . . . enabling me to choose, perhaps, to live in the north away from Dunedin memories.'[79] The official reason for the award of the annuity was 'services to New Zealand literature'. Understandably, however, Charles Brasch had raised the issue of Frame's health as a lever to help secure the award. The Cabinet paper that supported the proposition had stated that 'she has had a history of mental instability and such a person needs some security in order to work well'. Professor Wallace Ironside had added: '[Because] she keeps well largely through the psychological effects of writing, chronic anxiety over money would gravely threaten her health.'[80]

Frame described to Bill Brown what she saw as the implications of the annuity:

I don't expect to make any more visits out of New Zealand. I've realised that many of my flights . . . were the result of my being afraid to stay there when I was never certain I could provide for myself, but now that the NZ Govt has decided to dispense this (confidential) annuity I shall have no worries in that direction. It will be lonely but . . . And now that I am provided for I know that I need not stay in Dunedin . . . And when I get there I will be the one who is visited by friends from overseas, if they care to . . .[81]

The final days at Yaddo in the week before Christmas were lonely. 'We have Christmas wreaths on the doors, and the mail is full of parcels for everyone (except me) . . . [I've had] a last piano lesson . . . doing a Schubert Dance . . . I'm hopelessly ploddy, though I do love the music . . . I have found such warmth in this country . . . Or should it be that [here] I find myself capable of loving people?'[82]

In New York en route for Baltimore on 22 December Frame delivered the manuscript of *Daughter Buffalo* to Carl Brandt, whom she had now decided to retain as her American agent ('I can't cope with anthology queries etc').[83] She told Bill Brown that the new book 'had the usual acknowledgements [but] no dedication as the only one I can think of would be embarrassing'.[84] Those acknowledgements were 'to Sue and John Marquand, John Money, and the Yaddo Corporation, for their hospitality'.

Frame spent Christmas alone at Money's (he was, as usual, with his sister and her family in Canada); and she flew out of Baltimore in the New Year to California, where she spent several days with Brown and Wonner, all three making their common peace. For this visit she slept in a motel. She then flew from Los Angeles to Auckland, arriving on 7 January 1972. Impatient to be home, where she believed her untended garden would be rampant, she spent only four days with the Gordons before heading for Dunedin. There she was greeted by 'the brightness of the light . . . the sun's hotness and the shade's coolness . . . What life and light must have been like before pollution took over in American cities.' All she asked for now, she told Brown and Wonner, 'is quietness; and all I [ask] of you, my friends, is a visit now and again, from living quarters near or far'. She ended this letter, her first for 1972, with 'a sort of sad love'.[85]

CHAPTER TWENTY-THREE

# Away from Civilisation

$\mathcal{A}$FTER FIFTEEN YEARS OF BEING PUBLISHED IN NEW ZEALAND BY Pegasus, Janet Frame returned to Dunedin in January 1972 just as her new publisher, A.H. and A.W. Reed, released *Intensive Care* on the local market. To her surprise, the first newspaper she picked up, the *Evening Star*, described the novel as 'a tirade against the permissive society and its loose sexual morals'. It was 'amazing', she told Bill Brown, 'what people can read into one's writing! How typical of Dunedin.'[1]

That same week, her equilibrium was restored by a more perceptive review of the book in the *New Zealand Listener*, by her old friend Dennis McEldowney. 'It is almost impossible to judge a Janet Frame novel. Her books simply *are*, they arbitrarily exist (with whatever pains they are created) . . . [Her] characteristic theme . . . is death — the modes in which it appears, the games with which we while away the time until it does, the deceptions we practise to conceal from ourselves that this is what we are doing. *Intensive Care* is a characteristic Janet Frame experience.'[2] This observation and the review as a whole were especially acute. It did indeed seem that Frame's view of life and her writing style were forged by a deeply internalised tension that grew from a preoccupation with death. And Frame herself appeared to confirm this when she commented to Bill Brown that, in her opinion, 'the [very] function of the imagination depends on the foreknowledge of death'.[3]

Her more immediate preoccupation, however, was how to disengage from Dunedin, which she now found more disruptively noisy than Baltimore or New York. 'I'm going mad with all these penis-motormowers being worked in the weekend and everybody hammering and sawing,' she told John Money.[4] Even more intrusive, a quarry a mile away was now using a bulldozer whose sound and vibrations echoed back and forth across the valley throughout the day; at night, she listened to the 'nerve-destroying' whine of washing and drying machines from a laundry down in the gully below Evans Street.

As a temporary refuge from these assaults, Frame had a basement room insulated and lined, and then decorated it to suggest a smaller version of a Yaddo studio. And she bought a piano, 'a John Brinsmead upright which cost all my money — nearly four hundred dollars . . . I find the Schubert dances rather hard, but I can play the Chopin prelude and I can do a few easy minuets, and I'm working through that "easy" Beethoven sonata . . . It's a relaxation.'[5] For further relaxation she would soon enrol in a university extension music theory course, and she visited friends Ruth Dallas, Charles Brasch and Dorothy Ballantyne, whose second husband, Robert, played the flute for her after dinner.[6] In April Jacquie Baxter came to stay for ten days, her annual holiday, an experience both women enjoyed. Shortly afterwards she became a great-aunt for the first time with the arrival of William Gordon, son of her nephew Ian and his wife, Suzie.

Frame was, for the present, financially comfortable. Her new New Zealand publisher sold 850 copies of *Intensive Care* in the first month and sent her, unsolicited, a royalty statement and cheque — something Pegasus had rarely done. This encouraged Frame to write to Pegasus yet again to ask for money owing on sales of her earlier books, which produced a cheque for thirty-three dollars at the end of February and a further seventy-two dollars in April. April was also the month in which she began to receive her annuity, initially at a rate of sixty-four dollars a month. To her considerable amusement, these payments turned out to be administered by the war pensions branch of the country's defence forces, so that for several months she identified herself as a 'war widow', speculated about her eligibility for membership of the Returned Services Association and reflected on how pleased her father would have been by this development.[7]

Noise continued to be a source of distraction and torture at Evans Street, however, and her new basement room proved no better insulated than the rest of the house. This prevented the resumption of anything that resembled a serious writing routine. In May 1972, acting on impulse, Frame flew to Auckland to stay with the Gordons and to investigate the price of houses in rural districts north of the city. To her surprise, she discovered that they were cheaper than comparable properties in the vicinity of Dunedin. She reported to Peter Dawson:

[I've] found a little bach on the Whangaparaoa Peninsula which I'm selling my house here to buy . . . The place has electricity, and that's about all. Tank water, a bury-your-own toilet . . . and I shall probably have to get around by bicycle . . . I shall have to coddle anything I plant, as the place is exposed to sea-wind [and] the vegetation leans away from the wind . . . [There's] nothing like telephone and so on. I'm in the mood to get away from civilisation.[8]

She told John Money that she had a 'huge quantity' of manuscripts to burn before she left, though in fact she left most of them, in a trunk and two suitcases, in Otago University's Hocken Library, which hoped eventually to acquire all her papers.[9] As she packed, she was constantly amused by Negative ('Neg'), a white kitten which she had bought for company in May. 'She is very pretty and fluffy, and her eyes are being ruined [by] watching the tv.'[10] The purpose of the television, the first she had hired, was to watch the appearance of her brother-in-law, Wilson Gordon, in a locally made serial (*Section Seven*), to see music programmes (a Daniel Barenboim masterclass in Beethoven sonatas, for example) and to follow the American presidential election campaign.

Once Bill Brown and Paul Wonner learned of Frame's intention to shift, they offered to contribute to the cost of the new house and to the expense of installing a septic tank (they had just sold their home in Montecito and were themselves in the process of moving to Peterborough in New Hampshire). Frame sold the Evans Street cottage for $4500, almost twice what she had paid for it, and bought the Whangaparaoa property for $7000. Wonner sent a cheque for $US3000 to cover the difference and the costs of moving; and a second one for $US1300 for plumbing and fencing.[11] In the midst of all these arrangements and related correspondence, Frame was invited to attend her first literary festival, in Adelaide, South Australia, but declined ('I'm not that kind of person').[12]

Considering that she had lived there for seven-and-a-half largely contented years — longer than she had remained in any community apart from her childhood in Oamaru — Frame made the break from Dunedin with surprising ease. The determination to do so had firmed up at Yaddo the previous November. In the absence of the Baxters, the city no longer seemed to her to be a home base. Her remaining friends, with the possible exception of Ruth Dallas, were not ones with whom she felt she shared conspicuous intimacy. The persistent coldness of the climate, particularly of her uninsulated wooden cottage, now depressed her. 'Perhaps [it] reinforces an inner cold,' she suggested to Peter Dawson.[13] And Dunedin still held the residue of earlier, unhappy times which, now that she was no longer distracted by a passion for Bill Brown, seemed to rise up to greet her more frequently. The noise problem was only the last in what seemed to be an accumulation of disadvantages. By June 1972 Frame told Dawson that her only major regret about leaving the first home she had owned was that she was unable to take her plants with her.[14]

Charles Brasch was overseas when Frame took her leave of the city on 11 July. He told Sargeson by letter that he was 'very sad' though 'hardly surprised' by his protégée's move.[15] She *was* able to farewell Ruth Dallas and Dorothy Ballantyne, though she wounded Ballantyne with her comment that her departure was prompted by an absence of friends. Ballantyne, instead of saying something like, '"Ere, 'ere, what about me?' was offended and never again felt as close to Frame as she had done, though they would remain in communication.[16]

The offence that Frame inadvertently gave to Dorothy Ballantyne was in part, perhaps, a consequence of the difficulty the writer experienced in empathising with people who appeared to be strong and self-reliant. But it arose also from a florescence of enthusiasm for her new home. The house, a fibrolite bach like Sargeson's, only larger, stood high on a hill overlooking Shakespear Bay on Whangaparaoa Peninsula, forty-eight kilometres north of Auckland. Located near the easternmost point of the peninsula, it had ocean views in three directions and also looked out to distant islands to the north and south, and to Coromandel Peninsula on the far horizon. It was a panorama that well-travelled aficionados likened in the summer to that offered by the Aegean Sea. 'I can see the sea from everywhere except the west windows,' she told Brown and Wonner within days of moving in. 'I look out on to the bay as I write this. The tide is out. I can see [an] old shipwreck; and a solitary bird on the sand, and its tall shadow . . . [The beach] is good for shellfish — pipis and muscles and cockles and fishing itself . . . The nights are so quiet [that] I sleep till seven o'clock in the morning. The days are quiet too.'[17]

The 900-acre farm at the far end of the peninsula, owned by 'old Mr Shakespear, 92 and sans everything', was to be turned into a reserve and would never be developed.[18] A second farm to the west, behind Frame's house, was to be subdivided for housing, but this would occur gradually, over a period of years (she was told). Because of the spaciousness of their sections, the neighbours were some distance away, behind manuka hedges, and did not intrude. The nearest was Celtic, dark-eyed and handsome and, as Frame's father had done, occasionally played the bagpipes. 'I am isolated,' Frame told Peter Dawson, 'but less lonely.' Auckland and the company of Frank Sargeson and his friends, and of the Gordons, was only an hour and twenty minutes away by bus and less time by car. The nearest village, Manly, was six and a half kilometres from her house. A daily rural mail delivery also brought 'bread and newspaper and anything else within reason'.[19]

Frame's first expedition towards civilisation was not wholly successful. She set out to cycle to the Manly post office. Because the road ran along an undulating ridge, she walked the bicycle up the hills, then walked it down the other sides as well, frightened that she might reach uncontrollable speeds. In this manner the journey took an hour each way. Then the local librarian asked her kindly if she had ever borrowed books before, and Frame found herself unable to explain that she wrote them. 'So now I'm wondering how to masquerade.'[20] She subsequently had gears fitted to the bicycle to make the journey easier and quicker; later still she bought a motorcycle.

Her bus trips to Auckland were rather more successful. In the first month she went to the city to see an exhibition of surrealist painting, and to stay with Frank Sargeson and the Gordons. Sargeson was rejuvenated to have Frame living again within visiting distance and told a friend that it was 'extraordinary how well we hit it off in personal relations'.[21] Time with the Gordons, who had moved to a smaller house in the suburb of Glenfield, was more taxing, but had its compensations for a writer. 'One's family . . . is marvellous material, and I'm inclined to think the *only* material . . . because it supplies enough tension to last several lifetimes; and when their way of life is so different from one's own, it's like a free gift of several novels.'[22] Wilson Gordon was now managing a North Shore newspaper, and June teaching at a local kindergarten. The children had all left home. Frame's niece, Pamela, working as a librarian, was now involved with a young railways worker named Stephen Bailey, whom she would marry in 1973.

On the whole, though, Frame's social life was 'with books and music and the sea and the wailing wind from the sea', Frame told Bill Brown in August. 'I've had two fairly crank callers, one who came five miles to see me because she'd heard [mistakenly] I was a Rosicrucian . . . The other a woman who'd heard I was a writer and who [asked] me lots of questions which I did not answer . . . I'm really only interested now in people who work in the arts and who are outside the mainstream of living — the others are interesting, and useful, material, that's all.'[23]

'Material' was a commodity of which the Whangaparaoa Peninsula had an ample supply. It was unavoidable that Frame's observation of her neighbours eventually found its way into what little fiction she wrote while she was there, including this passage from a short story:

> Most . . . were retired, spending the days that at last belonged exclusively to them trying to improve the appearance and comfort of their house and land, adding a terrace here, a flamingo there, a rose-arch, an orchid-house, a new fence, new furniture, new rooms. Carriers and concrete contractors with their revolving grey-bellied mixers were forever arriving, unloading, turning awkwardly half on the road, half on the footpath; sometimes a small heap of concrete blocks would appear overnight as if a new kind of mammoth had passed by; or a bulldozer would be discovered in a den in a clump of manuka, or parked in a driveway lying in wait for the performance of a new trick of landscaping. How busy the people were, who had said goodbye to work . . .[24]

One such neighbour, deeply involved in the business of gardening and beautification, turned out to be Frame's former hospital superintendent Geoffrey Blake-Palmer.

Frame had set up her study in a middle bedroom overlooking Army Bay. But she did not establish a work routine until late August 1972. First she had had to oversee the installation of her septic tank, and of a telephone 'party line' shared with five other subscribers; then she planted out a vegetable garden and fruit trees. She was delighted to dig up kauri gum on the section, an indication that the peninsula had once been cloaked in giant trees. When she did resume writing, helped by the cat's daily demand for attention from 5 am, the new book turned out to be 'about water — not that you'd guess, it's so far from the point'.[25]

Her forty-eighth birthday, 28 August, was also publication day in the United States for her 'American' novel, *Daughter Buffalo*. In this book, a wealthy young doctor named Talbot Edelman, drawn to some extent from John Money's former student Dan Granoff, and a poet named Turnlung, with some affinities with Frank Sargeson, conduct separate and joint investigations into the nature of death. They also develop a need for each other, and 'meet, mate and die' in the heat of a New York summer. Edelman is sexually excited by Turnlung's physical decline; and Turnlung, as he disintegrates, adopts a young buffalo from Central Park Zoo as his daughter.

For most of the American publications that reviewed it, the mix was perhaps too rich and too ripe, but rewarded the effort required to read and digest it. Josephine Hendon in the *New York Times Book Review* described it as 'a poem to the union of the living dead, a *Liebestod* based on common mutilation and common need. Pathetic and ugly, sad and destructive, it has the grim power of life drawn up as a suicide pact.'[26] *Time* said that Turnlung's flashbacks to his New Zealand origins suggested 'autobiography, and their effect . . . is like the Japanese puppet shows in which the puppeteer is camouflaged in black but just visible . . . a subtle reminder to viewers that their puppets are not their own masters.'[27] The *New Yorker* reviewer said 'one resists a book that can be so clear in presenting its theme and yet so obscure in developing it'.[28] While Robert Ostermann in the *National Observer* asserted that 'Miss Frame is difficult to track, but she marks her trail; the signs are there if you look for them. Indisputably, she is worth the trouble . . .'[29]

The only one of these reviews on which Frame commented in her correspondence was that of Josephine Hendon, which she described as 'good' and 'thoughtful'; but she was amused that Hendon thought the idea of working with 'sexually unfinished children' — one of John Money's specialities — was a figment of her imagination.[30] To Money himself, Frame described *Daughter Buffalo* as 'an imaginative study based on a few facts gathered and put into an imaginary pattern . . . [It] was really inspired by Dan Granoff . . . I hope he doesn't read it, or his family. O treacherous authors!'[31] It was Granoff's father, Henry, who had engineered grants from his charitable trust, the Henry Foundation, to support her work in the United States.

That same month, September 1972, Frame received her advance for the American edition of *Daughter Buffalo*. Braziller's $1500 had been reduced $450 by taxation, and $225 by agency commission, to a total of six hundred New Zealand dollars. Frame was especially annoyed that Brandt and Brandt had increased the percentage of their commission so soon after she had returned to them as a client.[32]

Towards the end of September Frame had a foretaste of what the character of her neighbourhood would be in summertime. '[It] was a warm weekend . . . There were about fifteen cars at the entrance to the beach, with parties coming and going all day, people boating and swimming and so on. It wasn't noisy [but] I stayed indoors, and Neggy stayed in too. Later, when the people had gone . . . I went out into the balmy air and planted six feijoa bushes which will form part of a hedge. They . . . have fruit [which] tastes like guavas.'[33]

That same week she heard from Sargeson that he had run into Jim Baxter in Takapuna, 'and he looked much healthier than I've seen him for many years — apparently he's eating better. I pushed a couple of dollars on to him. Token resistance.'[34] Baxter had left his community at Jerusalem and may not have intended to return; and he had just completed what would prove to be his last collection of poems, *Autumn Testament*.[35] He was based for the time being in Auckland, though Frame had not seen him since the week she overlapped with him in Ngaio in January the previous year.

On 24 October, less than a month after Sargeson's letter, Frame wrote to Brown and Wonner:

Jim Baxter has just died of a heart attack. He was forty-six. How arrogant I am to have thought that I could keep death in books, lure it there so it would not stray into life's business . . . While I'm thinking of you, I have the thought of Jim's death, and all those other thoughts which Death (who demands personification) so generously and busily hands out; you know . . . the fears for those we love. Once again the instant mourning in music and poetry and painting is there to help.

Jacquie is coming to stay with me when it is all over and the 'mules' praises and brays', of which there will be many, some sincere, some not so, have ceased.[36]

She wrote the following day with further information.

[Television] news showed Jim Baxter's funeral. The Maoris gave him the funeral they would have accorded a chief, and he was allowed to be buried on Maori land just outside the house where he set up the commune . . . The body lay in state on the marae (meeting place), the coffin open, and though the tv cameras had obviously been used with discretion, a sudden film showed Jim lying in his coffin, as if he were asleep, with flowers strewn over him. In the background, at the head of the coffin, guarding him according to Maori custom, Jacquie sat . . . looking like stone, absolutely immobile. I hated myself for only half-living, for watching on tv the funeral of someone I loved, but I could not bear to go to see him, and can't even believe that he is dead . . . [For] all my fancy writing about death I end up watching it on tv . . . There is a Requiem Mass today in the Cathedral but, again, I shan't go, although it is good, I think, to engage in formal mourning . . . I'm feeling a bit lonely, without sharing.[37]

Frame expressed that loneliness by writing five long letters to Brown and Wonner in the week of Baxter's death. Parts of these were intensively evocative descriptions of her immediate surroundings and doings.

It is early morning, pearl-grey sea and sky, Neggy setting a blowfly at my feet for my breakfast. Mr Shakespear's lambs seem perpetually reborn, are crying out; and the spring birds are singing their summer songs. The small lemon tree is covered in sweetest blossom, the orange tree has one orange growing, the feijoas are beginning to bloom their crimson flowers which I'm told are edible . . . I was given a lift by my neighbour Jim Aicheson and young Mr Shakespear. They had been fixing old Mr Shakespear's yacht [which] he's had for 67 years . . . for sailings around the gulf and the islands . . . It was my first meeting with [young] Mr Shakespear. He is fresh-faced [and] resembles one of the clowns out of *A Midsummer Night's Dream*.[38]

Other pages were reminiscences prompted by a sharply awakened sense of nostalgia:

Suddenly I am walking down Madison Avenue . . . to 74th Street. Or I am walking from 74th Street down to the Marquands' old place in W. 57th Street, and I go down Fifth Avenue because I know Stravinsky lives somewhere there and he has just died . . . [And] I walk down through the Zoo, and there's the little buffalo I saw . . . Perhaps it just appeared that day because Stravinsky died. I never dreamed it would come to be written about! So I'm walking to the apartment and I go up there for lunch of yoghurt, boysenberry, with Sue, and we play roulette for which I have a 'system'; and Sue is ill, and the city pollution is especially bad and everyone's eyes are smarting as if they were filled with pieces of glass and one's stomach churns with nausea. Good old New York . . .[39]

Frame's nostalgia, though, did not embrace Dunedin. 'I'm not at all homesick for [there], though I do miss my secretive friends . . . Here, there's no one to talk to unless I want what I'm saying to be repeated. No Secret Sharers. But I'm glad I'm here.'[40]

The rest of the year tailed off in further expeditions to the Gordons' and Frank Sargeson's ('he tells me all the literary gossip and a few dirty stories which I forget'),[41] a visit to an exhibition of Californian paintings and drawings (which included work by Paul Wonner and Don Bachardy), and further failed attempts to work — Baxter's death had 'knocked my writing . . . I feel so tired'.[42] This tiredness was reinforced by news of other deaths: John Pascoe, a poet and archivist and friend of Sargeson who had walked up to her in the street one day in Wellington and kissed her out of sheer admiration for her novels; and Jess Whitworth, who was released from her senility within weeks of Baxter's death. 'Dear Jess!' Frame exclaimed to Peter Dawson, 'I knew her only at what would be the tail end of her life, yet she stocked me with enough emotional riches and memories to last beyond my lifetime.'[43]

For Frame, the only positive feature of the latter part of the year was the election of a Labour Government on 25 November 1972, ending twelve years of conservative rule by the National Party and military involvement by New Zealand in the now-winding-down Vietnam war. She told correspondents that she admired the intelligence and compassion of the country's new Prime Minister, Norman Kirk, 'though I fear he hasn't enough imagination — perhaps it will develop now he is in power'.[44] Like other New Zealand writers, Frame had been heartened by Kirk's promise to introduce public lending right payments for authors to compensate them for the use of books in libraries; and the New Zealand Authors Fund was duly set up in late 1973, the first such scheme in the English-speaking world. It immediately lifted Frame's annual income by around $3000 (her first payment from the fund, sent to her in March 1974, was for $2994.66, based on New Zealand library holdings of fourteen Frame titles).

The long hot summer of early 1973 opened large cracks in the ground around her house. Frame responded by tossing sunflower seeds, date stones and peach stones into these gaps, 'having a memory of tales of strange plants emerging from the earth at such times'.[45] She also ordered a new tank with a capacity of 850 gallons to make it less likely that she would run out of household water.

She continued to report an inability to write ('what I am working on now . . . I haven't even begun'; 'it's taking a long time for me to settle'; 'work has been very little'; 'I keep losing my manuscript').[46] Superstitiously, she attributed this aridity at least in part to the deaths of the previous year. And the sense that these losses were in some way associated with her 'death novel' intensified when *Daughter Buffalo* was published in New Zealand by Reed in May 1973. Charles Brasch died the same month. 'Death has crept around a lot in the past year,' she told John Money. 'I [had] enough of it in *Daughter Buffalo* . . . The most recent recruit [is] Charles Brasch . . . a big shock to the frail art world of New Zealand.' To another friend she wrote, 'Charles' death is a great loss . . . He was a noble man.'[47]

Brasch's absence from Dunedin when she had left in July of the previous year meant that Frame had been unable to take a formal farewell of her friend and patron of nearly thirty years. Her pain that this should have been so was eased when Alan Roddick, his literary executor, sent her a copy of a poem that Brasch had written, literally, on his death bed:

With You
(To Janet Frame)

Can you hear me Whangaparaoa?

Listen to your seas, listen to your tides,
To the moon pulling the deep.

I am there, under the waters,
In the winds, in the leaf that sighs.

I am there, sleeping in the rocks,
Under the houses, below the promontories.

I am the sea, I am the wind,
Everything and nothing, with you.[48]

A fortnight after Brasch's death Frame was reporting to Peter Dawson that *Daughter Buffalo* 'has had nasty reviews here; this has rather depressed me, yet I don't feel too bad as the book was set in America . . . and I have had very perceptive reviews [there]'.[49] On the whole, this was true. Even Dennis McEldowney, an admirer of Frame's work, had called it 'an artistic failure . . . but not one I have the heart to deplore'.[50] Despite more understanding reviews in the literary journals *Landfall* and *Islands*,[51] and despite the fact that the novel won the Hubert Church Award and came second in the 1973 Wattie Book of the Year Award, it was the largely unfavourable consensus of newspaper and magazine notices that preyed on Frame's mind and gave her — again — a feeling that she was viewed more sympathetically abroad than she was in her own country.

In the same letter in which she reported her depression to Dawson, Frame announced that she planned to apply for the Katherine Mansfield Fellowship, a recently established bursary that enabled the recipient to live and work in Menton in the South of France for six months. Previous fellows had included C.K. Stead and James McNeish. 'I'd like to be out of this country again,' she told Dawson. 'I find myself turning against it.'[52]

This feeling was intensified by the fact that the threatened subdivision of the farm behind her at Army Bay was now taking place. The construction of houses — with attendant noise, vibration and visual distraction — was shredding her days and giving her further excuses for an inability to write anything more sustained than poems and short stories. Perhaps she could arrange her movements, she told John Money, so that she was out of New Zealand for the most intensive period of house-building, and return when it was over. 'Unfortunately this area has suddenly boomed . . . If, by the time I get back, things are not less noisy, I'll leave.'[53]

A further source of distress in the middle of 1973 was a temporary falling-out with Frank Sargeson over the similarities between himself and the Turnlung character in *Daughter Buffalo*. Margareta Gee, wife of the writer Maurice Gee, borrowed Sargeson's copy of the novel before he had read it. When she returned it she told him that she was sure that Turnlung was based on him.'He couldn't believe it, and then was rather put out.'[54] Sargeson himself wrote to Phillip Wilson on 17 June:'[In] my view she doesn't present portraits of people, but it's part of her . . . slant on things to collect items about people she knows which she apparently has no second thoughts about using. In her time she has taken bits of hide off her sister, Karl Stead, Ruth Dallas, and (now) Charles Brasch or myself . . . take your pick . . . I don't mind for myself, but it's a sheer bastard when she involves a third party.'[55]

Sargeson *did* mind, of course, and his annoyance at what he regarded as Frame's misuse of information about her friends and family led him in the following months to resort to the kinds of irritated remarks about her writing that he had made before the publication of *The Adaptable Man*. 'I can't read *Daughter Buffalo* — exactly the same pattern . . . since *Owls Do Cry*, a page beautifully done with all sorts of profound and moving sentences — and then the next page just schoolgirl's rattle or prattle, the bright *literateur* of the fifth form. Well, take it or leave it, but for me without too much regret I leave it.'[56]

To Canterbury University academic Winston Rhodes, who had written a critical biography of him for the American Twayne World Authors series, Sargeson went further. 'Meeting her "instability" in life, I don't take much to finding it in her books . . . For her there may be something therapeutic in her death theme but [over] the years it has come repeatedly freakish, a tiresome reiteration of her refusal to admit there are people in the world *as such*, not just a gallery of monsters transformed *into such* by her Boschian imagination . . . I always hoped for some line which would derive from her little story "The Day of the Sheep". In that she is *not* writing about herself . . . [For] me it is significant that you cannot mention that story to her without her immediately closing up. I deduce from this that one view of her work could be that it is a long elaborately worked out self-indulgence.'[57] Another view could be that Frame was simply not writing the kind of social realist fiction of which Sargeson approved — and hence that *her* imaginative world was not in harmony with his.

Sargeson's acerbic brew of personal and professional considerations, aggravated by discomfort from rheumatism and a bad back, had receded by the end of the year. But, in the interim, it was corrosive enough for him to change his will to make Christine Cole his sole beneficiary; in reaching this decision, however, Sargeson was mindful of the fact that Frame now had her annuity and the imminent prospect of Authors Fund payments, and that she was unlikely to be as destitute again as she had been in earlier years of her writing career.

In mid-September 1974 Frame was required to go into hospital for surgery on a cartilage problem in her knee. Sargeson's wounded feelings had recovered sufficiently for him to invite her to stay at Esmonde Road after the operation. A fortnight later, in early October, the French Ambassador to New Zealand announced at the James Cook Hotel in Wellington that Frame had been awarded the Katherine Mansfield Fellowship. She would sail for Europe on the Chandris Line vessel *Ellinis* on 30 November and return by air in the second half of 1974. Frame attended the function, her first in the capital city, in the company of Jacquie Baxter. For this to occur, the *New Zealand Listener* reported, Frame had had to be 'found by a literary world, by the people who drink cocktails'.

> [It] was a formal occasion. She mixed among the formality, camouflaged . . . Enveloped in a yellow brown dress with dolman sleeves, her feet in dilapidated brown shoes, a dull green velvet bag over her arm she stood, moving from one foot to another, while people congratulated her and made speeches. Her hair shot up in a frizzy mass from her head, her face was completely devoid of make-up. She was the most important person in the room, and she was probably . . . also the poorest . . .
>
> [Her] turn to speak. She thanked those present and those not, mentioned the nightmare trip she had experienced the night before on the train journey from Auckland to Wellington . . . 'This is very important to me,' she said then, in reference to the award. 'If you look up the word "important" in the dictionary you will understand all its connotations. That is all.'
>
> Clapping, approval, more congratulations — she wrote her signature for someone on the page of one of her books. She talked vaguely of things and eventually turned to her companion, Jacquie Baxter, and suggested it was time to leave.[58]

The following afternoon Frame sat in the office of the new *Listener* editor, Ian Cross, who, in a previous career incarnation as a novelist, had been the first Burns Fellow at the University of Otago. Cross had suggested to his reporter Jill McCracken that Frame might better endure the trial of being interviewed if she was able to type her responses to questions rather than answer them orally.

> An easy question and she would turn to the typewriter, a delighted smile across her face, pound the keys and then talk, answering both by the written and the spoken word . . . [The] two-page 'manuscript' she produced [had] small holes in the paper where the o's and full-stops should be . . .
>
> 'Why now to France?'
>
> 'I thought the time was right,' she explains . . . 'I was there fifteen [*sic*]

years ago, I would like to see it again.' She turns to the typewriter, at ease, the ground is safe, there is no need to fight for answers that don't want to be given. 'But I want to hurry back, to live here, settle . . .'

She would like to write something on the ship — maybe begin the journal she has never kept since the diary of her youth . . . Her plans for Menton are vague — 'If I talk about them they'll dissolve,' she says, her hands floating in front of her eyes as she tries to think of something else to say. She keeps looking at the clock, 'I can't stay long,' and at Jacquie, 'Shall we go home soon? Let's go home.'[59]

The arrangements for Menton came together as planned — at least at the New Zealand end of the journey. In addition to the $290 per month which Frame would receive as the fellowship stipend, she had also won $650 for her Wattie Award. As a result of engaging a firm of accountants recommended by Charles Brasch, she had secured her first tax refund from the United States, of $400. Small sums of royalties dribbled in from Pegasus, W.H. Allen and Braziller; and her first Authors Fund payment would arrive while she was away. Her annuity would continue to be paid into her local bank account. She would not be destitute when she returned home. She also arranged to let the Whanga-paraoa house for twelve dollars a week to a 'giant-sized ginger-bearded painter' who ran an art gallery on the peninsula. This tenant would bring his own cat and undertook to look after Neg.[60]

On 29 November, the night before she boarded the *Ellinis*, Frame slept at Esmonde Road. Sargeson, reconciled to his protégée, told a friend what ensued the next day. 'I took the morning off work [to ensure] everything that had to go with her was suitably packed. But at noon she decided to go to the boat from her sister's place . . . So I put all the packings and herself into a taxi after I had searched the house and nothing had been overlooked. Alas, at her sister's things came unpacked — including the spectacles she can never be without. And [so] she leaves behind a most essential tool of trade.'[61] Faithful Wilson Gordon, however, dashed from the wharf back to Glenfield and delivered the spectacles to a purser just as the *Ellinis* was ready to pull out.

Then followed a month at sea, spent in a single cabin without facilities on the top deck. As she had feared, Frame spent much of this time seasick. The vessel travelled to the Netherlands via Tahiti, Cristobal, Curaçao and Ponta Delgada, arriving at Rotterdam on 30 December. From there Frame travelled by train to Paris, which she found 'little changed' from the city she had seen seventeen years earlier.[62] After two days she took an overnight train to Menton, where she arrived on 3 January 1974.

CHAPTER TWENTY-FOUR

# The Mansfield Connection

KATHERINE MANSFIELD LEFT THE COUNTRY OF HER BIRTH AS A YOUNG adult in 1908 and died in France in 1923. And yet for decades after her death she remained to the world beyond New Zealand that country's sole literary reference point. Writers of apparent promise who emerged from there between the 1930s and the 1960s — James Courage, Frank Sargeson, Dan Davin, Janet Frame — found their names linked with her as British publishers and reviewers sought to convince a disbelieving reading public that worthwhile literature could originate from the Antipodes. 'No writer of comparable stature has come from the Dominion since Katherine Mansfield,' John Lehmann trumpeted on the jacket blurb for his London edition of Sargeson's stories in 1946.[1]

Frame too was the subject of this kind of puffery from W.H. Allen and George Braziller in the 1960s: 'the most talented writer to have come out of her country since Katherine Mansfield' became a kind of mantra, initiated by her publishers and taken up by reviewers and interviewers, especially in London. For her, it became an unwelcome and a misleading refrain. For she was in no way influenced by her better-known compatriot; and there were far more respects in which her life and writing differed from Mansfield's than resembled it.

Where Frame's mother's family, the Godfreys, were descended from minor English gentry who had gone *down* in the world in an imperial colony, Katherine Mansfield was descended from yeomanry on their way up through the ranks of the middle class. Mansfield's father, Harold Beauchamp, was a bumptious merchant with an eye for the main chance who was eventually knighted. She herself was the product in part of a Wellington private school and a London ladies' college and came from a family whose outlook and values were closer to those of the English middle class than to those of her fellow countrymen. Indeed, one critic has characterised Mansfield's fictionalised family as 'smugly riddled with the certainties of a class for whom the rest of society exists in a tributary role'.[2] While many of her most successful stories were set in New Zealand, their characters and themes bear little relation to those of mainstream New Zealand life of the time. And when Mansfield moved out of her class to write, for example, of working people, those were her least successful ventures into characterisation. The style of her writing too reflected European movements of thought and the preoccupations of the London literary world. She left New Zealand as a barely formed young adult and never returned, except in thought. And New Zealanders, at least up to the 1960s, offered her little recognition as one of their own.

Janet Frame, by contrast, was the product of a 'blue-collar' family whose upbringing of their children, at least in material terms, was as unprivileged as Mansfield's had been privileged. Where the Frame girls slept in a heap of sisters in a sheetless bed, Mansfield and her sisters had linen, bedrooms of their own as they grew towards adulthood, and domestic servants. And where Mansfield had left New Zealand for a finishing school in London at fourteen, Frame did not venture abroad until she was thirty-two. The characters and themes of Frame's stories and novels arose initially from the milieux she encountered in her railway family, the provincial town of Oamaru and New Zealand mental hospitals of the 1940s and 1950s. She began to make a literary reputation in her own country with a book of stories that, apart from the effects of her wide reading, owed little to the fashions of metropolitan culture on the other side of the globe.

Frame's only authentic associations with Katherine Mansfield were the fact that her mother had worked in Picton for the writers' grandparents; and that she herself had resisted reading Mansfield's stories precisely because Lottie Frame had recommended them with such fervour. The alleged connection of her writing to Mansfield's came out of no shared tradition or social milieu. It was simply a ploy on the part of publishers to give British and American readers an incentive to take seriously a writer who, by virtue of her country of origin, might otherwise be thought to be of merely provincial interest and value.

In New Zealand, Katherine Mansfield became a kind of literary icon, if only — as one critic has said — a 'qualified' one.[3] Her name did not become widely known, nor her reputation weighty, until the very years that Frame was making her way as a writer. Mansfield's strongest early promoters in New Zealand were members of the New Zealand Women Writers' Society. This guild of largely (but not wholly) undistinguished authors and would-be authors regarded her as the godmother of New Zealand literature. They sought to heighten her local profile by memorialising her place of birth in Wellington, raising funds to help the Alexander Turnbull Library accumulate a collection of Mansfield papers, and persuading the Bank of New Zealand, of whose board Mansfield's father, Sir Harold Beauchamp, had been a former chairman, to sponsor a national short story award. Then, in the late 1960s, this same group of women coordinated private endowments to establish a Katherine

Mansfield Memorial Fellowship, known initially as the Winn-Manson Menton Fellowship after its principal benefactors.

This bursary, which Frame was awarded for 1974, was New Zealand's only overseas literary fellowship. Launched in 1970, it aimed to give writers who might otherwise not be able to afford it some experience of living in Europe; and it sought to commemorate Katherine Mansfield's association with France, and in particular with the town of Menton on the French–Italian border, where she had enjoyed what some critics had regarded as the most fruitful period of her creative life.[4] Staying there at the Villa Isola Bella in 1920 and 1921, Mansfield had written such stories as 'The Daughters of the Late Colonel', 'The Stranger', 'The Lady's Maid', and 'Poison'. She had praised the location saying that Isola Bella would be forever engraved, like pokerwork, on her heart.[5] The owners of the house in the 1960s and 1970s were not interested in being part of any commemorative arrangement. But they allowed the municipality of Menton to buy a cellar under the house so as to convert it into a Katherine Mansfield Memorial Room. And it was in this room that the visiting New Zealand writers would be expected to work. Four Katherine Mansfield fellows had preceded Frame to Menton, including Karl Stead in 1972; and the condition of 'the room' and the adequacy of of the fellow's stipend had become matters of controversy within the New Zealand writing community. No one wanted to 'go public' on the subject, however, lest the already fragile arrangements by which the fellowship operated should collapse altogether.

Janet Frame was warned about potential difficulties by a previous fellow, Margaret Scott, who had gone to Menton in 1971 to further her work on an authoritative edition of Mansfield's letters.[6] And it was to Scott that Frame unburdened herself after her arrival in Menton on 3 January 1974.

Unfortunately all your predictions . . . have been realised . . . The voyage by sea was a nightmare, as I was seasick all the way. The ship was crowded — deck music all day and so on . . . When I arrived in Menton I found that promises to have money waiting for me had not been kept, and nothing came until the end of January, and then only after [the New Zealand Ambassador in Paris] had telephoned the solicitor for the Trust. I had been led to believe that delays were the fault of banks here; I now know that the money had simply not been sent* . . . [The solicitor] does not even have the courtesy to answer a letter I wrote to him a month ago asking could *all* the [stipend] be sent and have done with it.

---

* The money problem led Frame to write:

> A gullible writer once Wenton
> a voyage (her money was Senton).
> Alas at the bank
> there wasn't a franc,
> and now she's Repenton in Menton

As for the room! . . . I couldn't work [there]. The lack of lavatory and running water is my chief problem. I'm trying to do all I can to see that this state of affairs doesn't go on as it has done for — five? — years now.[7]

In a novel written later in the decade Frame gave a fictional account of her first sight of the memorial room beneath the Villa Isola Bella in Garavan, a suburb on the eastern side of Menton, adjoining the Italian border:

I walked up a narrow street beneath a railway bridge and up another street that had once been a Roman Road, and on the left I saw the plaque . . . giving the date of [KM's] birth and death . . . and a list of her writings. The garden was overgrown with weeds, the stairs leading to the small room were thick with sodden leaves and fragments of paper thrown off the street . . . [I] pushed open the sun-blistered wooden door which . . . 'dropped' like an old used womb. I walked in. I opened the tiny windows, pushing back the branches that crowded against them. The room slowly became 'aired' like old stored linen . . . There was an air of desolation . . . A water-spotted plaque inside gave further details of [KM's] career. There were a few straight-backed vicarage-type chairs . . . and a desk and a bookshelf . . . and layers of cold along the bare tiled floor . . . [There] was the kind of peace that one feels walking among the dead and listening, as the dead may, at a great distance from the world and its movement and noise.

I went to explore the small garden and found a green garden seat which I cleared, brushing away the bruised ripe loquats fallen everywhere from the huge loquat tree; and I lay down, half in sun, half in shadow, looking up at the lemon tree in the neighbouring garden of the Villa [Louise]. I closed my eyes . . . I fell asleep. And when I woke I shivered with cold. The mountains were harsh and grey with fallen used daylight, softened in the crevices with the blue of distance and evening.[8]

One reason for falling asleep on that first visit to the 'stone chamber' was that Frame had arrived in Menton with influenza. She spent the first week based at the Villa Louise, a pension next door to Isola Bella, which she described as 'so *fin de siècle* that I feel as if I'm living in a film or fiction. The guests grow more & more to resemble the marble of the staircases . . . The meals are tremendous & go on & on — if you saw the film *Death in Venice* you'd get the setting.'[9] A literary pilgrim from Paris who shared Frame's table at the pension gave her a glimpse of how highly Mansfield was revered by her French readers. This woman came to Menton every year on the anniversary of the writer's death (9 January). When Frame suffered a fit of coughing, a consequence of her flu, this woman said to her, 'Have you read the journal of Katherine Mansfield? She was from New Zealand and had a cough like yours.'

Frame *did* read Mansfield's journal that week, in French, 'and found it so much more moving . . . than in English . . . [I feel] more admiration for her now. She really was an exile . . . and all her happiest dreams were of Wellington; whereas I, when I have nightmares, they are always of New Zealand.'[10]

Also in Menton at the time of Frame's arrival were two of the fellowship's major New Zealand patrons, Cecil and Celia Manson, and their thirty-year-old son, Bill. They advanced her money to compensate for the non-appearance of the stipend, and wined and dined her in some of the town's best restaurants. Cecil looked like 'a faded English colonel. I get on very well with him & I'm moved by his obvious devotion to his son & his pride in him; & the son is so gentle & sympathetic to his parents, in spite of his embarrassment at their pride . . . The mother is very intelligent & slightly bewildered, with a powdered face.'[11] In café conversation with Bill and his partner, Carlita Foss, Frame pointed to a young man passing in the street and said, 'If I'd had a son that could be him.' They misunderstood her to say that she *had* a son of that age, which led subsequently to a rumour to that effect in New Zealand; and to at least one rosy-cheeked, red haired man claiming to be that son.[12]

The other favour the Mansons performed was to help establish Frame in what they hoped would be her permanent accommodation in the town, a tiny one-room apartment in Garavan, which would cost six hundred francs a month, half her stipend. Her initial plan was to work in the memorial room and to eat and sleep in the bed-sitter. The next problem, however, was that the typewriter which had been left in the room by the first fellow, Owen Leeming, was now 'battered and useless . . . the legs go down and won't go up'.[13] Continental typewriters would be no substitute, because the keyboard placings were different from those on an 'English' typewriter. Eventually, however, she found a second-hand model that was satisfactory.

In the third week in January, shortly after the Mansons had left and before she had been able to settle to work, Frame was sought out and 'rescued' by another New Zealand writer, Anton Vogt, who was temporarily resident in Menton. Vogt, as he liked to tell anyone who was listening, had been conceived in the Argentine, born in Norway, and educated in England, Switzerland and South Africa.[14] He had come to New Zealand with his family in his early teens and developed there into a poet, gifted teacher and controversialist. It was he who had put John Money in touch with Denis Glover in 1946 to arrange publication of Frame's first book; and he had been one of the judges who awarded her the Hubert Church prize in 1952. Vogt too had featured with Frame in the first Oxford University Press anthology of New Zealand stories, and he had written to the *New Zealand Listener* in defence of *Owls Do Cry* when that novel was given a less than wholly enthusiastic review. He was in Menton in 1974 on sabbatical leave from Simon Fraser University in Vancouver. He and his wife, Birgitte, had bought and were redecorating two houses there, one to live in after his retirement and the other to rent out for income.

When they found Frame, both Vogts were appalled by the state of the memorial room ('It's degrading [for] Janet Frame to work there');[15] and by the claustrophobic and expensive nature of her accommodation. In the last week in January 1974 they invited her to live in their rental property, a green-shuttered cottage alongside their own house in Avenue Cernuschi, about twenty minutes' walk from Garavan.

Frame was delighted to accept. 'There's no suggestion of squalor as there was inclined to be in the other place. Everything is new and fresh and Birgitte has put all the housewifely touches to it . . . I have my own yard and table-in-the-sun, and my own two storeys in the house . . . My bedroom is downstairs, with lavatory, shower and two washbasins . . . while upstairs is the big sitting-room looking out over Italy with two divans, a kitchen . . . and a bathroom with [a] huge bath . . . [It] is right in Menton, but in a *cul de sac*, literally an oasis, with all the palm trees.'[16] All this would cost her no more than she had previously paid for the single room.

Frame was also delighted by the Vogts' company. They brought her to their house for occasional lunches and dinners; and she reciprocated. They also took her on periodic outings in their open-topped sports car — across the Italian border to Ventimiglia, up to mountain villages in the Alpes Maritimes, to places of cultural and historical interest such as Eze, La Turbie, and Roquebrun, where W.B. Yeats had died in 1939. 'They [are] careful to respect my privacy and I . . . theirs. It's just the kind of good fortune that I seem to have from time to time,' she told Bill Brown.[17] There were also echoes of Oamaru, albeit exotic ones.

[Yesterday] I went exploring . . . up the back of the Vogts' land where they have never been yet, and I was so pleased to come back with an armful of wild freesias. It's really lovely up there — big pine trees, mimosas, a eucalyptus, and a wild growth of little olive trees and broom, and grass to lie in and really feel alone in the world; and far out is the sea, and the coast of Italy. I know where to find some peace and aloneness — it's very much the feeling of being a child again and (as the womb is locked and chained) finding a secret place in the grass.[18]

By mid-February Frame was contentedly settled and beginning to work — in the cottage, not the memorial room. 'After writing six short stories I have finally (cross fingers and hearts) begun a novel which I have planned to finish . . . about the end of June.'[19] She was trying out what she called her 'adventures' in the French language on shopkeepers, and on the family of Bernard Tardy, the town's genial and handsome director of tourism, who was responsible for local administration of the Katherine Mansfield Fellowship. '[Although] my conversation is pretty awful, when I read French I have a feeling as if I'm doing it from the "inside" with it surrounding me like a kind of lining, whereas before I was "outside" and had to tear the material to get in.'[20] She also wrote a considerable number of poems in French, including one for the Tardys' ten-year-old son, Etienne, which read in part:

> Etienne, Etienne.
> Il a dix ans.
> Il pique comme les abeilles qu'il attrappe.
> Etienne, Etienne.
> C'est certain qu'il est sur le Massif Central,
> Etienne, la turbie, la bise, le mistral,
> et les abeilles mortes, suffoquées,
> qui faisent, il était une fois,
> le miel de jasmin.[21]

Frame never ceased to be charmed by the character of Menton and its environs. 'It has rained for days now, with a heavy low grey sky and no wind and the mountains — the tail end of the Alps — seen from here are wonderfully mysterious, wrapped in mist . . . Anton and Birgitte asked me if I would like to . . . visit St Agnes, the highest mountain village on the coast. So [we] went on a very pleasant excursion [and] talked to an old man who is 115 . . . He was sitting on a stone seat, out in the cold, with the snow on the mountains above him, and he wore a bright blue nylon raincoat. He was blind.'[22]

Other Menton residents offered her hospitality, including a retired English Member of Parliament, John Martin, who had been a friend of John Middleton Murry at Oxford, and his wife, Dorothy. 'He is quite old [in his eighties], she a little younger . . . [Their] apartment is overrun with books — Virginia Woolf lying beside D.H. Lawrence on the coffee table! They pressed books upon me . . . and I came home with Keats' Letters, some of Somerset Maugham's stories, French poetry and Proust in French . . . Longtemps je me suis couchée de bonne heure . . . What a lovely beginning.'[23]

Late in February John Money came to stay for a few days after attending a conference in Geneva. He shared both Frame's delight in the Côte d'Azur and the Vogts' indignation at what seemed to be the poor administration of the fellowship (Frame had received only her first month's stipend payment from Wellington) and the condition of the memorial room. As soon as he was back in Baltimore he fired off a letter to the *New Zealand Listener*. The Katherine Mansfield Room, he pointed out, had neither 'water, gas nor electricity. It is furnished with a portable burner for heating, a small table, chair and portable typewriter, and a kerosene lamp. The lamp is needed even at midday, as the small apertured window does not permit sufficient illumination, and the climate does not always permit the door to be kept open. There are no toilet facilities . . . [Made] aware of these conditions, New Zealanders will, I hope, in haste do something to correct them.'[24]

To complement this letter, Anton Vogt wrote a feature for the *Listener* in which he elaborated on Money's description of the room and added historical background. He also commented: 'Few New Zealand writers would expect to live in the luxury to which Katherine Mansfield was accustomed . . . Nevertheless, some things can be done to make a fellowship in her honour an honour . . . One is not to ask any writer to occupy the cell. Another is to provide a living wage of not less than 2000 francs per month . . . A third might well be to forget the romantic allegiance to Isola Bella, except as a mausoleum; and to buy a small apartment or flat nearby for perhaps 100,000 francs, to be available rent-free to subsequent Fellows.'[25]

In reply, Karl Stead referred to Vogt's piece as an 'extravagant overstatement' of the shortcomings of the room and the fellowship, and accused him of 'selective malice . . . [In] view of the fact that renovations are planned and money promised for them [by the municipality of Menton], his attack — which amounts to an attack on the Fellowship — seems quite pointless.' Cecil and Celia Manson also responded, pointing out that the state of the room was the responsibility of the authorities in Menton, not the New Zealand fellowship committee. Embarrassingly for Frame, they quoted her as saying, when they had told her about the promised renovations, 'Oh, what a pity! I love the room as it is.'[26]

By this time, May 1974, Frame was close to abandoning the fellowship. Not because of the state of the room, but because her payments from Wellington were still overdue; and the organising committee was not replying to her requests for the remission of the whole stipend, nor to her queries about whether she was permitted to fly home via the United States. Eventually the rest of the money did arrive, four months late. 'But,' said Frame, 'they'll never know how much I have been put off my work, waiting.'[27] As for the published opinions about the state of the memorial room, Frame pronounced them all to be 'equally truthful . . . If I'd been a ghost with no bodily functions and no need of light I'd happily have made the room my headquarters. I'm pleased [to hear] that future Fellows may have the advantage of . . . improvements.'[28] The public airing of criticism produced a salutary result. The French Embassy in Wellington put pressure on the Menton municipality to carry out its undertaking to upgrade the memorial room and to install a bathroom. Work on these alterations had begun before Frame left Menton in August 1974.*

---

* There was a side-bar to this controversy. Frank Sargeson wrote to a friend that he was 'much troubled by the Vogt–Money stuff in the *Listener* . . . I feel I may be lucky to have escaped criticism for the sort of place [my] hut was to inhabit.' (Sargeson to Winston Rhodes, 8/5/74, SP 4261/208.)

There were further interruptions to Frame's proposed work schedule. George Braziller made a 'lightning visit' in May. He hired a car from Nice Airport, collected Frame, and drove her 'to St Agnes in the mountains, and then into Italy, just outside San Remo, for dinner . . . In the morning I went with him to the Picasso Museum at Antibes — how lovely that was, with all the flowers out in the sculpture garden by the sea! Braziller then left on the plane and I took a bus home.'[29]

Later that same week she finally met the French scholar who had been stalking her for six years, Victor Dupont. Professor Dupont had written from Toulouse to say that he still hoped to meet the author to whom he had devoted so many years of study; and to invite Frame to a 'round-the-table discussion about your work at the University of Toulouse and [to] an international Commonwealth Literature Conference in Belgium [where I] shall make so bold as to read a paper on "Janet Frame's *Intensive Care*: the lost, the unhappy and the kind"'.[30] Frame declined the invitations but allowed Dupont to visit her in Menton in May, hoping that by talking to him she could steer him away from some of the inaccurate views he had expressed in print, such as references to her 'diseased mind', her 'recurring suicidal impulses', and his conviction that she had 'never recovered from the shock of seeing her sister burned in a rubbish fire'.[31]

After the visit, Frame told Bill Brown the professor had been 'quite charming', and also courageous, because he was subject to 'un tremblement', probably a symptom of advancing Parkinson's Disease. 'I do feel somewhat resentful as he seems to feel my books belong to him, that he has read me and I am his "creation". I didn't have time to convince him that I *was* crazy. I should have suddenly drawn a knife from my bosom, widened my eyes, cried Ha — and proceeded to peel an apple.'[32]

Instead, Frame sent the professor away with a copy of a letter she had elicited for this purpose from Bob Cawley. It read:

Miss Janet F. Clutha has told me that a number of literary scholars and editors of anthologies are publishing biographical comments which refer to her previous state of mind as sick or disordered. I understand that some people are going so far as to suggest that her creative ability is in some way related to a history of mental illness.

Miss Clutha was under my care between 1958 and 1963, and I saw her frequently during that time. She and others have kept me informed about her activities since then. She has been seen by a number of eminent psychiatrists all of whom agree with my opinion that she has never suffered from a mental illness in any formal sense. She went through a long period of unhappiness before making various decisions about how to spend her life.

I have told Miss Clutha that in my opinion any writer who publishes comments referring to her 'disordered mind' or 'mental illness' is running two risks. One is of public ridicule at the hands of scholars more know-ledgeable and informed about these matters. The other is litigation.[33]

This letter was written on Maudsley Hospital letterhead ('Patron: HRH Princess Alexandra') and signed 'R.H. Cawley, Physician'. It was a warning to Professor Dupont, and Frame was to feel that she had cause to send it to other literary critics in the coming decade.

Throughout May distractions multiplied and any possibility of resuming writing 'flew out the window'. In the middle of the month Frame travelled by train to Florence, for what she called her 'one and only glimpse into Italy' apart from the brief expeditions to Ventimiglia and San Remo. 'I' was quite stupefied and overcome by the marvels of the Uffizi Gallery . . . I've never seen anything like that . . . Whatever happened to painting after Florence? I didn't see half of what I wanted to see, and I began to suffer from looking-indigestion, the chief symptom of which is that you look and don't see any more . . . I was haunted all the time by the marvellous colour, compassion, intimacy . . . I had thought I was too old to travel alone but found I enjoyed it and it would have been twice as exhausting with company.'[34]

In the first week in June Frame flew from Nice to London to spend two days in that city (and to see Bob Cawley and Mildred Surry); then a week in Norfolk with Peter Dawson, who would celebrate her eightieth birthday in September. They ate 'fresh raspberries, freshly gathered honey, fat broad beans and peas, and [cycled] in still deserted lanes'.[35] Then Frame flew to Paris to meet Jacquie Baxter, who was making her first visit to Europe and would travel through France and Spain before heading to Morocco, where her sister lived. The two women spent four days together in the French capital, seeing galleries, historical buildings and the cathedral at Chartres, before travelling by train to Menton, where Baxter stayed with Frame in the shuttered cottage until 5 July.

According to Anton Vogt, who drove them to Monte Carlo, Frame and Baxter were like a couple of peasant women who communicated non-verbally in a series of nudges, changes of expression and giggles.[36] They enjoyed them-selves together seeing the tourist sights around Menton, including civic rooms decorated by Jean Cocteau, and crossing the Italian border to visit Ventimiglia, where they shopped in the market and had a restaurant meal. Baxter, like Frame, took an almost childlike delight in features of French life that were different from New Zealand, such as being able to ring a bell on the beach and have icecreams lowered from the roadside in a little basket.[37]

Baxter's eventual departure for Spain, however, provoked a 'certain hysteria'. As usual, Frame was anxious about the possibility of missing the train, so they arrived at Menton station hours too early. 'As we waited for the 8.30 train to Barcelona, it whizzed by, scarcely stopping, and only half there, leaving [Jacquie] and me shocked and horrified . . . Some time later we learned that the train had been cut in half at Pisa, and the other half, with my friend's coach on it, came by at ten o'clock.'[38]

Only two-and-a-half weeks now remained before Frame's own departure from France. Her novel had come to a halt and seemed beyond revival in the time available, so she wrote further poetry instead. She prepared an ambitious farewell meal for the Vogts — oven-roasted chicken, with eggplant stuffed with mushrooms, tomatoes and peppers — in gratitude for the fact that they, like the Baxters in Dunedin, had accepted her as she was and given her a sense of being part of a family. And she told Bill Brown that, apart from the Vogts, the people in Menton she would miss most would be 'the shopkeepers [and] the workers . . . my butcher, my baker, my second-hand bookstore dealer, my grocer. And the policemen — so fantastically handsome and happy.'[39] She would also miss the feeling that 'to go for a walk is not to be stared at as if one were crazy . . . Whenever the sun comes out . . . people still promenade [with] everybody smiling.'[40] And yet, and yet . . . 'Somehow it is too romantic for me, too colourful . . . I tend to like [best] the drab gray world without the colour within, though I'd never have missed the oleanders.' [41]

Not until 19 July did she get an answer from the fellowship committee about her request to fly home via America; they told her that this was not permissible, and enclosed a ticket booked through Asia, which Frame then discarded, as she had made her own arrangements at her own expense in the interim. She left Menton on 24 July, flew from Nice to London, and then spent a further week-and-a-half with Peter Dawson in Norfolk, which she enjoyed for its contrasts with the South of France: 'incredible peace, greenness, a countryside deserted by all but pheasants and ripening corn'.[42]

On 6 August Frame flew on to New York, where the George Washington Hotel on Gramercy Park appeared now to have been taken over by Mafiosi and drug dealers. The compensations, however, were spending time with a still attentive George Braziller and attending a concert by Lili Kraus, the Hungarian-born pianist who had been interned by the Japanese during the Second World War and subsequently taken New Zealand citizenship.

Frame then made her way to Baltimore for a week with John Money who, in addition to his 'quadruple locks', had also been forced to install a burglar alarm. 'I nearly died of fright when in the early morning I went into the kitchen to make some coffee . . . and suddenly it began to scream, sensing my presence.' On this visit, East Baltimore seemed deserted. '[Half] the shops are boarded up; the same goodies are displayed in the bakeshop — I swear no one has bought them for years; and the funny little uniform shop is still displaying strange-looking tennis outfits in an area where no one plays tennis.'[43] She reported to the Vogts, however, that Money was mellowing with age (he was now fifty-three, three years older than Frame), and that a pleasant time had been made more pleasant by the presence of one of his nieces, Sally Hopkins, whose father was a cousin of W.H. Auden.[44] She would later become Money's secretary and buy a house next door to him in East Madison Street.

On 19 August Frame flew to San Francisco to spend a week with Bill Brown and Paul Wonner, who had abandoned 'out east' in favour of returning to California, where they were now established at Berkeley. 'The house is lovely,' Frame reported to John Money, 'and I have a bathroom to myself and a nice room overlooking . . . Berkeley, Oakland and San Francisco, this morning wreathed in mist . . . I'm enjoying myself greatly [and] I'm continually amazed at the way one moves to newer relations with people.'[45]

She left San Francisco for Honolulu on 25 August, and from there reached Auckland on the twenty-eighth, her fiftieth birthday. Any inclination to celebration was crushed by a series of shocks. One was that the houses that were being built when she left Whangaparaoa nine months earlier were still under construction. And a second, more serious, was to find that her tenant had failed to pay rent, trashed the house and run up enormous electricity and telephone bills. 'He proved to be a kind of rogue and liar . . . Everything in the house that could be broken or trampled on has been . . . Some of the furniture has been taken out of the house and left in the rain; the crockery and cushions have gone. I've had to clear up filth including shit . . . [He] broke into both the locked room and the locked wardrobe and removed . . . anything he fancied . . . My plants are either dead or arrested in growth . . . [Neighbours] knew all this was going on but . . . didn't like to worry me.'[46]

There was more to come. Three days after she confronted this domestic chaos Norman Kirk, the country's fifty-one-year-old Prime Minister who had so impressed her with his 'intelligence and compassion', died in Wellington. And Anton Vogt's son John rang June Gordon with news that his father, still five years away from his planned retirement, had had a stroke which left him blind in one eye and partially paralysed.[47] Frame's own blood pressure was found to be dangerously high and her doctor said she would need monthly checks to monitor it.

All these developments made her homecoming disappointing and unsettling. Frame told Bill Brown that she was uncertain about whether she would stay on in her now violated house. 'As I write this it's raining, the tide is in, and the seagulls are wheeling and crying . . . as huge as planes. I can see both sides of the peninsula and there's not a soul anywhere in view . . . [But] sooner or later there are going to be two houses in front of me, quite near . . . "We shall see," as parents and grandparents say . . .'[48] The good news, the *only* good news, it seemed, was that Neg the cat was well, having been taken in and cared for by a sympathetic neighbour.

CHAPTER TWENTY-FIVE

# In Search of Silence

*F*RAME SPENT THE REMAINING MONTHS OF 1974 TRYING TO RECOVER A
sense of privacy and security at Whangaparaoa. In September she paid a local
labourer to tidy the section, re-establish the vegetable garden and install a gate.
Then she ordered sufficient timber, cut to size by the local hardware shop, to
erect a six-foot-high fence around the perimeter of the property and built it
herself through October and November. At the height of this surge of confidence and self-reliance, she bought a 60 cc motorcycle to solve the problem of
bringing provisions and mail from the village four miles away (the rural delivery
service had ceased while she was in Menton).

By December 1974 she was able to report to John Money that she was
self-reliant in vegetables. The garden was now producing spinach, tomatoes,
cucumber, cabbages, runner beans, lettuce, potatoes, kumara, sweetcorn and
sweet peppers, and mint, thyme and caraway. She surrounded these with
marigolds and asters. There was no sign of the sunflowers whose seeds she had
dropped into cracks in the earth the previous summer ('they went down to
Spain'); so she planted more seeds around her concrete water tank, and the
plants and flowers shot up luxuriantly.[1]

Although Frame had moved her *Landfall* desk, assertively, to the centre of
the living room — 'making a stand, so to speak'[2] — writing took second place
to the schedule of home and property improvements. As late as December
1974 she was still reporting that 'I haven't yet started my novel'. And there was
now a further impediment to what she referred to as 'brain work'. Medication
for her blood pressure left her mentally fatigued. 'The doctor says it's the only
way to stop my having a stroke in a few years' time but I'm beginning to think
I'd rather just go ahead and be un-exhausted. It seems to remove sexual feeling
too. As if I want it here — but [after all] one is human and one likes to
appreciate other people in all one's senses.'[3]

She had some hope that her writing might be kick-started by rereading the novel she had begun to write in Menton. When it arrived in Whangaparaoa by surface mail in October, she was disappointed. 'I now don't feel "related" to it, yet I don't feel, as I have done with other interrupted work, that I'll cast it away . . . [It's] the stirrings of something . . .'[4]

Frame did succeed, however, in writing a commissioned essay for the journal *Education* on a book which had impressed her as a child. She chose *Grimms' Fairy Tales*, which she had borrowed from Poppy Firman and was, she said, the first book she could remember reading. 'I found [it] so satisfying, I think now, in the convention of its story-telling, the journeys, meetings, the matter-of-fact descriptions of marvels, the talking animals and trees, and in the way the stories had their heart in a family — brothers, sisters, mothers, fathers, rich and poor, whose goodness and wickedness had been found out and described without fear. Any act was possible . . . Nothing was forbidden.'[5] Oddly, this piece was accompanied by a photograph of the Maori writer Keri Hulme who would, a decade later, win the British Booker Prize for her novel *the bone people*. In 1974, however, Hulme was little known; her only resemblance to Frame was frizzy hair and a liking for shaded spectacles.

A writer who *was* well-known, the English poet Jon Silkin, arrived in Auckland on a British Council-sponsored tour in October and expressed a wish to visit Frame, whom he had met briefly in London in 1959. '[We] spent a very enjoyable afternoon here and on the beach, with an unusual kind of penguin-like bird appearing for his benefit, and a magnificent sea creature being stranded at his feet — I've never seen such before or since and I couldn't find reference to it in the encyclopaedia. As meetings are . . . it was tremendously rich and interesting . . . I delicately refrained from mentioning his former wife or wives in front of his new [one]. The young lecturer who drove them here is the daughter of [Phillip Wilson] . . . I'd met her before when she and her father came up to visit one afternoon. Her name is Janet. Her father has just dedicated his new book to me [*New Zealand Jack*] and though it's very flattering, I don't quite know how to take it.'[6]

Nor did she know, a fortnight later, how to take the news that a New Zealand academic proposed to write a critical biography of her for the Twayne World Authors series (which had previously featured Sargeson and his work). Patrick Evans of the University of Canterbury had been interested in Frame since his mother had persuaded him to read *Owls Do Cry* in 1957, when he was thirteen. In 1971 he had published *An Inward Sun*, a study of Frame's novels written primarily for schools.[7] Evans had incorporated Frame's fiction into his courses at university and he had written substantial reviews of her books and broader assessments of her work.[8] He was the first literary critic in New Zealand — or, apart from Victor Dupont, elsewhere — to regard her writing as worthy of serious study.

Evans had not sought Frame's permission to work on her life and writing; nor did he need to; nor did he do so now. But, informing her of the Twayne commission, he did say that he would not proceed if Frame expressly forbade him to. She did not. Instead, writing to Evans, Frame addressed what she saw as an implication in *An Inward Sun* that much of her fiction, especially her three first novels, was autobiographical. Evans had written, for example, about 'the more obvious autobiographical sources of her art'; and referred to *Faces in the Water* as 'a more detailed and extensive treatment of Daphne's (and Janet Frame's) experiences in mental hospitals'.[9] If these statements were to be believed, Frame felt, then there was a danger that Evans's analyses of her characters could be read as comments about members of her family (Chicks, for example, whom Evans describes as 'a shallow pretentious social climber concerned only with money and status').[10]

Frame's letter to Evans, which was both warning and smokescreen, thanked Evans for his interest in her work and expressed admiration for his ability. She went on to say:

It is an occupational risk of authors that their work is confused with their life . . . A review of *The Adaptable Man* in USA said 'the author is living in London and married to a failure' . . . One can be amused and perhaps flattered by this. In many of my stories, and in *Owls Do Cry*, I invented a childhood which I am almost persuaded to believe was my own childhood, because others believe it and I believed it while I was writing the stories and the book. I do not keep on writing a book if I stop believing in its reality . . . I was startled to find that Charles Brasch believed that I had a sister burned in a rubbish dump fire. Unfortunately, my 'Beginnings' in *Landfall*, necessarily concentrated, helped perhaps to strengthen a myth.

I find myths very useful. I'm rather troubled, though, by the suggestion that I myself . . . have been 'insane'. The story of many years of my life is a sad comment on New Zealand society and institutions and my escape from New Zealand to the Northern Hemisphere was a social and not a literary refuge. I shan't go into details . . . because writing fiction (and not writing my autobiography) is my pastime.

One postscript to this letter said Frame was troubled by the thought that *An Inward Sun* suggested 'facts about my life which are not true'; a second told Evans that the name Istina Mavet from *Faces in the Water*, which he had written 'appears to be a name invented', was taken from the Serbo-Croatian word for truth and the Hebrew word for death. She also enclosed a copy of the letter from Bob Cawley which she had sent previously to Victor Dupont.[11]

On the basis of this response, Patrick Evans went ahead with the critical biography. Not wishing to disturb Frame any further, he approached Janet Gibson, Frank Sargeson and John Money, all of whom provided him with biographical information relating to the periods of Frame's life with which they were familiar. To Money, Evans wrote: 'I want you to know that I am not a critical peeping tom, with ball-point and sandshoes. I stand at the hinge between art and life, much more interested in the influence of Rilke and Shakespeare and Hardy on her writing than whether or not she played ping-pong while at university.'[12]

Evans also dredged Frame's own autobiographical writings and interviews, especially the 'Beginnings' essay; and he researched data on the Frame family through the office of the registrar of births, deaths and marriages. Frame, meanwhile, unsettled by the exchange of letters with Evans, dismissed his project from her mind and then forgot about it — until she saw the Twayne study on the shelves of the Stratford Public Library in 1978.[13]

Frame was also troubled in November 1974 by correspondence with another literary 'middleman', a neighbour and associate of Frank Sargeson's named Phoebe Meikle. Meikle, editor for the Auckland educational publisher Longman Paul, was compiling a series of short story anthologies for use in schools. One of these contained work written between 1935 and 1960, in which 'the post-Mansfield story in New Zealand as a serious literary form took on important characteristics and reached maturity'.[14] Meikle had hoped to include Frame's work in this volume, but Frame had not replied to any of the publisher's letters (written in July and August 1971, when she was in the United States).

Three years later Meikle tried again. Her *Stories Four* was to be published the following year, and she asked if she might use 'two or three' examples of Frame's work. 'I know which stories would be right for the kind of balance and tone I'm after but I so much want to include Frame stories that I should try to meet your wishes over choice.'[15] In reply, Frame explained that she sometimes had not answered mail which had been sent to her when she was overseas and was often many months old by the time it caught up with her. 'Other times I am so shocked at the suggestion that stories and poems I don't like are to be reprinted that I don't answer the letters . . . My problem is that although I do not publish stories and poems, I write many, and requests to include stuff written so long ago are usually met with distaste.'[16]

Despite this warning, Meikle regarded the very fact that Frame had written to her on this occasion as encouragement and she specified which stories she wanted to use. She also told Frame that 'you write of death (and of madness) in a more sensitive, unsentimental and honourable way than any other New Zealand writer I know'.[17] To Frame's ears, this did not sound like a compliment. Instead of an agreement to publish, Meikle received a refusal, and a copy of Bob Cawley's warning about Frame's alleged 'madness'. Meikle reacted by describing herself 'shocked and distressed . . . for you as much as for me . . . It hit me hard to receive . . . a nasty variant of a typical Frame theme: the rich/popular/socially correct girl boasts of her possessions to the poor/unpopular/socially inferior girl . . . as though she may share. Then, after a long delay — designed to make the disappointment greater — she snatches them away . . . Of course I ponder . . . your reasons for allowing OUP to publish in their anthologies stories which you insist are no good and which you "don't show" to anyone.'[18]

This overreaction expressed the sharp disappointment editors would often feel when Frame, virtually alone among the authors they dealt with, was unwilling to have her work appear in anthologies. But it was so much a misreading of her position that Frame arranged a visit to Meikle's home in Milford, on Auckland's North Shore, to explain more fully her feeling that she was reluctant to allow what she regarded as inferior work to appear again outside its original context; and that her preference was for whole books, especially her novels, to remain in print. Meikle was mollified by this visit, but remained disappointed that she had been unable to persuade Frame to relent.

The month Frame began this correspondence with Phoebe Meikle she had also written to Pegasus to tell Albion Wright that, now that they were out of print, New Zealand rights for *Faces in the Water*, *The Edge of the Alphabet*, *Scented Gardens for the Blind*, *The Reservoir*, *The Adaptable Man*, *A State of Siege* and *The Pocket Mirror* had all reverted to her.[19] To her annoyance, she was unable to reclaim local rights to *Owls Do Cry* because the Sun Books paperback published in Melbourne was apparently not out of print, even though Frame had received no royalties from the publisher for twelve years nor seen any sign of the edition on sale in New Zealand.[20] All this, including the Longman Paul anthology request, was the kind of business that ought to have been handled by an agent; and, with the exception of Brandt and Brandt in New York, Frame now had no agent. (At her request, however, A.M. Heath in London wrote to Sun Books in Melbourne and extracted payments from them of thirty-nine pounds and sixty-two pounds, which they forwarded to Frame — only to discover subsequently that fifty percent of that sum should have been paid to Pegasus Press.)[21]

The year 1974 ended with the customary influx of good and bad news. The 'good' news was that Frank Sargeson was awarded an honorary doctorate in literature from his alma mater, Auckland University, in November. 'When they asked him was he going to make a speech, he said no, his tom cat did not make a speech when it was "doctored",' Frame told Bill Brown.[22] To Sargeson himself she wrote: 'Dear Doctor Sargeson, Do you make house calls? . . . I have this jam in my word . . . [They] said you've performed some marvellous sentences, in fact you were sentenced long before you were doctored . . . [Are] your clause cut? I hope your syntax still fits . . . Have patients . . .'[23]

In December, Maurice Duggan died of cancer at the age of fifty-one. In earlier years he had been regarded as Sargeson's most promising protégé and Frame had met him at Esmonde Road in 1955. She was to tell his biographer that she had been thinking of Duggan as she took public transport into Auckland on 11 December. 'As the bus passed what she thought of as a particularly barren corner, she was stricken with a sudden feeling of unease, a panicky sense that nothing was connected to anything any more.'[24] She learned later that this was about the time that Duggan had died. 'I looked upon him as our greatest writer of prose,' she told Bill Brown. 'After years of struggle, depression, mental hospital, alcohol etc . . . he was beginning to write again.'[25]

This was dismal enough. But in the last week of December came the nightmare she feared most. Frame found herself in the centre of a crowd of noisy holiday-makers. 'People occupy every bit of land . . . There's a family in a tent just over the back hedge, and when they talk it's as if they were in the room here, and how they talk, on and on.' Then: 'An awful machine has started up. A boat-sanding thing. At half-past six in the morning.'[26] And finally: 'Two men arrived on to the property in front and began building a house. It's about ten feet from the boundary. I can hear every word they say, and of course every hammer-blow . . . I have to think seriously of moving . . . perhaps [to] Takapuna in a "settled" area where there will still be motor mowers and so on but the building is finished.'[27]

While she dithered for another month over whether to do anything about these circumstances, she made a determined effort to master driving the motorcycle she had bought in 1974. She had taught herself how to take it to pieces and put it together again; and she had passed her provisional licence — the theoretical one — 'with flying colours'.[28] But she was too frightened to take the machine out on the roads. 'It is so powerful and alive . . . One has to be tall, dark, lean and masterful, like the heroes of the serials in women's magazines.'[29] After a false start in January 1975, when she 'walked' the scooter to and from the village, she began to practise in the nearby park until she had developed the confidence of a speedway rider and felt able to apply for, and to pass, her full licence. Then she used it on the peninsula roads and was soon enjoying the sensation of controlled speed. She wore a helmet and visor, and carried groceries and mail in a basket fixed over the front mudguard.

In mid-January Frame had an opportunity to voice publicly her preoccupations about noise. She was interviewed by the *North Shore Gazette*, a local paper managed by her brother-in-law, for a series called 'North Shore Notables'. It quoted her as saying:

[In] New Zealand concrete mixers start up at seven in the morning, motor mowers and chainsaws whine. These intrusions hit the silent worker, the writer . . . [Writers] are not plumbers or carpenters . . . and their long silent hours in their houses, their solitary prowlings in the street and the lack of visible evidence of their working, are all the objects of unsatisfied curiosity and speculation, of superstition and rumours . . . [They] work without a building permit and sometimes their boundaries come too close for comfort . . .

It is the invisibility of the material — ideas, dreams, feelings — that arouses wonder. The inspiration is in the discoveries the writer makes on the imaginative journey — darkened landscapes are suddenly drenched with light, you know how the novel will go and where it will end.

The eye — and the pen — of the journalist also came 'too close for comfort'. Frame would not be pleased about the reporter's assessment of her circumstances and personal history.

> In her small house . . . Janet Frame wears her fame incognito. The scrubbed face, tatty house dress and orange jandals give nothing away. Only the house itself with its outside toilet and interior chaos makes one wonder about the owner. The random dumping of books, clothing and belongings is the work of an intellectual cyclone. Obviously she is concerned with the realm of the mind — not the realm of suburbia . . .
>
> Occasionally in periods of depression or exhaustion Janet Frame has voluntarily admitted herself to mental institutions for rest periods and gained there material for her poignant and haunting descriptions.[30]

This last comment was inaccurate. And, in Frame's opinion, the appearance of the interview as a whole, the first she had ever granted 'at home' in New Zealand, came close to an invasion of her privacy.[31] It would make her wary of repeating the experience. And it was perhaps unfortunate that a little over a week after its publication she was participating in a similar exercise with a film crew. Late in 1974 she had agreed, for a fee of five hundred dollars, to appear in a programme initially designed to commemorate the United Nations-instigated International Women's Year. A crew from Endeavour Films came to Whangaparaoa early in February 1975 to film Frame talking about her life as a writer. She told Bill Brown that she had spent 'eight solid hours being filmed and today I'm sunburnt on my face and my eyes and my lips and there's the usual reaction after such experiences . . . I appeared as what I am, a complete ninny with not a word in my head.'[32]

In the resulting documentary, shown in 1977 as a stand-alone programme incorporating the interview and dramatised excerpts from *Owls Do Cry*, Frame seemed at ease and articulate. She told the interviewer, Michael Noonan, about her mother's love of poetry and about winning the year's subscription to the Oamaru Athenaeum. Questioned about where her stories came from, she said, 'they arise, one uses one's feelings', and gave as an example the visit to the dentist at Camberwell, which had led eventually to the characters and plot of *The Adaptable Man*. 'Of course one doesn't write unless one is haunted. I don't write unless . . . an idea haunts me.'

Frame spoke also of how her work had been energised by time in America, and said she believed that her writing had 'developed a little' over time. 'When I wrote *Owls Do Cry*, for instance, I'd never been to bed with a man. I'd never had all these experiences that I've had since . . . One learns a tremendous lot by living these things.' Only when she was asked, finally, if she had considered the proposition that she might be one of the great writers of the century, did she falter and appear flummoxed. 'Well, that seems to me . . . Well, it doesn't reach me,' she replied.[33]

At about the same time Frame was approached by the poet and university lecturer Riemke Ensing and asked if she would allow some of her work to appear in an anthology of New Zealand women's poetry, also planned to commemorate International Women's Year. Frame replied curtly, asking Ensing if she was also planning an anthology of men's poetry — which the editor took to be a refusal.[34] The anthology, *Private Gardens*, was eventually published in 1977 without work from Frame or Ruth Dallas. Dallas had told Ensing that 'poetry should stand or fall on its own merits; and whether it is written by women or men seems to me to be irrelevant'.[35]

The week of the film interview also brought to Whangaparaoa a renewal of construction noise and holiday partying that welled up again in the last days in January, a public holiday weekend. And this disturbance precipitated a decision about the Whangaparaoa property. 'Yesterday I got in touch with a land agent and put this place on the market for $19,500,' Frame told Brown and Wonner, 'far more than we paid for it . . . I'm searching for a place which is (ha ha) secluded, quiet . . . cheap as possible, where shops, offices, library, cinema are not too far away.'[36]

In the event Frame did not sell the house, but swapped it for another in Glenfield, the suburb where June and Wilson Gordon had been living for the previous year. She bridged the $6000 gap between the valuations of the two properties by drawing out her savings and her previous year's Authors Fund payment, and she moved in on 12 March, during the tail end of a tropical cyclone.

The house at 276 Glenfield Road was 'twenty years old and has more character than more recent places,' she told Brown and Wonner, 'though it is the usual box-type house you find here, a version of the children's drawing house . . . [It] has a big kitchen (a bit battered) with room to sit down and eat in, and a big sittingroom with a brick fireplace . . . three bedrooms, a bathroom, and separate lavatory and outside a brick carport . . . and a brick barbecue with seats . . . [It] is about half the land I had before, but full of rich rich soil, with three peach trees, a sweet orange, a lemon tree, and the neighbouring gardens also full of trees (apples and figs are blown on to the back lawn).'[37]

There was a small shopping centre and a park with native bush minutes' walk away; and Auckland city was only ten minutes over the harbour bridge by bus or car. 'The snag is that there's a very busy noisy road outside, though at night the traffic quietens to a Whangaparaoa hush.'[38] After dismissing the months of the past summer as 'coasting', Frame planned 'a winter of very hard work at my writing' in Glenfield.

First, however, there was an unavoidable hiatus as she unpacked and organised her chattels and books. Then the Gordons came to stay in April, having sold their house prior to moving to Stratford in Taranaki, where their daughter, Pamela, and son-in-law, Stephen Bailey, had bought an old house and three acres of rural land. Then, in late April, Jacquie Baxter arrived to stay over the Anzac Day holiday weekend, the first time the two women had seen each other since Menton.

By chance, Frame had moved to an address close to the house where Jim Baxter had collapsed and died two-and-a-half years before, after coming to the door and asking if he might use the telephone.[39] Jacquie Baxter was certain that 'fate or something has taken a hand in my being [here] . . . She had been wanting to visit the people who took him in and we walked along the street, and called on the people who gave us the grim story blow by blow. It was an uncanny sort of experience.'[40]

For the first three months in Glenfield Frame was again subject to the corrosive stress of anxiety about money. Payment for the new house had cleared her savings. Then, in late March, her nineteen-dollars-a-week annuity mysteriously dried up. 'I [felt] suddenly desolate and abandoned . . . It wasn't very pleasant trying to find out what had happened to it because the office girls in the Welfare Department were rather haughty and impatient.'[41] All that had occurred, however, was that the file had been 'lost'; in May it was 'found' again, and payments resumed. Peter Dawson meanwhile had come to the rescue by sending Frame one thousand pounds sterling, which translated in to $NZ1780. The arrival of this sum in her savings account, she told Dawson, was a considerable relief.

Work did not go well. In addition to worries about money, there were problems with her kidneys and a lingering bout of winter influenza. The specialist investigating her kidneys told her that she had 'mirror organs', confirmation that she had been conceived and begun to develop as an identical twin.[42] Frame told Peter Dawson in August that everything she had tried to write had seemed 'stale . . . and all I want to do is sleep, or at least recline in a daze'.[43] She told a Braziller editor in New York that none of her recent manuscripts had 'set' properly.[44] She did manage to write a story called 'The Painter' for the *New Zealand Listener*, however, inspired by the do-it-yourself activities of the man next door, who had distracted her for days by scraping paint off his house. It could also be seen as a form of score-settling with her Whangaparaoa holiday neighbours:

> Some families are forever discussing, announcing (I'm going to do the washing now; I'm going out to the car), or calling to each other, like birds, if they are in different rooms or out in the garden. A small moment apart creates a ravine of distance that has to be bridged at once or all is lost.[45]

It was not until late September that Frame began to write what would turn out to be her next publishable — and published — novel. She told John Money that it was about 'two memories of Baltimore — of my first visit and the snowy night when I was sure I heard a wolf howling; and then of the time you wound your watch . . . forward through years of minutes to get the right time. Remember?'[46] With the arrival of spring and the diminution of ill-health, her spirits lifted. '[My] peach and plum and apple trees are in blossom . . . I [also] have silver beet . . . spinach, kumaras, pumpkins, cucumber, lettuce, sunflowers, scarlet runner beans; and two cream carnations . . . I look out of the window from my sittingroom and see vegetation moving, which is always a balm to my spirit.'[47]

A batch of invitations at about this time helped to make Frame feel valued. Sue Marquand suggested a return visit to the east coast of the United States; the organisers of the Adelaide Festival made a second request for her attendance, this time in March 1976; and Bill Brown proposed that she take an apartment near his and Wonner's house in Berkeley in the middle of 1976, to work, and to recreate with her Californian friends. The spectacle of June and Wilson Gordon departing in September 1975 for their first trip abroad, to stay with their son Neil in Massachusetts, made her wish that she was travelling with them — not so much for the excitement of the journey ('I get sick on anything that moves'),[48] but because they would be in the United States in the middle of winter. 'I get homesick for the cold. That is, provided there is always the assurance of inside warmth . . . New Zealand is too extroverted a country for me. We just can't help our outdoorsness.'[49] This was in part a reaction against the resumption of noisy suburban activity; and partly against the fact that a general election at the end of the year had tipped out the Labour Government and returned a National one which, Frame told John Money, 'embraces most fascist-tending ideas: there may be some nasty developments here'.[50]

One such development was a warning that her annuity might be up for annual review, in a climate of slashing public expenditure;[51] another that the new government had undertaken to resume sporting contacts with South Africa. These prospective changes would cause Frame emotional distress in the coming year, especially the notion that her annuity might be reduced or abolished (a large part of its value to her was that it freed her from long-term financial anxiety — an effect which annual reviews threatened to erase).

Frame spent Christmas 1975 on her own, 'reading David Copperfield and other books and falling in love again with Dickens . . . I'd really forgotten that David actually grew up. In the same way I used to think of Jane Eyre as just a girl at boarding school. I do resent the denial, in our school teaching, of adulthood . . . [This] tendency is also in our government, with its film and book censorship: trying to protect everyone from the facts of adult life.'[52]

By New Year 1976 Frame had decided to decline the Adelaide Festival invitation ('I found I had to be more "sociable" than I at first thought');[53] but to accept Brown's proposal to look after a neighbour's apartment in Berkeley while the owners were in Europe. 'The apartment is rent-free, and although Bill offered to pay my fare, I insisted on paying half . . . I shall be [there] for

May and June . . . I'm treating it as a kind of Western Yaddo, taking my typewriter and hoping to have a manuscript at the end of two months. It's pretty unthinkable that I should then go home without visiting the east coast, but . . . I have no plans to do so . . . I'm feeling at the moment more like working and I can't face the idea of travelling across the continent.'[54]

In the meantime she was busy judging a 'first book award (prose)' for the New Zealand branch of the writers' organisation PEN. 'I quite look forward to the task but I did tell them it was a betrayal . . . of Author's Rights when they ask an author to judge without remuneration.'[55] She did enjoy the experience and found much to admire in the books, however; and she awarded first prize to an emerging Maori author, Patricia Grace, who was, she said, a 'genuine writer'.[56] To raise additional money over this period she sold her motorcycle. She had been too timid to use it on Glenfield Road which, with the opening of a north-harbour bridge, had become a major feeder road into Auckland and the North Shore.

Frame's own writing continued to trouble her. 'My . . . work is so awful just now, in both senses,' she told Bill Brown in February. 'I'm so awed by the . . . tremendous thoughts that come into my head that I first get excited, then delighted, then I flee. Thank God for self-deception.'[57] She did not make any substantial progress until she started work in California in May.

Her visitors in the early months of 1976 included the novelist Phillip Wilson, who had moved to Auckland; her nephew Ian, whose first marriage had just ended and to whom she felt especially close at this time; and June and Wilson Gordon, who returned from the United States in February. 'Neg and I took a few days off to recover from the whirlwind of them, their son, and their daughter and husband and child who all came to meet them and bring them back here, and everyone was so excited.'[58] In March Frank Sargeson came to the house for the first time. 'I talk to him about once every two weeks on the phone but he . . . is wary about my meeting any of his friends, "in case you write about them". Poor Frank.'[59] Now, however, Sargeson was hopeful that one of those friends, Clarence Tucker — elderly, alcoholic and 'a kind of urchin man'[60] — might be able to stay in the house while Frame was in California, and he came to look it over. It passed muster, though Sargeson said it reminded him of a brothel. In the event, Tucker stayed with Sargeson at Esmonde Road.

In April, Frame checked Neg into a cattery five miles out in the country, 'where to my shame I wept after I saw her big-eyed with panic, into her seemingly too small cage in a big room without green and with nowhere to look at the view . . . a state too unhappy to bear'.[61] Ian Gordon then drove her south to Stratford, where she stayed a week over Easter and liked what she saw of this country town where her sister and niece had settled so contentedly. She returned to Auckland by bus in time to fly to Los Angeles at the end of the month. Frame arrived in San Francisco on 2 May, where Bill Brown was waiting to take her first to his and Wonner's house; and then to the apartment in Keeler Avenue, Berkeley, that would be her home and workplace for the next two months.

With the exception of the periods when she wrote *A State of Siege* in Auckland in 1964 and *The Rainbirds* in Dunedin in 1965, all Frame's most intensive and fruitful spells of writing since *Owls Do Cry* had occurred while she was working outside New Zealand. This pattern was sustained in California in May and June and the early part of July 1976. While there she wrote a large part of the first draft of *Living in the Maniototo* which, when it appeared in 1979, would end a seven-year gap in the publication of her books. She weaved into its narrative the circumstances in which she found herself in Berkeley — living in a borrowed house while its owners were in Italy — and combined these with memories of Baltimore, and of Glenfield, which, in the novel, she would call 'Blenheim' and make a sister city of Baltimore.

Frame wrote to Frank Sargeson just over a week after her arrival:

I've settled into the house [which] is small and pleasant with lots of marvellous books on architecture, art, music, as well as such inviting things as Evelyn's *Diary* [which had been edited in six volumes by Charles Brasch's cousin Esmond de Beer], Izaac Walton, complete Greek drama, Chaucer etc . . . [The] owner [is] a city planner, author of *The San Francisco Bay Area, American City Planning* . . . His wife is a landscape gardener . . .

It's so quiet here, day and night. And there are trees everywhere, and a young redwood outside the window . . . [The] only complaint of the people in this privileged place is that the deer keep trespassing in their gardens and eating the plants . . . [A] skunk and a racoon came to the door the other evening. I love the wildlife and the birds. I think there's a hummingbird nesting in the redwood [and] there are the red squirrels chattering away.[62]

To her niece Pamela, Frame added:

[The] climate is marvellous, with a sea-mist keeping the day temperature to mild and sunny and the nights (pleasantly for me) cool, and the humidity only half what it is in Auckland. More like a Stratford climate . . . Every night I have dinner and spend the evening at Bill's and Paul's, and I go in my summer dress with a cardigan . . . [We] play scrabble — very innocuous — but relaxing and pleasant. And of course Bill plays the piano — late Schubert and *Tristan and Isolde* these days. And I'm reading aloud Orwell's *Essays*.[63]

Frame made rapid advances with the novel and outlined her progress to her eternally patient American publisher George Braziller on 19 June. 'I have written a couple of works since I gave you *Daughter Buffalo*, but they've not been satisfactory . . . What I'm doing now is something I began [in earnest] last month after I'd settled down here, and because conditions are so quiet and I have almost no interruptions, I'll be finished my first draft before I leave . . . I'll retype as soon as I get back to New Zealand. You should have a typescript by the end of September . . . I have a title but I'm reluctant to say it just now, as . . . it will diminish the power which the work has over me . . . [There] has to be this relationship between the writer and the writing, a kind of mutual self-deception and enclosure.'[64]

Because of the intensity of the writing, Frame confirmed that she would not fly east to see the Marquands, nor John Money and George Braziller. 'I must keep to my original intention to work,' she told Money. 'It's appalling to think that I had to leave New Zealand for a couple of months to get the necessary quiet. And now I have it . . . I am seizing the opportunity to get [the] book done.'[65] She added that she felt 'more and more unwilling to face the terrible strain of flying which . . . needs such tremendous counter-fear programming on my part . . . When Christ comes back to earth I'm going into business with him, getting the patent for walking on water.'[66]

Instead, John Money flew west to see her, and Frame and Paul Wonner collected him from Oakland Airport and took him back to Berkeley for a long weekend in June. It was the first time Money had met Brown and Wonner, who put on a dinner party the night of his arrival. Afterwards Frame told him that it had been good to see him, especially 'in the world where I'm most at home and where you've never seen me before'.[67]

This California sojourn was over, it seemed to Frame, all too soon. On 4 July her two friends threw a small party, and they watched an Independence Day fireworks display over the San Francisco Bay. A week later Frame left and she was back in Auckland by 12 July, feeling for the first time in seven years that she had accomplished some sustained and worthwhile writing. It would be another two years before Braziller saw a manuscript, however; and even longer before it reached her British and New Zealand publishers.

Frame's single source of anxiety in California had been the welfare of her cat, condemned to spend more than two months in the company of strangers, far from her favourite haunts. She got home, however, to find that, after a few days of grieving, Neg had 'made herself Queen of the Cattery and controlled the other [seven] cats, putting each one in its place . . . [She] ate more, played more, and did everything else more than the others . . . Mrs Montefiore fell in love with her and didn't want to part with her.'[68]

As for the Glenfield house, it now seemed 'smaller than I imagined it [and] cramped with too much furniture, and the bedrooms are only as big as cupboards, and it all seems as if I spent my childhood here and have now returned'.[69] Despite her wish to get on with the second draft of the novel, she found the first few weeks without daily contact with Brown and Wonner lonely. Frank Sargeson rang and told her he had become a television star in her absence. He had appeared on a live talk show with a chimpanzee and a group of dancers dressed as Wombles. So well had he performed that he had been asked to reappear in October 'with an overseas visitor whose name he can't say at the moment' (it turned out to be Malcolm Muggeridge).[70]

Frame's only visitors through July and August were Phillip Wilson ('he sat at the kitchen table and I sat at the kitchen table and we ate — raisins, dates, bread, cheese, and drank tea and [he] went home about two hours later');[71] and a visiting Australian academic, John Beston, and his American wife, who were en route for Hawaii. Frame found Beston, who would subsequently compile a bibliography of her work and write about her fiction, 'a very gentle unassuming person . . . They told me news of Patrick White, whom they had been visiting, and they were enthusiastic about his humanity and compassion . . . [When] I told them about my letter from him, still unanswered, they said I must answer it.'[72] Apart from these callers, there was 'a small boy aged ten-and-a-half who keeps knocking on my door and wanting to talk'.[73]

Other distractions were not long in coming. As Frame had feared, the new National Government swung politics sharply to the right. The country's rugby team was allowed to visit South Africa to play apartheid-segregated teams, which resulted in an African boycott of the Montreal Olympics. Pacific Islanders were dragged from their homes in a series of dawn raids around Auckland and questioned about their right to live in New Zealand. Frame told Peter Dawson that these occurrences made her feel ashamed. The new Prime Minister, Robert Muldoon, 'has repeatedly insulted the third world [and now] we await the arrival of nuclear ships from the USA . . . when our last government voted for a nuclear-free Pacific'.[74]

There were more obtrusive distractions closer to home. To her puzzlement and then mounting annoyance, Frame began to receive telephone calls from people wanting fire extinguishers serviced or repaired. It turned out that the national distribution company had stamped her number instead of their own on thousands of extinguishers. Eventually the manager rang and offered to pay her for answering the calls and referring customers to the correct number.[75] More ominously, she began again to be plagued by neighbourhood noise. The man next door worked away from his house during the day and used his power tools at home every night.

'He and his two sons have been building and sanding another boat for the summer. As they never seem to go away on the water . . . I don't quite know what their purpose is. In desperation I have arranged for a man to put up a six-foot fence to screen me from them and them from me.'[76] The fence went up in late October 1976. No sooner was it in place than the neighbour knocked out the wall of his house that faced Frame's property and installed floor to ceiling glass, which had the effect of increasing the noise level and giving

Frame the feeling that she was being observed. This was, for her, the proverbial last straw. There was an inevitability about her next move.

'On Thursday I rashly put this house on the market and yesterday [10 September] I sold it [for] $26,000 . . . I'm moving to an official quiet zone — the same street my sister lives in, in Stratford, so I shall be in a kind of Yaddo situation.'[77] June and Wilson Gordon, feeling a little isolated in Taranaki despite the proximity of their daughter and her family, were delighted to be able to entice Frame south and found her a house two doors away from their own, which Frame bought unseen for $12,500. A few necessary alterations would bring its total cost to about $15,000. Frame would be able to invest the balance left over from the sale of the Auckland property. She spent the rest of September packing up her chattels for carriers to move; then the Gordons came to collect her and the cat for the three hundred mile journey to Taranaki.

By the first week in October she was in her 'new old house'. The entire transaction, from decision to resettlement, had taken three weeks. She was fast becoming, she admitted to Brown and Wonner, a 'dab hand' at upping stakes and moving rapidly. Her work, of course 'goes by the board for a time. I suspect I have arranged it this way and I hate myself for it . . .'[78]

## Chapter Twenty-Six

# State of Siege

$\mathcal{S}$TRATFORD, A RURAL TOWNSHIP OF SOME 5000 SOULS, LAY IN THE centre of one of the country's most prosperous dairying regions and was bisected by a river — not the Avon, whose name had already been appropriated by Christchurch, but the Patea. Stratford's streets, however, were named after Shakespearean characters and locations. It was a consolation, Frame told George Braziller, to know that she would be posting her letters in Prospero Place.[1] Her own address was Miranda Street. 'It's like being back in the old home town without the old home town's unpleasant memories.'[2]

To John Money she reported that her house was similar to that in which she had grown up in Eden Street, Oamaru — 'somewhat too like my Dunedin house except that it's about fifteen years younger and in better condition, though full of borer; and the ceilings are wooden with fancy squiggles, and very high, as they used to be. I have two chimneys . . . There's a quarter acre with hedges all around, and many shrubs including camellia and tulip trees [and] a vegetable garden.'[3]

The town was spread out over the eastern slope of a dormant volcano, Mount Egmont, from whose Maori name, Taranaki, the district as a whole took its name. Frame could see the snow-covered cone from four of her rooms. It had special interest for her because one of the two first Europeans to climb the mountain, in 1839, had been James 'Worser' Heberley, who later married her great-grandmother Charlotte Joyce. From the back of the house Frame could see two other volcanoes, Ruapehu and Ngauruhoe, which were intermittently active in the centre of the North Island. 'The Maoris say that all three volcanoes used to live together, but they quarrelled and [Taranaki] was flung as far away as possible in a battle. This story seems quite real as you . . . see the fields full of huge boulders, as if there had been a stone throwing session.'[4]

Frame reported to Bill Brown with some satisfaction that Stratford's location ensured 'fresh mountain air. The streets . . . are wide and there are many old houses which, had they been in Auckland, would have been demolished many years ago . . . [The] shops are a walk away, across the river and through a park. The library is old and spacious, very much like the library I knew as a child . . . and is housed in the municipal buildings, upstairs, along a corridor lined with portraits of past town dignitaries and dead soldiers.' New Plymouth, the nearest city, was a forty-eight kilometre bus ride away. 'The area is not so silent that one thinks one is in the grave, but it is blissfully quieter than where I *was* living . . . I'm starting to work again.'[5]

This quiet was guaranteed, she hoped, by the fact that the Stratford Hospital lay along the opposite side of her street. The neighbours behind were also quiet and had a trampoline on their lawn. Occasionally Frame glanced over the hedge 'to see them bouncing away, thrillingly'.[6] Though the Gordons were only two houses away and the sisters often spoke by telephone, Frame felt 'as if I'm in my own little world . . . nothing disturbs me'.[7] Indeed, she even went so far as to say that the location of Stratford was little short of inspirational for a writer.

It was not simply the effect of the Shakespearean place names, but the fact that the town's history was 'one of the bloodiest in New Zealand'.[8] Taranaki Maori had been punished for allegedly rebelling against the Crown in the 1860s, and the region had been 'scoured' by British troops who attacked and burned twenty-eight Maori settlements. Stratford was built on land confiscated from Maori, and Jacquie Baxter was a descendant of people disinherited by this act. Baxter's own tribe was named Taranaki and regarded itself as descended from the mountain. In the face of this background, Frame told Bill Brown, Stratford's 'Englishness' was little short of extraordinary — and provocative.[9]

Despite her intention to begin work at once, Frame found the resumption of a writing routine difficult. '[From] time to time I have intimations that send me into a state of shock about the enormity of everything.'[10] And she was too easily distracted by novelties in the early months in the new house. She read Frank Sargeson's second volume of memoirs, *More Than Enough*, which she had had since the previous year. She had postponed opening it, however, because she knew that it covered the period of her occupation of 14 Esmonde Road, and she was anxious about how Sargeson may have treated that, especially in view of their falling-out over *Daughter Buffalo*. But her fear was misplaced. Sargeson had dealt with the episode briefly and restrainedly:

> It is for Janet Frame to tell the story of her days in my hut if she chooses, and tell it with surprising dignity and grace I do not doubt. But for the record I can say that . . . she settled to write her novel *Owls Do Cry*, which besides demonstrating again her very extraordinary gifts promised the work which now becomes more and more known . . .[11]

Frame thanked Sargeson for his own grace; and also read and admired an illustrated biography of him which Dennis McEldowney had written, *Frank*

*Sargeson in His Time*, which appeared in November 1976. McEldowney, Frame told Sargeson, was 'trustworthy, has taste, and is a fine prose writer'.[12] She at once sent a copy to Brown and Wonner along with Allen Curnow's *Collected Poems*, and explained that she had bought both in New Plymouth, where she had been pleasantly surprised by a fine bookshop and an excellent art gallery, which was showing an exhibition of drawings from the Courtauld Institute.[13] In the same month she attended Stratford's Agricultural and Pastoral Show, and said that such events always reminded her of *Madame Bovary* — 'the displays of cattle, pigs and so on. And like this old house with its garden of lilac, the shows are part of my childhood.'[14]

Another reminder of her childhood was that, while contact was by no means daily, she was seeing more of her relatives than she had done since Oamaru days: the Gordons at least once a week; and visits to and from her niece, Pamela Bailey, and her family. Of particular concern to all of them was that Pamela and Stephen's daughter, Josie, appeared, at the age of three, to be arrested in her development. '[She] is a strange, beautiful child, either severely handicapped mentally or emotionally, or so bright that her own world contains her,' Frame wrote to Brown. '[She's] very advanced physically as far as balance [is] concerned, quite a little gymnast; but . . . she does not speak, scarcely responds.'[15] By the following year Josie had been diagnosed as 'probably autistic'. This came as a shock to Frame, who had introduced an autistic girl, Milly Galbraith, into *Intensive Care*; it was a reminder of things she had written in *Owls Do Cry* and *The Edge of the Alphabet* which had seemed to anticipate actual events. Doctors asked Pamela if there were any 'eccentric solitary people in the family', Frame told Bill. 'Enough said!'[16] By this time Pamela was pregnant with her second child, Daniel, who would be born in July 1977.

When Christmas 1976 arrived, Frame felt that she had been seeing rather too much of family, and too concentratedly, and she opted for Christmas dinner on her own. 'June, however, brought me a dish . . . and I did not object to that . . . Afterwards I went and sat for about half an hour with the family . . . Then Stephen planted some native trees on my property and Ian paid me a visit . . . [We] get on well. The topic of our conversation is usually philosophy-of-life.'[17]

After Christmas Frame and June, driven by Wilson Gordon, visited their mother's seventy-eight-year-old sister, Joyce Mills, who was in hospital in Wanganui, seventy-seven miles away. 'It was all very sad . . . [She] is expected to die there as she has had several strokes . . . I last saw her about six years ago when she and her other sisters, all widows, were still as beautiful and full of life as they ever were, really blooming. Her eyes are hauntingly full of vitality . . . she looks very like my mother.'[18]

In January 1977 Jacquie Baxter came to stay for five days and brought with her a revelation. 'I found out that, as usual,' Frame wrote, 'my moving here has strange associations with the Baxters.'

Jacquie was born . . . near here and her mother died [and] is buried by the sea . . . June and Wilson took us to see the place, Opunake, although Jacquie and I did not say exactly what we were seeing . . . We came to the small cottage hospital where Jacquie was born and, almost next door, the graveyard . . . of Jacquie's tribe . . . [And] what a beautiful place to lie, with the mountain on one side and the sea on the other — the cemetery was right on top of a cliff . . . The day was brilliant and hot and the combination of mountain light mixed with snow, and sea light and blue sky made the place seem like heaven . . .

[On] one other day we climbed to the snowline on the mountain, past the forest, and then scrub, and then the snowgrass and the blue and yellow and white mountain flowers. The rest of the time we just lazed about in the sun here at home and talked and read and listened to music.[19]

In the course of this visit, when both women's thoughts had been focussed on mortality (even when they climbed the mountain, because a young man fell down a precipice that day),[20] Sue Marquand died in New York. Frame knew nothing of this until John Marquand wrote to her in February, though she had been 'very worried about her without knowing why'.[21] Marquand said his wife had been stricken with bacterial meningitis in August 1976, then recovered. But just as she appeared to be returning to health she developed difficulty in swallowing, and was found to have cancer of the oesophagus.

[Surgery] was ruled out because of the precarious location of the tumour so close to the aorta . . . [We] lived on hope and she had a sufficient remission to be able to leave the hospital and be home for Christmas. For her last three weeks she was surrounded by the love and attention of all of us . . . [It was] the best and most affecting Christmas Sue and I ever spent together in 22 years. Then a few more happy days . . . and she died in her sleep.[22]

Marquand went on to say that his wife had loved Frame very much. 'You were her friend through many difficult times . . . Thank God, it was largely due to [her] suffering that Sue and I discovered the true depths of our attachment to each other.'[23] Frame confessed to Bill Brown that this news had been 'a terrible shock . . . I suspect it is more painful [for me] because she is one of the few people in the world who let me know that I was needed . . . Her feeling of urgency about everything, which no one really understood, can now be explained . . . She was only forty-four.'[24]

In February too the Gordons moved to a smaller home in another part of Stratford. They were planning to take a 'grand tour' of Britain and Europe with the proceeds of their 'down-sizing'. 'I'm quite pleased they are a little further away,' Frame told Brown.[25] 'They are so different from me in so many respects. I'm [mostly] glad that I've had the opportunity and privilege of living alone, because in that way I can explore so many aspects of thinking which

. . . two people living together or in a family [would] never have the chance to do.'[26]

The fact that the Gordons would soon be travelling, however, made Frame nostalgic for the northern hemisphere. 'It's funny,' she wrote to John Money, 'but even here in a mildly wintry New Zealand, in the marvellously cool air blowing from the sea . . . I can feel the opposite Spring air in the north; and the unusual autumnal air of the south also — I have such a strong feeling of standing beneath those huge hemlock trees of Yaddo, feeling the chill wind in the woods and watching the leaves fall.'[27] For the next two months she vacillated between a determination to complete the next novel and an inclination to travel as 'a kind of escape from my work, [which] scares me'.[28]

In April 1977 Frame was invited to a conference at the University of Hawaii on the interaction of Eastern and Western Culture in literature. She decided to accept and to use the fifteen hundred dollar gift from Peter Dawson to take in a rapid visit to England and mainland America before the conference in October. This would enable her to see Dawson, who was approaching her eighty-second birthday, for what Frame imagined would be 'a last visit before she too [like Sue Marquand] catches the train . . . it would be nice to share a meal in the waiting room'.[29] There was a 'rub', however. She would have to prepare a conference paper. But the more she thought about the subject the more the idea appealed. 'I've decided to try one, and also try to hide my meagre knowledge by inventing things,' she told John Money on 10 May. 'I've written a summary . . . and sent it to the professor.'[30] If she developed her customary anxieties about delivering it, 'I can always, like the Queen . . . be confined to my room with a heavy cold.'[31]

While this news was a surprise to her friends, she had an even more dramatic announcement the following month. 'I've been experimenting with the idea of joining the Catholic Church . . . I've arrived at the stage where I can no longer ignore and not praise "continually" a creator, named or nameless.'[32] This development was not as sudden as it may have seemed. Her niece, Pamela, married to a Catholic, was taking instruction and would become a Catholic that year. And Frame herself had been further influenced by her proximity to the local place of worship, the Church of the Immaculate Conception, which stood close to her home in Miranda Street. 'I like to go there,' she told Bill Brown, 'because it's not far to walk, and it's nice and peaceful inside . . . I guess I've exchanged my old habit of sitting quietly in cemeteries for sitting quietly in churches . . . I [also] enjoy the changed concept of time that a church gives one. It's such a pleasure to be able to know the date, not just by the day the man came to read the meter . . . but by the birthdays of the Saints . . . [My] birthday is the day of St Augustine.' She was not without reservations, though. 'I have to be sure of their teaching on sex — I believe and hope their attitude is more tolerant . . . than it used to be. My niece assures me it is.'[33]

Pamela, her husband, Stephen, and their now two-week-old baby boy accompanied Frame to Wanganui in July to explore the Catholic bookshop there. 'Unfortunately in spite of travel pills I was pretty ill [and] in such a state that I could hardly take advantage of all those goodies in the shop — tripping over priests and nuns. I bought the papers of Vatican Two, which are interesting and enlightening and enlightened . . . And I bought the *Letters of St Teresa* to give my niece for her birthday . . . but such was my ignorance I bought the wrong St Teresa.'[34]

While Frame was making plans for her British and American visits in September and October — and further neglecting the languishing novel — an invitation arrived to represent New Zealand 'as a guest of honour' at the International PEN Congress to be held in Sydney in December 1977. Again, contrary to previous inclination and behaviour, Frame surprised family and friends by accepting. Having avoided all such occasions up to her fifty-fourth year, she was now to attend two gatherings of writers in the space of two months.[35]

John Money passed through Stratford to see her in August, en route for a medical conference in Australia. 'I think he had a relaxing stay,' Frame told Brown, 'but a few days later I saw him on tv and he looked toothless and shrunken — like the rest of us.'[36] That same month came news that a New Zealand producer, Patrick Cox, wanted to make a feature film of *Owls Do Cry*. Frame was to be offered an advance payment of five hundred dollars, with a notional advance of five thousand dollars to be left in the film as a private investment. If agreement was reached to proceed on this basis, Pegasus would print another hardback edition of the book.[37] Frame, however, was uncomfortable with the idea of that particular book being made into a commercial film, as she had been when another producer, John O'Shea, had approached her ten years earlier; and she could not help but be aware of family sensitivities to the portrayals of Chicks and Toby. She put off making any decision on the proposal until after she returned from England and the United States.

By contrast, she did authorise two students from the School of Fine Arts at Canterbury University, Timothy White and Vincent Ward, to make a 'non-commercial' film from their adaptation of *A State of Siege*. She did this because she was impressed by the perception and sensitivity of their proposal, because she had a weakness for serious-minded young people seeking a career in the arts, and because the resulting film would be shown to student audiences and film societies. On this basis she neither asked for nor expected income from the film.

On 13 September she travelled to Auckland by bus, then flew out to Los Angeles on the sixteenth. She spent two days on the west coast of America before flying on to London, which she reached on 19 September. After two days there and a meeting with Mildred Surry (Bob Cawley was away), Frame travelled up to Norfolk for four days with a now fragile Peter Dawson. She then returned to London and flew to New York on 28 September, where she stayed at the fraying George Washington Hotel on Gramercy Park, in spite of George Braziller's warning that it had become a nest for criminals and drug addicts.[38]

In what was a new element in her travelling, she seasoned the itinerary with visits to Catholic churches and bookshops. In London, for example, she went to Mass at Westminster Cathedral — 'a beautiful place with various haunts like little churches within the big church [and] priests & nuns, from youthful to elderly, lurking in the shadows. One kneels on cushioned velvet.'[39] In New York she explored a Catholic bookshop on 43rd Street. George Braziller's warnings about the hotel proved to be well-founded, however. The bathroom in Frame's room had a hole where the shower had been ripped from the wall, the bath had no taps, the television would not work, and her door kept jamming shut. After reporting these defects to the desk clerk, who seemed unmoved, Frame was attempting to leave her room when the heavy ventilator unit above the door fell and struck her on the side of her head. This accident, which stunned her, caused her to miss an appointment with George Braziller and left her with severe headaches in the succeeding weeks. She went to John Money's in Baltimore for two days to recover; and he had her examined by a doctor, in case she decided to seek compensation from the hotel (in the end she did not, because of the difficulties of initiating litigation from New Zealand).

From Baltimore Frame flew to San Francisco, where Bill Brown and Paul Wonner were installed in a new residence, a Victorian house in an old part of the city. 'It's very pleasant, with a village-like atmosphere [and] little shops . . . There's a library across the road and a post office near by, and it is all so *quiet* . . . compared to Stratford. I'm afraid that spacious New Zealand landscape magnifies all sound.'[40] At her request, Wonner accompanied her to Mass at the local Catholic church, St Philip's; and the three friends went to a Tennessee Williams play and a Rudolph Valentino film.

By 15 October Frame was in Honolulu for her 'first conference'. Rather to her surprise she found it an exhilarating experience. 'All the others who are used to conferences declared it was the best they'd ever been to because the time was spent not in reading the papers . . . but in discussing.' Frame's own paper, which, like the others, had been circulated in advance of the gathering, was called 'Some Recognitions of the Cross-Cultural Encounter in Literature'. Transactions between literatures, she had written, were endless and age-old.

[If] one, as a writer, has been influenced by these, one has a special affection for the particular circumstances. I think of Rilke's visit to France, his embracing of the French language [and] his poems written in French, *Les Vergers* . . . [For] I believe that the poets do not 'take' the pulse of another culture, they become its pulse. One thinks [also] of the West Indian novelists who, living and working and writing of another land, in their English, yet seem to record, as if it were an underground stream flowing through their writing, the life of the West Indies.

She noted also that, in every cross-cultural encounter, there was 'a dominance, a submission, a merging or a resistance'.

[When] my earlier books were printed in the United States, I was surprised and horrified to find many of my words 'translated' into American English, often with little knowledge of the original meaning. 'Kerosene box' which, in a rural community without electricity, where I spent my early years, meant the large wooden box which had held the bulk supply of kerosene for the lamps . . . became in the American edition of my book 'gasoline shed': meaningless . . .

We want our words. If I write of a *bach* by the sea, I do not want it to be turned into a bungalow or cottage or mansion. If we write of a *tangi*, we mean just that: a *tangi*. This absorption . . . of another culture means a form of imprisonment for able-bodied words which languish and could die exiled from the literature, never having the opportunity to work within it and enrich it. How much more magnified this imprisonment and exile may be in a world-setting, when countries high in literacy and publishing opportunities, reinforced by an abundance of exported films, can almost vacuum-clean, overnight, another culture and language.[41]

Describing the conference to Brown and Wonner, Frame said they would not be surprised to learn that she became known as the 'quiet one'.

[But] I did get bolder . . . and on the last day when the professor went round the table asking everyone to speak I actually had something to say, and I kept on saying, 'Oh, and one more thing' . . . [which] marks the career of a talker . . . who goes on, and on, and on. We all grew so fond of one another and there really were tears at the end, mostly from the lovely emotional 'Eastern' people, some of whom [may] be imprisoned or shot on their return home.

Well it was nice . . . an international Yaddo.[42]

Frame had got on especially well with the Nigerian poet and dramatist Wole Soyinka (who would win the Nobel Prize for Literature in 1986), the Indian poet Nissam Ezekiel, the Samoan writer Albert Wendt and John Beston, who had visited her in Glenfield. And she made an important discovery. 'I'm quite good at reading (with the use of a micophone) to an audience. This . . . does promise something. I used to give speeches years ago at school . . . and I have often wished that I hadn't lost that confidence . . . [Well] I haven't . . . I [was] very calm and in complete command.'[43]

Back in Stratford early in November 1977, Frame found members of her family in the news. Josie Bailey had been chosen to present a cheque to the mayor of money raised for intellectually handicapped children's activities. The local paper ran a photograph of her snatching the cheque back after she had handed it over.[44] And June Gordon was selected to stand as Labour candidate for the Waitotara electorate in the 1978 general election. She was the first woman in the region nominated by a major political party to stand for Parliament. Frame was proud of her sister but worried about her health. 'The work-load . . . is too much and I feel she's already cracking under the strain.'[45]

Frame herself was feeling a certain amount of strain in the knowledge that she would be home for only one month before heading to Sydney for the PEN Congress. In the interim, however, there was time to recuperate, if not to undertake serious work. 'Life at Stratford is sweet-smelling and quite lovely,' she told Bill Brown. 'All the flowers are out . . . the bushes and the beautiful bronze irises. The lawn is covered with daisies . . . [Mornings] and evenings are lighter, and summer is a-comen in.'[46] She began formal instruction classes at the Catholic presbytery, but found them 'rather juvenile' and began to have second thoughts about 'converting'. 'I really can't accept their focus on so-called "sins of the flesh", nor the reward and punishment aspect of their beliefs. Rewards and punishments appear to me to be a human invention.'[47]

Early in December 1977 Frame flew from Wellington to Sydney, carrying a virus with her which went into remission for the week-long congress. Again she enjoyed being among fellow writers, helped by the fact that her friend Ruth Dallas was another guest of honour. 'I reminded her how Charles [Brasch] had said to us once, Some day you and Ruth must go to one of those literary festivals in Australia . . . One of the organisers was Charles's cousin, a woman who rather resembled him.'[48]

Delegates and guests stayed in a Kings Cross hotel which had views of the harbour and of the Sydney Opera House. 'I found the Eastern people and the African and South Pacific . . . writers most interesting . . . and got on well with them. It could be that I am an inverted racist . . . [The] Europeans appeared to be in a state of emotional constipation and rather drained of life.'[49] She tried to attend all sessions of the congress until it became 'too much for me . . . I gradually learned not to go to everything.' Sydney residents appeared to her 'more leisurely' than New Zealanders — 'gentle and kind and sensitive . . . I'd love to go back there without being "bound"'.[50] She told Bill Brown that she had not seen Patrick White. 'Although I had his address I forgot to take it with me, and I heard that he abhors all forms of conferences, interviews and so on, and lives in seclusion.'[51] Another Australian writer, Judah Waten, greeted her warmly and asked her to convey warm regards to Frank Sargeson, with whom he had got up to high jinks in Auckland in 1939.[52]

Frame stayed with Jacquie Baxter on the way home and renewed her friendship with the whole family. John Baxter was there with his wife, Karen, who was about a week off giving birth to their daughter Jessica. 'He's been earning a living by selling (very readily) his batik wall-hanging designs and has become interested in wood-sculpture. What a clear-sighted young man he is!

He was always, even when he was a child, so much wiser than his father — as if he were father of the man.'[53]

Once she was home again in Stratford the virus returned and Frame collapsed into bed for two weeks, including Christmas. Feeling depressed and bad-tempered, she asked a Stratford solicitor to reject, on her behalf, the memorandum of agreement sent by the producer who wanted to make a film from *Owls Do Cry*. The whole issue, including the legal agreement, seemed fraught with too many potential complications.[54] And she did not feel comfortable with the thought of that particular story and set of characters being reshaped by other hands on the basis of commercial imperatives. So ill was she that she did not even see the Gordons until the New Year, and she had to struggle to keep to herself 'the doom and gloom predictions which I always feel about their lives'.[55]

There was good news, though. The vice-chancellor of the University of Otago had written to tell her, in confidence, that it was the university's wish to confer honorary doctorates in literature on her and Ruth Dallas in May 1978. Frame accepted the proposal; so, to her relief and delight, did her friend.

In January 1978 Frame took stock of her circumstances and found them wanting. Writing to Frank Sargeson on New Year's Day she confessed to being 'dissatisfied with my work, for a while now . . . I used to live in a tent but now the walls . . . have been removed as if in an earthquake and I can see the landscape for miles and the weather gets in . . . You probably understand.'[56]

She could not, like the princess of her fairy story, wave a wand over the 'rags' of her manuscripts and transform them into a beautiful gown. But she could change her working conditions. She became convinced that difficulties in completing her current novel were directly related to the fact that her place of work was now as noisy as any she had encountered elsewhere. The hospital lawns across the road were cut with tractor mowers which, in all but the winter months, seemed to operate all day, most days. Her nights were disturbed by the sound of trains at the railway marshalling yards less than a kilometre away. Locomotive engines seemed to throb for hours at a time and she could hear wagons being loaded, unloaded and shunted. With the opening up of New Plymouth as a container port, Stratford had become the railway depot for the whole region.

'I work with earplugs in my ears,' she told Bill Brown, 'ear muffs and white noise on the [gramophone] . . . I visited a seaside town about thirty miles from here, to look at houses . . . but they all had too much to be done to them.'[57] Just over a week later, on 10 February, she made an announcement. 'I'm moving to another part of town, not to a quiet part but to one maybe slightly quieter . . . [It] is beside the railway line, although the trains go straight past and don't stop and throb all night . . . as they do here.'[58]

The 'new' house, in Juliet Street, was about one hundred years old. She was able to buy it for $14,000 after selling the other for $13,000. 'It needs a new roof and various other things but it is nice inside [and] romantic, with all sorts of hideyholes . . . [Outside] is another dwelling, a little bedroom and sitting-room with a small verandah. I suppose I'm crazy as usual, but I could be indulging in other vices . . . It is very private and when I go outside nobody sees me — that's my ideal world . . . The fact that I'm moving from Miranda to Juliet seems rather untimely — it should be the other way . . .'[59] She was not unduly daunted by the fact that the surname of the previous owners was Death.

Frame was settled in Juliet Street by 8 March 1978 and told Frank Sargeson that the move was 'definitely my last before the last . . .'[60] After what she referred to as 'my middled-aged wandering' — and after a quick trip to Wanganui to see the Baileys, who had shifted there in a effort to ensure better prospects for Josie — Frame's priority for the remainder of the year was to be 'work, work, and only work . . . My pile of manuscripts grows, and soon I'll get rid of some of it to suitable quarters.'[61] She now revealed to her correspondents that, far from concentrating on a single book, she was experimenting with 'two or three mixed-up novels' which had grown out of the manuscript conceived in Menton and what she had been able to write since, in California and New Zealand.[62] The fact that her writing focus was less concentrated than usual further postponed an immediate conclusion to current work.

Frame was determined to discard other distractions. She now relinquished her pursuit of Catholicism, 'because when it comes to the crunchy crunch I can't be ruled over by an institution . . . I haven't the energy to submit myself to that kind of house-cleaning . . . [The] only cleaning which suits me is in the institution of language, spoken, written, unspoken . . .'[63] She remarked to her niece on an oddity: no sooner did she stop attending Mass at Immaculate Conception than she also stopped running into priests in the street — she simply never saw them again.[64]

Frame remained concerned about her niece's daughter, whom she described as 'this lovely child who is a stranger in a foreign world'.[65] She wrote to her former Dunedin psychiatrist Wallace Ironside to ask if he could suggest where Josie's parents might look for understanding and support.[66] The fact that she felt some rapport with her great-niece's 'social deficiency' was made clear in a letter to another medical practitioner whom Pamela Bailey had already consulted.

When I was visiting my sister, [the family would arrive] all in a hullabaloo of greetings, and each time I found myself in the corridor with Josie because both she and I had left the roomful of people. Even I, in my mature years, still leave a room if people arrive, and I avoid being in a room where there are more than about two people. I recognise this trait in Josie . . .

I have sometimes thought that I had an allergy to people, or that I have some chemical which is in short supply and which is needed to go through the usual process of being sociable, that a large 'dose' of people exhausts the supply which must be built up again before the next 'dose', and while the supply is being built up there is an aversion, a turning away, an avoidance of people, as if one had been seasick and couldn't face the thought of food . . . [Josie] has this avoidance of contact to such an extreme degree that she has not acquired the spoken language of people, whether through some deficiency in perception [or] as part of the avoiding process.[67]

Because of her own need to retain her 'necessary isolation' from family, Frame was not displeased when June and Wilson Gordon suggested that they too, like their daughter, might move to Wanganui. But they would wait until after the election.[68]

Frame declined to contribute an essay to a special issue of the literary journal *Islands* which commemorated Frank Sargeson's seventy-fifth birthday on 23 March 1978. But she sent her friend a birthday poem in which the first letters of each line spelled out his name (beginning 'For Rage A Noble Keelage'); and, a little later in the year, a warm letter in which she paid tribute to his unequalled contribution to New Zealand letters by way of example and mentoring:

The Great Irrigation Scheme of NZ literature is having marvellous results — remember the narrow channel you made, all alone, into that part of the land where everyone said nothing would grow? And remember the struggle you had to get people to accept that it was necessary? You can look at all those creeks and canals that followed . . . and see the orchard. What an orchard. I'm as excited as you about the flowering talent.[69]

As far as Sargeson was concerned, they had made their peace. And, in the month of his birthday, he reinstated Frame as a beneficiary in his will.[70]

One distraction she could not deflect, and did not want to, was the conferral of her honorary doctorate in Dunedin on 6 May 1978. Coincidentally it came only weeks after her nephew Neil Gordon returned from the Massachusetts Institute of Technology with his own doctorate, in science. The Gordons drove her south and en route they visited relatives on both sides of the family: her father's sister Aunty Polly Curtis in Wellington, and Lottie Frame's sister Grace Hislop in Kaikoura. 'They were both very entertaining in their different ways, and of course resembled Mother and Father very much.' At Kaikoura, the Hislop clan were spread around the district but assembled to see their famous relative. Frame was especially engaged by her unmarried cousin, Archie, 'who has a commune that looks like MacDowell . . . with studios and caravans [and] a huge garden, and then the beehives and the flour-grinding equipment

. . . [When] my niece, rather disgruntled, said to me, "Archie had eyes only for you", I, of course, felt gruntled.'[71]

Dunedin, Frame found, was 'as formal as ever with those dinner parties and fancy foods and formal conversations . . . I had to go to a certain number of receptions, and it was all very tiring, but quite fun getting dressed up (like in a secret society) in red gown and pink hood and being fitted with a trencher.'[72] She wandered around the university, remembering 'all the misery of once being a student, and how I used to pore through the *University Calendar*, reading the lists of past students and graduates'.[73] Her guests at the capping ceremony, in addition to the Gordons and Pamela Bailey, were Dorothy Ballantyne and her husband, Robert. The citations for Frame and Ruth Dallas were written and read by Alan Horsman, in his role as the university's Public Orator. Thirty-five years after she had first enrolled there as a student, he called Frame forward to receive her degree as 'a writer who identified unexpected human treasure'.[74] A highly gratifying day ended with a dinner for the family at the Ballantynes.

Home again in Stratford, Frame told John Money that she now had the option of calling herself Dr Frame or Dr Clutha. She would do so 'when I want to impress the plumber and the grocer and suchlike, for these are the people with all the power and wealth these days'.[75]

That same week in mid-May 1978, she wrote an angry letter. The Australian academic John Beston, who was now at Harvard, sent her a biographical note that he intended to publish with a bibliography of Frame's work. It contained several errors, and Beston said that he had derived most of his information from Patrick Evans. He meant from Evans's book in the Twayne World Authors series, *Janet Frame*, which had been published the previous year. Frame had not seen the volume and assumed that Beston had communicated directly with Evans at the University of Canterbury. She herself now wrote to Evans:

> As you've never had the courtesy to submit facts about my life and work to me for correction, I'm unable to say whether the several inaccuracies are yours or John Beston's. He has at least sent me his note for correction.
>
> Perhaps you feel that inaccuracies of fact don't matter? . . . Perhaps you feel that writers should inhabit as well as write their fiction? Or perhaps in a subtle way you are making a comment on the ever-lasting topic of capital-lettered Life and Art? One of the Porlock people, maybe?[76]

Mention of the 'Porlock people' referred to the person who interrupted Samuel Taylor Coleridge when he was trying to write 'Kubla Khan', and seemed to imply that activities such as Evans's critical writing interfered with

Frame's own ability to work, and hence with the artistic process itself (although Frame was also aware of Stevie Smith's poem 'Thoughts about the Person from Porlock', which suggested that Coleridge *wanted* to be interrupted).[77] Certainly her discomfort over the Evans book was magnified when, later in the year, she found it in the Stratford Library and — glancing around to ensure no one was watching her — took it off the shelf to read it. There she found a serious and respectful analysis of the elements of and influences on her fiction; and one which would boost the stature of her work as a worthy subject for further study. But she also found factual inaccuracies in addition to those in the draft Beston bibliography which would prejudice her against the writing of critical biography in general.[78] She would have corrected the errors, as she had done with John Beston's script, had she seen the text before publication. Evans had not submitted it to her, however, because she had failed to make her attitude to the book clear to him when he had written to her about it, and because he had been unwilling to disturb her work or her peace of mind. By acting as he did, he had achieved inadvertently the very result he had thought — and sought — to avoid.

Another source of anxiety at this time was the knowledge that there was now a gap of six years since the publication of her previous book, and that all her books were in effect out of print in New Zealand. Her income from royalties had now virtually dried up. Her annuity and Authors Fund payments alone were now insufficient to support her, and she had been able to pay her way only by eating into the profit she had made on the sale of the Glenfield house. The annuity was frozen at its original value of $1000 per year. The widow's benefit, with which it had been commensurate in 1972, had since risen to $2536 per annum. She had spent the nest egg from E.P. Dawson on her trip to England and the United States the previous year. While she now worried about future prospects, she remained adamant that the one project in the offing which could have earned her some money, the filming of *Owls Do Cry*, should not proceed. 'The idea of such a film as a commercial venture is [distasteful] to me, as is the idea of the film itself,' she told Albion Wright on 24 August, after he had urged her to reconsider her position.[79]

That same month she had a visit from Timothy White, the student who had produced the School of Fine Arts film of *A State of Siege*, and who turned out to be young (twenty-two), frail, and 'fallen-from-outer-space looking'.[80] He brought with him a print of the fifty-two-minute film and showed it to Frame in the local high school lecture theatre. She was stunned by it and called it 'a very fine work of art . . . The actress [Anne Flannery as Malfred Signal] was superb also.'[81] She elaborated to Pamela Bailey:

I was most impressed . . . by the way the makers understood the book. It was an agreeable change to see the character portrayed as she was — an artistic virgin venturing forth, rather than as a neurotic sexual virgin. Even the attempted seduction in the fern-house was that of the Muse!

As for that scene by the sea, with the tremendous waves! The film was a poem in its own right.[82]

This verdict turned out not to be Frame's alone. On the film festival circuit it received high praise from critics. Michael Heath, for example, writing in Wellington's *Evening Post*, called it 'a landmark in New Zealand film making . . . the most intelligent film that has ever been made in New Zealand'.[83] It was taken to film festivals abroad and won gold medals in Chicago and Miami. The director, Vincent Ward — whom Frame met later in Wanganui — was to go on to an internationally successful career with such films as *Vigil*, *The Navigator* and *Map of the Human Heart*.

For most of the second half of 1978 Frame was wrestling to produce a single coherent novel from the 'two or three' manuscripts on which she had been working. As a general rule she was at her desk from six in the morning until noon. '[Writing] is a boon, analgesic and so on,' she told Sargeson. 'I think it's all that matters to me. I dread emerging from it each day.'[84] She had returned to the 'Baltimore story' which she had begun three years earlier. Mindful of her difficulties with Frank Sargeson, she now asked John Money how he would feel about his house, neighbourhood and friends appearing, 'disguised', in a novel. 'It's what I want to write, and I've never been able to write anything except what I want to write.'[85] By November she was able to assure him that the novel had now 'solved itself . . . helped by your not minding some Baltimore references'. To Frank Sargeson she said, 'Every time I'm writing a book, I remember . . . your saying how after the hundredth page everything falls into place. It does of course, while before the hundredth everything falls apart.'[86] She described what was emerging as 'a strange book', and said she would be posting the manuscript to Braziller after Christmas, when the surge of mail was over.[87]

November was also the month of the country's national election. June Gordon was canvassing full time and addressing audiences, with Wilson acting as her campaign manager. Frame went to support her sister at a meeting in Stratford addressed by the former Prime Minister and now Opposition leader, Bill Rowling. 'June spoke a few words — the first time I'd heard her. She was very emotional and passionate . . . I've advised her to try to stay calm . . . [When] someone asked her how she planned her campaign, she said, The campaign manager and I plan it in bed together . . .'[88] On election day, 25 November 1978, the National Government was returned to office and June Gordon failed to take Waitotara from the sitting member, Venn Young. But she polled over 4000 votes and came a creditable second. The following month she and Wilson joined their daughter and her family in Wanganui.

Frame's major source of excitement in December was a cable from George Braziller announcing that he would visit New Zealand in January 1979, if she planned to be in the country. She did. Although Braziller indicated that the object of his trip was to investigate New Zealand writing, this was not primarily so. His major purpose would be to determine whether or not Frame herself was writing and whether her work was indeed approaching a publishable state, as she assured him it was. [89]

'I've almost finished typing the final copy of my book,' Frame told Dawson on 21 December, 'and will be making carbon copies when [George] arrives . . . I'm hoping that if [he] likes my book . . . he will boost my finances. I have . . . two more books to write at once, though I'd have to choose which to do — as you know, writing breeds writing.' Commenting on the Gordons' absence in Wanganui she noted that 'it's delicious to be alone'.[90]

Frame and George Braziller's sense of anticipation about meeting in Stratford was mutual and intense. He had been her publisher for two decades; and he was now, for better or for worse, her *only* assured publisher. Pegasus had formally severed links with her only months earlier;[91] and Frame had heard nothing for years from her British and most recent New Zealand publishers (indeed, the only scrap of information she was to glean about Reeds in the coming months was from a broadcast in which their senior editor, Arnold Wall, made it clear that the company was reluctant to publish any more fiction).[92] Braziller, by contrast, had a profound respect and affection for his New Zealand author, kept alive by her intermittent visits to New York. Like her New Zealand friends, however, he was genuinely worried that the eight-year drought since her delivery of the manuscript of *Daughter Buffalo* in 1971 presaged the close of Frame's writing career. The joy he would eventually feel in taking possession of the manuscript of *Living in the Maniototo* would be both personal and professional.

The conjunction of publisher and manuscript would be delayed for a further two months, however. Frame reported to Bill Brown on 10 January that 'there's no sign of Geo Braziller. Mysterious.'[93] It was not until her telephone account turned up in early February that Frame discovered that the cable she thought she had sent to Braziller in December, assuring him of her presence and his welcome, had for some reason never left Stratford Post Office. 'At the time of my sending it they seemed to be so muddled and inefficient . . . that I had my doubts.'[94] It was a typical Frame-type plot scenario of the message sent but never received, with all the attendant complications that made possible.

Instead she posted the manuscript to New York in mid-February, saying as she did so that it was 'not a literary achievement but an environmental one — being able to work against NZ motor mowers and chainsaws'.[95] She added: 'The theme of the book is not original but it is one that fascinates me — the process of writing a novel, given the manifold (Kant's definition) and all the avoidances, interruptions, irrelevancies, and so on, plus the terrible everlasting substantiality of the manifold.'[96]★ The title, she told Dorothy Ballantyne, had come from her visit to the Ballantynes in Dunedin the previous year. 'I have

---

★ In Kant's philosophy, the manifold is the sum of the particulars furnished by the senses before they have been unified by understanding.

been haunted . . . by the phrase which was often used in your household . . . I remember an aunt [Isy Renwick] who used to say, "When I was up Central, in Middlemarch," and the image I had was absolutely haunting . . . The same thing happened to me with "When I was in the Maniototo" . . . You both seemed caught up in its magic, and you netted me.'[97]

To Bill Brown Frame reported that the new novel was 'technically foul, because . . . my chief pet aversion in the literary world is the craze for the use of the historic present tense. It's vivid, "now" and it lures the reader, but the more it is used the more I resent it . . . I've even gone pluperfect . . . with much straight narrative, simply because I can't bear the artificial emphasis on the *present* . . . [The] history of my life has been a rebellion against everything "in fashion".'[98]

Braziller sent a telegram at the end of February to say that the manuscript had arrived. Then Frame hunkered down for what she imagined would be a long and nerve-racking wait for news of acceptance or rejection; she suffered all her usual misgivings and second thoughts. The verdict arrived only days after acknowledgement of the manuscript, however. Braziller cabled again to say that he liked it; then he telephoned Frame in the second week in March to say that he would publish the novel 'this coming northern fall . . . Even though I don't earn any money from his way of marketing and my way of writing,' Frame told Brown, 'the personal touch [is] worth all the financial earnings I don't get.'[99] What she would get was an advance on royalty earnings that would convert to $NZ1600.

The very week this good news arrived it was undercut by another blow to her well-being. 'An awful thing has happened,' she told Brown on 14 March 1979. '[The] two houses next door, at the back, are being demolished and three are being built in their place.'[100] The coming months would be a cacophony of 'thuds and thumps and saws and bulldozers' — and that would be just the demolition; construction noises would follow.[101] In addition, Juliet Street was made into a bypass for heavy traffic, and so the sound of stock trucks and milk and petrol tankers rumbling past was added to the discord and continued throughout the night.

Frame's immediate reaction was to put a For Sale sign outside the gate of 9 Juliet Street. She was angry, and incredulous that, yet again, noise had sought her out; and she was fed up with Stratford and now dismissed the notion that she might find peace in a small town. The thing to do, she decided, was to move to a provincial city, such as Wanganui or Palmerston North, where she could be more certain of finding a house outside an industrial area and away from major traffic routes. Wanganui appealed most, because of what she had seen of the Gordons' and Baileys' lives there. And, as she always did when she had not seen her relatives for a time, she missed their occasional company.

Within weeks of putting the property on the market, however, an unexpected obstacle became apparent. Early offers made it clear that she was unlikely to sell it for more than the valuation of $13,000 — in other words, at a loss. To re-establish herself in Wanganui or Palmerston North she would need a further ten to fifteen thousand dollars to acquire accommodation comparable to that which she now enjoyed. With her savings exhausted, and her annuity and Authors Fund income barely adequate to support her daily living expenses, where would she find the additional money? In April 1979 she wrote to the head of the Department of Internal Affairs, which administered the Authors Fund and the Literary Fund.

> When I was a student we used to talk of 'selling our body to the Medical School' in exchange for an immediate cash payment . . . Would it be possible for me to complete some kind of legal document whereby I exchange my literary property for an immediate cash grant of enough for me to find a quiet place to live so that I may continue writing? . . . I have several [books] which have been 'waiting in the queue' . . . and which I hope will be able to win the terrible battle with the chain saw, the stereo, the heavy truck — not to mention the motor mower.[102]

The Secretary of Internal Affairs passed the letter to the Literary Fund, whose secretary replied that the agency most likely to be interested in Frame's papers was the Alexander Turnbull Library in Wellington, which had bought Sargeson's letters and manuscripts. She would explore the extent of their interest and report back to Frame.[103] Investigations revealed that the value of Frame's papers to the library could be anywhere from four to ten thousand dollars, depending on their content, quantity and condition; the secretary also undertook, confidentially, to ask the Department of Social Welfare if Frame's annuity could be increased in line with the widow's benefit.

Frame now had a further reason for wanting to abandon Stratford that she did not communicate to Internal Affairs. She was deeply unhappy about the performance of the doctor who was supplying prescriptions for her blood pressure medication. Early in 1979 she had written to him:

> On Friday I was very sick and in a state of collapse. I was able to crawl to the telephone and phone your number. The receptionist answered and suggested that I drink boiled water . . . [She] said, Oh it's going about — or something to that effect . . .
>
> [I] accept the fact that one day I might collapse and die — after all, it's been 'going about' and has been for centuries. But you, as a doctor, have prescribed me certain tablets which I take, following your directions. I do think that . . . you should show some professional interest in the effect of the tablets . . . instead of practising medicine as diagnosis by receptionist.[104]

In response to accusation, the general practitioner concerned pointed out that Frame had been speaking to a nurse, not a receptionist; and that the advice she had given would have been adequate for someone with viral gastroenteritis.[105]

In April 1979, however, Frame had cause for even greater displeasure, as she told Frank Sargeson. On a visit to the doctor for a repeat prescription, he 'talked in the present tense of "my illness"."What illness?""Your mental illness." I had such a shock and scare to be faced, after sixteen years of being home in NZ, with an old-style Seacliff Hospital mentality where difference is a disease to be cured . . . I got *such* a shock that, after dismissing the idea of leaving the country, I put this house up for sale.' When she repeated the conversation by letter to Bob Cawley, he undertook to write to the doctor.

After Frame had eventually and reluctantly agreed to omit a lengthy epilogue in poetry, the galley proofs for *Maniototo* arrived from Braziller in the same month. They were largely 'clean', apart from the fact that she had to change spellings altered by the New York editor back to their New Zealand form ('beaut', for example, meaning 'great' or 'fine').And she was pleasantly surprised at the effect of the typeset text. '[Reading] it is rather like discovering what looks like a corpse and then watching it slowly come to life and warmth . . . I could feel the gradual flowing of blood that appeared at first to be frozen.'[106] She was encouraged by Carl Brandt's description of the novel as 'extraordinary'; and John Money's 'a great Zealandic saga [with] a magnificent mental interior'.[107] Asked by her Braziller editor to state, for the jacket blurb, what she had been doing since *Daughter Buffalo* appeared, Frame replied, 'writing and suffering'.[108]

While she waited in hope for a house buyer and a favourable response to her appeal to the Department of Internal Affairs, Frame attempted to shut out the continuing noise from next door so as to grapple with the idea she had for her next novel. Her intention was to explore 'a theme which has haunted me [ever] since I took an extra-mural course in music theory: the teaching of music in New Zealand'.[109] A story she had sent to the *Listener* the previous year, 'Two Widowers', was published in June 1979 and praised by Sargeson as producing a quintessentially 'Frame' effect.[110] She toyed also with the idea of putting together a 'miscellany' of stories and poems which she held in draft.

In August 1978, to the surprise of organisers, she agreed to attend a writers' conference in Wellington sponsored by PEN. She had decided to go, she told Anton Vogt, because it was the first national gathering of writers since 1959. 'I remember that almost every writer I used to meet used to talk of that conference as something special, and so many of these writers are now dead. I'm going as a kind of private memorial gesture.'[111] Those who were *not* dead and who would be participating included poet Allen Curnow, past and current *Listener* editors Monte Holcroft and Ian Cross, and Karl Stead, who would deliver what turned out to be the most seminal paper of the conference, on 'modern and modernist in recent New Zealand poetry'.[112] Sargeson, invited as a guest of honour, declined to attend because of poor health. Stead, aware of some residue from his spat with Frame over 'The Triumph of Poetry' sixteen years earlier, suggested that they meet for lunch in the course of the weekend.[113]

She went first to Wanganui, to spend a week with her sister and brother-in-law, and then on to Wellington, where she stayed again at the Baxters. She attended only two sessions of the conference, and scuttled away when the chairman of one of these good-heartedly but disastrously drew the audience's attention to the fact that she was present and welcomed her.[114] As she told Bill Brown, however, she came away feeling 'in love with Wellington'. She enjoyed the company of the Baxter family, as she always did, and the meal with Stead. 'We are friends again and we get on very well together. He is . . . still happily married to the same wife with the same children.'[115]

August was also the month in which her seven-year book publishing drought broke with the appearance of *Living in the Maniototo* in the United States. It was dedicated to 'my dear friends living and dead who will know'. As on previous occasions, the first review to come to the attention of New Zealand readers was that in *Time*. Seeing it, Sargeson told one of his friends that Frame had been a worry to him for years on account of being 'a non-publishing writer . . . However — never to be calculated on as usual — there she is with two pages in *Time*, her photograph and a "rave" review headed "The Diary of a Mad Widow" . . . Please God may this time the public . . . cotton on.'[116]

It was an exaggeration to describe the notice by R.Z. Sheppard as a 'rave'. But it was, as Sargeson noted, the lead review, surmounted by a desert landscape painted by Yves Tanguy, and favourable. The Maniototo might be a desert-like plain in Central Otago, Sheppard noted, but it was also a region in the 'wonderfully deranged mind of the novel's narrator, herself a chimera of identities. She is, at various stages, Violet Pansy Proudlock, a ventriloquist; Mavis Barwell, widow of a plumber; a Mrs Halleton, widow of a French teacher turned debt collector; and Alice Thumb, a novelist.'

The far-flung settings of the book are straightforward. A suburb of Auckland, New Zealand, is dominated by a North American-style shopping mall called Heavenfield — 'a huge windowless pretense, as much an insinuation of Elsewhere as its own name or that of the city or of the restaurant, Manhattan, at its entrance'. Baltimore, Md., death place of Edgar Allan Poe, is recognisable, with its gray asphalt, red brick and black iron gratings, as are the affluent hills of Berkeley, 'passing through a "wilderness" phase where it was fashionable to let meadow grass and herbs grow as they pleased, and the wild creatures come and go in the gardens and on the hillside roads.'

There, in the guise of novelist Alice Thumb, the narrator accepts an invitation from an elderly couple to use their house while they vacation in Italy . . . Suddenly it all belongs to Alice. A lawyer calls to say that her hosts have been killed in an Italian earthquake and that she is the sole heir. She is also advised that the departed had invited four others to use the house, and that it would be kind if Alice let them come. When they arrive, she becomes distracted from her work in progress and and writes instead about her guests . . .

The review concluded that Frame's art 'shows little shyness. It boldly confronts the isolation and private logic of madness, and shows how aberration, anguish and longing can be turned into lucid fiction . . . Visions of brave new worlds are many, but Frame makes them newer with a brew of personal lyricism, broad cultural allusion and sudden chills.'[117]

All of which could have been said to constitute a triumphant return to the publishing stage. But Frame, as she had done in the past, became fixated not on the compliments but on the elements of the review that annoyed her, particularly the 'Mad Widow' headline. That would contribute to her difficulties with doctors, she told John Money, 'for their first idea is my "reputation" of being dotty . . . [But] I'm so desperate for money that if it brings sales, who cares? . . . I liked the illustration of the desert painting — he's a favourite painter of mine. And, secretly, I do feel rather proud that I wrote about the desert [in the novel] and I've never been to it.'[118]

Other reviews contributed to the most respectful and favourable consensus she had yet achieved in the United States. Margaret Atwood in the *New York Times Book Review* called the book's voice 'quirky, rich, eccentric, nervous and sometimes naive, like a cross between Patrick White's novels and Stevie Smith's poems. It is also, in its own terms, authentic, [leaving] the reader feeling that the author has pulled it off.'[119] The *New Yorker* deemed it 'a clever, high-spirited performance . . . that [keeps] her readers happily alert to the cross-currents of her intellect, her imagination, and her memory'.[120] Elizabeth Wheeler in the *Los Angeles Times* said the book was 'not an easy [novel] but a good one'. And *Kirkus Review* called it a 'playful, deft work . . . by a writer of eccentric strengths'.[121]

Closer to home, Karl Stead, who had borrowed Frame's advance copy of the novel to write the review for the *Melbourne Age*, said that *Maniototo*, for all its diversity, was 'a coherent single work, because in all its parts and through all its registers there is consistently the quality of Frame's mind, a rare and beautiful intelligence'. He went on to suggest that, in her hands, fiction 'challenges its own genre, questions its own "reality", and finally collapses in upon itself'.[122]

In a letter to Frame, Stead said that he had enjoyed the novel greatly and was having fun 'identifying' some of the characters: he recognised elements of James K. Baxter, the deceased Taranaki writer Ronald Hugh Morrieson, and Katherine Mansfield, and, in the 'Watercress family', traces of the Mansons, sponsors of the Katherine Mansfield Fellowship. 'All irrelevant, I know, but I'm enjoying these little prizes you planted . . . for your local readers.' After Sargeson had read the book, he told a friend that Frame 'finally clinches her hold on the literary world with a masterpiece. God knows where her comic genius derives from, but there it is, staggeringly original, disturbingly probing . . .'[123]

Stead's enthusiasm led him to suggest that he and Frame should jointly write a novel that would begin with what had transpired at Sargeson's house twenty-five years earlier. '[I] would be Curl Skidmore; you would be Cecelia Skyways. Frank would figure as Melior Fabro, or the old master . . . I would write the first 20 pages and send it back to you and then you would write the next 20 . . .'[124] Frame thought the idea a good one. 'Seriously, that time should be recorded before it's forgotten.'[125] But neither writer again raised the suggestion of collaboration and Stead wrote the novel *All Visitors Ashore* on his own, published to some controversy in 1984.

There was still no sign of would-be publishers for *Living in the Maniototo* in England or New Zealand. Frame told the Vogts that she had written to Reeds saying she had a new book, but that 'they didn't give me much hope about their prospect of publishing it'.[126] Her now sole agent, Carl Brandt in New York, undertook to try to find a London publisher; and to do this he enlisted the help of A.M. Heath as sub-agents, even though, officially, they no longer acted for Frame. It would be a further eighteen months before anything was arranged for these markets. In the meantime, there were no proposals from any quarter to bring earlier work back into print.

After the conference in Wellington, Frame, tired of waiting on Internal Affairs for a decision about financial assistance and, still unable to work uninter-ruptedly because of the noise bombarding her property, decided to spend her Braziller advance for *Maniototo* on a quick trip to England with her sister. After all, she told John Money, she was now fifty-five years old. '[According] to the pattern of longevity, I have only about ten more years to live . . . so why not fling?'[127] More seriously, she was worried about Peter Dawson, now in her eighty-sixth year, who had just written to Frame in her role as friend and beneficiary of her estate. 'I sensed in her letter a need to have — perhaps — a final talk over affairs to set her mind at rest . . . I plan to do all I can to make the old lady cosy & warm for the coming winter — like in a fairy tale . . .'[128] Frame and June Gordon would leave from Auckland on 28 September, stay two nights in Los Angeles (from where she would telephone Brown and Wonner), then fly on to London, arriving on 1 October. They would stay a week in the capital, then a week in Norfolk with Dawson, then return to London until 23 October. They would be back in New Zealand less than a month after their departure.

It was the first time that the sisters had travelled abroad together and — for the most part — they enjoyed the trip as an opportunity to get to know each other again, away from the demands and distractions of other family members. 'We didn't quarrel and we laughed a lot,' Frame reported to Bill Brown, though she said she had been disturbed by what she viewed as a sense of competitiveness on June's part. '[This] could make her say a simple sentence like, "I wake up at four", and imply a better person, a better world and the superiority of waking up at four beside all other hours.'[129] The very fact that Frame noticed and commented on such behaviour, of course, meant that the competitiveness was mutual — and normal between siblings.

In Norfolk Frame stayed in the caravan at Dawson's and June in an adjacent hotel. They found the old lady 'still amazing, cycling to and fro into town'. Frame spent concentrated time with her old friend, reading, and meditating, at Dawson's suggestion, on the Lord's Prayer. Those meditations, she told Dawson afterwards, 'exhausted you and me, yet something intangible came out of them, and the kind of memory that one cherishes for its richness. It's like the memory of books read for the first time.'[130]★

In London, Frame was distressed that when she and June visited the A.M. Heath office, nobody seemed to know who she was, or to care — which strengthened her conviction that her previous professional relationship had been with Patience Ross rather than with the agency. This setback was compensated for by the length and quality of the time she was able to spend with Bob Cawley. 'He appeared to be so well, and happy, more so than . . . I've ever seen him . . . [He's] suggested I write a number of autobiographical essays which, together with numerous notes, [he hopes] to make into a book which might help give me some kind of income.'[131]

Indeed, Cawley proposed a series of essays by Frame 'to be followed by comments and miscellany from documents in my [Cawley's] possession. I should think a "notebook" form is very suitable . . . I suggest that you do not at this stage write to Seacliff, Sunnyside or Avondale . . . If we need anything from them I could . . . write if you felt you would rather not.'[132] So enthused was Cawley about this idea, as a means by which his star patient could finally clear away all misunderstandings about her 'illness' *and* generate more substantial income, that he wrote for advice to Iris Murdoch, a friend of a friend. Murdoch replied cautiously: 'Much would depend on how long the case history section was and how it cohered with the rest . . . [Any] publisher might take it . . . if it was vivid enough . . . I wish Miss Frame luck.'[133]

This was an idea that Frame would very soon pursue. And her appetite to pursue it had been sharpened by the behaviour of her general practitioner in Stratford and by the 'Mad Widow' headline in *Time*. But all immediate thoughts of future work were postponed by the fact that when she got home there was a reply from the Department of Internal Affairs to her appeal for financial assistance.

What the department offered her was not the purchase of her literary papers,

---

★ Continuing their joint reflections on the prayer, Frame sent Dawson this quotation from Simone Weil when she returned home: 'The Our Father contains all possible petitions; we cannot conceive of any prayer which is not already contained in it. It is to prayer what Christ is to humanity. It is impossible to say it once though, giving it the fullest possible attention to each word, without a change, infinitesimal perhaps but real, taking place in the soul.' (JF to EPD, 27/2/80.)

but a straight grant of $7500 towards buying another house in quieter surroundings. '[So] my dream of denouncing everyone and leaving has fallen through,' she told Bill Brown, 'and now that the buying is sort of "official", "government-sponsored", as it were, I have to go carefully.'[134] But she was relieved; and she now, with the help of her sister and brother-in-law, mounted an intensive search in Wanganui for a house that met her requirements and was affordable.

In a little over a month she managed to sell the Stratford property (to the local postman) and buy another in Wanganui for the exact sum of money she had available from the sale and the grant. The new house — and this time it *was* newer than the one she was vacating — was a 1950s bungalow with a stucco exterior. It stood on a corner section in a suburb, Gonville, that was dominated by box-like state houses and retired couples or families on low incomes. The street, Andrews Place, was a cul-de-sac, and the property had 'a huge palm, a pohutukawa [in flower when she moved in], two apple-laden trees, a laden lemon tree [and] an oleander . . . all on a small piece of land halfway between the city (only 38,000 population) and the sea, and at night I can hear the surf of the Tasman (so much wilder than the Pacific)'.[135]

Frame was ensconced before Christmas 1979 and — while Wanganui was also the home of the Gordons, the Baileys and a cousin on the Godfrey side, a music teacher named Barbara Lewis — she did not feel crowded. 'The city is big enough for all of us,' she told John Money, 'and I enjoy being tucked away . . . in the corner.'[136] She also enjoyed, she admitted, a restoration of local telephone access to her sister, which cost nothing. On Boxing Day, twenty-one seagulls circled the street and then landed on her neighbour's roof. 'It looked like a scene from that movie *The Birds*. Then they flew away back to the sea, which is only a mile or two from here.'[137] This proved to be an excess of romanticism. The birds, as she would soon learn, came from the Balgownie Swamp and the municipal rubbish dump, which lay behind a row of trees a few hundred yards away, considerably closer than the sea. But the birds did provide an illusion of proximity to the natural world; the misunderstanding was a metaphor worthy of a Frame novel.

# A Change of Direction

$\mathcal{W}$ANGANUI HAD BEEN A COMMUNITY ON THE FRONTIER OF Maori–European contact and conflict in the nineteenth century. It developed near the mouth of the Whanganui River in the 1840s as an 'overflow' settlement from the town of Wellington. Relations between the two races there were at times cooperative, at times acrimonious. Fighting higher up the river in the mid-1860s forced local Maori to take positions for or against the Crown. Resulting divisions between and among the communities along the Whanganui River were still apparent in the twentieth century; and many Maori were offended by a monument in the city, at Moutoa Gardens, that exalted those who had 'died in defence of law and order against fanaticism and barbarism'.[1]

Wanganui became a city in 1924. It had grown initially as a port, and as a service centre for the region's farms (predominantly sheep and cattle, but some dairying too). Secondary industries grew out of these primary ones: a meatworks at Gonville, within smell, if not sight, of Frame's home in 1980; plus a meat-packing plant at Castlehill, flour mills, cake and pastry manufacturers, and dairy and biscuit factories. Many of these industries employed Maori. But the importance of the city declined through the twentieth century as land transport replaced coastal shipping. The association between Maori and Pakeha remained uneasy; and it became more uncomfortable through the 1980s as government economic restructuring reduced employment opportunities and a national renaissance of Maori culture made the indigenous people more assertive about what they saw as their rightful place in the community. Frame would encounter reverberations from this volatile social equation.

As it had done in Glenfield and Stratford, Frame's choice of residence turned out to have particular significance for the Baxter family. Jim Baxter had been buried near the site of his commune at Jerusalem, which was on the bank of the Whanganui River, sixty-eight kilometres upstream from the city. And it was Jacquie Baxter, arriving to stay in the New Year of 1980, who became

Frame's first guest in the new house. Pamela and Stephen Bailey drove Baxter and Frame up the river road to visit the grave. 'Jim lies on a hilltop overlooking the river, under the kind of big branching walnut tree that I haven't seen since I was a child. We came home laden with ripe wild plums, a gift from the Maori family [there] — and we left with promises to return when the chestnuts on all the huge chestnut trees had ripened.'[2]

It was soon after this that Frame made contact with Maori in the city. Deciding that her lawns and garden had been too long unattended since the previous owners had departed, Frame rang a local trust, Mahi Tahi, which ran a work skills and activities programme for young unemployed people, most of whom were Maori. She had spotted the trust's advertisement in a local paper. A gang of workers arrived under the direction of Piki Takiari, an energetic volunteer and mother of six in her late thirties.

When the job was done, Takiari went to the door of Frame's house, curious that all the blinds were down in the middle of the day. Frame opened the door just wide enough to pass through an envelope containing payment. Takiari was having none of that. She put her foot forward to keep the door open, then invited herself into the house to meet and talk with the owner. After a confused discussion, which included mention of Frame's most recent book being published in North America, Takiari came away with the impression that the occupant of 3 Andrews Place was a travel writer from Canada, and that she liked her.[3]

Over the succeeding months Takiari and Frame became friends, despite this initial misunderstanding. Takiari persuaded her to enrol in classes in Maori culture at a local intermediate school; and it was when she was introducing her to another friend, arts administrator and writer Derek Schulz, that both Takiari and Schulz suddenly realised who Frame was. Schulz impressed on Takiari that 'this lady has an international reputation'; and for a time Takiari was nervous of her new friend.

Nervousness evaporated in the face of Frame's relentlessly unintimidating behaviour, however. Frame and Takiari, along with Takiari's children, Schulz and his partner, Jill Studd, and their son, Christopher, began meeting for lunches at Andrews Place. And Frame accepted invitations to accompany them to the Mahi Tahi Centre in the city; to local marae, including that at Kaiwhaiki, home of Takiari's family; and on a visit to Kaitoke Prison, where Frame read poems to the inmates, initially to the accompaniment of hoots and wolf-whistles. Frame's correspondence was soon peppered with references to activities with these friends (she told Bill Brown that Schulz and Studd were 'young, sensitive, loving');[4] and to the topics of her conversation with Takiari. She wrote to John Money, for example, that, like her, Takiari felt she was a fraud: but for a different reason — as part of a people who had undergone so much pressure to become Pakeha, but who had never been able to carry off the pretence satisfactorily.[5] To Sargeson, she said that her own style of participation at a hui was simply to go to bed and watch and listen. '[And] I hear such wonderful tales of life "up the river" in "the old days". One such tale, Takiari's, was about the time when 'breakfast was a big dish of flour sprinkled in hot water [with] mussel shells provided for spoons'.[6]

It was as a result of these experiences, Frame said later, that she had been engaged and encouraged by the resurgence of interest in Maori language and traditions. 'There has always been interest, yet too often it has been the interest of the living directed towards the presumed dead. I think it marvellous . . . that, however slowly . . . people banished to sleep, to a silence that equates with death, are [coming] alive, speaking and writing their own language and sharing its riches.'[7]

Before, after and in the course of such activities, Frame found that she was able to work. In February 1980 she announced to Peter Dawson that she had begun to write the autobiography 'which RHC talked over with me and which (he hoped) will provide daily bread that is visible'.[8] And in April, in the same letter in which she discussed her friendship with Takiari, Frame told Dawson that she had encountered resistance within herself to the act of writing autobiography. '[Yet] when I overcome the resistance, I'm enjoying it immensely, particularly the new insights and the glimpse of the pattern, the *absolute pattern* of my life, which I think would be true for everyone's life. The *wholeness* of being alive, of past present future ("because I do not hope to turn again" or "because I *do* hope to turn again"), is quite overwhelming.'[9]

At the same time there were changes occurring, in her life and in the lives of people associated with her. Frank Sargeson reported that he had had a stroke and regretted that he had not been 'knocked clean out'.[10] A deterioration became evident in the content and clarity of his letters. Denis Glover, her first publisher, *was* knocked clean out and died in Wellington in August 1980 after a further descent into the irrationalities and indignities of alcoholism. June and Wilson Gordon, to be near whom she had in part moved to Wanganui, decided in July 1980 to shift to Levin, where they had set up in practice as hypnotherapists ('specialising in providing relief from nervous tension and distressing habits . . . blush, travel sickness, bed wetting, shyness').[11] Frame appeared slightly embarrassed by this development in their lives. Meanwhile the Government, as a consequence of representations from the Literary Fund, increased her annuity to $1500 a year (just under $30 per week).[12] And the fund itself decided to award Frame $2000 a year for four years from its own budget, to provide her with what they judged to be a more adequate level of support until she became eligible for superannuation in 1984.[13]

No sooner had Frame digested the news of these increases in income than she learned that *Living in the Maniototo* had won the $2000 New Zealand Book Award for fiction, even though it had yet to be published in New Zealand (a fact which led subsequently to a change in the conditions of the competition). Delighted, she used the windfall to buy another motorcycle, this time a Suzuki F50. And the award became the occasion for her first interview by the local daily paper, the *Wanganui Chronicle*, which Frame used to voice her standard complaints about noise. 'You wouldn't let a stranger into your house without knocking, so why let noise come in uninvited?' Her favourite among all her books, she remarked, was *Mona Minim and the Smell of the Sun*, which had so far been published only in the United States. 'Editors who decide what children's books should be published . . . are all women and they've got a thing about insects. They don't like them. I've been told, "Well, if you'd written about rabbits" . . .'

> She won't say what she is working on at present. Her front door stays locked at all times and the room where she writes is out of bounds to all comers. It's the most private place of a very private house and she plans to keep it that way . . . [None] of her books is in print in this country. The novel which won her this week's award . . . was published in America and she doesn't know if it will ever appear on the shelves of local bookstores.[14]

This last comment voiced her major worry at this time: the lack of any planning or rationale in her publishing career. Although Braziller reprinted *Scented Gardens for the Blind* and *A State of Siege* for the American market in 1980, New Zealand editions of her books were out of print and — in addition to the absence of sales — she was concerned that library holdings of her work would diminish as worn-out volumes could not be replaced, and her Authors Fund payments would drop accordingly. There were still no plans to publish *Maniototo* in Britain or New Zealand; but the Women's Press in London, which had been established in 1977 by a young New Zealand-born publisher, Stephanie Dowrick, had told Carl Brandt that they were keen to republish *Faces in the Water* and 'one other' Frame novel. There was still no sign of income from the Australian paperback of *Owls Do Cry*, even though it was still in print.

What Frame needed, of course, was an energetic literary agent to coordinate and promote publication of her books, old and new. All she had was Brandt and Brandt in New York, who were not in a favourable position to sell her work outside the United States nor, really, within that country, so long as George Braziller had a stranglehold there on all Frame's books. And, with Patience Ross gone from A.M. Heath, and that company's failure to recognise her when she had called at the London office in 1979, Frame was reluctant to allow her former agents to act in any way for her, even as sub-agents for Brandt and Brandt.[15]

Eventually it was Stephanie Dowrick's personal enthusiasm for Frame's fiction that broke the pack-ice in which her career outside the United States had been frozen. Dowrick, thirty-three years old in 1980, had read *Owls Do Cry* and *Faces in the Water* before she left New Zealand in 1964. She had found them 'deeply mysterious, enormously attractive and unforgettable'. When, as publisher for the Women's Press, she discovered that there were virtually no editions of Frame's work available in Britain and the Commonwealth, she felt 'a useful feeling of outrage that someone as talented as that should be so overlooked and marginalised'.[16] So she inquired of W.H. Allen about *Faces in the Water*, and this led to her negotiations for that book with Brandt and Brandt and (on their behalf) A.M. Heath. A contract was signed in September 1980 for a paperback edition of *Faces*, with an advance to Frame of three hundred and fifty pounds; and this led the Women's Press to bid also for British and Commonwealth rights to *Living in the Maniototo*, for which a contract for a hardback edition was signed in March 1981, with an author's advance of five hundred pounds. The Women's Press had an agent in New Zealand, Hutchinson, who would initially distribute editions of Frame's books there.

This association of Frame, the Women's Press and Hutchinson led to their publishing, in addition to *Faces* and *Maniototo*, *Scented Gardens for the Blind* in 1982, *You Are Now Entering the Human Heart* (stories, 1984), and *Owls Do Cry* (1984), all in paperback; and all three of Frame's autobiographies in hardback in, respectively, 1983, 1984 and 1985. And, from 1984, Hutchinson, under a succession of name changes (Century Hutchinson, then Random House), became and remained Frame's publisher in New Zealand.

While republication of *Faces in the Water* was being negotiated between agencies and publishers (it would appear in London before the end of 1980), Frame continued work on her autobiography — but far more slowly than she had anticipated. Part of the difficulty was a recurrence of her old problem: neighbourhood noise. Other occupants of the cul-de-sac, whose hobby was 'fixing up' cars and motorbikes, made themselves a tight motorcycle track on the front of their section and drove round it 'day in, day out. I'm sure I invite this kind of thing in some mysterious way.'[17]

She was also dismayed that the autobiographical book 'seemed to get longer and longer, and I'm lonely for fiction'.[18] Frame had begun the narrative at the beginning of her life and written down everything she could remember. What seemed like near-total recall began to alarm her, so she stepped back to plan the book in a series of sequences and chapters, and then wrote to this plan. By the latter part of 1980 she had concluded that what she had envisaged as a single book was likely to be far too long and to absorb too much of her time. So she then began to think in terms of a multi-volumed work, possibly as many as five books. By November she was admitting that there were 'days and days when I do anything rather than face it; and I'm only up to my twenty-second year . . . Last evening, however, I swallowed my distaste . . . and read this first volume [and] although I know it is a complete bore . . . a picture did emerge . . .'[19]

Her intention now was to complete volume one and several rewrites of the manuscript, then reward herself with a quick trip to England and the United States from April to June 1981. If she stayed away longer than three months her annuity payments would stop.

She was pleased when National Radio in New Zealand commissioned readings of *A State of Siege* by the fine actress Pat Evison, for which she as author was paid $275. And this broadcast and its subsequent availability to schools on tape led to negotiations for an Australian edition of that novel from Angus and Robertson (eventually published in 1982). Dealing with arrangements for the cassette broadcast led Frame to exclaim to one of the Braziller editors that, 'I get so weary of business correspondence because it interferes with my ordinary work, and I do tend to put things out of my mind to give myself some peace from all these decisions and answerings of mail.'[20]

Less than a fortnight after writing this, in July 1980, Frame received a letter from Ray Richards of Auckland, a former publisher who was now acting as New Zealand's sole literary agent. 'If it would be helpful to you to have the services of [an] agent I would be pleased and honoured to assist, without commission or charge to yourself, and without anyone else knowing that such an arrangement had been made.'[21] This good-hearted offer initially seemed to Frame to be simply one more unwelcome piece of business requiring her attention. But it generated a correspondence which helped her concentrate on ways in which her publishing affairs might be reorganised in the interests of simplicity and financial advantage, and she told Richards more than once that it was a considerable relief to have someone 'help with these matters. Such worries do interfere with daily work.'

Frame had two trips out of Wanganui in the second half of 1980: to Wellington in August, to see a visiting John Money ('he has a perm and his hair looks wild and curly, which [gives] him a frenzied air');[22] and to Auckland in November, largely to spend time with an increasingly frail Frank Sargeson. '[He's] isn't seeing anyone, because he's embarrassed about certain disabilities the strokes have brought . . . He does need some kind of help with domestic things, but I know that only a man would have some offer like that accepted.'[23] At this time too she announced that she had fallen in love again with Auckland — 'chiefly because the trees have grown [and] the place is not so barren-looking . . . [If] I could, I'd return to live on the North Shore.'[24]

One reason she considered such a move at this time was a conviction that Sargeson did not have long to live. The letters they wrote to each other in the wake of the 1980 visit were especially tender, with no residue of the issues or spats that had once divided them. '[My] own brand of inspired lunacy has a relationship to your own, which until lately I hadn't been aware of,' Sargeson wrote in November. 'Of course I could never come within cooee of what you do in Maniototo . . . [But] when I think of your future years and career . . . Well!!!'[25] He was even able to joke that he saw himself turning into a character in one of her novels.[26] Frame responded by reminding him that she was 'forever grateful for the help you gave me . . . and if there's anything, even the littlest or biggest thing that I can do for you, just say so, please'.[27]

Frame still took time off work to make occasional visits to Piki Takiari and her team at the Mahi Tahi centre in town; and to provide lunches at Andrews Place for the Takiaris and Derek Schulz and Jill Studd and their children —

'raspberry and Boston buns, sandwiches and lots of gossip'.[28] She also took recreation on her new motorcycle, using it cautiously at first for shopping expeditions, then with increasing confidence and enjoyment on Wanganui's back roads. 'You [become] a projectile and suffer enormous loss of body temperature and so, without knowing it, can have hypothermia. I think that is the cause of much erratic . . . riding — you become euphoric. Even at forty k's an hour, with warm clothes on, I [feel] myself becoming reckless.'[29]

After Christmas, which she spent alone and in bed with a virus, Frame attempted and achieved her most ambitious ride ever: from Wanganui to the Gordons in Levin, and — after a bus trip to and from Wellington — home again on the motorcycle. She had ridden a total of 264 kilometres, all at 'a steady 30 km an hour . . . [It] was like sailing on the sea whenever a huge lorry passed farting its wind-wave on my face. I managed to keep upright.'[30] In Wellington she had stayed with the Baxters and visited her Aunty Polly, now aged ninety and confined to hospital; the old lady died the following month and Frame returned to Wellington by bus for the funeral. 'Like most of the family,' she told John Money, '[Polly] never had much to do with the little horrors that the Frames [became], and so when she gave up trying to teach us etiquette, we didn't know her very well.'[31]

Back home Frame pressed on with the 'autobiographical essay'. She had now decided to close volume one with the end of her school days in Oamaru. By February 1981 she was on to her second typing of the manuscript, which she estimated would run to about seventy thousand words. The usual distractions plagued her. An official from the Ministry of Foreign Affairs wrote seeking permission to publish one of her stories, 'The Lagoon', in an anthology to be published by the Australia New Zealand Literary Society of Japan. Because the book came into the category of 'cultural promotion', there would be no fee. Frame declined permission for the use of her story, but went on to say that she hoped her fellow writers would receive payment for the inclusion of *their* work. 'It is, after all, their profession, and their annual income is on the lowest scale in this country. If they are to become a charitable institution, then might it not be wise for the Inland Revenue Department to exempt them from tax?'[32]

A more serious problem was that the Department of Internal Affairs was four months late issuing cheques for the previous year's Authors Fund payments. Waiting to find out what she *would* be paid, Frame told Sargeson, was torture.[33] And in this state of mind she wrote a miserable letter to George Braziller.

I'm beginning to wonder why I bother getting my work published . . . [It] is arrogant of me ever to have supposed that I might make a living from it. When your statements come in from Brandt they are only depressing as I note that . . . I have still not made up the advance on books published nearly twenty years ago . . . My total [American] earnings are about $150 a year . . . I'm giving serious thought to making changes in my publishing 'career' . . . dispensing with or changing the agent and [having books] published in New Zealand at the same time as anywhere else.[34]

This last decision was reached as a result of her correspondence with Ray Richards, who had worked out that even her publishing arrangements with the Women's Press unnecessarily disadvantaged her. Because the editions of *Faces in the Water* and *Living in the Maniototo* being published in London were Commonwealth ones, her income from New Zealand sales was paid at a lower 'export rate'; in addition, because money was channelled from London, to Brandt and Brandt in New York, and finally to New Zealand, she was liable for taxation in all three countries, including on money earned from New Zealand sales. Ray Richards' advice was that she should have publication of future work initiated from New Zealand; and that she should retain a local agent rather than an American one. Carl Brandt agreed, and he wrote to Tim Curnow, son of poet Allen Curnow, who ran the Curtis Brown office in Sydney, and asked if he would act for Frame.[35] Curnow was delighted to agree — the more so because of his slight family association with her (they had met when Frank Sargeson brought Frame round to the Curnow household in Takapuna in 1955). Ironically, Curnow also knew Ray Richards, who had given him a job in publishing and then sent him to Australia to represent A.H. and A.W. Reed, where he had been recruited for Curtis Brown.[36]

Frame then had to explain to Ray Richards that, despite his good advice offered free of charge over the previous year, she had decided to sign up with Curtis Brown for the usual agency commission arrangements. 'I do have to protect myself, as I have so little confidence . . . in the area beyond my desk and my typewriter . . . [For] me, the ideal condition would be never to submit a manuscript anywhere, let alone to anyone in my own country, as one's fellow countrypeople, being "family", tend to be insensitive in their statements.'[37] This last remark was a reference to Richards having referred to *Mona Minim* as an 'old book'. The upshot was, Frame was saying, she felt that she could cope with an agent living as far away as Sydney, but not one living as close as Auckland. She was also, inevitably, influenced by the fact that Carl Brandt recommended Curtis Brown because he knew of Tim Curnow, whereas he had never heard of Richards. And so, by the end of 1981, Frame would be a Curtis Brown author, whose business was administered from the agency's Sydney office. This would prove to be a sound move for her 'career'.[38]

Frame's reputation and sales were given another potential boost by the publication of a brief but admiring book on her fiction by Margaret Dalziel, her former colleague at the University of Otago. This was part of an Oxford University Press 'New Zealand writers and their work' series aimed at the education market, which had already produced volumes on James K. Baxter, Charles Brasch, Denis Glover and Frank Sargeson.[39] The placing of Frame in this company was further recognition that she was now seen as holding a place in the country's literary canon. Its value to Frame was potential rather than actual, however, given that all her books other than *Owls Do Cry* were unavailable in New Zealand except through libraries.

Meanwhile, to boost her sagging morale, Frame decided to accept another offer of a plane ticket from Bill Brown and to make a three-month trip to England and the United States beginning in April 1981. En route for Auckland by bus, however, she became ill with her customary motion sickness, and with what appeared to be a severe panic attack. She cancelled the trip within days of flying out to San Francisco. 'It's an awful disappointment,' she told Peter Dawson. 'I had *suspected* that my travelling days were over but I'd been unwilling to face the fact . . . I'll mourn the loss of seeing you, and of never again seeing Dr Cawley, my beloved RHC.'

> I have a very curious feeling about all this . . . [The] Maori people I know gave me a lovely farewell before I set out, and at the last moment one of them came forward and put a whalebone ornament which belongs to them around my neck, saying it was full of mana and very precious and ordinarily stayed in Wanganui, but they were handing it to me so that it would see me safely through my travels until I returned . . . Maybe the ornament wanted to go home? 'The fault, dear Brutus, is not in our stars but in ourselves . . .'[40]

And so she remained in Wanganui for a winter of writing; and to become involved in the most tumultuous period of civil unrest that her country had seen since the days of the Great Depression.

The mid-year months of 1981 came to be known as New Zealand's Winter of Discontent. It was the time of the last visit of a Springbok rugby team in the apartheid era; and views on the desirability and morality of the tour split the country into two vigorously opposed factions. Frame was against the tour — because it implied participation in South Africa's racist policies, because of the degree of acrimony it generated within New Zealand, and because of the damage done to the country's reputation abroad.

'Things are in rather a turmoil here,' she told Bill Brown, 'the twentieth century has caught up with us at last and the next few months may be violent.'[41] On 3 July an anti-tour mobilisation campaign drew 75,000 people into the streets nationally. In Wanganui 300 turned out for the march, Frame among them. 'She wore her multi-coloured hand-knitted hat and scarf,' Derek Schulz noted in his journal. 'She positively glowed, looking as if she had stepped off an Oamaru street [on] Friday night.' The march was peaceful, with demonstrators spread four- or five-wide across the main street. At the close of speeches, however, Frame was 'suddenly recognised, which set up a buzz in the crowd as people began to gather around to talk to her. At first she was okay, but then suddenly [turned] in a panic to ask if she could be taken home.'[42]

A month later Frame was describing to Brown the manner in which the tour itself was unfolding.

[There] have been large demonstrations as each match is played, with every rugby ground arranged by the army as a kind of prison camp, and countless police shoulder to shoulder ringing the ground and within it: an awfully depressing sight. Last week the police set to and beat *peaceful* demonstrators about the head with their batons — gashed heads, blood flying, screams and so on . . . The awful shame is that today the team is playing my town, Wanganui, which is a fairly sleepy conservative place, but yesterday the team and the police (800–1500 from out of town) arrived and suddenly the town is a police state with the rugby ground being protected. There's to be a silent vigil which mightn't be all that peaceful as the rugby heavies are out to 'get' the protesters. I'm hoping a radical group of demonstrators will successfully stop the tour and let us get on with our lives.[43]

Frame attended the vigil with Pamela Bailey, and they were both disappointed when protesters from outside Wanganui took it over and used megaphones to hurl abuse at tour supporters. Frame was more comfortable with other forms of protest action. She sent a telegram to the government, asking them to show 'vision and imagination' by cancelling the tour;[44] and she wrote a ballad for the *Wanganui Chronicle* ostensibly sung by a man named Footy Pool, who bore some resemblance to the chairman of the New Zealand Rugby Union. It ended:

> But I am only an ordinary bloke
> more ordinary than most
> my freedom is such that I'm not really free
> to count the human cost.
> I repeat that I'm only an ordinary bloke
> and I wouldn't ask for more,
> so please don't give me responsibility,
> just give me the rugby score.[45]

The tour ground on. By the time the final match was over on 12 September, it had provoked 'more than 200 demonstrations in 28 centres involving in excess of 150,000 people [and] over 1500 people were charged with tour-related offences'.[46] The spectacle had left Frame drained and unnerved. Long after the Springboks had gone she pronounced herself to be 'still recovering' from it. [47]

To her embarrassment, when the Women's Press edition of *Living in the Maniototo* had arrived at last in New Zealand in August 1981, it shared the booksellers' best-seller list with *The Encyclopaedia of New Zealand Rugby*. The novel had attracted generally favourable reviews in Britain two months earlier, with especially enthusiastic notices in the *Daily Telegraph* ('a many-layered palimpsest of a book . . . as near a masterpiece as we are likely to see this year') and the *Guardian* ('puts everything else that has come my way this year right in the shade').[48] The New Zealand reception too was admiring, though somewhat muted, possibly because it had won the fiction section of the New Zealand Book Awards a year ahead of its availability (a fact some reviewers mentioned in what sounded like aggrieved tones).

Frame's attention, however, was concentrated now on the autobiography; and by August 1981 she was working on volume two, 'my student days . . . The quality of my memory deteriorates, unfortunately, after my shock treatments in hospital.'[49] She warned John Money that he would feature in the current book, but said that she would give him a pseudonym, as she had done for her brother in volume one, so as 'to not draw attention to him as a living person'.[50] By late August, however, she had returned to volume one, to type it for the third time. Rather than wait until all three volumes were ready, she now decided to despatch the first one so as to generate some much needed income.[51] She had promised it to the Women's Press, though asked that it be published simultaneously 'in New Zealand', so that local sales would not be treated as British earnings. The first person to whom she sent the manuscript, however, now tentatively titled 'Children of the Is-Land' and running to 65,000 words, was George Braziller. And because it was her first non-fiction book, she awaited his response with more than usual trepidation. When it came, it moved her greatly:

> Finishing your manuscript I burst into tears. What were the tears for? Was it for myself or was it for the joy and privilege of sharing your life and experience over the many years? I was once asked about my epitaph. I replied [that] I wanted to be known as the publisher of Janet Frame.[52]

The Women's Press was now headed by Ros de Lanerolle (Stephanie Dowrick had moved to Australia, but remained involved in the company as a director). In November 1981, maintaining Dowrick's intention to bring more of Frame's earlier work back into print, de Lanerolle proposed a three-book contract that would result in the republication of *Scented Gardens* and *Owls Do Cry* and the production of a new book of stories.[53] Within weeks of this news Tim Curnow took over as Frame's agent and steered these proposals, and future ones, through the processes of negotiation and publication.

Curnow wrote to Frame on 9 December, reminding her of their meeting in his childhood and expressing delight that they would now be working together. '[We] will use the Sydney office and the London office to represent you in the British Commonwealth market . . . [Our] long term strategy would be to find a publisher . . . prepared to keep the bulk of your work in print with the better selling titles supporting some of those which may not sell as well.'[54] He asked to see the manuscript of the autobiography as soon as possible; and he confirmed that Frame's previous American agency arrangements with Brandt and Brandt would continue.

By this time Frame was ready for relief from a chain of circumstances that she had found gruelling — the Springbok tour, interrupted work on the two manuscripts and a general election that had confirmed the National Government in office. Despite the collapse of her travel plans earlier in the year she decided to attempt another American trip, taking advantage of Bill Brown's renewed offer to pay her fare. To her delight, she was accepted for a place at Yaddo in February and March 1982, and she determined to get herself there to work on volume two of the autobiography and — she hoped — on some new fiction.[55] She would spend the preceding month with Brown and Wonner in San Francisco. In preparation for these new ventures, she sold her motor cycle and bought a new typewriter.

In the weeks before her departure at the end of December, she had two pleasant experiences. One was that Piki Takiari's Mahi Tahi group asked her to be their patron; the second was a 'farewell lunch' with her Wanganui friends just before Christmas. Derek Schulz recorded:

> [Janet] had loaded two tables with food. On the one, rare and subtle tasting farm baked pioneer foods, meat loaf and jellied carrot and salad and date loaf, all carefully measured for their calories; and on the other table the 'pig it down' creams and pastries. Jan and I between us polished off a complete plate of cream puffs one after the other as she talked . . . She sat in her chair amidst the clutter of her small living room, dashing out for another bottle of drink for [the children] . . . Young, good humoured and quiet Debbie Noble sat on the sofa and said not a thing . . . Then Piki arrived with two others and her children, piling even more food on the tables and sitting on the floor cross-legged and serious. Finally we left, Jan seeing us out to the car, suddenly intimate, almost taking Jill by the arm and smiling with affection and sadness. One wave and she disappears . . .[56]

Frame headed for the Gordons in Levin on 30 December to spend New Year with them. Then on 4 January she travelled by train to Auckland, from where she would leave for San Francisco on 8 January. In Auckland, however, she was dismayed to discover that Frank Sargeson had been taken to North Shore Hospital on 21 December, and was declining rapidly from what turned out to be a combination of heart disease, prostate cancer and senility. She visited him for short periods over three days, and he rallied occasionally to joke and talk of literary matters. But it was apparent that his faculties were shutting down. At the end of one of her visits Sargeson gestured towards the hospital reception desk and said, 'Some time we must have a Chinese meal from this place.'[57]

'I sincerely feel that if I can be of any help even in brief daily hellos I would cancel my trip or shorten it,' Frame wrote to Sargeson's neighbour, Kath Tremain, 'for I more or less owe Frank my life — that sounds dramatic, but it's true'.[58] To Karl Stead she reported that 'I'm thinking of him all the time . . . Is there any way that he can not be so separated from his old surroundings?'[59] Hospital staff assured her that Sargeson's current condition might remain unchanged for many months; and that there was nothing really that she could do by remaining there. Other friends, including the Steads, would visit; and Christine Cole Catley, Frank's executor, was due shortly from the South Island, where she had just buried her own husband. And so, Frame concluded, 'What better can I do but continue the tradition of writing and spend the time writing?'[60] With frequent backward glances over her shoulder and concern about what lay ahead for her old friend, she flew to San Francisco at the end of the first week in January 1982. She knew that she was unlikely to see Sargeson again.

Frame's pleasure in being with Bill Brown and Paul Wonner was undercut by the awareness of Sargeson's plight, and by the acquisition of a back injury and a virus in the two weeks she stayed in San Francisco. 'I dare not seek help in this medically expensive land,' she wrote to Pamela Bailey. 'I'm just hoping they will go away.'[61] They did not. She was still ill, and still hobbling, when she reached Boston on 20 January to stay with her nephew Neil Gordon (a visiting professor at the Massachusetts Institute of Technology) and his wife, Jenny; and when she got to Rutland, Vermont, to stay with John Beston, with whom she had remained in communication since they had last met at the East West Centre conference in Hawaii. Beston and his wife, Rose Marie, kept her with them until the virus abated: Yaddo did not allow guests to arrive with any kind of communicable illness.

By 9 February she was installed at the colony, in Elizabeth Ames' old bedroom in Pine Garde, the only building open in the depth of winter. 'From my window I have a view over the pine grove and the mountainous heaps of snow . . . There are only five artists here — a young woman Japanese–American painter, another young woman painter, a young male writer, Roland Flint, a painter turned writer who is very well known here, Tobias Schneebaum, and myself.'[62] Frame was given a sharp sense of the passage of time when one of the women painters told her she reminded her of her mother.

The fellow colonist with whom she formed the closest relationship was Schneebaum, two years older than her, who had grown up in Brooklyn, had a distinguished career as a painter, and then become increasingly interested in writing after living in Mexico and Peru. He had attracted considerable attention in the United States for his book *Keep the River on Your Right*, which arose from experience in South America. Each morning at Yaddo Schneebaum and Frame arrived at the breakfast table at 7.55 am. He remembered:

> This left us alone . . . for forty minutes. On the rare occasions when one of the other guests showed up early Janet kept within herself, not saying a word. At the breakfast table, she whispered. I am also soft-spoken. We talked mostly about the personal side of our lives, with Janet talking a great deal about her time in hospital . . . She looked magnificent with her hair haloing her head. She was . . . wonderfully innocent even though she was no virgin. She was very articulate and had a splendid memory. Sometimes she said nothing but while eating was thinking out the chapter she was working on . . . In the evening she was quite different, more voluble; just a bit louder and more willing to take part in conversations. I liked her immensely.[63]

The book in question was the second volume of autobiography; and she had finished the first draft, which took her life up to the time she left New Zealand in 1956, by the first week in March 1982. That same week she received news that Frank Sargeson had died peacefully in his sleep shortly before midnight on 1 March, three weeks short of his seventy-ninth birthday. She spent the remainder of her time at Yaddo, until 17 March, writing a two-thousand-word memoir of him for the literary journal *Islands*, which took the form of a letter and overlapped in some respects with ground covered in the volume of autobiography just completed.

> You were so much a part of your many friends that it took me some time to see that you were a man apart, finally alone, on your literary estate that spilled back and forth between the printed page and your life. You were the Squire without a feudal bone in your body. Yet I sometimes thought that you were everybody's servant, maintaining command only over the inhabitants of your true literary estate — the words of the English language.[64]

To Bill Brown she wrote: 'I'm beginning to believe he organised his death very well, with a true beginning, middle and end, a Forsterian literary death following *Aspects of the Word*. As for myself, I've often wondered how it would be without Frank — the blast from the cold world enters now.'[65]

Because the effects of the virus continued to debilitate her, Frame decided to leave Yaddo early and cancel the English visit. Before departing on 17 March

1982, however, she indulged in a little whimsy. She placed on the community noticeboard a bogus guest list, supposedly of the next Yaddo intake. It read: Mary Ann Evans, Samuel Clemens, Paul Picasso, Wolf Mozart, Leonard Vinci, John Bach, Lottie Brontë, David Thoreau, Berthe Grimaulte, Willa Cather, Alex Pope, John Keats, Vincent Gogh, and Emily Dickinson ('visit cancelled for personal reasons').[66] And she sent John Money a piece of doggerel about his major professional interest:

> Be polite to your hermaphrodite
> don't beat him when he sexes
> or send him packing from your sight
> to Tennessee or Texas.
>
> A little spark though he may be
> his current surely flows
> directly or alternately
> or maybe both of those.
>
> So interfere not with his fuse
> but watch his wattage flower.
> You never know when you may lose
> your own electric power.[67]

She then spent four days in New York, where she had dinner with George Braziller and went to a film with him, *The Brothers*; and one evening with John Marquand and his companion, Susan Martin. 'I was especially sorry to miss James, who is at Harvard studying among other things History of the Middle Ages (of nations, I imagine).'[68] From there she went briefly to John Money's in Baltimore, then to Los Angeles for two nights, before flying to Auckland on 2 April. Because of her lingering illness, the Gordons met her at the airport and drove her home to Wanganui on 6 April. By compressing the trip to three months she had not forfeited her annuity payments.

At Andrews Place, things were not as satisfactory as Frame might have hoped. The gardener paid in advance to take care of her property had not done so, and was 'found out' by her early return. A neighbour's house had been burgled but not, thankfully, Frame's. Another neighbour had begun major house alterations, which promised a season of hammering and sawing. And Neg the cat came home from the cattery 'fur and bone' and weighing a mere eighteen ounces. The woman who owned the establishment offended Frame irreparably by describing her pet as 'geriatric' and 'better dead'.[69] To work off the anger generated by these combined circumstances Frame cleaned up, burned paper and threw away 'half my possessions'.[70]

Sargeson's executor, Christine Cole Catley, wrote to inform Frame that she had been left a bequest of $500 in the writer's will, news which gave her 'a boost of confidence'. Cole Catley also reported that she was setting up a charitable trust to administer the estate; and that Frank's assets would be used, with an expected government subsidy, to set up a residential writer's fellowship and preserve his house in Esmonde Road. That way he could go on helping writers 'beyond the grave'; and those who were interested would be able to view the property on which he worked with such monastic dedication for half a century. 'How eerie it will be,' Frame told Bill Brown. 'Frank didn't want this, but he knew (he once told me) that Christine would do it anyway. It will be nice to think that, as long as that part of the world exists, there will be writers . . . coming and going still where they used to, in Frank's "day". And people who used to come from all over the world to see Frank will still come.'[71]

That news cheered her. Almost at once, however, she was dashed to hear that John Money had been mugged in Baltimore while walking between Johns Hopkins and his home — 'broken nose, bashed face, injured eye . . . he appears to be recovering'.[72] Simultaneously the noise from the neighbour's alterations became louder and more disruptive and Frame was forced to turn up the volume of her record player to block it out. Other neighbours tormented her with radios and the revving of engines associated with car repairs. 'It's times like this that I think I will have to move from here.'[73] Instead, when the din became too obtrusive, Frame went for rides on her new second-hand push-bike; and, when her advance arrived from George Braziller for the American edition of her autobiography, she decided to spend it on the postponed trip to England and to take her sister with her. When she was able to work, she began to type the second draft of the second volume of memoirs. There was still no sign of advance copies of volume one.

The middle of the year was blighted for Frame by another bout of influenza. But by late August 1982 she was ready to fly to England from Auckland. June Gordon was unable to accompany her on the beginning of the trip but would join her several weeks later in London. In the meantime she and Wilson agreed to look after Neg, to avoid the unpleasant consequences of another stay in the cattery. By 2 September Frame was with Dawson at Itteringham Common after an uneventful non-stop journey. 'I really could not rest until I had seen what I could do for Miss Dawson, apart from celebrate her eighty-eighth birthday,' she wrote to Brown and Wonner.

I came armed with the usual senseless ideas and advice and suggestions, only to find that all were pretty well useless, that she has got herself into a marvellous order in the midst of marvellous disorder and is best left to carry on, even to sleep . . . up those twisty, witch-stairs, and hope she

*Carl Brandt, Frame's New York agent: young, attentive and urbane.* (Carl Brandt)

*Frame's studio in the basement of John Money's house, Baltimore.* (John Money)

Left: *Sue and John Marquand on Salt Cay: American patrons and friends.* (James Marquand)

Below: *Frame in her studio at MacDowell, New Hampshire, October 1969.* (Bill Brown)

Right: *William Theophilus Brown, gifted painter and musician and, for Frame, 'the chief experience of my life'*. (Bill Brown)

Below: *Frame with Paul Wonner, Montecito, December 1969.*
(Bill Brown)

*Menton on the French-Italian border.* (Alexander Turnbull Library)

*John Williams and
E. P. Dawson admire a
copy of* The Lagoon
*for the camera.* (Janet Frame)

Above: *Frame with John Money in Baltimore, March 1982.* (John Money)

Below: *Geordie Frame comfortably ensconced in his Willowglen house, 1987, the year before it burned down.* (Oamaru Mail)

*The four Janets: Frame on the set of the Jane Campion film* An Angel at my Table, *August 1989; with (from left) Karen Fergusson, Alexia Keogh and Kerry Fox.*
(Bridget Ikin)

Above left: *Frame with her friend Ruth Dallas, joint honorary doctors of literature, Otago University, May 1978.* (Janet Frame) Above right: *Walking the Janet Frame Heritage Trail, Oamaru, 1998.* (Michael King)

*With biographer, Michael King, Auckland 1997.*
(Anita McNaught)

Above: *Modelled in clay for an Anthony Stones head, St Clair, December 1998.* (Reg Graham)

Below: *Sibling survivors: Frame and her sister June Gordon, St Clair Beach, Dunedin, July 1999.* (Reg Graham)

won't fall . . . She is quite batty, as we all are, only it's fairly well uncovered with all the neighbours alienated and not understanding that her accusations are part of the vagaries of age, and the marvellous manoeuvre which we younger folk dare not practise, of blaming all the world for every misfortune — even the old woman next door who has somehow managed to creep in and cast a spell which makes Miss Dawson unable to ride her bike after all these years. For me, it's an exercise in lonely patience, and I'm trying to do what practical things I can such as repairing worn electric plugs and cords and clearing those everlasting English nettles.[74]

Through Dawson Frame met another local writer, John Cannon, who had just had a book published on the Brontës, *The Road to Haworth*. Frame found it 'fascinating', and reported that Cannon lived with 'his wife, his two infants, her or his senile mother, his daughter and her husband, and his ex-wife . . . We had an interesting exchange of reminiscences about Ibiza, where he used to live.'[75] Frame distracted herself from Peter Dawson's plight by 'roaming the lovely country lanes on a bicycle under the marvellously looming Norfolk sky'.[76]

In mid-September Frame returned to London to meet June Gordon, and they spent a few days together in the city before returning to Norfolk, where June stayed in a hotel close to Dawson's cottage. Then, after a further week together in London, the two sisters flew back to New Zealand via Los Angeles, from where they rang Brown and Wonner.

The very week that Frame passed through the United States on her way home, *To the Is-Land*, the book that would re-launch her career and bring her a whole new range and generation of readers, was published there. The first review, in fact, appeared in the *San Francisco Chronicle* on the very day that Frame and and her sister rang Brown and Wonner from Los Angeles. The reviewer, thriller writer Dorothy Bryant, called Frame 'one of the great writers of our time' and quoted May Sarton to the effect that the New Zealander was a genius. Why, then, was she so little known in the United States?

> I could guess at several reasons for public neglect . . . starting with geography. Writers from Canada, Australia, New Zealand and other places far from the center of publishing are often labelled 'regional', whatever that means . . . Frame does not write conventional page turners — she largely ignores the traditional plotline — but she is not hard or 'literary'. Her strengths — poetic, visual, psychological and moral — quickly reward readers who open up to them. Such readers will find . . . vivid descriptions of outer and inner weather, passages that beg to be read

aloud as poetry, a deep probing of the human psyche and a clear devotion to saving that psyche from the fate that overtakes most of us — that of drowning in our own fears and evading the challenges of life.[77]

Helen Bevington in the *New York Times Book Review* had more to say about the book itself, explaining that 'is-land' was Frame's childhood pronunciation of 'island' — but that even after she was corrected she went on thinking of it as the 'land of is', not the past or the future. In the autobiography the 'is-land' became the place of her childhood and adolescence.

It is a wistful tale, honestly and believably told, of the puzzling encounters of childhood, the recognition, the gain and the loss . . . [One] closes the book aware that if one is to know Janet Frame better . . . one must consent to follow her on her journey to as many Is-lands as there are. Yet this vivid first volume is in a real sense complete, satisfying not merely as Chapter One but as an account of the making of a writer from the beginning possessed by words.[78]

Most other American notices echoed this verdict. Elizabeth Ward in the *Washington Post Book World* said the volume was 'unpretentious yet curiously haunting' and caused the reader to 'shiver with the sense of yesterday . . . [It] is precisely the freshness with which she writes of a particular place and childhood which accomplishes this, rather than the genuinely profound concerns with time and death and language which underlie the book.'[79] The oddest comment came from *Publishers' Weekly*, which described the book as 'impressionistic; inferential; at times wryly funny; a memory bank, with only a hint of Maori . . .'[80]

The American reviews of *Is-Land* added up to a more favourable consensus than those for any of Frame's books published previously in the United States. But there were not as many of them as there generally had been for her novels, which was probably another symptom of Braziller's half-hearted attempts at promotion. Frame would achieve broader recognition there, and wider sales; but not until the release of a film based on all three volumes of her autobiography nearly a decade later. In the meantime, the reception accorded volume one could be considered a harbinger of better things to come.

Frame arrived in Wanganui on 18 October to learn that Albion Wright, her second publisher, had died early in the month after being hospitalised for asthma; and to find her home city being rocked by a series of earthquakes and waiting, she reported, 'for the big one . . . It's like being at sea, with the creaking timbers and the swaying motion . . . [We] have been told to have a supply of water, food etc. ready. Some people have left town. There is a Maori superstition that whenever British royalty visits New Zealand there is a national disaster . . .' The current visitor, she went on to explain, was Queen Elizabeth's youngest son, Prince Edward, who had just taken a tutoring position at Wanganui Collegiate school.[81]

That same week Piki Takiari and her family took Frame back to their home village of Kaiwhaiki, twenty-one kilometres from the city up the Whanganui River road. She told Bill Brown that this small community was now flourishing.

> A few years ago one might drive anywhere in the country and someone might point out a place in ruins — 'There used to be a Maori pah there.' Now the Maoris are returning to their villages which are not much different in structure from a tiny English village, or maybe a Scottish camp where one clan lives. There are several acres of land, with each member of the family or tribe having its own house and land, all centred on the meeting-house, a large hall with cooking and washing facilities, and room for about sixty people or more to sleep . . . The tiny children get their education pre-school from the elders in the meeting-house. The land is communally owned by the tribe . . . and any move made must be decided by a committee appointed by the tribe.[82]

Several weeks later Frame was playing host rather than guest as she waited for a visit from Sargeson's executor, Christine Cole Catley. She told Brown that documents establishing the Sargeson Trust would be signed before Christmas; and that Cole Catley had asked her, Frame, to apply for the first Sargeson residential fellowship as soon as applications were sought. 'I'm looking forward (with some awe) to Chris's stay, for I feel she is the nearest to Frank now, and it's nice to have a live link . . . As Frank told me . . . "If anyone can get things done it's Chris." Practical, energetic, extrovert . . .'[83]

That month, December 1982, Frame's other news was that Pamela Bailey and her family had moved to Wellington in the hope of finding better care for Josie. '[So] I am now on my own here, except for my cousin Barbara, the music teacher . . . and of course my Maori friends and the young folk at the Gallery. Derek is doing some serious writing and Jill some sculpture . . . I'm [still] working hard on my second volume of autobiography . . . Despair sets in. "The tangled tree stems scored the sky like strings from broken lyres . . ." More difficult than the single-bud simple first volume.'[84]

The next two volumes of autobiography, she told the Vogts, were being written primarily 'to set the record straight' — in particular the record of her so-called illness. '[Yet] even as I write I realise that's impossible, that records are born crooked and twisted.'[85] To John Money, she said she was incorporating the 'big impression' he had made on her when she was at university. 'For a quivering student longing for identity and aspiring to be a poet, to be given the idea . . . that most poets were "mad", to be told "when I think of you I think of Hugo Wolf, of Van Gogh . . ." gave me a certainty of direction, particularly when I found out that [they] suffered from schizophrenia.'[86]

On Christmas Day 1982 Frame was 'inevitably alone, having declined to mix and mingle . . . so it's early on Christmas morning and I've had a light breakfast, my usual, fruit and coffee and a piece of whole wheat toast; and Neg's out in the street . . . waiting to tease or be teased by passing cats . . . Inside it's cool and fresh since I made my do-it-yourself insect screens . . . to allow some relief from the summer heat and the mosquitoes from the Balgownie Swamp [and] rubbish dump . . . which now has a car crusher for use . . . eleven hours a day, six days a week, like an industrial orchestra.'[87] Frank Sargeson had once said to her that it was her fate to live next to railway lines or rubbish dumps and, at the close of 1982, that view seemed to Frame like a prophecy fulfilled.

In addition her blood pressure was up again, well over 200 over 120 — what her doctor called 'killing range'. He believed it was caused in part by her unremitting but unsuccessful attempts to write in a neighbourhood that was now full of noise. Again, she told her sister, she was contemplating a move. She was even tempted, once more, to abandon New Zealand and retreat to Peter Dawson's sanctuary in rural Norfolk.[88] Before making a decision, however, she would wait and see what the New Year brought with it.

CHAPTER TWENTY-EIGHT

# Gathering Fame

$\mathcal{T}$HE YEAR 1983 WAS A HINGE ONE FOR JANET FRAME'S CAREER AS A New Zealand author. In the New Year, despite the fact that her first book had been published more than three decades previously, she was still a reclusive writer living in a small New Zealand city, known to and read by a minority of aficionados. Apart from *Owls Do Cry* and *Faces in the Water*, her novels had sold in modest quantities only — editions of two to three thousand copies — over long periods. She remained unrecognised and unhonoured by the community at large. By the end of the year, however, she was a nationally known figure, a best-selling author and holder of one of the country's highest civic awards. The temptations she had voiced the previous year to relocate herself in England now withered before what seemed like a blaze of acclaim, which both gratified and alarmed her.

The year began quietly enough, however, with lunch at the Nobles', family of a surgeon who worked at Wanganui Hospital and lived in 'the oldest Wanganui house by the river [with] tennis courts, bush-trees, swimming pool [and] opossums living in the walls of the house'.[1] The whole family was 'brilliant', Frame told Bill Brown, with interests in music, photography, glass-blowing and architecture. But her special concern was for a younger daughter, Debbie, who had had psychiatric problems and an inclination towards suicide. Like Audrey Scrivener's family, the Nobles hoped that Frame, as someone who had survived treatment in psychiatric hospitals, could help Debbie. Frame, with a different view of her own past, was not so sure; but she could and did offer understanding and friendship.[2]

Her own source of anxiety in the early months was that her first volume of autobiography was to appear in New Zealand — and the United Kingdom — in April; she had still not received copies of the American edition, which she wanted to give to members of her family 'to let them fret and fume *before* the book is published here . . . this is especially important for my brother who has two children of vulnerable age'.[3] Nor was she looking forward to a series of newspaper, magazine and radio interviews which the Women's Press had asked Hutchinson to arrange so that they could be quoted in publicity for the book in the United Kingdom.

News that pleased her, however, was that *To the Is-Land* would be published as a joint Women's Press/Hutchinson New Zealand imprint, which would make it eligible for local awards; and that as the stress associated with publication and publicity increased, her blood pressure went down again.[4] Copies of both the Braziller and the Women's Press editions of the autobiography finally arrived together, in early March. Frame told Tim Curnow that the English version was well printed; but she found the cover — a lurid picture of three sisters in bed, which looked like an illustration from a *Girls' Annual* — 'rather odd'.[5]

The scheduled round of interviews began in February, and then appeared in a series of stories in the local and national press over succeeding weeks. The first was a New Zealand Press Association story from Washington about American reviews of the book and was carried in newspapers throughout the country with headlines such as 'New Zealand author a "neglected genius"'.[6] The best of those that followed were a profile by Tony Reid in the *New Zealand Herald* and a broadcast interview by Elizabeth Alley on Radio New Zealand's Concert Programme, repeated on the National Programme.

In the *Herald* story Frame complained about the misuse and misinterpretation of her 'Beginnings' essay in *Landfall*.

This extremely rare insight into her personal life has been misinterpreted. Partly the fault of scholars who 'don't speak to me and then wrongly state my personal position and preferences'. And partly her own fault. 'I didn't explain properly and I was too melodramatic.'

The point she was making was that when she had written in 'Beginnings' about having to chose between 'this world' and 'that world', 'that world' referred not to 'dream, disturbance or insanity', but to the realm of the imagination. Reid also asked Frame about May Sarton's characterisation of her as a genius.

She smiles. 'Yes, I know that some are saying that. It pleases me. But it's not so. I know my limitations. The only thing I have is a clear way of seeing something. However, my expression falls short. I'm constantly embarrassed by my small vocabulary of vital words.'

The famous, elusive lady sitting in the high-backed chair is friendly, shy, but assured. Her voice reveals the continuing, looming presence of an extended adolescence — it has the clear, light, bell-like tone of a wise child. . . . she also has an old-fashioned penchant for giggles.[7]

That 'bell-like tone' was evident in her answers to Elizabeth Alley's questions on what was only the second radio interview Frame had done. What she wanted to emphasise, she said, was that the autobiography was *her* say. 'I wanted to write my story, and . . . to correct some of the things which had been taken as fact and are not fact. My fiction is genuine fiction. And I do invent things. Even in *The Lagoon* . . . the children are invented, and the episodes are invented — but they are mixed up so much with part of my early childhood . . . [This] is the first time I've written the *true* story.'[8]

The one question Frame felt she dealt with poorly in an otherwise successful interview was one about the imagination. 'I looked on imagination as something I had to possess if I were to be a writer,' she told Alley in a subsequent letter. '[And] I think that wanting to *be* a writer comes from the family preoccupation with writing as a natural way of expressing feeling, observations, etc. I think my own extra desire to write was prompted by a need to have "my place" — an escape if you like — undisturbed by outward pressures and expectations.'[9]

Frame had found the exchanges with Reid and Alley stimulating. The other interviews, however, were 'awful, the kind of questions the narrow-minded people of the narrow-minded world keep asking me'. (The *Woman's Weekly* wanted to know if she made her own clothes.)[10] Once it was over, her verdict was emphatic: 'Never again. The whole experience has temporarily stopped writing, corresponding, everything, and left me with the sort of shame one felt (meaning me) when I first started to masturbate . . . [Also] with a revulsion to the printed word.'[11]

What mattered far more to Frame than 'promotion' of *To the Is-Land* was knowing how her brother and sister reacted to it. She reported to Bill Brown in March that Geordie Frame had written 'a long letter full of his own reminiscences, including some interesting notes about our early childhood. He told me that he learned only recently that our neighbours . . . had boarded the local priest who one night crept into bed with the neighbour's wife. I'm chiefly glad that my brother has no apparent objections . . . Relatives *can* be so difficult . . .'[12]

Geordie Frame, in fact, *was* difficult: but not in communication with his sister. He told the *Oamaru Mail* that a lot of things were 'wrong' in the autobiography — including the suggestions that he was called 'Robert' and 'Bruddie' (which Janet had resorted to so as to protect him), and that he was not with his mother when the doctor brought news of Myrtle's death. He also felt that his sister had not given him credit for being, in his view, the person responsible for Frame family finances. 'They can't fool me, 'cause I can remember all my life since I was two. I remember all Janet's life . . .' He was not mollified by June Gordon's assurance that none of this mattered, because the book was 'Janet's version'.[13]

June Gordon too, inevitably, had reservations about the autobiography. But hers were based largely on the fact that some elements in the family story which she remembered were not there: and some she did remember had, she believed, occurred in a manner rather different from her sister's recollection. She did not tax Frame directly about disagreements, but subsequently wrote her own version of the story of their childhood years, titled 'Dance before the Tide', and offered it to the Women's Press in London. She dedicated it, in part, 'to my sister Janet, for her fine example'.[14]

Frame, of course, had anticipated family reactions to 'versions' of experience; and to the fact that everybody 'owned' their own versions. '[Memories] do not arrange themselves to be observed and written about,' she said in *Is-Land*. '[They] whirl, propelled by a force beneath, with different memories rising to the surface at different times and thus denying the existence of a "pure" autobiography and confirming, for each moment, a separate story accumulating to a million stories, all different and with some memories forever staying beneath the surface.'[15]

In April 1986, when *To the Is-Land* went on sale in New Zealand and Britain, there were further reactions — from reviewers, and from some of those who had shared the life of the Frame family in Oamaru and elsewhere. This time the reviews were nearly unanimous, praising the book's 'accessibility' and 'artistry' and bandying about words such as 'genius' and 'masterpiece'. According to Vincent O'Sullivan in the *New Zealand Listener*:

> Frame's autobiography charts the constant play between two forces. On one side there is poverty, failed aspirations, death and the daily fare of physical shame, the simple lines of childhood gradually blurring and changing ground. On the other side there is her mind growing in confidence to call its own tune, to reach the point of saying . . . that reality may appear to be like this, but *I* shall make it otherwise. Imagination, the act of writing, a gift with words — as the book progresses, their claims are strengthened.

O'Sullivan went on to say that the writing of Frame's words was 'not a matter of plot, or of moving pieces according to set rules . . . It is a matter, rather, of creating designs, sequences of images overlaid and underpinned, characters set by the language that is given them — the pattern in the dance. The autobiography is more muted than the fiction. But we recognise familiar methods.'[16]

Lawrence Jones in the *New Zealand Times* said that the outer circle of Janet Frame's world in the autobiography was 'a world which tries to deal with Time, Sex and Death by repressing any overt reference to them, a world symbolised by the imprisoning grey school tunic, becoming more constrictive each year'. But it was also a world from where 'the special vision' of the writer 'can shine upon the worlds of Nature and Society, bringing out the lights and shadows, revealing what is really there in all its beauty and its terror'.[17]

English reviewers as a group were only a little less enthusiastic. Anne Chisholm in the *Times Literary Supplement* noted that Frame managed to 'invoke past innocence, and show how stories, legends and poetic images were for her the magic keys to understanding and expression. . . . This autobiography provides many clues to the working of her mind and talent, for despite a certain overwroughtness she is a writer of originality and power.'[18] Faith Evans, writing in the *Observer*, was one of several reviewers to make the point that the autobiography would bring Frame a wider audience of readers and admirers outside New Zealand.[19] Only A.L. McLeod in *World Literature Today* suggested that Frame's talent did not encompass autobiography and claimed that the book was 'poorly edited'.[20]

In Oamaru the local paper's review, by writer Owen Marshall, was as warmly favourable as any. 'Almost every town, moor, lake, city, street or railway station has its reference in British literature; famous or obscure, but an aura all the same. I had a strong feeling as I read this first volume of Janet Frame's autobiography, that it is such books which are enriching the literary associations of our own country and in this instance our own town of Oamaru. . . [This] book has special piquancy and adds in a subtle way to our relationship with the place in which we live.'[21]

In the town itself, however, not everybody shared this view. Miss Iris Romans, one of Frame's former teachers at Waitaki Girls' High School, stood up at an old girls' meeting and 'expressed disappointment that . . . Janet chose to be critical of those who helped her in her Oamaru years'.

> The years following the Depression were difficult for many other young people and in fact Mr Frame was employed while many parents were without work. She felt it was sad that Janet appeared to be unable to come to terms with the fact that she was by no means the only Waitaki girl who was poor and disadvantaged. Miss Romans also felt that while Janet Frame had undoubted ability New Zealanders tended to place her on a pedestal. It was important, if we wished to gain a balanced picture of her achievements, to view her work alongside that of her contemporaries, world wide, and this was not always easy to do in our position of isolation.[22]

Such responses, or at least public expression of them, were rare. The survivors of Frame's Waitaki Girls' High School days who chose to write to her, such as Katherine Bradley, were full of warmth and praise. 'She described [the book] as everything she had always wanted to know about how other people felt about things nobody talked about, and was afraid to ask.'[23] The Firman family, however, were displeased that Frame had named Ted Firman as the boy who tried to 'do it' with Myrtle in the pine plantation; and hinted that there were further dark secrets omitted from the autobiography.[24] And the descendants of Ma Sparks were indignant that Frame alleged that their grandmother had not worn underwear.[25]

Sales of *To the Is-Land* were unexpectedly brisk in New Zealand. The entire Hutchinson edition of 3000 hardbacks was sold out by October and the publisher ordered a paperback edition of 7000 copies to meet the continuing demand, 4000 of which were sold by February 1984. Moreover the success of the book and the highly favourable publicity surrounding it gave sudden momentum to Frame's career as a whole.

The month that *Is-Land* appeared, Curtis Brown closed a deal with Victoria University Press for a new selection of Frame's stories, *You Are Now Entering the Human Heart*, which would be published before the end of the year in an edition of 3500 copies and with an advance for Frame of $1500. It was made up of some work from her previous story volumes, and stories written since *The Reservoir* which had not been previously 'collected'. The book would be dedicated to her Wanganui friends, 'Piki, Jody Anne, Derek, Jill, Christopher and Amy, with love'. A co-edition by the Women's Press would be published in London the following year. In addition to this her agents also arranged a French edition of *Owls Do Cry*; a film contract with an Australian company, Barker Productions, for *Faces in the Water*, with an advance of $1500; a small edition of *The Lagoon*, bound from previously printed pages set by Caxton in the early 1960s; and a serialisation of *To the Is-Land* for reading on Radio New Zealand (author's fee $528). While these deals were being negotiated, Tim Curnow also wrote to all Frame's publishers of out-of-print books outside the United States to arrange the formal reversion of rights to the author; this would eventually allow a systematic planning of new editions of all her novels with the exception of *The Edge of the Alphabet*, which Frame did not want reprinted in English in her brother's lifetime. Her own 'favourites' as candidates for re-issue were *Daughter Buffalo, Intensive Care* and *The Adaptable Man*. [26]

Honours and rumours of honours began to appear in this *annus mirabilis*. In May a Sunday paper revealed that the writers' organisation PEN had been annually nominating Frame for the Nobel Prize for Literature for the previous five years, and 'have high hopes of her success this year because of the enthusiastic response in America to her . . . autobiography'.[27] Just over a month later it was announced that Frame had been awarded the CBE (Commander of the Most Excellent Order of the British Empire) in the Queen's Birthday honours list. 'I'm pleased to be honoured for myself,' Frame told Elizabeth Alley, 'and for other writers, for it is a way of accepting writers into the esteemed company of athletes and accountants and thus recognising them as part of our daily life.'[28] She admitted a modicum of regret to Bill Brown that she had not achieved 'Dame Frame' and that — as her mother would have said — 'that's my wack'.[29]

In August 1983 she completed the rewriting and retyping of her second volume of autobiography and sent copies of the manuscript to Tim Curnow, and to Anthea Morton-Saner of Curtis Brown London. At first she planned to call it 'Tricks of Desperation' (from *The Tempest*) but then opted for *An Angel at My Table*, a title taken from Rilke's French poem, *Les Vergers*, which she had discovered and studied with Bill Brown fourteen years previously and which, she said subsequently, represented 'the story of my life' (and, she might have added, the importance of angels in the cosmology she had inherited from her Christadelphian mother):[30]

Reste tranquille, si soudain
l'Ange à ta table se décide;
efface doucement les quelques rides
que fait la nappe sous ton pain.

Stay still, if the angel
at your table suddenly decides;
gently smooth those few wrinkles
in the cloth beneath your bread.

Tu offriras ta rude nourriture
pour qu'il en goûte à son tour,
et qu'il soulève à sa levre pure
un simple verre de tous les jours.

Then offer him your own rough food
so he can have his turn to taste,
so he can raise to that pure lip
a simple, common glass.

Ingénuement, en ouvrier céleste,
il prête à tout une calme attention,
il mange bien en imitant ton geste,
pour bien bâtir à ta maison.

Ingenuous celestial carpenter,
he lends all a calm attention,
he eats well, imitating your gesture,
so he can build well on your house.[31]

This new manuscript covered the years from her enrolment at teachers' college to her departure for London in 1956 and included the periods of hospitalisation. It was about the same length as volume one; and as the wordage she planned for volume three, 'Tomorrow's Palace', on which she began to work at once. She told Bill Brown that the fourth volume would be for posthumous publication and the fifth, for publication in her lifetime, 'will be in verse and set in the hereafter . . . then I [shall] do several volumes of a fiction. Then stories and poems. So I have an awful lot of work on my plate.'[32]

George Braziller accepted *An Angel* at once and arranged payment of an advance. But there were unexpected problems. In September a new Braziller editor 'performed gross indecencies . . . on my manuscript, in the way I'd heard about but have never met. I was so shocked and depressed by his intrusion into *my* province that I almost felt like giving up . . . I wrote to the editor about my feelings [while] I felt my confidence ebbing lower and lower.'[33]

That confidence was given a boost at the end of the month by the news that *To the Is-Land* had won the Wattie Book of the Year award which, at $6000, was the country's largest literary prize. The best she had done previously was to come second in 1973, with *Daughter Buffalo*. Frame, with memories of not enjoying her reception for the Menton award in 1973, chose not to attend the function; but she did show up the following week with the Gordons for her CBE investiture at Government House in Wellington on 6 October 1983. She told Bill Brown that the Governor-General had pinned on her 'a huge gold and blue medal . . . made by the Queen's goldsmith, and set in a handsome black box containing a neck ribbon, instructions on how to wear the medal, and noting that on death [it] is not surrendered but the Orders of Knighthood in London must be notified'.[34] The Gordons, she noted, 'like all true family . . . hobnobbed with the governor and made me ashamed of their boldness . . . They're good souls, though, and I think we all get better as we get older and realise we're all in Together.'[35]

Home in Wanganui, Frame received a letter from George Braziller to say that he had taken the offending editor 'off' her manuscript. It would, as usual, be published as submitted. Relieved by this news, and by the knowledge that her $6000 Wattie Award, her Braziller advance, and a further $3000 from her film option money, provided an opportunity to escape from Wanganui, Frame put the house on the market and organised the Gordons to help her find a suitable replacement in Levin. Her determination to act was strengthened by notification that a natural gas pipeline was soon to be laid within metres of her property; and by the fact that Piki Takiari had moved out of Wanganui and back to her home village of Kaiwhaiki. '[They've] set up a community on tribal land . . . growing their own food, keeping goats, hens, pigs and so on [and] she takes kids who would otherwise end up in jail.'[36]

A little over a fortnight later her move was organised. She had sold the Andrews Place property at a loss, but managed to buy a more expensive one in Levin by using her windfall money. She would move house on 15 November. 'I'm looking forward to being nearer Wellington,' she told John Money, 'also [to] being able to walk to the shops. . . . Levin to me has always meant Tolstoy and characters from *Anna Karenina*. I like a town to have literary associations. And not far south is Plimmerton and Karehana Bay, pure New Zealand Glover.'[37]★

The name Levin derived, in fact, from one of the directors of the Wellington and Manawatu Railway Company, which had laid a railway line between Wellington and Palmerston North in the 1880s. By 1983 it was a modest sized community, population around 15,000, and a servicing centre for a variety of secondary industries. It reminded Frame of 'small-town America . . . it's on the main highway, it has many eating-places, shopping malls and so on. The library is pleasant and good but there's no public art gallery.'[38]

Her new home in Bowen Street was another box-like model with a tiled roof, built in the 1950s, with two of the 'boxes' forming an L-shape, 'like a big new apartment with two wings, one for working and sleeping, the other for eating, sitting, washing, cooking etc'.[39] The view from her window 'is all Eudora Welty Curtain of Green, with grapefruit hanging like . . . "golden lamps in a green night"'.[40] The Gordons lived around the corner in the same symmetrically organised block of houses. 'The days here,' Frame told Bob Cawley, 'alternate between blue [ones] burning to the touch, and inexplicably grey days when clouds . . . drift down from the mountains, the Tararuas, part of the chain which is the "backbone" of the North Island.'[41]

------------

★ This is a reference to Denis Glover's 'Threnody' which begins:

> In Plimmerton, in Plimmerton,
> The little penguins play,
> And one dead albatross was found
> At Karehana Bay.

She had not 'solved' the noise problem, but reported that Levin seemed to have an 'upper silence which tends to muffle strident sound. I play piano records softly, and just now I'm trying out those suitable for long hours of work . . . Schubert's Impromptus and Schumann's Forest Scenes and Schubert's Piano Sonata in A. Just now it is Beethoven's Diabelli Variations and Haydn's Piano Trio . . . all played just on the outskirts of the ear.'[42] With such insulation, and the usual 'quiet Christmas of my own choosing', Frame spent most of December and January 1984 judging seventy 'finalist' entries in the inaugural American Express Short Story Award (culled from 700 submissions). She did not resent the fact that it was time away from the third volume of autobiography. In fact, she told Tim Curnow, 'I'm a short story addict, both reading and writing them, and I always keep hoping for the perfect story (in reading these).'[43]

Her 'career' (Frame always referred to it in inverted commas) now seemed to be surging forward, partly because of the unexpected success of *Is-Land* and partly because of an extraordinary degree of activism on Frame's behalf by Curtis Brown staff. Hutchinson in New Zealand agreed to pay her a total of $6000 as advances on the paperback edition of *Is-Land* and the forthcoming hardback edition of *An Angel at My Table*, for which they would print 6000 copies. The Women's Press handed over £750 as their advance for *Angel*, and a further £600 advance on their edition of the *Human Heart* stories. The first printing of the Women's Press edition of *Is-Land* (3000 copies) sold out in Britain and was followed by a 3000-copy paperback edition. George Braziller announced that he would print 5000 hardback copies of *Angel* for the American market, his largest-ever print run of a Janet Frame book. And all this occurred while Frame saw out the summer in Levin, read the short stories for the American Express competition, then (in February 1984) took up the threads of the third volume of her autobiography. She did allow herself one luxury: using a little of her unanticipatedly luxuriant income, she bought an 'electronic self-correcting' typewriter which, she told Tim Curnow, 'is rather startling to work on and tends to anticipate my mistakes'.[44] Her one addition to the text of *An Angel at My Table*, provision of an appendix by Bob Cawley 'testifying' to her sanity, she was persuaded by Curtis Brown to withdraw — Tim Curnow felt strongly that it was superfluous; and it was out of harmony with the rest of the book.

Early in March 1984 Frame travelled to the South Island to take part in the Christchurch Festival. On the way she visited Picton, her mother's home town, and rediscovered it as 'the most beautiful place I've seen, at the end of winding fiords, beautiful blue water — marvellous'.[45] Her cousin Archie Hislop, the former commune leader, now lived there on a yacht. In Christchurch Frame gave what was billed as 'her first public reading in this country'. The session, with three other writers, drew an audience of 1200 people and had patrons queuing for a block and a half outside the Christchurch Town Hall. One of the local newspapers reviewed the performance:

Janet Frame's shyness and reticence in public is well known yet her light fragile voice was carefully controlled with clear enunciation and charm. Her delivery of the nearly 20 poems she read was even and unforced. Her touch was light and lacked deliberate stress to emphasise humour or change of atmosphere.

'The Landfall Desk' was an early favourite as the poem described the ambivalent attitudes of the writer to a desk given to her when a *Landfall* editor retired. The desk became the personification of the literary critic — stalking the arid phrase and dominating its environment.

Most of the poems were concerned with the theme of change.[46]

The audience gave Frame a prolonged standing ovation, increasing her confidence in her own judgement that, if she *had* to appear in public, reading was the kind of performance she was most able to carry off successfully.

Home again in Levin Frame received a letter from two twenty-nine-year-old apprentice film makers, Jane Campion and Bridget Ikin. Both admired *To the Is-Land* and sought television rights to make a 'collaborative' three-part film of the book. 'We are both very conscious of the highly personal nature of the autobiography and for this reason the idea of a television version may be something that you are completely averse to. But because we both consider the work to be a classic of New Zealand literature, we are both insistent that if the project is to be done at all, it should be . . . conceived with the highest standards of quality and commitment, with the aim of making it, too, a classic. . . Our attitude is one of the production of quality films [with] commitment, dedication and a strong sense of the value of the *ideas* you are working with.'[47]

As she had been with Timothy White and Vincent Ward, Frame was impressed by the serious-mindedness of their proposal; but the idea of a television series did not appeal to her. After writing an acknowledgement to these 'enterprising talented women', she asked Tim Curnow to write a formal reply. 'Janet . . . would prefer individual films based on the three volumes of her autobiography . . . [We] feel it is premature to consider the assignment of film or television rights in an unfinished three-part [work].' He suggested that they write to Curtis Brown at the end of the year, when they would have had an opportunity to assess all three volumes. In the meantime, the agency would not option film or television rights elsewhere.[48] Privately, Curnow thought Campion and Ikin 'a couple of dreamers' and did not expect anything to eventuate from their proposal.[49]

It was now Frame's intention to resume serious work on volume three of the autobiography. Inevitably, however, there were distractions. *An Angel at My Table* was released in New Zealand in May 1984 (and in the UK in August, and the United States in September). This time Frame did not make herself available for interviews; but she could not avoid reading reviews, some of which appeared in publications she bought; others were sent to her by Curtis Brown or well-meaning family and friends. There were no negative ones in New Zealand, however, and hence no unpleasant surprises — only a harmonious chorus of admiration.

'As her fiction is the work of a rare imagination,' wrote Lydia Wevers in the *New Zealand Listener*, 'so her autobiography is a work of rare intelligence . . . many literary autobiographies concentrate on the development of a refined sensibility and an illustrious group of friends at the cost of a sense of the real life from which talent has drawn its material. But Janet Frame . . . recalls her past selves with such honesty that it seems to illuminate one's own life.'[50] And Bill Manhire in the *New Zealand Times* concluded: 'It is impossible to read this book without admiring, as well as her honesty, the extraordinary artistry with which Janet Frame has put her life on paper. She has a marvellous sense of the pace and patterns of experience . . . It would be hard to overpraise [it] . . .'[51]

Writing to Charles Brasch in 1964, when she had just completed her 'Beginnings' essay for *Landfall*, Frame spoke of what was then an unfulfilled ambition: 'Some day I'd like to write [about my life] from "within" instead of from "without".'[52] By mid-1984 there was a consensus among reviewers and critics that she had achieved this ambition; and that the achievement was marvellous and rare.

It was, perhaps, both fortuitous and fortunate for Frame that *An Angel at My Table* was published, reviewed and read in New Zealand when it was. Unbeknown to her, one of the country's few cultural philanthropists, a Wellington manufacturer named Fred Turnovsky, had set up a trust to award an occasional Turnovsky Prize for Outstanding Achievement in the Arts. Worth $20,000, this award was offered for the first time in 1984. There were ninety-one nominations from such varied sectors of the arts as music, dance, opera, painting, sculpture and photography — and literature. And the announcement was made on 8 June that the inaugural winner of the prize was Janet Frame, 'New Zealand's finest artist in words.'[53] The money was to be tax free; there were no requirements nor 'strings attached'.

Frame, superstitiously almost frightened by what seemed to be a continuum of good fortune, said she would accept the award as an opportunity 'to pay tribute to [the] authors who inspired her, especially fellow New Zealand writers'.[54] She went to Wellington to attend a dinner in her honour on 9 July, staying with Jacquie Baxter and wearing a long dress she had bought for the occasion for $1.50 from the Salvation Army shop. She also wore a cicada pendant, given to her by Bill Brown, and, she reported to him, it was much admired. At the dinner, in the capital's Michael Fowler Centre, she sat between Fred Turnovsky (and loved him for his 'love of Schubert') and the Governor-General, Sir David Beattie. Directly opposite was the Minister for the Arts Allan Highet, and his painter wife, Shona McFarlane. In this company, Frame sat 'all ears and eyes, absorbing'.[55] After dinner, replying to Sir David Beattie's presentation of her award, Frame read the final part of her short story 'Swans' and her verse 'Poets' ('to make [people] think about artists in New Zealand').[56]

As a finale to an extraordinary week — which included a 'snap' general election, in which the National Government was defeated and replaced by a Labour one — she learned that she had won the New Zealand Book Award for non-fiction, a prize of $2000 for *An Angel at My Table*; and a prize called the Buckland Award, privately endowed for 'literary excellence', which was worth $600. This latter was a late 1983 recognition of *To the Is-Land*, and she had won it previously in 1967, 1972 and 1980. Her cup, she told Brown, 'runneth over'.[57] But there was a dismal development too, as if to protect her from hubris: French secret agents sank the Greenpeace vessel *Rainbow Warrior* in Auckland harbour on 10 July, New Zealand's first instance of 'international terrorism'; and she returned to Levin to find changes in the neighbourhood. 'Two doors away a man has begun a car-wrecking business; & the man next door has suddenly built a powerful motorbike & goes round and round his lawn on it. . . . It's a great relief to know I've got $20,000 in the bank; if the worst comes and I have to move again.'[58]

August 1984 brought Frame's sixtieth birthday, and with it some public acknowledgements. Radio New Zealand marked the occasion by broadcasting on their concert programme nine of the twenty-five stories from *You Are Now Entering the Human Heart*, introduced by Professor Margaret Dalziel. Tapes of the readings would be delivered to New Zealand embassies and high commissions so that the stories would be heard around the world, the programme's producer announced (before such an arrangement had been negotiated or even discussed with the author or her agent).[59] Only weeks prior to this, National Radio had followed their broadcast of *To the Is-Land* with readings from *An Angel at My Table*.

In Oamaru, the Waitaki Writers' Group in association with the public library organised a weekend of Frame-related activities, the first time her old home town had mounted a commemoration or appreciation of this kind. Frame was invited to attend, but declined. In her absence the organisers would screen the *Janet Frame* film shot in 1975, Patrick Evans would give an address titled 'Janet Frame: Her Life and Art', there would be a guided tour of Oamaru places featured in Frame's fiction and autobiography, and the library would mount an exhibition of Frame books and memorabilia, including her letter declining to attend the festivities. Most dramatically, Geordie Frame would make himself available to answer questions about the Frame family and about his famous sister. According to Patrick Evans, the session with Geordie, which was not on the original programme, had been 'arranged at the last minute to accommodate his threat to gatecrash proceedings'. Evans described what transpired:

> George sits enthroned before the audience and with a lip-licking relish answers the questions the audience has written on slips of paper . . . An impression of doughty impenetrability [exudes] from him . . . He sits with his hands in his lap as the questioner reads [each] question aloud and then passes it to him. There is a pause, as he reads it carefully with his

specs on the tip of his nose . . . George's lips move slightly, and then after half a minute he throws his head back and begins to bawl . . . This procedure is followed for each question, with a long, tense pause between the reading-aloud of each question and his reply. Quite often the message-from-Mars quality of this interchange is scrambled by George's adding an unexpected coda to some of his replies at the same time as the interviewer is reading out the next question. At moments like these the audience becomes almost uncontrolled, and at one point a couple of gasping librarians flee into a back room . . . [George has become] the centre of the evening, his sister marginalised with an ease that seems natural and habitual, as if no one could possibly have the slightest interest in her. 'No, I wouldn't say we're exactly what you'd call close,' he says cautiously when questioned about their current relationship. 'When she's in town she calls in, of course.'⁶⁰

There was a sequel to this event. The following month, the Dunedin playwright and former Burns Fellow Roger Hall suggested that the Oamaru Borough Council place a plaque on the Frame home at 56 Eden Street and, for long-term commemoration, buy the house and preserve it. The proposal was supported editorially by the *Otago Daily Times* but ridiculed in Oamaru itself. Nothing further was done to promote it.⁶¹

Frame's own sixtieth birthday celebration involved visits from family, and from her Wanganui friends Piki Takiari, Derek Schulz and Jill Studd. As she told Tim Curnow, however, she had organised a treat for herself. She would take another overseas trip in September to visit London and Norfolk, then New York and Toronto. In Toronto she would participate in the International Authors' Festival and stay a week at the Toronto Hilton, at the expense of the festival. After that she would travel to Baltimore and San Francisco, aiming to be back in New Zealand by late November. She hoped to complete the final typing of the third volume of autobiography before she left; but, if not, she would work on it in England and the United States.⁶²

Curnow immediately alerted his London colleagues to this itinerary because Frame was planning to be in England at precisely the time that *An Angel at My Table* and *You Are Now Entering the Human Heart* were to be published there by the Women's Press. Publisher and agents hoped that she might be persuaded to take part in some effective but undemanding promotional activities, such as newspaper interviews.

Before Frame departed on 19 September with her sister June, who would accompany her on the England leg of the trip, a curious controversy erupted around a new novel by Karl Stead. Called *All Visitors Ashore*, it was the same book Stead had suggested that he and Frame co-author, based on their mutual experience and memories of Takapuna in 1955.⁶³ While Frame had called that suggestion 'a good idea' in 1979, Stead had gone on to write the book alone, though he set it in 1951, the year of New Zealand's seminal Waterfront Dispute, which led to severe restrictions on the freedom of speech and sparked an earlier 'snap election'. The characters Stead had proposed five years before were there, however: a narrator called Curl Skidmore, a poet turned professor; a mentor figure called Melior Farbro who, like Sargeson, was homosexual, changed his name, had a bach at Takapuna, and grew tomatoes and peppers; and an apprentice writer in Farbro's hut, Cecelia Skyways, an 'electrified . . . ex-nun' who is writing her first novel, *Memoirs of a Railway Siding*. It was perhaps inevitable, given the appearance of this novel in the same year as *An Angel at My Table*, which described similar characters and some similar events in an autobiographical manner, that New Zealand readers and reviewers would make connections between the two books. It was probably also inevitable that more erudite readers would link publication of the novel with Frame's story 'The Triumph of Poetry'. Indeed, there is a glancing reference to the story in *All Visitors Ashore*. As Cecelia Skyways leaves New Zealand by ship and expresses a degree of resentment about the character based on Kay Stead, the author has her thinking: 'One day she will write a story about it . . . [she] smiles a small smile and turns her mind to the prospect of Spain.'[64]

The literary editor of the *New Zealand Listener* was concerned that Frame might be hurt by the appearance of the book and contacted her to ask if his magazine ought to review it. And a *Listener* journalist, David Young, after speaking with both Frame and Stead, wrote:

> Frame acknowledges that more than 25 years ago Stead took exception to a short story which has been collected into a George Braziller edition of her work . . . It is a slight piece, 'not a very good short story' in Frame's estimation and some of its elements are also found in *All Visitors*. It is about an indifferent poet, first a student who becomes a balding, compromised academic and about his relationship to his lover and later wife.
>
> Told in a sardonic detached tone, two of the story's central concerns, the sense of friends packing up and departing by ship for distant shores and an abortion sequence, are also found in Stead's book. Frame is adamant the story, written during her first visit to Britain, was never about Stead or his wife, Kay. At that time she was living out her own experiences, years and thousands of miles from New Zealand.
>
> For all his [and her] disclaimers, the reader is left not just with 'a masterpiece of creative writing' as Frame herself describes the work but with a sense that maybe there are some old scores being settled here. For all its clearly fictional character, the novel is, at least, an act of literary one-upmanship. . . .[with its] dedication on the opening page: 'To whom it may concern'.[65]

Frame's attitude to the flutter of conversation and comment about this dimension of *All Visitors Ashore*, largely confined to the literary community, was resigned. Stead's explanation for the basis of his characterisation ('They are not allusions to her. They are allusions to a character who bears some resemblance to her') was no different from hers for work of her own. And the consequences of that earlier story about the poet in decline meant that the appearance of a character based in certain aspects on her own life was simply something that had to be endured. And so it was; and the incident did not substantially affect a re-established friendship with the Steads.

In London Frame and her sister stayed in a 'hole-in-the-wall and hole-in-the-pocket hotel', a dreary rooming house near Victoria Station.[66] They attended a small reception organised by Curtis Brown on 25 September and another — after their visit to Norfolk to see Peter Dawson in a rest home in Sheringham — at New Zealand House on 9 October. The latter was sponsored by the Women's Press and included reviewers and journalists, one of whom — Jill Neville of the *Sunday Times* — wrote about the occasion.

> Seeing her now at her publisher's party — frizzy haired, face open and porous, strangely young for her 60-odd years, wearing meek country-women's shoes, one could sense she is not in her element . . . [There] was a barely perceptible twitch from time to time as adoring fans from the Women's Press gazed up at her, a Suffering Female Artist. She may have sensed that adulation and her gathering fame could undo her if she didn't rush back to the New Zealand fastness pretty soon . . . [67]

Reviews of *An Angel at My Table* and *You Are Now Entering the Human Heart* appeared in the British press while Frame was in England or shortly after she left on 10 October. Most gave wholehearted praise to the autobiography and qualified approval to the stories. Some, like that by Fleur Adcock in the *Times Literary Supplement*, assessed both books in a single feature. Adcock, a former New Zealander and a poet, concluded:

> Her fictional and autobiographical writings are so closely interrelated that to read one work creates an appetite for the others; her various treatments of any subject enhance, rather than diminish, each other. Everything she presents is illuminated and thrown into sharp focus by the limpid clarity of a highly individual vision; she can be detached and passionate at the same time. The autobiography lacks the occasional flamboyance of some of her fiction — it is a deliberately subdued exercise in establishing the facts — but it is irresistibly readable, commendably honest, and, as a lesson in how courage and the will to survive defeated the effects of a ghastly mistake, inspiring.[68]

Such a view was echoed by others, including Naomi Mitchison in the *New Statesman*, who said that Frame had given readers 'a new and authentic picture of her own country . . . New Zealanders are proud of her; they should be. She has shown, so quietly, a mastery of the English language which dazzles one beyond ordinary praise.'[69]

On her own now, Frame carried on to New York for two days; and then to Toronto for the seven-day International Authors' Festival. To her surprise she found the eagerly anticipated Hilton Hotel 'rather a desert';[70] and she was grateful to be rescued for outings by John Money's sister and brother-in-law, Joyce and Humphrey Hopkins. She attended all the authors' readings (four each evening by luminaries such as Margaret Atwood, Nadine Gordimer, V.S. Naipaul and Yevgeny Yevtushenko) and gave her own performance on the final night. For this she had chosen the story 'Two Sheep' and an extract from the autobiography about Aunty Isy's chocolates. In this way she gave publicity to the new books, both of which would be published by Braziller in North America that month. By this time she was stricken with a cold and her reading voice was 'croaky'.[71]

She then spent three convalescent days with the Bestons, who now lived in Rochester in upstate New York; then travelled to John Money's in Baltimore where, over the next eleven days, she finished typing *The Envoy from Mirror City*, her third volume of autobiography, and sent copies off to her publishers in New York, London and Auckland. She completed her tour with nine days in San Francisco with Brown and Wonner, and arrived back in Levin on 23 November 1984.

In New Zealand she found incontrovertible evidence that her 'career' no longer required her own presence or direction to maintain its gallop. *An Angel at My Table* had come third in the Wattie Book of the Year Award and sold 5000 copies in hardback since April. Hutchinsons had also sold out of their paperback edition of *Is-Land* and were reprinting a further 3000; and they planned to release *Angel* in paperback in April 1985 with a print-run of 6000 copies. Victoria University Press, who had exhausted their edition of *Human Heart*, were also reprinting. Then, within weeks of her return home, George Braziller rang to say that he would publish *The Envoy from Mirror City*; and Hutchinson agreed to do so in New Zealand with an advance of $4000. Hutchinson had also signed a contract for a new New Zealand edition of *Owls Do Cry* and were to pay a $3000 advance on this book. Meanwhile Curtis Brown in London were negotiating for a French edition of *An Angel at My Table* (advance 7500 francs) and a German edition of *Maniototo*. Frame could scarcely keep track of these developments, even though she was well informed by Tim Curnow — who wrote on 3 December to say that he had had a meeting in Sydney with Jane Campion, who now wanted to film a three-part mini-series for television based on all three volumes of Frame's autobiography; and Curnow recommended that Frame should meet with Campion and discuss this proposal.[72]

The only disadvantage inherent in all these arrangements arose from the fact that the new Labour Government had imposed a surtax on the additional income of superannuitants: the government would take 58 cents in every dollar Frame earned above $6500. 'My new-found wealth,' she exclaimed to John Money, 'has vanished . . . [and] just when I thought I had no money worries for the first time in my life'.[73] This was to some extent compensated for by the fact that the government had also declared the country 'nuclear free' so that the passage of nuclear-armed and nuclear-propelled vessels through its ports had been banned. What the government took away with one hand it appeared to give, at least morally speaking, with the other.[74]

Another problem, and to Frame's mind a more serious one, concerned Neg the cat, about to enter her fourteenth year. She was showing the effects of age and needed veterinary attention more frequently than previously. She had slowed considerably and was developing cancers on both ears. And, when Frame reclaimed her from the Gordons after the English–American trip, Neg took some time to adjust to being back in Bowen Street. Each morning she trotted along the road, 'approaching every door to find if she lived there — while I had to drive her like a cow or goat along the street back home'.[75] But Frame was unable to bear the thought that she might be parted from her pet. '[She] continues to find joy in living, dancing around like a kitten . . . I expect/hope to find her quietly dead one day as she lies in the sun.'[76] So long as she exhibited that joy, her owner was not going to be responsible for extinguishing it.

Film maker Jane Campion, New Zealand-born but now Sydney-based, came to see Frame just before Christmas 1984. Although they had not met previously, Frame was well aware of Campion's family. Her parents had both trained at the Old Vic in London and founded the New Zealand Players, a travelling professional theatre, in the 1950s. Edith Campion, Jane's mother, had shared one half of the book *Tandem*, in which Frank Sargeson's last novella had been published in 1979. In addition Frame had recently been introduced to Jane's godmother, Margaret Gordon, who lived in Levin.

At the meeting the two women got on well. Campion reiterated that she believed adaptation of the autobiographies for television made more logical and logistical sense than making a cinematic film. Frame, however, was still not prepared to commit herself. She told Campion she preferred to wait until the books were 'published and done with' (*The Envoy from Mirror City* was due out in New Zealand in June 1986). But she remained interested in the Campion/Ikin proposal and agreed that it should have priority consideration when the time came for dealing with film and television rights. The other film previously under consideration — Lynn Barker's proposed adaptation of *Faces in the Water* — had lapsed because of Barker's inability to raise the necessary money.[77]

There were other visitors over the early months of 1985. Jacquie Baxter and Piki Takiari came to stay in January, sleeping in an 'unroadworthy' caravan

that Frame used as a spare bedroom. She had a lavatory and wash basin installed
in the back porch of the house so that such visitors could be 'self-contained'.[78]
In February she agreed to speak to a reporter from the *Wall Street Journal* on
tour in New Zealand; and to a doctoral student from Sydney University, Gina
Mercer, who was doing a thesis on Frame's fiction. But she warned Tim
Curnow that she did not welcome such encounters. 'It really interferes terribly
with my writing day when people come to see me, for it takes two or three
days or longer before the event and some days after for me to return to an
even keel on my writing sea — the arrival of people really affects me like a
storm.'[79] On top of this came the usual summer lawn mowing and revving of
car engines. 'I've now contracted to have double windows put on my study,
and a kind of brick-cladding around the outside of the house.'[80] These
renovations, along with the earlier installation of additional bathroom facilities,
represented luxuries she could never have afforded in previous years. They
were among the fruits of the spectacular increase in her income in 1984.

Frame had hoped — and promised her agent and publishers — that she
would apply herself to serious work on the new novel in March 1985. It was a
'crazy book', she told Tim Curnow. 'A tentative [title] is "Housekeepers of
Ancient Springtime". A mouthful.'[81] By March, however, 'it was not going at
all well . . . because it scares me [and] I keep trying to escape from it'.[82] Then,
total disaster: 'My year is going to be sadly disrupted . . . they're uprooting my
street during April and May.'[83] This was for the laying of the gas pipeline,
whose earlier encroachment had forced her to abandon Wanganui. She wrote
to Pamela Bailey in May:

> [The] giant machines are now in Quinn's Road, and are advancing next
> into Bowen Street. I play my record-player with a small pair of
> headphones attached, and as the machines and their noise advance, I
> choose the more dramatic pieces. This morning I have the Emperor
> Concerto (always a great silencer), the Agnus Dei side of Mozart's
> Requiem (always a great melter of stony hearts) and the slow movement
> of B.'s Ninth symphony (which makes machines invisible and takes me,
> anyway, to within range of the unknowable, at least to the boundary of
> the knowable.)[84]

The one element of delight in the pipe-laying saga was the discovery that the
digging machines were called 'Ditch Witches'.

One source of distraction from the noise was to write '"poetry" — I put it
in inverted commas because I make no claims . . . that I'm a "poet" or that it *is*
"poetry". I only know it's fun and it leads me into interesting places. I sometimes "fit it in" to my book, or even use it as an introductory quote.'[85] When
one of her Labour Party heroes, Joe Walding, died in London in June 1985,
she wrote a poem about him for the *Listener* that was published the following
month ('Did you see at the races young Joe Walding, barefoot,/selling pies —

mud, custard, sweet apple/with the Timaru trademark and a red label?').[86]

Another distraction was wrestling with an early computer, her second, a Commodore 64, which she bought in May 1985 — another benefit of her enlarged income. 'I feel I am betraying artists by venturing into the computer world,' she told Bill Brown, 'but I love it — I am hooked . . . [It produces] a look-no-hands kind of letter when I could be using a turkey or goose quill dipped in a pot of ink. Oh how I long for all past ways and days, like in the medieval world among the highwaymen and the silence and the dark nights that are gone forever . . .'[87]

She was no Luddite, however. She rapidly mastered a word-processing programme, Easy Script, and she used her television screen to display her own text. She had trouble for several months managing margins and spacing; and she worried about her printer, which at times sounded as if it had asthma. But she was, as she had said to Brown, hooked on the technology; and for the rest of her working life she would progress at the most advanced level, upgrading computers and programmes as more sophisticated options became available. She continued for some time to write her book manuscripts on a typewriter, however, because she had grown accustomed to the 'resistance' of the keys.

Computer expertise gave her common ground with an Inland Revenue officer who came to her house in July to instruct her on the workings of the new Goods and Services Tax, which required all 'sole traders' earning more than $25,000 a year to charge an additional ten percent for their 'services' within New Zealand, including writing. This woman too had a Commodore 64, and 'I showed mine when she told me about hers . . .'[88] Frame's favoured working place, by this time, was in a corner of the sitting room. Unfortunately, this entailed an inescapable disadvantage, she told Bill Brown. 'That's where people (the dread species) come & go & I can't bear the presence of people in my working area.'[89]

*The Envoy from Mirror City* was published in New Zealand, as scheduled, on 10 June 1985 (and in the United States in September and the UK in November). It covered the years from her arrival in England in 1956 to her return to New Zealand after the death of her father in 1963. As with the previous volumes, the dominant tone of reviews in all markets was one of respect and admiration — more so since Frame indicated that, contrary to her original plan for five volumes, *Envoy* was the final book in a trilogy. She used the image 'mirror city' as a metaphor for the world of imagination, and the 'envoy' for the imagining self or the muse. In writing the autobiographies, she said, her 'imagined treasures [had] faded in the light of this world, in their medium of language they have acquired imperfections [and] lost meaning that seemed, once, to shine from them and make your heart beat faster with the joy of discovery of the matched phrase or cadence, the clear insight. Take care. Your recent past surrounds you, has not yet been transformed. Do not remove yet what may be the foundation of a palace in Mirror City.'[90] The clear implication was that she was turning from autobiography back to the more challenging but potentially more satisfying task of writing fiction.

Dennis McEldowney in the *New Zealand Listener* viewed this final volume as giving further shape and sense to the preceding ones, resolving 'what has seemed a discontinuity between the reasonably "normal" childhood of the first volume and the emotional and institutional horrors of the second'.

> The Envoy, the power of the imagination, led the revolt against the role of the 'good child' whose life was determined by the expectations of other people. The revolt issued in bizarre, attention-getting behaviour; this led to a diagnosis of schizophrenia, which once made was never re-examined. Schizophrenia then became the 'reason' for the behaviour, which during her long incarceration she perfected from text-books and observation.[91]

In volume two Frame had shown *how* she came to be diagnosed as schizophrenic; in volume three she described the process by which doctors at the Maudsley had rejected that label. Thus she fulfilled the major purpose with which she had begun the venture, after discussion with Bob Cawley: to clear her name, once and for all, of the stigma of madness. In this she succeeded, as reviews and letters from a wide variety of sources — including some members of the psychiatric profession — would now attest. But in writing too about the life of a writer and the ways in which the imagination draws from and transforms the raw material of human experience, she had achieved something far more ambitious. And that 'something' was voiced for many readers by English biographer Michael Holroyd writing in the London *Sunday Times*. Frame, he said, had told a heroic story, 'and told [it] with such engaging tone, humorous perspective and imaginative power, that . . . I feel sure it is one of the greatest autobiographies written this century'.[92] Similar unsolicited testimonies came from other writers such as Lawrence Durrell and Patrick White. White went so far as to declare the biographies 'among the wonders of the world', and to propose Frame to the Swedish critic Ingmar Bjorksten as a candidate for the Nobel Prize (although as David Marr, White's biographer, noted, he was probably wrong in assuming that Bjorksten had influence in such matters).[93] Perhaps the final indication that superlatives were not misplaced was the fact that by midway through the following year, the three volumes of the autobiography had sold in total more than 52,000 copies worldwide.[94]

The gravity of the autobiographies' success continued to draw other books of Frame's back into print. Hutchinson in New Zealand, now Century Hutchinson as a result of a merger of publishers in the United Kingdom, paid $4000 as an advance on royalties for a new edition of *Daughter Buffalo*; and the company's New Zealand publishing director, David Ling, announced plans to follow that with new editions at the rate of one a year of *The Lagoon*, *The Adaptable Man*, *A State of Siege*, *The Rainbirds* and *Intensive Care*. *The Edge of the Alphabet* was excluded because Frame continued to worry about its likely effect on the life of her brother in Oamaru. Radio New Zealand had broadcasting rights for *Envoy*, but this time paid $1000 — considerably more than they had for earlier readings, recognising the fact that Frame's burgeoning reputation had enlarged even the local market value for her work. The Women's Press in London sold the paperback rights to the autobiographies in Commonwealth editions to Grafton Books, a subsidiary of Collins, with an advance for Frame of £6300.

Nor was there any let-up in the succession of prizes which the autobiographies had attracted like iron filings to a magnet. In September *The Envoy from Mirror City* won the $7000 Wattie Book of the Year Award for 1985, the third consecutive year in which Frame's work had featured in the top three placings. This result attracted the kinds of headlines that had now become commonplace in New Zealand: 'Frame Scores Again' and 'Frame Again a Winner'.[95]

The adulation and the accumulating bank balance (despite the superannuation surtax) had a curious effect on Frame. She felt no exultation; just a kind of emptiness, which seemed to intensify with each new chapter of good news. 'The autobiography is *for me* gone and forgotten,' she told Bill Brown, 'which is what I wished to happen . . . I feel as if I am walking in a strange new territory, a dreamworld, and I think I'm sending my novel down the drain and replacing it with poems which I can't write.'[96] And, on another occasion: 'I am at my desk of nothingness, with weights on my mind.'[97]

As an antidote to this numbness, which continued to inhibit work on the new novel, Frame decided in November 1985 to take her niece Pamela Bailey on a two-week trip to Sydney. This was a postponed treat. Frame was conscious of how much care of Josie had absorbed Pamela's time and energy, and she had proposed joint holidays on previous occasions which, for one reason or another, never occurred. Aunt and niece had also seen little of each other since Pamela had shifted to Wellington in 1982, so the Sydney jaunt would give them a chance to rekindle an intimacy that had become diluted with distance. Frame had pleasant memories of Sydney from the time of the PEN Congress in 1977; and she wanted to explore the city with company of her choice and with more leisure than the previous visit had allowed.

They stayed in a hotel in Pott's Point with a sweeping view of the city. They made excursions out to parks, bookshops and the zoo; and they wandered curiously and alertly around the Kings Cross 'red light' district. At the zoo they discovered a compatibility that they had not suspected previously: each of them preferred to stand and look for a long time at individual animals rather than rush through and attempt to observe everything. To their simultaneous horror and delight they saw a snake devour a rat. They also bought clothes, in pale pastel colours, which they subsequently referred to as their 'doctors and nurses outfits'.[98] And Frame went to the Curtis Brown office for a 'business' session with Tim Curnow.

Inevitably, however, there was a degree of strain involved in being cooped up in a smallish hotel room for two weeks, and in the fact that Pamela smoked and her aunt did not. It surfaced when Frame was interviewed for the *Sydney Morning Herald* by her original Women's Press publisher, Stephanie Dowrick, who had decided to live in Australia and pursue a writing career of her own (her first novel, *Running Backwards over Sand*, based in part on her New Zealand childhood, had appeared that year). Responding to intelligent and sympathetic questions, Frame revealed more about herself than was customary for her. She told Dowrick that she had the image of a whole novel before she began writing it. 'But, of course, once I start the actual mechanism of writing the sentences — it produces a whole new world. You still have the original idea, but it changes.'

> She writes four or five versions of everything. The first several versions are littered with notes to herself in brackets: (*My God, improve*). 'I'm terribly critical of what I've done. I say it all aloud. I speak it . . . The "dream" is never quite grasped. But I like that. I like the vision. I think that's what sustains one.'
>
> The last version is written on a computer. Frame enjoys the surprise this information produces. 'People *are* surprised by this. I play chess on it — and don't always win! I also have a flight simulator. I'm terrified of flying but anything that will get me closer to controlling a plane . . . !'

Dowrick made reference to the fact that the autobiographies, with their apparent simplicity, had provided a new and larger audience for Frame's work, and that the writer had received an enormous volume of correspondence from readers 'telling me things about their lives and remembering things they hadn't thought of before'.

> This enlarged audience is a mixed blessing for Frame who values anonymity, winter cold and darkness. 'Writing was and is so much a means of survival, and anything which interferes with that, which makes me waver, is, for me I feel, quite dangerous. I always feel I have to have this strong sense of being myself. It's not something you get and keep — and you have to keep renewing it.'[99]

The question that triggered friction between aunt and niece was Dowrick's request that Frame tell her about her family. 'I have no family,' Frame replied firmly, cutting off that line of discussion. She meant, of course, no immediate family. Pamela felt that she and *her* family had been repudiated, and she and Frame quarrelled after Dowrick's departure. Partly to defuse the tension, Pamela decided to visit her brother-in-law, Richard Bailey, in the Blue Mountains. In the confusion at Sydney Railway Station she boarded the train without Bailey and his companion, and ended up alone in Katoomba for several hours while her brother-in-law searched for her and imagined that she had been abducted. This episode became the subject of a lengthy Frame verse, to be sung to the tune of 'Frankie and Johnny': 'Pam caught her train, but she caught it wrong'. Frame also recorded an interview with Gina Mercer for the radio programme *Books and Writing*. And, on their last day in Sydney, she tried to ring Patrick White, to thank him for his unacknowledged letter of two decades previously. She spoke to White's companion, Manoly Lascaris, who told her that White was too ill to come to the phone. And so Frame wrote to him instead:

> When your letter came twenty-two years ago I was so much over-whelmed that I couldn't think how to answer it. It has now become part of my life (private) as 'the letter' & has perhaps assumed a literary life of its own. As the years passed I found it harder to answer. I'm using the left-over courage needed on a jet flight to Sydney, to greet you [and] to say thank you for your encouragement and for your wonderful writing . . . there's no need to acknowledge [this] letter.[100]

White *was* unwell at this time. According to his biographer, there was a further extenuating circumstance at work in his refusal to see or speak to Frame. 'I think he didn't want to disturb the very detailed fantasy he'd come to have of her . . . as mad, shy etc. It was violation enough of that image that she had crossed the Tasman . . . The vision would have collapsed if she'd crossed the threshold and sat down to tea. He didn't want her to be ordinary . . . so he fobbed her off.'[101]

One of the topics Frame discussed with Tim Curnow on this visit was the Campion–Ikin proposal for a film based on the autobiographies. Negotiations for the project accelerated in the latter weeks of 1985 and an agreement was signed on 16 January 1986. This gave Hibiscus Films and Jane Campion a three-year option on the books, to produce from them a mini-series for television. Frame would be paid $1000 for each year the option was exercised, this sum to be deducted from an eventual total payment of $72,815; and she would receive a small percentage of any profit. Although the agreement specified 'up to six films', Ikin and Campion thought it likely that they would make three ninety-minute programmes, that script writing and pre-production would take two years, and that the films would be shot in 1988. Frame would have the right to approve the scripts and would be consulted about the casting of major roles. The films would aim to be 'a quality television series, designed to create a wider market for the autobiographies (and by implication the other works of Janet Frame), and to appeal to those who are already familiar with the books'. Bridget Ikin hoped too that a new edition of the autobiographies would be published to coincide with transmission of the films.[102]

Frame pronounced herself 'happy to go ahead with it' and signed the agreement.[103] The only point at issue between them was that Ikin and Campion wanted to dramatise hospital scenes from *Faces in the Water*, to compensate for the absence of such material from *An Angel at My Table*. Frame agreed to this reluctantly, pointing out that *Faces* was 'autobiographical but not autobiography' — and that, in particular, the narrator, Istina Mavet, was a fictional character (and based on several people, including Audrey Scrivener, rather than Frame herself).[104] Campion and Ikin also asked Frame if she had any family photographs, which would help them visualise Southland and Otago at the time of Frame's childhood and such details as clothing and bathing costumes. Frame produced a shoebox full of such pictures. 'Why weren't any of these in the autobiographies?' asked Ikin. 'Well, the publisher never asked for them,' Frame told her.[105] A selection of the photographs *was* used in subsequent editions of the books.

The 'post-autobiography' stagnation that made it difficult for Frame to write imaginatively also reduced the volume of her personal correspondence. In what was becoming a rare event she wrote to Bill Brown in the New Year of 1986 to bring him up to date with her activities and to say that she had had a 'non-eventful' Christmas and a Christmas cake which she still had not touched. '[As] usual for New Year I read Pepys [diary] of 1664, where he is describing — believe it or not — what seems to be Halley's Comet — "a great arch of fire in the sky"; it's no wonder it is [associated] with disaster when it appeared during the Great Plague and Fire of London.'[106] The point was, of course, that the comet was appearing again in 1986; and Frame would eventually sight it, a 'long-haired blond star' — but its size and character were disappointingly reduced in comparison with previous appearances.[107]

Frame told Brown that she had two engagements planned in the coming months. She had agreed to read at the International Festival of the Arts in Wellington in March; and she wanted, again, to go to Norfolk to visit Peter Dawson in the rest home, having heard that she was considerably weakened. 'I can't bear not to make a last visit to someone who has been such a good friend and who is now quite alone and unvisited except for an ancient sister.'[108]

The festival performance, like her appearance at the Christchurch Festival two years before, was a considerable success. 'Some 2000 people turned up to hear Frame read [from *Intensive Care*], a task she had not relished, but accomplished with great style and expression,' the *New Zealand Listener* reported.[109] Every seat in the spacious Renouf Foyer at the Michael Fowler Centre was taken, and additional patrons lined the walls two or three feet deep. Again, she took confidence from a good performance, and from the standing ovation that it produced.

Frame was *not* confident, however, when she set out for the first leg of her rapid excursion to England on 2 April. En route for Auckland by train she became ill — motion sickness, her old bugbear — and when she got to Auckland she cancelled the trip. News that Peter Dawson's health was worsening, however, and that she herself was to be made an honorary member of the American Academy and Institute of Arts and Letters, impelled her to rebook the journey for May and June 1986, this time travelling first to Baltimore and New York.

In New York on 21 May Frame attended the American Academy's lunch and ceremony at its headquarters on Broadway, overlooking the Hudson River. In the absence of John Money, who had other commitments, Frame was accompanied by his sister and niece, Joyce and Sally Hopkins. At lunch she sat at the same table as Norman Mailer and John Updike, and was girlishly pleased to be hugged by the former. At the mid-afternoon presentation ceremony she was escorted by John Kenneth Galbraith and given a citation that read:

> Janet Frame's writing is quite singular in directness of tone and assumptions of shared mental experience. Concentration of observation in the author is returned to the readers with matching precision and power and her writing sets off small explosions in the mind and imagination. As the body of her work has enlarged, one comes to understand it not just as a series of extraordinary insights into suffering and thought, but as a mighty exploration of human consciousness and its context in the natural world.[110]

Unbeknown to Frame, one week before this ceremony, when she was flying from Los Angeles to Baltimore, Peter Dawson had died in Sheringham. When she got to England in the last week in May, all Frame could do was visit a freshly dug grave at Itteringham and the rest home where her friend had spent her last two years ('The Dales'); and then go back to the cottage at Itteringham Common which now belonged to her. 'It may have to be sold to pay the [fees] at the Dales,' Frame told John Money. 'I'd dearly like at least to write a book there, maybe next year . . . If I were as rich as Ngaio Marsh used to be, I'd spend six months here, six months there . . .'[111] She was not 'rich', however; or at least not *that* rich. She would sell the cottage in the following year, and pass some of the proceeds to her brother. In June 1986, however, Frame spent two more days in London, where she learned that Bob Cawley had married the previous year. His wife, Ann Doris, was a London social worker whom he had known for twenty-seven years. Frame did not meet her on this occasion, but flew back to New Zealand via San Francisco, where she spent four days with Brown and Wonner.

Home on 18 June she found a letter informing her that she had again won the New Zealand Book Award for non-fiction, this time for *The Envoy from Mirror City*. Her New Zealand publisher David Ling would drive her to Wellington the following week for the awards ceremony in the New Zealand Parliament's Beehive Building, where the Minister for the Arts, Peter Tapsell, would present her with a cheque for $4000. According to the press, Frame appeared 'slightly overwhelmed' by the occasion (she was in fact suffering from another bout of influenza). She declined to make a speech but did say to the gathered reporters it was a pity that more writers could not share the prize. 'I really think that instead of just one award they should spread it, say, among ten authors. I think that would be better.'[112] Non-fiction writers present, who had been subject to three consecutive years of unexpected competition for their prize from a novelist, expressed relief and gratitude that Frame had limited her autobiography to a trilogy.

In Levin she discovered that she had won yet one more prize: an iced cake raffled by her local savings bank. As if this was insufficiently excessive, the cake was delivered personally by the manager of the branch, whose name turned out to be Mr Biggs (Frame misheard it as 'Mr Big'). 'Wonders will never cease,' she exclaimed to Bill Brown. But cessation of wonders was precisely what she wanted. What she needed now, almost desperately, she said, was a period of quiet normality without functions, awards, and other distracting commitments falling upon her. 'It's so hard to be separated from one's work as I feel I have been these past [months]. It's the feeling, I think, that religious people have when they are separated from their God; an alienation; when the world around seems excessively squalid and stupid, simply because one is not in one's own "home" . . .'[113]

What remained of the New Zealand winter she would spend in both her 'homes', the literal and the metaphorical, regaining that sense of self of which she had spoken to Stephanie Dowrick the previous year; and she would regain it, and renew it, by doing something of which she had had precious little experience in the previous seven years: writing fiction.

# CHAPTER TWENTY-NINE

# Ascending Angel

$O$NE MARK OF FRAME'S DETERMINATION TO RESUME A MONASTIC working routine in the winter months of 1986 was that she had arranged for an additional sound-proofed room to be added to the Levin house while she was overseas in May and June. By July 1986 it was ready for occupation. '[It] does provide a measure of buffer for the whole house,' she told Bill Brown, 'although it's smaller than I thought.'[1] She also bought an answerphone, so that she could confine dealing with telephone calls to a time of day that suited her. This innovation she found 'marvellous'.[2]

Other protective steps were needed. She declined all further invitations — one was to a Melbourne Arts Festival in October; another to participate in a television programme called 'On the Couch', in which 'Basil James, Psychiatrist, interviews well-known people . . . to discover the human being behind the public face.'[3] Given that Frame did not *want* a public face, she had all the more reason not to want to reveal the person supposedly behind it. The most difficult invitations to refuse, however, were those issued for what she called for 'cultural' occasions. She told Bob Cawley:

> There is a certain amount of pressure here for me to attend literary functions, with the kind of blackmailish threat — 'It's important to New Zealand, a historic occasion' etc., implying that 'if you don't come it means you don't think it's important to N.Z. how arrogant of you!' . . . They don't happen often but too often for me. We are . . . [soon] opening a new National Library which is indeed a historical event. But do I have to *be* there? 'It is an important event you know.' . . . I've said, not, 'I'll be there' but 'I'll *try* to be there.' What a difference that one word has made. I'm [now] not worrying about the occasion . . .
>
> It seems that I am always being grateful to *words*.[4]

Despite these measures, writing did not come easily. In reply to a query from Tim Curnow in September 1986 Frame wrote: 'I can't say how my work is going because it's so deadly . . . I won't elaborate.'[5]

One invitation she did accept, though for the following year. The Sargeson Trust had at last set up its Sargeson Fellowship, and would soon call for applications in 1987. The trust's chairperson, Christine Cole Catley, invited Frame to apply for it, and hence to be the inaugural Sargeson Fellow, based in a studio in a converted stables building on the edge of Albert Park in Auckland. Frame agreed to apply, 'for Frank's sake', though said she would take it for two-and-a-half months only. Following that spell, she told her correspondents, she would travel to England in May for a final stay in Peter Dawson's cottage before she sold it.[6]

Curtis Brown continued to arrange her literary affairs, overseeing the programme of reprints and processing an increasing number of requests for her work — fiction and poetry — to be anthologised. One source of mild irritation to Frame was the Women's Press's refusal to reissue *Daughter Buffalo* on the ground that the leading characters were men. So the British and Commonwealth rights in the book were sold to Picador instead.[7] Behind the scenes, Tim Curnow and Carl Brandt discussed strategies for steering Frame's next novel, which they hoped was imminent, away from George Braziller and towards a publisher such as Random House, who could be expected to promote Frame's books in the United States more energetically. In the latter part of the year Anthea Morton-Saner from Curtis Brown's London office toured New Zealand and visited Frame's publisher Century Hutchinson, and Frame herself.

The one notable development in an otherwise uneventful period was the death of Frame's cat of fifteen years early in November 1986. 'Neg's absence,' she wrote to Bill Brown, 'is devastating. I know I invested too much of myself in her — it's hard not to when one lives alone and has one cat. I resolve never [to have one] again, at least not while I'm absent from home from time to time.'[8] And to John Money she added: 'For one emotionally [restricted] like me, the loss of an animal has been grimmer than the loss of those creatures called people . . .'[9]

The new New Zealand edition of *Daughter Buffalo* was published by Century Hutchinson in November and the following month precipitated one of the few uncomprehending, even hostile, reviews to which her fiction had been subject in recent times. It was, if nothing else, an indication that the relative fame and understanding of her work that the autobiographies had brought was by no means universally accepted. 'Janet Frame's later writings have become a specialist taste for a few,' it said, 'known paradoxically enough as an avant garde — the last of the faithful.'

> Some readers gamely followed her passed [*sic*] those previous landmarks in New Zealand literature *Owls Do Cry* and *Faces in the Water*. But the deliberate, or inadvertent, contrivance of a concentration and

preoccupation with the bizarre lost her followers.

When a reader's perception of where the writer is going is made unduly difficult because of the obscurity of the author's verbal or mental wanderings, then the failure of communication lies with the writer, not the reader. And some have found Janet Frame's novels increasingly demanding: the gift she has of sharpening our mental faculties can be too harshly won. There is doubtful compensation for accompanying her down the depressing paths of bleakness or melancholy, festooned with macabre, illustrative incidents.

Janet Frame's insights may well be too allusive, too esoteric for the form of the novel. Echoes of T.S. Eliot possibly point to a more appropriate medium for her writing — that of the incantatory voice of the poet consumed with his or her vision — rather than that of the prose-writer.[10]

Frame's publishers and friends did not send her that notice. It was the kind of review that, in earlier days, would have entirely deflated her confidence. Everybody close to her who cared about her, professionally or personally, was concerned to ensure that she was given the opportunity to write uninterrupted by distractions of the 'Porlock' variety; and unsympathetic reviews very definitely came into this category.

After her customarily quiet Christmas and New Year, Frame moved to Auckland in late January 1987 to become the first Sargeson Fellow. She was delighted with the Sargeson Trust's studio in Albert Park — both with its quiet location and its Spartan but comfortable facilities. She reported to Tim Curnow:

> My visit to Auckland was everything I hoped (rather desperately) it would be. For nearly nine weeks I had complete privacy, reasonable quiet, and above all aloneness — no neighbours, only trees; with the city at hand for me to wander in when I needed reminding that other people existed — without having to be *talked to*. The conditions in the spacious flat were ideal for me. I scrapped everything but the idea, the feeling that's haunted me, and I began and finished my novel. With two or three re-typings it will be ready by September . . . I plan to work on it in Norfolk . . . The former tentative title, 'Housekeepers of Ancient Springtime' appears in the book but I have decided against it . . . My new tentative title is *Gulliver Everywhere*. And I'm afraid the novel is crazy, slight, with one small spark and a few possibilities . . .[11]

She told Bill Brown that, in Levin, she had been 'sinking deeper and deeper into the mire . . . [But] in Auckland, I am renewed: this city . . . is as seductive as ever and I'm beginning to think that . . . I may end up shifting back here again. The drawback, however, is the inflation of property values — half a million dollars for a shack — Alas alas. The light and sky are lovely, though, and I'll enjoy them while I may.'[12]

She said to poet Gregory O'Brien, who visited to interview her for a book on New Zealand writers, that she was enjoying being away from the day-to-day trappings of her house and life in Levin. 'Freed from belongings and domestic chores, she was able to channel all her energy into her work . . . She writes a final draft [continuously]. This enables her to achieve unity of time and expression, while leaving room for those *moments of invention,* surprises that crop up along the way . . . She goes to bed at night "wrapped in it". Her sleep is often interrupted, sometimes hourly, by the continuous flow of ideas and words.'[13]

In Auckland, Frame heard from Peter Dawson's lawyer that Flint Cottage was now 'uninhabitable'. '[That] could be,' she told John Money, 'if rain and snow have damaged the electrical wiring . . . The ceiling upstairs has fallen in under the weight of snow, and there was one window on that side broken in a storm, and the little caravan is no longer weatherproof . . . I think I can make a stay of it for a few weeks but not for the three months I wanted.'[14] When she heard that John Money would be in England at the time she was there, Frame asked if he could collect her on 7 June and drive her and her luggage to London.[15]

She returned to Levin on 10 April and prepared for the trip to England, which she believed would be her last. The one factor that helped her travel with an easier mind was that there was no cat to worry about. On 7 May she flew out of Auckland in the company of the Gordons, who were travelling with her as far as London then going on a tour of their own around the United Kingdom and Eastern Europe.[16]

At Itteringham Common in the second week of May 1987 Frame found her cottage in as bad a condition as the lawyer had said — worse, in fact, because a water pipe had burst inside a week before she arrived and inundated the downstairs. Being Frame, however, she found consolation even amid the desolation. '[Every] time I go to the lean-to to use my toilet bucket, I apologise to the swallows nesting there . . . the two birds come and go through an opening in the top of the door.'[17]

She told Bob Cawley that the garden was 'in ruins and in blossom — the two apple trees, the raspberry canes, and the gooseberry bushes; and the nettles. I have broken a path . . . dug a hole for burying and hitched up a clothesline.'[18] The goods she had consigned from New Zealand, including her typewriter, had not arrived, and consequently her manuscript languished, awaiting attention. But she found usable bedding in the caravan; and she was as enchanted as ever by the Norfolk landscape and light.

During my earlier stays here, mostly in September–October, I was always impressed by the Norfolk dark. Now, at night, the world is grey *all night* & it's not a twilight grey . . . but the grey of Gustave Doré's illustrations of Dante's woods of Hell (the outlook of the cottage is upon trees & 'thicket' — firs, chestnut, yew, cypress) . . . During the night I get up & draw the curtain & look out at the strange eerie grey world with all its bones showing.[19]

On 29 May the cottage was auctioned for £30,000. Frame stayed on for another week, writing some poems, but mainly reading some of the sixty or so books that remained in the house. Despite the isolation, mail was delivered twice a day and groceries brought to the door from local shops. She told Bob Cawley that the neighbourhood was 'extraordinarily rich in character, with a higher proportion of courage than is usual where I live . . . I suppose this is . . . because Antipodean courage is embellished by and perhaps lost in the sweetness and light of climate and comfort — whereas here their life, like the summer dark, is exposed and unadorned.'[20]

Frame's final task was to put a wooden cross on Dawson's grave at Itteringham. Elspeth Barker, wife of poet George Barker, organised one of her son's friends to carve it. Then Frame gave her Dawson's old bureau and her own Olivetti typewriter — which arrived from New Zealand the day before she left — and sent the remaining books to the library at the Maudsley Hospital.[21]

On 7 June John Money, an English cousin, and a doctor friend, drove her back to London. A major chapter in her life had closed and Frame would never return to Norfolk. Nor did she expect, even, to return to England. In London she saw Karl Stead and walked with him through Hyde Park; and Bob Cawley. Her letter of thanks to Cawley had all the features of an elegiac farewell. 'At [our] age the goodbyes increase, goodbyes encompassing anything from people to thoughts to pets to places to dreams . . . Because I am a solitary person, my hellos are limited . . . I find also that while I am sometimes lonely, it is not the kind of loneliness that is healed by people, in fact I grow more unwilling to venture among people . . .'[22]

Back in Levin on 17 June, Frame opened piles of mail, which she then placed in boxes labelled 'unanswered May June 1987', to join all the other boxes similarly labelled for the previous months and year. Then she settled to rewrite the manuscript of the new novel, which had travelled around the world with her unread and untouched. 'I have retyped only five chapters out of thirty-five,' she told Bob Cawley on 7 July, 'but given the winter peace and quiet I should have retyped the book twice by late September, to fit it into shape. Apart from the world of my work — I mean the preoccupation of the book — the real world (except for . . . sky, snow-covered mountains, spring flowers, trees) seems very bleak.'[23]

It seemed even bleaker later that month when Geordie Frame, visiting Wellington, had a heart attack and was taken to hospital. He gave June Gordon's name as his next of kin; and the Levin police came to the Gordons' house to tell them the news. June and Wilson then drove to Wellington Hospital to visit him. Early in August 1987, when Geordie was to be discharged, the hospital rang June and asked her to take him home to her place. At this point June felt her brother was manipulating her and asked the hospital to contact Geordie's eighteen-year-old son, George Frame jnr, who lived in Oamaru. She and Janet then composed a to-whom-it-may-concern letter, initially for Wellington Hospital:

> For personal and medical reasons, my sister Janet Frame and I, June Gordon, have been strongly advised to keep our lives completely separate from that of our brother George Frame. We have followed this advice for the past twenty to thirty years.
>
> While we are concerned about his illness, our complete separation from him must remain, and any communication must be from a distance only. George is aware of this. His son Mr George Frame Junior lives at 32 Stour Street, Oamaru, and is next of kin.[24]

Geordie's exploits would continue to perplex and worry his sisters. Scarcely a year went by that he was not reported in the press for some newsworthy escapade; and those reports always identified him as 'brother of author Janet Frame'. Earlier in 1987, under the heading 'Sporran Rifled', the New Zealand Press Association filed a story nationally about Geordie collapsing on the Southerner train and being taken to Timaru Hospital. When he got there he alleged that the sporran, which he was wearing with kilt and tam-o'-shanter, had been unzipped and $150 and a starting pistol removed from it. Asked about the purpose of the starting pistol, he said he carried it so that he could attract attention if he needed help.[25] Two months later he placed an advertisement in the personal column of the *Otago Daily Times* which read 'If you find me collapsed and lying on the road, don't send for ambulance, don't take me to hospital.'[26]

At the end of the year, realising that they had a larger-than-life character on their doorstep, the *Oamaru Mail* ran a two-part feature on Geordie headed 'George Frame Remembers'. In this he gave his own version of Frame family history and criticised his writer sister for giving him 'little credit' in her autobiographies.

> George too has dabbled in the art of writing and has written several poems and short stories over the years but has never had any published. His bad spelling is the main reason for publishers turning his work down, he says.
>
> Now living alone at Willowglen, George's bad heart limits the amount of things he can do. Often seen around Oamaru wearing his kilt, George does not wear it because he has Scottish origins, but rather to prevent him from working in his yard. 'I wear my kilt so that I don't get tempted to do work around the yard. There's a lot of work you can't do when you're wearing a kilt.'
>
> Because of his indisposition George is considering selling Willowglen

and buying a smaller property as it has got to the stage where he can not cope with the work the place demands.[27]

The extent of that work was made clear in a photograph accompanying this feature, which showed Geordie lying in bed amid a degree of disorder that had literally to be seen to be believed. All this squalor went up in flames eight months later, when the house and possessions were destroyed by fire. Geordie survived with only the pyjamas he was wearing and the bicycle he used to support his escape. Everything he lost was uninsured.[28]

Once the immediate crisis involving her brother was resolved in August 1989, Frame decided to move to a smaller house and property five streets away, in Rugby Street. She bought a semi-detached flat, separated from its neighbour by a double garage and a stone wall. She described it to Bill Brown as 'wooden, with a New Zealand iron roof, but . . . sturdy with old-fashioned windows that don't show you sitting at your breakfast table, head to toe. There are two bedrooms, one of which I'll use as a study.'[29] She could not move into it, however, until she finished retyping the novel in November. At about the same time she acquired another cat from the local vet ('free to a good home') and called her Penny — 'short for Penelope, a variant of Fenella . . . an old Irish name meaning white shoulders'.[30]

She finished typing the final version of the novel in the last weekend in October, and posted copies off to Hutchinson in Auckland, Tim Curnow in Sydney, Anthea Morton-Saner in London and Carl Brandt in New York. After further vacillations ('Housekeepers of Ancient Springtime'? 'The Orchard of Puamahara'? 'The Memory Flower'?) she settled on *The Carpathians* as a title (from the Slavonic word for mountain used for the East European range extending from Poland to Romania). It drew heavily on her recollections of the Marquands in New York and the Bahamas (and both locations featured, as well as Levin, which was called Puamahara, the 'memory flower'). Frame described the book to Tim Curnow as a 'coded dream';[31] and she told George Braziller that it was the first of a planned series of novels.[32] Hutchinson agreed rapidly to publish it in New Zealand (they would print 4000 copies initially and pay an advance of $3000); and Braziller took it in America, despite the agents' hope that it would be offered elsewhere. In England, however, Curtis Brown recommended that it go to Bloomsbury, a new firm run by Liz Calder, a publisher who had lived in New Zealand, because of a number of dissatisfactions with the performance of the Women's Press. This provoked an anguished letter from Ros de Lanerolle, who told Frame that she found it 'hard to believe that you felt so unfriendly towards us, and suspect your agent of a bit of double dealing'.[33] Frame replied that she felt no hostility towards the Women's Press, only that she wanted to be published by a 'general' publisher. 'When I learned that you did not want to republish *Daughter Buffalo* because its main characters were men, I felt that I wanted to be published or not using other criteria.'[34]

Frame moved into the Rugby Street flat in November 1988, and took much of the summer to unpack and organise her books and papers — a more difficult task this time, because she had less space than before. And, after dutifully lugging it about for two decades, she gave away the crippled and cumbersome *Landfall* desk to Bowen Street neighbours. In December and January she read Laura Jones' scripts for the film series of the autobiographies, and pronounced them 'clever and faithful . . . I prefer to make as little comment as possible, because it's not *my* script and the whole must belong to the person writing it. I would like music and sky (in various countries) and the quality of light and death to be "characters" which continue with me through the series, otherwise the film may become a series of episodes with myself as the only developing character. Although this is a true picture of my life among people, it needs to include the rich "other" life.'[35]

To Bridget Ikin, Frame wrote in the New Year that the scripts were 'quite luminously beautiful'. But she expressed disquiet about the hospital scenes derived from *Faces in the Water*. '[For] me, they don't fit into the autobiography . . . [That] time is a film in itself and ought to be portrayed as a period of years and years rather than a "dipping into" to get a taste . . . [It was] a time of the seemingly everlasting nightmare . . . which still haunts me.'[36] She eventually came to an agreement with Ikin and Jones about which of these scenes should be used, and how; and she made other useful suggestions about idiom, costuming and furniture which the script writer and producer were only too happy to incorporate. She also sent, on tape, her own version of childhood rhymes and songs which provided further touches of authenticity. Most of all, Ikin, Campion and Jones were grateful for Frame's recognition that the film was ultimately *their* property rather than hers; and for trusting them sufficiently to allow them to make their own artistic decisions.[37]

By mid-year 1988, Ikin was able to tell Frame that pre-production work on the films would begin in February 1989, when Campion would have finished directing her first feature film, *Sweetie*, in Australia. Filming on the Frame project would occur over July to October 1989, and the series should be ready to go to air in March 1990. Television New Zealand, the Australian Broadcasting Corporation and Channel Four in Britain bought the series in advance.[38]

Frame, meanwhile, was restless in the new flat. The summer was hot and humid; and Rugby Street seemed to be as noisy with suburban holiday activities as any place in which she had lived. And she felt compressed by the size of the building and lack of storage space. When she saw in the local paper a property advertised for sale near Shannon, a 'dying' community thirty-three kilometres from Palmerston North and seventeen from Levin, she asked the Gordons to drive her there to inspect it. What she found was a seventy-year-old farm house whose owners, the Moynihans, had built a new house over the hill from the old one. The old house sat on an acre of land, surrounded by paddocks. As Frame told Bill Brown, '[When I] sat beneath the 120-year-old Australian pepper tree, listening to the wind . . . singing in the grass and not a neighbour in sight . . . I knew I'd found "my place".' She had decided to buy the house and live there for eight months, to see 'whether I can cope with dreams realised . . .'[39] But she would retain the town flat for the period, and return there if country living turned out not to be to her liking.

She paid $56,000 for the property, most of which came from proceeds from the sale of Peter Dawson's cottage, and moved there on 8 March 1988. It lay three kilometres from Shannon, a small servicing centre that was in decline because of the effects of economic restructuring on industry and a sharp downturn in income from farming. The valley that contained Frame's acre was one of 'rich grasslands framed by the jagged range of the Tararuas'.[40] The house had been well maintained and had high ceilings and spacious rooms with one open fireplace, one enclosed, and both an electric and a coal range in the kitchen. The kitchen also had, Frame noted in an excess of nostalgia, 'a pulley clothes-drier — [and] there's a bootscrape at the back door'.[41] As she had done in Stratford, she felt she was returning to scenes from her early childhood, and she added to this feeling by taking over the Rhode Island red chickens which came with the house and acquiring a goose and gander to graze the grass and act as 'watchdogs and creatures to be watched'. Penny the cat was transformed rapidly into a farm animal and caught rats with panache, and played happily in and around trees and grass.[42]

'I have golden fields, trees, sky, a river and silence except for the sound of the wind [and] the numerous birds — pukeko squawking, tiny wrens piping, magpies galore, a few kingfishers, wood pigeons. I'm at home,' Frame told John Money after six weeks in the house.[43] It was a taste of Willowglen life, only more spacious, more comfortable, and without family stress. The only major drawback was that the post office and grocery shop were three kilometres away, and Frame had to cycle there and back, which would present problems in winter. So she began to study the road code and take driving lessons from a Shannon instructor, with a view to buying her own car.

Frame's first visitor, apart from family, arrived in mid-May. He was Douglas Wright, a gifted young dancer who 'fell in love' with Frame through her books when he was a schoolboy in South Auckland in the late 1960s, and came to regard her as 'an imaginative elder'. He conversed with her by telephone when she was in Stratford. In 1983, when Wright was part of the Paul Taylor Dance Company in New York, he met Tobias Schneebaum, Frame's friend from her 1982 stay at Yaddo. He and Wright became friends, because of their mutual association with Frame. Back in New Zealand Wright visited Frame at Levin and at Shannon; and in May 1988 brought with him videos of three of his new dances. Later in the year, he would return with Schneebaum. Frame enjoyed Wright's company and admired his dancing and choreography. For his part, he would say that his work 'exists partly because of her'; and that he was always engaged by the 'odd, startling and true things' each conversation with her threw up.[44]

The following month Jacquie Baxter came to stay. 'I made a rabbit pudding which in the old cookery book was printed next to "Pork pie with Figgy Pastry" . . . I cooked [it] in layers of mushrooms, bacon, tomatoes, herbs from the garden, and enclosed in pastry . . . Neither Jacquie nor I had tasted rabbit for years . . . [The] local butcher gave it to me free, I don't know why.' Frame reported also that John Baxter, one of her favourite protégés, was now starting on a Diploma in Maori Studies at Victoria University 'and doing very well'.[45]

Frame too was doing well with her driving lessons. She assured John Money that 'I really am very watchful, but I haven't yet got the skill to see *everything* at once . . . Sometimes I leave the choke out [and] forget to notice the temperature.'[46] She passed her learner's licence none the less, on 4 July 1988 — a month short of her sixty-fourth birthday. And she bought herself (appropriately enough for a writer of fiction) a small Daihatsu Charade which, as her confidence grew, she would drive conscientiously at a steady 75 to 80 km/h — mostly to the local shops, but eventually to Levin; and to Palmerston North, where June and Wilson Gordon moved to in the course of the year.

The impending publication of *The Carpathians* in New Zealand in September brought further visitors. Marion McLeod, wife of poet Bill Manhire, came to Shannon in August 1988 to interview Frame for the *Listener*. And Elizabeth Alley followed soon after to record another radio interview. McLeod's story described the setting for her conversation with Frame:

> An old wooden farmhouse, white with a brown roof, standing alone in the valley — a child's drawing with smoke coming out of the chimney. Clumps of wild daffodils by the double farm-gates and what could be a sprightly farmer's wife (grey and white handknit jersey, red tights) coming down the long drive to greet us . . . the aureole of frizzly red hair now grey and close-cropped. Nobody, these days, would suggest [Frame] have it straightened.

Passing through the author's house, McLeod noted 'the big living room with a large table and a comfortable couch covered with a homely tartan rug. The crocheted hat of many colours on the table is her own work: "I do them on aeroplanes — hats and Henry James, both very soothing."'

> Adjacent to the couch is a tray with a board set up for chess. 'I have this special little chess computer. I used to play against the big computer but I always won.' Frame plays three or four games a day against this little specialist machine, always set at the hardest level, naturally. 'I often beat it. I always play white so that I can start. I like to make unusual moves — it gets confused.'[47]

In the broadcast interview with Elizabeth Alley, which she submitted to with 'much grace but some discomfort', Frame spoke more of the process of writing. '[The] hope is always that the imagination comes home to rest in invisible places. The bee comes here and leaves on each word traces of honey that we've never had before — that kind of thing.'

Writing *The Carpathians*, Frame said, had placed her in some kind of whirlpool.

[And] after I'd written it . . . I felt those reading it to be within this whirlpool; the whole world with everything broken by the gravity star, but not lost. Everything was to be renewed — rebuilt, selves, thought, language, everything. It was a death but only in the sense that death is a horizon to be travelled beyond . . . In the first part of the book Mattina is collecting detail, and her object is to . . . perfect her love; and the second part of the book is where she carries all this detail away, . . . everything reaches this horizon and is . . . broken into pieces like a whirlpool . . . she has become two-dimensional and three-dimensional, she even . . . has these experiences which are repeated in a . . . so-called Novella (the 'imposter' novel) . . . So she sort of finds herself sliding along in . . . going down into the whirlpool. But there's this sense of unease, I did feel it when I re-read it . . . I felt what on earth's happened, everything's gone, it's like a death, but it's not a death, it's not really gloomy.[48]

Oddly, while the novel's legendary 'memory flower' was a fiction, the idea of a pervasively influential 'gravity star' was not. Frame quoted at the front of the book from a Press Association report she had read in the *Dominion* newspaper: 'A survey of distances to galaxies has revealed something that at first seemed implausible: a galaxy that appears to be both relatively close and seven billion light years away . . . [The] paradox is being interpreted as being caused by the focussing of light from a distant quasar (starlike object) by the gravity of an intervening galaxy.'[49] The use of the name Carpathians — for a range of hills in New Zealand known in real life as the Tararuas — was another metaphor for the simultaneous distance and proximity signified and made possible by the gravity star.

Frame's employment of this almost 'science fictive' possibility to determine the shape and content of the new novel led Alley to ask her if she was becoming more interested in surrealism. 'Perhaps', Frame replied. 'I could define [surrealism] as what is beyond the real . . . It becomes like staring at an x-ray of the real and the visible. *That's* what I'm interested in.'[50]

The appearance of *The Carpathians*, in New Zealand and Britain in September 1988, and in the United States in December, made clear the relevance of this discussion, and — perhaps — the need for it. It was almost universally seen as a 'difficult' novel, exploring as it did 'the problematic relationship between the claims of self, fiction and the activity of writing'. Michele Leggott outlined the Chinese box nature of the 'plot':

> Inside the novel written by Janet Frame is one written by John Henry Brecon, son of wealthy New Yorker Mattina Brecon and her writer husband, Jake. Mattina's story is being told 'in the third person' — with an initial disclaimer by Brecon jun. that the events of his novel bear any relation 'to actual persons living or dead'.
>
> Within the story of Mattina's two-month trip to Puamahara . . . is a usurping type-script, shown to Mattina by her 'imposter novelist' neighbour, that takes over a third of its parent novel, before releasing Mattina into a terrifying account of the apocalypse of human language.
>
> She survives, though mortally ill, faced with the task of getting her story out through these fictive layers (reality boxes?) to husband Jake, who will tell it to son John Henry, who has written it as fiction, read by us reading Janet Frame's 11th novel . . .[51]

There were parallels here with the lives of the Marquands: John, who, like Jake, had been struggling to write his second novel; Sue, like Mattina, the wealthy New York wife with an elderly Nanny or housekeeper, to whom she is closely attached; and James, like John Henry, the son who has ambitions himself of being a writer — to say nothing of locations in New York and the Bahamas that bore a close resemblance to the Marquands' households in both places.

Opinions in the New Zealand reviews were sharply divided on the question of whether or not Frame had 'succeeded' in conveying her artistic vision. Margaret Scott in the *Sunday Times* and Michele Leggott in the *Evening Post* felt that she had;[52] Tony Reid in the *New Zealand Herald* and David Ballantyne in the *Otago Daily Times* felt that she had not.[53] Patrick Evans in the *Listener* exposed the subtleties of the novel's many layers and spoke disparagingly of Frame's 'house style', and her 'evasions and displacements'. In *The Carpathians*, he wrote, she reverts 'to her basic posture as a writer, to a kind of late provincialism that is common to New Zealand writers of her generation. This involves a distaste for her immediate environment, a deep conviction that, however hard the writer may pretend, life in this country was never made to be written about.'[54]

Reviews in the United Kingdom were equally mixed, with some, such as Fleur Adcock in the *New Statesman & Society*, excavating the complexities and concluding that they added up to 'good fiction';[55] and others, such as David Nokes in the *Observer*, seeing the whole exercise as 'more than a little forced'.[56] Robert Nye in the *Guardian* voiced what was probably the most common verdict: 'Frame seems to me to be misleading her own talent when she has moral and philosophic designs on the reader. Her successes come when she is concerned simply to imitate experience in fiction, to create a continuum where life is going on.'[57]

In the United States there were markedly fewer reviews than for Frame's previous novels and the autobiographies, perhaps reflecting the fact that Braziller's promotion — again — was minimal, and this despite his promise to mount 'major promotion' as a condition for retaining publishing rights to Frame's work. *Time* ignored it, as did many of the journals of stature. Most of those that did review it, such as the *San Francisco Chronicle*, were of the view that 'Frame's magical writing ultimately leaves us disappointed by the novel's failure'.[58] The one exception to all this was Nancy Wartik in *The New York Times Book Review*, who said that *The Carpathians* was 'fascinating, frustrating, obscure, complex, with a deceptively haphazardous plot and confoundingly shifting points of view . . . But it is a small masterpiece of literary craftsmanship, the work of an original thinker with a poet's ear for the sound and cadence of language.'[59] Unexpectedly, the place where the reviews were almost uniformly admiring was Australia, where Frame was building up a small but strongly loyal following of readers and reviewers.[60]

In November 1988 Frame decided to remain in the Shannon house — despite a September flood which had lapped the front door — and sell the flat in Levin. She gave most of the proceeds to her brother, to enable him to buy another house after his own was destroyed by fire in October. Writing from the verandah on a 'grey-calm day', she told John Money that she had become, again, a country person. 'I'm learning to accept the torture that is part of animal life and I've come to look on these sheep and cattle as noble souls far superior to us human beings . . .'[61] With her 'full' driver's licence she was enjoying use of the car, though she took it more frequently to Palmerston North than to Levin, whose approach road from Shannon was 'treacherous'. Her one source of anxiety, she said, was that she seemed unable to write since publication of *The Carpathians*. 'It's a cause of some despondency and a sad feeling of one whose work has "come to nothing" — a grim questioning: Is this the end then?'[62]

She was experiencing her customary 'post-book blues', this time intensified by a strain of influenza which kept going into remission and returning over the next six months. She was also disappointed by the puzzled and unfavourable reaction of so many reviewers to *The Carpathians*. 'Some understand, some don't,' she told Tim Curnow. 'I can only do my best.'[63] She was depressed too that, as usual, she had heard nothing from Carl Brandt or George Braziller about American publication of the book and had not received her author's advance copies let alone reviews. And in the United Kingdom, where many of the reviews had been favourable, there was disappointment that the novel failed to achieve nomination for the Booker Prize, which fellow New Zealand writer Keri Hulme had won in 1985. Perhaps the most graphic example of the manner in which the new novel had been misrepresented and misunderstood was a request from the German publisher Argument Verlag to be allowed to publish it in their 'crime suspense thrillers'.[64]

By January 1989, Frame herself was feeling more optimistic about future writing. She told Tim Curnow that *The Carpathians* was 'the first of three or four (or five novels) based on the makeup of the novel, although each one will not be so confiding and obvious . . . I will keep quiet about this.' She also said that a volume of stories was possible — 'fifteen await writing as outcrops from (though unrelated to) *The Carpathians* . . . The process of writing [stories] is very strange . . . more like chasing butterflies or mosquitoes than netting a swarm of words . . . I "capture" them by writing down their titles.'[65]

This return of confidence was welcomed by her agents and publishers. But it was her earlier comment that proved the more prescient. Frame would produce no further books in the coming decade, neither fictional nor autobiographical. What remained of her writing career would be carried on the wings of reputation, and of work already completed.

January 1989 brought a further setback. Geordie Frame, 'brother of author Janet Frame', got himself again into very public trouble. On this occasion he had been taken into police detention after falling asleep in a Christchurch bus shelter. According to him, police had twisted his arms behind his back, handcuffed him, roughed him up, and tossed him in a cell. 'There was blood all over the cell floor because my toe was bleeding. They didn't bring my bag with the medicine I've got to take, they refused when I asked for a doctor, and they refused me a lawyer.' He told the *Dominion* newspaper that the way he had been handled was 'worse than the way he was treated by Russian authorities when he was arrested in Berlin as a suspected American spy . . . [Asked] why he was behind bars, he was told [it] was because he had been intoxicated. This was the last straw for Mr Frame because he was a Mormon elder before losing his hearing in a riding accident 27 years ago. "I don't drive," he said . . . "I may be deaf, but I'm not dense. I've been around the world a bit . . ."' Not unexpectedly, police denied the allegations, and Geordie Frame declined to make a formal complaint.[66]

February brought news that poor reviews had had an effect on sales of *The Carpathians* in New Zealand. Out of 5000 hardbacks released onto the market in September 1988, only 3000 had sold. This was a considerable drop on previous recent sales figures; and Frame's New Zealand publisher, David Ling, hoped that the trend would be rectified by favourable publicity for the coming round of literary awards. This optimism seemed well-founded when, a month later, *The Carpathians* was declared to be a finalist in the fiction section of the New Zealand Book Awards. Century Hutchinson were also sufficiently confident in the long-term 'bankability' of their star author to release a

4000-copy single volume edition of the autobiographies at the end of March 1989.[67]

Other good news concerned the film. Bridget Ikin's company Hibiscus Films had been successful in raising finance for the television series. Ikin confirmed that shooting would begin on 7 August. Everyone associated with the project took considerable heart from the fact that, in the same month, Jane Campion's film *Sweetie* was selected for competition at the Cannes Film Festival.[68]

By mid-year *The Carpathians* had won the New Zealand Book Award for fiction, but failed to gain a place in the better-funded (and better promoted) Wattie Book of the Year competition. Just as Frame's New Zealand publisher began to express annoyance at this latter outcome news arrived of a potentially more rewarding prize. Frame was named winner of the South-East Asian and South Pacific section of the Commonwealth Writers Prize. This was worth £500; and regional winners were eligible to win the Commonwealth-wide award, worth £10,000. The result would be announced at a dinner in Sydney in November 1989. All of this was good for morale; though Frame's flu had recurred throughout the year and, in addition, she developed a lung infection. These problems in combination severely undermined her stamina for work or even for writing letters.

She was well enough to go to Auckland for a week in August, however, to watch the actors and film crew at work on *An Angel at My Table*. Frame travelled north by train with Margaret Gordon, a Levin friend of her sister and brother-in-law, who was also Jane Campion's godmother. They stayed at a motel in Herne Bay with Laura Jones and the cast and crew and went out with them each morning to observe filming. Much of the shooting was being done in a warehouse in Mt Albert, where indoor sets had been constructed of the Eden Street and Willowglen houses. And it was there that John Maynard, the film's co-producer, photographed the four Janets: Kerry Fox, who played the adult Frame; Karen Fergusson, the adolescent; Alexia Keogh (the child); and Frame herself.

Frame enjoyed the week immensely. 'All those red-wigged Janets running around!' she told Bill Brown. 'I'm full of admiration for the talent and dedication of all the crew.'[69] She was almost persuaded to appear in the film as an extra, in a scene where 'sympathetic neighbours' arrive to mourn the loss of Myrtle and admire the photograph of her reconstructed arm. Frame was especially admiring of actress Kerry Fox who, she thought, supplied the right nuances of her adolescent and young adult creativity and vulnerability.

Coincidentally, at the very time the Hibiscus film was being shot in and around Auckland, seventh form students of Waitaki Girls' High School were making a forty-two-minute video entitled *Janet Frame's Waimaru*, in which they filmed Oamaru locations mentioned in Frame's fiction and autobiography. They added voice-over commentary about the author's life and work and — without permission — included extracts from the books; local short story writer Owen

Marshall, who taught at Waitaki Boys' High School, rounded off the programme with an assessment of Frame's career. One of the students involved in the production was Frame's niece, also Janet, Geordie's daughter. The video was subsequently made available as an 'educational aid' for Otago schools.

Meanwhile Curtis Brown continued their efforts to bring Frame's work back into print in as many markets as possible. A contract was signed with Pandora in London to republish *Daughter Buffalo* in a 12,000-copy print run (of which 4000 would go to Australia). This brought Frame an advance of £1500. In New Zealand she earned another $4000 as an advance on a Century Hutchinson edition of *The Lagoon and other stories*, republished almost forty years after Caxton's original printing. And arrangements were set in train to publish the screenplay of the film of *An Angel at My Table*, with Frame and Laura Jones sharing the income.[70]

By October 1989 Frame had doubts about remaining in Shannon. While she enjoyed the quiet, she was beginning, after nineteen months, to regret the almost total absence of human activity within sight and sound of her house. In addition, in a year when her health had been poor, she found it a burden to commute to and from Palmerston North for medical care. She wrote to Bob Cawley to offer good wishes on his retirement and said that, because of sickness, she had 'lost the winter — although I suspect it will turn up somewhere'.[71] Early in the New Year, she said, she would return to town because, while she enjoyed peace, the country house was quieter than a grave. The specific decision she had to make was whether to return to Levin or move to Palmerston North, to be nearer the Gordons once more and to enjoy the wider cultural amenities offered by a 'university city'.

In November Frame was asked to attend the dinner at the Sydney Opera House at which the overall award for Commonwealth Writers Prize would be announced. She did not feel like travelling so she declined. When she was telephoned by one of the organisers and told she had won, and that they would appreciate her presence to add to the sense of occasion, Frame suggested they give the prize to one of the writers who *could* be there.[72]

Instead, Century Hutchinson publisher Lance Earney and Tim Curnow attended on Frame's behalf, and Earney accepted the envelope with her name on it. *The Carpathians* had won the award, the judges announced, because it was 'a novel of great visionary depth which added a new significance to the art of fiction'. Curnow was especially pleased because, earlier in the year, the Commonwealth Award for Poetry had gone to his seventy-nine-year-old father. Earney and Curnow believed that inside the presentation envelope would be a cheque for £10,000. But when they opened it, they found instead a hand-written note suggesting that Frame might like to fly to London to receive the cheque from the Queen at Buckingham Palace on 12 December.[73]

For Frame, this outcome represented good news and bad. She was pleased about the money (unlike her film fee, it would not be taxed), and about the distinction, especially the notion of a railway worker's daughter from Oamaru going to Buckingham Palace to accept an award from the Queen. She was *not* altogether thrilled about the idea of flying to and from England for such a short period of time. 'I think it's a shocking waste of money to be in London for five days,' she told Bob Cawley on 20 November. '[But] the occasion will be tolerable if there's a chance of saying hello to you . . .'[74] June Gordon was keen to accompany her sister.

By early December, however, the London trip was off. The organisers, the Commonwealth Foundation, noted Frame's dislike of travelling; and they noted that the Queen would be in New Zealand in February 1990, as part of the country's sesquicentennial celebrations. It was decided, therefore, to postpone the presentation and hold it at Government House in Wellington.

In December 1989 too Frame decided to vacate the Shannon house and move into Palmerston North. She bought a small brick unit in Alexander Street, and shifted there before Christmas. She did not dispose of the Shannon property, however. She left most of her books and papers there and told correspondents that she planned to let it, at a modest rental, to writers; and to return there herself to work from time to time. After her death, she said, she would turn it over to a trust to administer as a kind of mini-Yaddo, a sanctuary for artists and writers to work away from the distractions of normal domestic and suburban life.[75]

Two shocks in the course of the month were the death in Oamaru Hospital on 20 December in his sixty-eighth year of her brother, for whom she had always felt intense compassion despite the difficulties he had created for his sisters; and a letter from Bill Brown which arrived the same week, informing her that he had sold his papers, including her letters to him, to Pennsylvania State University library. Brown explained that he thought it 'better to place them now while I have control over them rather than leaving them for uncaring nieces and nephews to dispose of. They are such wonderful letters that I couldn't contemplate destroying them. The library offers protection . . . as no one can publish anything in them without our combined consent.'[76] This was a perfectly reasonable step to take. But, because of Frame's sense of privacy, she would still have preferred all her correspondents to destroy her letters rather than risk other people reading them and — at a later date — publishing their contents without necessarily providing a context which made sense of them.

Writing the following month to James McNeish, Frame emphasised that she had not yet sold her own papers to anybody, though Boston University had continued to make approaches to her (as recently as October 1985). 'Anything I have goes to the Hocken [Library] when I die but should I need money for my living years, I know that selling material is an option. [But] to end up overlooking the river Charles instead of the Leith . . .'[77]

Palmerston North in 1989 was the country's sixth largest city and provincial centre for the Manawatu region. Like Levin, it had initially grown as a service centre for farming and forestry activities, then grown with the spread of secondary industries in the twentieth century. The character of the city was conditioned by the presence of Massey University, which drew in a large population of staff and students and generated many of the cultural activities (theatre, film, music and bookshops) which orbited around a centre of higher learning. Frame's new home was in one of the city's outer suburbs, which was not greatly different in character from the streets in which she had lived in Levin.

As part of her plan for the long-term use of the Shannon house, Frame arranged in February to let the property to Frances Cherry, a Wellington writer who had just received an Arts Council grant to complete a second novel and needed somewhere quiet to work, away from domestic responsibilities. Frame herself settled into the Palmerston North flat and attempted to resume work on *her* new novel, but was interrupted too frequently over the summer — by visitors and 'business' correspondence — to make appreciable progress.

One of those interruptions was the visit to Government House in Wellington on 14 February 1990 to receive her Commonwealth Writers Prize, $21,000 in New Zealand currency, from the Queen. The occasion was part of a gathering of members of the Order of New Zealand, the country's highest civic award, restricted to only twenty members, which Frame now received in the 1990 New Year's honours (fellow writer members of the order were Allen Curnow and children's author Margaret Mahy). After being invested with the ONZ, Frame and Curnow each spent about twenty minutes in 'private audience' with Her Majesty.

The Queen was not at all put out that she and Frame faced each other in dresses of almost identical pattern and colour. Her Majesty showed an interest in the writer's diamond and ruby butterfly brooch, with one antenna missing, which Frame had inherited from Peter Dawson; and in her handbag ('Mrs Thatcher has one just like that'). The Monarch appeared not to have read any of Frame's books but she was, Frame noted later, 'well-briefed' about her work. They talked about autobiography, and the Queen said that so many of her ministers had written memoirs over the years, but when she came to read their account of things in which she herself had been involved, she often found them unrecognisable. She also lamented the fact that, everywhere one went these days, one was served a 'Continental' breakfast; no one seemed to make porridge any more (to which Frame's niece commented subsequently that if Her Majesty had had to make it herself, and clean the pot afterwards, she would understand why).[78] In all, Frame's impression of her Monarch was that of a likeable naïve woman who was almost innocent in her expectation that people would behave decently given half a chance; but, like Queen Victoria, she had clearly developed considerable political nous simply by 'being there' and associating with her ministers, starting with Churchill, over a long period. Her Majesty also confessed to Frame that she discussed affairs with 'the Duke', and found his advice helpful. The day ended with dinner at Orsini's restaurant, courtesy of the Commonwealth Foundation, which was attended by family (the Gordons) and friends (Jacquie Baxter, Piki Takiari, Derek Schulz, Jill Studd). All this had been immense fun, but, on top of moving house again, disruptive. Frame told Tim Curnow that *The Carpathians* and the Queen were partly responsible for the fact that all work on the new novel had come to a halt.[79] A further distraction, in April 1990, was the arrival of a videotape of the just completed television film *An Angel at My Table*, which she played and watched three times in rapid succession. She told a reporter subsequently that when she ran it through the first time she was too emotionally caught up in it to make a judgement. But by the third viewing she was pleased with the result. Indeed, she used the word 'thrilled . . . [Within] its own limits it found its own freedom and did [the job] splendidly,' she said. 'For me, that is a sign of excellence.' Her only mild reservation was about the effect of film as a genre rather than this film in particular. It was that when reality was altered for creative purposes, it tended to become as 'fixed' on film as it did in print. There were things that happened in the film that did not happen in her life which would now become part of the 'authorised version' of her life.[80]

Meanwhile the film now took on a life of its own, just as the books on which it had been based had done. The Sydney Film Festival screened the original three-hour version in June 1990 and it was voted the most popular film of the festival. It also generated reviews packed with superlatives. '[*An Angel at My Table*] is bound to appeal to audiences seeking an intelligent and compassionate study of a troubled but gifted woman . . . Campion and screenwriter Laura Jones have come up with a life-affirming celebration of the world of an eccentric, but obviously talented woman.'[81] The first New Zealand screenings followed at the Wellington and Auckland Film Festivals in July.

Encouraged by the responses to the film at these festivals, and after much heated discussion with the New Zealand Film Commission, Campion and Ikin agreed to convert the television version into a film for theatrical release. A round of further film festival invitations ensued, starting with a request to launch the film at the prestigious Venice Film Festival in September 1990 (the first time a New Zealand film had been so selected). It won eight awards there, including the Silver Lion and the Special Jury Prize. Then followed festivals in New York, Toronto, and many other cities over the following months. Theatrical releases were negotiated by the New Zealand Film Commission for New Zealand, Australia, the United States, Canada, the United Kingdom, France, Italy, Germany, Belgium, the Netherlands, Sweden, Spain and Japan. And the Women's Press moved rapidly to have a hardback edition of the autobiography ready for release in September 1990, when the film opened in British cinemas.

At the very time promotion and sales of the film were gathering momentum, however, Frame was in hospital. In mid-June she had a stroke.

She woke one morning to go to the toilet and found that the right side of her body was weak and she walked with a 'wobbly' gait. She was also nauseated and began vomiting. Wilson Gordon took her to the doctor, who had her admitted to Palmerston North Hospital. Overnight her condition improved rapidly and, in the opinion of medical staff, Frame had suffered 'no neurological deficits'. She was therefore discharged, with appropriate medication.

Back home, she 'informed' those who needed to know about this setback, and its impact on her life. The whole experience, she told Tim Curnow, had been 'a shock for me . . . [Yet] I think I'm almost fully recovered except possibly for a few more brain cells down the drain . . . I also have diabetes now and I've gone on a permanent diet and . . . have lost twenty pounds weight.' To her eventual biographer, with whom she was in correspondence about his biography of Frank Sargeson, she wrote that she was 'hoping to recover fully — until the next one!'[82] To occupy herself during the first weeks out of hospital she bought a laptop computer and 'laboured for at least a week' to master a new word processing program. She told David Ling that she was 'taking things quietly', although it was difficult to live *more* quietly than she had done previously.[83]

Frame now decided to simplify her life. She sold the car and the flat in Alexander Street and moved to a larger home, a thirty-year-old two-bedroom home in Dahlia Street, near the centre of the city (in the middle of town, but in a quiet pocket). She then also sold the Shannon property and had all her books, papers and chattels moved to the new house. Now she was located in an area close to shops, the post office, the doctor and the hospital. Over the weeks and months in mid-1990 that Frame made these arrangements, and began to recover her strength and confidence, the film continued to attract audiences, acclaim and awards, paralleling the history of the books on which *Angel* was based. It had opened to general audiences in London, where it earned £161,000 off one cinema in a single week; and in Sydney and Melbourne, where it took $250,000 from five screens in less than a fortnight. These were feats achieved by no previous New Zealand film. Then, as it opened progressively in other European centres, the film sparked an unprecedented demand for Frame's books, and her agents in London and Sydney were stretched to the limits to cope with an avalanche of requests about foreign language rights for the novels and the autobiographies.

By November 1990 Curtis Brown had organised Italian editions of the autobiographies and *Faces in the Water*, Spanish editions of the autobiographies plus *Faces* and *Maniototo*, Dutch editions of the autobiographies, Danish editions of the autobiographies and *Maniototo*, a Swedish edition of *To the Is-Land* and a Norwegian one of *Maniototo*. All these agreements brought with them advances on royalties for Frame, with the Italian and Spanish sums being especially high. The Australian distributor of the autobiography kept running out of stock and reordering from England (they were selling a thousand copies of each volume per month in October and November 1990); and Bloomsbury in

London paid Frame an advance of £3000 for a new edition of *The Lagoon*. Matters moved more slowly in the United States — not only because of George Braziller's apparent lethargy, but also because of extraordinary bad luck in the management of the film distribution: the film distributor went bankrupt, and the publicist died shortly after being appointed. Much of this lost ground was made up the following year, however, and Braziller would oblige with a new single-volume edition of the autobiography in anticipation of the American release of the film in May 1991.

Frame was staggered by the speed with which each one of the foreign rights agreements was followed by another.'I am amazed that [these] publishers have any faith in my work; and grateful,' she told Tim Curnow in November. 'I owe [it] to the work of Hibiscus Films, and (of course) the work of you faithful agents.' The news was not all good, however. In September she had suffered a mild cerebral 'episode' and reported to John Money, 'I'm only half as strong physically as I used to be, and goodness knows what moths have eaten into my brain.'[84]

By November she was feeling more confident; and in December she astonished her agents and publishers by accepting an invitation to visit Paris in April 1991, to help promote the film, provided Jacquie Baxter could travel with her. She also agreed to do 'a little bit of publicity' while there to promote the European editions of her books. By New Year 1991 she had gone cold on this idea, partly because she had been unable to secure a second airline ticket for Baxter. But she did hold out the hope that, 'in September or October, after I have surrendered my unwilling typescript, I may be able to travel to Europe and US and UK with my own funds, if I [still] have any . . .'[85]

In February 1991, Tim Curnow heard a rumour that the British Academy was promoting Frame for the Nobel Prize. '[Very] good news,' he told Carl Brandt. 'Our experience . . . is that such an award generates an enormous amount of interest in the entire body of an author's work.'[86] At the same time PEN New Zealand was continuing to nominate Frame annually for the award. Even as such rumours were mooted, however, and Frame's books going into foreign language editions undreamed of ten years previously, some commentators regarded her still as an 'unknown' and 'unappreciated' genius. Curnow felt obliged to write to Kerry Fox who, in the course of promotion for the film, had told a journalist that Frame was 'unfortunately not widely read beyond her homeland'.[87] And Oxford University Press in New Zealand turned down a manuscript on Frame's fiction by Gina Mercer, niece of the Australian poet A.D. Hope, on the ground that there was 'little interest' in Frame's work.[88]

And still the foreign editions accumulated: *Maniototo* went into Italian, and a Dutch publisher took *Faces in the Water* and *The Lagoon*; Norwegians published the autobiographies and *Faces*; *To the Is-Land* was published in French; Germans took the autobiographies and *Faces*; and there was a Japanese edition of the autobiographies and *Faces*. Century Hutchinson in New Zealand signed contracts with Frame for new editions of *The Adaptable Man, The Pocket Mirror* and *Mona Minim and the Smell of the Sun*. Bloomsbury in London put *The Lagoon* into paperback; and there were trade paperback editions of some of the earlier foreign language editions. For all these agreements, Frame received further advances on royalties. And on top of these sources of income there was additional money owed to her as a percentage of profit on the film (some $5000). News that the film would at last achieve cinema release in the United States in June 1991 promised to benefit sales of her books there, provided George Braziller could be persuaded to act. (And he *was* so persuaded, initiating select bookstore and radio promotions of the autobiographies — which did result in a small increase in sales, but nothing as spectacular as those which had occurred in New Zealand, Australia and the UK.)

It now became a matter of urgency for Frame to deal correctly with taxation arising from her multiple sources of substantial income. In April 1991 she consulted the Palmerston North office of the Department of Inland Revenue, and received what seemed to her to be the necessary advice and tax certificates. She also began to express doubts about whether *all* her previous work should be reprinted. With the death of her brother, reservations about republication of *The Edge of the Alphabet* were eliminated. But she now told Tim Curnow that she thought 'the earlier books (*Rainbirds, Adaptable Man, Edge of the Alphabet*) all have a subtly degrading attitude to women. They are of their time . . . pre-Feminist and narrow in outlook.' Any joy she took from them now, she added, came simply from her recollection of the pleasure of writing them.[89]

Writing was not something from which she was able to take pleasure in the second half of 1991. Since her stroke she lacked both physical and mental stamina and the medication she was taking to help control her diabetes and blood pressure seemed to intensify the lassitude. After speaking with her in July, Tim Curnow reported these problems to Curtis Brown in London with the verdict that there was no imminent prospect of a new Frame manuscript.[90] As she marked time, Frame experimented with a new computer and upgraded word processing software, sending out correspondence in a startling variety of shapes and formats and with unexpected graphics, such as a portrait of Mona Lisa.

In August she reported to John Money that the National Government, returned to power in 1990, had introduced a savage budget that slashed spending on beneficiaries and retained the surcharge on superannuitants, despite a pre-election promise to lift it. All this amounted to a 'collapse of the welfare state' and soon the old age pension would no longer be available as an entitlement. These measures were so severe, she said, that she would think about leaving New Zealand if she was able to build up sufficient funds from further advances and film earnings.[91]

Frame also brought Money up to date with family news. Wilson Gordon had had a serious heart attack, but appeared to be recovering, despite looking frail. Geordie's daughter, Janet, aged twenty-one, was about to marry a forty-six-year-old former ship's engineer in Oamaru; and Geordie's son, also known as Geordie, had become a father. 'Strange and significant the impetus of a father's death.'[92]

Her own progress was steady, and when Tim Curnow rang her from Auckland in October, he felt that his star New Zealand author was well on the way to recovering her health and resuming writing.[93] Almost at once, however, Frame was dealt another blow, which eroded any immediate prospect of writing. A letter arrived in the second week in October from an investigations officer of the Department of Inland Revenue.

> I have received instructions to examine your taxation returns forwarded to the Department. I would like you to call at this office on Thursday, 11 October 1991 at 10.00 am so that these returns can be discussed with you . . . Please have available the filing records . . . bank statements and cheque butts . . . cash-books, journals, ledgers and working papers . . . Invoices, receipts, vouchers, day books and any other business records . . . Full documentation relating to royalties received . . . Please also have your passport available at the interview.[94]

This was a considerable and wholly unexpected shock, coming as it did just over a year after one agency of the government had awarded her the country's highest civilian honour, and in the same year as what she viewed to be savage attacks on beneficiaries and the elderly. She was unable to locate and carry to the tax office all the documentation required by the due date. And so the investigating officer came to her and searched for and recovered the necessary documentation from 53 Dahlia Street.

Frame was persuaded to talk about the experience by the local newspaper, although she did not realise that what she said was being recorded and was regarded by the reporter as an 'interview'. The paper then claimed, with considerable inaccuracy, that the resulting story was Frame's 'first media interview for thirty years':

> 'The investigation has been a great shock to me. I can't understand it. I'm not an important person and I cannot write while this is going on.' She said the tax investigator came to her home looking for antique furniture and 'racehorses under the bed'. . . .
>
> Miss Frame said boxes of stuff had been removed from her house causing her a great deal of pain. 'I'm very sick.' [She] said she now had an accountant to look after her affairs. 'They were a little bit messy. But there is nothing wicked.'
>
> She said the taxman told her that just because she was famous didn't mean she didn't have to pay tax.[95]

The tax audit was carried out over four months. The investigations officer came and went from her home, each time bringing with him a further list of questions for Frame to answer and carrying away as many further papers as he had returned. For Frame, there was no diminution in anxiety. 'When I phoned [the taxman] yesterday,' she told Elizabeth Alley on 6 December, 'he said he had some queries about my not disclosing my full earnings, but when I asked him for details, he refused to give them, and made an appointment with me for 19th December. I suggested that in the meantime he write me a letter with details. He refused to do this. "Wait until 19th December." And as he has all my papers I can't even know what he is talking about, for I have indeed entered all my earnings. When it is "all over" I plan to deal with it in my own way.'[96]

The 'queries' which the investigations officer raised on this occasion, which implied fraud on Frame's part, turned out to be based on errors, or misunderstandings of her records. As word of the investigation spread, and of the length of time it was taking to complete, people including Frame's local Member of Parliament acted to try to have the proceedings halted. Her New Zealand publisher, David Ling, wrote to the Minister of Inland Revenue on 5 February 1992:

> I am writing . . . to express my concern at the effects that . . . [the] investigation . . . is having on her health and ability to continue writing. I imagine you are familiar with her Autobiography recently filmed as *An Angel at My Table*. The sensitivities that are the background to the creation of such outstanding literature, and that have been so frequently misunderstood by the 'outside world' have made Janet more vulnerable than most to this sort of intrusion into her affairs. . .
>
> [A] large number of her papers, including personal material [has] been taken from her home . . . She [has] found this profoundly disturbing, intrusive, and unsettling to the extent that she was unable to continue to work. . . Unfortunately they still haven't finished, despite the fact that Janet has maintained near-impeccable records, and a list of alleged discrepancies provided in December has since been shown to be the Department's errors.
>
> In addition to being overlong the investigation also seems overzealous. Janet has been asked to identify a sum as small as $25 [from John Money]. When told it was a gift from an overseas friend the investigating officer wanted to know who that person was. He has also asked her to identify a person he . . . saw her with when she came to collect a form from the Department.
>
> I don't mean to suggest that Janet's affairs cannot be questioned but the time that this is taking and the degree of intrusion are . . . too much. It is difficult to understand how we can award her the Order of New Zealand and then treat her with such a seeming lack of real under-

standing. Janet has told me that this is the most difficult time she has had since her time in hospital and is genuinely considering leaving the country as soon as this matter is resolved, in order to find some peace in which she can write again. I'm anxious to ensure that we do not lose our most distinguished living writer as a result of this situation.[97]

The standard reply to letters such as this was either to point out that no one was immune from the possibility of tax audits; or to say that the department was prevented from commenting on individual cases by requirements of confidentiality.

By March 1992 the only instance of the 'evasion' produced by the audit was a decision that Frame ought to have paid tax on the money inherited from the sale of Peter Dawson's cottage in 1987, an obligation of which she had been unaware; and on the Turnovsky Prize, which she had been advised at the time of the award was exempt from taxation. Inland Revenue now demanded that she pay $8000 in settlement of these obligations, which she did. At last the episode was over, and she ought to have been able to return to her writing.

In mid-March, however, she was confronted by a crisis of even greater magnitude. Her general practitioner asked if he could visit her at Dahlia Street after an investigation he had initiated for pain from an abdominal growth. He told her that the x-ray had revealed the presence of what appeared to be a fast-growing and malignant tumour, which indicated cancer of the ovaries or uterus or both. The outlook was not good, and it was possible that she had as few as nine months left to live. He arranged for her to see a gynaecological surgeon immediately, and it was likely that she would be admitted to Palmerston North Hospital for surgery that week. In the meantime, he said, it would be prudent to consider putting her affairs in order. What he did not say to her was that because of her existing medical problems, the operation itself would not be without risk.[98]

In the week of this visit Frame rang her sister, Jacquie Baxter, Bill Brown, John Money and George Braziller, to tell them the news. Baxter came at once to Palmerston North to help her prepare for her hospital admission on 17 March. The following day the surgeon removed a malignant cyst from her left ovary but decided that a hysterectomy would be 'hazardous'.[99]

Frame survived the operation, and it was then a matter of waiting to see if the cancer reappeared or spread and fulfilled her doctor's gloomy prognosis. She was not unaware of the irony inherent in this unexpected development: just when her income had increased to the point where she could look forward to living without the material anxiety that had always accompanied her, it now seemed that life itself was to be abbreviated. Surprisingly, this realisation brought no panic — only a feeling of resignation.

After she had told Jacquie Baxter about the cancer, her friend had responded in a letter-poem. 'There was,' she said,

in the changing
Timbre of your voice . . . an excited curiosity
As though you had already joined
The queue before the exit sign,
Poised to look back one last time
With raised hand, a traveller's
Flashing smile, before shuffling
Through the last gate
Eager to learn a new geography
Dwell in a different dimension.[100]

CHAPTER THIRTY

# An Allegiance to Origins

*E*VEN WHEN THEY APPEARED TO HAVE BEEN MANAGED SATISFACTORILY,
Frame's serious health problems in the early 1990s had enduring consequences.
Unsurprisingly, they left her with less physical and mental stamina than she
had enjoyed prior to the strokes and the surgery for cancer. This resulted in a
reduction in personal correspondence, which now shrank to exchanges of
cards, as well as a reduced capacity to work for lengthy and continuous periods
on fiction.

A second effect, however, was unexpected. As death had come to seem a
more likely and more proximate prospect, her dread of it — a burden she had
carried since adolescence — had diminished. When she had spoken to Jacquie
Baxter about her poor prognosis, her friend had been doubly shocked: at the
news itself; and at the near-eagerness with which it had been communicated.[1]
In the event Frame had survived. But, in the wake of illness, and in the relative
calm that followed, she found considerable difficulty returning to writing.
There would be no new books to follow *The Carpathians*, published four years
earlier. Despite this hiatus, however, her existing work continued to attract
recognition and honour. In March 1992, the day she entered hospital for
surgery, she was again made an honorary doctor of literature, this time by the
University of Waikato in Hamilton.

Elizabeth Alley, whom Frame had named as literary executor in a new will,
accepted the degree on the writer's behalf. The occasion was not designed to
rehearse the difficulties of Frame's life, Alley told the graduation audience.

> But even the distressing and debilitating investigation she has recently
> undergone at the hands of the Inland Revenue Department — quite
> unjustifiably as one might imagine — she has been able to turn to good
> account. Of that, and of her current illness, she was able to say to me . . .
> 'Whatever comes to the writer, good or bad, is all useful experience.'

That, I think, is the single most important focus of Janet Frame's life. That she is singlemindedly and unequivocally absorbed in the one thing that has profound meaning and continuity for her — interpreting the significance of the particular vision that enables her to write . . . to fix her focus on the coding of what is written to describe what has not yet been written.[2]

That 'Frame vision' was further described and discussed at length at the inaugural conference of the Association of New Zealand Literature in Dunedin in August 1992. This occasion was the first on which an entire conference was devoted to the significance of Frame's oeuvre. Scholars attended from New Zealand, Australia, Canada and the United Kingdom; and a paper arrived, without its author, from Italy. A journalist present noted that the participants considered Frame's writing 'from Freudian, Jungian, Kristevan, Irigarayan, Foucauldian, Bakhtinian and Marxist perspectives; allegorical, postmodern, postcolonial, feminist and Shakespearian readings were offered'. The non-academic section of the audience — 'those who had known Frame . . . or who have lived in or near Oamaru, were bewildered by the specialised language with which her words were interpreted'. Bewildered they may have been; but they were nonetheless eager 'to bask in the reflected glory of their heroine'.[3] Frame, unsurprisingly, declined to attend this celebration of her virtuosity.

Instead, she spent the mid-year months of 1992 convalescing from surgery. She had a second operation six weeks after the first, which revealed no further malignancy. 'After being told in March that I had six to nine months to live,' she wrote to Dorothy Ballantyne, 'they now think that I am "cured", although they wait five years for certainty . . . [I have] had the delight of several overseas visitors.'[4] These were Bill Brown and George Braziller, who made the long pilgrimage to Palmerston North for what they imagined were 'final visits' to salute and farewell their friend. They undertook this task with due solemnity; and they were delighted, if at first disbelieving, to hear subsequently that the crisis, though real enough, had vanished as abruptly as a plot twist in a Janet Frame novel.

By August 1992, the month of the Frame conference and of her sixty-eighth birthday, she felt sufficiently recovered to contemplate travelling abroad again the following year, even if her mood in announcing this intention had about it an air of farewell. First, though, she took a short South Island holiday with her sister, to prove to her doctor that she was sufficiently well to travel. Again, her mood was elegiac, and she told John Money that her view of the South Island had put her in mind of a poem by one of his ancestors, Oliver Goldsmith's 'The Deserted Village':

> Ill fares the land, to hastening ills a prey,
> Where wealth accumulates, and men decay;

Princes and lords may flourish, or may fade;
A breath can make them, as a breath has made;
But a bold peasantry, their country's pride,
When once destroyed can never be supplied.

This feeling, she said, was especially strong when she surveyed what had happened to the railways — 'stations falling to pieces, tracks uprooted, but trains . . . full of tourists'.[5]

If the trip had been devised, as she said, to test her stamina, then the outcome was ambiguous. Frame got as far as Dunedin, then succumbed to influenza. Instead of visiting widely (she saw only Ruth Dallas and Raymond and Joyce Ward), she took an early train home. She did promise, however, to return to the city for a writers' and readers' conference in March 1993, when John Money would be one of the invited guests, speaking on a panel of people who had been used as models in New Zealand fiction (in Money's case, as Brian Wilford in *Living in the Maniototo*).[6]

Back home in December Frame discovered that Sheila Leaver, the former Waitaki Girls' High School teacher who had organised the production of the student video *Janet Frame's Waimaru*, now wished to produce a book linking Frame's fictional and autobiographical writing to specific places in Oamaru. Frame wrote to both the would-be author and publisher to make it clear that she had objected to unauthorised quotations from her writing in the video; but that she had not taken action to prevent its distribution because it was an 'educational exercise'. She would, however, prohibit any such use of her work in book form. 'Comments, photos, yes, but not quotes.' She therefore declined permission for use of her copyrighted material. Frame also baulked at Leaver's suggestion that she should be 'memorialised' in Oamaru, but did say that she would not object to a proposal that a room in the Oamaru Public Library should be named for her.[7]

Over the summer of 1992/3 Frame returned to her desk and tried to coax the genesis of a novel back to life and growth, a kind of sequel to themes and characters in *The Carpathians*. But while it engaged her attention and met her need to renew herself daily in the act of writing, it did not develop to her satisfaction. At one point she told Tim Curnow that it was 'a crazy book, absorbing to write and quite impossible to solidify — it might vanish'.[8] In a sense it did vanish, in that while she continued to wrestle with it, she ceased to refer to it in correspondence and conversation. Future enquiries on behalf of Curtis Brown were politely parried.

It was not just that there were interruptions and distracting noises — these were constant. There seemed also to be an inability to relocate herself in that zone which Sargeson (quoting André Gide to her) had referred to as 'God's share'— that upwelling of patterns of words from the unconscious with which, in the past, she had been able to build paradigms of reality.[9] The content and style of her published fiction had always been forged from a deeply internalised tension. Was it true, as she had written to Bill Brown twenty years before, that 'the function of the imagination depends on the foreknowledge of death'?[10] More relevantly, was it true for her? And had she now, in a resigned acceptance of her fate, whatever that might prove to be, lost the taste of that foreknowledge? Whatever the cause, there was at this time no new writing of any substance that pleased her sufficiently to consider offering it for publication.

Earlier work continued to find new markets, however, through Curtis Brown's management of the continuing momentum generated by the autobiographies and the Campion film. Individual stories were being republished almost monthly. And, in a two-year period, she signed agreements for a Norwegian edition of *The Lagoon;* a Swedish edition of *Faces in the Water;* a Polish edition of *Faces;* Dutch editions of *Owls Do Cry* and *The Carpathians;* a French edition of *Owls;* Italian editions of *Owls, Scented Gardens,* and *Mona Minim;* a Hungarian edition of *Owls;* a Spanish edition of *Mona Minim;* and a Chinese edition of the autobiographies. Random House in New Zealand, who had taken over Century Hutchinson, published new editions of the autobiographies in single volumes, and *Mona Minim* and *Daughter Buffalo.*

The readers' and writers' festival came and went in March 1993 and Frame did not accompany John Money to Dunedin. She told him she had had a haemorrhage in one eye and also needed to remain at home while June Gordon underwent surgery for what was feared to be cancer but turned out to be a digestive problem.[11] She asked Money to come to Palmerston North, however, and he did so. Several months later Frame learned that Money too was facing a serious health problem, prostate cancer, for which he was given successful radiation treatment. Frame invited him back to Palmerston North to recuperate but her friend preferred to remain in Baltimore and gradually resume his work routine.[12] He did visit New Zealand for a family reunion in October 1993, however.

Honours continued to seek Frame out. At a special function in June the local university presented her with its highest award, the Massey University Medal. The accompanying citation said that Frame was 'in no small measure responsible for the fact that no one would [now] speak of New Zealand literature as if it were a shameful disease'.[13] In the same month Elizabeth Alley began to organise a kind of *festschrift* for Frame — a book of appreciation from friends and fellow writers — to be presented to her at the International Festival of the Arts the following year in a commemoration of her seventieth birthday. The gesture was originally planned as a surprise; but Alley eventually decided that she needed to consult Frame about the contributors and contents, in case that surprise turned out to be an unpleasant one (Alley was concerned, for example, about Bob Cawley's frank account of Frame's treatment at the Maudsley and she eventually removed some sections of the original script).[14]

Frame's ability to work in the latter months of 1993 was further undercut, first by a bout of double pneumonia, and then by her old nemesis — a resumption of construction noise. December was shattered by the sound of major repairs to Dahlia Street, with machinery 'pounding away all day'.[15] And then demolition work began on one of the houses behind her. To escape this, Frame accompanied the Gordons on a trip to and from the South Island, on which they went as far as Oamaru. Again, she was testing her stamina in preparation for an overseas trip scheduled now for 1994.

She put that capacity for endurance further to the test by attending, for only the second time, the readers' and writers' week of the International Festival of the Arts in Wellington in March 1994. Guests and speakers included a range of fellow New Zealand writers, plus such internationally known performers as Doris Lessing, Jung Chang, Roger McGough and Sharon Olds. The week was to close with a 'Tribute to Janet Frame in her Seventieth Year', at which the book of reminiscences and appreciations would be launched; and selected writers would read from her work or their own.

Everything about this week of writerly activities delighted Frame, from the well appointed hotel accommodation overlooking the capital's harbour, to the presence of old friends — George Braziller, Jacquie Baxter, Sheila Natusch, Dorothy Ballantyne, Karl Stead — to attendance at a number of sessions presenting the work of other writers. She was accompanied most of the time by Braziller, who was relieved to have an excuse to be away from New York in the week that he was publishing a book of essays by the death-sentenced Salman Rushdie. Frame had an especially rewarding exchange with Keri Hulme and gave the Maori writer the ivory cicada which Bill Brown had sent her, as a gesture of recognition and respect from one writer to another. 'We've been waiting for a long time for a writer like her to emerge,' she said, 'somebody founded in both our major cultures.'[16] And she had a joyful reunion with Dorothy Ballantyne and her daughter Vicky Feltham.

The day after meeting Ballantyne at one of the public sessions, Frame went with her to Vicky's house in the suburb of Brooklyn for lunch and an afternoon of conversation and hilarity. 'It was uncannily like the way we'd talked nearly thirty years before, as though intervening time had just fallen away.'[17] The encounter entirely eliminated any doubts Ballantyne may have had about the strength of her friendship and rapport with Frame and restored the sense of intimacy which they had lost when the writer left Dunedin in 1972. It also turned out to be their last opportunity to achieve this reconciliation. Ballantyne died the following February, without seeing Frame again.

As anticipated, the climax of the week was the birthday tribute on Sunday 13 March. Writers Karl Stead, Margaret Mahy and Barbara Anderson praised Frame's contribution to New Zealand letters; Lauris Edmond and Kevin Ireland read poems. George Braziller spoke of his encounters with Frame in Norfolk and the South of France, and said the one trip he still had to make with her was to Stockholm in Sweden for the award of the Nobel Prize for Literature.[18] Frame herself read her early story 'My Cousins who could eat cooked turnips' and an extract from *Daughter Buffalo*; and the atmosphere changed 'from mere anticipation to palpable excitement'.[19] One of the visiting writers described the reading as 'one of the most astonishing events I have ever witnessed'.[20] Elizabeth Alley then presented Frame with the *festschrift*, published as *The Inward Sun*, inadvertently echoing the title of Patrick Evans's small book of twenty-three years earlier. Contributors included Braziller, John Money, Bob Cawley, Karl Stead, Dennis McEldowney, Phillip Wilson, Keri Hulme, Tim Curnow and Alley herself. As Frame accepted her copy, the *Dominion* newspaper observed, 'the large crowd then broke into a spontaneous rendition of *Happy Birthday*'.[21] Frame returned home deeply fatigued; but feeling valued and respected. The whole experience, she told Alley, had been 'so much a pleasure'.[22]

Frame's appetite for further immediate socialising was reduced, however. She discouraged Random, her New Zealand publisher, from mounting any kind of function around the actual date of her seventieth birthday, in August; and she was dismayed that she seemed to have agreed to an interview with a New Zealand-born Australian journalist, Susan Chenery, in May 1994. 'I'm not having any more [interviews],' she told Chenery when the journalist arrived. 'This is my last interview. It is very difficult to have people calling, I don't have people calling. To write you must be with yourself and your thoughts.' Chenery, an enterprising journalist, used this comment to sell her story to at least two publications on the ground that it represented Frame's 'final word' and 'last interview'. And she persuaded her subject to speak of her experience of cancer. Frame told her:

> The profound experience was preparing to die. It turned my life around. It was a very rich time in some ways because I took advantage of it in noticing how things were and how I felt. I had a radio mended and the man who came to mend it said, 'it'll be good for two years'. I smiled to myself because I [thought I] was only good for five or six months. It was very, very hard preparing to leave, to say goodbye, to everything . . . I felt that I would miss the ordinary things. I would miss being alive and the day passing and tomorrow and tomorrow and so on. Then I had the operation and they removed it all . . . It is a bit of an anti-climax now.[23]

Her consciousness of death had been renewed, however, by a visit from Piki Takiari and one of her daughters. They came to tell Frame that Takiari's emphysema, which she had been battling for several years, was now advanced, and that it was likely to kill her soon; and she did indeed die, at home at Kaiwhaiki, in November 1994.

To Chenery, Frame also confessed to not feeling wholly secure in Palmerston North. 'When I think of a place I think of it in its layers of time. I find Palmerston North is very strong in its layers. The land really belongs to the river. It is built on a flood plain, a swamp. Now and again the river really wants its way, it wants to be what it used to be. I take refuge in the idea of the river underneath, waiting, biding its time.'[24]

Possibilities for serious work shrank further when, in mid-year, Frame developed an ulcer on one eye, which grew from a painful rash on her face and interfered for a time with her vision. She now looked to the planned trip to England, the United States and Canada in September and October 1994 to restore both her health and her morale. To make the long-haul sections of the flight more endurable she booked first-class seats for the first time in her life. She had hoped to persuade Jacquie Baxter to accompany her, but this turned out to be impossible.

Frame set out from Auckland on 31 August, alone, but in good spirits. She was looking forward to being 'on the road' again after a gap of seven years since her last expedition abroad; and she especially anticipated the prospect of seeing old friends again in all the countries she planned to visit. She only got as far Los Angeles, however, where she cancelled her forward travel and returned home. And the only friend she saw was Bill Brown, who travelled south from San Francisco to spend a couple of days with her. It was not clear precisely what had provoked this literal about-turn.

John Money, whom Frame rang from the west coast on 1 September, noted that her plane had experienced turbulence on the first leg of the flight and that this had shocked Frame, who had thought that first-class passengers would be somehow immune to such disturbance. Worse, the one real advantage of the first-class cabin had not appealed to her at all: she was unable to hear the engines and was several times convinced that they had stopped. '[What] she had to say added up to some premonitory danger of death if she didn't turn back.'[25] Frame herself believed that she had had 'some kind of heart attack', and this view was backed up by her doctor in Palmerston North who noted irregularities on an electrocardiogram reading. As a consequence he recommended that Frame wear a nitroglycerine patch on her shoulder to 'keep the blood flowing'. The insurance company doctor who examined her in Los Angeles reached another conclusion, however, and Frame was refused a refund on her unused ticket. She persisted nonetheless in her determination to return home; and she was back in Palmerston North by 10 September.

Apart from disappointing waiting friends in England and North America (one of whom, John Marquand, would die in April the following year), the major disadvantage of the cancelled trip was that she failed to meet her agents in New York and London. Anthea Morton-Saner had on her desk the manuscript of *The Janet Frame Reader*, which the Women's Press had commissioned an Australian academic, Carole Ferrier, to assemble and edit. It contained extracts from a range of Frame's published writings, with an analytical foreword and afterword. When Frame failed to appear in London in September 1994, nobody registered the fact that she had neither sighted the material nor approved the concept. The manuscript moved inexorably through the publication process and the first Frame knew of it was when proofs arrived in Palmerston North in January 1995.

Frame wrote at once to Kathy Gale of the Women's Press. '[The] typescript

. . . is alarming to me. I've . . . signed no contract for it, and I disapprove of others making a choice of work I myself would prefer to choose.'[26] To Tim Curnow she wrote:'Please, is there some way I can refuse this?'[27] The outcome was a compromise. *The Janet Frame Reader* was published in June 1995 in Europe and the United Kingdom only, and alterations and cuts were made in both the extracts and the commentary in an effort to accommodate Frame's reservations. A disclaimer facing the contents page advised, albeit in minuscule type, that 'the extracts . . . were selected by the Editor and should not be interpreted as having been selected or approved by Janet Frame'.[28]

Publications *about* Frame and her writing continued to appear: two major ones in 1992; three in 1994; another in 1997.[29] She felt ambivalent about such volumes, pleased that people cared sufficiently about her work to write them, but fearing'fury or perplexity or a sense of disbelief' if she actually read them.[30] Usually she did not, regarding even the best of them as 'work[s] of art with my own book lying as a shrivelled skin beside the newly-sprung essay'.[31] She made an exception of Palmerston North teacher Judith Dell Panny's book *I have what I gave, The Fiction of Janet Frame*. She read it because she had met the author, who had introduced her to Frances Cherry, the writer-tenant in her Shannon house; and because she appreciated it. The volume was, she told Elizabeth Alley, 'the result of extensive reading and scholarship . . . I thank Judith Dell Panny for noting that, far from being a random explosion or outburst, my books are the result of "patterning and purpose".'[32]

She would probably have found as much to praise and approve in Gina Mercer's 1994 book, *Janet Frame, Subversive Fictions*, which credited her with a 'wicked and powerful subversion of expectations' and of deliberately 'over-turning . . . fundamental thought and language structures'. She chose not to read this volume, however, possibly because of circumstances that occurred in the course of its composition. Mercer, an Australian academic, had treated Frame with great respect and interviewed her when the writer visited Sydney in 1985. It transpired, however, that the Hocken Library in Dunedin had given Mercer access to manuscripts which Frame had deposited there.These included drafts of four novels which were different in some respects from the versions published. Frame's intention had been that the papers were with the library for safekeeping only.They were not to be sighted, much less cited, by anybody for any purpose until after her death. This intention was both a reflection of her belief that it was the finished, published work that mattered, not preliminary and rejected drafts; and it was to prevent speculation that some versions of her novels may have been closer to autobiography than fiction.

When Mercer sought formal permission to include quotations from these manuscripts in her forthcoming book, she noted,'it was discovered that there had been a significant difference between what Janet Frame thought that Hocken Library had given me access to, and what they had actually made available . . . When I sent her copies of the material I had gathered, she was extremely unhappy.' Mercer dealt with what she rightly called 'a considerable muddle' by listing only details of and quotations from typescript material already available as a result of the publication of articles elsewhere.[33] Given that such earlier publication had resulted from Mercer's own research, and that what was said about the unpublished typescripts was more than Frame had wanted revealed, it was unsurprising that Frame remained unhappy about the outcome.

A potentially more troubling and troublesome book was set in motion in 1995. For two decades Frame had been approached by a succession of biographers or would-be biographers, largely academics, some New Zealanders and some from further afield, who wanted to write her life story or critical biographies, or to edit and publish her correspondence.[34] The whole notion was distasteful to her. Despite the measure of fame that came with recognition of her stature as a writer, she clung to the belief that what mattered was her published work, and that her own life was her private property and that of her family. This belief was strengthened when academics and journalists *had* written about her life without authorisation or assistance and, inevitably, got some facts wrong and misunderstood others. It was in part to forestall such projects, and to defuse the impact of revelations about her time in psychiatric hospitals, that she had written her autobiography.

Unexpectedly, however, the publication of her autobiographies and the release of the Jane Campion film had served to heighten interest in her life. They provided new texts on which commentators, whose ranks included some of the would-be biographers, could base speculation on her motives, on whether or not she had been 'truthful', on whether she was intent on concealing as much as she revealed, and on the supposed relationship between her life and her art. Patrick Evans, who had written two books about Frame and commented extensively on her writing in other publications, had spoken of *his* frustrations in a paper delivered at the Frame conference in Dunedin which he had called 'The Case of the Disappearing Author':

> I can think of only two other writers, Thomas Pynchon and J.D. Salinger, who have done more to sever the link between art and life than [Frame] has. Writers who hide away probably do so principally because they want to avoid meeting people like me; and this is something Janet Frame has done with great skill and cunning. Over the years she has turned me into a sort of critical *paparazzo* . . . always trying for that special, authentic shot as I stumble through the shrubbery of her life. It is supposed by some people that I have acquired some kind of special knowledge of, or intimate information about, her, but I haven't, not a word, and in fact we've never met, and barely corresponded, and everything I know is at second- or third-hand. My attempts to find first-hand information, most recently last year, have been vigorously and efficiently rebuffed, and as I have moved closer and closer to people who know her, the less and less is said. There is a remarkable taboo around Janet Frame, a remarkable desire to protect her from enquiry.[35]

Evans went on to speculate that his 'meddlings' might have been 'getting close to some kind of uncomfortable aboriginal truth, some skeleton in the oedipal closet . . .'[36] This was unlikely. Frame's resistance to his efforts had been of a passive rather than an active variety, and precipitated by Evans's reluctance to bother her with seemingly endless questions. To Frame, this well-intentioned considerateness had seemed like furtiveness; and, of course, she disapproved of the whole notion of the critical biographer. Indeed, she had been distressed by the knowledge that research on her life was being conducted without reference to her and this had led to her earlier characterisation of Evans as, perhaps, 'one of the Porlock people'.[37]

In 1994 George Braziller and Frame's executor, Elizabeth Alley, suggested to her that the best way to deal with such anxieties might be to authorise somebody she knew and trusted to write a biography with her cooperation. 'My feeling . . . is that [this] would keep some of the sharks at bay,' Alley advised.[38] Frame replied that the very thought was like having 'a beetle on my skin'.[39] On reflection, however, she came to agree that appointing a biographer would provide a way of distancing herself from applicants for the job whom she did not know, particularly those who lived in countries far enough away to make it difficult for them to understand the New Zealand context of her life. It might also be a means of correcting what she regarded as the errors and misconceptions in previously published biographical and critical works.

Her present biographer presented himself in the latter part of 1995, having just completed a biography of Frame's mentor and friend Frank Sargeson. She had been acquainted with him for fifteen years, then worked rather more closely with him on the Sargeson book.[40] She told him in August that she would endorse his application to write her biography; and she wrote a to-whom-it-may-concern letter to family and friends asking them to give him access to documents, photographs and recollections.[41] Most were surprised; the habit of non-disclosure of private information about Frame was deeply ingrained. But almost all would comply.[42]

By the end of 1995, any attractions which Palmerston North had once held for Frame had diminished. She now associated the city and the house in Dahlia Street with serious illness (and the earlier suspicion of diabetes had been confirmed when she was hospitalised in July), the debilitating tax audit and the apparent stalling of her writing career. Worse, her anxieties about flying in and out of the district in 'small planes' seemed suddenly better-founded when an Ansett passenger flight coming into the city crashed in June 1995 with the loss of four lives. It was scarcely a surprise to family and friends, then, that when June and Wilson Gordon shifted in September to Auckland, where their eldest son, Ian, still lived with his family, Frame followed early in November.

The Gordons settled into a Methodist retirement village in the suburb of Mount Albert. Janet bought a property in nearby Avondale on the bank of the Whau River.

While the move itself was understandable — Frame had been contemplating a return to Auckland for the past decade and the sisters still felt the need to be near each other — Frame's choice of a home seemed more than usually eccentric. The exterior was decorated with a large boomerang and the name of the house, 'Billabong'. Inside, the living room was taken up almost entirely with a full-sized pool table around which Frame and her guests had to edge their way to chairs (she soon swapped it for a large desk). One side of the house was bordered by one of Auckland's busiest and noisiest commuter routes and the Gordons experienced considerable difficulty entering and leaving the property by car. On the other side lay the Whau River which, a kilometre downstream, also passed the site of the old Avondale Mental Hospital. She was once again, as Frank Sargeson had put it more than forty years before, 'up the Wow';[43] only this time literally rather than figuratively.

Frame spent the early part of summer unpacking boxes of books and papers stored initially in the property's two commodious garages, entertaining members of her extended family and renewing contact with a small number of Auckland friends, including Douglas Wright, Phillip Wilson and Dennis McEldowney. Jacquie Baxter came to stay with her new partner, Peter Alcock. In February 1996 she began twice-weekly sessions with her biographer and to sort out relevant papers for him to read from the mountain of box files she had accumulated over three decades.

In April she spent a day with her biographer and Dennis McEldowney visiting her former homes on Auckland's North Shore. At Whangaparaoa her old bach was now jostled by new houses; but most of the timber fence she had built had withstood the gales of a quarter of a century. In Glenfield, where occasional mail still arrived for her after twenty years, the current owners invited her inside. 'The living room was furnished and ornamented . . . with 1950s kitsch,' McEldowney noted in his diary. 'In the laundry there were piles of crates of home brew, and on the fully concreted front yard an opulent caravan. Like a page from a Frame novel rather than her life.' At Sargeson's cottage at Takapuna, now preserved as a 'literary museum', Frame 'looked wistfully at the missing back garden where the army hut used to be . . . pointed to the patchwork quilt on the bed, which she had made, and did a vigorous tap-dance on the bare floorboards to demonstrate how she unwound from hours of writing'.[44] This last was, of course, a 'routine' dating back to the days in Oamaru when she and her sisters had prepared themselves for careers in Hollywood.

Even at this stage of her life occasional instances of misunderstanding and flashes of hostility towards Frame and her work still occurred. A locally published book by one Sophie Trevelyan made reference to her as an 'unreadable literary nutter. Should have been locked up years ago.'[45] More frequently, however, unsought and unexpected awards — indeed, awards she had never previously heard of — continued to find her. In late 1993 it had been the Italian Premi Brancati Prize, previously given to Ezra Pound, Alberto Moravia and Paul Bowles. Winning it brought her 'a surge of optimism'. In March 1996 it was a medal from the Chilean Government in honour of Gabriela Mistral, the country's first Nobel Laureate, in literature, in 1945. Frame herself was still frequently identified as a Nobel Prize contender, and the New Zealand Society of Authors, which had superseded PEN, faithfully forwarded her name to the Swedish Academy each year. Karl Stead, however, was of the opinion that the country's literary community had 'got into the habit of speaking about Frame, not just uncritically, but in hushed and reverent tones, as if we were gathered at her bedside'. [46]

The month that the Chilean award was announced came news of the large and ugly *Landfall* desk, which she had offloaded on neighbours in Levin and hoped never to see again. Now, she heard, Victoria University in Wellington had acquired it — still in two pieces, its leatherette surface frayed and ripped, its amputated legs still wobbling. It had taken on the status of a precious literary artifact. The university asked Frame to verify its provenance, and she confirmed its association with Charles Brasch and herself and accounted for its multiple mutilations. She was amused to learn that it was to be 'restored' and conserved and made available for the use of students studying and practising creative writing.

Oamaru, meanwhile, as a result of labours by a Janet Frame Recognition Group, had just opened a 'Janet Frame Heritage Trail'. This marked with signs and interpretative notices such places depicted in her fiction and autobiography as the old Athenaeum (now the North Otago Museum), the town baths where Myrtle had drowned, the Oamaru Gardens duck pond, the Garden of Memories, and the site of the now demolished house at Willowglen, on what was still the margin of the town. Alongside the last of these an animal park had been established and tourists in search of Frame associations found themselves confronted with disconsolate alpacas and wallabies. The Eden Street house, which, along with its plum and pear trees, had survived intact, could not be part of the trail out of consideration for the current owner. An earlier proposal that the borough council should buy the house and convert it into a museum to celebrate Frame's connection with the town or, at the very least, identify the property with a plaque, had met with local incredulity. [47]

Other communities, however, began to show a willingness to commemorate Frame's place in New Zealand letters. A street in Upper Hutt was called Janet Frame Way, though the dignity of the name was undercut by the added warning 'No Exit' on the signpost. A plaque which quoted one of her Dunedin poems was embedded in the footpath below Robbie Burns statue in the city's Octagon, as part of a 'Writers Walk' ('having been to church the people are good, quiet,/with sober drops at the end of their cold Dunedin noses . . .'). The residents of 61 Evans Street in Dunedin's North-East Valley had her poem

'At Evans Street' tastefully typeset, framed and displayed inside the front entrance. And niece Pamela, who was now 'unmarried' and had reverted to use of the Gordon surname, reported from Seacliff, where she was living in 1996, that the magnolia in the grounds of the former superintendent's garden mentioned in *Owls Do Cry* and *Faces in the Water* had recently been redis-covered, identified and stripped of covering vegetation. There were plans to mark it with a plaque and it would now be referred to locally as 'the Janet Frame magnolia'.[48] First editions of *The Lagoon*, of which Frame herself had none, were now highly sought after and one volume fetched $580 at auction in Wellington in 1998.[49]

Frame could see that recognition was preferable to non-recognition, especially when it came in forms that allowed her to preserve her personal privacy (and she still introduced herself to neighbours as Janet Clutha, in the vain hope that she would not be recognised as the person who wrote books). She acknowledged too that these gestures of respect were good-hearted in their intention. But the puritan in her was discomforted; and the experience of being memorialised in one's lifetime contributed to the sense of unreality she had always associated with her own life and career.

A combination of satisfactory drug and dietary regimes for her diabetes and the move to a warmer climate rejuvenated Frame. She felt well more often than she had in previous years; and she recovered more physical stamina. In the middle of 1996, with encouragement from her sister, she decided to attempt what two years before had seemed impossible: to travel again to the United States and England. She and the Gordons made the return trip in August and September. Taking advantage of some of the surplus income from her high-earning years they travelled business class. June arranged that they should be taken off their plane in wheelchairs. Although Frame's fear of flying was scarcely diminished, the greater space and comfort available to them helped ensure that there were no unpleasant incidents or accidents. June Gordon noticed, not for the first time, the surge of confidence that came over her older sister when she left New Zealand and became, again, the seasoned traveller.

Bill Brown flew down again from San Francisco with a poet protégé, Jamie Yates, to join them for three days in Los Angeles. Frame was awed and then a little alarmed to find that Yates knew most of her *Pocket Mirror* poems by heart. They spent the time together walking and talking and eating in local restaurants; and they made a shopping expedition to Santa Monica, where Frame bought copies of Donne and Keats poems for her friends. After the débâcle of the previous visit, Brown was relieved to find her back to what seemed like her former good health.

In London, Frame stayed at the Ibis Hotel near Euston Station and saw the Gordons off on a six-day bus tour of the south-west of England (largely uneventful but for their missing a bus at Brighton because they waited at the wrong pier). While they were away Frame rested to recover from the flight, and then visited Anthea Morton-Saner at the Curtis Brown office in Haymarket, where Tim Curnow too was visiting, from Sydney. She also saw her niece Janet Cutmore's mother-in-law, whom she had met in New Zealand; and Peter and Renate McKenzie, with whom she had stayed in John Williams's house nearly three decades previously, prior to his disappearance. Her major outings, however, involved Bob Cawley who, after a distinguished career, was still working as a consultant psychiatrist and still spry — in spite of serious heart problems — at seventy-two. He and his wife, Ann, whom Frame was meeting for the first time, took her to dinner at the Reform Club in Pall Mall. She revelled in the elegance and theatrical character of the experience. They treated the occasion as a celebration of friendship, drank champagne and were merry together.

The following Sunday Frame had lunch with the Cawleys in their Pimlico apartment overlooking the Thames near Vauxhall Bridge, opposite the new headquarters of MI6. As a former Londoner, Frame enjoyed all these sights and associations. But she especially enjoyed the company of one of her oldest friends, and the one who had done more than any other to equip her to abandon institutional living and make her independent way in the world as a writer. That they had both endured serious illness in recent years and survived served to make their encounter even more valued; as did the fact that, despite the length of their association, Frame felt that this was the first time that they were interacting simply as friends and wholly outside the context of doctor and patient. They ate their lunch with the doors and windows open to a benign summer's day, then looked at books and listened to George Butterworth's orchestral music and songs based on Housman's *A Shropshire Lad*. It was an afternoon all three would remember as deeply satisfying. Frame and Cawley would not meet subsequently.

Home again in September 1996, Frame was more aware of shortcomings in the location of the Avondale house. The immediate neighbourhood, she told Tim Curnow, had turned out to be 'hellishly noisy'.[50] One of the problems inherent in concealing her name and occupation as a writer was that people could not then be expected to exercise the kinds of consideration a writer would hope for — in particular, quiet. This distraction, combined with a continuation of conversations with her biographer, made it difficult to reconstruct a writing routine. In addition, the post office and supermarket were forty minutes' walk from the house and shopping expeditions were increasingly fatiguing. The Gordons, as always, were willing to help; but they were intimidated by the danger that four lanes of speeding traffic presented when they drove in or out of the property. By year's end she was again caught in the pattern that one friend identified as 'moving, loving, loathing, leaving'.[51] This time she bought a near-new house in Browns Bay on Auckland's North Shore, close to her former homes in Glenfield, Northcote and Takapuna. This seaside property was the most expensive she would own and securing it all but used up the resources which a decade of relatively high income had allowed her to accumulate.

Still Frame did not settle, however. The shops were considerably closer to the new house than they had been in Avondale and a pleasant beach was within easy walking distance. But a degenerative back ailment now made mobility increasingly difficult, especially walking uphill, which she had to do to return home. Some mornings she was unable to move at all until painkilling drugs took effect. This new difficulty and a succession of mid-year callers, including house guests Pamela Gordon and John Money in May, and Money's twice-widowed cousin Meredith Money, who spoke French with her (he had taught the subject at Waitaki Boys' High School) and commenced a visiting routine that bordered on courtship, ensured that she continued to postpone the return to a serious writing regime.

In October 1997 she relinquished the Browns Bay house and shifted temporarily to the Methodist retirement village in Mount Albert, into a unit close to that shared by the Gordons. In less than another month, finding the camaraderie and communal visiting there intolerable, she decided to return to Dunedin. Her niece Pamela Gordon was there teaching linguistics at Otago University; her cat Penny was there, taken in by Pamela when her aunt moved to the retirement village; her biographer was about to move there to take up the Burns Fellowship; and there were still friends there from her own Burns days, particularly Ruth Dallas. She told her biographer, perhaps only half-facetiously, that by returning to the city of her birth she would be giving her life a semblance of symmetry. She also looked forward, she said, to living again in a less temperate part of the country where the passage of seasons was more defined and the shadows more substantial.[52] More prosaically, the difference in property prices between Auckland and Dunedin enabled her to put aside a substantial surplus and gave her additional financial security at a time when her earnings from writing were again declining, though still considerably higher than in the pre-*Is-Land* days.

Frame's new home in South Dunedin was her fifth in two years. Opinion varied among family and friends as to whether she was not writing because she was moving so frequently, or moving because she was not writing. Some thought that she made the shifts for the same reason that she had previously travelled: because such arrangements gave her a feeling of control of her life, and excitement and novelty energised her. In Frame's view, however, there had been specific reasons for each relocation, as there had been for all fourteen shifts in the previous twenty-eight years. And this one, she felt sure, would be 'one of her last'.[53] Because of an absence of commercial prosperity, Dunedin seemed essentially unchanged from the times of her previous residences there. She felt a comforting sense of recognition of both the character of the city, and of her old ghosts there, with whom she now felt herself to be in harmony.

Her refurbished 1920s bungalow in the seaside suburb of St Clair had ample room for working, and for accommodating sporadic guests, such as Jacquie Baxter, who joined her for a few days in February 1998. It had a private back garden, where the previous owners had held barbecues. And it lay only a couple of hundred metres from Richardson Street, where the family lived when she was born seventy-three years earlier. The feeling of coming full circle was enhanced when the Gordons arrived in March 1998 and settled in nearby St Kilda. Observers could not help but notice that the two surviving siblings, who had looked so unalike in childhood and young adulthood, now bore such a strong resemblance that one was sometimes mistaken for the other.

Frame remained just over a year in St Clair. In the course of it she surprised organisers by turning up at celebrations to mark the fiftieth anniversary of the Burns Fellowship at Otago University in May 1998. As another writer in attendance said, her very presence on that occasion as an elder of the tribe gave her colleagues a sense of pride and security;[54] and she, as had become usual, was comfortable in the company of fellow writers. In November of that same year she allowed the sculptor Anthony Stones, whom she had first met at Frank Sargeson's forty-three years earlier, to come and go from the house over a fortnight while he modelled her head in clay for eventual casting in bronze. This permitted Stones to complete a sequence of work which had included heads of Sargeson, Allen Curnow, Denis Glover and Dan Davin.

In April 1999, her seventy-fifth year, Frame moved once more: to a slightly older and less gentrified house in the working-class suburb of St Kilda, more in accord with what had been the ambience of Eden Street, Oamaru, and within easy walking distance of her sister and brother-in-law, her niece, and of the shops. Here she continued to receive visits from friends and family; and to communicate by electronic mail with her oldest surviving associates, John Money, still in Baltimore, aged seventy-eight; and Bill Brown, now an octogenarian in San Francisco. It was here that she learned of Bob Cawley's death in London on 21 April 1999, an event she had anticipated so frequently in the past that its confirmation came almost as an anti-climax.

Here too she completed discussions with her biographer, telling her life in a tone that acknowledged past tragedies but seemed more frequently to tremble on the brink of laughter. Beyond the three score years and ten that her mother's *Bible* had promised, beyond an age that any of her immediate family had reached, beyond, now, her fear that she might cut short her life with her own hand — beyond all that, her voice and articulation remained bell-clear, almost childlike. Key words were hesitated over, as if she and her interlocuter should pause to marvel over the huge adventure they were engaged in: the possibility of recreating the past and finding meaning there through the device of linguistic communication. Talking *and* writing, she conveyed a vivid sense that reality itself is a fiction, and one's grasp on it no more than preposterous pretence and pretension. And that sense delights her, as it does her readers and listener.[55]

Behind locked doors and curtained windows, she makes a concentrated effort to return to writing, without the confrontation with extinction that animated so much of her previous work. As always, she feels most herself at the keyboard, transforming thought, feelings, dreams and memory, pushing the possibilities of language to their furthest limits in an effort to convey textures and nuances of experience that have largely eluded other writers and artists. Her face is most alive in the glow of the VDU where, via the Internet, electronic mail and her own word-processing facility, she rediscovers the world and engages with it, without the burden of social contact.

# Acknowledgements

I began work on this book in 1995, but seeds were sown considerably earlier. It was my friend Ruth Brassington who convinced me that literary biography was the most interesting genre to read or write. Anton Vogt told me in Menton in 1976 that Janet Frame was the most important writer New Zealand had produced and should be the subject of my 'next' biography. Other links in the causal chain were Frank Sargeson, Janet Frame herself (whom I met in 1979), Eric McCormick, Christine Cole Catley, Elizabeth Alley and Brian Boyd.

Tenure of two university fellowships gave me the resources to research and write the biography: the University of Auckland's Fellowship in Humanities and the University of Otago's Burns Fellowship. In addition to providing me with what Edmund Gosse defined as necessities for a writer — 'an assured income, a state of comparative isolation . . . and unlimited stationery' — these arrangements also gave me access to a supportive network of fellow scholars led by (respectively) Professors Terry Sturm and Jocelyn Harris. Creative New Zealand provided funds to permit research in England and the United States; and Air New Zealand assisted with travel expenses.

Four collections of papers made a disproportionate contribution to the structure and content of the book: Janet Frame's own letters and manuscripts; John Money's papers held in his office at Johns Hopkins University in Baltimore; William Theophilus Brown's papers at Pennsylvania State University; and Robert Cawley's papers held at his home in London. Other collections which were significant include those of the Alexander Turnbull Library in Wellington (the Frank Sargeson and Denis Glover papers); the Hocken Library in Dunedin (the Charles Brasch, James K. Baxter and E.P. Dawson papers); Canterbury Museum in Christchurch (the Pegasus Press papers); and McMaster University in Ontario (the Constance Malleson papers in the Bertrand Russell Archives). John Scrivener of Melbourne retains the letters from Janet Frame to his sister Audrey Scrivener; and George Braziller holds most of his business and personal correspondence with Frame. Other letters cited are held by recipients or their descendants.

For permission to quote copyright material I am indebted to Janet Frame, John Money, Ann Cawley, Bill Brown, Jacquie Baxter, Christine Cole Catley and the Frank Sargeson Trust, Alan Roddick (for Charles Brasch material), C.K. Stead, Ruth Dallas, Philip Roth and John Bayley. Frank Sargeson provided the book's title.

I owe a special debt of gratitude to Janet Frame herself (acknowledged in the Author's Note); and to her family, especially her sister June Gordon, her brother-in-law Wilson Gordon, and her niece Pamela Gordon. I also received help from Ian and Neil Gordon, Geordie Frame junior and Janet Cutmore. Considerable help was given by R.H. Cawley, John Money, Bill Brown, Patrick Evans, Dennis McEldowney, C.K. Stead and Heather Murray. Lynn Bogarde, Sally Garland and Anita McNaught carried out additional research for me in New York and London. Reg Graham copied photographs for me and took new ones especially for this book. And Tom and Trish Brooking, Peg Cadagan, Stephen and Margaret Baird, Reg and Judith Graham, and Paul and Heather Aubin provided homes away from home.

Among others who assisted me, and whom I herewith acknowledge and thank, are:

Denise Almao, Kathy Anderson, Louise Armstrong, Elspeth Barker, Kate Barker, Norma Barrett, Hilary Baxter, John Baxter, Gene Beach, Caroline Bennett, Henry Bennett, Joan Blackburn, Kenneth Blackwell, Tonya Blowers, Beverley Booth, Kenneth Bragan, Carl Brandt, George Braziller, Barbara Brookes, Tom Brooking, Sean Brosnahan, Margaret Brownlie, Warwick Brunton, Cyril Burt, Elizabeth Caffin, Hortense Calisher, Patric Carey, Simon Cauchi, John Cody, Roger Collins, Ann Cotton, Linda Cowan, Gert Christeller, Roger Culpan, Buddy de Graafe, Margaret Dalziel, Vicki Darling, Janine Delaney, Stephanie Dowrick, Ellen Ellis, George Emery, Fleur Erson, Ruth Fainlight, Jane Fasani, Vicky Feltham, Lorraine Fodie, Alex Frame, Phyllis Gant, Rose Leiman Goldemberg, Jane Goulden, Liz Grant, Andrea Grieve, George Griffiths, Gil Hanly, Kate Harris, Fiona Henderson, Tom Heyes, Michael Hitchings, Fred Hoffman, Gerard Hogg, Sally Hopkins, Marjorie Hore, Alan Horsman, Anthony Hubbard, Bridget Ikin, Kevin Ireland, Lawrence Jones, Geraldine Keith, Rachael King, Max Lambert, Sheila Leaver-Cooper, Alan Lelchuk, Barbara Lewis, Cybele Locke, David McDonald, James McLauchlin, James and Helen McNeish, Gregor Macaulay, Bill and Lita Manson, James Marquand, David Marr, Owen Marshall, Phoebe Meikle, Phyllis Metcalfe, Paul Miller, Joy Monteath, Geoffrey Moorhouse, Anthea Morton-Saner, Peter Munz, Sheila Natusch, Richard and Rachel Nunn, Gordon Ogilvie, Eric Olssen, Phillip O'Shea, Vincent O'Sullivan, Keith Ovenden, Annette Pacer, Leslie Paine, Wendy Patterson, Bill Pearson, Alan Phillips, Gillian Prowse, Alan Riach, Ray Richards, Rhys and Margaret Richards, Jonathan Riley, Katharina Ruckstuhl, Alison Rudd, Colin Salt, Margaret Scott, Derek Schulz, John

Scrivener, Tina Shaw, Alan Sillitoe, Jeffrey Simmons, Jean Smith, Jo-Anne Smith, Kay Stead, Sandra Stelz, Stuart Strachan, Kathleen Stringer, Jill Studd, Kiritahi Takiari, Michael Thomas, Jane Tucker, Merle Van de Klundert, Violet Walker, Anton and Birgitte Vogt, Albert Wendt, Reina Whaitiri, Iona Williams, Lorraine Williamson, May (Frame) Williamson, Janet Wilson, Kerry Neal Wilson, Phillip Wilson, Helen Woodhouse.

Finally, I thank my agent, Tim Curnow, my New Zealand publisher, Geoff Walker, and my wife Maria Jungowska, all of whom helped with this project far beyond the limits of duty and tolerance.

*Michael King*

# Bibliography of Janet Frame's Writing

(first publication)

## Novels

*Owls Do Cry*, Pegasus Press, Christchurch, 1957.
*Faces in the Water*, Pegasus Press, Christchurch, 1961.
*The Edge of the Alphabet*, Pegasus Press, Christchurch, 1962.
*Scented Gardens for the Blind*, Pegasus Press, Christchurch, 1963.
*The Adaptable Man*, Pegasus Press, Christchurch, 1965.
*A State of Siege*, Braziller, New York, 1966.
*The Rainbirds*, W.H. Allen, London, 1968.
*Intensive Care*, Braziller, New York, 1970.
*Daughter Buffalo*, Braziller, New York, 1972.
*Living in the Maniototo*, Braziller, New York, 1979.
*The Carpathians*, Braziller, New York, 1988.

## Stories

*The Lagoon and other stories*, Caxton Press, Christchurch, 1951 (1952).
*The Reservoir: Stories and Sketches*, Braziller, New York, 1963.
*Snowman, Snowman: Fables and Fantasies*, Braziller, New York, 1963.
*The Reservoir and Other Stories*, Pegasus Press, Christchurch, 1966.
*You Are Now Entering the Human Heart*, Victoria University Press, Wellington, 1983.

## Children's Prose

*Mona Minim and the Smell of the Sun*, Braziller, 1969.

## Poetry

*The Pocket Mirror*, Braziller, New York, 1967.

## Autobiography

*To the Is-Land* (Autobiography 1), Braziller, New York, 1982.
*An Angel at My Table* (Autobiography 2), Braziller, New York, 1984.
*The Envoy from Mirror City* (Autobiography 3), Hutchinson, Auckland, 1984.
*Janet Frame: An Autobiography* [combines the three volumes of autobiography], Century Hutchinson, Auckland, 1989.

**Articles**

'A Letter to Frank Sargeson' in *Landfall* 25, March 1953, p. 5 (an open letter to Sargeson, signed by sixteen New Zealand writers including Janet Frame).

'Review of Terence Journet's *Take My Tip*' in *Landfall* 32, December 1954, pp. 309–310.

'Review of *A Fable* by William Faulkner' in *Parsons Packet*, no. 36, October–December 1955, pp. 12–3.

'Memory and a Pocketful of Words' in *Times Literary Supplement*, 4 June 1964, pp. 12–3.

'This Desirable Property' in *New Zealand Listener*, 3 July 1964, pp. 12–3.

'Beginnings' in *Landfall* 73, March 1965, pp. 40–7.

'The Burns Fellowship' in *Landfall* 87, September 1968, pp. 241–242.

'Charles Brasch 1909–1973: Tributes and Memories from His Friends' in *Islands* 5, Spring 1973, pp. 251–253.

'Janet Frame on *Tales from Grimm*' in *Education*, Early Reading Series, 24, 9, 1975, p. 27.

'Departures and Returns' in G. Amirthanayagan (ed.) *Writers in East–West Encounter*, Macmillan, London, 1982.

'A Last Letter to Frank Sargeson' in *Islands* 33, July 1984, pp. 17–22.

# Bibliography of other works used or cited

Akenson, Donald Harmon, *Half the World from Home, Perspectives on the Irish in New Zealand 1860–1950*, Victoria University Press, Wellington, 1990.

Alley, Elizabeth (ed.), *The Inward Sun, Celebrating the Life and Work of Janet Frame*, Daphne Brassell, Wellington, 1994.

Barringer, Tessa, 'A Spiralled Be(com)ing: Language, Subjectivity and the (Im)possibility of Meaning in the Early Works of Janet Frame', thesis submitted for the degree of Doctor of Philosophy at the University of Otago, 1997.

Barringer, Tessa, 'Frame [D]: The Autobiographies', unpublished paper presented to Critical Theory Conference, University of Canterbury, 1993.

*Beginnings, New Zealand Writers Tell How They Began Writing*, Oxford University Press, Wellington, 1980.

Bell, Millicent, *Marquand, An American Life*, Little, Brown, Boston, 1979.

Beston, John B., 'A Brief Biography of Janet Frame' in *World Literature Written in English*, 17, 2, November 1978, pp. 565–69.

Beston, John B., 'A Bibliography of Janet Frame' in *World Literature Written in English*, 17, 2, November 1978, pp. 570–85.

Bragan, Kenneth, 'Janet Frame: contributions to psychiatry' in *The New Zealand Medical Journal*, vol. 100, no. 817, 11 February 1987, pp. 70–3.

Bragan, Kenneth, 'Janet Frame: Contributions to Psychotherapy' in *Australian Journal of Psychotherapy*, vol. 8, nos. 1 & 2, 1989, pp. 134–43.

Brasch, Charles, *Collected Poems*, Oxford University Press, Auckland, 1984.

Brasch, Charles, *Indirections, A Memoir 1909–1947*, Oxford University Press, Wellington, 1980.

Braziller, George, 'Thoughts on a 30 Year Journey' in Alley 1994, pp. 15–19.

Brooking, Tom, 'Sharing Out the Haggis: The Special Scottish Contribution to New Zealand History', unpublished Bamforth lecture, 1997.

Carey, Rosalie, *A Theatre in the House*, University of Otago Press, Dunedin, 1999.

Cawley, Robert, 'Janet Frame's Contribution to the Education of a Psychiatrist' in Alley 1994, pp. 4–11.

Chisholm, Donna, *From the Heart: A Biography of Sir Brian Barratt-Boyes*, Reed Methuen, Auckland, 1987.

Coxhead, Marian (ed.), *The Globe Theatre, A Celebration of 25 Years 1961–1986*, University of Otago, Dunedin, 1986.

Curnow, Allen (ed.), *A Book of New Zealand Verse 1923–45*, Caxton Press, Christchurch, 1945.

Curnow, Tim, 'Connections' in Alley 1994, pp. 25–33.

Dallas, Ruth, *Curved Horizon, An Autobiography*, University of Otago Press, Dunedin, 1991.

Dalziel, Margaret, *Janet Frame*, Oxford University Press, Wellington, 1980.

Davitt, Michael, *Life and Progress in Australasia*, Methuen, London, 1898.

Delbaere, Jeanne (ed.), *The Ring of Fire, Essays on Janet Frame*, Dangaroo Press, Sydney, 1992.

*Dorothy Neal White, A Tribute*, Friends of the Dorothy White Collection, Notes, Books and Authors No. 7, Wellington, 1998.

Elworthy, Sam, *Ritual Song of Defiance*, A History of Students at the University of Otago, OUSA, Dunedin, 1990.

Ensing, Riemke, *Private Gardens, An Anthology of New Zealand Women Poets*, Caveman Press, Dunedin, 1977.

Evans, Patrick, *An Inward Sun, The Novels of Janet Frame*, New Zealand University Press/ Price Milburn, Wellington, 1971.

Evans, Patrick, *Janet Frame*, Twayne Publishers, Boston, 1977.

Evans, Patrick, 'The Muse as Rough Best, The Autobiography of Janet Frame' in *Untold*, No. 6, Spring 1986, pp. 1–10.

Evans, Patrick, *The Penguin History of New Zealand Literature*, Penguin, Auckland, 1990.

Evans, Patrick, 'The Case of the Disappearing Author' in *Journal of New Zealand Literature*, no. 11. 1993, pp. 11–20.

Ferrier, Carole (ed.), *The Janet Frame Reader*, The Women's Press, London, 1995.

Ferris, Paul, *Dylan Thomas, The Biography*, Dent, London, 1999.

Gordon, June, 'Dance before the Tide, An Autobiography', unpublished typescript held by the author.

Goulden, Mark, *Mark My Words! Memoirs of a Journalist/Publisher*, W.H. Allen, London, 1978.

Grave, Shirley, *Waiting for the Sugar-Water*, Benton-Guy, Auckland, 1992.

Greenaway, Richard and Brocklebank, Norris, *Oamaru*, John McIndoe, Dunedin, 1979.

Haley, Russell, *Hanly, A New Zealand Artist*, Hodder & Stoughton, Auckland, 1989.

Holcroft, M.H., *Reluctant Editor, The 'Listener' Years, 1949–67*, Reed, Wellington, 1969.

Ikin, Bridget, 'An Assemblage of Janet' in Alley 1994, pp.141–5.

Johnson, Carol Morton and Morton, Henry, *Dunedin Teachers' College, The First Hundred Years*, Dunedin Teachers' College, Dunedin, 1976.

*Journal of New Zealand Literature*, no. 11, 1993 (Janet Frame Conference Issue), Department of English, University of Otago, Dunedin.

Kelly, Henry D., *As High as the Hills, The Centennial History of Picton*, Cape Catley, Picton, 1976.

King, Michael, *Hidden Places, a Memoir in Journalism*, Hodder and Stoughton, Auckland, 1992.

King, Michael, *Frank Sargeson, A Life*, Viking, Auckland, 1995.

King, Michael, *God's Farthest Outpost, A History of Catholics in New Zealand*, Penguin, Auckland, 1997.

Klein, Edward, *All Too Human, The Love Story of Jack and Jackie Kennedy*, Pocket Books, New York, 1996.

Leaver-Cooper, Sheila and Smith, Ian S., *Janet Frame's Kingdom by the Sea: Oamaru*, Lincoln University Press/Daphne Brassell, Canterbury, 1997.

Leitch, David and Scott, Brian, *Exploring New Zealand's Ghost Railways*, Grantham House, Wellington, 1998.

McCormick, E.H., *The Expatriate, A Study of Frances Hodgkins*, New Zealand University Press, Wellington, 1954.

McDonald, K.C., *White Stone Country, The Story of North Otago*, North Otago Centennial Committee, Dunedin, 1962.

McEldowney, Dennis, *Full of the Warm South*, McIndoe, Dunedin, 1983.

McEldowney, Dennis, 'The Pilgrim' in Alley, 1994, pp. 74–78.

McEldowney, Dennis, 'Publishing, Patronage, Literary Magazines', in Sturm (ed.) 1998, pp. 631–694.

McKay, Frank, *The Life of James K. Baxter*, Oxford University Press, Auckland, 1990.

Marr, David (ed.), *Patrick White Letters*, Random House, Sydney, 1994.

Meikle, Phoebe, *Accidental Life*, Auckland University Press, Auckland, 1994.

Mercer, Gina, *Janet Frame, Subversive Fictions*, Queensland University Press, St Lucia, 1994.

Milner, Ian, *Milner of Waitaki, Portrait of the Man*, John McIndoe/Waitaki High School Old Boys' Association, Dunedin, 1983.

Money, John, 'On Being Brian Wilford and John Forrest' in Alley 1994, pp. 20–4.

Morrell, W.P., *The University of Otago, A Centennial History*, University of Otago Press, Dunedin, 1969.

Murray, Heather, 'Dot's Little Folk, and Other Children's Pages' in *Kite*, 10, April 1996, pp. 11–12.

O'Brien, Gregory, *Moments of Invention, Portraits of 21 New Zealand Writers*, Heinemann Reed, Auckland, 1988.

Ogilvie, Gordon, *Denis Glover: His Life*, Godwit, Auckland, 1998.

O'Sullivan, Vincent (ed.), *Katherine Mansfield, New Zealand Stories*, Oxford University Press, Auckland, 1998.

Ovenden, Keith, *A Fighting Withdrawl, The Life of Dan Davin, Writer, Soldier, Publisher*, Oxford University Press, Oxford, 1996.

Panny, Judith Dell, *I Have What I Gave, The Fiction of Janet Frame*, Daphne Brassell, Wellington, 1992.

Ramsay, Atholea, Stead, Helen and Lindemann, Elspeth, *The Honour of Her Name, The Story of Waitaki Girls' High School 1887–1987*, Waitaki Girls' High School Centennial Committee, Dunedin, 1987.

Richards, Ian, *To Bed at Noon, The Life and Art of Maurice Duggan*, Auckland University Press, Auckland, 1997.

Richards, Trevor, *Dancing on Our Bones, New Zealand, South Africa, Rugby and Racism*, Bridget Williams Books, Wellington, 1999.

Robinson, Roger and Wattie, Nelson (eds), *The Oxford Companion to New Zealand Literature*, Oxford University Press, Melbourne, 1998.

Sargeson, Frank, *More Than Enough*, Reed, Wellington, 1975.

Shaw, Margaret S. and Farrant, Edgar D., *The Taieri Plain, Tales of the Years that Are Gone*, Otago Centennial Historical Publications, Dunedin, 1949.

Shaw, Peter, *Whitestone Oamaru, A Victorian Architectural Heritage*, Craig Potton, Nelson, 1995.

Sinclair, Keith, *A History of New Zealand*, Pelican, Auckland, 1959.

Stead, C.K., *In the Glass Case: Essays on New Zealand Literature*, Auckland University Press, Auckland, 1981.

Stead, C.K., *All Visitors Ashore*, Harvill, London, 1984.

Stead, C.K., *The End of the Century at the End of the World*, Harvill, London, 1992.

Stead, C.K., 'Allein auf dem Eis' in *Merian*, 8/8/96, pp. 56–9.

Stead, C.K., 'Janet Frame, Janet Clutha and Karl Waikato,' in *Landfall* 198, Spring 1999, pp. 217–32.

Sturm, J.C., *Dedications*, Steele Roberts, Wellington, 1996.

Sturm, Terry (ed.), *The Oxford History of New Zealand Literature in English*, Oxford University Press, Auckland, 1998.

Sutherland, Stuart, *Breakdown, A Personal Crisis and a Medical Dilemma*, Weidenfeld & Nicolson, London, 1976.

Tod, Frank, *Seacliff, A History of the District to 1970*, Dunedin, 1971.

Twain, Mark, *Mark Twain in Australia and New Zealand*, Penguin, Victoria, 1973.

Williams, Mark, *Leaving the Highway: Six Contemporary New Zealand Novelists*, Auckland University Press, Auckland, 1990.

Williamson, May, 'Janet Frame – New Zealand Writer' in *Northland* 23, vol. 6, no. 3, July 1963, pp. 5–11.

# Notes

Information on the location of collections of papers cited in these notes can be found in the Acknowledgements. The following abbreviations are used:

AW for Albion Wright; Autobiog. for Frame's *Autobiography*, with page numbers cited from the 1990 edition by the Women's Press; BB for Bill Brown; BBP for Bill Brown's papers; CB for Charles Brasch; CKS for C.K. Stead, known to Frame and Frank Sargeson as Karl; DG for Denis Glover; EPD for Elizabeth Pudsey Dawson, known to Frame and Sargeson as 'Peter'; FS for Frank Sargeson; int. for interview; JF for Janet Frame; JFP for Janet Frame's papers; JM for John Money; MK for Michael King; p.c. for personal communication (information conveyed in a less formal manner than by interview or letter); RHC for Robert Hugh Cawley, known also as Bob; TC for Tim Curnow; and WGHS for Waitaki Girls' High School.

### Chapter One: Railway People

1. Twain 1973 p. 287. He visited Dunedin in November 1895.
2. Autobiog. p. 69. For details of Frame family history I am indebted primarily to June Gordon, who collected relevant birth, death and marriage certificates in addition to family stories about relations and origins; Janet Frame too was a source of such stories. I have checked information about family movements in New Zealand from street directories, electoral rolls and — in the case of George Samuel Frame — employment records.
3. Brooking 1997 p. 3.
4. Sinclair 1959 p. 92.
5. Kelly, John Liddell, 'Heather and Fern', *New Zealand Times*, Wellington, 1902. The best of these Scottish–New Zealand poets, however, was the journalist Jessie Mackay, born in Canterbury in 1864.
6. Autobiog. p. 7.
7. Information about George Frame's railway career and movements associated with it are taken from relevant copies of the *Appendices of the Journal of the House of*

*Representatives* and the *New Zealand Gazette* lists of railway employees, and from the National Archives file R series 13, box 60.

8. For details of Godfrey family history I am indebted to Barbara Lewis (especially Barbara Lewis to MK, 20/11/95); and Kelly 1976.

9. All details of George Frame's war service come from his service file, WW1 4/2039.

10. Geordie Frame, *Oamaru Mail*, 28/12/87.

11. JF to BB, 14/6/77. In the *Autobiography* (p. 10) Frame identifies the doctor as Emily Siedeberg McKinnon. That too was her name, but not until after her marriage to James Alexander McKinnon in 1928. In the *Autobiography* Frame writes: 'I had a twin, which did not develop beyond a few weeks. Twins were hereditary in mother's family . . .' It could be tempting to relate the pre-natal loss of a twin sibling to the feelings of loss and depression with which Frame struggled throughout and beyond childhood. In Britain, a Lone Twin Network includes 'members who have lost their twin at [or before] birth and they . . . go through life feeling completely lost' (*New Zealand Herald* 7/2/98).

12. Shaw & Farrant 1949 p. 33.

13. JF to JM, 29/7/46.

14. Autobiog. p. 11; see also *Oamaru Mail* int. with Geordie Frame, 19/12/87.

15. Autobiog. pp. 13, 18 & 66. The Maniototo (in Maori, 'plain of blood') was to provide the adult Frame with a title of a novel (Frame 1979).

16. Autobiog. p. 13.

17. Ovenden 1996 p. 4.

18. JF to BB, 12/5/77; & Autobiog. p. 14.

19. Autobiog. p. 15. Frame gives another version of the same story in *Beginnings* p. 27. Patrick Evans comments (1977 p. 18) that Frame 'claims' to have composed this story and he describes it as 'probably insufficiently telegrammatic for a child of three'. Frame, however, was adamant that the story emerged as she recorded it (int. 16/4/96). Her recollection of telling it had been reinforced by repetition over many years by her parents and older siblings.

20. Autobiog. p. 22.

21. Ibid p. 15.

22. This time frame, somewhat different from that in the *Autobiography* (pp. 15–17), is reconstructed from George Frame's railway service file (R series 13, box 60). I believe Frame's recollection of unhappiness at Glenham inflated in her mind the length of time the family lived there and at Edendale. George Frame's appointment to Glenham was from 1/3/27 and that to Wyndham from 24/6/28. Certainly the family was at Wyndham by the time June Frame was born there on 30/6/28.

23. Autobiog. p. 16.

24. Ibid p.17.

25. Ibid p. 18.

26. Ibid pp. 22 & 20.

27. 'The First Crocus' by LCF, handwritten manuscript held in JFP.

28. Autobiog. p. 12.

29. Ibid pp. 27–8.

30. Ibid p.28.

31. Ibid p. 24.

32. Ibid p. 24.

33. Ibid p. 23.

34. Ibid p. 26.

35. *Beginnings* p. 27.

36. Autobiog. p. 23.

## Chapter Two: Kingdom by the Sea

1. There were major Maori communities in the nineteenth century to the north of Oamaru, at the mouth of the Waitaki River, and to the south, at Moeraki. There were ample signs that Oamaru had had small-scale Maori settlements in earlier times, however, including middens in the hill behind the Frames' rented home in Eden Street.

2. Shaw 1995 p. 4.

3. Two years later, after the collapse of the Bank of Otago, the building became the Oamaru branch of the National Bank of New Zealand.

4. Evans 1977 p. 16.

5. Shaw 1995 p. 13.

6. Davitt 1898 p. 353.
7. Autobiog. pp. 61 & 62.
8. May Williamson to MK, 26/2/96.
9. Autobiog. p. 29.
10. Ibid p. 103.
11. Ibid p. 31.
12. Ibid pp. 31–3.
13. Ibid p. 43.
14. Ibid pp. 43–4.
15. *Beginnings* pp. 28–9.
16. Autobiog. p. 33.
17. Ibid p. 34.
18. Williamson 1963 p. 6.
19. Autobiog. p. 38.
20. JM clinical notes, 22/7/46.
21. Autobiog. p. 39.
22. Ibid p. 39; Seacliff comment from int. JF, 8/3/98 & 13/6/98.
23. Autobiog. p. 45. Marjorie Hore, née Firman, interviewed in 1997, confirmed Frame's version of these events but said that the Firman children gave a 'different reason' for not being allowed to play any more with the Frames; she declined to elaborate (int. 21/3/97).
24. Autobiog. p. 39.
25. Up to the election of the Labour Government in 1935 primary schooling in New Zealand was free but secondary education was not.
26. A version of this sequence of events, using real family names, is given in Frame's story 'The Secret' (*The Lagoon*, pp. 12–8).
27. Mrs McGimpsey makes an appearance in *Owls Do Cry* as 'Mrs Mawhinney': see pp. 38 & 41.
28. Autobiog. p. 52.
29. Int. Marjorie Hore, 21/3/97.
30. A journalist writing about the town more than sixty years later referred to Oamaru's 'puritanical narrowness' and 'pinch-lipped respectability' (Anthony Hubbard, *Sunday Star Times*, 29/3/98).
31. JF, typescript for 'The Birds of the Air' (labelled in her hand 'a true story'), pp. 1–2, BBP.
32. JM clinical notes, 1/12/46; see also int. Marjorie Hore, 21/3/97.
33. JM clinical notes, 15/7/46.
34. Anonymous neighbour quoted in *Dominion Sunday Times*, 23/12/90.
35. Autobiog. p. 56. Frame refers to the inspector as 'Mr Crump'; this is incorrect.
36. See Autobiog. p. 172; Barbara Lewis, p.c. 20/11/95; May Williamson, p.c. 26/2/96.
37. Autobiog. p. 58.
38. Ibid p. 8.
39. Ibid p. 9.
40. JF, typescript for 'The Birds of the Air', p. 3. BBP.
41. Autobiog. p. 9.
42. *Landfall* 87, September 1968, p. 241.
43. The identification of the Frames' ways as 'batty' was made in a *Dominion Sunday Times* article of 23/12/90. Even as late as 1975 the then principal of Waitaki Girls' High School would write: 'Oamaru has its own idea of the roles people should play and also of who are the "right" people. At times I have felt that trial by fire and water sounded less barbaric than the much more subtle methods used now' (Joyce Jarrold to Patrick Evans, 22/7/75).
44. Violet Walker (Mrs Feathers' daughter) to her grandson Duncan, undated. Patrick Evans Papers.
45. Autobiog. p. 65.
46. JF to BB, undated (February 1972).
47. Autobiog. pp. 65 & 67.
48. *Beginnings* p. 29.
49. Autobiog. p. 71.
50. Ibid p. 66.
51. Ibid p. 66; & JF to JM, 5/2/61.
52. See for example *New Zealand Mercury*, vol. 3, no. 10, January 1936, p. 8; other publications for which Lottie Frame wrote poems include *Railways Magazine* and *New Zealand Mirror*.
53. JF writes (*Autobiography* p. 76) that the English vanity publishers Stockwells 'accepted' a book of Lottie Frame's verse; but they expected her to pay for the cost of publication – which, of course, she was unable to do.
54. Autobiog. p. 73.
55. Ibid p. 76.
56. Ibid p. 75.
57. *Otago Daily Times*, undated clipping (1936). JFP.
58. Evans 1977 p. 25. He was speaking of Frame's childhood verse published in

the *Oamaru Mail*; but his remarks are equally applicable to those published in the *Otago Daily Times*.
59. *Otago Daily Times*, 28/9/36.
60. *Otago Daily Times*, 2/8/37.
61. Autobiog. pp. 80–1.
62. Ibid p. 84.
63. June Gordon, unpublished autobiography, p. 76.
64. Autobiog. p. 85.
65. Coroner's report, National Archives J36 Cor 1937/319.
66. Autobiog. p. 86.
67. Ibid p. 86.
68. Edgar Allan Poe, 'Annabel Lee'.
69. Autobiog. pp. 88 & 89.
70. Ibid p. 101.

**Chapter Three: Like Cousin Peg . . .**
1. Autobiog. p. 98.
2. *Owls Do Cry*, p. 28; this is a fictional depiction of J.B. Wilson, but one that was recognised for its documentary quality by former pupils and teachers of WGHS.
3. Janet Frame and June Gordon each recited slightly different versions of this rhyme in June 1998.
4. Autobiog. p. 94.
5. WGHS records, 1937–42.
6. JF to BB, undated (December 1970); Frame also wrote about the experience of winning, and of *expecting* to win, school prizes in the story 'Prizes' (*The Reservoir*, pp. 19–26).
7. Int. Wendy Patterson, 5/5/98; Frame had written about the doll's house being on the lawn, but Patterson says that was not its normal location.
8. Autobiog. p. 100.
9. Ibid pp. 94 & 99.
10. The Group is the subject of Frame's story 'Hecate, You Look Angerly' in *The Reservoir*, pp. 53–62.
11. *The Reservoir*, p. 56.
12. Autobiog. p. 91.
13. Ibid p. 98.
14. Ibid p. 103.
15. JF to BB, 15/2/76.
16. See, for example, 'Mail Minor' pages for 23/2/40, 26/4/40, 14/6/40.
17. Autobiog. pp. 93 & 105–6.
18. JF to Elizabeth Alley, 21/2/83.
19. Autobiog. p. 113.

20. Autobiog. p. 132; & June Gordon, unpublished autobiography, p. 151.
21. Both Janet Frame and June Gordon had this comment thrown at them on more than one occasion. See also Janet Gibson to Patrick Evans, 11/7/75, and Janet Gibson to Jean Smith, 28/9/80. Patrick Evans Papers.
22. Autobiog. p. 95.
23. *Beginnings* p. 30; & JF to JM, 18/3/47.
24. Janet Frame diary for 1942, held by John Money. Frame handed this document to Money in 1945 with a note that read: 'An after-the-valley Diary (!) which escaped from the fire — how or why I do not know.'
25. Autobiog. pp. 120–1.
26. Ibid p. 122.
27. See Army Service Record no. 3/18/1569.
28. Autobiog. p. 124. Scott Memorial Day was observed each year at Waitaki Boys' High School to commemorate the fact that Oamaru was the first port of call for the *Terra Nova* bringing news of Scott's death from the Antarctic in 1913.
29. Autobiog. p. 133.
30. Ibid p. 133.
31. Ibid p. 129.
32. Ibid p. 130.
33. Ibid p. 112.
34. JF diary for 1942.
35. Examination results, WGHS records. Oddly, though, Frame scored high marks in English and French in that year's University Scholarship examinations (Janet Gibson to Patrick Evans, 11/7/75).
36. Int JF, 30/4/98.
37. Autobiog. p. 140.
38. Ibid p. 155.
39. Ibid pp. 151 & 153.
40. Ibid p. 152.
41. Ibid pp. 153–4.
42. Ibid p. 154.
43. See Sheila Natusch to MK, undated (1996); & Patricia Guest, review of *Faces in the Water*, YA radio programme, 1962.
44. Janet Frame, personal file, Dunedin College of Education.
45. Autobiog. p. 158.
46. Ibid p. 165.
47. Ibid p. 157.

48. See frontispiece of *The Great Painters, Giotto*, held by Janet Frame and won by her as a sixth form art prize in 1941.
49. Autobiog. p. 172.
50. Ibid p. 159.
51. June Gordon, unpublished autobiography, p. 209.
52. Autobiog. p. 52.
53. Ibid pp. 161 & 162. Frame wrote in the *Autobiography* that she had moved 'from the second person plural to a shadowy "I" . . .' She agreed in interview (23/7/98) that what she had intended to write was '*first person plural . . .*'
54. Ibid pp. 164 & 165.
55. Janet Frame, personal file, Dunedin College of Education.
56. Autobiog. p. 166.
57. Ibid p. 167.
58. Ibid p. 166.
59. JF to JM, 3/5/46.
60. Cyril Burt to MK, 1/5/98.
61. In the *Autobiography* Frame suggests that the shift to Willowglen occurred early in 1945; this is incorrect.
62. Autobiog. p. 179.
63. Ibid p. 181.
64. Ibid p. 180.

**Chapter Four: An Unravelling**

1. Autobiog. p. 168.
2. Ibid p. 170.
3. Ibid p. 170.
4. Ibid p. 171.
5. Ibid p. 172.
6. Ibid p. 172.
7. Ibid p. 172.
8. Ibid p. 173.
9. Ibid p. 174.
10. Ibid p. 173.
11. Judith Powell (former editor of *Te Rama*) to Patrick Evans, 19/8/75. Evans states (Evans 1977, p. 29) that Frame also submitted a children's story to *Te Rama*, and that it was rejected as being 'too gruesome'. Janet Frame, however, advises that this was the work of her sister Isabel, who had a 'wild imagination' (int. JF, 3/4/96).
12. Autobiog. p. 175. See also *Te Rama*, 1944, p. 16. I have used the version of 'Cat' published in *Te Rama*, which differs slightly from that in the *Autobiography*.
13. Autobiog. p. 175.
14. Int. Vicky Feltham (Dorothy Neal White's daughter), 7/12/96.
15. Autobiog. pp. 115–6.
16. Janet Frame, personal file, Dunedin College of Education.
17. Janet Frame's academic record, University of Otago.
18. Autobiog. p. 175.
19. Her address would be 12 Chamberlain St.
20. Autobiog. p. 183.
21. Ibid p. 183.
22. *Faces in the Water*, p. 118.
23. Autobiog. p. 183.
24. Ints Iona Williams & Norma Barrett, 26/4/99.
25. Autobiog. pp. 183–4.
26. Ibid p. 184.
27. Ibid p. 188.
28. Ibid p. 184.
29. JM to Ruth Money, 15/10/45.
30. Autobiog. p. 185.
31. Ibid p. 185.
32. Sheila Natusch to MK, undated (1996).
33. Autobiog. p. 188. In the *Autobiography*, Frame confuses the sequence of events over this period (pp. 187–91). John Money's clinical notes, written in 1945 and 1946, make it clear that Frame attempted suicide in the middle of the second school term of 1945 and came to see him as a consequence of writing about that attempt in a class assignment and then walking out of Arthur Street School in the course of an inspection in September 1945. Money then recorded (and dated) consultations with her from 19/9/45 to 21/6/47. My reconstruction of Frame's life in the latter part of 1945 is drawn largely from Money's contemporary notes, with occasional reference to the *Autobiography* in instances where I believe it to be soundly based.
34. Autobiog. p. 189.
35. Int. JM, 28/4/97.
36. Autobiog. p. 189.
37. JM to Ruth Money, 28/5/45.
38. JM, clinical notes, 19/9/45–3/10/45.
39. Ibid 21 & 24/9/45.

40. Ibid 24/9/45.
41. JF to JM, 3/3/47.
42. JM, clinical notes, 12/10/45.
43. Ibid 15/10/45.
44. JM to Ruth Money, 15/10/45.
45. JF to JM, undated (October 1945).
46. JM, clinical notes, 18/10/45.
47. Autobiog. p. 190.
48. JM to Ruth Money, 23/10/45.
49. Autobiog. p. 190.
50. JF's hospital notes, transferred with her to Seacliff Hospital in November 1945. JF's hospital file.
51. JM, clinical notes, 23/10/45.
52. Autobiog. p. 190.
53. Ibid p. 201.
54. Ibid p. 190.
55. Ibid p. 191.
56. JM, clinical notes, 30/10/45.
57. The Mental Defectives Act passed in 1911 and amended in 1928 defined seven classes of 'mentally defective' persons: persons of unsound mind who are incapable of managing themselves or their affairs; persons 'mentally infirm'; 'idiots'; 'imbeciles'; the 'feeble-minded'; epileptics; and persons 'socially defective'. Frame was at this time presumed to be in the first category.
58. The documents authorising this procedure are all contained in Janet Frame's hospital file.

**Chapter Five: Out of the Depths**

1. Although, as Warwick Brunton points out (p.c. 4/11/98), the Seacliff main building was in fact modelled on an English hospital, Hereford, not a Scottish one.
2. Tod 1971, p. 25.
3. *Appendices of the Journal of the House of Representatives*, 1943, H-7a, p. 3.
4. Reina Whaitiri to MK, 4/8/96. According to Ms Whaitiri, the Otakou chief Tuhawaiki had told a Crown agent, George Clark, in the 1840s: '[Here], and there, and there and yonder; those are all burial places, not ancestral burial places, but those of this generation. Our parents, uncles, aunts, brothers, sisters, children. They lie thick around us . . . [We] cannot part with this portion of our land.' The land *was*

acquired by the Crown.
5. Admission notes, Seacliff Hospital, Janet Frame's hospital file.
6. Autobiog. pp. 195 & 193.
7. Clinical notes November & December 1945, Janet Frame's hospital file.
8. JF to Sheila Traill, undated.
9. JF to RHC, 7/8/70.
10. JF to JM, 20/11/45.
11. JF to Sheila Traill, undated. Dr Kenneth Brogan comments (to MK, 30/4/99): 'This is a fine description of pathological attachment at a conscious level, but it does not grasp what goes on outside consciousness . . . it was not being aware of this that got Money into difficulties.'
12. JF to Sheila Traill, undated.
13. JF to JM, 20/11/45.
14. JF to JM, 21/1/48. Although this letter was written over two years later, it refers to Frame's first Seacliff admission (she was not readmitted there until 9/10/48).
15. Autobiog. pp. 193–4.
16. June Gordon, unpublished autobiography, pp. 248–9.
17. Autobiog. p. 193.
18. Clinical notes, December 1945, JF's hospital file.
19. Autobiog. p. 194.
20. Ibid pp. 194–5.
21. Ibid p. 195.
22. Ibid p. 196.
23. Ibid p. 196.
24. JF to JM, undated (January 1946).
25. In the *Autobiography* (p. 197) Frame says her wage was three pounds a week; at the time, however, she told John Money she was earning fifteen shillings a week (JM, clinical notes, 2/5/46).
26. Autobiog. p. 198.
27. Ibid p. 200.
28. Ibid p. 199.
29. Ibid p. 200.
30. Ibid p. 200.
31. Ibid p. 192.
32. Ibid pp. 192–3. The particular poems Frame refers to are Curnow's 'Time', ('dust and distance'), Curnow 1945 p. 156; Glover's 'The Magpies', p. 172; and Brasch's 'Great Sea'. p. 151. She also makes mention of Denis Glover

in a diary she kept briefly in 1946, held by John Money (see entry for 25/8/46).

33. Ibid p. 200.
34. Ibid p. 200.
35. JF to JM, undated (1946).
36. See 'University Entrance', *New Zealand Listener*, 22/3/46, pp. 18–9.
37. JF to JM, 5/2/61.
38. JF to JM, undated (late April 1946).
39. JM to JF, 29/4/46.
40. JM to Ruth Money, 5/7/46.
41. See JM clinical notes for 1946.
42. Autobiog. p. 201.
43. Ibid p. 201. A reading of John Money's clinical notes for Frame's visits at this time bear out this account of the pattern of Frame's behaviour and Money's response to it.
44. Autobiog. p. 201.
45. Ibid p. 201.
46. Ibid p. 200.
47. JM, clinical notes, 17/6/46.
48. JM, clinical notes, 28/6/46.
49. Autobiog. p. 201.
50. The manuscript copies of these stories are now held by the University of Auckland library (Mss & Archives B-7), gifted to that institution at Frank Sargeson's suggestion in 1960. According to dates written on the stories in John Money's hand they came to him in the following order: The birds began to sing (7/2/46 — although this is almost certainly in error, since Money did not begin to inquire about the stories until June 1946; the date should probably read 7/2/47); Treasure (5/7/46); The pictures (2/8/46); Miss Gibson and the lumber room and A note on the Russian War (12/8/46); Alison Hendry (13/9/46); On the car (27/9/46); My Cousins who could eat cooked turnips (30/9/46); The Secret (18/10/46); Summer (25/10/46); The Bedjacket and Dossy (4/11/46); My father's best suit and A beautiful nature (December 1946); Snap-dragons (January 1947); Keel and Kool (12/3/47). No date is given for Swans, The day of the sheep, Child, and Spirit. Manuscripts for The Park and My Last Story are missing. John

Money records (clinical notes) being given The Park on 28/6/46, so it is likely that this was the first of the stories he was shown. He also records that Frame gave him My Last Story on 5/7/46, the same day she handed over Treasure. Swans (entitled on the manuscript 'The Swans') was sent to Money in Pittsburgh on 2/7/48.

51. *Landfall* 2, June 1947, pp. 116–120. Oddly, when this story was republished in *The Lagoon*, editor and printer Denis Glover chose Frame's original nom de plume for the title, which made no sense in the context of the story.
52. JM to Ruth Money, 28/3/46. The comment about Baxter and Shakespeare was made by Money's (and Baxter's) friend Noel Ginn.
53. JM, clinical notes, 15/7/46.
54. JM, clinical notes, 4/10/46; & int. 28/4/97.
55. JM to MK, 4/8/98.
56. JF's hospital file.
57. JM, clinical notes, 29/11/46.
58. JM, clinical notes, 6/12/46.
59. Vogt, who had overlapped with Money at Wellington Teachers' College in 1939–40, had had one volume of poems, *Anti All That*, published by Caxton Press in 1940; a second collection, *Poems for a War*, had been published by the Progressive Publishing Society in 1943.
60. JM, clinical notes, 9/12/46. Frame continued to send Money stories in New Zealand until March 1947; and send further ones to him in the United States up to November 1949 (Tiger, Tiger).
61. Autobiog. p. 205.
62. JF to JM, 18/1/47. In the *Autobiography* Frame implies that the Stewart Island holiday occurred in 1945 (pp. 176–7). It did not.
63. DG to JM, 24/1/47.
64. DG to JM, 17/3/47.
65. JF to JM, 8/2/47.
66. JF to JM, 26/1/47.
67. Autobiog. p. 206.
68. JF to JM, 24/2/47.
69. See A.J. Hubbard to Janet Gibson,

23/7/75.

70. Coroner's report, National Archives J46 cor 241/47.
71. Autobiog. p. 209.
72. JM, clinical notes, 15/7/46.
73. JM to JF, 2/3/47.
74. Autobiog. pp. 209–10. John Money comments (to MK, 25/8/98) 'A "form letter" is one that comes off a printing machine and is distributed to many recipients. I wrote a personal letter of which there was only one copy.'
75. JF to JM, 3/3/47.
76. JF to JM, 4/3/47.

**Chapter Six: Except through Storm**

1. JF to JM, 20/3/47.
2. JM, clinical notes, 1/4/47.
3. JF to JM, 7/4/47.
4. *Otago Daily Times*, 8/5/47, p. 4. This letter is identified as Frame's in JM to JF, 13/5/47.
5. JF to Sheila Traill, 30/4/47.
6. JF to JM, 22/4/47.
7. JF to JM, 6/5/47.
8. DG to JM, 16/5/47.
9. *Landfall* 2, June 1947, pp. 116–20.
10. JM to JF, 3/8/47.
11. JM, clinical notes, 21/6/47.
12. JF to JM, undated (late May 1947).
13. JM, clinical notes, 21/6/47.
14. JF to JM, 3/7/47.
15. JF to JM, 17/7/47 & 3/7/47.
16. Autobiog. p. 211.
17. Autobiog. p. 212.
18. Ibid p. 212.
19. JF to JM, 7/10/47 & 30/10/47.
20. Autobiog. p. 212.
21. JF to JM, 13/11/47.
22. Autobiog. p. 203.
23. JF to JM, 7/10/47.
24. Int. JF, 23/4/99.
25. JF to JM, February 1948.
26. JF to James K. Baxter, undated (from Occidental Hotel), Baxter Papers, Ms 975/183 (Hocken Library).
27. Autobiog. pp. 212–3.
28. JF to JM, February 1948.
29. JF to JM, 18/3/48.
30. JF to JM, 7/10/47.
31. Note by JM on JF's letter to him of 7/10/47.
32. *Faces in the Water*, p. 10. What she said to Money at the time was: 'How can

I say it? Nothing near, nothing close. Everything hanging and strangled and mad' (JF to JM, February 1948).
33. JF to JM, 18/3/48.
34. JF to JM, 14/5/48.
35. JF to JM, 2/7/48.
36. JF to JM, 14/5/48.
37. Sutherland 1976, pp. 184–5. Frame too has made this comparison (int. JF, 14/10/98).
38. Autobiog. p. 213.
39. JF to JM, 14/5/48.
40. JF to JM, 14/5/48.
41. JF to JM, undated (from Sunnyside Hospital).
42. JF to JM, 18/3/48.
43. Autobiog. p. 213.
44. JF hospital records, 9/10/48.
45. JF to JM, 2/7/48.
46. JF to JM, 26/8/48.
47. *The Oxford Companion to English Literature*, 1985, p. 831.
48. This version is from the J.B. Leishman translation of Rilke (1957). Frame had an earlier edition of this volume, either the 1936 or 1946 printing. Coincidentally *Landfall* published an elegy from Rilke's *Duino Elegies*, translated by James Bertram, in *Landfall* 10, June 1949, pp. 109–11.
49. JF to JM, 26/8/48.
50. JF to JM, 26/8/48 & 10/8/48.
51. See *The Lagoon*, pp. 44–53. The story was sent to Money on 2/7/48. Frame commented: 'I send a story, formless, technically poor, slushy. I can't remember when I wrote it.'
52. JF to JM, 10/8/48.
53. JF to JM, 3/10/48.
54. JF hospital notes, 4/10/48.
55. JF hospital notes, 4/10/48.
56. JF hospital notes, 4/10/48.
57. JF hospital notes, 4/10/48.
58. JF hospital notes, 9/10/48.
59. Malcolm Brown to Lottie Frame, 27/10/48, JF hospital notes.
60. Autobiog. p. 213.
61. JF hospital notes.
62. Autobiog. pp. 213–4.
63. JF to JM, 14/11/48.
64. Autobiog. p. 239.
65. JF to JM, 1/3/49.
66. JF to CB, 30/4/49.

67. JM to JF, 15/5/49.
68. Although Denis Glover, writing to Sargeson in August 1949, made reference to one of his authors 'frothing in Seacliff, no less, partly because her stories are not yet out' (Glover to FS, 16/8/49).
69. JF to JM, 15/5/49.
70. Malcolm Brown to Lottie Frame, 8/6/49 & 27/7/49, JF hospital notes.
71. JF to JM, 14/2/50.
72. Autobiog. p. 214.
73. William Yates to JF, 17/11/50.
74. JF to JM, 12/5/49.
75. Autobiog. p. 215.
76. Richards 1977, p. 372.
77. Geoffrey Blake-Palmer to Michael Shepherd, 29/7/57, JF hospital notes. This letter summarises Frame's illness from the time of her admission to Avondale.
78. JF hospital notes, 2/1/51.
79. Sutherland 1976 pp. 187–8.
80. Autobiog. p. 216.
81. JF to JM, undated (February 1948).
82. Autobiog. p. 216.
83. JF hospital notes, 4/3/52.
84. Blake-Palmer, known to his subordinates as 'Snake-Charmer', did not begin to hyphenate his surname until he took up his position as medical superintendent of Seacliff Hospital.

**Chapter Seven: Into the World**

1. DG to JM, 16/7/52.
2. Autobiog. p. 216.
3. Ibid p. 216.
4. *Press*, 22/3/52.
5. Autobiog. p. 217.
6. *Listener*, 18/4/52.
7. Dorothy Neal White, 4YA review, June 1952.
8. Neal White to JF, 17/3/52.
9. *Landfall* 22, June 1952, pp. 152–3.
10. Davin (ed.), *New Zealand Stories*, OUP, London, 1953, pp. 315–21.
11. FS to Dan Davin, 16/4/52.
12. See FS to Maurice Duggan, 3/6/52; FS to EPD, 20/3/52; Dennis McEldowney, Diary, 20/4/52.
13. See, for example, Barbara Anderson quoted in *Kite* 7, December 1994, p. 5; & Meikle 1994, p. 153.

14. Katherine Bradley to Dorothy Neal White, 19/5/52 & 19/11/52.
15. Janet Gibson to Patrick Evans.
16. Ogilvie 1998, pp. 274–5.
17. Autobiog. p. 217.
18. Ibid p. 219.
19. Ibid p. 200.
20. JF hospital notes, 9/5/52.
21. Autobiog. p. 221.
22. *Faces in the Water* (1961).
23. Autobiog. p. 221.
24. Int. JF, 23/8/98.
25. Autobiog. p. 221.
26. Ibid p. 222.
27. JF to JM, 24/12/52.
28. JM to JF, 6/2/53.
29. JF hospital notes, 31/1/51.
30. JF hospital notes, 20/12/52.
31. *Appendices of the Journal of the House of Representatives*, 1949, Vol. 3, H-7, p. 14.
32. Sutherland 1976, p. 189.
33. See various papers including *New Zealand Herald*, 27/12/52; *Oamaru Mail*, 26/12/52; *Evening Star*, 26/12/52.
34. The Hubert Church Award was established by private endowment in 1945 in memory of a poet, novelist and critic who had died in 1932; PEN New Zealand administered this award, and the Jessie Mackay Poetry Award, inaugurated in 1940.
35. Autobiog. pp. 222–3.
36. Ibid p. 223.
37. JF hospital notes.
38. Autobiog. p. 223.
39. JF to JM, 19/8/52.
40. Autobiog. p. 223.
41. JF to Dorothy Neal White, 12/3/54.
42. This visit and the gift of the photograph is fictionalised in *Faces in the Water* (p. 211), where Neal White appears as 'Eunice'.
43. Autobiog. p. 218. In this book Frame locates these events as occurring prior to her long period of hospitalisation in 1952 and 1953. In discussion, she agreed that they had occurred after her release from Seacliff in November 1953.
44. Autobiog. p. 241.
45. *Landfall* 25, March 1953, p. 5.
46. *New Zealand Short Stories*, OUP, London, 1953.

47. *Listener*, 18/12/53.
48. Autobiog. p. 225.
49. This review was carried in the same issue of the *Listener*, 18/12/53, which had the editor's unfavourable comments about Frame's story in *New Zealand Short Stories* — which raises the possibility that one might have been intended to compensate for the other.
50. JF to JM, 22/4/54.
51. CB to JF, 1/3/54.
52. JF to CB, 1/4/54.
53. CB to JF, 2/9/54.
54. *Landfall* 32, December 1954, pp. 309–10.
55. 'Lolly-Legs' was in the *Listener* for 15/10/54; and the poems in the same journal, 13/8/54.
56. JF to JM, 4/10/53.
57. *Historic Places*, no. 49, September 1994, p. 33.
58. Autobiog. p. 230.
59. Ibid p. 229.
60. Ibid p. 231.
61. Ibid p. 233.
62. JF to JM, 7/6/54.
63. Autobiog. pp. 235–6.
64. Ibid pp. 236–7. Frame writes as if this was her first contact with Charles Brasch since her time in Seacliff. Their correspondence makes it clear, however, that they had been exchanging letters since 1/3/54.
65. Ibid p. 229.
66. Ibid p. 232.
67. Frame's hospital admission and discharge dates are as follows:
18/10/45–3/11/45: Dunedin Public Hospital
3/11/45–21/12/45: Seacliff Mental Hospital
April–June 1948: Sunnyside Mental Hospital
9/10/48–20/2/49: Seacliff Mental Hospital
30/5/49–6/2/50: Seacliff Mental Hospital
8/4/50–16/9/50: Seacliff Mental Hospital
2/1/51–19/3/52: Auckland Mental Hospital (Avondale)
9/5/52–29/11/53: Seacliff Mental Hospital
14/12/54–1/3/55: Seacliff Mental Hospital.
68. Blake-Palmer, 25/11/54, in JF hospital notes.
69. JF to CB, 9/12/54.
70. JF hospital notes, 14/12/54.
71. JF hospital notes, 14/12/54–1/3/55.
72. JF hospital notes, 1/3/55.
73. Autobiog. p. 226.
74. Ibid p. 241.
75. Ibid p. 240.
76. Ibid p. 240.
77. Ibid p. 242.
78. Ibid p. 243.

**Chapter Eight: Sorcerer's Apprentice**

1. Autobiog. p. 215.
2. *Landfall* 25, March 1953, p. 5.
3. *Listener*, 18/4/52.
4. JF to Dorothy Neal White, 2/11/52.
5. Dennis McEldowney to MK, 9/6/95.
6. Int. June Gordon, 3/10/97.
7. Autobiog. p. 243.
8. FS to Dennis McEldowney, 27/3/55.
9. Autobiog. pp. 244–5.
10. Ibid p. 246.
11. Ibid p. 247.
12. Ibid p. 252.
13. Ibid p. 252.
14. Stead 1999, p. 218.
15. Autobiog. pp. 252–3.
16. Ibid p. 255.
17. Stead 1984, pp. 76–8. Stead's comment to me on 18/10/98 was that the episode described in this passage had occurred; Frame confirmed this on 17/9/99. The compressed nature of the passage I have quoted might have the effect of over-emphasising the sexual dimension of the encounter.
18. JF to MK, 27/7/86.
19. Autobiog. pp. 253 & 254–5.
20. FS to Dennis McEldowney, 27/6/55.
21. Autobiog. p. 249.
22. JF to JM, 19/5/55 & 15/5/49.
23. Autobiog. pp. 250–1.
24. Copy in JFP.
25. John Lehmann to FS, 27/7/55; Frame gives a slightly different version of this story in the *Autobiography* (p. 260).
26. Autobiog. p. 256.
27. JF to JM, 14/9/55.
28. Autobiog. p. 257.

29. Ibid p. 258.
30. Ibid p. 259.
31. FS to MK, 23/3/78.
32. Copy in JFP.
33. Copy in JFP.
34. JF to AW, 10/9/55.
35. AW to JF, 27/9/55.
36. Autobiog. p. 261.
37. See the poem 'Waiting for Daylight' in *Landfall* 39, September 1956, pp. 196–7; 'The Wind Brother' in *School Journal* 51, part 3, no. 1, autumn 1957, pp. 57–67; 'The Friday Night World' in *School Journal* 52, part 3, no. 1, autumn 1958, pp. 58–67; 'I Got a Shoes' in *Listener*, 2/11/56, pp. 26–7 & 31; & 'Face Downwards in the Grass' in *Mate*, 1/9/57, pp. 6–12.
38. FS to CKS, 17/3/56 & FS to DG, 17/3/56.
39. *Parsons Packet*, no. 36, October–December 1955, pp. 12–13.
40. Maurice Duggan to JF, 1/1/57.
41. Maurice Duggan to Dan Davin, 14/9/55.
42. McEldowney 1994, p. 77.
43. Lottie Frame to JF, 20/11/55.
44. Lottie Frame to FS, 6/11/55. 'Chinese gooseberries' were later renamed kiwifruit.
45. JF to JM, 24/12/55.
46. Autobiog. pp. 261–2. June Gordon (p.c. 6/6/98) points out that Sargeson was not on the telephone at this time. Information about Lottie Frame's death had been rung through to Wilson Gordon at work; he came home to tell June; then both Gordons went round to Esmonde Road to tell Frame. It is difficult to see how else the news could have been conveyed to her.
47. Autobiog. p. 262.
48. Ibid p. 263.
49. Ibid p. 265.
50. SP (432/164).
51. Autobiog. p. 249.
52. Sargeson Papers (432/164).
53. FS to CKS, 22/4/56.
54. JF to JM, 24/12/55.
55. Autobiog. p. 266.
56. Ibid p. 267.
57. JF to JM, 10/2/62.
58. JF to DG, 3/1/56.
59. JF to DG, 12/1/56.
60. JF to DG, 12/1/56.
61. See, for example, AW to DG, 15/3/56; & DG to AW, 13/6/56.
62. DG to AW, undated (April 1956).
63. In a letter to DG (3/3/56) Sargeson refers to two Pelican Books, *To Define True Madness* and *Psychiatry Today*.
64. FS to DG, 3/3/56.
65. DG to FS, 9/4/56.
66. FS to DG, 3/3/56.
67. FS to EPD, 16/5/56.
68. DG to FS, 30/5/56.
69. See, for example, FS to EPD, 10/5/55.
70. Autobiog. p. 270.
71. Ibid p. 274.
72. Ibid pp. 269 & 273.
73. Ibid p. 276.
74. Ibid p. 274.
75. Ibid p. 271.
76. Ibid p. 272. The 'Mediterranean' quotation is from Shelley's *Ode to the West Wind*.
77. Ibid p. 276.
78. Ibid p. 276.
79. Ibid pp. 278–9.
80. JF to Audrey Scrivener, 6/7/56.
81. FS to Dan Davin, 20/7/56.
82. FS to William Plomer, 5/7/56.
83. FS to AW, 27/7/56.
84. JF to JM, 11/7/56. John Money did visit Sargeson later in the year.
85. JF to FS, undated (July 1956).
86. FS to EPD, 26/7/56.
87. FS to Dan Davin, 9/9/56.
88. Autobiog. p. 415; & JF to EPD, July 1963.

### Chapter Nine: Traveller's Joy

1. Autobiog. pp. 284–5.
2. Ibid p. 287.
3. Ibid p. 282.
4. JF to Audrey Scrivener, 13/8/56.
5. Autobiog. p. 295.
6. Ibid p. 298.
7. Ibid p. 295.
8. Ibid p. 298.
9. Ibid p. 300.
10. Ibid p. 301.
11. JF to FS, 31/8/56. Sargeson and Plomer, a South African who had lived in London since 1929, were pen friends. The ballad to which Frame refers is about a scholar who uses the reading room in the British Museum:

'Off he goes on gouty feet . . . Off towards Great Russell Street' (see Plomer, *Collected Poems*, Jonathan Cape, London, 1973, pp. 108–9).

12. JF to FS, 31/8/56, & to JM, 15/11/56.
13. 'Patrick Reilly' is not the man's real name. He was still living in London in 2000 and I exchanged letters with him. He played hide and seek with me when I attempted to interview him in 1997 and, in spite of his advanced years, outwitted me at every turn.
14. The figure of 27/6 comes from a letter to Audrey Scrivener, 3/10/56; in the *Autobiography* (p. 301), Frame says the rent was 17/6 per week.
15. Autobiog. p. 302.
16. 'Patrick Reilly' to MK, 4/2/99.
17. Autobiog. p. 306. Some of the biographical information about 'Patrick Reilly' in the *Autobiography* (pp. 302–6) is wrong. I am indebted to 'Mr Reilly' for corrections in letters to me, 9/1/97 & 14/12/98. He, in turn, however, had some erroneous notions about Janet Frame's personal history which I had to reject on grounds of demonstrable inaccuracy and improbability.
18. See Evans 1986.
19. Autobiog. p. 303.
20. Ibid p. 315.
21. Ibid p. 306.
22. JF to FS, 5/9/56.
23. JF to FS, 5/9/56.
24. Autobiog. p. 306.
25. The Keats quotation is the first stanza of 'La Belle Dame Sans Merci'.
26. Autobiog. pp. 307–8.
27. Ibid p. 308.
28. Ibid p. 313.
29. Ibid p. 308.
30. 'Waiting for Daylight', *Landfall* 39, September 1956, pp. 196–7.
31. FS to EPD, 3/10/56.
32. JF to FS, 5/9/56.
33. Autobiog. p. 312.
34. JF to FS, November 1956.
35. Autobiog. pp. 314–5.
36. Ibid pp. 317–8.
37. Autobiog. p. 317.
38. Ibid p. 318.
39. Ibid p. 319.
40. Ibid pp. 309–10. The Underground station that caved in was Bank on the Central Line, bombed on 11/1/41.
41. Ibid p. 310.
42. Ibid p. 315. The 'beaker' quotation is from Keats's 'Ode to a Nightingale'.
43. Ibid pp. 315–6.
44. Ibid pp. 320–1.
45. JF to FS, 26/12/56; & Autobiog. p. 322.

### Chapter Ten: In the Warm South

1. Autobiog. pp. 322–3.
2. Ibid p. 323.
3. Ibid p. 323.
4. Frame implies in the *Autobiography* (p. 325) that she met Greville Texidor and her husband, Werner Droescher, in the course of this first visit to Barcelona; her correspondence at the time, however (for example JF to FS, 17/11/56), makes it clear that she did not.
5. Autobiog. pp. 324–5.
6. JF to FS, undated (November 1956).
7. Haley 1989, p. 57.
8. Autobiog. pp. 326–7.
9. Ibid p. 327.
10. In the *Autobiography* (p. 328) Frame is vague about the whereabouts of El Patron. But a letter to her from Harvey Cohen, an American who later shared the house, indicates that the owner had been away from Ibiza at the time Frame was there and returned in April 1957 (Harvey Cohen to JF, 22/4/57).
11. Autobiog. p. 329.
12. See, for example, letters to FS, 11/11/56 & 17/11/56; & to JM, 15/11/56.
13. JF to JM, 15/11/56.
14. JF to FS, 11/11/56 & 17/11/56.
15. Autobiog. pp. 329–30. Oddly, the same William Monk wrote to Frame late in 1957 seeking her help in securing a British Arts Council grant (William Monk to JF, undated (1957).
16. JF to FS, 6/12/56 & 3/1/57.
17. Autobiog. pp. 331–2.
18. JF to FS, 6/12/56.
19. FS to Dennis McEldowney, 4/12/56.
20. See, for example, FS to Dennis McEldowney, & to DG, 4/12/56; to

the Steads, 7/12/56; to Dorothy Neal White, 8/12/56; and to AW, 18/12/56.

21.  FS to DG, 4/12/56.
22.  DG to FS, 9/12/56.
23.  JF to FS, 26/12/56.
24.  The *Landfall* poem was 'Waiting for Daylight', *Landfall* 39, September 1956, pp. 196–7.
25.  JF to FS, undated (January 1957).
26.  JF to JM, 13/3/57.
27.  JF to JM, 26/12/56.
28.  JF to FS, 3/1/57.
29.  In Greek mythology, Pylades was son of the Phocian king Stophius, and friend of Orestes, whose sister Electra he subsequently married. Frame never offered this manuscript for publication and, when asked, declined to outline its content and themes.
30.  JF to FS, 3/1/57.
31.  JF to CB, 28/12/56.
32.  FS to AW, 21/11/56.
33.  JF to FS, undated (January 1957); & Autobiog. p. 335.
34.  Autobiog. p. 336.
35.  JF to James Beasley, 6/1/57.
36.  JF to JM, 26/12/56.
37.  JF to FS, 6/12/56.
38.  JF to JM, 13/3/57.
39.  JM, memorandum on meeting JF in London, 1961.
40.  JF to FS, undated (February 1957).
41.  Autobiog. p. 341.
42.  Ibid p. 341.
43.  JF to FS, undated (February 1957); & Harvey Cohen to JF, 22/4/57.
44.  Autobiog. p. 343.
45.  JF to FS undated (February 1957).
46.  JF to JM, 3/3/57.
47.  JF to JM, 3/3/57.
48.  JF to JM, 3/3/57. Conscious at the time only of her own deceit, Frame had no idea of the extent of Parlette's deceptions. He was in fact four years younger than he claimed to be (and three years younger than Frame); he was not, as he alleged, a history teacher; and he had shown no ambition to be a poet until he met Frame. According to a member of his family, 'his bending of the truth was most likely so that she would feel that they had everything in common' (p.c., 16/11/99).

49.  JF to FS, 7/2/57.
50.  JF to FS, undated (February 1957); & to JM, 3/3/57.
51.  JF to FS, undated (January 1957).
52.  JF to JM, 12/2/57 & 13/3/57.
53.  JF to JM, 13/3/57.
54.  Autobiog. p. 353.
55.  See, for example, JF to FS, undated (January 1957, 7/2/57,& undated (February 1957).
56.  JF to FS, undated (March 1957).
57.  JF to FS, undated (February 1957), & undated (March 1967).
58.  Autobiog. p. 354.
59.  JF to JM, undated (March 1957).
60.  JF to JM, undated (March 1957).
61.  JF to FS, undated (April 1957).
62.  Greville Texidor to FS, undated (March 1957).
63.  Autobiog. pp, 354–5.
64.  JF to FS, 16/4/57.
65.  JF to Audrey Scrivener, undated (April 1957).
66.  JF to FS, undated (April 1957).
67.  Autobiog. p. 358.
68.  JF to FS, undated (April 1957).
69.  See, for example, FS to EPD, 7/5/57.
70.  Autobiog. p. 359.
71.  Ibid pp. 360–1.
72.  Ibid p. 361.
73.  Forty years later, John Money believed that Frame had been raped in Ibiza and had subsequently had an abortion in Barcelona (JM to MK, 14/12/98).
74.  JF to FS, 16/5/57; & Autobiog. p. 363.

**Chapter Eleven: Towards Sanctuary**

1.  The miscarriage occurred in the second week in April 1957; *Owls Do Cry* was published on 9/4/57 (see AW to JF, 9/4/57: 'Review copies are now being sent out').
2.  The scene was loosely based on a passage in which Toby walks through a fictionalised version of Auckland, which is not, of course, a 'small' town (*Owls Do Cry*, p. 149).
3.  CKS to FS, 27/5/57.
4.  FS to Roy Parsons, 4/11/56.
5.  Meikle 1994, p. 153.
6.  JF to AW, 17/6/57.
7.  These comments from the *Southland*

Times, the *Free Lance*, and the *Press*
(Christchurch), all held in Pegasus
Press file 3/11.

8. H.Winston Rhodes in 'Bookshop' (YA
radio book review programme), Pegasus
Press file 3/11.

9. *Free Lance*, 7/6/57. See also Maurice
Duggan's review in *Here and Now*,
September 1957; Bruce Mason's in
*Education*, vol. 6, no. 3, November
1957; & H. Winston Rhodes in
*Landfall* 44, December 1957, pp. 327–
31.

10. *Listener*, 31/5/57. It could be noted
too that David Hall was virtually the
only reviewer of New Zealand
fiction in the *Listener* at this time and
was the more influential for that
reason.

11. *Listener*, 14/6/57.
12. *Listener*, 28/6/57.
13. *Listener*, 8/9/57.
14. JF to JM, 19/6/57.
15. JF to JM, 21/6/57.
16. JM to JF, 18/7/57.
17. CKS to FS, 27/5/57.
18. Int. June Gordon, 15/3/97.
19. Interviewee who requested
anonymity, Oamaru, 21/3/97.
20. Williamson 1963, p. 7.
21. JF to Sheila Natusch, undated (June
1956).
22. FS to CKS, 5/9/64.
23. JF to FS, 16/5/57.
24. JF to AW, 17/6/57.
25. JF to JM, 21/6/57.
26. JM, memoir written after seeing
Frame in London, 1961.
27. JF to FS, 16/5/57 & 16/6/57.
28. Quotation is from the jacket blurb of
*The Edge of the Alphabet* (1962).
29. 'The Dead' in *Landfall* 42, June 1957,
p. 148; & 'The Wind Brother' in
*School Journal* 51, part 3, no. 1,
autumn, 1957, pp. 57–67.
30. JF to FS, 16/5/57.
31. JF to JM, 12/8/57.
32. JF to FS, 16/5/57; & Autobiog. pp.
368–9.
33. JF to Audrey Scrivener, 11/6/57.
34. JF to FS, 16/6/57.
35. JF to FS, 16/6/57.
36. JF to JM, 19/6/57. The reference to a
'Shield Match' is to a game for a
New Zealand provincial rugby

football trophy, the Ranfurly Shield.
37. Curtis Brown declined to take on
either the stories or *Owls Do Cry*;
but they asked to see future work of
Frame's (see letters to JM of
31/7/57 & 26/8/57). Money also
submitted one story, 'Gorse Is Not
People', to *Mademoiselle* magazine,
who returned it.
38. WP to FS, 21/5/57.
39. JF to FS, 16/6/57; Frame is echoing
the title of Sargeson's first book,
*Conversation with My Uncle* (Unicorn
Press, Auckland, 1936).
40. Curtis Brown to JF, 18/7/57.
41. Autobiog. p. 370. In fact e.e.
cummings' work was handled by
Heath's American associates, Brandt
and Brandt. In England the agency's
better known clients included
George Orwell, and Radclyffe Hall,
whose celebrated novel *The Well of
Loneliness* was successfully prosecuted
in the late 1920s for obscene libel.
42. There was a belief among former
Pegasus Press staff members in 1998
that Frame had approached A.M.
Heath because that company was
already Pegasus's own agent in the
United Kingdom. In fact, as Albion
Wright's correspondence with
Patience Ross makes clear, Pegasus's
association with the firm came about
subsequent to and because of
Frame's involvement (see, for
example, AW to Patience Ross, 2/2/
59).
43. Int. Michael Thomas, 22/5/97.
44. Autobiog. p. 370.
45. JF to FS, undated (January 1957).
46. JF to FS, 23/7/57.
47. JF to FS, 23/7/57.
48. Gene Beach to MK, 21/9/98.
49. JF to JM, 21/6/57.
50. JM to JF, 4/2/57.
51. JF to JM, 1/4/57.
52. JM to JF, 29/1/57 & 18/7/57.
53. JF to FS, 4/7/57.
54. JF to JM, 10/8/57.
55. JF to JM, 11/7/57.
56. JF to JM, 23/7/57.
57. JF to JM, 23/7/57.
58. JM to Michael Shepherd, 29/7/57.
59. Michael Shepherd to JM, 23/7/57; &
to the 'Physician-Superintendent' of

Seacliff Hospital, 23/7/57.
60. JF to RHC, 9/10/82.
61. JF to JM, 12/8/57.
62. JF's Maudsley admission notes, copy held in her New Zealand hospital notes.

### Chapter Twelve: A Home in the Maudsley

1. Autobiog. p. 371.
2. Ibid pp. 367 & 373.
3. JF to JM, undated (September 1957).
4. Autobiog. p. 374.
5. JF to FS, 22/8/57.
6. JF to EPD, 5/9/57.
7. JF interviewed by RHC, 9/10/82.
8. Ibid.
9. Autobiog. p. 374.
10. JF to JM, undated (September 1957).
11. JF hospital notes (on discharge), 12/2/58.
12. Autobiog. p. 374.
13. Autobiog. p. 375. Although Frame makes reference to 'Sir Aubrey Lewis', Lewis was not knighted until 1960. For the date 18/10/57 for the decisive meeting of consultants, I am indebted to Dr R.H. Cawley.
14. Autobiog. p. 375.
15. JF hospital notes, 12/2/58.
16. JF hospital notes, 12/2/58.
17. Autobiog. p. 377.
18. AW to JF, 29/1/58.
19. FS, reporting JF's reaction to AW, 9/2/58.
20. 'Face Downwards in the Grass' in *Mate* 1, September 1957, pp. 7–12.
21. JF to EPD, undated (September 1957).
22. Autobiog. p. 377.
23. Ibid p. 377.
24. FS to CKS, 15/12/57.
25. CKS to FS, 28/1/58.
26. CKS to FS, 4/3/58.
27. Stead 1996.
28. JF to FS, 2/3/58.
29. Autobiog. pp. 378 & 379.
30. AW to JF, 11/3/58.
31. Autobiog. p. 378.
32. JF to JM, 4/8/58.
33. JF to AW, 31/3/58.
34. This was 'The Friday Night World', *School Journal* 52, part 3, no. 1, autumn 1958, pp. 59–67.
35. JF to JM, 21/3/58.

36. JF to Audrey Scrivener, 15/4/58.
37. Autobiog. pp. 379–81.
38. Ibid p. 380.
39. Dan Davin to JF, 17/2/58.
40. Carl Brandt to JM, 25/4/58, in reply to JM's letter of 11/4/58.
41. See Alan D. Miller to JM, 2/6/58.
42. JF to FS, 18/6/58; & to JM, 9/8/58.
43. CKS to JF, undated (1958).
44. JF to JM, 4/8/58.
45. JF to FS, 18/6/58. This scholar may have been Joseph McLeod, who also published poetry in Scotland under the name Adrian Drinan.
46. Autobiog. p. 379.
47. Alan Miller to JM, 2/6/58.
48. Autobiog. p. 381.
49. JF to JM, 16/6/58; see also JF to FS, 18/6/58 & 4/7/58.
50. JF to JM, 4/8/58.
51. JF to JM, 4/8/58.
52. Autobiog. p. 382.
53. JF to FS, 11/9/58; & to JM, undated (September 1958).
54. Autobiog. p. 383.
55. Cawley 1994, p. 5.
56. Int. RHC, 13/5/97.
57. Cawley 1994, p. 6.
58. Ibid pp. 5–6.
59. Autobiog. p. 384.
60. Ibid p. 383.
61. Cawley 1994, pp. 9–10.
62. RHC to Anthony Claire, 16/10/90.
63. Int. RHC, 13/5/97.
64. JF to JM, undated (November 1958).
65. JF to FS, 11/9/58.
66. JF to FS, 28/12/58.
67. JF to JM, 11/1/59.
68. Cawley 1994, p. 8.
69. See JF's acknowledgement of his letter, undated (September 1968), JF hospital notes.
70. JF to FS, 9/10/58; oddly, it was to be another six months before the Literary Fund communicated this news to Frame.
71. JF to FS, 28/12/58.
72. See Geordie Frame to JF, 12/1/59 & undated (1959).
73. Geordie Frame to JF, 12/1/59.
74. JF to EPD, 1/12/58. Persephone was the daughter of the brother and sister Zeus and Demeter. She was obliged to spend one-third of each year in the darkness of the Lower World.

Persephone therefore became a
metaphor for seeds, which remain
underground part of the year then
germinate and grow towards the
light, bringing nourishment to
animals and humankind.
75. JF to JM, 17/12/58.
76. Int. RHC, 13/5/97.
77. Int. RHC, 13/5/97.
78. Autobiog. p. 384.
79. JF to FS, 4/6/59.
80. JF to Audrey Scrivener, 13/6/59.
81. Neither Brandt and Brandt's nor
George Braziller's early records were
available for inspection at the time of
writing this book; this date for the
contract signature for *Owls Do Cry*
comes from A.M. Heath's JF file.

**Chapter Thirteen: A Career Resumed**
1. Braziller 1994, pp. 15–6.
2. Carl Brandt to JM, 4/8/59.
3. Patience Ross to AW, 7/8/59.
4. In the *Autobiography* the other
inhabitants of the house are referred
to as Ted and Joan Morgan, Myra
and Tilly (p. 385).
5. Autobiog. p. 385.
6. Ibid p. 386.
7. Ibid p. 386.
8. JF to FS, 11/10/59.
9. JF to FS, 22/8/60.
10. JF to FS, 11/10/59.
11. Autobiog. pp. 387–8.
12. See letters of 22 & 26/1/60 in
Pegasus JF file; also Michael Thomas
to AW, 3/1/61.
13. JF to JM, 2/10/59.
14. Autobiog. p. 388.
15. JF to JM, 2/10/59; & int. RHC, 13/
5/97.
16. JF to JM, 2/10/59.
17. JF to JM, 29/6/60.
18. Autobiog. p. 390.
19. JF to FS, 10/6/60.
20. JF to JM, 2/10/59.
21. JF to JM, 6/8/62.
22. Int. JF, 22/8/98; the poem could not
be found among JF's papers, and an
inquiry to Jon Silkin's executor also
drew a blank.
23. JF to JM, 25/4/60.
24. RHC to MK, 9/11/97.
25. JF to Audrey Scrivener, 27/6/60.
26. JF to FS, 10/4/60.

27. JF to Audrey Scrivener, 29/11/60.
28. Autobiog. p. 391.
29. Ibid p. 387.
30. JF to FS, 10/4/60.
31. JF to Patrick Evans, 13/11/74.
32. Autobiog. p. 388.
33. Handwritten note by JF on JM's
copy of *Faces* manuscript.
34. JF to JM, 25/4/60.
35. JF to JM, 1/6/60 & 29/6/60.
36. JF to JM, 1/6/60.
37. JF to AW, 17/6/60; & to JM,
29/6/60.
38. *New York Times Book Review*,
31/7/60.
39. *New York Herald Tribune*, 14/8/60.
40. *New Yorker*, 13/8/60.
41. *Esquire* 55, April 1961.
42. See JM to AW, 1/7/60; & Carl
Brandt to AW, 12/9/60.
43. JF to JM, 28/7/60.
44. JF to JM, 29/9/60.
45. Patience Ross to AW, 26/1/60.
46. George Braziller, press release for
*Owls Do Cry*, copy from Pegasus
Press JF file.
47. Ints. George Braziller, 17/6/97;
Jeffrey Simmons, 20/5/97; & letter
from Michael Thomas to AW,
15/11/60. Mark Goulden's own
account of this sequence in his
autobiography *Mark My Words!* (see
Goulden 1978) is wildly inaccurate.
48. JF to EPD, 4/1/61. Pipis are a New
Zealand bivalve shellfish which
Frame had eaten at both Sargeson's
and Dawson's. The reference to
Sargeson's pipi recipe is from his
autobiographical 'Up On to the
Roof and Down Again' originally
published in four parts in *Landfall*
16–20, December 1950-December
1951.
49. JF to Audrey Scrivener, 27/6/60.
50. JF to JM, 19/7/60.
51. JF to JM, 29/9/60.
52. JF to JM, 29/9/60.
53. JF to EPD, 6/10/60.
54. See, for example, George Frame to JF,
14/9/59.
55. See JF to EPD, 21/3/60; & to Audrey
Scrivener, 22/7/60.
56. JF to JM, 6/5/62.
57. In the *Autobiography*, Frame writes
that she re-met Patrick Reilly on a

bus (p. 395); a letter from him in her papers (26/9/60), however, makes it clear that contact was resumed by correspondence.

58. Autobiog. pp. 396–7.
59. JM to JF, 23/12/60.
60. JF to Audrey Scrivener, 8/1/61.
61. JF to FS, 4/1/61.
62. JF to Audrey Scrivener, 8/1/61.

**Chapter Fourteen: On the Rock of Her Self**

1. JF to JM, 14/3/61.
2. JF to JM, 25/5/61.
3. JF to Audrey Scrivener, 23/5/61.
4. JF to JM, 24/4/61.
5. JF to FS, 30/4/61.
6. JF to Audrey Scrivener, 21/5/61.
7. JF to EPD, 29/5/61.
8. FS, regaling the story to Patrick Evans, 18/10/75.
9. JF to EPD, 29/5/61.
10. RHC to MK, 9/11/97.
11. Autobiog. p. 389.
12. *Times Literary Supplement*, 22/7/61. *TLS* reviews were not signed at this time, however.
13. *New Statesman*, 14/7/61.
14. *Sunday Telegraph*, 16/7/61.
15. *Sunday Times*, 16/7/61.
16. Autobiog. p. 393.
17. See, for example, letters from David Bolt of David Higham Associates, 3/8/61; & Thomas Hill of Houghton Mifflin, 10/3/62.
18. JF to Audrey Scrivener, September 1960.
19. JF to JM, 31/5/61.
20. RHC to MK, 9/11/97.
21. JF to JM, 7/7/61.
22. RHC to MK, 9/11/97.
23. JM, notes of visit to JF in London, July/August 1961.
24. JM to Carl Brandt, 28/8/61.
25. Carl Brandt to JM, 30/8/61.
26. 'Prizes' was published in the *New Yorker* on 10/3/62, pp. 44–6; 'The Reservoir' in the same magazine on 12/1/63, pp. 31–6; & 'The Red Currant Bush' in *Mademoiselle*, April 1962, pp. 183–6.
27. She delivered this manuscript to him on 8/9/61 (RHC to MK, 9/11/97).
28. C.A. Sharp to AW, 8/3/61.
29. JF to JM, 10/6/61.
30. See *Faces in the Water*.
31. Arnold Wall, 'Bookshop', 2YA radio station, 23/8/61. This review was written from an advance copy of the novel.
32. *Landfall* 16, June 1962, p. 196.
33. *Listener*, 3/11/61; *NZ Monthly Review*, 19/12/61; *Southland Times*, 14/10/61; *Fernfire*, 9/8/62.
34. Patricia Guest, a former fellow teachers' college student was one of these.
35. See, for example, John Griffin (UBS Dunedin) to AW, 10/5/61.
36. See Albion Wright to A.M. Heath, 31/8/66; J.O. Mackie to MK, 2/4/98 & 7/4/98; & int. Margaret Brownlie, 3/9/98.
37. A former Seacliff psychiatrist who requested anonymity to MK, 6/4/98.
38. David Stenhouse to MK, 20/11/97.
39. J.O. Mackie to MK, 7/4/98.
40. John Cody to MK, 6/7/97.
41. Geordie Frame to JF, 20/3/62.
42. Geordie Frame to JF, 20/3/62; & JF to JM, 6/5/62.
43. Janet Gibson to Jean Smith, 1/10/61.
44. Shirley Gilles (school friend) to JF, 24/5/62.
45. AW to Jeffrey Simmons, 26/10/61. Pegasus eventually took 440 copies in addition to their original order of 2000 — and would have taken more from W.H. Allen had they been available.
46. See Pegasus JF file for 17, 18 & 19/10/61; & for 10 & 21/4/61. These putative foreign language editions of *Owls Do Cry* seem never to have been published; but the French edition of *Faces*, *Visages Noyes*, appeared in 1963.
47. Kurt Heinrich Hansen to JF, 30/11/61.
48. This meeting appears to have taken place in August 1961. See Patience Ross to AW, 15/8/61; JF to AW, 6/12/61; & Patience Ross to AW, 9/1/62.
49. AW to JF, 28/8/61.
50. See JF to AW, 28/5/61, 8/7/61 & 19/7/61.
51. Carl Brandt to JM, 3/5/61.
52. *Time*, 22/9/61.

53. *NewYork Times Book Review*, 8/10/61.
54. *Atlantic Monthly* 208, October 1961.
55. *Esquire* 56, October 1961; *Life*, 18/8/61; & *Harper's Magazine*, September 1961.
56. JF to JM, 22/10/61.
57. JF to EPD, 12/10/61.
58. JF to JM, 26/7/61 & 29/12/61.
59. JF to JM, 21/11/61.
60. JF to JM, 6/12/61.
61. JF to FS, undated (December 1961).
62. JF to EPD, 30/1/62 & 25/12/61.
63. JF to FS, undated (December 1961).
64. All this Peter Dawson revealed to Sargeson, not at this time to Frame.
65. JF to EPD, 30/1/62.
66. Autobiog. p. 392.
67. *Weekend Observer*, 11/2/62.
68. *Times Literary Supplement*, 26/1/62.
69. *Spectator*, 19/1/62.
70. *Sunday Times*, 11/3/62.
71. *Guardian*, 19/1/62.
72. Autobiog. p. 392.
73. JF to FS, 2/3/62.
74. JF to FS, 2/3/62.
75. JF to FS, undated (December 1961).
76. Autobiog. p. 402.
77. JF to JM, 31/5/62.
78. JF to JM, 10/2/62.
79. JF to JM, 23/3/62.
80. JF to JM, 23/3/62.
81. JF to JM, 23/3/62.
82. JF to FS, 2/4/62.
83. Patience Ross to JF, 16/4/62. This letter establishes the sequence of publication, not the actual dates.
84. Patience Ross (16/4/62) speaks of four hundred pounds; and there would be a half-share of $US625 to come from Pegasus for the Continental editions of *Faces*.
85. The Braziller edition of stories came out in 1963 in two boxed volumes, *The Reservoir, Stories and Sketches* and *Snowman Snowman, Fables and Fantasies*.
86. JF to FS, undated (December 1961).
87. JF to JM, 6/5/62.
88. JF to JM, 6/5/62.

## Chapter Fifteen: A Roots Crisis

1. Frame, ever alert to portents, was struck by the juxtaposition of the name of the village, Eye, the fact that the cottage owners worked in an eye hospital, and that her recently completed manuscript was titled *Scented Gardens for the Blind*.
2. Autobiog. p. 405.
3. JF to JM, undated (July 1962).
4. JF to FS, 25/8/62.
5. Autobiog. pp. 407–8.
6. Ibid p. 415.
7. JF to JM, 15/9/62.
8. JF to FS, 25/8/62.
9. Autobiog. pp. 407 & 408.
10. JF to FS, 11/9/62.
11. JF to JM, 1/7/62.
12. JF to JM, 6/8/62.
13. Karen Sweeney (A.M. Heath) to JF, 30/8/62; the story appears not to have been published.
14. Robert Hemenway to Carl Brandt, 8/6/62; this letter was forwarded to Frame.
15. See JF to AW, 2/7/62.
16. JF to AW, 16/6/62.
17. EPD to JF, 22/7/62.
18. June Gordon to JF, 25/5/62 & 10/7/62. June Gordon's manuscript was not accepted for publication; and the outcome of the court case involving her brother is recorded in an undated clipping from the *Oamaru Mail*, April 1963, held by MK.
19. Mark Goulden to JF, 1/8/62.
20. Autobiog. p. 401. In 1933 Goulden, as editor of a small newspaper, the *Sunday Referee*, had been the first publisher to print a Dylan Thomas poem. The following year the paper sponsored *18 Poems*, Thomas's first published collection of verse. According to Thomas's biographer, Goulden insisted on meeting Thomas in 1934, because he suspected that he had been the victim of a con-trick. 'He met Thomas and was satisfied that he was genuine [but] later he lost interest in him "because he became a disreputable person".' (Ferris 1999, p. 93.)
21. Goulden 1978, pp. 189–90. It has to be said that Goulden's account of Frame's 'life story' is so garbled and full of errors that it casts doubt on the reliability of everything else that

he writes about her.
22. Ibid p. 191.
23. Mark Goulden to AW, 21/8/62.
24. Int. JF, 29/6/99.
25. See, for example, Carl Brandt to JM, 5/11/62.
26. JF to FS, 25/8/62.
27. JF to JM, 15/8/62.
28. JF to JM, 15/9/62.
29. JF to Audrey Scrivener, 1/4/62.
30. JF to EPD, undated (March 1963).
31. Int. JF, 27/3/98.
32. George Braziller to JF, 1/11/62.
33. JF to JM, 31/10/62.
34. Autobiog. p. 410.
35. JF to EPD, undated (November 1962).
36. JF to EPD, 1/11/62.
37. Geoffrey Moorhouse to MK, 7/2/98.
38. Ashton-Warner's *Spinster* (1958), Hilliard's *Maori Girl* (1960), and Cross's *The God Boy* (1957).
39. Geoffrey Moorhouse, 'Out of New Zealand', *Guardian*, 16/11/62.
40. JF to EPD, undated (October 1962).
41. *Time*, 26/10/62.
42. *New York Times Book Review*, 23/9/62.
43. *Commonweal* 77, 19/10/62.
44. *Times Literary Supplement*, 23/11/62.
45. *New Statesman*, 23/11/62.
46. *Times Literary Supplement*, 23/11/62.
47. JF to EPD, 21/11/62.
48. Geoffrey Moorhouse to MK, 7/2/98; & JF to Geoffrey & Janet Moorhouse, 1/1/63.
49. JF to EPD, undated (November 1962).
50. JF to EPD, undated (October 1962).
51. JF to EPD, 2/1/63.
52. Int. RHC, 18/5/97.
53. JF to EPD, 2/1/63.
54. JF to Geoffrey & Janet Moorhouse, 1/1/63.
55. FS to EPD, undated (February 1963).
56. JF in int. with RHC, 9/10/82.
57. Constance Malleson's first letter to JF was dated 24/11/62; the others from L. Phillips, 4/12/62, & Winifred Gardner, 3/1/63.
58. Constance Malleson to JF, 24/11/62.
59. JF to Constance Malleson, 28/11/62.
60. JF to Constance Malleson, 27/1/63.
61. Constance Malleson to JF, 28/1/63.
62. JF to Constance Malleson, 30/1/63.
63. Patrick White to Ben Huebsch, 17/

2/63, *Patrick White Letters* ed. David Marr, Sydney, 1994, pp. 218–9. This letter may have sparked a sequel. When George Braziller met Huebsch for the first time at the latter's retirement party in New York, he said, 'I don't think you know me . . .' Huebsch looked at him and replied at once, 'But I do know you. You are the publisher of Janet Frame.' (Braziller 1994, pp. 17–8.)
64. Patrick White to Duttons, 17/3/63, quoted in David Marr to MK, 23/4/97.
65. Patrick White to Mickey Parker, quoted in David Marr to MK, 23/4/97.
66. JF to Patrick White, 22/11/85. I am grateful to David Marr for locating this letter.
67. JF to EPD, 12/2/63.
68. JF to JM, 23/2/63.
69. JF to JM, 23/2/63.
70. JF to JM, 25/2/63.
71. C.A. Sharp to JF, 1/4/63.
72. See letters from Trans-Pacific Passenger Agency to JF, 26/3/63 & 1/4/63.
73. JF to Constance Malleson, 13/4/63.
74. Int. June Gordon, 31/5/96.
75. JF to JM, 27/4/63.
76. JF to JM, 27/4/63.
77. JF to EPD, 21/3/63.
78. 'The Islands', see Charles Brasch's *Collected Poems* (1984), pp. 16–7.
79. See AW to JF, 20/2/63.
80. *Listener*, 8/3/63.
81. *Landfall* 66, June 1963, pp. 193 & 194.
82. JF to EPD, 21/11/62.
83. JF to EPD, 23/2/63.
84. JF to EPD, 14/3/63 & undated (March 1963).
85. Ruth Fainlight to MK, 31/8/99.
86. Autobiog. pp. 411–2.
87. Ruth Fainlight to MK, 31/8/99.
88. JF to Constance Malleson, 5/4/63.
89. Constance Malleson to JF, 31/3/63.
90. JF to Constance Malleson, 26/5/63; & Constance Malleson to JF, 3/7/63.
91. JF to EPD, undated (June 1963).
92. JF to EPD, undated (April 1963).
93. JF to JM, 23/2/63.
94. JF to JM, 30/6/63.
95. JF to EPD, undated (June 1963).

96. JF to Constance Malleson, 30/6/63.
97. Int. JF, 29/6/99.
98. JF to EPD, undated (May 1963).
99. JF to EPD, undated (June 1963).
100. JF to AW, 20/3/63.
101. JF to Constance Malleson, 23/7/63.
102. *Times Literary Supplement*, 2/8/63.
103. *The Times*, 25/7/63.
104. *New Statesman*, 19/7/63.
105. *Sunday Times*, 14/7/63.
106. *Observer*, 10/10/82.
107. JF to EPD, 23/7/63.
108. *Landfall* 68, December 1963,
    pp. 386–9.
109. *Listener*, 16/8/63.
110. *Time*, 20/9/63.
111. *New York Times Book Review*,
    18/8/63.
112. Autobiog. p. 413.
113. Ibid p. 413.
114. JF to JM, 11/8/63.
115. Autobiog. p. 414.
116. JF to JM, 18/8/63.
117. JF to JM, 11/8/63.
118. JF to Constance Malleson, 26/8/63.
119. See Patience Ross to JF, 12/8/63; &
    Mark Goulden to JF, 22/8/63.
120. Int. RHC, 18/5/97.
121. Autobiog. p. 416.
122. JF to FS, 27/8/63.
123. June Gordon to JF, 28/8/63.
124. JF to Constance Malleson, 26/8/63.
125. JF to JM, 27/8/63. In the
    *Autobiography* Frame implies (pp.
    414–5) that she had made a decision
    in September 1963 to return to New
    Zealand permanently; her letters
    contradict this — at the time she left
    London she was determined to
    return the following year.
126. Autobiog. p. 420.

## Chapter Sixteen: Return of the Prodigal

1. JF to JM, 23/9/63.
2. JF to EPD, 23/10/63.
3. Autobiog. pp. 420–1.
4. JF to EPD, 23/10/63.
5. Autobiog. p. 421.
6. Ibid p. 421.
7. See, for example, JF to EPD,
   21/4/61.
8. FS to Dorothy Neal White,
   8/2/57, in which he says: 'The
   situation would be that four people
   undertook to look after her, each for
   three months in each year. I gladly
   undertake to do my share . . . [No]
   non-psychotic can be expected to
   endure the situation for more than
   three months at a time.'
9. Autobiog. p. 422.
10. See clippings in JFP dated simply
    'Wellington January 1963'; the first is
    by NZPA correspondent Susan
    Vaughan; see also *Northland Magazine*,
    July 1963, p. 11.
11. *New Zealand Herald*, 15/10/63.
12. Autobiog. p. 422.
13. JF to EPD, 23/10/63.
14. See FS to JF, 13/10/63; AW to JF, 15/
    10/63; May Williamson to JF, 21/10/
    63; Sheila Natusch to JF,
    15/10/63; W. Farrell, Oamaru Jaycees,
    to FS, 25/9/63; *Woman's Weekly* to JF,
    16/10/63; Kendrick Smithyman to JF,
    undated (October 1963).
15. JM, notes on a visit to NZ, 10/1/64.
16. JF to EPD, 23/10/63.
17. JF to FS, 27/8/63.
18. FS to JF, 3/9/63 & 13/10/63.
19. Autobiog. p. 423.
20. JF to EPD, 23/10/63.
21. Autobiog. p. 423.
22. Sargeson, quoted in King 1995, p. 360.
23. Autobiog. p. 424.
24. Ibid p. 425.
25. See, for example, FS to Dan Davin,
    undated (October 1963).
26. June Gordon to JF, undated (August
    1963).
27. See Geordie Frame to JF, 2/4/64 &
    30/4/64.
28. Autobiog. p. 426.
29. *Oamaru Mail*, 1/11/63.
30. Autobiog. pp. 426, 427 & 428.
31. Ibid p. 432.
32. JM, notes on a visit to NZ, 10/1/64.
33. Janet Gibson to Jean Smith,
    10/11/63.
34. Janet Gibson to Patrick Evans.
35. Autobiog. p. 430.
36. JF to Dorothy Neal White,
    10/11/63.
37. McEldowney 1991, p. 575.
38. CB to JF, 2/1/64 & 24/6/64.
39. CB to JF, 15/11/63. In fact other
    New Zealand publishers had similar
    contractual clauses, rarely activated
    because of the rarity with which

locally published books were taken up outside the country. The proposed *Landfall* essay, eventually entitled 'Beginnings', was published in *Landfall* 73, March 1965, pp. 40–7. It was the second in the series. It would be republished in *Cornhill Magazine* 175, pp. 189–197; and again in book form in *Beginnings, New Zealand Writers Tell How They Began Writing*, Oxford University Press, Wellington, 1980, pp. 26–34.

40. AW to Michael Thomas, 11/11/63.
41. These offers were repeated in a letter to Frame, 5/2/64.
42. JF to CB, 2/1/64.
43. Patience Ross to JF, 3/10/63 & 23/12/63.
44. The *Press*, 10/12/63. Although this story was published in December 1963, Frame and Pegasus had had unofficial news of the award the previous month (AW to A.M. Heath, 11/11/63). The award was initially announced as being to the value of five hundred pounds. Subsequent correspondence between Frame and the Literary Fund established that this was an error (C.A. Sharp to JF, 27/1/64).
45. JF to EPD, 3/1/64.

**Chapter Seventeen: Exiled at Home**
1. JF to CB, 31/12/63 (this letter incorrectly dated 1964).
2. JF to JM, 20/1/64.
3. Dennis McEldowney, Diary, 13/12/63.
4. JM notes on a visit to NZ, 10/1/64.
5. JM notes on a visit to NZ, 10/1/64.
6. JM notes on a visit to NZ, 10/1/64.
7. JF to EPD, 13/2/64.
8. Roger Culpan to JF, 5/2/64.
9. Roger Culpan to JF, 5/2/64.
10. Roger Culpan to RHC, 28/8/63.
11. JF to Roger Culpan, 31/1/64.
12. *Landfall* 68, December 1963, p. 388.
13. JF to CB, 2/1/64.
14. JF to CB, 29/1/64.
15. CB to JF, 2/2/64. Among the other authors Brasch commissioned pieces from for this series were Sargeson, Maurice Duggan, James K. Baxter, Ruth Dallas and Raymond Ward. The last three of these would

become friends of Frame in Dunedin over the next two years.
16. *Landfall* 73, March 1965, p. 46.
17. FS to Rhondda Coleman, undated (February 1964).
18. JF to MK, 30/10/90.
19. EPD to JF, 22/1/64.
20. JF to EPD, 2/2/64.
21. JF to JM, 17/2/64; the similar letter to EPD was written on 9/2/64. According to Roger Culpan, the problem turned out to be 'cystic hyperplasia of the breasts' (Roger Culpan to RHC, 9/10/64).
22. JF to JM, 27/2/64.
23. JF to EPD, 3/3/64.
24. JF to EPD, 21/2/64.
25. JF to EPD, 3/3/64.
26. The book on which McNeish was working at this time was a biography of Danilo Dolci, *Fire under the Ashes*, published in London in 1965.
27. James McNeish to MK, 22/7/97.
28. FS to Patrick Evans, undated (July 1975).
29. By the late 1990s the address of the house was 82 Queen's Drive, Oneroa.
30. JF to JM, 11/5/64.
31. *Times Literary Supplement*, 4/6/64, p. 487. Frame was paid thirty-four pounds for this contribution.
32. JF to EPD, 11/5/64.
33. JF to FS, undated.
34. Text of radio talk published in *Listener*, 3/7/64.
35. Janet Gibson to Jean Smith, 13/6/64.
36. *Listener*, 3/7/64.
37. They were 'The Joiner', 'The Senator Had Plans' and 'Scott's Horse', *Landfall* 71, September 1964, pp. 209–11.
38. Ibid p. 211.
39. CB to JF, 16/6/64.
40. JF to FS, 8/6/64; & to CB, 27/5/64.
41. JF to JM, 11/10/66; but composed on Waiheke. This fragment of verse is an echo of the rhythm and rhyme scheme of Arthur O'Shaughnessy's 'Ode', which begins: 'We are the music makers, / And we are the dreamers of dreams . . .' *The Oxford Companion to English Literature* calls this piece 'a characteristic example of Victorian escapist verse'. (1945, p.

723).

42. See JF to JM, 5/10/64.
43. JF to JM, 16/9/64.
44. The *New Leader* 47, 31/8/64, p. 85.
45. See, for example, Peter Buttenhuis in the *New York Times Book Review*, 16/8/64; & *Harper's Magazine*, September 1964. Frame herself did not find out that the book had appeared in New York until October 1964.
46. JF to JM, 15/7/64.
47. Howard Gotlieb to JF, 27/8/64.
48. See JF to JM, 16/9/64.
49. This story was subsequently republished in the second series of *New Zealand Short Stories*, 1966, which Stead edited for Oxford University Press; see pp. 325–353.
50. FS to CKS, 30/8/64. The South African-born poet Roy Campbell had caused considerable controversy with his attacks on friends and associates in his book *The Georgiad* (1932), an assault on the Bloomsbury group; and in his two volumes of autobiography.
51. Note handed over with the story volumes, held by CKS.
52. JF to 'Karl Waikato' (CKS), 5/9/64.
53. Stead 1999, p. 224.
54. CKS to JF, 16/9/64; Stead 1999, p. 224. The story *was* published in New Zealand, unchanged, in *The Reservoir and other stories*, Pegasus, 1966, pp. 215–240.
55. The phrase 'tinged . . . with feminine jealousies and hopes' is from Frame's letter of 5/9/64.
56. JF to JM, 16/9/64 & 5/10/64.
57. See JF to JM, 5/10/64.
58. JF to CB, 7/10/64.
59. RHC to JF, 11/10/64.
60. JM to JF, 8/10/64.
61. JF to Audrey Scrivener, 23/10/64.
62. JF to JM, 30/9/65.
63. JF interviewed by Endeavour Films (1975); and her notes in preparation for this interview.
64. JM, notes from JF's 1964 visit to New York and Baltimore.
65. FS to CKS, 7/10/64.
66. Endeavour Films int. with JF (1975).
67. JM, notes from JF's 1964 visit to New York & Baltimore. So enthusiastic was Beasley senior about

meeting Frame that he described himself to Money as 'wanting a little more of that white pussy'.
68. JF to FS, 22/10/64.
69. Int. JF, 3/4/96.
70. JF to Audrey Scrivener, 23/10/64.
71. JF to JM, 12/12/64.
72. CB to JF, 24/12/64.
73. J.W. Hayward (Registrar) to JF, 20/11/64.
74. JF to FS, 23/1/65; & to JM, 17/1/65.
75. JF to JM, 17/1/65 & 6/2/65.

**Chapter Eighteen: Dunedin and the Messrs Burns**

1. Such as D.P. Kennedy in 1937, and John Child in 1947. See Elworthy 1990.
2. See King 1995, p. 357. 'Strait Is the Gate' was subsequently produced by the Globe Theatre in Dunedin in the 1980s; see Carey 1999, p. 149.
3. From 'Envoi [to "University Song"]', *Collected Poetry* (1980), p. 52.
4. *The Pocket Mirror*, pp. 3–4.
5. *The World Regained* (1957); and *Donald Anderson, A Memoir* (1966).
6. JF to JM, 15/8/65.
7. JF to Margaret Dalziel, 7/10/64.
8. JF to Constance Malleson, 25/1/65.
9. JF to FS, 23/1/65; & to EPD, 2/2/65.
10. FS to MK, March 1978.
11. JF to FS, undated (March 1965).
12. JF to Constance Malleson, 30/1/65.
13. Frame in *Landfall* 87, September 1968, p. 241.
14. JF to FS, 6/4/65.
15. JF to JM, 6/2/65.
16. *Otago Daily Times*, 13/2/65.
17. JF to JM, 14/3/65.
18. JF to FS, 2/3/65.
19. *The Pocket Mirror*, p. 5.
20. JF to Roger Culpan, 5/3/69.
21. JF to Sheila Natusch, undated (March 1965).
22. JF to FS, undated (March 1965).
23. Alan Horsman, citation for JF's honorary doctorate, 6/5/78.
24. *Critic*, 19/3/65.
25. JF to Dorothy Neal White, 13/2/65.
26. Int. Vicky Feltham, 7/12/98.
27. JF to FS, 2/7/65.
28. EPD to FS, 8/11/65.

29. JF to FS, undated (March 1965).
30. JF to FS, undated (May 1965).
31. Dennis McEldowney, Diary, 7/5/65.
32. Dennis McEldowney, Diary, 15/6/65.
33. Dennis McEldowney, Diary, 22/6/65.
34. JF to FS, 28/6/ 65; & to EPD, 8/11/65.
35. JF to FS, 28/6/65 & 3/7/65.
36. JF to FS, 28/6/65.
37. JF to FS, 3/7/65.
38. JF to JM, 20/6/65.
39. See, for example, JF to JM, 15/8/65.
40. JF to FS, 22/6/65.
41. JF to JM, 3/9/65; *Landfall 75*, September 1965, pp. 225–30.
42. JF to AW, 20/3/65.
43. AW to JF, 26/4/65.
44. JF to FS, 21/7/65 & 16/8/65 & 9/7/65; & to JM, 15/8/65.
45. JF to JM, 15/8/65.
46. JF to FS, 23/3/65.
47. JF to FS, 7/5/65.
48. JF to EPD, 9/5/65.
49. JF to JM, 11/4/65 & 30/5/65.
50. Int. Vicky Feltham, 7/12/96.
51. Int. Vicky Feltham, 7/12/96. Such cremations of manuscripts took place on more than one occasion.
52. JF to EPD, 27/8/65.
53. *The Pocket Mirror* (1967), pp. 56–7.
54. Ibid p. 11.
55. *Time*, 6/8/65.
56. JF to FS, 5/8/65.
57. Dennis McEldowney, Diary, 5/8/65.
58. JF to JM, 5/8/65.
59. JF to JM, 5/8/65.
60. Carl Brandt to JM, 10/9/65.
61. *New York Times Book Review*, 8/8/65.
62. William Plomer to FS, 24/10/65.
63. *Times*, 21/10/65; the *Times Literary Supplement*, 21/10/65; & the *Listener*, 11/11/65.
64. The *Press & Herald Tribune* reviews from undated clippings in Pegasus Press files; David Hall in *Listener*, 17/12/65.
65. *Landfall 77*, March 1966, pp. 93 & 94.
66. FS to EPD, 22/12/65.
67. JF to FS, 12/8/65.
68. JF to JM, 30/9/65.
69. CKS to FS, 8/10/65.
70. JF to FS, 26/10/65.
71. See 'The Reservoir' in *New Zealand Short Stories* (1966), pp. 170–186.
72. JF to FS, 12/10/65.
73. JF to RHC, 19/9/65.
74. JF to FS, 16/10/65.
75. JF to JM, 20/9/65.
76. J.W. Hayward (Registrar) to JF, 14/10/65.
77. JF to JM, 15/10/65.
78. Alan Horsman to J.W. Hayward, 19/10/65.
79. JF to FS, 12/9/65; & to JM, 19/10/65.
80. Autobiog. p. 434.
81. JF to EPD, 22/10/65.
82. See *Settler and Stranger: Poems*, Caxton, 1965.
83. Dennis McEldowney, Diary, 29/10/65.
84. JF to EPD, 18/11/65.
85. JF to EPD, 18/11/65.
86. Dennis McEldowney, Diary, 7/12/65.
87. Dallas 1991, pp. 148–9.
88. Dennis McEldowney, Diary, 30/9/65.
89. This was published in *Landfall 80*, December 1966, pp. 349–57. It was also broadcast at a later date.
90. JF to Alan Horsman, 3/11/65.

**Chapter Nineteen: Home and Away**

1. JF to JM, 26/4/66.
2. JF to EPD, 15/1/66.
3. JF to CB, 24/11/65.
4. JF to RHC, 24/1/66.
5. JF to RHC, 22/2/66.
6. See JF to EPD, 24/2/66; to RHC, 22/2/66; & to JM, 27/1/66.
7. JF to JM, 3/3/66.
8. JF to RHC, 16/1/66.
9. 'For All the Saints', *New Zealand Short Stories* (1966), pp. 211–220. Jacquie Baxter would have a book of stories published in 1983, *The House of the Talking Cat*; and a book of poems, *Dedications*, in 1996, using her maiden name of Sturm.
10. JF to EPD, 20/8/66.
11. JF to EPD, 6/8/66.
12. JF to FS, 2/4/66.
13. James K. Baxter, 'The Cattle Shed (for Janet)', unpublished poem in JFP.
14. 'The Reply', *The Pocket Mirror*, pp. 54–6.
15. Ibid p. 56.
16. JF to FS, 8/4/66; Frame had swapped this squib with the Baxters.

17. Int. John Baxter, 13/2/97.
18. JF to EPD, 20/8/66.
19. JF to RHC, 7/6/66.
20. JF to Dick White, 4/8/66.
21. JF to FS, 3/5/66.
22. CB to JF, 26/4/66; Stead 1999, p. 225.
23. Phillip Wilson, unpublished memoir on JF, undated (1998).
24. *New Yorker*, 29/3/69, pp. 134–8.
25. Int. JF, 4/11/98.
26. 'A Boy's Will', *Landfall* 80, December 1966, pp. 314–23.
27. See Carl Brandt to JF, 28/4/66.
28. *New Zealand Monthly Review*, no. 67, May 1966, p. 24.
29. JF to Alan Horsman, 6/5/66; & further note, 21/10/66.
30. See JF to FS, 2/4/66; *New Statesman*, 11/3/66 & *Times Literary Supplement*, 28/4/66. This *TLS* review appears *not* to have been written by Dan Davin.
31. *Listener*, 29/7/66.
32. *Landfall* 79, September 1966, pp. 290–2.
33. JF to FS, undated (September 1966).
34. *New York Times Book Review*, 11/9/66.
35. *New York Times*, 21/7/66.
36. J.H. Silversmith Junior, president, National Jewish Hospital at Denver, to JF, 28/7/66.
37. Dr Robert I. Zanthe to JF, 25/5/66.
38. JF to EPD, 6/8/66.
39. Dennis McEldowney, Diary, 29/7/66 & 10/8/66.
40. JF to FS, undated (September 1966). The reference is to W.H. Auden's 'Miss Gee', see *Collected Poems* (1976), pp. 132–4.
41. JF to FS, undated (September 1966); & Dennis McEldowney, Diary, 21/9/66.
42. JF to FS, 17/10/66.
43. See insert in *Landfall* 80, December 1966. The journal continued publication and was nearing issue 200 at the time this book went to press.
44. JF to JM, 11/10/66.
45. Patience Ross to JF, 23/9/65.
46. JF to Alan Horsman, 21/10/66.
47. JF to George Braziller, 10/11/66.
48. JF to George Braziller, 24/11/66.
49. George Braziller to JF, 28/12/66.
50. JF to JM, 13/11/66.
51. JF to RHC, 17/11/66.
52. See JM to JF, 4/12/66.
53. JF to JM, 4/1/67.
54. JF to JM, 24/1/67.
55. Dennis McEldowney, Diary, 28/1/67.
56. Dennis McEldowney, Diary, 1/2/67.

## Chapter Twenty: Utopia Discovered and Postponed

1. JF to FS, 24/2/67.
2. See JM to Henry Granoff, 29/1/67.
3. JF to FS, 24/2/67.
4. JF to FS, 24/2/67.
5. JF to EPD, 6/3/67.
6. JF to Dorothy Neal White, 14/3/67.
7. JF to Dorothy Neal White, 14/3/67.
8. JF to FS, 21/3/67.
9. JF to EPD, 16/4/67.
10. JF to EPD, 16/4/67.
11. JF to JM, 21/4/67.
12. JF to FS, 18/4/67.
13. JF to FS, 18/4/67.
14. JF to JM, 17/4/67.
15. JF to JM, 21/4/67.
16. Jeffrey Simmons to AW, 15/3/67.
17. See Jeffrey Simmons to AW, 15/3/67; & AW to Jeffrey Simmons, 22/3/67.
18. JF to EPD, 9/7/67.
19. Int. JF, 24/4/98.
20. JF to EPD, 14/5/67.
21. JF quoted in *Listener*, 27/7/70.
22. Int. JF, 28/3/96.
23. Klein 1996, pp. 18 & 107.
24. The Jules Feiffer quote is from an unidentified obituary for John Marquand in the possession of his son, James Marquand.
25. JF to JM, 16/5/67 (misdated 'March').
26. Barbara Epstein, p.c., 6/5/98.
27. JF to EPD, 22/7/67.
28. JF to JM, undated (July 1967).
29. See *Listener*, 27/7/70.
30. JF to RHC, 17/9/68.
31. JF to FS, 9/7/67.
32. Int. JF, 5/6/99.
33. Int. JF, 5/6/99. Frame wrote a story (unpublished) arising from this incident.
34. JF to Pamela Gordon, 1/7/67.
35. *New Yorker*, 31/1/70, pp. 37–9.
36. JF to JM, 12/7/67.
37. Hortense Calisher to MK, 15/4/98.
38. JF to JM, 14/8/67.

39. JF to JM, undated (August 1967).
40. JF to EPD, 22/7/67.
41. JF to JM, undated (August 1967); & to EPD, 22/7/67.
42. See John Barkham, 'Shy Writer Has Love–Hate Attitude', *Daily Press*, Hampton, Va, 21/5/67.
43. C.K. Stead in *Contemporary Poets* (ed. James Vinson), New York, 1975, p. 509. See also J.R. Willingham in *Library Journal*, 15/5/67, p. 1938; S. Stepanchev in *New Leader*, 14/8/67, p. 20; & Jack Bevan in *Southern Review*, Summer 1970, p. 872.
44. JF to EPD, 22/7/67.
45. See EPD to FS, 17/3/68.
46. JF to Dorothy Neal White, 17/9/67.
47. JF to Constance Malleson, 29/10/67.
48. JF to RHC, 19/9/67.
49. JF to RHC, 19/9/67.
50. JF to JM, 26/10/67.
51. JF to JM, 28/10/67.
52. JF to Audrey Scrivener, 29/10/67.
53. JF to EPD, 28/11/67.
54. JF to EPD, 17/12/67; & to FS, 29/12/67.
55. JF to EPD, 17/12/67.
56. JF to EPD, 17/12/67.
57. JF to FS, 29/12/67.
58. Patience Ross to JF, 2/1/68.
59. JF to Gordons, 8/1/68.
60. JF to JM, 22/1/68.
61. JF to JM, 22/1/68.
62. JF to JM, 20/2/68.
63. JF to Audrey Scrivener, undated (early March 1968).
64. JF to FS, 4/3/68; & FS to EPD, 9/3/68.
65. JF to AW, 30/3/68; the poem is in *The Pocket Mirror*.
66. JF to JM, 29/4/68.
67. Int. Vicky Feltham, 7/12/68.
68. JF to JM, 29/3/68.
69. JF to JM, 27/4/68.
70. JF to EPD, 16/6/68.
71. JF to FS, 29/4/68.
72. JF to JM, 13/5/68.
73. JF to JM, 27/4/68.

**Chapter Twenty-one: Cherishing America**

1. *Listener*, 29/3/68.
2. Royalty statement dated 29/2/68, received in March 1968.
3. P.G. Rogers (Pegasus Press) to JF, 10/4/68.
4. JF to AW, 29/4/68.
5. AW to JF, 2/5/68.
6. JF to AW, 29/5/68.
7. JF to FS, undated (May 1968).
8. AW to JF, 2/5/68.
9. JF to JM, 25/7/68.
10. JF to FS, undated (May 1968).
11. JF to RHC, 4/7/68.
12. JF to JM, 13/5/68.
13. JF to EPD, 29/7/68.
14. JF to JM, 13/5/68.
15. JF to EPD, 16/6/68.
16. See J.C. Sturm, *The House of the Talking Cat* (1983).
17. JF to Audrey Scrivener, 22/8/68; & to FS, 29/7/68.
18. JF to JM, 6/8/68.
19. JF to EPD, 16/9/68.
20. JF to EPD, 20/10/68.
21. JF to JM, 5/10/68.
22. *Otago Daily Times* (undated clipping, September 1968), JFP.
23. JF to RHC, 4/7/68.
24. JF to EPD, 20/20/68.
25. Int. Jacquie Baxter, 13/2/97.
26. JF to JM, 5/10/68.
27. Henry Granoff to JM, 4/11/68.
28. It would be published there on 29/3/69, pp. 134–8.
29. JF to JM, 19/11/68.
30. JF to JM, 21/12/68.
31. JF to BB, undated (September 1971), referring to her 1968/69 visit.
32. Int. JF, 16/4/96.
33. Int. JF, 16/4/96.
34. JF to BB, 26/11/69.
35. JF to FS, 24/2/69.
36. JF to EPD, undated (January 1969); & to FS, 24/2/69.
37. *New York Times*, 3/2/69.
38. *New York Times Book Review*, 9/2/69.
39. *Time*, 21/3/69.
40. *Harper's Bazaar* 102, June 1969.
41. JF to JM, 25/2/69 & 31/5/69.
42. Alan Lelchuk to MK, 1/5/98.
43. See, for example, JF to JM, 25/2/69 & 2/3/69.
44. Alan Lelchuk to MK, 1/5/98.
45. JF to JM, 11/3/69.
46. JF to JM, undated (March 1969).
47. Philip Roth to JF, 2/4/69.
48. JF to FS, 12/4/69.
49. JF to EPD, 2/4/69.

50. JF to JM, 5/5/69.
51. *New York Times Book Review*, 9/11/69.
52. JF to JM, 10/6/69. Nothing came of this proposal.
53. James Mellow to JF, undated (June 1969).
54. EPD to FS, 13/8/69 & 5/10/69.
55. JF to FS, 9/8/69.
56. Int. JF, 16/4/96.
57. Rhys Richards to MK, 8/8/99. John Williams contacted the author indirectly in January 2000 and asked that he not be 'discussed' in this biography.
58. *Landfall* 89, March 1969, p. 93; JF to JM, 8/8/69.
59. JF to FS, 13/10/69.
60. Int. JF, 16/4/96.
61. Int. JF, 16/4/96.
62. BB to MK, 15/11/97.
63. JF to FS, 13/10/69.
64. JF to JM, 29/10/69.
65. JF to JM, 29/10/69; see also letters to FS, 13/10/69, & EPD, 21/10/69.
66. BB to MK, 15/11/97.
67. BB to MK, 15/11/97.
68. JF to JM, 15/11/69.
69. JF to EPD, undated (January 1970).
70. JF to BB, 17/11/69.
71. JF to BB, undated (November 1969).
72. JF to BB, undated (November 1969) & 26/11/69.
73. JF to FS, 21/4/70.
74. BB to MK, 15/11/97.
75. JF to EPD, undated (December 1969).
76. JF to BB, undated (December 1969).
77. JF to May Sarton, 3/12/69.
78. JF to May Sarton, 10/1/70.
79. JF to BB, undated (December 1969).
80. JF to EPD, 25/1/70.
81. JF to EPD, 29/1/70.
82. JF to BB, undated (late December 1969).
83. JF to BB, undated (December 1969).
84. JF to BB, 8/1/70.
85. JF to BB, 8/1/70, & undated (January 1970).
86. JF to BB, undated (late January 1970).
87. JF to BB, undated (late January 1970).
88. JF to BB, undated (December 1969).
89. JF to BB, 20/1/70.
90. JF to BB, undated (January 1970).
91. JF to BB, undated (January 1970).
92. JF to BB, undated (mid-February 1970).
93. JF to BB, undated (January 1970). Coleman's autobiography appears not to have been published.
94. See JF to BB, 5/2/70.
95. JF to BB, 5/2/70.
96. JF to BB, undated (mid-February 1970).
97. JF to BB, undated (late-February 1970).
98. JF to EPD, 26/4/70.
99. JF to FS, undated (March 1970).

## Chapter Twenty-two: Lonely for Her Own Kind

1. JF to BB, undated (March 1970).
2. JF to BB, undated (March 1970). Jess Whitworth died on 14/9/72.
3. JF to BB, undated (March 1970).
4. JF to BB, 11/4/70.
5. Chisholm 1987, p. 135.
6. JF to BB, undated (1971).
7. JF to BB, 31/3/70.
8. JF to BB, 4/4/70.
9. Later published in *How You Doing? A Selection of New Zealand Comic and Satiric Verse*, 1998, pp. 75–6.
10. JF to BB, 11/4/70.
11. JF to BB, 21/5/70.
12. JF to RHC, 9/7/70.
13. CB to JF, 25/7/69 & 18/12/69.
14. JF to BB, 21/5/70.
15. The preceding novel, *The Rainbirds*, had lacked a dedication.
16. *Time*, 18/5/70.
17. *New York Times*, 23/4/70.
18. Quoted in Braziller advertisement in *New York Times Book Review*, 3/5/70.
19. *New York Times Book Review*, 3/5/70; and JM to Julian Moynahan, 14/5/70.
20. JF to BB, undated (December 1970).
21. CB to JF, 16/8/70.
22. Joan Stevens, 'The Art of Janet Frame' in *Listener*, 4/5/70; previously broadcast on the YC radio network on 29/3/70.
23. JF to BB, 21/5/70.
24. *Listener*, 27/7/70; interview previously broadcast on the National Programme 11/6/70.
25. JF to May Sarton, 4/6/70.
26. JF to RHC, 7/8/70.
27. JF to BB, 21/5/70. For example: 'I think within the stink of ink. Do

you faint in the unrestraint of paint?
I believe it is a common complaint
which causes both inner saint and
outer sinner and outer saint and
inner sinner either to become a
quaint clouter and shouter or to faint
and day by day grow thinner. (The
Auckland summer is all shimmer.)' JF
to BB, undated (December 1970).

28. JF to FS, undated (June 1970).
29. JF to BB, undated (early 1971).
30. JF to BB, undated (early July 1970).
31. Victor Dupont to JF, 1/9/69.
32. JF to FS, undated (July 1970).
33. JF to RHC, 9/7/70.
34. JF to RHC, 9/7/70.
35. JF to FS, 29/7/70.
36. Int. Michael Thomas, 22/5/97.
37. Richard Dunbar (vice-consul,
    American Embassy) to JF, 9/8/70.
38. Testimonial from Charles Neider,
    27/11/70.
39. JF to RHC, 7/8/70.
40. See chapter 12.
41. JF to RHC, 7/8/70.
42. JF to JM, undated (August 1970).
43. JF to BB, 25/10/72.
44. JF to JM, 5/9/70.
45. JF to JM, 15/10/70.
46. See Gwen Wales in Coxhead (ed.)
    1986.
47. JF to JM, 24/11/70.
48. *Listener*, 25/1/71. The television
    production, by Wayne Tourell, was
    recorded in Dunedin on 4/3/71.
49. JF to BB, undated (mid-December
    1970).
50. JF to BB, undated (January 1971).
51. AW to JF, 8/1/71.
52. JF to AW, 24/1/71.
53. JF to JM, undated (January 1971).
54. JF to FS, undated (March 1971).
55. See undated 1971 clipping in JM
    papers.
56. JF to FS, undated (March 1971).
57. JF to BB, undated (March 1971); &
    to FS, undated (March 1971).
58. JF to BB, 1/3/71.
59. JF to FS, 20/4/71.
60. JF to FS, 3/6/71.
61. JF to BB, undated (June 1971), &
    undated (July 1971).
62. JF to FS, 3/6/71.
63. JF to BB, undated (June 1971).
64. JF to BB, 16–18/6/71.

65. JF to BB, 16–18/6/71.
66. JF to BB, undated (July 1971).
67. JF to JM, undated (July 1971).
68. JF to JM, 20/8/71.
69. JF to FS, undated (August 1971).
70. BB to MK, 15/11/97.
71. JF to BB & Paul Wonner, 7/11/71.
72. JF to BB & Paul Wonner, undated
    (September 1971).
73. *Guardian*, 25/9/71.
74. *Times Literary Supplement*, 17/9/71.
75. JF to BB, undated (September 1971).
76. JF to FS, 25/10/71; & to BB, undated
    (October 1971).
77. JF to BB, 20/11/71.
78. JF to BB, 7/11/71.
79. JF to BB, 18/11/71.
80. Cabinet Paper (71) 1120, Office of
    Veterans' Affairs. See also Fred
    Hoffman to MK, 14/9/99. An
    appendix to the Cabinet paper gave
    an estimate of Frame's income for
    the previous seven years as: 1964,
    $2580; 1965 (no figure available);
    1966, $2000; 1967, $600; 1968, $1000;
    1969, $1900; 1970, $1500; 1971
    (estimated), $500. 'For the years
    1957–63, Miss Frame's income
    averaged less than $600 . . .'
81. JF to BB, 21/11/71.
82. JF to BB, undated (December 1971).
83. JF to JM, 21/11/71.
84. JF to BB, undated (December 1971).
85. JF to BB & Paul Wonner, 16/1/71.

**Chapter Twenty-three: Away from
Civilisation**

1. JF to BB, 16/1/72. The review was in
   the *Evening Star*, 15/1/72.
2. *Listener*, 10/1/72.
3. JF to BB, undated (February 1972).
4. JF to JM, 12/3/72.
5. JF to JM, 5/2/72.
6. JF to BB, 5/3/72.
7. See, for example, JF to BB, undated
   (April 1972).
8. JF to EPD, 1/6/72.
9. JF to JM, 2/6.72. The Hocken
   Library did acquire all her papers, in
   August 1999.
10. JF to JM, 2/6/72.
11. See JF to BB, undated (June 1972).
12. JF to BB, 30/6/72.
13. JF to EPD, 23/7/72.
14. JF to BB, 23/6/72.

15. CB to FS, 6/7/72.
16. Ints. Kerry Neal Wilson, 22/5/97; & Vicky Feltham, 7/12/96.
17. JF to BB, 19/7/72.
18. JF to FS, undated (July 1972).
19. JF to BB, 19/7/72.
20. JF to EPD, 23/7/72; & to BB, undated (July 1972).
21. FS to Winston Rhodes, 6/8/72.
22. JF to BB, undated (August 1972).
23. JF to BB, undated (August 1972), & 28/7/72.
24. 'They Never Looked Back', *Listener*, 23/3/74.
25. JF to BB, 3/10/72.
26. *New York Times Book Review*, 27/8/72.
27. *Time*, 11/9/72.
28. *New Yorker*, 30/9/72.
29. *National Observer*, 28/10/72.
30. JF to JM, undated (September 1972).
31. JF to JM, undated (September 1972).
32. JF to JM, 22/9/72.
33. JF to BB, 25/9/72.
34. FS to JF, 23/9/72.
35. *Autumn Testament*, Price Milburn, Wellington, 1972.
36. JF to BB & Paul Wonner, 24/10/72.
37. JF to BB & Paul Wonner, 25/10/72.
38. JF to BB & Paul Wonner, 25/10/72, & undated (October 1972).
39. JF to BB & Paul Wonner, 2/11/72.
40. JF to BB & Paul Wonner, 2/11/72.
41. JF to BB, undated (November 1972).
42. JF to BB & Paul Wonner, 2/11/72.
43. JF to EPD, 3/1/73. Pascoe died on the same day as Baxter, 22/10/72, & Whitworth on 14/9/72.
44. JF to EPD, 3/1/73.
45. JF to Neil & Jenny Gordon, 9/3/73.
46. See, for example, letters to EPD, 3/1/73; & to JM, 15/1/73.
47. JF to Margaret Scott, 23/11/73.
48. See Charles Brasch, *Collected Poems*, OUP, Wellington, 1984, p. 204.
49. JF to EPD, 8/6/73.
50. *Listener*, 21/5/73.
51. *Landfall* 106, June 1973, pp. 159–163; *Islands* 3 (Spring 1974), pp. 335–8.
52. JF to EPD, 8/6/73.
53. JF to JM, undated (April 1973).
54. Margareta Gee to MK, 13/5/95 & 13/4/96.

55. FS to Phillip Wilson, 17/6/73.
56. FS to Phillip Wilson, 17/6/73. Later in the year Sargeson wrote to Charles Brasch's executor, Alan Roddick: 'My relations with [Frame] for complicated reasons are very difficult at present' (FS to AR, 14/10/73).
57. FS to Winston Rhodes, 11/11/73.
58. *Listener*, 27/10/73.
59. *Listener*, 27/10/73.
60. JF to JM, 3/11/73.
61. FS to Dorothy Sutherland, 16/12/73.
62. JF to FS, 2/1/74.

**Chapter Twenty-four: The Mansfield Connection**

1. *That Summer and Other Stories*, John Lehmann, London, 1946.
2. O'Sullivan 1998, p. 9.
3. Roger Robinson in Robinson & Wattie (ed.) 1998, p. 341.
4. Vincent O'Sullivan in Robinson & Wattie (ed.) 1998, p. 340.
5. Letter to John Middleton Murry, 12/11/20; see *Collected Letters of Katherine Mansfield*, vol. 4, 1920–1921, Clarendon Press, Oxford, 1996, p.107. The quotation is on a plaque with an incorrect date attached to the Katherine Mansfield Memorial Room in Menton.
6. Eventually co-edited with Vincent O'Sullivan and published by Oxford University Press in five volumes, of which the first appeared in 1984.
7. JF to Margaret Scott, 2/4/74.
8. *Living in the Maniototo* (1979), pp. 226–7.
9. JF to BB, 5/1/74 & 14/1/74.
10. JF to BB, 10/1/74.
11. JF to BB, 10/1/74.
12. Int. JF, 12/7/99. Bill & Carlita Manson had no recollection of this incident in 1999 (Carlita Manson to MK, 1/8/99).
13. JF to JM, 13/1/74.
14. See King 1992, pp. 124–7.
15. *Listener*, 13/4/74.
16. JF to BB, 9/2/74 & 2/2/74.
17. JF to BB, 9/2/74.
18. JF to BB, 30/3/74.
19. JF to BB, undated (February 1974).
20. JF to BB, 26/3/74.
21. Manuscript held by JF; she never

offered any of these French poems
for publication.

22. JF to BB, 2/2/74 & 9/3/74.
23. JF to BB, 9/3/74,
24. *Listener*, 20/4/74; the letter was dated
    11/3/74.
25. *Listener*, 13/4/74.
26. Stead's & the Mansons' responses to
    the Vogt article were published in the
    *Listener*, 18/5/74.
27. JF to BB, undated (May 1974).
28. JF's undated draft of a letter to the
    editor, *Listener* (JFP). She did not
    submit it for publication until she
    returned to New Zealand in August
    1974.
29. JF to BB, 19/5/74.
30. Victor Dupont to JF, 9/2/74.
31. JF to BB, 30/3/74; & to Victor
    Dupont, 8/3/74.
32. JF to BB, 4/5/74.
33. Letter from RHC quoted in JF to
    BB, 4/5/74.
34. JF to BB, 19/5/74.
35. JF to BB, 30/7/74.
36. Anton Vogt to MK, p.c., May 1976.
37. Int. Jacquie Baxter, 13/2/97.
38. JF to BB, 7/7/74.
39. JF to BB, 20/7/74.
40. JF to BB, undated (1974).
41. JF to BB, 30/7/74.
42. JF to BB, 11/8/74.
43. JF to BB, 11/8/74.
44. JF to Vogts, 4/9/74.
45. JF to JM, 26/8/74; & to Vogts,
    4/9/74.
46. JF to BB, 1/9/74 & 8/9/74.
47. JF to BB, 1/9/74.
48. JF to BB, 8/9/74.

### Chapter Twenty-five: In Search of Silence

1. JF to JM, 27/12/74.
2. JF to JM, 5/11/74.
3. JF to JM, 27/12/74.
4. JF to BB, 14/10/74.
5. *Education*, vol. 24, no. 9 (1975), p. 27.
6. JF to BB, 29/10/74.
7. Patrick Evans, *An Inward Sun*, New
   Zealand University Press/Price
   Milburn, Wellington, 1971.
8. Evans 1971, p. 21.
9. Ibid p. 15.
10. Ibid p. 11.
11. JF to Patrick Evans, 13/11/74.
12. Patrick Evans to JF, 4/8/75.
13. Patrick Evans, *Janet Frame*, Twayne
    Publishers, Boston, 1977.
14. Meikle 1994, p. 232.
15. Phoebe Meikle to JF, 10/11/74.
16. JF to Phoebe Meikle, 13/11/74.
17. Phoebe Meikle to JF, 19/11/74.
18. Phoebe Meikle to JF, 10/1/75. Frame
    had two further stories, 'The Bath'
    and 'Winter Garden' in the third
    series of *New Zealand Short Stories*
    which, edited by Vincent O'Sullivan,
    appeared from Oxford University
    Press in 1975.
19. JF to AW, 9/11/74.
20. JF to AW, 31/10/74.
21. See Michael Thomas to AW, 5/5/76.
22. JF to BB, 20/11/74.
23. JF to FS, undated (November 1974).
24. Richards 1997, p. 412.
25. JF to BB, 22/12/74.
26. JF to BB, 26/12/74.
27. JF to BB, 27/12/74.
28. JF to the Vogts, 14/1/75.
29. JF to BB, 6/1/75.
30. *North Shore Gazette*, 22/1/75.
31. Frame wrote a letter of protest to the
    paper (JFP) but did not post it.
32. JF to BB, undated (February 1975).
33. Soundtrack, *Janet Frame*, Endeavour
    Films, 1977.
34. Reimke Ensing to MK, 9/8/99.
35. Ensing 1977, p. 16.
36. JF to BB, 29/1/75.
37. JF to BB & Paul Wonner, 27/2/75; &
    to EPD, 18/3/75.
38. JF to EPD, 18/3/75.
39. Frame had bought 276 Glenfield
    Road; Baxter had died at no. 544.
40. JF to BB, 1/5/75.
41. JF to EPD, 17/5/75.
42. JF to EPD, 2/6/75.
43. JF to EPD, 26/8/75.
44. JF to Minda Tessler (Braziller),
    6/4/76.
45. *Listener*, 6/9/75, p. 20.
46. JF to JM, 8/10/75.
47. JF to JM, 8/10/75, & 15/11/75.
48. JF to Baileys, undated (January 1976).
49. JF to Baileys, undated (January 1976).
50. JF to JM, 23/12/75.
51. JF to BB, 18/2/76.
52. JF to BB, 3/1/76,
53. JF to EPD, 17/11/75.
54. JF to JM, 18/3/76.

55. JF to JM, 23/12/75.
56. JF to BB, 1/4/76. The book was *Waiariki*, Longman Paul, Auckland, 1975.
57. JF to BB, 19/2/76.
58. JF to BB, 9/2/76.
59. JF to BB, 1/4/76.
60. King 1995, p. 395.
61. JF to BB, 14/4/76.
62. JF to FS, 12/5/76; & Baileys, undated (May 1976).
63. JF to Baileys, undated (May 1976).
64. JF to George Braziller, 19/6/76.
65. JF to JM, undated (June 1976).
66. JF to JM, undated (June 1976).
67. JF to JM, 19/6/76.
68. JF to BB, 20/7/76.
69. JF to BB, 14/7/76.
70. JF to BB, undated (August 1976).
71. JF to BB, undated (August 1976).
72. JF to BB, undated (August 1976). See John B. Beston, 'A Brief Biography of Janet Frame' & 'A Bibliography of Janet Frame' in *World Literature Written in English*, vol. 17, no. 2, November 1978, pp. 565–585; and 'The Effect of Alienation upon the Themes of Patrick White and Janet Frame' in Daniel Masa (ed.), *Individual and Community in Commonwealth Literature*, University of Malta Press, Malta, 1978, pp. 131–39.
73. JF to BB, 27/7/76.
74. JF to EPD, undated (July 1976).
75. JF to BB, 6/8/76.
76. JF to BB, undated (August 1976).
77. JF to BB, 11/9/76.
78. JF to BB, 15/9/76.

**Chapter Twenty-six: State of Siege**
1. JF to George Braziller, 11/10/76.
2. JF to EPD, 6/11/76.
3. JF to JM, 5/10/76.
4. JF to BB, 15/9/76.
5. JF to BB, 4/10/76 & 9/10/76.
6. JF to BB, 9/10/76.
7. JF to BB, 9/10/76.
8. JF to BB, 17/10/76.
9. JF to BB, 11/12/76.
10. JF to BB, undated (January 1977).
11. Sargeson 1975, p. 154.
12. JF to FS, 3/12/76.
13. JF to BB, 30/11/76.
14. JF to BB, 11/11/76.
15. JF to BB, 11/11/76 & 30/3/77.
16. JF to BB, 17/4/77.
17. JF to BB, 9/1/77.
18. JF to BB, 9/1/77.
19. JF to BB, 1/2/77.
20. JF to JM, 17/2/77.
21. JF to BB, 23/2/77.
22. John Marquand to JF, 14/2/77.
23. John Marquand to JF, 14/2/77.
24. JF to BB, 23/2/77 & 7/5/77; & to JM, 30/3/77.
25. JF to BB, 1/2/77.
26. JF to EPD, 31/3/77.
27. JF to JM, 5/5/77.
28. JF to EPD, 7/3/77.
29. JF to BB, undated (April 1977).
30. JF to JM, 10/5/77.
31. JF to BB, 18/7/77.
32. JF to BB, 14/6/77.
33. JF to BB, 18/7/77.
34. JF to BB, 22/7/77.
35. JF to BB, 10/8/77.
36. JF to BB, 23/8/77.
37. AW to JF, 5/8/77.
38. JF to BB, 2/9/77.
39. JF to the Baileys, 29/9/77.
40. JF to JM, undated (October 1977).
41. Frame in Amirthanayagan 1982, pp. 85–94.
42. JF to BB, 10/11/77.
43. JF to JM, 2/11/77.
44. JF to JM, 2/11/77.
45. JF to BB, undated (November 1977).
46. JF to BB, 18/11/77.
47. JF to BB, 3/1/78.
48. JF to BB, 30/12/77.
49. JF to BB, 3/1/78.
50. JF to BB, 30/12/77.
51. JF to BB, 3/1/77.
52. JF to FS, 1/1/78. According to Sargeson, Waten and his friend Noel Counihan had 'robbed and wrecked the local English Public Schools Club, in fact put it out of action for ever' (King 1995, p. 392).
53. JF to BB, 3/1/78.
54. See Robert Saley to Scott Hardie Boys Morrison & Co, 21/12/77.
55. JF to BB, 3/1/78.
56. JF to FS, 1/1/78.
57. JF to BB, 30/1/78.
58. JF to BB, 10/2/78.
59. JF to BB, 10/2/78 & 15/2/78; & to

FS, 9/3/78.

60. JF to FS, 9/3/78.
61. JF to JM, 8/3/78.
62. This is mentioned in letters to BB & JM.
63. JF to BB, undated (1974).
64. JF to BB, 23/6/78.
65. JF to Pamela Bailey, undated (March 1978).
66. JF to Wallace Ironside, 17/6/78.
67. JF to Kay Bradford, 26/7/80.
68. JF to JM, 7/4/78.
69. JF to FS, 21/9/78.
70. See copy of FS's final will, signed 7/3/78.
71. JF to JM, 15/5/78; & to BB, 29/5/78.
72. JF to JM, 15/5/78.
73. JF to JM, 7/4/78.
74. Alan Horsman, citation for JF's doctorate in literature, 6/5/78.
75. JF to JM, 15/5/78.
76. JF to Patrick Evans, 14/5/78.
77. See Stevie Smith, *Selected Poems* (1962).
78. The errors were largely in matters where Evans's sources had been at fault — a common phenomenon in an 'unauthorised' work. He says, for example, that 'Frame was known in her early years as Jean, the second name of her older sister' (p. 18); in fact Myrtle's second name was Joan. He attributes to Frame a gruesome children's story written at Dunedin Teachers' Training College (p.29), which was actually written by Isabel Frame.
79. JF to AW, 24/8/78.
80. JF to BB, undated (August 1978).
81. JF to BB, undated (August 1978).
82. JF to Pamela Bailey, 21/8/78. Frame wrote a commendation of the film in similar terms for use by the New Zealand Film Commission in promoting it.
83. *Evening Post*, 29/7/78.
84. JF to FS, undated (November 1978).
85. JF to JM, 2/7/78.
86. JF to FS, undated (November 1978).
87. JF to JM, 7/11/78.
88. JF to BB, 7/11/78.
89. Int. George Braziller, 17/6/97.
90. JF to EPD, 21/12/78.
91. AW had written to JF on 29/8/78: 'All your books published by us are now out of print so with regret we now close our 21-year association with your work.'
92. JF to FS, 14/2/79.
93. JF to BB, 10/1/79.
94. JF to BB, undated (February 1979).
95. JF to JM, 14/2/79.
96. JF to George Braziller, 3/3/79.
97. JF to Dorothy Ballantyne, 15/2/79.
98. JF to BB, 10/1/79.
99. JF to BB, 14/3/79.
100. JF to BB, 14/3/79.
101. JF to FS, 3/7/79.
102. JF to Secretary of Internal Affairs, 9/4/79.
103. Pat Stuart to JF, 19/4/79.
104. JF to her Stratford GP, undated (1979).
105. Stratford GP to MK, 27/8/99.
106. JF to Elizabeth Hock (Braziller), 19/4/79.
107. Carl Brandt to JM, 12/6/79; & JM to Carl Brandt, 21/6/79. These verdicts were relayed to JF by JM.
108. JF to Elizabeth Hock, 19/4/79.
109. JF to Literary Fund committee, 14/9/79.
110. FS to JF, 6/6/79. The story was in the *Listener*, 9/6/79.
111. JF to Anton Vogt, 14/8/79.
112. Published in *Islands* 27, November 1979, pp. 467–86; & in Stead 1981, pp. 139–59.
113. CKS to JF, 13/8/79.
114. The chairman was Wiremu Parker; the session was on Maori and Polynesian writing.
115. JF to BB, 15/9/79.
116. FS to Ralph Bodle, 12/8/79.
117. *Time*, 6/8/79.
118. JF to JM, 14/8/79; & to Vogts, 14/8/79.
119. *New York Times Book Review*, 16/9/79.
120. *New Yorker*, 17/9/79.
121. *Los Angeles Times* 21/10/79; & *Kirkus Review*, 15/6/79.
122. CKS in *Melbourne Age*, November 1979; reprinted in Stead 1981, pp. 130–6.
123. FS to Ralph Bodle, 18/11/89.
124. CKS to JF, 13/8/79.
125. JF to CKS, undated (August 1979).
126. JF to Vogts, 14/8/79.
127. JF to JM, 14/2/79.
128. JF to BB, 20/8/79.

129. JF to BB, 7/11/79.
130. JF to EPD, 10/11/79.
131. JF to EPD, 10/11/79.
132. RHC to JF, 22/11/79.
133. Iris Murdoch to RHC, 23/11/79.
134. JF to BB, 7/11/79.
135. JF to John Marquand, 28/1/80.
136. JF to JM, 29/12/79.
137. JF to BB, 27/12/79.

## Chapter Twenty-seven: A Change of Direction

1. See King 1997, p. 89. The name of the city is Wanganui; and of the river and tribes, Whanganui.
2. JF to John Marquand, 23/1/80.
3. Derek Schulz to MK, 3/5/99.
4. JF to BB, undated (June 1980).
5. JF to JM, 1/7/80; see also JF to JM, 2/4/80, & to EPD, 27/2/80.
6. JF to JM, 3/9/80.
7. *Listener*, 24/9/88.
8. JF to EPD, 27/2/80.
9. JF to EPD, 2/4/80. The quotation is from T.S. Eliot's 'Ash-Wednesday'.
10. FS to JF, 25/3/80.
11. June & Wilson Gordon's business card.
12. JF to Vogts, 17/6/80.
13. See Pat Stuart, memo to Literary Fund Advisory Committee, 25/7/80.
14. *Wanganui Chronicle*, 5/7/80.
15. JF to Tish O'Connor (Braziller), 15/7/80.
16. Int. Stephanie Dowrick, 25/7/97.
17. JF to BB, 17/8/80.
18. JF to BB, 1/7/80.
19. JF to BB, 26/11/80.
20. JF to Tish O'Connor (Braziller), 15/7/80.
21. Ray Richards to JF, 26/7/80.
22. JF to FS, undated (September 1980).
23. JF to BB, 20/11/80.
24. JF to JM, 20/11/80.
25. FS to JF, 16/11/80.
26. FS to JF, 16/12/80.
27. JF to FS, 12/11/80.
28. Derek Schulz to MK, 3/5/99.
29. JF to FS, 4/3/81.
30. JF to FS, undated (February 1981).
31. JF to JM, 27/2/81.
32. JF to Ministry of Foreign Affairs, 13/2/81.
33. JF to FS, 4/3/81.
34. JF to George Braziller, 8/3/81.
35. Carl Brandt to TC, 18/3/81.
36. Int. TC, 15/11/96.
37. JF to Ray Richards, 5/5/81.
38. Int. TC, 15/11/96. An objective appraisal of Frame's publishing record from the time she joined Curtis Brown can only support this assessment.
39. *Janet Frame*, Oxford University Press, Wellington, 1980. Despite the imprint year of publication being given as 1980, the book appeared in 1981.
40. JF to EPD, 5/4/81.
41. JF to BB, 15/7/81.
42. Derek Schulz, Journal, 6/6/81.
43. JF to BB, 7/8/81.
44. JF to BB, 7/8/81.
45. *Wanganui Chronicle*, 3/8/81.
46. Richards 1999, p. 3.
47. JF to BB, 18/9/81.
48. For *Daily Telegraph* & *Guardian* reviews, see undated clippings held by JF.
49. JF to JM, 15/7/81.
50. JF to JM, 3/2/82.
51. JF to BB, 23/8/81.
52. George Braziller to JF, 17/11/81.
53. See Michael Thomas to JF, 24/11/81.
54. TC to JF, 9/12/81.
55. JF to BB, 2/10/81.
56. Derek Schulz, Journal, 26/12/81.
57. JF to MK, 22/5/95.
58. JF to Kath Tremain, undated (January 1982).
59. JF to CKS, 9/1/82.
60. JF to JM, 10/1/82.
61. JF to Pamela Bailey, 13/1/82.
62. JF to BB, undated (February 1982); & to the Mahi Tahi Centre group, 21/2/82.
63. Tobias Schneebaum to MK, 16/4/98.
64. 'A Last Letter to Frank Sargeson', *Islands* 33, July 1984, p. 17.
65. JF to BB, 29/3/82.
66. Notice held in JFP.
67. The verse echoes, of course, Lewis Carroll's rhyme from *Alice in Wonderland* which begins: 'Speak roughly to your little boy,/And beat him when he sneezes . . .'
68. JF to BB, 29/3/82.
69. JF to BB, undated (April 1982).

70.  JF to JM, 20/4/82.
71.  JF to BB, 22/4/82.
72.  JF to BB, 2/6/82.
73.  JF to JM, 1/6/82.
74.  JF to BB, 14/9/82.
75.  JF to BB, 14/9/82.
76.  JF to BB, 7/9/82.
77.  *San Francisco Chronicle*, 14/10/82.
78.  *New York Times Book Review*, 21/11/82.
79.  *Washington Post Book World*, 2/1/83.
80.  *Publishers' Weekly*, 27/8/82.
81.  JF to BB, 30/10/82; & to Keith Goldsmith (Braziller), 29/1/83.
82.  JF to BB, 30/10/82.
83.  JF to BB, 3/12/82.
84.  JF to JM, 3/12/82; & to BB, 25/12/82.
85.  JF to Vogts, 20/12/82.
86.  JF to JM, 12/12/82.
87.  JF to BB, 25/12/82; & to Keith Goldsmith (Braziller), 29/1/83.
88.  JF to EPD, 22/1/83.

**Chapter Twenty-eight: Gathering Fame**
1.  JF to Gordons, undated (February 1983); & to BB, 25/12/82.
2.  JF to JM, 20/1/83; & to Keith Goldsmith, 29/1/83.
3.  These interviews would be with the *New Zealand Herald*, *New Zealand Woman's Weekly*, the *Wanganui Chronicle* and Radio New Zealand.
4.  JF to Gordons, undated (February 1983).
5.  JF to TC, 8/3/83.
6.  See undated clipping of NZPA story in JFP.
7.  *New Zealand Herald*, 12/2/83.
8.  Elizabeth Alley int. with JF, YC Programme, broadcast 30/4/83.
9.  JF to Elizabeth Alley, 21/2/83.
10.  JF to BB, 3/2/83.
11.  JF to BB, 17/4/83.
12.  JF to BB, 8/3/83.
13.  *Oamaru Mail*, 28/12/87.
14.  See June Gordon, unpublished autobiography.
15.  See Autobiog. p. 131.
16.  *Listener*, 9/4/83.
17.  *New Zealand Times*, 16/10/83.
18.  *Times Literary Supplement*, 8/7/83.
19.  *Observer*, 3/4/83.
20.  *World Literature Today*, Spring 1983.
21.  *Oamaru Mail*, 18/6/83.

22.  WGHS centennial committee minutes.
23.  JF to June Gordon, 14/9/83.
24.  Int. Marjorie Hore, 21/3/97.
25.  Lorraine Fodie to MK, 26/4/99.
26.  JF to TC, 6/4/84.
27.  *New Zealand Times*, 29/5/83.
28.  JF to Elizabeth Alley, 7/7/83.
29.  JF to BB, 16/6/83.
30.  MK to Roger Horrocks, 11/11/96, reporting a conversation with JF that had occurred that day.
31.  From Rilke's *Les Vergers*.
32.  JF to BB, 16/6/83; & to RHC, 11/1/84.
33.  JF to BB, 26/10/83.
34.  JF to BB, 26/10/83.
35.  JF to BB, 26/10/83.
36.  JF to BB, 4/3/85; & to JM, 28/1/85.
37.  JF to JM, undated (October 1983); & to TC, 25/10/83.
38.  JF to BB, 28/11/83.
39.  JF to BB, 26/11/83.
40.  JF to BB, 15/2/84.
41.  JF to RHC, 11/1/84.
42.  JF to RHC, 11/1/84.
43.  JF to TC, 20/1/84.
44.  JF to TC, 6/4/84.
45.  JF to BB, 28/3/84.
46.  Undated clipping, JFP.
47.  Jane Campion & Bridget Ikin to JF, 26/3/84.
48.  TC to Jane Campion & Bridget Ikin, 19/4/84.
49.  TC to JF, 13/4/84.
50.  *Listener*, 21/7/84.
51.  *New Zealand Times*, 5/8/84.
52.  JF to CB, 29/1/64.
53.  Turnovsky Endowment Trust press release, 8/6/84.
54.  *Evening Post*, 10/7/84.
55.  JF to BB, 11/7/84.
56.  *Evening Post*, 10/7/86.
57.  JF to BB, undated (August 1984).
58.  JF to BB, undated (August 1984).
59.  *Evening Post*, 23/8/84. The overseas distribution proposal was not carried out.
60.  Evans 1986, pp. 8–9. This event, called 'Focus on Janet Frame', occurred on 14 & 15 September 1984.
61.  See *Oamaru Mail* & *Otago Daily Times* for 19/10/84.
62.  JF to TC, 14/8/84.

63. CKS to JF, 13/8/79.
64. Stead 1984, p. 117.
65. *Listener*, 13/10/84. *Listener* writer David Young discussed *All Visitors Ashore* with Frame in September 1984, before she left for London.
66. JF to JM, 11/10/84.
67. *Sunday Times*, 14/10/84.
68. *Times Literary Supplement*, 9/11/84.
69. *New Statesman*, 19/10/84.
70. JF to JM, 30/10/84.
71. JF to JM, 2/11/84.
72. TC to JF, 3/12/84.
73. JF to JM, 2/12/84 & 28/1/85. The basis for the surtax would change several times over the following years and it was removed a decade after its imposition.
74. JF to BB, 28/1/85.
75. JF to BB, 2/12/84.
76. JF to BB, undated (1985).
77. JF to BB, undated (1985) & 19/8/85.
78. JF to TC, 11/1/85; & TC to JF, 1/2/85.
79. JF to JM, 28/1/85.
80. JF to TC, 15/1/85.
81. JF to BB, 28/1/85.
82. JF to TC, 21/8/85.
83. JF to BB, undated (March 1985).
84. JF to Pamela Bailey, 2/5/85.
85. JF to Pamela Bailey, 2/5/85.
86. 'June 1985' in *Listener*, 20/7/85.
87. JF to BB, undated (June 1985).
88. JF to the Gordons, 31/7/85.
89. JF to BB, 19/8/85.
90. Autobiog. p. 434.
91. *Listener*, 7/9/85.
92. *Sunday Times Review*, 8/12/85.
93. Lawrence Durrell's view was communicated to TC by Anthea Morton-Saner who, in addition to being Frame's agent in London was also Durrell's (see TC to Anthea Morton-Saner, 27/8/85); & White's comments were in a letter to Ingmar Bjorksten, 3/12/85. David Marr's opinion of Bjorksten's influence on Nobel Prize decisions is in a letter to MK, 23/4/97.
94. The *Evening Post* of 9/7/86 reported that 40,000 copies had been sold in New Zealand alone; sales by this time in the United Kingdom and the United States totalled over 12,000 copies.
95. *Manawatu Evening Standard*, 21/9/85; & *Waikato Times*, 20/9/85.
96. JF to BB, 20/9/86.
97. JF to BB, 19/12/85.
98. Int. Pamela Gordon, 2/11/96.
99. *Sydney Morning Herald*, 21/11/85.
100. JF to Patrick White, 22/11/85. Copy of letter held by David Marr.
101. David Marr to MK, 22/11/97.
102. Agreement between Janet Clutha & Hibiscus Films, 16/1/86; & Bridget Ikin to TC, 1/9/85.
103. JF to TC, 11/10/85.
104. Int. Bridget Ikin, 14/1/97; & Bridget Ikin to TC, 27/2/86.
105. Int. Bridget Ikin, 14/1/97.
106. JF to BB, 13/1/86.
107. The comet Pepys saw was almost certainly not Halley's: wrong year.
108. JF to BB, 13/1/86.
109. *Listener*, 18/10/86.
110. *New Zealand Update*, August 1986, published by the New Zealand Embassy, Washington.
111. JF to JM, 9/6/86. New Zealand thriller writer Ngaio Marsh (1895–1982) spent many years of her life commuting between homes in England and New Zealand.
112. *Evening Post*, 9/7/86.
113. JF to BB, undated (August 1986).

**Chapter Twenty-nine: Ascending Angel**

1. JF to BB, 14/7/86.
2. JF to BB, 14/7/86.
3. Information included in letter to TC, 18/9/86.
4. JF to RHC, undated (1986).
5. JF to TC, 18/9/86.
6. JF to BB, 20/9/86; & to JM, 9/12/86.
7. Anthea Morton-Saner to TC, 25/4/86; & TC to David Ling, 1/5/86. The Pandora edition of *Daughter Buffalo* was published in 1990.
8. JF to BB, 6/11/86.
9. JF to JM, 9/12/86.
10. The *Press* (Christchurch), 13/12/86.
11. JF to TC, 3/5/87.
12. JF to BB, undated (February 1987).
13. O'Brien 1988, pp. 139 & 143.
14. JF to JM, undated (May 1987).
15. JF to JM, undated (May 1987).
16. Int. June Gordon, 4/8/96.

17.  JF to Derek Schulz & Jill Studd, 20/5/87; & to JM, 15/5/87.
18.  JF to RHC, 26/5/87.
19.  JF to RHC, 26/5/87.
20.  JF to RHC, 26/5/87.
21.  Other books, especially Dawson's collection of New Zealand literature, had earlier been sent to Dawson's *alma mater*, Royal Holloway College in London.
22.  JF to RHC, undated (June 1987).
23.  JF to RHC, 4/7/87.
24.  'To-whom-it-may-concern' letter by June Gordon & JF, 12/8/87.
25.  The *Press* (Christchurch), 29/1/87.
26.  *Otago Daily Times*, 28/4/87.
27.  *Oamaru Mail*, 28/12/87; matching feature in an earlier edition of the paper on 19/12/87.
28.  *Otago Daily Times*, 23/8/88.
29.  JF to BB, 19/8/87.
30.  JF to BB, 19/8/87.
31.  JF to TC, undated (October 1987).
32.  JF to George Braziller, undated (November 1987).
33.  Ros de Lanerolle to JF, 1/9/88.
34.  JF to Ros de Lanerolle, 11/9/88.
35.  JF to TC, 28/12/87.
36.  JF to Bridget Ikin, 7/1/88; & to TC, 30/1/88.
37.  Int. Bridget Ikin, 14/1/97.
38.  Bridget Ikin to JF, 1/9/88.
39.  JF to BB, undated (February 1988).
40.  Introduction to Elizabeth Alley int. with JF, broadcast 19/10/88.
41.  JF to JM, 2/5/88.
42.  JF to JM, 2/5/88.
43.  JF to JM, 2/5/88.
44.  Douglas Wright to MK, 5/4/98; & JF to BB, 16/5/88.
45.  JF to JM, 29/6/88; & to BB, 14/6/88.
46.  JF to JM, 29/6/88.
47.  *Listener*, 24/9/88.
48.  Elizabeth Alley int. with JF, broadcast 19/10/88.
49.  *The Carpathians* (1988), p. 7.
50.  Elizabeth Alley int. with JF, broadcast 19/10/88.
51.  *Evening Post*, 10/9/88.
52.  See *Sunday Times*, 18/9/88; & *Evening Post*, 10/9/88.
53.  *New Zealand Herald*, 24/9/88; & *Otago Daily Times*, 5/10/88.
54.  *Listener*, 24/9/88.
55.  *New Statesman & Society*, undated clipping in JFP.
56.  *Observer*, 23/10/88.
57.  *Guardian*, 28/9/88.
58.  *San Francisco Chronicle*, 8/1/87.
59.  *New York Times Book Review*, 22/1/89.
60.  See *Sydney Morning Herald*, 22/10/88; *The Age*, 10/12/88; the *Weekend Australian*, 17–18/12/88; & *Melbourne Herald*, 23/12/88.
61.  JF to JM, 26/11/88.
62.  JF to JM, 26/11/88.
63.  JF to TC, 27/1/89.
64.  See TC to David Ling, 21/11/88.
65.  JF to TC, 27/1/89.
66.  *Dominion*, 11/1/89.
67.  David Ling to TC, 25/2/89.
68.  See various communications from NZ Film Commission to JF, 1988/89.
69.  JF to BB, 18/8/89; & to TC, 30/8/89.
70.  JF to TC, 8/8/89.
71.  JF to RHC, 12/10/89.
72.  TC to Anthea Morton-Saner, 14/11/89.
73.  Int. JF, 6/6/98.
74.  JF to RHC, 20/11/89.
75.  See JF to Purdy & Holley (EPD's solicitors), 4/12/89; & to BB, 14/12/89.
76.  BB to JF, 11/12/89.
77.  JF to James McNeish, 29/1/90.
78.  JF to MK, 15/4/98.
79.  JF to TC, 17/4/90.
80.  JF to Lindsay Shelton, NZ Film Commission, 20/9/90.
81.  *Dominion*, 28/6/90.
82.  JF to MK, undated (June 1990).
83.  David Ling to TC, 20/7/90.
84.  JF to JM, 20/10/90.
85.  JF to TC, 11/2/91.
86.  TC to Carl Brandt, 12/2/91.
87.  TC to Kerry Fox, 21/6/91.
88.  TC to Peter Rose (OUP Melbourne), 5/12/90. Mercer's book, *Janet Frame, Subversive Fictions*, was subsequently published by University of Queensland Press & University of Otago Press in 1994.
89.  JF to TC, 28/2/91 & 29/7/91.
90.  TC to Anthea Morton-Saner, 18/7/91.
91.  JF to JM, undated (August 1991); & to TC, 2/8/91.

92. JF to JM, undated (August 1991).
93. TC to Anthea Morton-Saner, 10/10/91.
94. G. Ogilvie (for IRD) to JF, 4/10/91.
95. *Evening Star*, 20/6/92.
96. JF to Elizabeth Alley, 6/12/91.
97. David Ling to Wyatt Creech, 5/2/92.
98. Int. JF, 4/8/96.
99. Int. JF, 4/8/96.
100. 'Under Threat, for Janet' in Sturm 1996, p. 26.

## Chapter Thirty: An Allegiance to Origins

1. Int. Jacquie Baxter, 13/2/97.
2. Elizabeth Alley to University of Waikato graduation audience, 17/3/92.
3. Valerie Sutherland, *Melbourne Age*, 3/10/92.
4. JF to Dorothy Ballantyne, 5/12/92.
5. JF to JM, 15/12/92.
6. JF to Dorothy Ballantyne, 15/12/92.
7. JF to Sheila Leaver, 15/12/92; & to Daphne Brassell, 22/12/92. The book was eventually published as *Janet Frame's Kingdom by the Sea*, Daphne Brassell/ Lincoln University Press, Canterbury, 1997. Leaver, soon to become Leaver-Cooper, circumvented the problem of copyright by rewriting the quotation material in indirect speech. Frame was not happy about the result.
8. JF to TC, 8/11/93.
9. Gide's expression about 'God's share' had been one of Sargeson's favourite and most frequently quoted maxims when Frame was at Esmonde Road in 1955–56.
10. JF to BB, undated (1972).
11. JF to JM, 4/3/93.
12. JF to JM, 18/8/93.
13. *Manawatu Evening Standard*, 15/6/93.
14. JF to Elizabeth Alley, 17/10/93; & Elizabeth Alley to TC, 16/11/93.
15. JF to JM, 15/12/93.
16. JF to MK, 28/3/96.
17. Int. Vicky Feltham, 7/12/96.
18. Int. JF, 4/8/98.
19. Elizabeth Alley to MK, undated (August 1999).
20. Elizabeth Alley to MK, undated (August 1999).
21. *Dominion*, 14/3/93.
22. JF to Elizabeth Alley, 16/5/94.
23. *The Australian Magazine*, 6–7/8/94. Another publication which took Chenery's story was the *Sunday Star Times*, 25/9/94.
24. *The Australian Magazine*, 6–7/8/94.
25. JM memo, 1/9/94.
26. JF to Kathy Gale, 27/1/95.
27. JF to TC, 25/1/95.
28. Ferrier 1995, p. IV.
29. See Panny 1992 & Delbaere 1992; Mercer 1994, Alley (ed.) 1994, & *Journal of New Zealand Literature*, no. 11, a special issue arising out of the 1992 Frame conference in Dunedin (although dated 1993, it appeared in May 1994); & Leaver-Cooper 1997. Ferrier 1995 could also be considered part of the group.
30. JF to Elizabeth Alley, 24/8/92.
31. JF to Elizabeth Alley, 24/8/92.
32. JF to Elizabeth Alley, 24/8/92.
33. Mercer 1994, p. 287.
34. See, for example, Susan Ash (Dept of English, Edith Cowan University, Perth, W.A.) to TC, 11/4/94. Other would-be biographers from the United States, Germany, Switzerland and New Zealand approached Frame or her agents at various times throughout the 1990s.
35. *Journal of New Zealand Literature*, No. 11, 1993, p. 16.
36. Ibid p. 17.
37. JF to Patrick Evans, 14/5/78.
38. Elizabeth Alley to JF, 14/4/94.
39. JF to Elizabth Alley, 16/5/94.
40. See King 1996.
41. JF to MK, 17/8/95.
42. Of a total of nearly forty of Frame's friends or acquaintances approached for assistance, only two declined to cooperate.
43. FS to Dan Davin, 16/4/52.
44. Dennis McEldowney, Diary, 18/4/96.
45. Sophie Trevelyan, *The Ultimate Book of New Zealand Insults*, Hodder Moa Beckett, Auckland, 1997. This text was probably intended to be tongue-in-cheek; but it is difficult to be sure.
46. Stead 1999, p. 231.
47. See Margaret Wallis, letter to *Listener*, 19/8/91; also Anthony Hubbard, *Sunday*

*Star Times*, 29/3/98.

48.  Pamela Gordon to MK, undated
     (1996); & *Star Weekender*, 23/2/97.

49.  Max Lambert to MK, undated
     (February 1999).

50.  JF to TC, 27/9/96.

51.  Dennis McEldowney to MK,
     undated (1999).

52.  JF to MK, 4/11/97.

53.  JF to MK, 15/12/97.

54.  The comment was made by Witi
     Ihimaera to MK, 25/5/98.

55.  This whole paragraph was suggested
     by a perceptive and richly suggestive
     passage written by C.K. Stead, which
     I originally intended to quote in full.
     As I transcribed the quotation,
     however, I realised that it did not
     quite convey what I wished to
     communicate, and I rewrote it
     accordingly. Stead's original
     paragraph (from his typescript for the
     article 'Allein auf dem Eis', published
     in *Merian*, 8/8/96, pp. 56–9) reads:
         'An anecdote . . . is always told by
     Frame in a tone that seems to
     tremble on the brink of laughter.
     Her voice and articulation are bell-
     clear, almost child-like, and key
     words are hesitated over, as if she and
     her interlocuter should pause to
     marvel over the huge pretence they
     are engaging in, behaving as if they
     can hold chaos in check by the
     device of linguistic communication.
     The same sense of marvelling at
     itself, at times mocking itself,
     pervades the best of her writing. It
     represents . . . a scepticism native to
     post-colonial societies, where
     national identity is insecure and the
     social imprint faint. Add Frame's
     mental history to her New Zealand
     background and, with the accident
     of literary genius, you get this vivid
     sense that reality itself is a fiction; or
     that our grasp on it is no more than
     a linguistic pretence.' An almost
     identical passage appears in Stead
     1999, p. 229.

# Index

*Note:* JF = Janet Frame. Works listed are by Janet Frame unless otherwise indicated. The recipients of quoted letters are not indexed.

*Adaptable Man, The:* advance for, 235; composition of, 241, 245, 254, 255–6, 273, 291, 300; NZ publication, 291, 296; UK publication, 291, 296; US publication, 291, 294–6; out of print, 396; reissue of, 456; new NZ edition announced, 470; JF's reservations about, 498; new editions, 498
Adcock, Fleur, 465, 488
A.H. and A.W. Reed, 360, 367, 375, 422, 438
'Alison Hendry' (short story), 84–5, 92
*All Visitors Ashore* (Stead), 278, 428, 463–5
Alley, Elizabeth, 452, 452–3, 486–7, 503–4, 506, 508
A.M. Heath Ltd (literary agency): JF chooses, 177–8; handles or places JF's works (*Owls Do Cry*, 191, 201, 203, 204, 209; *Faces in the Water*, 207; *The Edge of the Alphabet*, 214; JF's short stories, 219, 220, 233, 264, 306; *The Adaptable Man*, 254, 273, 291; *The Rainbirds*, 311, 334; *The Pocket Mirror*, 317; *Mona Minim and the Smell of the Sun*, 325) and Sturges' ('Trespassers on Earth', 248, 293, 300); commissions charged, 204, 223, 342; handles JF's contracts with Pegasus, 223; JF dismisses, 357; staff fail to recognise JF when she calls, 429, 434; Women's Press negotiates with, 435; mentioned, 237, 263. *See also* Ross, Patience
American Academy and Institute of Arts and Letters, 474–5
American Express Short Story Award, 459

Ames, Elizabeth, 317, 320, 337, 347, 443
Anderson, Barbara, 507
Andorra, 166, 168–70
*Angel at My Table, An* (Campion film), 448, 460, 466, 467, 473–4, 484, 491, 492, 495, 496, 498, 511
*Angel at My Table, An* (second volume of autobiography): editing of, 457, 458; US publication, 459, 460, 466; UK publication, 460, 463, 465–6; NZ publication, 460–1; radio readings, 462; wins New Zealand Book Award, 462; foreign language editions, 466, 496, 497, 506; NZ sales, 466; third in Wattie Book of the Year Award, 466; Commonwealth paperback rights sold, 471. *See also* Autobiography (Frame's)
Angus and Robertson, 436
Annesley, Mabel, 242
Argument Verlag, 490
Arnold, Matthew, 184
'Art of Janet Frame, The' (radio talk by Joan Stevens), 354–5
Arthur Street School, 62–3, 66, 85, 285, 305
Ascherson, Neal, 239
Ashton-Warner, Sylvia, 238
Association of New Zealand Literature: inaugural conference (Dunedin, 1992), 504, 511–12
'At Evans Street' (poem), 514–15
*Atlantic Monthly*, 224
Atwood, Margaret, 427, 466
Auden, W.H.: JF reads or alludes to, 53, 309, 551*n*40

Autobiography (Frame's): composition of, 433, 435, 437, 441, 444, 446, 449–50, 456, 457, 459, 460, 463; Tim Curnow asks to see, 442; worldwide sales, 470; photographs included in later editions, 474; single-volume editions, 490–1, 497, 506; new hardback edition, 495. *See also Angel at My Table, An; Envoy from Mirror City, The; To the Is-Land*

Avondale (mental hospital): JF committed to, 105–6

Bachardy, Don, 345
'Back to the Oil Pipe-Line' (short story), 306
Bagatti, Mrs (landlady), 170, 239
Bailey, Daniel (great-nephew), 409, 411–12
Bailey, Josie (great-niece), 141–5, 409, 417–18, 471
Bailey, Stephen, 371, 400, 409, 411–12
Baileys (Pamela and Stephen, as married couple), 400, 411–12, 417, 430, 432, 449. *See also* Bailey, Stephen; Gordon, Pamela (*also* Bailey, niece)
Ballantyne, David, 122, 488
Ballantyne, Robert, 351, 352, 368, 419
Baltimore: JF visits or stays in, 279–80, 314–15, 320, 325–6, 327, 336, 340, 345, 346–7, 349, 362, 363–4, 365, 466; riots of 1968, 328–9
Barcelona, 144, 156, 167
Barker, Elspeth, 340, 481
Barker, George, 53, 60, 340, 341
Barker, Lynn (of Barker Productions), 456, 467
Barkham, John, 322, 552n42
'Bath, The' (short story), 291, 306
Battersea Polytechnic Hotel, 153
Bauer, Jerry, 228
Baxter, Archibald, 303, 312, 358
Baxter, Hilary, 302, 304, 312, 332, 334, 351
Baxter, Jacqueline (née Sturm): Money counsels, 86n; collection of stories, 332; accompanies JF to Christchurch, 378; in France with JF, 389–90; associations with Stratford, 408; visits JF, 358, 368, 409–10, 431–2, 467–8, 486, 513, 518; JF stays with, 415–16, 426, 437; accompanies JF to Michael Fowler Centre, 461; at celebratory dinner with JF, 494–5; letter-poem to JF, 501–2; at International Festival in Wellington, 507; mentioned, 509
Baxter, James Keir: early poetry, 79, 285; JF reads, 79, 80; JF's first meeting with, 85–6; JF's letters to, 94–5; unable to reconcile legacies of the two Burnses, 284–5; Burns Fellowship, 292, 298, 302, 312; friendship with JF, 302–3; literary seminar, 305–6; David Hall criticises, 309; goes to Jerusalem, 351; at home in Wellington, 360; death, 373–4; buried at Jerusalem, 431, 432; mentioned, 133, 330, 438
Baxter, John, 302, 304–5, 312, 351, 415–16, 486
Baxter, Lenore, 312
Baxter, Millicent, 303, 312
Baxter, Stephanie, 334, 351
Baxter, Terence, 312
Baxters (James K. and Jacquie, or Jacquie and children), 302–3, 309, 312, 330, 332, 351, 359
Beach, Gene (née Powell), 111, 178
Beacham, Dr Arthur, 290
'Beanman, Mr', 239
Beattie, Sir David, 461
Beauchamp, Arthur, 15, 381
Beauchamp, Harold, 15, 380, 381
Beauchamp, Jeanne, 15, 381
Beauchamp, Leslie, 42
Beauchamp, Mary, 14–15
'Beginnings' (*Landfall* essay), 263, 268–9, 394, 395, 452, 461, 548n39
Bell, Millicent, 307–8
Bertram, James, 42, 307
Beston, John, 405, 414, 419, 443, 466
Bevington, Helen, 448
'Big Bill' (poem), 288
'Birds of the Air' (short story), 337
Bjorksten, Ingmar, 470
Blake-Palmer, Dr Geoffrey, 106, 107, 108, 112, 113, 118, 119, 197, 207, 222, 257, 267, 371
Bloomsbury Press, 483, 498
Bock, Frederick, 318
*Book of New Zealand Verse, A* (ed. Curnow), 79
Booker Prize, 489
Bosch, Hieronymus: JF's works compared to, 355, 377
'Boston lure', 275, 308–9
Boston University, 275, 493
Botting, Ethel, 22
Bowen, Elizabeth, 226
Boyd, Warren John, 71
Boyle, Kay, 242
'Boy's Will, A' (short story), 306
Bradley, Katherine, 47, 52, 55, 82, 87, 94, 455

Bradley, Nancy, 55, 82, 87, 94
Brandt and Brandt (literary agency):
handles or places JF's works (short
stories, 191, 219, 337; *Owls Do Cry*, 191,
200, 201, 204, 208, 209; *Faces in the
Water*, 207, 210, 223–4, 224; *The Edge of
the Alphabet*, 214; *Scented Gardens of the
Blind*, 275; *The Adaptable Man*, 295; *The
Rainbirds*, 311; *Daughter Buffalo*, 365;
*Living in the Maniototo*, 428; *The
Carpathians*, 483); JF dismisses, 357; JF
returns to, 365; commission charged,
372; JF's only agent, 396, 434; Women's
Press negotiates with, 435; continue as
JF's American agents, 442. *See also*
Brandt, Carl
Brandt, Carl: on JF's talent, 191;
investigates possibility of fellowships for
JF, 314, 317, 333; JF visits, 339; on *Living
in the Maniototo*, 425; agrees to JF's
change of agent, 438; does not favour
Braziller as publisher, 478; mentioned,
219, 235, 320, 434. *See also* Brandt and
Brandt (literary agency)
Brandt, Carol, 320
Brasch, Charles: JF reads, 80; founds
*Landfall*, 85; JF's first meeting with, 92–
3; JF has tea with, 117; JF's letters to,
118, 161, 267, 278; helps JF financially,
142, 197; 'The Islands' (poem), 245; JF
sees again, 263; pension scheme for JF,
263, 265, 268–9, 274, 281, 290, 292, 352,
365; helps to endow Burns Fellowship,
283; JF in awe of, 285; JF socialises with,
289, 290, 297, 305, 306, 352; offers rug
for JF's house, 299; retires as editor of
*Landfall*, 310; offers JF private support
from 'various people', 352–3; letter of
appreciation to JF for *Intensive Care*,
354; asked about JF by French professor,
357; JF visits, 368; death, 375; and *Owls
Do Cry*, 394; mentioned, 15, 42, 122,
332, 369, 438. *See also Landfall*
Braziller, George: publishes JF's works in
USA (*Owls Do Cry*, 199, 200–1, 208,
209; short stories, 235, 251–2; *The Pocket
Mirror*, 311, 317; *Yellow Flowers in the
Antipodean Room*, 331; *Mona Minim and
the Smell of the Sun*, 348; *Intensive Care*,
353; *Living in the Maniototo*, 422–3; *An
Angel at My Table*, 457, 466; *The Envoy
from Mirror City*, 466; *You Are Now
Entering the Human Heart*, 466; *The
Carpathians*, 483, 489; single-volume
edition of JF's autobiography, 497); has

interest in innovative fiction, 200; not
good at promotion, 209, 448, 489;
contributes to cost of Kensington flat,
235; meetings with JF, 237, 249, 280,
321, 327, 339, 388, 390, 421–2, 445; JF
sends poems to, 311, 348; invites JF to
dinner, 315–16; organises
accommodation for JF, 316, 336; JF
remains loyal to, 332, 341, 357; royalty
payments, 379; publicity material for JF,
380; warns JF about George
Washington Hotel, 412, 413; JF's
miserable letter to, 437–8; makes 'final'
visit to JF in NZ, 504; at International
Festival in Wellington, 507; contributor
to *The Inward Sun* (1994), 508;
mentioned, 211, 254, 312, 404, 412, 434
Braziller, Marsha, 249, 316, 321, 327, 336
'Brecon, Jake', 488
'Brecon, John Henry', 488
'Brecon, Mattina', 488
British Museum Library: JF visits, 225
Brontës: Frame daughters identify with,
46
Brooke, Jocelyn, 296
Brown and Wonner: JF visits, 345, 361,
365–6, 391, 402, 413, 466; Buddhists,
349; JF proposes to settle in with, 357,
358; pay JF's fare to California, 359; end
of JF's Grand Passion, 363; worrying
about JF, 364; help JF financially, 369;
entertain John Money, 404; JF sends
Sargeson biography to, 409; mentioned,
442, 447. *See also* Brown, William
Theophilus (Bill)
Brown, Ed, 315
Brown, John Macmillan, 284, 303
Brown, Maitland, 70
Brown, Dr Malcolm, 69, 70, 71, 78, 101,
103, 106, 112
Brown, William Theophilus (Bill): at
MacDowell colony, 343–7; JF's letters
to, 344ff. *passim;* JF 'hooked on', 347;
weekend with JF in Baltimore, 362, 363;
helps JF financially, 438; makes 'final'
visit to JF, 504; sees JF in Los Angeles,
509, 515; now an octogenarian, 518. *See
also* Brown and Wonner
Browning, Robert: JF's parody of, 328
Bryant, Dorothy, 447–8
Bryant, Laurie, 289
Buckland Award, 462
Bullock, Florence, 208
Burge, Maud, 156
Burke, Kenneth, 347

Burns Fellowship, 278, 282, 283–6, 292, 298, 300, 330, 378, 517, 518
Burns, Robert, 283–4
Burns, Thomas, 284
Burt, Cyril, 111
Buttenhuis, Peter, 549n45

Calisher, Hortense, 321, 364
Cambridge (UK): JF visits, 215
Cameron, Donald, 66
Cameron, Gregor, 53, 275–6, 277, 286–7
Campion, Edith, 467
Campion, Jane, 460, 466, 467, 473–4, 484, 491. *See also Angel at My Table, An* (Campion film)
Campion, Richard, 467
Cannon, John, 447
Canterbury (Kent): JF visits, 215
Capote, Truman, 317
Cardiff: JF visits, 178
Carey, Patric, 359
Carey, Rosalie, 359
*Carpathians, The:* composition of, 481, 483; NZ publication, 486–8; UK publication, 488–9; US reviews of, 489; NZ sales, 490; wins New Zealand Book Award, 491; wins Commonwealth Writers Prize, 492; foreign language editions, 506
Carroll, Lewis: JF parodies, 445
Carson, Josephine, 343, 344, 348–9
Carson, Mark, 349
'Case of the Disappearing Author, The' (Evans, conference paper), 511–12
'Cat' (poem), 60
Catley, Christine Cole, 126, 377, 443, 446, 449, 478
'Cattle Shed, The' (Baxter poem), 303
Cawley, Ann, 516
Cawley, Dr Robert Hugh: psychiatrist assigned to JF, 194–6; 'conversations' with JF, 195, 198–9, 205–6, 225, 232, 237–8, 240, 249, 254, 325; JF beats at chess, 196; rejects schizophrenia diagnosis, 197; JF's books dedicated to, 199; interest in JF's writing, 204, 207, 210, 214, 273, 277; JF's letters to, 218, 270, 301–2, 352ff. *passim*; appointed to University of Birmingham, 237–8; JF's relationship with, 249–50, 256; 'reassurance letters' to JF, 267; JF consults about travel plans, 278; JF sees again, 281, 429, 340, 389, 481, 516; heart attack, 293; asked to support JF's US visa application, 358; letter stating that

JF 'has never suffered from a mental illness', 388–9, 394, 395; letter to Stratford GP, 425; proposes book of essays and documents, 429; JF regrets not seeing again, 439; unpublished appendix to *An Angel at My Table*, 459; marriage, 475; contributor to *The Inward Sun* (1994), 506, 508; death, 518; mentioned, 235, 288, 312, 412
Caxton Press, 79, 85, 87–8, 94, 107, 210, 299
Central Park Zoo, New York, 316
Century Hutchinson, 435, 470, 478, 483, 490, 497–8, 506
Charter, May (née Godfrey, aunt), 88
Chenery, Susan, 508
Cherry Farm (mental hospital), 297
Cherry, Frances, 494
Chicago, JF in, 321
*Chicago Sun-Times Book Week*, 354
Chisholm, Anne, 454–5
Christchurch: JF in, 92–8, 108; JF's public reading at Festival, 459–60
Christeller, Grete, 86, 87, 92, 95, 96, 98, 345
Clark, Russell, 81
'Clock Tower, The' (poem), 291
Clutha River, 56, 192
Cohen, Harvey, 162–4, 166, 176
Cole, Christine. *See* Catley, Christine Cole
Cole, John Reece, 114, 122, 126
Coleman, Elnora, 343, 348, 349, 363, 364
*Collected Stories* (Sargeson), 266
Colquhoun Ward, Dunedin Public Hospital, 69, 186
*Commonweal*, 239
Commonwealth Writers Prize, 491, 492, 494–5
Cooper, William, 217
*Corinthic:* JF sails on, 255–6
Cornwall: JF in, 227–9
'Cousin Peg' (who was a teacher in Canada), 38, 43, 57
Cox, Patrick, 412, 416
Craddock, June, 39
'Crane, Ma', 239
Crawford, Thomas, 245–6
Cross, Ian, 238, 285, 378, 425
Crumb, Albert, 32
Crutwell, Patrick, 227
Culpan, Roger, 267, 288
cummings, e.e., 177, 178
Cunningham, Kevin, 305
Curnow, Allen, 79, 80, 133, 134, 310, 425, 492, 494

Curnow, Tim, 438, 441–2, 452, 459, 466, 471, 473, 478, 492, 508, 510, 516. *See also* Curtis Brown (literary agency)

Curtis Brown (literary agency), 176, 177, 438, 456, 459, 460–1, 465, 478, 483, 492. *See also* Curnow, Tim

Curtis, Polly (aunt), 119, 144, 418, 437

Curtis, Vere (uncle), 119, 144

*Daily Express*, 250

*Daily Telegraph*, 441

Dallas, Ruth: Sargeson recommends *The Lagoon* to, 110; socialises with JF, 290, 297, 305, 368; and Southland, 294; finds Opoho house for JF and helps furnish it, 299; signs page in Brasch's honour, 310; Burns Fellow, 330; Dunedin friend, 352, 517; on funerals, 358; JF farewells, 369; does not contribute to *Private Gardens*, 399; guest of honour at Sydney PEN congress, 415; honorary doctorate, 416; JF visits, 505; mentioned, 332

Daly, Norman, 318

Dalziel, Margaret, 286, 288–9, 290, 291

*Daughter Buffalo:* composition of, 314, 343, 347, 348, 353, 363, 364–5; acknowledgements in, 365; US publication, 372; NZ publication, 375, 376; Hubert Church Award, 376; falling-out with Frank Sargeson over, 377, 408; reissue of, 456; British and Commonwealth rights sold, 478; new NZ edition, 478–9; Pandora edition, 492; JF's public reading from at Festival, 507–8; mentioned, 457, 484

Davies, W.H., 255

Davin, Dan: includes 'The Day of the Sheep' in anthology, 109, 122; signs *Landfall* letter for Sargeson, 114; proposes meeting with JF, 191; reviews JF's works in *TLS*, 217, 226, 239, 250–1, 364; mentioned, 134, 143

Davitt, Michael, 25

Dawson, Elizabeth Pudsey ('Peter'): JF reads, 80; and JF's first will, 132; has JF to stay at Mount Maunganui, 140–2; helps JF financially, 142, 176, 197, 225, 400; JF wears her slacks, 161; JF's letters to, 184ff. *passim;* returns to England, 225–6, 233; JF stays with in Norfolk, 236–7, 250, 281, 340, 341, 389, 390, 412, 428, 429, 446–7, 465; JF proposes to live with, 246, 248–9; stays with JF, 252, 253; appoints JF as executor, 269; JF regrets

not seeing again, 439; JF considers retreating to, 450; failing health, 474; death, 475; bequest of Flint Cottage, 480–1, 485; mentioned, 110, 151, 160, 312, 323

Dawson, Rachel, 252, 253

'Day of the Sheep, The' (short story), 109, 114–15, 122, 377

Day, Paul, 221

de Beer, Dora, 283

de Beer, Esmond, 283, 403

de Beer, Mary, 283

de Lanerolle, Ros, 441, 483

Dempsey, David, 252

Dickey, James, 322

Dimick, Reuben Eutycus ('Gussy'), 34–5

Dixon, Michael, 206

Doherty, Buddy, 111, 257

Dos Passos, John, 314

Dostoevsky, 98, 272

'Dot's Little Folk', 37, 175, 211

Doubleday, 316

Dowrick, Stephanie, 434, 434–5, 441, 472, 476

Dudding, Robin, 310

Duff, Oliver, 81, 126

Duggan, Barbara, 126, 134

Duggan, Eileen, 263

Duggan, Maurice, 110, 114, 122, 126, 134, 285, 396–7

Dunedin Public Hospital, 69, 85, 118, 186

Dunedin Teachers' Training College, 50, 51–3, 57, 58–9, 61–2, 285

Dupont, Professor Victor, 356–7, 388, 389

Durrell, Lawrence, 470

Earney, Lance, 492

'Edelman, Talbot', 372

*Edge of the Alphabet, The:* composition of, 210, 212, 213, 214; UK publication, 214, 225, 229, 238, 239; US publication, 214, 225, 229, 238, 238–9; NZ publication, 225, 229, 233, 245–6; Patrick White reads, 242–3; NZ sales, 264; out of print, 396; not to be reprinted in brother's lifetime, 456, 470; JF's reservations about, 498; mentioned, 409

Edinburgh: JF and Jess Whitworth visit, 216, 286

Edmond, Lauris, 507

*Education*, 393

El Botti Mario (fellow boarder in Andorra), 168, 169–70

'Electric Blanket, An' (short story), 129

Eliot, T.S., 53

Elizabeth II, Queen: JF meets, 494–5
*Ellinis:* JF sails on, 378, 379
Ellis, Havelock, 242
Emery, George, 207
Ensing, Riemke, 399
*Envoy from Mirror City, The* (third volume
    of autobiography): significance of title,
    159; composition of, 466; US
    publication, 466, 469, 470; NZ
    publication, 467, 469–70; UK
    publication, 469, 470; radio readings,
    470–1; Commonwealth paperback
    rights sold, 471; wins Wattie Award, 471;
    television rights sought, 473–4; wins
    New Zealand Book Award,
    475–6; foreign language editions, 496,
    497, 506. *See also* Autobiography
    (Frame's)
Epstein, Barbara, 335
Epstein, Jason, 335
*Esquire,* 208, 224
Evans, Faith, 455
Evans, Patrick, 192n, 393–5, 419–20, 488,
    511–12
*Evening Post,* 421, 488
*Evening Star,* 367
Evison, Pat, 436
Ezekiel, Nissam, 414

*Fable, A* (Faulkner), JF reviews, 134
'Face Downwards in the Grass' (short
    story), 187, 542n20
*Faces in the Water:* composition of, 199, 205,
    207, 214; NZ publication, 210, 220–3;
    UK publication, 210, 225,
    226–7; US publication, 210, 220, 223,
    223–4; sale of foreign language rights,
    223, 229; NZ sales, 223; JF's landlady
    reads, 287; earnings from, 291–2; out of
    print, 396; possible reprint considered,
    434; paperback edition, 435; proposed
    film adaptation, 456, 467; used as source
    for hospital scenes in film of *An Angel
    at My Table,* 473–4; foreign language
    editions, 496, 497, 506
Fainlight, Ruth, 247, 247–8
Faulkner, William, 115, 135, 217, 239, 355
Feathers, Violet, 34, 110
Feiffer, Jules, 338
Fels, Sara, 15
Fels, Willi, 15
Ferguson, Henry, 67, 68
Fergusson, Karen, 491
Finlayson, Roderick, 114
Firman family, 455

Firman, Marjorie (Poppy), 27–8, 30, 34, 393
Firman, Ted, 30, 455
'Fitting Tribute, A' (Stead), 276
Flannery, Anne, 420
Flaubert, Gustave, 324
Flint Cottage: JF's inheritance and sale of,
    480–1, 485, 501
Flint, Roland, 443
Florence: JF in, 389
Foss, Carlita, 384
Fox, Kerry, 491
Frame, Alex (South Hill cousin), 26
Frame, Alex (South Hill uncle), 26, 287
Frame, Alexander (grandfather), 11–13, 26,
    29, 33
Frame, 'Big Bill' (cousin), 117, 287–8, 353
Frame, Bill (uncle), 117, 287
Frame, Bob (uncle), 54, 79, 88, 285
Frame, Charlie (uncle), 211, 298, 353
Frame, Dolly (aunt), 287
Frame, George (Geordie, brother): born,
    16, 17; at school, 18, 26; epilepsy,
    29–30, 32, 110; deafness, 30; excluded
    from childhood games, 32; relations
    with father, 45, 54, 56–7, 78, 98, 174;
    one of 'Dot's Little Folk', 37; unfit for
    military service, 49; drinking,
    49–50; father's will, 131; and 'Toby
    Withers', 173, 197, 210, 211–12, 239,
    245; in London, 174–5; writing
    ambitions, 197, 211; on *Owls Do Cry,*
    222; arrest and conviction, 233–4, 243;
    accident, 244, 245; arrives unannounced
    in Auckland, 244; joint owner of
    Willowglen, 253, 259; marriage, 261–2;
    at cousin's funeral, 288; daughter's
    death, 309; stays with JF in Dunedin,
    310; arrives uninvited at JF's, 328; writes
    threatening letter, 357; on *To the Is-Land,*
    453; at Oamaru commemorative
    weekend, 462–3; heart attack, 481; on
    JF's autobiographies, 482; house
    destroyed by fire, 483, 486; JF helps
    financially, 486; arrested, 490; death, 493;
    mentioned, 134, 211, 451–2
Frame, George (Geordie, nephew), 452,
    482, 499
Frame, George Samuel (father): early life,
    13–14; railways career as fireman and
    engine driver, 14, 16, 17–18, 19, 22, 25–
    6, 44; agnosticism, 15; relations with
    wife, 15–16, 33, 130; war service, 15–16;
    falls in love with nurse, 16; amusements,
    18, 19–20, 33, 34, 39; employed
    throughout Depression, 21, 32; relations

with JF, 22, 114, 211; relations with Myrtle, 30, 31; character, 33–4, 45, 212; difficulty coping, 34, 110; union secretary, 36, 44; seen weeping after Myrtle's death, 39; Labour Party member, 44; relations with son, 45, 54, 56–7, 78, 98, 174; army reservist, 49; buys Willowglen, 56–7; falling-out with Renwicks, 59; and JF's suicide attempt, 67; farewells JF in Wellington, 143, 144; retirement, 211; death, 253; and 'Tom Livingstone', 353; mentioned, 107, 134

Frame, Han (aunt), 50, 54, 79, 285, 291, 352

Frame, Isabel May (sister): born, 17; shares double-bed with sisters, 26; childhood games, 32; one of 'Dot's Little Folk', 37; writing, 46; Wellington visit, 48; character, 50; at school, 54; at Willowglen, 56; attends Dunedin Teachers' Training College, 57, 58–9, 61–2; and JF's suicide attempt, 67; teaching, 78; death, 88–9; heart defect, 89, 211

Frame, Janet (aunt who died in early infancy), 29

Frame, Janet (*later* Cutmore, niece), 452, 492, 499

Frame, Janet Paterson:
CHILDHOOD AND EARLY LIFE: birth, 11, 16; embryonic identical twin, 16, 400; first words, 17; family picnics and camping holidays, 18, 21, 22, 34, 39; first story, 18, 19; at primary department, Wyndham District High School, 22; reputation as thief, 22, 23; at Oamaru North School, 26, 34–5; reading, 28–9, 35, 37–8, 40–1, 46; games, 32; at junior high school, 35, 36, 38; school prizes, 35, 44, 46, 49; writing, 35–8, 45–8; at Waitaki Girls' High School, 38, 42–4; death of sister Myrtle, 38–41, 49, 50, 144; Dunedin Teachers' Training College, 50, 51–3; attends Otago University, 52

EMPLOYMENT: Playfair St, Caversham, 78–9; Occidental Hotel, Christchurch, 93, 122; Grand Hotel, Dunedin, 116–18; TransTasman Hotel, Auckland, 120; Masonic Hotel, Devonport, 137; Battersea Polytechnic Hotel, 153; Regal Cinema, Streatham, 176

FINANCIAL AND BUSINESS MATTERS: beneficiary under father's will, 131; writes will, 131–2; changes name by deed poll, 191–2; on National Assistance, 198, 202–3, 206, 225; Pegasus contracts, 203–4, 209, 233, 263, 264; advances and royalties, 225, 229, 240, 264, 265, 311, 330–1, 331–2, 334, 341–2, 348, 353, 372, 423, 436, 458, 459, 461, 471, 475, 494, 498; tax problems, 240, 342, 349, 498, 499–500; joint owner of Willowglen, 253, 259; executor of father's estate, 259; Brasch's 'civil list' pension proposal, 263, 265, 268–9, 274, 290, 292, 352, 365; appointed Dawson's executor, 269; banking difficulties, 269; 'Boston lure' and variants thereof, 275, 308–9; Otago University grant, 298; buying, letting and selling houses, 298–9, 334–5, 369, 379, 391, 399, 406, 416–17, 423–4, 430, 458–9, 484–5, 489, 493–4, 496, 513, 516–17, 517–18; Brasch's offer of private support, 352–3; US immigrant visa application, 357–8; annuity, 365, 368, 377, 379, 400, 401, 420, 424, 433, 435, 445; Authors Fund income, 375, 377, 379, 420, 424, 437; considering sale of papers, 424; grant from Internal Affairs, 429–30; Literary Fund grants, 433; superannuation surtax, 467, 471; instructed in GST, 469

HEALTH AND MEDICAL TREATMENT: decaying teeth, 49, 93–4, 95; depression, 50, 301–2, 306, 328; suicide attempt, 64–5; schizophrenia diagnosis, 70, 78, 83–4, 139, 179, 186–7; ECT, 94–7, 101, 104; outpatient at mental clinics, 99–100, 118; insulin shock therapy, 105; 'prefrontal leucotomy' (lobotomy) proposed but not carried out, 111–12; pregnancy, 167; miscarriage, 169; suicidal impulses, 198; much better, 219–20; breast tumour, 270, 278; virus, 301–2, 415, 416, 443, 444, 445; meningitis, 323–4, 328; convalescence, 324–5; medical examination, 325; knee surgery, 378; high blood pressure, 391, 392, 424, 450, 498; influenza, 400, 446, 475, 491; kidney problems, 400; ; unsatisfactory Stratford GP, 424–5; back injury, 443; common cold, 466; lung infection, 491; diabetes, 498, 515, 496, 498; cancer, 501–2, 503, 508; strokes, 503, 495–6, 497; convalescing from surgery, 504; double pneumonia, 506; haemorrhage in eye, 506; ulcer on eye, 509; back ailment, 517

HOSPITALISATIONS: admitted to psychiatric ward, Dunedin Public Hospital, 69, 302, 328; admitted to

Frame, Janet Paterson: HOSPITALISATIONS
(*continued*)
Seacliff, 71, 73–7, 100, 110, 118; released
on probation, 77, 102, 104, 108, 114;
discharged, 86, 118, 119, 189, 199, 240,
302, 329; admitted to Sunnyside, 96–8;
committed to Avondale, 105; admitted
to Maudsley Hospital, 179–82, 183–9,
194–9, 240; fear of recommittal to
hospital, 256
NAMES (other than Janet Frame): Jean,
11, 22, 23, 54; Nini, 11, 28, 54, 191;
Clutha, 56, 191–2, 315; K.K.A., 60;
Santie Cross, 130; Nene, 191
PERSONAL LIFE: first dance, 116; good at
chess, 196, 472, 486; appearance, 128,
144, 234, 338, 465; 'roots crisis', 243–6;
experiments with marijuana, 318;
proposal of marriage, 340; buys and
learns to drive motorcycles, 392, 397,
402, 433, 437, 442; considers joining
Catholic church, 411–12, 413, 415, 417;
voice, 452, 518, 564n55; sixtieth birthday,
463; buys new typewriters, 442, 459;
acquires computer skills, 469, 472, 498,
518, 519; family photographs, 474;
driving lessons, 485, 486; ownership and
use of a car, 486, 489, 496. *See also*
Brown, William Theophilus (Bill);
Parlette, George; Reilly, Patrick; Stead,
C.K.
PLACES OF RESIDENCE: Dunedin, 16, 51–
4, 55, 57, 58–71, 78–87, 116–18, 282–3,
283–312, 327–9, 330–5, 351–9, 367–9,
505, 517–19; Glenham, 17–20, 293–4;
Edendale, 20, 293–4; Wyndham, 20–3,
293–4, 328; Oamaru, 24–50, 87–90,
114–15, 118, 130–1, 259–62;
Christchurch, 92–8; Kentish Town,
189–91; Camberwell, 199, 201–3, 205,
214–15, 218–19, 228, 229, 241, 398; East
Suffolk, 230, 231–6, 241; Kensington,
234–6, 237; Devonport, 265–6, 268, 270;
Waiheke, 270–1, 273–5; Opoho, 298–9,
334–5, 369; Whangaparaoa, 369–71, 379,
391, 392, 397, 399; Glenfield, 399–401,
404–6; Stratford, 406, 407–9, 416–17,
423–4; Wanganui, 430, 431–42, 445–6,
448–50; Levin, 458–9, 460, 462, 463,
466–8, 476, 477; near Shannon, 484–6,
489, 496; Palmerston North, 493–4;
Avondale, 513, 516; Browns Bay, 517
WRITING CAREER: juvenilia, 35–8, 45–8;
longing to write novel, 102–3; Hubert
Church Award, 112, 114, 275, 376, 384;

signs *Landfall* letter to Frank Sargeson,
114; staying in Frank Sargeson's army
hut, 124–30, 131–40; poems, 138, 264,
289, 291, 309, 311, 347, 348; award for
achievement, 197, 348; press interviews,
256, 257, 259–60, 433–4, 452–3, 486,
508; scholarship in letters, 259, 264, 269;
Burns Fellowship, 278, 292, 298, 300;
effect of negative reviews, 295, 354, 489;
signs page in honour of Brasch, 310;
radio interviews, 355–6, 452–3, 486–7;
pursued by French graduate student,
356; Wattie Book of the Year Awards,
376, 379, 457, 458, 466, 471; Katherine
Mansfield Fellow, 378–9, 382–7;
misleadingly compared with Katherine
Mansfield, 380–1; books out of print,
396, 434, 439; attends conference in
Honolulu, 413–14; honorary doctorates,
416, 418–19, 503–4; New Zealand Book
Awards, 433, 441, 462, 475–6, 490, 491;
Sargeson Fellow, 449, 478–9; CBE, 456,
457; nominated for Nobel Prize, 456,
470, 497, 514; Turnovsky Prize, 461, 501;
Buckland Award, 462; Commonwealth
Writers Prize, 491, 492, 494–5; Massey
University Medal, 506; presentation of
*The Inward Sun* (1994), 506, 507–8;
foreign honours, 514; civic
commemorations, 514–15; head
modelled for Anthony Stones bronze,
518
Frame, June. *See* Gordon, June (née Frame,
sister)
Frame, Lottie Clarice (née Godfrey,
mother): character, 14, 18, 21–2, 26, 29,
32–3, 45; meets future husband, 14;
Christadelphian beliefs, 15, 21–2, 40,
349, 456; relations with husband, 15–16;
children born, 16; amusements, 18, 19,
39; *Bible* readings, 21, 31; poetry
writing, 21, 31, 36, 39; reading, 21, 35,
279, 280, 320; relations with children,
21, 35, 37; cares for dying relations,
22–3, 33; rejects Seacliff for her
children, 30; poor household
management, 31, 32–3; devotion to
duty, 33; relations with son, 40; falling-
out with Renwicks, 59; persuaded to
sign Seacliff application form, 71, 100;
apprehension over JF diminished, 77;
death of daughter Isabel, 88–9;
helplessness, 98; seeks news of JF from
Seacliff, 101, 103; heart attack, 110;
persuaded to sign letter of consent for

leucotomy, 112; wants JF to stay at home, 114; thinner and more frail, 130; cheery correspondence, 134; death, 134–6, 141; mentioned, 107
Frame, Margaret (aunt), 29, 33
Frame, Mary (née Paterson, grandmother), 12–13, 17, 22–3, 26, 33, 191–2
Frame, May (South Hill cousin, *later* Williamson), 173, 257
Frame, Myrtle Joan (sister): born, 16; at school, 18, 26, 35; sees grandmother dead, 23; shares double-bed with sisters, 26; disciplined, 30; ambitions, 30–1; heart defect, 31, 39, 211; leaves school, 31; and JF's poetry, 36; one of 'Dot's Little Folk', 37; death, 38–41, 88, 146; character, 50; tenth anniversary of her death, 88
Frame, Polly (aunt), 31, 35, 38, 43
Frame, Robert (no relation), 341
Frame, Zarene Rose (niece), 297, 309
Frame, Zelda (née Chalmers, sister-in-law), 261, 288, 297, 309, 310, 328
*Frank Sargeson in His Time* (McEldowney), 408–9
Frank Sargeson Trust, 446; JF inaugural Sargeson Fellow, 449, 478–9
Frank, Stella, 226–7
'Frankie and Johnny': JF's parody of, 472
Frazer, James, 60
*Free Lance*, 172
Freud, Sigmund, 60
'Friday Night World, The' (short story), 190, 542*n*34
Friern Barnet Hospital, 193, 194

Galbraith, John Kenneth, 475
'Galbraith, Milly', 409
Gaskell, A.P., 114, 122
Gee, Margareta, 376
Gee, Maurice, 285
George Washington Hotel, New York, 390, 412, 413
Gibson, Janet, 110, 222–3, 262, 273, 394
Gilling, C.D., 63, 66
Giotto, JF's poem about, 53
Glasgow: JF and Jess Whitworth visit, 216, 286
Glover, Denis: JF reads, 80; publishes *The Lagoon*, 87–8, 92, 107; brief meeting with JF, 94; Brasch sends one of JF's stories to, 102; at Pegasus Press, 115; pal of Albion Wright, 133; suspects Sargeson's hand in *Owls Do Cry*, 138; writes JF a contrite letter, 138; on

Literary Fund committee, 139, 141, 160; grew up in Dunedin, 285; signs page in Brasch's honour, 310; death, 433; mentioned, 438
Godfrey, Alfred (grandfather), 14
Godfrey, Billy (uncle), 14
Godfrey, Jessie Joyce (grandmother), 14, 337
Godfrey, John (great-grandfather), 14
Godfrey, Dr John (great-great-grandfather), 14
Godfrey, Lance (uncle), 15, 16
Goldsmith, Oliver, 272, 504–5
Goldwater, John, 144, 152
Gordimer, Nadine, 466
Gordon, Ian (nephew), 108, 119, 120, 301, 350, 368, 402, 409, 512
Gordon, June (née Frame, sister): born, 20; shares double-bed with sisters, 26; childhood games, 32; remembers 'print starvation' at family home, 35; one of 'Dot's Little Folk', 37; death of sister Myrtle, 39, 40; Wellington visit, 48; character, 50; at school, 54, 78; at Willowglen, 56; JF writes to, 74; visits JF in hospital, 76; accompanies JF to Picton, 77; marriage, 97, 98, 104; gift to JF of Shakespeare's *Works*, 102; accompanies JF to Christchurch, 108; and father's will, 131; and mother's death, 134, 135; writing ambitions, 233; brain haemorrhage, 244, 245; encourages JF to sell Willowglen, 259; recovery from stroke, 266; undergoes surgery, 327, 506; asked about JF by French professor, 357; graduation from Kindergarten College, 359–60; Labour candidate for Waitotara, 415, 421; accompanies JF on trip to England, 428–9, 463; joins JF in England, 447; response to *To the Is-Land*, 453–4; memoir of childhood years, 454; mentioned, 257, 299, 391. *See also* Gordons (June and Wilson, as married couple)
Gordon, Margaret, 467, 491
Gordon, Neil (nephew), 108, 119, 120, 301, 306, 350, 359, 360, 401, 418, 443
Gordon, Pamela (*also* Bailey, niece): birth, 119–20; heart surgery, 211, 233, 323; childhood, 301, 321, 339; marries Stephen Bailey, 371; at Otago for JF's honorary degree, 419; accompanies JF on protest vigil, 440; taken by JF on trip to Sydney, 471–3; reports

Gordon, Pamela (*also* Bailey, niece) (*continued*)
   rediscovery of Seacliff magnolia, 515; teaching at Otago University, 517; visits JF, 517. *See also* Baileys (Pamela and Stephen, as married couple)
Gordon, William (great-nephew), 368
Gordon, Wilson (brother-in-law): marriage, 98, 104, 131; JF knits scarf for, 113; brings JF package from Albion Wright, 138; buys caravan for JF, 257; appearance in television serial, 369; manages North Shore newspaper, 371; retrieves JF's spectacles, 379; manages *North Shore Gazette*, 397; wife's campaign manager, 421; takes JF to doctor, 496; heart attack, 498–9
Gordons (June and Wilson, as married couple): shift to Auckland, 98; JF stays with, 104, 119–20, 122–3, 264, 275, 281, 301, 312–13, 327, 335, 350, 359–60, 366, 368, 402, 442; bring JF news of mother's death, 134; help JF financially, 160; Geordie arrives unannounced, 244; meet JF at wharf, 257; inspect Waiheke bach, 271; first home in Evans Street, 299; living in Glenfield, 399; living in Stratford, 399–400, 408, 410–11; overseas trip, 401, 402; help JF shift to Stratford, 406; JF sees regularly, 409; take JF on visit to Wanganui, 409; drive JF to Dunedin, 418; living in Wanganui, 421, 430; living in Levin, 433, 458; hypnotherapy business, 433; look after Neg, 446, 467; accompany JF to Government House, 457; and Geordie's exploits, 481–3; at celebratory dinner with JF, 494–5; living in Auckland, 512–13; accompany JF on trip to England, 515–16; living in St Kilda, 518; mentioned, 265, 299, 370, 410, 418, 492. *See also* Gordon, June (née Frame, sister); Gordon, Wilson (brother-in-law)
'Gorse is not People' (short story), 115
Gosse, Edmund, 300
Gotlieb, Howard, 275, 292
Götz, Sir Leon, 264
Goulden, Jane, 236, 237, 246–8, 316
Goulden, Mark, 209, 234–5, 237, 238, 241, 249, 256, 316–17. *See also* W.H. Allen
Graham, John, 126
Grand Hotel, Dunedin, 116–18
Granoff, Dan, 372
Grattan, C. Hartley, 208

'Gravy Boat, The' (short story), 115
Gray, Marjorie, 44
*Grimms' Fairy Tales*, 28, 393
*Guardian*, 227, 238, 239, 307, 364, 441, 488–9
Guest, Patricia, 109, 132

Hall, David, 172, 173, 221, 245, 251, 296, 307, 309
Hall, Roger, 463
Hardy, Thomas, 184, 290–1, 395
Harnack, Curtis, 321, 364
*Harper's Bazaar*, 233, 306, 337
*Harper's Magazine*, 224, 549n45
Harty, Eric Robin, 71
*I Have What I Gave: The Fiction of Janet Frame* (Panny), 510
*Hawke's Bay Herald Tribune*, 296
Hawthorne, Nathaniel, 35
Heath, Michael, 421
Heberley, James 'Worser', 14, 407
Hemenway, Robert, 233
Hendon, Josephine, 372
Henry Foundation, 314, 333, 334, 372
Hicks, Dorothy, 347
Hicks, Granville, 347, 354
Highet, Allan, 461
Hilliard, Noel, 238
Hindemith, Paul, 346
Hislop, Archie (cousin), 418–19, 459
Hislop, Grace (aunt), 211, 418
Hocken Library, Otago University, 369, 493, 510–11
Hodgkins, Frances, 156
Hodgkins, Michael, 141
Holcroft, Monte, 114–15, 425
Holman, Mr (Streatham cinema manager), 239
Holroyd, Michael, 470
Honolulu: JF attends conference at, 413–14
Hope, Francis, 226
Hopkins, Gerard Manley, 53
Hopkins, Humphrey, 466
Hopkins, Joyce, 466, 475
Hopkins, Sally, 391, 475
Horsman, Professor Alan, 286, 288–9, 290, 300, 302, 304, 307, 311, 419
Horsman, Dorothea, 290, 297, 302, 304
'Housekeepers of Ancient Springtime' ('crazy book'), 468
Hubert Church prize, 112, 114, 275, 376, 384
Huebsch, Ben, 242
Hulme, Keri, 489, 507, 508

Humphries, Barry, 276
Hunter, Mr (Education Board inspector), 66
Hutchinson, 435, 452, 466, 470
Hyde, Robin, 124, 270
Hyman, Stanley Edgar, 275

'I Got a Shoes' (short story), 160
Ibiza, 131, 144, 152; JF in, 156–67
Ikin, Bridget, 460, 473–4, 484, 491
Illingworth, Michael, 302
'In Alco Hall' (short story), 306
*Intensive Care*: composition of, 321, 332,
    333, 337–8, 340; advance for, 353;
    dedication of, 353; NZ publication, 353,
    354, 360, 367; UK publication, 353, 364;
    US publication, 354; NZ sales, 368;
    reissue of, 456; new NZ edition
    announced, 470; JF's public reading
    from, 474; mentioned, 409
International Women's Year, 399
*Inward Sun, An* (Evans, 1971), 393–4
*Inward Sun, The* (ed. Alley, 1994), 506, 507–8
Ireland, Kevin, 126, 187, 507
Ironside, Wallace, 288, 292, 352, 365, 417
Isherwood, Christopher, 343, 345
*Islands*, 376, 418, 444
'Islands, The' (Brasch poem), 245

Jack (English physics teacher), 151–2
Jacques, Robin, 339
*Janet Frame* (Dalziel), 438–9
*Janet Frame* (Evans), 393–5, 419
*Janet Frame* (film, shot 1975), 398–9, 462
'Janet Frame: Her Life and Art' (address by
    Evans), 462
*Janet Frame Reader, The* (ed. Ferrier), 509–10
*Janet Frame, Subversive Fictions* (Mercer),
    510–11
*Janet Frame's Waimaru* (video by Waitaki
    GHS students), 491–2
Jennings, Elizabeth, 227
John, Augustus, 156
*John O'London's Weekly*, 150
Jonathan Cape (publishing house), 176
Jones, Laura, 484, 491
Jones, Lawrence, 454
Joseph, Michael, 296
Joyce, Charlotte (great-grandmother), 407
Joyce, James, 53, 239
Jung, Carl, 60, 86

Kafka, Franz, 115
Katherine Mansfield Memorial
    Fellowship, 376, 378–9, 382–3, 386–7
Kazin, Alfred, 347, 348

Kazin, Ann, 347, 348
Keats, John, 149–50, 184
'Keel and Kool' (two stories so titled), 60
'Keenan, Pat', 210, 239
Keogh, Alexia, 491
King, Martin Luther, 328, 336
King, Michael, 512, 513
Kirk, Norman, 375, 391
Kirkness, J.C., 173
Kirkness, Jessie Banks (née Wilson), 42, 43,
    44, 46, 173, 262
*Kirkus Review*, 427
Knox, Grace, 207
Kozubei, David, 153–4, 190–1, 225
Kraus, Lili, 390

'Lagoon, The' (short story), 437
*Lagoon, The* (volume of short stories):
    composition of, 84; Caxton edition,
    106, 107–10, 114, 122, 456, 515; Hubert
    Church prize awarded for, 112, 114, 384;
    German translation, 203, 210; reprinted,
    210; JF's broadcast readings from, 311;
    later editions, 470, 492, 497; foreign
    language editions, 497, 506; paperback
    edition, 498; mentioned, 138
Lake District: JF holidays in, 215–16
Lamming, George, 176
*Landfall*: Brasch founds, 85; JF's actual or
    proposed contributions to, 84, 92, 102,
    115, 134, 151, 160, 175, 273–4, 291, 306;
    reviews of JF's works in, 109, 221, 245–
    6, 251, 267, 296, 307, 376; letter to
    Sargeson, 114, 122; Brasch retires as
    editor, succeeded by Dudding, 310;
    historic desk, 310–11, 351–2, 392, 460,
    483, 514; John Money's letter, 341;
    mentioned, 287. *See also* Brasch,
    Charles
'Landfall Desk, The' (poem), 351–2, 460
Lascaris, Manoly, 473
'Last Letter to Frank Sargeson, A'
    (memoir), 444
Leaver, Sheila, 505
Leeming, Owen, 251, 267–8, 384
Leggott, Michele, 488
Lehmann, John, 122, 130, 150, 380
Lehmann, Rosamund, 226
Lelchuk, Alan, 338
Leonard, John, 337, 354
'Letter to a Sculptor' (projected novel), 233
Lewis, Professor Aubrey, 184, 186
Lewis, Barbara (cousin), 430, 449
*Life*, 224
'Liftman, The' (poem), 115

Lindsay, Catherine, 36, 37, 262
Ling, David, 470, 475, 490, 500–1
*Listener*, 296
Literary Fund: Pegasus applications for
    subsidy, 133, 140, 220, 221; JF's
    application for travel grant, 139, 140,
    141–2, 160; Sargeson's efforts to gain
    extra funding for JF, 160, 188; award for
    achievement for *Owls Do Cry*, 197;
    awards JF scholarship in letters, 197,
    264; JF invited to apply for assistance,
    244; award for achievement for *The
    Pocket Mirror*, 348; mentioned, 263
*Living in the Maniototo*: fictional account of
    Isola Bella, 383, 555n8; composition of,
    400–1, 403, 403–4, 421; advance for,
    423; US publication, 425, 426–7; awards,
    433, 441; NZ publication, 435, 441;
    paperback edition, 435; UK publication,
    435, 441; foreign language editions, 466,
    496, 497
Livingston, Iona, 50, 62, 79, 305
'Livingstone, Leonard', 353
'Livingstone, Tom', 353
Llobera, Miguel Costa, 159–60
'Lolly-Legs' (short story), 115
*London Magazine*, 130, 150
Longfellow, Henry Wadsworth, 35, 233, 279
Longman Paul, 395–6
Los Angeles: JF in, 509, 515
*Los Angeles Times*, 427
Loudon, Agnes, 140

Macaulay, Miss (Waitaki GHS
    schoolteacher), 47, 81
McCahon, Colin, 266
McCarthy, Mary, 178
McCormick, Edna, 265
McCracken, Jill, 378
McCullers, Carson, 317, 339
MacDowell Colony, 333, 340, 342–5, 355,
    358
McEldowney, Dennis: has story included
    in Davin's anthology, 114, 285; JF
    socialises with, 266, 285, 290, 297, 299,
    305, 313, 513; on JF's reviews, 295; signs
    page in Brasch's honour, 310; reviews
    JF's works, 367, 376, 470; *Frank Sargeson
    in His Time*, 408–9; contributor to *The
    Inward Sun* (1994), 508; mentioned, 110,
    123, 128, 160
McEldowney, Margery, 299
McFarlane, Shona, 461
McGimpsey, Mrs, 31, 173
McKellar, Peter, 64, 65, 68

McKenzie, Peter, 340, 516
McKenzie, Renate, 340, 516
McLachlan, Dr, 100, 101
McLennan, Mrs (mother of Aunty Han),
    79
McLeod, A.L., 455
McLeod, Joseph (translator), 542n45
McLeod, Marion, 486
Macmillan Brown, John. *See* Brown, John
    Macmillan
MacNeice, Louis, 53
McNeish, James, 271, 376
*Mademoiselle*, 220
Mageur, Norma, 62
Mahi Tahi group, 432, 442
Mahy, Margaret, 494, 507
Malleson, Lady Constance, 241–2, 243,
    244, 251, 293, 300
*Man and His Wife, A* (Sargeson), 141
Mander, Rita, 197
Manhire, Bill, 170n, 461
Mansfield, Katherine, 15, 37, 114, 121n, 217;
    contrasted with JF, 380–1
Manson, Bill, 384
Manson, Cecil, 384, 387
Manson, Celia, 384, 387
'Maria' (short story by Dawson), 80, 140–1
Marquand, James, 319, 322, 326, 335, 339,
    445, 488
Marquand, John Phillips, junior: meets JF
    at Yaddo, 318–20; writes to inform JF of
    Sue's death, 410; JF meets, 445; death,
    509
Marquand, John Phillips, senior, 318, 319,
    320
Marquand, Susanna (Sue, née Coward),
    meets JF, 320; shares apartment with JF,
    321; arranges accommodation for JF,
    361–2; ill in hospital, 362, 363; invites JF
    to Baltimore, 401; death, 410
Marquands (John and Sue, as married
    couple): JF staying with, 321–2, 326–7,
    335, 339; pay JF air fare, 333; offer to pay
    JF's air fare, 358–9; JF borrows
    apartment, 340; JF visits, 349; and *The
    Carpathians*, 488
Marsh, Ngaio, 96
Marshall, Owen, 455, 491–2
Martha's Vineyard: JF at, 321–2
Martin, John (retired English MP), 386
Mason, R.A.K., 284, 285
Masonic Hotel, Devonport, 137
Massey University Medal, 506
*Mate*, 134, 187, 310
'Maude, Reverend Ainsley', 294–5

Maudsley, Henry, 183
Maudsley Hospital, 179–82, 183–9, 194–9, 240, 256
'Mavet, Istina', 203, 207, 220, 394, 474
'Mawhinney, Mrs', 173
Maynard, John, 491
Mayne, Richard, 217
Meikle, Phoebe, 171, 395–6
Mellow, James, 339–40
*Memoirs of a Peon* (Sargeson), 227, 258, 266
'Memory and a Pocketful of Words' (*TLS* article), 271–3
Menton: JF in, 380–90
Mercer, Gina, 468, 473, 497, 510, 510–11
Mexico City: JF in, 314, 335
Milford cottage: JF considers living in, 270
'Mill Belongs to Sandy, The' (fragment absorbed into *Intensive Care*), 307, 311, 315, 318, 324, 337–8
Miller, Dr Alan D., 185, 186, 187, 188, 189, 192, 193, 212
Miller, Esme, 44
Miller, Marguerite, 39
Miller's Flat: JF has vacation work in, 55–6
Mills, Joyce (née Godfrey, aunt), 409
Mills, Tom, 45
Milner, Frank, 42, 49
*Mona Minim and the Smell of the Sun* (children's story), 321, 325, 331, 337, 339, 337, 339, 434, 498, 506
Money, John: JF's teacher of psychology, 63–4, 65; counselling of JF, 65–6, 67–8, 82–4, 85–7, 96; visits JF in hospital, 69; JF's letters to, 74ff. *passim;* and JF's psychology paper, 77; and JF's schizophrenia diagnosis, 83; interest in JF's writing, 84–6, 87–8, 92, 176, 191, 200, 201, 207, 210, 214, 220, 223, 277; attempts to introduce Baxter to JF, 85–6; letter to JF on Isabel's death, 89; moves to USA, 92, 93; JF sends poems to, 102; return visit to New Zealand, 143; helps JF financially, 161, 176; and JF's admission to Maudsley Hospital, 179–82, 184; writes to JF, 203; and *Owls Do Cry*, 209; meets JF in London, 218–19; remarks on JF's improved health, 219–20; visits NZ and sees JF, 266–7; passes on US book reviews to JF, 275; invites JF to Baltimore, 278; shows JF New York, 279; tells JF of Boston University writer-in-residence scheme, 292; stays with JF in Dunedin, 309–10; secures grants for JF, 314, 333; JF staying with, 314–15, 340; JF accompanies to Buffalo, 320; knows John Williams, 323; negotiates with Pan Am over JF's postponed flight, 325–6; letter to *Landfall*, 341; JF writes that they are 'far apart in interests', 346–7; ever the loyal consort, 354; testimonial for JF, 358; worrying about JF, 364; visits JF, 386, 404, 412, 436, 517; gives Evans biographical information about JF, 394; and *Living in the Maniototo*, 421, 425; mugged, 446; JF's memories of, 449–50; and 'Brian Wilford', 505; contributor to *The Inward Sun* (1994), 508; JF communicates with by electronic mail, 518; mentioned, 107, 235, 281, 282, 363, 481, 506
Monk, William, 157, 159
Montecito: JF in, 345, 349, 363, 365–6
*Monthly Review*, 307
Moorhouse, Geoffrey, 238, 239, 243
Moorhouse, Janet, 243
Mortimer, John, 226
Morton-Saner, Anthea, 456, 478, 483, 509, 516
Moynahan, Julian, 354
Muir, Hillary, 109
Muldoon, Robert, 405
Murdoch, Iris, 429
Murray, Rosie, 111
'My Cousins who could eat cooked turnips' (short story), 507

Naipaul, V.S., 466
Nannen-Verlag, 203, 210
Nash, Charlotte (great-grandmother), 15
National Health Service, 184
National Jewish Hospital, Denver, 308–9
*National Observer*, 372
Natusch, Gilbert, 282
Natusch, Sheila (née Traill): friendship with JF, 52, 64, 69, 82, 94, 257, 285; JF's letters to, 74, 75, 92, 111–12, 115, 173; on *Time* review of *Faces in the Water*, 224; JF visits, 282; at International Festival in Wellington, 507
Neal White, Dorothy. *See* White, Dorothy Neal
Neg (JF's white cat), 369, 371, 391, 402, 404, 406, 445–6, 446, 450, 467, 478
Neider, Charles, 358
Nene, Tamati Waka, 28, 191
Nesbitt, Lowell, 279
Neville, Jill, 465
*New Leader*, 275

*New Statesman*, 150, 217, 239, 251, 296, 307
*New Statesman & Society*, 488
*New York Herald Tribune*, 208, 209
*New York Review of Books*, 335
*New York Times*, 308, 337, 354
*New York Times Book Review*, 208, 209, 224, 239, 252, 295–6, 307–8, 337, 339, 354, 372, 427, 448, 489, 549*n*45
*New Yorker*, 208, 220, 225, 233, 240, 306, 321, 334, 337, 347, 372, 427
New Zealand Authors Fund, 375, 377, 379
New Zealand Book Awards, 433, 441, 462, 475–6, 490, 491
New Zealand Broadcasting Corporation, 311
*New Zealand Herald*, 257, 452, 488
*New Zealand Listener:* JF's contributions, 65, 81, 84, 134, 160, 273, 400, 425, 468–9; reviews of JF's works, 114–15, 172, 221, 245, 251, 296, 307, 367, 454, 461, 464, 470, 488; Vogt's response to unfavourable review, 172, 384; controversy over Katherine Mansfield room in Menton, 386, 387; text of Joan Stevens's radio talk, 354–5; review of dramatisation of *A State of Siege*, 359; JF interviewed for, 378–9, 486; on JF's reading at International Festival, 474; mentioned, 126, 306, 308
New Zealand Literary Fund. *See* Literary Fund
*New Zealand Short Stories* (ed. Davin, 1953), 109, 114–15, 285, 384
*New Zealand Short Stories* (ed. Stead, 1966), 297, 302
*New Zealand Times*, 454, 461
New Zealand Women Writers' Society, 381
'New Zealand writers and their work' series (OUP), 438–9
Niagara Falls: JF views, 320–1
Nobel Prize: JF nominated or proposed for, 456, 470, 497, 514
Noble, Debbie, 442, 451
Noble family, 451
Nokes, David, 488
Noonan, Michael, 398
Norfolk: JF in, 236–7, 281, 340, 341, 389, 390, 412, 428, 429, 446–7, 480–1; JF proposes to live in, 246, 248–9; JF considers retreating to, 450
*North Shore Gazette*, 397–8
*Northland Magazine*, 256
Nweze, Clement, 151
Nye, Robert, 364, 488–9

Oamaru, 24, 462–3, 514. *See also* Frame, Janet Paterson: PLACES OF RESIDENCE
Oamaru Hospital, 212, 297
*Oamaru Mail*, 259–60, 482–3
Oamaru Public Library, 505
Oates, Joyce Carol, 337
O'Brien, Gregory, 480
*Observer*, 226, 251, 455, 488
Occidental Hotel, Christchurch, 93, 122
'Ode' (O'Shaughnessy): JF's parody of, 274
Oliver, W.H., 172
Orwell, George, 206
Ostermann, Robert, 372
O'Sullivan, Vincent, 454
*Otago Daily Times*, 37–8, 45, 175, 211, 463, 482, 488; JF's letters to, 92, 333
Otago University, 52, 278, 416
Outram, 16–17
*Owls Do Cry* (originally 'Talk of Treasure'): composition of, 129, 130, 398; NZ publication, 132–3, 139, 140, 142, 143, 161, 171–4, 187, 189; Sargeson sends copies to overseas publishers, 176; NZ sales, 179, 187, 264; UK publication, 191, 209, 216–18; award for achievement for, 197; US publication, 199, 200–1, 203, 203–4, 207, 208, 209; foreign language editions, 203, 208, 210, 506; foreign language rights, 223, 456; royalties from, 223, 225; Patrick White reads, 242–3; JF invited to lecture on, 289; paperback edition, 307, 396, 434, 435; Patrick Evans reads, 393; proposed films of, 412, 416, 420; proposal to republish, 441; new NZ edition, 466; mentioned, 409
Oxford University Press, 109, 114–15, 285, 297, 302, 384, 438–9, 497

'Painter, The' (short story), 400
Palmerston North, 423–4, 486, 492, 493, 494
Panny, Judith Dell, 510
Pare, Dr Michael, 192–3
Paris: JF in, 155–6, 389–90
'Park, The' (short story), 84
Park, Mrs T., 78
Parker, Dorothy, 208, 224
Parlette, George, 164–6, 170
Parry, Doris, 201, 202, 206, 212, 213
Parry, Richard, 201, 202, 206, 213
Parry, Ursula, 201, 202
*Parsons Packet*, 134
Partridge, Eric ('Party'), 51
Pascoe, John, 374–5

Patterson, Cristina, 156, 157
Patterson, Keith, 156, 157
Patterson, Wendy, 32, 44, 49
Payne, Arthur 'Agony', 61
Pegasus Press: publishes JF's works in NZ
  (*Owls Do Cry*, 132–3, 187, 201; *Faces in
  the Water*, 207–8, 222; *The Reservoir and
  other stories*, 291, 307; *A State of Siege*,
  307); applications for Literary Fund
  subsidies, 133, 140, 220, 221; advances to
  JF, 142, 160, 188, 189; JF's contracts with,
  203–4, 209, 233, 263, 264; royalty
  payments, 291–2, 330–1, 353, 357, 368,
  379; severance of connections with,
  357, 422; mentioned, 115, 179, 223. *See
  also* Wright, Albion
PEN, 402, 412, 415, 425–6, 456, 497, 514
*Penguin New Writing*, 122, 340
Penny (JF's second cat), 483, 485, 517
Pepys, Samuel, 240, 272, 474
Philadelphia: JF in, 321
Phillips, Alan, 255, 281–2
Phillips, John. *See* Marquand, John Phillips,
  junior
Picador, 478
Pick, Robert, 224
Picton: JF visits, 459
Pinder, Rona, 52, 87
'Place, The' (poem), 294
Plath, Sylvia, 339
Platts, Una, 126
Plomer, William, 147, 176, 176–7, 296,
  338*n*
*Pocket Mirror, The* (poems): US publication,
  311, 317, 322; UK publication, 317; NZ
  publication, 330, 348; advances on, 331;
  out of print, 396; new editions, 498;
  Jamie Yates knows many poems by
  heart, 515
Poe, Edgar Allan, 40, 279, 280
*Poetry Review*, 150
'Poets' (verse), 461
Poore, Charles, 308
Porter, Louise, 177, 228
*Portnoy's Complaint* (Roth), 338
Potter, Beatrix, 141
Powell, Gene, 111, 178
Premi Brancati Prize, 514
*Press*, 108, 296, 478, 561*n*10
*Private Gardens* (ed. Ensing), 399
'Prizes' (short story), 220
'Problems of the Newly Born, The' (short
  story), 307
Proust, Marcel, 202
*Publishers' Weekly*, 448

'Quick as a Bream' (short story), 115

*Rainbirds, The*: composition of, 291, 300,
  307, 328; UK publication, 311, 325, 331,
  334; advances on, 331; NZ publication,
  331; new NZ edition announced, 470;
  JF's reservations about, 498. *See also
  Yellow Flowers in the Antipodean Room*
Rama, Te, 60, 62
Ramsay, Professor Herbert, 53, 287
Ramsay, Noreen, 111
Random House, 435, 506, 508
Rawlings, Peggy, 201, 202, 213
'Red-Currant Bush, The' (short story),
  220
Regal Cinema, Streatham, 176
Reid, J.C., 330
Reid, Tony, 452, 488
Reilly, Patrick, 147, 148, 152, 154, 161, 170,
  176, 187–8, 210, 212–13, 225, 239
'Reminders' (short story), 306
Renwick, George (Aunty Isy's husband),
  50, 51, 54, 55, 59
Renwick, Isabella (née Frame, 'Aunty
  Isy'), 31, 35, 50, 51, 53, 55, 57, 58, 59, 285
Renwick, Molly ('radio aunt'), 30, 51
'Reply, The' (poem), 304
'Reservoir, The' (short story), 220, 233
*Reservoir, The, and other stories* (Pegasus and
  W.H. Allen, 1966), 264, 291, 307; out of
  print, 396
*Reservoir, The: Stories and Sketches* (Braziller,
  1963), 229, 235, 251–2, 264, 275
Rhodes, Winston, 172
Richards, Ray, 436, 438
Riding, Laura, 53
Rilke, Rainer Maria, 98, 345, 349, 356, 395,
  413, 456–7
Robert Burns Fellowship. *See* Burns
  Fellowship
Roddick, Alan, 375
Rolo, Charles, 224
Romans, Iris, 455
Rosenzweig, Saul, 92
Ross, Patience: JF sees, 177–8, 281, 312; JF
  gets on well with, 227; lends JF holiday
  cottage, 227–8; outlines JF's publishing
  programme, 229; considers Goulden's
  proposal 'idiotic', 235; farewells JF at
  Victoria, 254; advice to JF on *The
  Rainbirds*, 311; visits JF in hospital, 324;
  distressed when JF dismisses A.M.
  Heath, 357; gone from A.M. Heath,
  429, 434; mentioned, 191, 312. *See also*
  A.M. Heath Ltd

Roth, Philip, 338
Rothschild, Phillippe de, 350–1
Rowlandson, Rebie, 271, 274
Rowling, Bill, 421
'Royal Icing' (short story), 233
*Ruahine:* JF sails on, 142, 143, 144, 144–5
Russell, Bertrand, 241, 242

Salt Cay: JF at, 326–7, 333, 334, 335–6
San Francisco, 279, 391, 401–2, 443
*San Francisco Chronicle,* 447, 489
Santa Barbara: JF in, 345, 349, 363, 365–6
Sargeson, Frank: and *The Lagoon,* 108–9,
    109–10, 122; *Landfall* letter, 114, 122;
    army hut, 120, 122–4, 387n; meets JF
    and invites her to stay in his army hut,
    120, 122–4; relations with JF, 122–43,
    296–7; and JF's will, 132; and JF's
    schizophrenia diagnosis, 139–40; and
    *Owls Do Cry,* 143, 171, 176; advice to JF
    on travel, 144, 146, 155; and JF's writing,
    151, 187, 190, 191, 210, 425, 427–8; JF's
    letters to, 159ff. *passim;* inclination to
    panic, 160, 169; writes to donors, 160;
    and C.K. Stead, 188; comments on JF's
    Lake District holiday, 216; meets JF
    again on her return to NZ, 257–9; has
    civil list pension, 263; collected stories,
    266; JF visits, 266, 313, 350; praises *An
    Adaptable Man,* 296; diplomatic
    intervention between JF and Stead, 297;
    JF does library research for, 300; Yate–
    Butler dialogue, 300; yarns about
    Frame, 306; signs page in honour of
    Brasch, 310; JF's gratitude to, 325;
    jealous of JF, 338; on *Portnoy's
    Complaint,* 338n; worrying about JF, 364;
    and 'Turnlung', 372, 377, 408; bequest
    to JF, 377, 418, 446; response to *Daughter
    Buffalo,* 377; gives Evans biographical
    information about JF, 394; honorary
    doctorate, 396; visits JF in Glenfield,
    402; television appearance, 405;
    memoirs, 408; McEldowney's
    biography of, 408–9; seventy-fifth
    birthday, 418; suffers stroke and health
    declines, 433, 436, 442–3; death, 444;
    favourite Gide phrase, 505; mentioned,
    219, 279, 370, 415, 425–6, 438. *See also*
    Frank Sargeson Trust
Saroyan, William, 79
Sarraute, Nathalie, 200, 315–16
Sarton, May, 343–4, 346, 447, 452
*Scented Gardens for the Blind:* composition
    of, 214, 220, 229; UK publication, 229,

250–1; US publication, 229, 235, 251,
    275; NZ publication, 251, 267–8, 275;
    'trick' ending, 275; Hubert Church
    Award, 275; James Mellow's letter of
    appreciation, 339–40; out of print, 396;
    reprinted in US, 434; paperback
    edition, 435; proposal to republish, 441;
    foreign language editions, 506
Schneebaum, Tobias, 443, 444, 485
*School Journal,* 28–9, 134, 175, 190
Schoon, Theo, 92
Schulz, Amy, 456
Schulz, Christopher, 432, 456
Schulz, Derek, 432, 436–7, 449, 456, 463,
    494–5
Schwartz, Delmore, 317
Scott, Margaret, 382, 488
'Scott's Horse' (poem), 273–4
Scrivener, Audrey: leucotomy, 113, 242; and
    'Istina Mavet', 207, 474; JF's meetings
    with, 266; JF visits, 313
Scrivener, Len, 113
Seacliff (mental hospital), 69, 72–3, 85, 106;
    JF's experience of, 71, 73–7, 118, 222
Seath, David, 274
Sedgwick, Sally, 336
Shadbolt, Maurice, 285, 291
Sheed, Wilfred, 308
Shepherd, Dr Michael, 179, 180, 181, 184,
    185, 186, 187, 195
Sheppard, R.Z., 426, 426–7
Siedeberg, Dr Emily, 16
'Signal, Malfred', 274, 308, 359, 420
Silkin, Jon, 205, 393
Sillitoe, Alan, 209, 247
Simmons, Jeffrey, 209, 235, 317
Sinclair, Keith, 126
Smith, Jean, 262
Smith, William, 239
Smithells, Philip, 359
Smithyman, Kendrick, 126, 257
'Snowman Snowman' (fable), 228, 252
*Snowman Snowman: Fables and Fantasies,*
    228, 229, 235, 251–2, 264
Solomon, Hyde, 339
'Some Recognitions of the Cross-Cultural
    Encounter in Literature' (conference
    paper), 413–14
'South Pacific' (Manhire), 170n
Soyinka, Wole, 414
Spark, Muriel, 355
Sparks, Ma, 455
*Speaking for Ourselves* (ed. Sargeson), 79, 80,
    117, 123, 140
*Spectator,* 226

Spender, Stephen, 345
Springbok rugby tour (1981), 439–40
Springfield, New Hampshire: JF in, 348
Stanford, Ann, 318, 327
State Literary Fund. *See* Literary Fund
*State of Siege, A:* composition of, 271, 274, 291, 300, 307; UK publication, 307, 317; US publication, 307, 307–8; NZ publication, 322; sales, 330–1, 331; advances on, 331; adapted for stage and television, 359; out of print, 396; 'non-commercial' film of, 412, 420–1; reprinted in US, 434; radio readings, 435–6; Australian edition, 436; new NZ edition announced, 470
Stead, C.K.: charged and indeterminate meeting with JF, 126–8; on *Owls Do Cry*, 171, 173; visits JF in hospital, 188–9, 197; on JF's name 'Clutha', 192; and 'The Triumph of Poetry', 276–8, 464–5; seeks permission to anthologise 'The Reservoir', 297; at literary seminar, 305–6; JF socialises with, 306; signs page in honour of Brasch, 310; Sargeson speaks of, 313; judgement on JF's poetry, 322, 552*n*43; Katherine Mansfield Fellow, 376, 382, 387; at Wellington PEN conference, 425–6; reviews *Living in the Maniototo*, 427; JF sees in London, 481; at International Festival in Wellington, 507; contributor to *The Inward Sun* (1994), 508; deprecates uncritical reverence of JF, 514; mentioned, 131, 160, 279
Stead, Kay, 126, 131, 160, 188, 189, 197
Stenhouse, John, 112
Stevens, Joan, 59, 354–5
Stewart Island: JF in, 87
Stewart, William Downie, 92
Stockport: JF in, 243
Stone, Robert, 318
Stones, Anthony, 126, 518
Stowe, Harriet Beecher, 279
*Strait Is the Gate* (R.A.K. Mason), 284
Stravinsky, Igor, 343, 346
Stroud, James Jesse, 36
Stuart House, 59
Studd, Jill, 432, 436–7, 449, 456, 463, 494–5
Sturges, Joan, 241, 242, 293
Sturm, Jacqueline. *See* Baxter, Jacqueline (née Sturm)
Styron, William, 335, 361
Sun Books, 307, 396
'Sunday Afternoon at Two O'Clock' (poem), 285

*Sunday Telegraph*, 217, 306
*Sunday Times*, 217, 226–7, 251, 465, 470
Sunnyside (mental hospital), 96–8
Surry, Mildred, 190, 191, 196, 204, 225, 240, 254, 281, 312, 324, 389, 412
Sussman and Sugar (publishing house), 176
'Swans' (short story), 99, 461
Sydney, 412, 415, 471–3
*Sydney Morning Herald*, 472

*Take My Tip* (Journet): JF reviews, 115
Takiari, Piki, 432, 433, 436–7, 449, 456, 458, 463, 467–8, 494–5, 508
'Talk of Treasure' (prose fiction). *See Owls Do Cry*
Tanguy, Yves, 426
Tapsell, Peter, 475
Tardy, Bernard, 385
Tardy, Etienne: JF's poem for, 386
Texidor, Greville, 122, 131, 144, 167, 168, 287
'That Summer' (Sargeson), 122
'This Desirable Property' (radio talk), 273
Thomas, Dylan, 53, 60, 209, 217
Thoreau, Henry David, 343
*Time* magazine, 208, 223, 224, 251–2, 294–5, 307, 337, 372, 426, 489
'Timely Monologue, A' (poem), 307
*Times, The*, 227, 251, 296
*Times Literary Supplement*: reviews of JF's works, 150, 217, 219, 226, 239, 250–1, 296, 307, 364, 454–5; JF's commissioned article for, 271–3
*To the Is-Land* (first volume of autobiography): US publication, 447–8, 451–2; NZ publication, 451, 452, 454, 455–6; UK publication, 451, 452, 454–5, 459; NZ sales, 455–6, 466; paperback edition, 455–6, 459, 466; radio readings, 456, 462; wins Wattie Book of the Year award, 457; advance for, 459; television rights sought, 460, 473–4; wins Buckland Award, 462; Commonwealth paperback rights sold, 471; foreign language editions, 496, 497, 506. *See also* Autobiography (Frame's)
Todd, Garfield, 50
Toronto: JF attends conference in, 466
'Torrence, Colin', 353
Tovey, Gordon, 60
'Towards Another Summer' (unpublished novella), 245, 248, 273
TransTasman Hotel, Auckland, 120
Tremain, Kathleen, 136, 443
'Trespassers on Earth' (Sturges), 241–2, 248, 253–4, 255–6, 293, 299–300

Trevelyan, Sophie, 513
'Triumph of Poetry, The' (short story), 275, 296, 306, 426, 464
Tucker, Clarence, 402
'Tunnel Beach' (poem), 60
'Turnlung', 372, 376
Turnovsky Prize for Outstanding Achievement in the Arts, 461, 501
Twain, Mark, 35, 279, 358
Twayne World Authors series: Evans's book on JF, 393–5, 419
'Two Sheep' (short story), 466
'Two Widowers' (short story), 425

'Uncle Pylades' (abandoned novel), 161, 166, 176, 187, 190, 233
'University Entrance' (short story), 65, 81, 84
University of Hawaii: conference at, 411
University of Waikato, 501–2

Vernarelli, Lucia, 318
Victoria University Press, 456, 466
Vietnam War, 293, 375
Villa Isola Bella, 382–3
Vogt, Anton: Money shows JF's stories and poems to, 87; signs *Landfall* letter for Sargeson, 114; JF in Menton sought out and 'rescued' by, 384–5; defends *Owls Do Cry*, 172, 384; disparages Katherine Mansfield Room, 387; comment on JF and Jacquie Baxter in France, 389; stroke, 391
Vogt, Birgitte, 384–5
Vogts (Anton and Birgitte), 385, 386, 390

Wadsworth, Elizabeth, 62, 69, 285
*Wahine* storm, 328
Waitaki Boys' High School, 42
Waitaki Girls' High School, 42–4, 155, 455
'Waiting for Daylight' (poem), 151, 160
'Waitresses, The' (poem), 115
Walding, Joe: JF's poem on, 468–9
Wall, Arnold, 360, 422
*Wall Street Journal*, 468
Walsh, Bluey, 48
*Wanganui Chronicle*, 434, 440
Ward, Elizabeth, 448
Ward, Joyce, 299, 505
Ward, Raymond, 287, 299, 505
Ward, Vincent, 412, 421
Wartik, Nancy, 489
*Washington Post Book World*, 448
Waten, Judah, 415
Wattie Book of the Year Award, 376, 379, 458, 466, 471, 491, 457
Wellington, 48, 143, 144, 281–2, 351, 359; JF's public reading at Festival, 474, 507–8
Wellington Hospital, 481–2
Wells, H.G., 242
Welty, Eudora, 178, 317, 339
Wendt, Albert, 414
Wevers, Lydia, 461
W.H. Allen: publishes JF's works in UK (*Owls Do Cry*, 209, 216; *Faces in the Water*, 210, 223; *The Adaptable Man*, 254, 291; *A State of Siege*, 307, 317; *The Pocket Mirror*, 317; *The Rainbirds*, 331; *Intensive Care*, 353); organises portrait session for JF, 228; undecided about stories and fables, 264; JF remains loyal to, 357; royalty payments, 379; publicity material for JF, 380; mentioned, 234, 237, 325. *See also* Goulden, Mark
Wheeler, Elizabeth, 427
Whitcombe and Tombs, 330–1
White, David Renfrew, 281
White, Dick, 262–3, 282, 305, 312
White, Dorothy Neal (*later* Ballantyne): recommends high mark for JF's student work, 61; reviews *The Lagoon* on Dunedin radio station, 109; visits JF in hospital, 114; reviews JF's reading of 'The Gravy Boat', 115; named in JF's will, 132; JF renews acquaintance with, 262–3; on Burns Fellowship committee, 278; JF becomes friends and socialises with, 285, 289, 293, 297, 305, 328, 332, 352, 368; widowed, 312; keeps eye on JF's house and tenants, 335; helps retrieve *Landfall* desk, 351; marries again, 351; JF inadvertently offends, 369; and *Living in the Maniototo*, 422–3; at International Festival in Wellington, 507; happy last meeting with JF, 507; mentioned, 282, 419
White, I.G. (Ida), 281, 287, 295, 309–10
White, Kerry, 263, 289, 305, 312, 328
White, Patrick: fan letter to JF, 242–3, 344, 405; does not meet JF, 415, 473; on JF's autobiography, 470; JF at last answers his letter, 473
White, Timothy, 412, 420–1
White, Vicky (*later* Feltham), 263, 289, 293, 297, 305, 312, 507
Whitman, Walt: JF reads or alludes to, 40, 272
Whittier, John Greenleaf, 35, 279
Whitworth, Jess: friend of Sargeson's, 126;

advice to JF on travel, 142, 144, 147, 150, 155; visits JF, 196–7, 215; visits Glasgow and Edinburgh with JF, 216, 286; JF visits, 257, 313, 350; death, 375; mentioned, 286

Wiegard, William, 239

'Wilford, Brian', 505

Wilkinson, Iris. *See* Hyde, Robin

Willemstad: JF in, 145, 255

Williams, John (medical researcher), 323, 324–5, 340–1, 553*n*57

Williams, John (professor of economics), 305

Williamson, May (née Frame, South Hill cousin), 173, 257

Willowglen, 56–7, 253, 259, 260–1, 514

Wilson, Colin, 217

Wilson, Janet, 393

Wilson, Jessie Banks. *See* Kirkness, Jessie Banks (née Wilson)

Wilson, Phillip, 114, 306, 355, 402, 508, 513

Winn–Manson Menton Fellowship. *See* Katherine Mansfield Memorial Fellowship

'Winter Garden' (short story), 306, 337, 347

'With You (To Janet Frame)' (Brasch poem), 375–6

'Withers, Chicks', 173, 394, 412

'Withers, Francie', 173

'Withers, Mr and Mrs', 173

'Withers, Toby', 173, 197, 210, 212, 239, 243, 412

*Woman's Weekly*, 453

Women's Press, 434–5, 438, 441, 452, 456, 463, 465, 471, 478, 483–4, 495

Wonner, Paul. *See* Brown and Wonner

Woolf, Virginia, 53, 217, 226, 355

*World Literature Today*, 455

Wright, Albion: Glover writes to, 138, 139; sends package to JF by Wilson Gordon, 138; sends advance on royalties, 142; JF's letters to, 161, 190, 250, 331; and Geordie's book proposal, 197, 211; publishes *Owls Do Cry*, 201; contributes to cost of Kensington flat, 235; welcomes JF on her return to NZ, 257; JF's meeting with, 263–4; interest in JF's poems, 287, 291; withholds royalty payments, 291–2; hurt letter from, 360; death, 448–9; mentioned, 160. *See also* Pegasus Press

Wright, Douglas, 485–6, 513

Wylie, C.M.J., 207

'Wyndham' (poem), 294

Yaddo artists' and writers' colony, 317–20, 324, 333, 334, 337–40, 347–8, 355, 364, 442, 443–5

Yates, Jamie, 515

*Yellow Flowers in the Antipodean Room*, 325, 331–2, 336–7. *See also The Rainbirds*

Yevtushenko, Yevgeny, 466

'You Are Now Entering the Human Heart' (short story), 321, 334, 337

*You Are Now Entering the Human Heart* (volume of short stories): paperback edition, 435; proposal to publish, 441; advance for, 456; dedication of, 456; NZ publication, 456, 466; UK publication, 456, 463, 465–6; radio readings, 462; US publication, 466

Young, David, 464

YWCA, 216, 315, 323, 344

Zanthe, Dr Robert I., 309, 551*n*37

*Zeit, Die*, 223